Christianity and Rabbinic Judaism

A Parallel History of Their Origins and Early Development

SECOND EDITION

EDITED BY HERSHEL SHANKS

BIBLICAL ARCHAEOLOGY SOCIETY

WASHINGTON, DC

Library of Congress Cataloging-in-Publication Data

Christianity and rabbinic Judaism: a parallel history of their origins and early development/
edited by Hershel Shanks.—2nd ed.

p. cm.

Includes bibliographical references and index.

1. Christianity—Origin. 2. Church history—Primitive and early church, ca. 30-600. 3. Judaism—History—Talmudic period, 10-425. 4. Judaism—History—Medieval and early modern period, 425-1789. 5. Judaism—Relations—Christianity. 6. Christianity and other religions—Judaism.

I. Shanks, Hershel.

BR129.C44 2011

261.2'609015—dc23 2011022582

4710 41st Street, NW
Washington, DC 20016

Printed in the United States of America

Design by AURAS Design

ISBN 978-1-935335-52-8 (hardcover)

ISBN 978-1-935335-51-1 (paperback)

ON THE COVER: The sixth-century C.E. Madaba mosaic map
with depiction of Byzantine Jerusalem highlighted.
Photo by Garo Nalbandian.

Table of Contents

Illustrations

Color Plates

Maps

The Authors

Harold W. Attridge is the Reverend Henry L. Slack Dean of Yale Divinity School and Lillian Claus Professor of New Testament. He has made numerous scholarly contributions to New Testament exegesis and to the study of Hellenistic Judaism and the history of the early Church. His publications include *Hebrews: A Commentary on the Epistle to the Hebrews* (Fortress Press, 1989) and *Nag Hammadi Codex I: The Jung Codex* (Brill, 1985), as well as numerous book chapters and articles in scholarly journals. He has edited 11 books, most recently, with Margot Fassler, *Psalms in Community* (Brill, 2004).

James H. Charlesworth is George L. Collord Professor of New Testament Language and Literature at Princeton Theological Seminary and also serves as director of the Princeton Theological Seminary Dead Sea Scrolls Project. He is a specialist in the Apocrypha and Pseudepigrapha of the Old and New Testaments, the Dead Sea Scrolls and the historical Jesus. Among his many books are *The Bible and the Dead Sea Scrolls* (Baylor University Press, 2006), *Resurrection: The Origin and Future of a Biblical Doctrine* (T & T Clark, 2006) and, most recently, *The Good and Evil Serpent* (Yale University Press, 2010), winner of *Christianity Today*'s award for best new work on biblical studies.

Shaye J.D. Cohen is the Littauer Professor of Hebrew Literature and Philosophy in the department of Near Eastern Languages and Civilizations at Harvard University. Before arriving at Harvard in 2001, he was the Ungerleider Professor and Director of Judaic Studies at Brown University. A specialist in the emergence of Rabbinic Judaism, he has written or edited several books and many articles, including *From the Maccabees to the Mishnah: A Profile of Judaism* (Westminster Press, 1987; second edition, 2006) and *The Beginnings of Jewishness* (University of California, 1999).

James D.G. Dunn is Emeritus Lightfoot Professor of Divinity in the department of Theology and Religion at Durham University in England. An expert on the origins and development of the early Christian movement, he has written extensively on the life and mission of Jesus and of the apostle Paul. His more recent works are *Jesus Remembered* (Eerdmans, 2003) and *Beginning from Jerusalem* (Eerdmans, 2009), the first two volumes of the trilogy *Christianity in the Making*, which explores Christianity's beginnings, particularly its first-century C.E. Jewish context.

Louis H. Feldman is Abraham Wouk Family Professor of Classics and Literature at Yeshiva University in New York. He is an authority on Josephus and Josephus scholarship and has written or edited 17 books and numerous articles on the subject. Most recently he wrote *Josephus's Interpretation of the Bible* (University of California Press, 1998) and *Philo's Portrayal of Moses in the Context of Ancient Judaism* (University of Notre Dame Press, 2007). He also published the translation and commentary *Flavius Josephus, Judean Antiquities 1–4* (Brill, 2000).

Isaiah M. Gafni holds the Sol Rosenbloom Chair of Jewish History at the Hebrew University of Jerusalem. He has published extensively in both Hebrew and English on the political, social and religious life of Jews during and after the Second Temple period, both in Palestine and in the Diaspora. His books include *The Jews of Talmudic Babylonia: A Social and Cultural History* (Jerusalem: The Zalman Shazar Center, 1990) and *Land, Center and Diaspora: Jewish Constructs in Late Antiquity* (Sheffield, 1997).

Dennis E. Groh is university chaplain emeritus and retired professor of humanities and archaeology at Illinois Wesleyan University. Formerly, he spent almost three decades as professor of the history of Christianity at Garrett-Evangelical Theological Seminary and The Graduate Faculty of Northwestern University in Evanston, Illinois. A seasoned field archaeologist, he has authored, co-authored or co-edited over a hundred publications, including six books, on the history of early Christianity and the archaeology of the Roman and Byzantine periods in Israel.

Lee I.A. Levine is professor emeritus of Jewish history and archaeology at the Hebrew University of Jerusalem. Among his many publications are *The Rabbinic Class of Roman Palestine* (Jewish Theological Seminary, 1989), *Jerusalem: Portrait of the City in the Second Temple Period (538 B.C.E.–70 C.E.)* (Jewish Publication Society, 2002), *The Ancient Synagogue: The First Thousand Years*, rev. ed. (Yale University Press, 2005) and *Visual Judaism in Late Antiquity: Historical Contexts of Jewish Art* (Yale University Press, forthcoming).

E.P. Sanders is retired Arts and Sciences Professor of Religion at Duke University, specializing in the development of Judaism and Christianity in the Greco-Roman world, with a particular emphasis on the Jewish context of Jesus and the earliest Christians. He is the author of numerous books, including *Judaism: Practice and Belief, 63 B.C.E.–66 C.E.* (SCM Press, 1992), *The Historical Figure of Jesus* (Penguin, 1993) and *Paul: A Very Short Introduction* (Oxford University Press, 2001).

Hershel Shanks is founder and editor of *Biblical Archaeology Review*. He has written numerous books on the Bible and biblical archaeology, including *The Mystery and Meaning of the Dead Sea Scrolls* (Random House, 1998), *Jerusalem's Temple Mount* (Continuum, 2007), *Jerusalem: An Archaeological Biography* (Random House, 1995) and *The City of David: A Guide to Biblical Jerusalem* (Tel Aviv: Bazak, 1973; reprinted many times). A graduate of Harvard Law School, he has also published widely on legal topics. His autobiography, *Freeing the Dead Sea Scrolls and Other Adventures of an Archaeology Outsider*, was published by Continuum in 2010.

Geza Vermes is fellow of the British Academy and director of the Oxford Forum for Qumran Research at the Oxford Centre of Postgraduate Hebrew Studies. He is also professor emeritus of Jewish studies at Oxford University, where he taught from 1965 to 1991. He is the editor of the *Journal of Jewish Studies* and has authored and edited numerous books on both the Dead Sea Scrolls and the Jewish background of the historical Jesus, beginning with *Jesus the Jew* (Fortress Press, 1973) and continuing with his most recent works, *Jesus: Nativity-Passion-Resurrection* (Penguin, 2010) and *The Story of the Scrolls* (Penguin, 2010). His widely-acclaimed *The Complete Dead Sea Scrolls in English*, available in the Penguin Classics series, will celebrate its golden jubilee in 2012.

Abbreviations

AGAJU	***Arbeiten zur Geschichte des Antiken Judentums und des Urchristentums***
AJA	***American Journal of Archaeology***
AJSR	***Association for Jewish Studies Review***
Antiquities	Josephus, ***Antiquities of the Jews***
Apion	Josephus, ***Against Apion***
ANRW	***Augstieg und Niedergang de römischen Welt,*** *H. Temporini and W. Haase, eds.*
ATR	***Anglican Theological Review***
ASOR	American Schools of Oriental Research
BA	***Biblical Archaeologist***
BAR	***Biblical Archaeology Review***
BASOR	***Bulletin of the American Schools of Oriental Research***
BHT	***Beiträge zur historischen Theologie***
BR	***Bible Review***
BS	***Byzantine Studies***
BT	**Babylonian Talmud, or Bavli**
BZNW	***Beihefte zur Zeitschrift für die neutestamentliche Wissenschaft***
CBA	Catholic Biblical Association
CBQ	***Catholic Biblical Quarterly***
CSCO	***Corpus Scriptorum Christianorum Orientalium***
Eccles. Hist.	Eusebius, ***Ecclesiastical History***
EJ	***Encyclopaedia Judaica***
HDR	***Harvard Dissertations in Religion***
HTR	***Harvard Theological Review***
HUCA	***Hebrew Union College Annual***
IEJ	***Israel Exploration Journal***
IES	Israel Exploration Society
JAAR	***Journal of the American Academy of Religion***
JBL	***Journal of Biblical Literature***
JJS	***Journal of Jewish Studies***
JJML	***Journal of Jewish Music and Liturgy***
JPS	Jewish Publication Society
JQR	***Jewish Quarterly Review***
JSJ	***Journal for the Study of Judaism***
JSNT	***Journal for the Study of the New Testament***
JSOT	***Journal for the Study of the Old Testament***
JSP	***Journal for the Study of the Pseudepigrapha***
JSS	***Jewish Social Studies***
JT	**Jerusalem Talmud**, or Yerushalmi (Palestinian Talmud)
JTS	***Journal of Theological Studies***
JTSem	Jewish Theological Seminary
LNTS	***Library of New Testament Studies***
Life	Josephus, ***Life***
Loeb	***Loeb Classical Library*** *(Cambridge, MA: Harvard University Press)*
NEAEHL	***The New Encyclopedia of Archaeological Excavations in the Holy Land,*** 5 vols., ed. Ephraim Stern (Jerusalem: IES and Carta, 1993; vol. 5, 2008)
NPNF	***A Select Library of Nicene and Post-Nicene Fathers,*** *P. Schaff and H. Wace, eds. and trans.*
n.s.	new series
NTTS	***New Testament Tools and Studies***
OEANE	***The Oxford Encyclopedia of Archaeology in the Near East,*** ed. Eric M. Meyers (Oxford: Oxford University Press, 1997)
o.s.	old series
PAAJR	***Proceedings of the American Academy of Jewish Research***
PG	***Patrologia Graeca,*** J. Migne, ed.
PL	***Patrologia Latina,*** J. Migne, ed.
REJ	***Revue des Études Juives***
SBL	Society of Biblical Literature
SC	***The Second Century***
SPCK	**Society for Promoting Christian Knowledge**
Suetonius	***Lives of the [Twelve] Caesars***
TAPA	***Transactions of the American Philological Association***
War	Josephus, ***The Jewish War***
WUNT	***Wissenschaftliche Untersuchungen zum Neuen Testament***
ZNW	***Zeitschrift für die neutestamentliche Wissenschaft***

BRITAIN
ATLANTIC
OCEAN
Rhine R.
GAUL
Lyons
Rhone R.
Milan
Ravenna
SPAIN
ITALY
Adriatic Sea
Rome
Elvira
SICILY
Carthage
Mediterranean
NORTH AFRICA
0
500 mi

THE ROMAN WORLD
Caspian Sea
Black Sea
ARMENIA
BITHYNIA
Chalcedon
Nicaea
PARTHIA
Edessa
ASIA MINOR
Tarsus
Tigris R.
Ephesus
Aphrodisias
Athens
Antioch
Apamea
Dura
Europos
Babylon
Rhodes
SYRIA
Cyprus
Damascus
Euphrates R.
Crete
JUDEA
Jerusalem
Alexandria
SINAI
EGYPT
Oxyrhynchus
Nile R.
ARABIA
Red Sea
Nag Hammadi

Timeline

Roman	Jewish	Christian
Augustus (Octavian), 31 BCE–14 CE	Herod, 37–4 BCE	Jesus, c. 6/4 BCE–30/33 CE
Tiberius, 14–37 CE	Philo, c. 15 BCE–c. 50 CE	Paul, d. c. 62 CE Vision of Jesus, c. 34 CE Mission to gentiles, c. 50 CE
Caligula, 37–41 CE	Agrippa I, 37–44 CE King of Judea, 41–44 CE	
Claudius, 41–54 CE	Agrippa II, 53–mid-90s CE	
Nero, 54–68 CE		Pauline epistles, 50–62 CE
	First Jewish Revolt, 66–70 CE	Gospel of Mark, c. 68 CE
	Destruction of Temple, 70 CE Fall of Masada, 73/74 CE	
Vespasian, 69–79 CE		
	Yoḥanan ben Zakkai Academy of Yavneh, c. 70 CE Beginnings of Rabbinic Judaism	
Titus, 79–81 CE	Josephus, 37–c. 100 CE *Jewish War*, 75–81 CE	Gospels of Matthew, Luke and John, c. 70–100 CE
Domitian, 81–96 CE	Gamaliel II Emergence of patriarchate, c. 90 CE	
Trajan, 98–117 CE	Diaspora revolt, 115–117 CE	
Hadrian, 117–138 CE	Second Jewish Revolt, 132–135 CE Simeon, d. 135 CE Rabbi Akiva, c. 50–135 CE Jerusalem rebuilt as Aelia Capitolina, c. 135 CE Judea becomes Syria-Palestina	*Didache*, c. 2nd century CE
	Academy moved to Galilee, c. 140 CE	Justin Martyr, c. 140–165 CE
Marcus Aurelius, 161–180 CE	Judah ha-Nasi, flourished 175–220 CE Growth of patriarchate	Irenaeus, flourished 175–c. 195 CE

Roman	Jewish	Christian
Severan Dynasty, 193–235 CE		Origen, c. 185–253 CE
	Completion of Mishnah, 200–220 CE	
Decius, 249–251 CE		
	Emergence of rabbinic academies in Babylonia Rav and Samuel, c. 220–250 CE	
Diocletian, 284–305 CE Empire divided into East and West	Galilean synagogues, late 3rd/4th centuries CE	Beginning of monastic movement, late 3rd century CE
		Empirewide persecution of Christians, 305–311 CE
Constantine, 306–337 CE Battle at Milvian Bridge, 312 CE		Eusebius of Caesarea, 260–340 CE *Ecclesiastical History*, 303–324 CE
		"Edict of Milan," 313 CE Religious freedom for Christians
		Christianity declared official religion, 324 CE
Constantius, 337–361 CE	Gallus revolt, 351 CE	Council of Nicaea, 325 CE Nicene Creed Arian Controversy, 318–381 CE
Julian the Apostate, 361–363 CE	Establishment of permanent Jewish calendar—Patriarch Hillel II (c. 359 CE)	Council of Constantinople, 381 CE Doctrine of Trinity John Chrysostom, 354–407 CE
	Julian's abortive attempt to rebuild the Temple, c. 363 CE	St. Augustine, 354–430 CE *The City of God*
Theodosius I, 379–395 CE	Jerusalem Talmud, c. 400 CE	Christianity becomes official religion of empire, 392 CE
		Sack of Rome by Visigoths, 410 CE
	Disappearance of patriarchate, c. 425 CE	Council of Carthage, 419 CE New Testament canon adopted
Justinian, 527–565 CE	Babylonian Talmud, c. 500/600 CE	Council of Chalcedon, 451 CE Nicene Creed acknowledged Definition of Faith
MUSLIM CONQUEST, 634–640 CE		

Acknowledgments

CREATING THE SECOND EDITION OF *CHRISTIANITY AND RABBINIC Judaism*, which is appearing nearly 20 years after the book's initial publication, represented a major scholarly and editorial challenge. For the contributing scholars, their already masterfully written and researched chapters had to be updated to incorporate the most important finds and insights from the past two decades of archaeological and historical research. We are especially grateful to Professor James D.G. Dunn, who appears in this edition for the first time, for his wholly new treatment of Chapter III.

The task before the book's editors and designers was no less daunting, having to manage the editing and inclusion of so much new material while maintaining the quality and readability that made the first edition such a success.

Biblical Archaeology Society president and *Biblical Archaeology Review* publisher Susan Laden laid the groundwork for this project and skillfully guided it from start to finish. The overall editing of the volume was ably handled by *BAR* assistant editor G. Joseph Corbett. He was assisted by *BAR* administrative editor Bonnie Mullin who communicated with authors, answered questions and proofed and edited the book's extensive endnotes. Thanks also go to *BAR* managing editor Dorothy D. Resig who produced the informative maps that have been included in this new edition, as well as to production manager Heather Metzger who oversaw the final stages of the book's publication. All were supported in their efforts by Connie Binder who was responsible for the book's indexing. Finally, the book's design and layout is the work of Rob Sugar and his staff at AURAS Design, especially Andrew Chapman. My thanks to all for making this second edition such a stellar accomplishment.

Hershel Shanks

Foreword

WHAT IS HERE PRESENTED TO THE PUBLIC IS AN INVITATION TO ruminate on the larger themes of history. It is an ongoing task. This is now the second edition of this widely used book, appearing nearly two decades after the first edition was published. I suspect in another two decades it will need updating again—and probably even earlier than that.

No single scholar could have written this book. No single scholar controls the vast and often arcane sources that comprise its subjects. Typically, Jewish history and Christian history are taught by different teachers; they are even considered different disciplines. As Oxford don Geza Vermes points out in his introduction, this book is unique; it is a parallel history of early Christianity and Rabbinic Judaism, an attempt to trace their stories side by side. This is what beckons us to ruminate on larger questions.

Paradoxically, these two stories have a common source; they grew out of the same soil—Second Temple Judaism. Yet their stories are very different. No figure in Rabbinic Judaism is as central to it as Jesus is to Christianity. A chapter in this book is devoted to the life of Jesus. There is no comparable chapter on a figure in Rabbinic Judaism.

Judaism started out as a nation in this story; it twice rebelled against its Roman overlords; twice it was defeated. Early Christians sometimes suffered persecution, but there is no comparable strand of Christian history.

Christianity started out as a little, off-beat Jewish sect—and conquered the West. Judaism, from being a nation, became a tiny minority in larger, often hostile cultures.

For Christianity, the questions were of doctrine and institutionalization; for Judaism, of adapting for survival as a people without a place. No wonder their histories—their stories—are so very different. No wonder they took such divergent paths.

Even the sources are very different. Rabbinic Judaism can point to nothing parallel to the Gospels or Paul's letters. The Mishnah and the Talmudim are not only very different from the earliest Christian documents, but they were compiled much later. And they are methodologically so arcane that it takes years of study to penetrate them competently—something few scholars of Christian history have done. The patristic literature of Christianity is also unique. Few scholars of Jewish history control this vast literature which, simply in its quantity, threatens to overwhelm us.

All this cannot help but make us stop and puzzle over how to achieve an understanding of the critical early centuries of Rabbinic Judaism and Christianity. This book—parallel histories—is not simply a compendium of summaries and generalizations. Here the reader will find the details, too, the basic evidence (and, for the student who wishes to pursue any particular subject, the references and citations).

As I again studied, chapter by chapter, each of the new chapters as they came in with their fresh material and revisions for this second edition, I had renewed respect for each of the authors. Each of these chapters is a little gem, a book in itself, a concise but detailed and authoritative treatment of its subject. Again and again, I was astounded at the erudition—at the capacity of these senior scholars to control all the details, yet tie all the strings together in a meaningful whole.

On the other hand, we have worked very hard to make these sometimes recondite stories as understandable and readable as possible. For this I must also express gratitude to the authors for their long and sometimes lonely labors—and for their patience and understanding when we continued to request clarification and, sometimes, simplification. I hope they—and, more importantly, the reader—will agree that the result has been worth all the effort.

Hershel Shanks
July 2011
Washington, D.C.

Introduction
Parallel History Preview

Geza Vermes

THIS COLLECTIVE ENTERPRISE, A PARALLEL HISTORY OF JUDAISM and Christianity that covers a period of over six centuries crucial to the development of both, is unprecedented in the annals of scholarship. Histories of the Jews of early Christianity abound at every level, from the rudimentary to the highly sophisticated, but so far no one has attempted to set out, side by side, two autonomous accounts, written by leading experts for the benefit of all, the learned and the learner alike. It is my great privilege to offer here a preview and a foretaste of the chapters that follow. Being myself a student of Judaism, I will be judging matters primarily from a Jewish historical vantage point; the balance will be provided by a Christian overview at the end of the volume (Chapter IX).

It should be observed that during the opening decades of the period surveyed, say until the middle of the first century C.E., no *parallel* history is conceivable because it was only then that Christianity began to appear as distinct from Judaism, especially because of the larger number of gentiles among its ranks. This was well after the death of Jesus, who was crucified about 30 C.E. Indeed, even the Judaism—or as it is nowadays fashionable to say, the Judaisms—of the first 70 years of the common era (outlined by Professor Louis H. Feldman in Chapter I) was (or were) different from that based on the Mishnah and the Talmud because of the then-prevailing multiparty religious system. First-century Pharisees, Sadducees, Essenes, etc., seem to have coexisted in a spirit of tolerant hostility in clear contrast to the progressively standardized "orthodoxy" of later ages. Also, if the often asserted claim that before its destruction in 70 C.E. the Temple of Jerusalem was the "central focus of the Jewish religion" is accepted as true (in fact, for most Jews living beyond easy reach of the Holy City, the Temple was more an idea than a tangible reality), the sanctuaryless Judaism of the post-destruction, rabbinic age must be seen in practice as a fresh departure.

Jesus of Nazareth belonged to pre-orthodox Judaism, not to "Christianity." I find Professor E.P. Sanders's Chapter II, outlining Jesus' life and message, to be both judicious and informative, but I do not expect conservative Christians to agree with the definition of Jesus as a Jewish charismatic prophet, healer and teacher, though this description is very close to that of the first-century Jewish historian Flavius Josephus, who described Jesus as a "wise man" and a "performer of paradoxical deeds" (*Antiquities* 18.63). Unlike many of his fellow New Testament scholars, Sanders believes that a great deal can be discovered in the Gospels about the historical Jesus "if we are content with a broad outline"—for example, that he was associated with John the Baptist, was accompanied by disciples, expected the "kingdom," went from Galilee to Jerusalem, threatened the Temple and soon thereafter was tried and crucified. Professor Sanders interprets the episode of Jesus' overturning the money-changers and merchants' tables as an actual attack on the Temple, but it could just as well have been the instinctive reaction of a hot-blooded rural Galilean holy man at the sight and sound—in sacred precincts—of what must have resembled a Levantine bazaar. In other words, if Jesus was responsible for an affray in the Temple court, it was probably inspired, not by hostility, but by reverence for the "house of God."

The spread of Christianity from Jerusalem to Rome during the years 30–70 C.E. is brilliantly outlined by James D.G. Dunn in Chapter III. The chapter offers a critical presentation of the information garnered from the Acts of the Apostles, the letters of Paul and the epistle of James. Dunn sketches first the emergence of the nascent church community centered on Jerusalem, which still exhibited all the Jewish characteristics of behavior and worship characteristic of the period, including participation in Temple cult. Common Jewish religiosity was accompanied by the peculiar institutions of the Jesus movement: the initiation rite of baptism, the Thanksgiving meal and life out of a common purse administered by the apostles, not unlike the religious communism practiced by the Essenes.

The bulk of the chapter is devoted to the spread of Christianity throughout the Holy Land, especially among Jews, with the occasional admission of gentiles. After Paul's joining the community, however, the new religion spread among non-Jews in Antioch in Syria and, as Paul undertook his missionary journeys, to the cities of Asia Minor and Greece. Professor Dunn displays an admirable critical grasp of Paul's teaching, which laid the foundation of the gentile church beyond the boundaries of Judea and Galilee, ensuring its survival after the death of Paul and the destruction of Judaism's central symbol, the Temple. Seventy C.E. marked the demise of the Judeo-Christian church and Jerusalem's role as the mother community of the infant movement. Thereafter, as James Dunn aptly remarks, the Jewishness of Christianity was lost largely by default.

Jewish history from the destruction of Jerusalem to the defeat of the Bar-Kokhba Revolt (70–135 C.E.) is discussed in Chapter IV by Professor Lee I.A. Levine. He correctly observes that the lost war against Rome hurt but did not break Judaism, and analyzes the non-rabbinic writings dating to the late first or early second century C.E.—the Apocalypse of Baruch, 4 Ezra and pseudo-Philo's *Book of Biblical Antiquities*—before turning to the work of Yoḥanan ben Zakkai and the assembly of the sages at Yavneh which resulted in the swift and successful restructuring of Jewish religious life in conformity with the new circumstances created by the sack of the Temple by the Romans. Such a smooth reorganization would be hard to understand if the cultic worship in Jerusalem had genuinely played as important a part in real Jewish life as many scholars presume.

The history of the Church from the fall of Jerusalem in 70 C.E. to the conversion of Constantine to Christianity (312 C.E.) is the subject of a well-documented presentation by Professor Harold W. Attridge in Chapter V. Starting with the non-Pauline New Testament documents and continuing with second-century polemical authors (pseudo-Barnabas, Justin Martyr and Bishop Melito of Sardis), Attridge explains that one of the paramount aims of Christianity was to define itself against Judaism. It was claimed not only that the Church inherited all the divine promises and privileges formerly granted to Israel, but also that Jewish rejection was foreseen and predicted by the biblical prophets. In the course of the second century, the heresy of Gnosticism was confronted and overcome, and subsequently, during the late second and early third centuries, the great Alexandrian church fathers—Clement and Origen—set out to lay the teaching of the Gospels on philosophical foundations that eventually gave birth to a thoroughly Hellenized Christian theology. Prior to triumphing over pagan Rome, Christians shared the experience of religious persecution and martyrdom, as did the Jews in the age of the Maccabees in the 160s B.C.E. and under Hadrian during and after the Bar-Kokhba Revolt in the 130s C.E. But the suffering inflicted on the Church by the last Roman imperial persecutors—Decius, Diocletian and Galerius, in the second half of the third and at the beginning of the fourth centuries—was soon overshadowed by the power and glory of the Christian empire inaugurated by Constantine the Great.

The period between the defeat of Bar-Kokhba (135 C.E.) and the death of Rabbi Judah the Patriarch (c. 220 C.E.) saw the reorganization of Jewish life in Galilee. The presence of Jews was no longer welcome in Judea, renamed Syro-Palestina, and Jerusalem was transformed by the victorious emperor Hadrian into a pagan city called Aelia Capitolina. This period saw not only the strengthening of the patriarchate to head the communal rabbis and represent Jewry before the imperial authorities, but also the compilation of the Mishnah in six orders, or divisions, and 63 tractates. This complex of topics is succinctly but powerfully sketched by Professor Shaye J.D. Cohen in Chapter VI. He seeks to navigate a middle course among the conflicting theories regarding the nature of the Mishnah. Discarding the traditional but superficial definition of it as a law code, and the recent theory that it is essentially the expression of a philosophical worldview, Cohen sees in the Mishnah a radically new venture, a book of laws containing conflicting opinions attributed to named sages without, as a rule, any reference to the Bible, and apparently bestowing complete autonomy on human reason. The main problem with such a thesis, as Professor Cohen himself realizes, is that the same Mishnaic rabbis, when they comment on the Torah, or are quoted in the Talmud, do not seem to agree with it.

The development of a literary formulation of Jewish law and lore, which began with the Mishnah around 200 C.E., was further pursued during the subsequent four centuries in Palestine and Babylonia and resulted in the Jerusalem, or Palestinian, Talmud (c. 400 C.E.), the Babylonian Talmud (c. sixth century) and the early Bible commentaries dating to approximately the same period. These are outlined in Chapter VII by Professor Isaiah M. Gafni, together with what is known of the history of the Jewish people during the talmudic age. By that time, Christians had become demographically significant, so much so that in the sixth century they formed the majority of the population of the land of Israel. Jewish sources sporadically include polemics thought to be directed against Christian teachings. Rabbi Abbahu of Caesarea in particular is seen as inserting anti-Christian twists into his interpretation of the Bible. But the main topic of the chapter is the study of anti-Jewish legislation in the Christian Roman Empire prohibiting mixed marriages, Christian participation in synagogue worship, the building and restoring of synagogues and pressure by Jewish authorities on would-be converts to Christianity. With the political upheavals in the Roman-Byzantine world, Jewish messianic expectation was reborn, whereas the Jews in Mesopotamia remained satisfied with Persia and accepted the secular "law of the kingdom." Apparently they even occasionally managed to persuade Christians to embrace Judaism, and there was little concern about conversion in the opposite direction.

The age from Constantine to the Arab conquest (312–640 C.E.), expertly portrayed by Professor Dennis E. Groh in Chapter VIII, saw within the Christian Church a series of major doctrinal conflicts relating to fine theological distinctions concerning the nature of the divine Christ. Propounders of heresies, Arius and Nestorius, were fought by ecclesiastical dignitaries, Athanasius and Cyril of Alexandria, and in councils of bishops at Nicaea (325 C.E.) and Chalcedon (451 C.E.). Christian monasticism flourished, and great theologians, among them Augustine of Hippo in North Africa and Jerome, translator of the Bible into Latin—after learning Hebrew from a rabbi in Lydda (Lod)—and outstanding Greek church fathers, erected the monumental edifice of theology. John Chrysostom was fulminating against the Jews in Antioch and Constantinople; but in Palestine, despite hostile imperial legislation and the anti-Jewish preaching of bishops, splendid synagogues with beautiful mosaic floors continued to be constructed. In the West, Roman power gave way before a barbarian onslaught; and in the East, the armies of Islam curtailed the power of Byzantium.

By the time this parallel history ends, Christianity and Judaism are definitely two distinct and distant religions.

A bird's-eye view of these 600 years of Jewish and Christian history, concerned first and foremost with mutual contacts and attitudes, cannot fail to note some curious but significant phenomena.

First, the relationship between Judaism and Christianity is not fully reciprocal. This is of course easy to understand; Judaism is fully comprehensible in itself, whereas Christianity, originally a Jewish religious subgroup, by necessity had to define itself *against*, and distance itself from, Judaism.

Second, this basic inequality is manifest throughout the various periods surveyed in this volume. The earlier layers of rabbinic literature, now that the myth of the specifically anti-Christian intent of the late first-century C.E. curse of the heretics (*minim*) in the synagogal prayer (*Amidah*) is revealed for what it is, contain no statements against, indeed hardly any allusion to, Christianity. Christianity, definitely in its gentile form, seems to touch Jewish consciousness only from the third, and especially the fourth, century onward, by which time it was fast becoming the official religion of the Roman Empire. Open and deliberate doctrinal conflict on the Jewish side had to wait until the Middle Ages, whether in the form of the crude and popular caricature of the Gospel story in the various versions of the *Toledot Yeshu* (Life of Jesus) or in the theological and philosophical polemics of a higher order.

Third, apart from such theologically nonsensitive matters as the identity of the plant (gourd or ivy) under which Jonah sat (Jonah 4:6)—on which an early fifth-century bishop of Oca in Libya was happy to consult the Jews according to a letter of Jerome to Augustine—a civilized and peaceful dialogue is a post-Holocaust phenomenon. A collaborative venture such as this parallel history would have been inconceivable even half a century ago. It is a remarkable achievement.

To finish on a lighter note, an anecdote recorded in the Babylonian Talmud (*Menahot* 29b) portrays Moses as seeking permission from God to attend in spirit a lecture given by Rabbi Akiva. He is allowed to slip into the classroom and sit inconspicuously in the back row. There he listens attentively to the exposition and the lively questions and answers, but Moses has absolutely no idea what the teachers and pupils are talking about until Akiva discloses that he is expounding a *halakhah* (legal teaching) brought down by Moses from Mount Sinai.

One may well wonder whether Jesus of Nazareth would have been equally dumbfounded had he been given a similar chance to eavesdrop incognito on the sessions of the Council of Nicaea where his nature was the subject of much heated debate.

ONE

Palestinian and Diaspora Judaism in the First Century

LOUIS H. FELDMAN

PERHAPS NO CENTURY IN THE ENTIRE HISTORY OF JUDAISM SAW more revolutionary changes than the first century of the common era. In this relatively short period of time two great religions developed—Rabbinic Judaism and Christianity. During this period the man Christians consider the Son of God lived and was crucified. During this period his greatest apostle wrote the canonical epistles to struggling new churches. During this period the Jewish Temple was destroyed. With the destruction, major changes occurred in the role of the high priests. Apocalypticism, proselytism and sectarianism, all of which had flourished before the destruction of the Temple, declined. This period also produced the two most outstanding Hellenistic Jewish writers—the philosopher Philo and the historian Josephus. Finally, this period laid the foundations for the Jewish academies that debated the law and ultimately led to its codification in the greatest Jewish work since the Bible—the Talmud.

In this chapter, we shall examine the political, economic, social, religious and cultural factors that lie behind these developments, as well as the events that presaged them, both in Palestine and in the Diaspora.

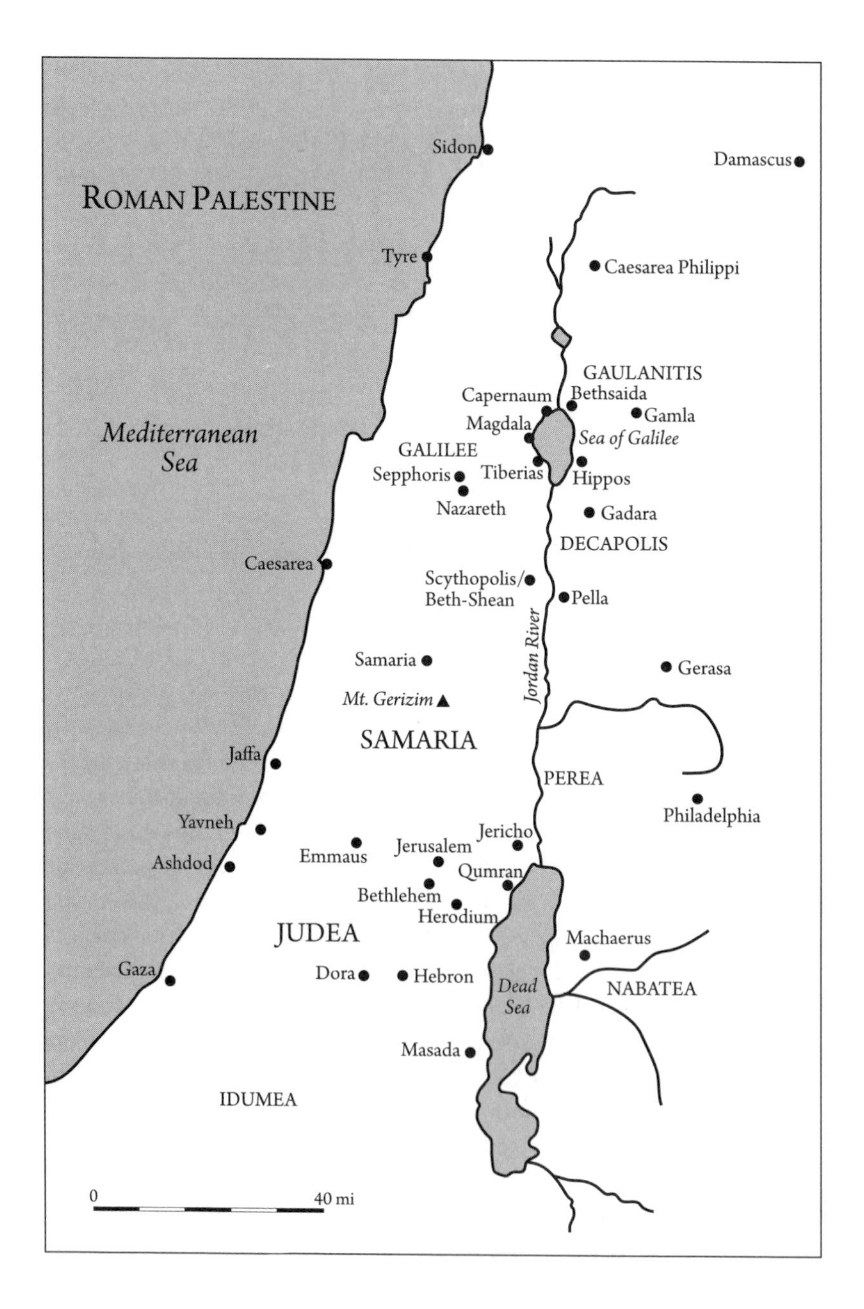
ROMAN PALESTINE
Sidon
Damascus
Tyre
Caesarea Philippi
GAULANITIS
Capernaum
Bethsaida
Gamla
Magdala
Sea of Galilee
Mediterranean Sea
GALILEE
Sepphoris
Tiberias
Hippos
Nazareth
Gadara
DECAPOLIS
Caesarea
Scythopolis/ Beth-Shean
Pella
Jordan River
Samaria
Gerasa
Mt. Gerizim
SAMARIA
Jaffa
PEREA
Philadelphia
Yavneh
Jericho
Emmaus
Jerusalem
Ashdod
Qumran
Bethlehem
Herodium
JUDEA
Machaerus
Gaza
Dora
Hebron
Dead Sea
NABATEA
Masada
IDUMEA
0
40 mi

I. The Palestinian World

The political background: The Augustan age

After a century of almost continuous civil strife, Rome finally achieved what historians call the *Pax Augusta*, or *Pax Romana* ("The Roman Peace"). Under the emperor Augustus (he called himself *Princeps*, that is, "First Citizen"), who ruled from 31 B.C.E. to 14 C.E., the empire (except for the Jews) enjoyed a measure of tranquility that lasted for two centuries. Augustus was a kind of preview of Napoleon after the French Revolution. His contemporaries looked upon him as a benefactor, deliverer, savior, almost messiah.[1]

At the time, Judea was considerably smaller than the present state of Israel. Herod (his father Antipater was Idumean, his mother may have been Nabatean), whose long reign lasted from 37 to 4 B.C.E., had brought relative peace and prosperity to the tiny principality. Visitors to present-day Israel will see ample evidence of Herod's building activities—at Jericho, Masada, Caesarea and, above all, Jerusalem, where he solved the problem of unemployment by establishing a kind of WPA, giving employment to thousands of workers who completely rebuilt the Temple. Ironically, it was a king of non-Jewish descent who rebuilt the Temple. According to the fourth-century church father Epiphanius, Herod himself was believed by some to be the Messiah. His popularity was doubtless due in part to the strong-arm measures he instituted to deal with muggers who roamed the city streets as well as the countryside—evidence of considerable social unrest. Herod made it safe for senior citizens to walk the streets at night.[2]

To be sure, Herod's personal problems would have required a team of psychiatrists. In the end, he ordered his wife Mariamne, her brother Aristobulus, her mother, Alexandra, and his two sons by Mariamne, Alexander and Aristobulus, to be killed. He also resisted the advances of the notorious Cleopatra.[3] Yet he managed to win the confidence of such excellent and diverse judges of responsible administration as Julius Caesar, Marc Antony, the Roman general Agrippa and Augustus himself. Indeed, considering the uprisings that broke out in Palestine after his death, we may well conclude that his repressive policies actually saved thousands of lives and preserved the Jewish state from extinction for a century.

When Herod died, his kingdom was divided among three of his sons. The major part, consisting of Judea, Samaria and Idumea, was bequeathed to Archelaus, his son by a Samaritan woman.[4] Archelaus so antagonized both his Jewish and Samaritan subjects that they complained to the Roman emperor. As a result, he was deposed and Judea was organized as a Roman province

(6 C.E.) under a Roman procurator, who, in turn, was under the jurisdiction of the governor of Syria.[5]

Syria was a key Roman province in the East, responsible for protecting the border with Rome's greatest and most persistent rival throughout the next centuries, Parthia (Persia). The governor of Syria was often the most distinguished of the Roman emperor's administrators. The inhabitants of his province could expect careful and fair consideration of their complaints by a man who had considerable clout even in the halls of the emperor in Rome.

The procurators of Judea, however, were neither so fair, nor so talented. One of them, Tiberius Julius Alexander (born 14/16 C.E.), was even an apostate Jew,[6] a fact that hardly ingratiated him with his Jewish subjects. Between 6 C.E., when Judea became a Roman province, and 66 C.E., when the First Jewish Revolt against Rome broke out, there were 14 Roman procurators, who served for an average of only four years. Obviously they often suffered from lack of experience, but if this were not bad enough, they also sought to make money during their brief incumbency by accepting bribes.

The most notorious of these procurators, Pontius Pilate, remained in office for ten years (26–36 C.E.), a tribute either to his efficiency or to Tiberius's deliberate policy not to replace administrators lest the new ones sap the economic strength of the province.[7] The last of the procurators, Gessius Florus (64–66 C.E.), was friendlier to the more Hellenized urban non-Jews than to those Jews who were concentrated in the farming areas and the small towns of Judea. The Roman historian Tacitus, who was no friend of the Jews, tells us that the Jews' patience lasted until Gessius Florus became procurator.[8] After Gessius Florus, the revolt broke out.

The rule of the procurators was interrupted briefly—between 41 and 44 C.E.—when the kingship of Judea was given to Herod's grandson, Agrippa I, who had helped Claudius to become emperor.[9] Because of his connections in Rome, Agrippa was apparently regarded as the leading vassal king in the East. When he attempted to convene a number of other petty rulers in Tiberias, however, the Roman governor of Syria, Marsus, was quick to break up the conference,[10] presumably because he suspected they might revolt or join the great national enemy of the Romans to the east, the Parthians. Shortly thereafter Agrippa died.[11] Some suspect that the Romans poisoned him—with arsenic, the standard poison of the time. The Romans were presumably uneasy about his great popularity with both the rabbis[12] and the masses. Agrippa was not only generous to the people, he also scrupulously observed the tenets of Judaism.[13]

One source of tension between the Jews and the Romans stemmed from a frequent request by the Jews for a limited autonomy equal to that of non-Jews.

This issue arose both in Caesarea on the Mediterranean coast of Palestine and in Alexandria in Egypt. Non-Jews regularly opposed this request; indeed, it was clashes between the Jews and non-Jews in Caesarea over this issue that sparked the Great Jewish Revolt against Rome in 66 C.E.

An additional factor that fueled the Jewish revolutionaries was the gradual assumption of political power in Rome by anti-Jewish freedmen of Greek origin. They gave aid and comfort to the non-Jewish elements in their strife with Jews in cities such as Caesarea.[14]

The economic background of the Jewish revolt against Rome

Since the time of Julius Caesar (100–44 B.C.E.), the Jews had been granted special privileges—exemption from quartering troops, exemption from military service, exemption from worshiping the emperor, permission to assemble and reduction of taxes. One may well wonder why the Jews of Palestine should have revolted against the Romans. Josephus places the chief blame on the Fourth Philosophy,[15] a movement that started in 6 C.E. in opposition to a tax on property in Judea instituted by Quirinius, the Roman governor of Syria. The followers of the Fourth Philosophy proclaimed that they could accept the overlordship of no one except God himself.

Other economic factors also played a role.[16] The Temple collected vast sums of money each year from Jews throughout the world and was a veritable bank, supporting large projects and giving employment to thousands. When the Temple rebuilding project (instituted much earlier by Herod the Great) was completed in 64 C.E., all the people who worked on it were thrown out of work. Unrest soon followed.

Moreover, the high priests, usually lackeys of the Romans, sent slaves to collect tithes and even beat people with staves when they failed to pay.[17]

Other economic factors were also significant in triggering the revolt. The heavy burden of taxation became even greater as a result of the extravagance of Agrippa I (41–44 C.E.). Strife developed between the owners of large estates and the landless. Poorer Jews hated wealthier Jews who had befriended the Romans, especially absentee landlords who exploited lowly Galilean peasants.[18] One of the first acts of the revolutionaries when the revolt broke out was to burn the records of debts.[19] Pervasive poverty was aggravated by restriction of the average Jewish peasant's holding, resulting from the vast increase in population. The struggle for cultivatable land became intense. Josephus tells us that there were 204 cities and villages in the Galilee,[20] the smallest of which had 15,000 inhabitants,[21] indicating a total of at least three million people. He also tells us that 1,100,000 Jews were killed in the revolt.[22] Though these figures may be vastly exaggerated, they nevertheless give some

ZEV RADOVAN/WWW.BIBLELANDPICTURES.COM

Coin of the First Jewish Revolt. *Minted by Jews who revolted against Roman rule in 66 C.E., the coin's obverse bears a chalice and the value—a half-shekel. Above the chalice are the letters* shin *and* bet. Shin *stands for* shenat, *or year (in the construct form);* bet, *the second letter of the Hebrew alphabet, has the numerical value 2. The letters date the coin to the second year of the insurrection, or 68 C.E. The other side of the coin depicts either a stem with three pomegranates or, as others have argued, the blossoming of Aaron's staff (Numbers 17:8). Surrounding the image are the words "Jerusalem the Holy" written in archaic Hebrew characters.*

indication of a great growth in population from the time when the Jews returned from the Babylonian captivity in the sixth century B.C.E.

But the dissatisfaction with Roman rule was not restricted to the lower classes. This is reflected in the fact that the aristocratic Jewish leaders refused to identify the culprits who had insulted the procurator Gessius Florus by passing around a basket as if they were begging on his behalf,[23] and in the fact that Florus loosed his soldiers against the upper classes with particular severity.[24]

Strangely enough, there is reason to believe that the economic situation in Judea actually improved during the first century, certainly for the inhabitants of Jerusalem. If nothing else, the fact that so many Jews—according to Josephus, at the outbreak of the revolt there were 2,556,000 Jews in Jerusalem[25]—came to Jerusalem and stayed for considerable periods of time indicates a tremendous tourist trade. Moreover, the outstanding success of Jewish proselytism meant that vast sums of money continued to pour into the Temple for all kinds of capital improvements.

The religious background of the revolt

We know of at least two instances in the first century when the Romans offended Jewish religious sensibilities by attempting to bring into Jerusalem busts of the emperor attached to military standards, once during the procuratorship of Pontius Pilate (c. 26 C.E.)[26] and again during the governorship of Vitellius (37 C.E.).[27] On another occasion (40 C.E.), the Roman authorities tried to place a statue of the emperor Caligula in the Temple.[28] In each case, the vigorous protests of the Jews forced the authorities to rescind the orders. But the insult lingered.

The Jews were also in constant conflict with the Samaritans.*[29] The Samaritans not only had a different text of the Torah, but they did not accept the books of the Prophets nor the third segment of the Hebrew Bible, known as the Writings. The Samaritans also refused to recognize the Oral Torah (the rules that ultimately became codified in writing in the Talmud), and they had a different calendar. Finally, the sacred mountain the Samaritans recognized was Mount Gerizim, not the Temple Mount in Jerusalem.† The bitterness between Jews and Samaritans was exacerbated when the Roman procurator Cumanus (48–52 C.E.), having been bribed by the Samaritans, failed to take action when some Jews on their way to Jerusalem for a religious festival were attacked by Samaritans. Similar incidents between the two groups could be multiplied.

Moreover, the high priests provided the Jews with no real religious leadership.[30] Since the Persian control of Palestine in the sixth century B.C.E., the high priesthood had become simply a political plum. In the Roman period, it was dominated by a few families, closely supervised by the Romans. Moreover, there was little continuity, as high priests were constantly being replaced. Tension existed even between the high priests and ordinary priests. Significantly, one of the first acts of the revolutionary Zealots when they occupied the Temple during the First Jewish Revolt against Rome was to choose by lot a high priest.[31]

The rise of messianism also contributed to Roman uneasiness during this period.[32] The first messianic claimant of whom we hear is the infamous Herod, as already noted. Suetonius[33] and Tacitus,[34] as well as Josephus,[35] mention a widespread messianic-like belief that a man, or men, coming from Judea would rule the world. The Romans were particularly wary of charismatic, messianic-like leaders who managed to attract large crowds. The fact that huge crowds came to Jerusalem for the three pilgrimage festivals (Passover, Weeks and Tabernacles) provided ample opportunity for charismatic leaders to cause trouble for the Romans (according to Josephus, as we have noted, there were more than 2.5 million people in Jerusalem at Passover when

* See Richard Pummer, "The Samaritans: A Jewish Offshoot or a Pagan Cult?" *BR*, October 1991.

† Yitzhak Magen, "Bells, Pendants, Snakes & Stones: A Samaritan Temple to the Lord on Mt. Gerizim," *BAR*, November/December 2010.

the revolt broke out).[36] According to Josephus, in about 44 C.E., a certain Theudas professed to be a prophet and persuaded masses of people to take up their possessions and follow him to the Jordan River,[37] which, he asserted, would part at his command. The Roman procurator Fadus slew Theudas and many of his followers.

The events surrounding Jesus' death would seem to be somewhat similar. The first question put to Jesus after his resurrection, according to Acts 1:6, was whether he would restore the kingdom to Israel, that is, whether he would create a state independent of the Romans.

The vast expansion of Judaism through proselytism may also have made the Romans nervous that their ancestral religion would be overwhelmed. According to Baron, who bases his estimate on biblical and archaeological data, Judea in 586 B.C.E., prior to the destruction of the First Temple, had no more than 150,000 Jews. By the middle of the first century C.E., he estimates, the world Jewish population had risen to about eight million, with approximately two to three million living in Palestine.[38] Even if these figures are inflated, it is clear that the increase in Jews throughout the empire could not have been achieved by natural birthrate alone.

Religious developments in Palestine

Before the Roman destruction of Jerusalem in 70 C.E., the central focus of the Jewish religion was the Temple.[39] It was much more than a religious symbol; it was also a powerful economic force, as we know from the fact that it was plundered of its riches from time to time. Jews throughout the world annually contributed vast sums to the Temple. Not surprisingly, the various revolutionary groups contended for control of it during the revolt against Rome.

The high priest, as the person in charge of the Temple, had great power. From a social and economic point of view, Josephus is quite justified in calling the government of Judea a theocracy,[40] a term which, incidentally, he apparently invented. After the reigns of Herod and Archelaus, Josephus tells us, "the high priests were entrusted with the leadership of the nation."[41] Nonetheless, in 59 C.E., bitter enmity between the high priests, on the one hand, and the ordinary priests and the populace of Jerusalem, on the other, erupted in ugly violence.[42]

The supreme political, religious and judicial body of the Jews in Palestine was the Sanhedrin (from the Greek *synedrion*, "a sitting together," or "session").[43] According to the Mishnah, a collection of debates on Jewish religious law assembled in about 200 C.E., the Sanhedrin had jurisdiction in trials of tribes, false prophets and false priests, as well as a number of other matters;[44] it could declare that a scholar was rebellious and it could choose a king or a high priest.[45] Whether this is a description of an ideal Sanhedrin or whether the Sanhedrin actually exercised all these functions is a matter of scholarly debate.[46]

Another scholarly dispute concerns the composition of the Sanhedrin. According to rabbinic sources,[47] the Sanhedrin was composed of Pharisaic scholars headed by the two foremost among them, the *nasi* (administrative or legislative head) and the *av beth din* (judicial head). In the Gospels (Matthew 26:57ff.; Mark 14:53ff.; Luke 22:54), the Sanhedrin is said to be headed by the high priest. Numerous other discrepancies exist between the description of the Sanhedrin in the Gospels and in rabbinic sources: In the Gospels (Mark 14:53; Matthew 26:57–58; Luke 22:54; John 18:13,24), the Sanhedrin met in the home of the high priest; the rabbinic sources (Mishnah *Sanhedrin* 11:2) indicate that it met in the Chamber of Hewn Stone. In the Gospels (Mark 14:53–54; Matthew 26:57ff., 27:1–2), it tried Jesus at night; in the rabbinic sources (Mishnah *Sanhedrin* 4:1), the Sanhedrin was not allowed to try criminal cases at night. According to Mark (14:64), Jesus was convicted on the same day he was tried; according to the Mishnah (*Sanhedrin* 4:1), in capital cases it was not permissible for a verdict of guilty to be reached on the same day. According to the Gospels (Matthew 26:64-65; Mark 14:62–63; Luke 22:70–71), Jesus was convicted on his own testimony; according to rabbinic law (Tosefta *Sanhedrin* 11:1), a person may not be convicted by his own testimony.

One solution to these discrepancies is to deny the historicity of the Gospel accounts; indeed, the Gospel of John says nothing about an assembly of the Sanhedrin and declares that the Sanhedrin lacked jurisdiction to put anyone to death (John 18:31). According to Josephus, however, in 62 C.E. the Sanhedrin did order the execution of James, the brother of Jesus.[48]

Another solution is to stress that the Mishnah, which is our earliest rabbinic source [See "The Rabbinic Sources," pp. 10–11], is a Pharisaic work dating to the end of the second century. Some of the high priests in the first century, it is argued, were Sadducean,[49] and the membership of the Sanhedrin (at least according to Acts 23:6) was composed in part of Pharisees and in part of Sadducees. According to this view, the trial of Jesus was conducted in conformity with Sadducean law, rather than Pharisaic law. Still another solution suggests that the Sanhedrin mentioned in the Gospels justified its violation of the rules of procedure by appealing to the principle that this was permitted in cases of emergency. Still another solution postulates two Sanhedrins, one political and one religious.[50] Or the Sanhedrin before which Jesus appeared may have acted simply in an advisory capacity to Roman authority.[51]

The Rabbinic Sources

There are no written rabbinic sources dating from the first century. The oldest extant code of Jewish law is the Mishnah, edited about 200 C.E. by Rabbi Judah the Prince. It is a legal code of 63 tractates, dealing with agricultural matters, with the law of persons and property, with legal procedure and with ritual. Accordingly, we should not expect and, indeed, do not find, except very incidentally, references to contemporary or historical events. The same is true of the Tosefta, a supplementary collection of interpretations of the Oral Torah (of which the Mishnah is the core). The Tosefta was edited, according to tradition, by Rabbi Hiyya bar Abba, a pupil of Judah the Prince, but it never achieved the status of the Mishnah. Of the rabbis who are most frequently quoted in both the Mishnah and the Tosefta, the overwhelming majority date from the second century.[1]

The traditional Jewish view of the Mishnah is that it is part of a divinely revealed Oral Law, which is to be interpreted as part of a chain of tradition culminating in rabbinic discussions called the Gemara. Jacob Neusner has challenged the usefulness of the Mishnah as a historical source for any period prior to its completion in about 200 C.E.[2] He has argued vigorously that the Mishnah is to be viewed as an independent work by a small group of men, reflecting the age in which it was composed, and that the views ascribed to various rabbis are to be viewed not as those of the rabbis but rather as those of the redactors (editors).

The rabbinic discussions based on the Mishnah and known as the Gemara originated in both Palestine and Babylonia. The Palestinian Gemara was eventually edited about 400 C.E.; it constitutes, together with the Mishnah itself, the Jerusalem Talmud. The Palestinian Gemara on most but not all of the 63 tractates of the Mishnah has been preserved. The same is true of the Babylonian Gemara, which was edited about 500 C.E. and which, together with the Mishnah, constitutes the Babylonian Talmud.[3] The Gemara in the Babylonian Talmud is fuller than that in the Jerusalem Talmud, and there are even more digressions, but there is little pertaining to historical or contemporary events.

Rabbinic tradition of a homiletic type known as *midrash* (plural, *midrashim*) consists of exegesis of biblical passages. Forerunners of *midrash* are found in the commentaries discovered among the Dead Sea Scrolls. The golden age of *midrashim* begins with *Genesis Rabbah*, which was not edited until perhaps the fifth century.[4] Many midrashic elements are, however, embodied in the Septuagint[5] and in Josephus's *Antiquities of the Jews*.[6] Some otherwise lost *midrashim* have been preserved by the church fathers, notably Origen and Jerome.[7] Only one rabbinic work of midrashic nature even purportedly contains historical data, the *Seder Olam Rabbah*, ascribed to the second-century sage Yose ben Ḥalafta; but it contains many late additions, and in any case is more of a chronology than a history.

As to the reliability of rabbinic sources for the history of the period before they were compiled, Shaye Cohen has argued that Josephus's traditions are older and more original than those of the rabbis, that in not a single case is there a compelling reason to assume the contrary and hence that Josephus provides a "control" for the study of rabbinic texts.[8] However, the rabbis have at least one great advantage over Josephus, in that they represent many different points of view and present their comments only in passing, and hence with no particular historiographical mission in mind.

Two small details indicate that the rabbis in the centuries that followed the Roman destruction of the Temple at least tried to be historically accurate: (1) A talmudic saying tells us that "Whoever reports a saying in the name of its originator brings deliverance to the world."[9] (2) A recently discovered manuscript of one of the tractates of the Talmud (*Avodah Zarah* 8b) clearly indicates that an *early* second-century sage wrote down the laws pertaining to fines;[10] hence, these laws, at least, are considerably earlier than the time of the compilation of the Talmud in which they were included.

It is sometimes forgotten that long before the destruction of the Temple, the synagogue was an important religious institution. The earliest references to synagogues in Palestine are in the New Testament (Matthew 13:54, in Nazareth; Mark 1:21, in Capernaum; Acts 6:9, in Jerusalem) and in Josephus—he mentions synagogues in Caesarea, Dora and Tiberias.[52] The Jerusalem Talmud notes that there were 480 synagogues in Jerusalem

COURTESY ISRAEL ANTIQUITIES AUTHORITY

Magdala Synagogue Stone. *This roughly 3-foot-long engraved stone with an early depiction of a seven-branched menorah and elaborate floral and heart designs was discovered in the recently excavated synagogue of Magdala along the shores of the Sea of Galilee. The synagogue is dated to the first century C.E. or earlier, making it one of the oldest synagogues ever found and was in use while the Jerusalem Temple still stood. Its halls may have seated some of Jesus' earliest followers, including Mary Magdalene. The precise function of the stone remains uncertain; some believe it may have served as a table on which Torah scrolls were rolled out.*

at the time of the destruction of the Temple;[53] the Babylonian Talmud gives the number as 394.[54] These need not be exaggerations; many of the ancient synagogues that have been excavated were quite small, and many others probably operated out of private homes, leaving no archaeological trace. Even the Temple had a synagogue.[55] The earliest synagogues unearthed by archaeologists—at Masada, Herodium, Gamla and now Magdala*—date

*For Magdala and other recent synagogue discoveries, see Joey Corbett, "New Synagogue Excavations in Israel and Beyond," *BAR*, July/August 2011.

from the first century C.E. and possibly earlier. An inscription from Jerusalem refers to a synagogue that had been built before the turn of the era.[56] Hence, when the Second Temple was destroyed in 70 C.E., the spiritual vacuum was hardly as great as it had been after the destruction of the First Temple by the Babylonians in 586 B.C.E.

The synagogue served not only as a house of prayer but also as a house of study, as a meeting house and as a guest house.[57] The synagogue inscription already referred to, known as the Theodotus inscription,[58] speaks—in Greek—of a synagogue built for the reading of the Torah, for the teaching of the commandments and as an inn for those who come from abroad, presumably for the pilgrimage festivals. That this synagogue was built by a single individual suggests that it, like many synagogues, was really nothing more than, in effect, a private club, often operating out of a private house. There were no rabbis for these synagogues, and they were not joined in any kind of umbrella organization.

In a remarkable statement, Elias Bickerman declares that the Roman general Titus, by destroying the Temple and, in effect, putting an end to

Theodotus Inscription. *"Theodotus son of Vettenus ... rebuilt this synagogue for the reading of the law and the teaching of the commandments ..." reads the beginning of this first-century C.E. inscription discovered in 1914 south of Jerusalem's Temple Mount. Dating to the time of Herod the Great, the inscription is written in Greek and appears on a 25-by-17-inch limestone plaque. Though the synagogue Theodotus referred to has not been found, the inscription shows that synagogues existed even when the Temple was standing.*

the sacrificial system, was the greatest religious reformer in history.[59] Most historians look upon the rabbinic period as beginning in 70 C.E. and regard the shift from Second Temple Judaism (prior to the destruction of the Temple) to Rabbinic Judaism as a monumental change. The fact is that Judaism could never have survived such a traumatic experience had not alternative and supplementary institutions, such as prayer, the synagogue and the academy, already been in existence. Unfortunately, the earliest extant rabbinic work of note, the Mishnah, dates from more than a century after the destruction of the Temple. Josephus, whose life is almost evenly divided between the period before and the period after the destruction of the Temple, has almost nothing to say about the impact of this destruction on the rabbis and on their method of study or, indeed, about the impact of the loss of the Temple on Judaism generally. This may be because Josephus is interested primarily in political and military, rather than religious and cultural, history; but the fact remains that he says almost nothing about the effects of this allegedly traumatic event. Surely if the effect on the rabbis and their academies was so traumatic, we would expect that Josephus would give us at least a clue that this was the case.

By the first century B.C.E., the great sages Hillel and Shammai had established what were, in effect, rabbinic academies. Hillel is said to have held the office of patriarch (*nasi*) for 40 years[60] until approximately 10 C.E. He was not merely a great scholar and model of virtue, but he was also the founder of a school of legal religious thought (Beth Hillel). In addition, he was the founder of a dynasty that led Jewish life in Palestine for the next four centuries. His liberal attitude toward the admission of proselytes[61] had a profound influence upon the attitude of the later rabbis. According to talmudic tradition, Yohanan ben Zakkai, who is usually regarded as the key figure in the metamorphosis of Judaism after the destruction of the Temple (see pp. 150–153), was one of Hillel's disciples.[62] Hillel's grandson, Rabban Gamaliel the Elder, who lived in the first half of the first century C.E., is said to have been a teacher of Paul (Acts 22:3).

We should say something about the position of women in Jewish life in Palestine. Unfortunately, the evidence is scant. Josephus, at any rate, had a derogatory view of them, if we may judge from his comment about the woman at Masada whom he describes as superior in sagacity and training to most women, as if women can be praised only when compared with other women.[63] In an addition to the Bible, he says that the testimony of women is inadmissible in Jewish law because of their levity and boldness.[64] However, pseudo-Philo, Josephus's presumed contemporary, has considerably greater respect for them.[65]

Arch of Titus. *Standing in Rome near the Colosseum, the Arch of Titus celebrates the emperor's destruction of Jerusalem and the Temple in 70 C.E. One of the arch's carved panels (see detail below) depicts a triumphal procession in which Roman soldiers carry the looted Temple treasure, including the menorah.*

Jewish sects

The Jerusalem Talmud tells us that there were 24 sects of heretics[66] at the time of the destruction of the Temple.[67] Josephus tells us about three schools of thought (the Greek word he uses, *hairesis,* has given rise to our "heresy," although it had no such connotation in the original).[68] These three schools are represented by the Pharisees, the Sadducees and the Essenes. In a subsequent discussion, Josephus adds another school of thought, the Fourth

Philosophy,[69] which sought to establish an independent theocratic Jewish state. Philo describes still another, the ascetic Therapeutae,[70] who flourished near Alexandria. The Herodians are mentioned in the Gospels (Mark 3:6, 12:13; Matthew 22:16) as a political party which, after the death of Herod, may have regarded him as the Messiah.[71] In any event, they sought to reestablish the rule of Herod's descendants over an independent Palestine. The Samaritans constituted still another faction, and, of course, the Christians (if they may be grouped together) another. Perhaps we should add the *averim*,[72] who, through their meticulous observance of the laws of purity and of tithes, separated themselves from the unlearned rural masses known as the *'amme ha'aretz* (people of the land) and would not eat with them.[73]

The views of the Pharisees have survived in the rabbinic literature. Unfortunately, we have no writings of the Sadducees or of the Essenes (unless we identify the Dead Sea sect with the latter, as most scholars do). Accordingly, we must rely on Josephus for much of our information about these movements. We also have some writings of the Samaritans, but they come from a later period.

The movements that were active in first-century C.E. Palestine may perhaps be divided into two groups: those that attempted to make a mass, egalitarian appeal (the Samaritans, Pharisees, Sadducees and the Fourth Philosophy) and those that were separatist, monastic, utopian, ascetic, esoteric and preoccupied with ethics (the Essenes and/or the Dead Sea sect and the Therapeutae). The *averim* have some but not all of these latter qualities. Christianity would seem to have elements of both.

A major common denominator of the Samaritans and the Sadducees was their rejection of the Oral Torah, which greatly expanded and interpreted the Written Law. While a rejection of the Oral Torah made it easier for Samaritans and Sadducees to understand their religious tenets, since the Oral Torah was much more complicated than the written Torah, it also deprived them of the flexibility that the Pharisees gained through their liberal interpretation of the written Torah.

Though many of these movements originated before the first century C.E., they seem to have flourished particularly in the period just before the destruction of Temple. All of these groups, with the exception of the Pharisees, the Christians and a far smaller number of Samaritans, apparently disappeared with the destruction of the Temple.[74] This, then, is a clue that much of the controversy centered around the Temple, its ritual and its purity laws.

The Sadducees,[75] though few in number,[76] seem to have had considerable influence because their power base was the Temple[77] and because they included men of the highest standing.[78] Sadducean support of Jewish nationalism was undoubtedly a major attraction for the many influential Jews who joined the party, including the important Hasmonean ruler of Judea, John Hyrcanus, who switched his allegiance from the Pharisees to the Sadducees in the second century B.C.E.

So long as the Temple stood, its vast treasury enabled those who controlled it to exercise considerable political, economic and religious power. We may guess that one reason the high priests of the Temple had such short terms of office was that the Romans would not tolerate the nationalism that was so integral a part of their Sadducean orientation. The Pharisees, on the other hand, recognized the value of the *Pax Romana*. The first-century Pharisaic sage Hanina Segan ha-Kohanim enjoined Jews to "pray for the peace of the ruling power, since but for fear of it men would have swallowed each other up alive."[79] Indeed in 62 C.E., the Pharisees brought a formal accusation before the Roman procurator against the Sadducean high priest Ananus, accusing him of arbitrary action in convening the Sanhedrin to condemn James, the brother of Jesus, to death;[80] the Sadducean high priest was removed from office. Eventually, it was the Pharisees' acceptance of Roman rule that caused a split in their ranks and gave birth to the Fourth Philosophy; as Josephus observes, the Fourth Philosophy agreed in all things with the Pharisees, except that they would not accept foreign rule.[81]

If the relationship between the Pharisees and the Sadducees was as bitter as would seem to be the case from Josephus and from later rabbinic writings, one wonders why we never hear of the excommunication of the Sadducees, especially in view of the fact that they refused to accept the Oral Torah, so central in Pharisaic thinking.[82] On the contrary, the Pharisees and the Sadducees seem to have managed to serve together in the Temple and in the Sanhedrin. The fact that the Sadducees are not even mentioned in the voluminous works of Philo (see "Who Was Philo?" pp. 30–31) or in the Apocrypha* or Pseudepigrapha† would appear to indicate that the division between them and the Pharisees was not as sharp as one would gather from Josephus. Indeed, Josephus himself hints that the division was perhaps not so great when he reports that the Sadducees "submit to the formulas of the Pharisees, since otherwise the masses would not tolerate them."[83]

As to the Fourth Philosophy, there was apparently some connection

*These books are considered deuterocanonical by the Roman Catholic Church and are included as part of the Catholic Bible. They are designated as apocryphal in Protestant Bibles, but are not included in the Hebrew scriptures.

†A body of Jewish religious texts written between 200 B.C.E. and 200 C.E., incorrectly attributed to people mentioned in the Bible or to authors of biblical books, similar in nature to biblical books but not recognized as part of the canon of the Bible or the Apocrypha.

between their ideology and that of the militant Maccabees in the second century B.C.E. Both fought against a great power (the Maccabees fought against the then-ruling power, the Syrians) in order to establish an independent state.[84] Indeed, Josephus ascribes to the Fourth Philosophy all the troubles that eventually befell the Jews of Palestine. Those who subscribed to the Fourth Philosophy refused to pay tribute to the Romans; they advocated rebellion on the ground that they could acknowledge only God as their master. Unfortunately, Josephus provides us with hardly any history of the movement (and he is our only source), except that it began in 6 C.E. in opposition to the census of Quirinius, the Roman governor of Syria. When Josephus gives us a catalogue of the five revolutionary groups, he does not even mention the Fourth Philosophy;[85] perhaps he regarded it as an umbrella group for all the revolutionaries, or perhaps he identified the Fourth Philosophy with the Sicarii, another militant group.[86] Until relatively late in the revolt, there appear to be no traces of intraparty conflict among the revolutionaries, although this may indicate only that the early incidents were largely spontaneous and not managed by any organized party.[87]

Messianism undoubtedly played an important role in the revolt, judging from the fact that Menahem, the leader of the Sicarii, appeared in Jerusalem at the beginning of the revolt "like a veritable king"[88]—that is, like a messianic leader. He was murdered while wearing royal robes.[89] Another revolutionary leader, Simon bar Giora, was captured, after the destruction of the Temple, in a white tunic with a purple (that is, royal) mantle;[90] he was said to have arisen out of the ground at the very spot where the Temple formerly stood. But Josephus appears to suppress the messianic ideals of the revolutionaries, perhaps to avoid the wrath of the Romans, who regarded a belief in a messianic ruler as treason. In the last books of his *Antiquities of the Jews*, however, Josephus mentions at least ten leaders who probably were regarded as messiahs by their adherents, though Josephus himself (except in the case of Jesus, in a passage[91] that is probably interpolated by a later editor*[92]) avoids calling them messiahs.

The meaning of the term "messiah" was apparently flexible enough to accommodate these various careers. Indeed, though Josephus presents Eleazer ben Dinai as a mere revolutionary,[93] the rabbis call our attention to his messianic pretensions.[94] We may also note that two later Jewish revolts against Rome, that of 115–117 C.E., led by Lukuas-Andreas in Cyrene on the North African coast (see p. 158) and that of 132–135 C.E., led by Bar-Kokhba in Palestine, were both definitely headed by messianic claimants.

*See John P. Meier, "The Testimonium: Evidence for Jesus Outside the Bible," *BR*, June 1991.

Of the minor sects, the Essenes were of the greatest interest to Josephus. Whether the Essenes were the Dead Sea sect whose library was discovered in our own day in the cliffs of the Wadi Qumran on the northwestern shore of the Dead Sea is still a matter of debate among scholars. But whether the Essenes and the Dead Sea sect are the same or just similar in some respects, one or both reached their height in the first century C.E.*

The Temple Scroll, the longest of the Dead Sea Scrolls, was (according to its modern editor, Yigael Yadin) regarded by the sect as a veritable Torah of the Lord. In it God himself gives commands as part of his original revelation to Moses. The quotations from the Bible in the Temple Scroll differ somewhat from the Masoretic text (the standard Hebrew text), from the Septuagint (an early Greek translation) and from the Samaritan Pentateuch. Apparently,

DUBY TAL/ALBATROSS

Qumran. *The first Dead Sea Scrolls were found in caves in this arid wilderness by Bedouin shepherds in 1947. In the foreground of the photo are the ruins of Khirbet Qumran, home of the sectarian Jewish community that most scholars believe hid the scrolls. The Dead Sea is in the distance. Of the more than 900 scrolls discovered thus far, only about a dozen are intact; the rest are mere fragments. The scrolls include biblical commentaries, prophecy, rules for the community and parts of every book of the Hebrew Bible except Esther and Song of Songs.*

*James C. VanderKam, "The People of the Dead Sea Scrolls," *BR*, April 1991.

the author of the Temple Scroll had a different version of the Hebrew Bible.

In another text, known as MMT (for *Miqsat Ma'aseh ha-Torah*, "Some Precepts of the Torah"),[95] the sect appears to agree with the Sadducees in a number of controversies it had with the Pharisees. It appears more and more likely that the Dead Sea Scrolls, as they are collectively called, reflect the thinking of more than one sect or splinter group. Several of the scrolls, such

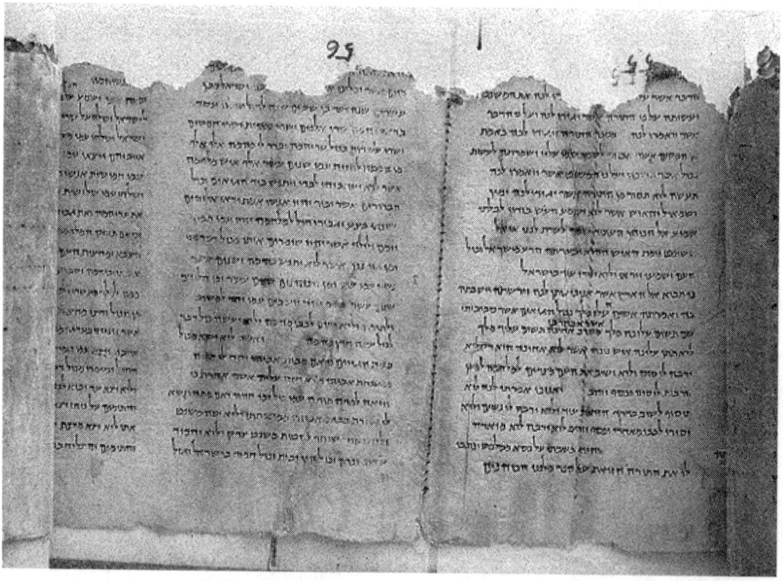

Temple Scroll. *The longest of the Dead Sea Scrolls from the caves of Qumran, the Temple Scroll contains detailed instructions for building the Temple not found in the Pentateuch, the first five books of the Bible. It is written in the first person with God himself giving the commands as part of his original revelation to Moses. The Dead Sea sect probably regarded it as sacred scripture on a par with the Torah itself.*

as the Testaments of Levi, Judah and Naphtali, belong to the Pseudepigrapha. Some scrolls contain apocalyptic sections, as well as messianic references. Indeed, with the cessation of prophecy, according to tradition, at the time of the destruction of the First Temple in 586 B.C.E.,[96] apocalyptic visions of the mysteries of creation and of the secrets of the end of days, in effect, replace prophetic visions. Books containing such visions have a close connection with the biblical Book of Daniel; like Daniel, they stress the impossibility of a rational solution to the problem of theodicy (explaining undeserved evil in light of a beneficent God) and the imminence of the day of salvation, to be preceded by terrible hardships, presumably reflecting the then-current historical setting. Such works had particular influence on early Christianity.

The question arises as to whether the Gnostic systems, some of which go back to the first and second centuries C.E., are related to the collapse of the apocalyptic strains in Judaism when the Temple was destroyed in 70 C.E. (On Gnosticism, see pp. 189–191.) It is highly doubtful that there is any direct Jewish source for this Gnosticism (from the Greek *gnosis*, "secret knowledge"); but some characteristic Gnostic doctrines are found in certain groups of apocalyptic first-century Jews, particularly the Essenes (or the Dead Sea sect). Gnostic-like doctrines are also found, to some degree, in such works as the first-century *Biblical Antiquities* of pseudo-Philo:[97] the dichotomy of body and soul and a disdain for the material world, a notion of esoteric knowledge and an intense interest in angels and in problems of creation.

Cultural developments in Palestine

The effect of Hellenism on Palestinian Judaism cannot be denied.* Whether it was as intense as in the Diaspora is a matter of scholarly controversy. Some scholars have gone so far as to suggest that we should stop differentiating in this respect Palestinian Judaism from Judaism in the western Diaspora.[98] Admittedly, both show Greek influence, an influence that is said to be manifest at a much earlier point than has been previously thought—in fact, at least a century before the beginning of the Maccabean revolt in 168 B.C.E. Still, I believe there are differences between Palestine and the Diaspora in this respect. Let's look at some of the evidence.

The coins of the Hasmonean rulers of Palestine in the second and first centuries B.C.E. bear legends in Greek and Hebrew; those of the Herodians in the first century B.C.E. and the first century C.E. are in Greek alone—presumably because at least for commercial purposes Greek was the *lingua franca* of Palestine. Undoubtedly, the tremendous number of Greek-speaking Jews from the Diaspora who came to Jerusalem for the three annual pilgrimage festivals—Pesach (Passover), Shavu'ot (Weeks) and Sukkot (Tabernacles)—brought with them not only the Greek language but also some elements of Greek culture. In addition, the tremendous success of the Jewish proselytizing movement must have brought to Palestine many converts whose native language was Greek. Yet Greek travelers, on the whole, seem to have ignored Judea, possibly because they feared being robbed by highwaymen; they visited the coast primarily, where Jews were not concentrated.[99] Moreover, though Greek is often found in tombstone inscriptions, perhaps to deter non-Jews from molesting the graves, the level

*For a useful overview of the Jewish encounter with Hellenism, see Martin Goodman, "Under the Influence: Hellenism in Ancient Jewish Life," *BAR*, January/February 2010.

of Greek in these inscriptions is very elementary.[100]

The fact that in 64 C.E., Josephus, a mere youngster of 26, was chosen for an extremely important and delicate mission to the Roman emperor, presumably because he knew Greek (and perhaps because he had connections at the imperial court), is evidence that the general knowledge of Greek was not deep. Josephus himself, never one to refrain from self-praise, admits that though he labored strenuously, he was unable to acquire a thorough knowledge of Greek because of his habitual use of his native language, Aramaic. To be proficient in other languages, principally Greek, was a skill common to freedmen and even slaves, Josephus remarks, the implication being that it was not common among free-born people.[101]

Indeed, it is clear from many sources—letters, contracts, documents, ossuary inscriptions, Pseudepigrapha, Dead Sea Scrolls, the New Testament and rabbinic works—that the predominant language of the Jews in Palestine from the time of the Babylonian captivity in 586 B.C.E. until well after the Arab conquest of Palestine in 640 C.E. was not Greek, but Aramaic. Thus when Titus sought to get the Jews to surrender Jerusalem, he sent Josephus to speak with them in their "ancestral language," presumably Aramaic.[102] Again, when Paul addresses the Jews in Jerusalem he speaks not in Greek, but in Hebrew (or in Aramaic) (Acts 21:40, 22:2).

It has been suggested that Greek was the language only of the upper classes, such as the Herodian princes who were educated in Rome, or Josephus; Aramaic, so the argument runs, was spoken by the uneducated, especially in rural areas. But the poor quality of the Greek on expensive ossuaries (bone depositories) from Jerusalem (presumably used by the wealthy), as well as the continued use of Aramaic by Josephus in the first century, indicates that such a distinction is not defensible.

Moreover, the archaeological evidence indicates that before the destruction of the Temple in 70 C.E., virtually all Jews refrained from any attempt at painting or sculpture, presumably in deference to a literal interpretation of the biblical prohibition against graven images (Exodus 20:4). Indeed, so great was the opposition to such art that at the outbreak of the First Jewish Revolt in 66 C.E. the Jewish forces in Galilee were ordered by the Jerusalem assembly to press for the destruction of the palace of Herod Antipas in Tiberias simply because it contained representations of animals.[103] So this aspect of Hellenism does not appear to have taken hold in Judea.

Erwin R. Goodenough in his magisterial 13-volume work concluded that Christianity spread so rapidly because Judaism had already been thoroughly Hellenized.[104] But we now know that it did not spread so rapidly, certainly not at first, as compared with, for example, the later spread of Mithraism or

DAVID HARRIS

Ossuaries. *An ossuary—literally, a bone box—is a rectangular box, usually carved from limestone and measuring about 2 feet long, in which bones were reinterred a year or so after an individual's death. The person's name was often scratched into the soft stone, sometimes in Greek but more frequently in Aramaic, indicating the widespread use of that language from the time of the Babylonian captivity in 586 B.C.E. until well after the Arab conquest of Palestine in about 640 C.E.*

even of Judaism itself before the destruction of the Temple.

Within Palestine were 30 Greek cities[105] where Hellenization was far advanced, as suggested by the archaeological evidence. But, remarkably, not a single Greek urban community was founded in Judea. Nor did Hellenism become deeply rooted in Samaria or Idumea. Moreover, unlike modern Jews, who live primarily in cities, only a small percentage of the Jews during the first century C.E. lived in cities such as Jerusalem (with probably fewer than 100,000 inhabitants)* or Caesarea on the coast (where contacts with non-Jews in commercial and governmental matters, and hence with the Greek language and culture, were more frequent). The great majority of Jews, as is clear from Josephus and rabbinic literature, were farmers, most of whom tilled very small tracts of land.

Jews were particularly numerous in Galilee, where, as we have noted, there were 204 cities and villages,[106] the smallest of which had 15,000 inhabitants[107]—giving Galilee, if Josephus is to be believed, approximately three times as many inhabitants as it has today. Not until the second century do we find Greek inscriptions in Galilean synagogues. Moreover, we must draw a distinction in degree of Hellenization between Upper and Lower Galilee. Upper Galilee is almost devoid of Greek epigraphic remains from the first and second century; the iconography is limited to menorahs, eagles and simple decorative elements. Lower Galilee, on the other hand, had several sizable urban centers that were linked to the more cosmopolitan and Greek-speaking West.

It is in Lower Galilee, significantly, that Jesus spent most of his career. The snide remarks of the later talmudic sages about first-century Galilee and some of the clichés in the New Testament are comments on the degree of accommodation to Hellenism in Lower Galilee.[108] Yet, real contact with non-Jews must have been slight; we know of only one occasion when Jesus refers to non-Jewish practices: Gentiles, when praying, he remarks, heap up empty phrases (Matthew 6:7).

What about literature in Greek by Jews in the first century? Josephus's rival, Justus of Tiberias, wrote *A Chronicle of the Jewish Kings* and *A History of the Jewish War*, neither of which has survived. Josephus grudgingly admits that Justus was not unversed in Greek culture.[109]

Of course, the supreme example of Hellenization in literature of a Jew from Palestine is Josephus.[110] (See "Who Was Josephus?" pp. 26–27.) However, he concedes that he needed assistants to help him with the Greek of the *Jewish War*,[111] which he originally wrote in his native Aramaic.[112] When

*Magen Broshi, "Estimating the Population of Ancient Jerusalem," *BAR*, June 1978.

he did not have these assistants, as apparently was the case in *Antiquities*, his style suffered considerably. Moreover, Josephus addressed his *magnum opus, Antiquities*, primarily to non-Jews; he believed that the entire Greek world would find it worthy of attention.[113]

In summary, Hellenization in Palestine, particularly in Upper Galilee, could hardly have been profound. The rabbis, in the talmudic tractate *Avodah Zarah* ("Idol Worship"), did not regard idolatry as an immediate problem. We hear of few apostates; on the contrary, there were apparently far more non-Jews who were attracted to Judaism either as proselytes or "sympathizers." Contacts with Greek culture were frequent only in the larger cities, where relatively few Jews lived. As for the alleged Greek influence on the rabbis, unlike the case in the medieval period, we know of none who distinguished themselves in philosophy or who wrote any treatise in Greek; nor are there any Greek philosophical terms in the talmudic corpus. Indeed, one wonders about the Greek philosophical influence upon people who regard the obscure Oenomaus of Gadara (c. 120 C.E.) as the greatest gentile philosopher of all time.[114]

II. The Diaspora World

The political background

In the first century C.E., the chief centers of Jewish population outside of Palestine were in Babylonia (under the Parthians), and in Syria, Asia Minor and Egypt, each of which, according to Salo Baron's estimate, had at least a million Jews.[115] That these Jews had sunk deep roots in their environment is clear from the fact that, except for a contingent from Adiabene (in Mesopotamia), we hear of no Jews from the Diaspora joining the revolt against the Romans in 66 C.E.

In Babylonia, in the early part of the first century, we hear of two Jewish brothers, Asineus and Anileus, of very ordinary background, who established an independent robber-state[116] and even, for a time, routed the Parthians. The brothers were defeated in 35 C.E., however, and the Babylonians then vented their longstanding hatred on the Jews. The Jews sought refuge in Seleucia on the Tigris River, but the Syrian and Greek inhabitants there slaughtered more than 50,000 of them.[117]

In Syria, the largest Jewish community lived in Antioch, the capital of the province. There, King Seleucus Nicator had granted civic rights to the Jews in the third century B.C.E.;[118] in all probability, this meant only that they were given the privilege of organizing themselves as a community. Josephus makes a special point, however, of their numbers and wealth.[119] In particular, he notes

Who Was Josephus?

Flavius Josephus (37–c. 100 C.E.)[1] is our chief source of historical information about the Jews from the period of the Maccabees (168 B.C.E.) to the Roman destruction of the Temple (70 C.E.).*

Josephus was born in Jerusalem of a distinguished priestly family. On his mother's side, he was descended from the royal Hasmonean house.[2]

According to his own account, he showed such precocity that at the age of 14 the chief priests and the leading men of the city constantly consulted him for information about Jewish law.[3] From age 16 to 19, he spent gaining personal experience, living successively as a Pharisee, a Sadducee and an Essene, after which he became a disciple of a hermit named Bannus.[4] Finally, he began to engage in public life, following the school of the Pharisees. When he was only 26, by gaining the ear of the emperor Nero, Josephus succeeded in freeing some priests who had been imprisoned in Rome.[5]

When the First Jewish Revolt against Rome began in 66 C.E., the 29-year-old Josephus, who apparently had no previous military experience, was entrusted by the Jewish leaders with the generalship of Galilee, the most important theater of the war at that time.[6] His military career is clouded by the fact that after a few months Josephus surrendered to the Romans[7] after all but one of his companions had killed each other rather than be captured. Brought before the Roman general Vespasian, Josephus, like Rabbi Yoḥanan ben Zakkai after him,[8] predicted that Vespasian would become emperor. After the war, Vespasian gave Josephus lodging in his former home in Rome, as well as a pension and Roman citizenship.[9]

It was in Rome that Josephus composed his four works, the *Jewish War* (79–81 C.E.)[10]—originally written in Aramaic,[11] then translated into Greek with the help of assistants[12]—covering the period from Antiochus Epiphanes's intervention in Judea in 170 B.C.E. to the capture of Masada in 74 C.E.; the *Antiquities of the Jews* (93–94 C.E.), covering the period from the creation of the world

*See Steve Mason, "Will the Real Josephus Please Stand Up?" *BAR*, September/October 1997.

to the outbreak of the revolt against Rome; the *Life* (c. 100 C.E.), the first extant autobiography from antiquity, largely a defense of his generalship in Galilee; and the treatise *Against Apion* (c. 100 C.E.), a defense of Judaism against the attacks of a number of critics of the Jews.[13]

As to the reliability of Josephus, modern scholarship gives Josephus mixed grades.[14] He is generally reliable in the topography and geography of the land of Israel, but he is far from infallible, as on-the-spot observation and archaeology have shown. As a political and military historian, especially when he is not involved personally, he is generally reliable in the instances where we can check him against other sources. But he can be a propagandist, especially in his defense of Judaism, in his appeal to pagan intellectuals and in his stance against Jewish revolutionaries. Inasmuch as almost all of classical literature is lost and inasmuch as scientific archaeology is still a new discipline, it is seldom that we are able to verify or refute Josephus in the mass of his details.

that they had been successful in winning proselytes and "sympathizers."[120] This success undoubtedly alarmed the non-Jewish inhabitants. That the Jews in Syria were hated is clear from the fact that at the outbreak of the revolt against Rome in 66 C.E., a general uprising against the Jews occurred.[121] Only in Antioch, Sidon and Apamea were the Jews spared.[122] After the fall of Jerusalem in 70 C.E., when Titus passed through Syria on his way home, the inhabitants of Antioch entreated him to expel the Jews from their city.[123] When this petition was denied, they requested him, though unsuccessfully, to revoke the privileges of the Jews.

Already in the first century B.C.E., Cicero indicates the large number of wealthy Jews in Asia Minor by noting the huge amount of money that had been collected from them for the Temple.[124] In city after city in Asia Minor, decrees were issued during the first century B.C.E. and the first century C.E.[125] permitting the Jews to send money to the Temple, exempting them from military service, excusing them from appearing in court on the Sabbath or in the late afternoon on Friday[126] and allowing them to form corporate groups. These concessions often aroused jealousy and hatred. Although the Romans were particularly sensitive to the charge that money sent to the Temple by the Jews was draining the state of money, the Roman authorities nevertheless pressured at least eight cities in Asia Minor to stop harassing their Jewish population.

The most important Jewish settlement in the Diaspora was in Egypt. Josephus tells us that Julius Caesar set up a bronze tablet in Alexandria declaring that the Jews were citizens;[127] Philo likewise speaks of Jewish citizens.[128] Nevertheless, in light of the so-called London Papyrus 1912, in which the emperor Claudius in the middle of the first century clearly contrasts the Alexandrians and the Jews and speaks of the Jews as living "in a city not their own," most scholars have concluded that the Jews possessed not citizenship but equal status as a community.[129]

The special privileges granted to the Jews, as well as the Jews' political and economic influence, aroused resentment among the Greek residents. When the Jews refused to participate in the state cults (having been granted a special privilege not to do so), they were accused of being unpatriotic.

In 38 C.E., the tetrarch Agrippa, who was later appointed by Caligula to be the king of Judea, visited Alexandria. The ostentatious display of his bodyguard of spearmen, decked in armor overlaid with silver and gold, aroused the envy of the Greek residents, who dressed up a lunatic with mock-royal apparel and saluted him as *marin,* the Aramaic word for lord. This was quite clearly intended to imply that the Jews were guilty of dual loyalty and constituted themselves as a state within a state. Even though Agrippa had considerable influence with the mad Roman emperor Caligula, Flaccus, the Roman governor of Egypt, thereafter deprived the Jews of their civic rights, denounced them as foreigners and herded them into a very small area—the first ghetto in history. The mob, in its fury at the Jewish status as a state within a state, burned Jews alive and did not spare even their dead bodies. The Jews were accused of storing arms, presumably plotting a revolution—perhaps in conjunction with Palestinian revolutionaries. That Flaccus was recalled in disgrace and eventually executed is evidence that the Jews' influence with the powers-that-be in Rome was still strong, but not strong enough to have prevented the massacre at the outset.[130]

Shortly after this incident, the Alexandrian Jews sent a delegation, headed by Philo (see "Who Was Philo?" pp. 30–31), to the emperor Caligula in Rome to ask him to reassert the traditional Jewish rights granted by the Ptolemies and confirmed by Julius Caesar and Augustus.[131] The opponents of the Jews also sent a delegation to Rome, headed by the grammarian and intellectual Apion. Here, as Victor Tcherikover has aptly remarked, the "Jewish question," for the first time in history, was discussed before a high tribunal.[132] Apion's argument was that the Jews were unpatriotic, since they did not pay the honors due the emperor. Philo, in his treatise *Legatio ad Gaium,* describes the ridicule which the emperor poured upon the Jewish delegation. Shortly thereafter, however, Caligula was assassinated; and when factional war was renewed between the Jews and their opponents, the new emperor, Claudius, issued an edict reaffirming the civic rights of the Jews.[133]

When the First Jewish Revolt against Rome broke out in Palestine in 66 C.E., a second major eruption of violence against Jews occurred in Alexandria.[134] When a mob of Greeks seized three Jews with the intention of burning them alive, the whole Jewish community rose to their rescue. In the resulting riot, ruthlessly put down by the Roman governor, Tiberius Julius Alexander—a nephew of Philo and an apostate Jew—50,000 Jews were said to have been massacred.[135] The fact that the Romans were not without casualties would seem to indicate that at least some Jews were armed; and the fury of the Roman assault, which knew no pity even for infants, would seem to indicate that the Jews fought tenaciously. As for the Greek mob, so intense was its hatred that considerable effort was required to tear them from the corpses. The date of the massacre may be significant; it coincided with the outbreak of the revolt against Rome in Palestine. One of the reasons for the viciousness with which the Romans crushed the Alexandrian Jews may have been to assure that they would not assist the Jews of Palestine.

Rome too was a major center of Jewish population, although it was not so large as Alexandria. As early as 59 B.C.E., Cicero remarks—to be sure with the exaggeration of a lawyer defending his client—how numerous the Jews in Rome are, how they stick together and how influential they are in informal assemblies.[136] Julius Caesar, in return for the aid the Jews of Palestine and Egypt had given him during the civil war against Pompey, conferred many special privileges on the Jews, as we have already noted. According to Suetonius, it was the Jews above all who in 44 B.C.E. mourned Caesar's death, flocking to his funeral pyre for several successive nights.[137] Augustus not only renewed his granduncle's edicts, but he added the additional privilege that if the monthly distribution of money or grain to the populace happened to fall on a Sabbath, the distributors were to reserve the Jews' portion for the following day.[138]

Especially in the reign of Tiberius (14–37 C.E.) do we find Jewish influence in high places. The Jewish king Agrippa—later to be the key figure in arranging the accession of Claudius—and his mother Berenice were unusually influential with the Roman royal family.[139] Agrippa's son (Agrippa II) was actually brought up in Claudius's household. Agrippa II's sister, also named Berenice, later lived in Rome as the mistress of the emperor Titus; it was even said that he promised to marry her (she was 12 years

Who Was Philo?

Philo was a Jewish philosopher and theologian who lived in Alexandria during the first century C.E. His extant works provide considerable information regarding Jewish life during this time.

Little is known of his life. Even the date of his birth is uncertain, though we may guess that he was born sometime between 15 and 10 B.C.E.[1] To judge from his frequent citations of many classical Greek authors, he must have had an excellent education in the liberal arts and was particularly well versed in music.[2] As we can see from his frequent allusions, he often attended the theater, was a keen observer of boxing contests, attended chariot races and participated in costly suppers with their lavish entertainment.

He tells us nothing of his Jewish education, which must have been weak, since he apparently knew little or no Hebrew.[3] Moreover, the only Jewish schools of which he speaks met on the Sabbath for lectures on ethics.[4] That Philo was personally observant, at least as he understood the law, seems clear from his vigorous denunciation of the extreme allegorists who deviated from the traditional observance on the ground that the ceremonial laws are only a parable.[5]

After the popular outbreak against the Jews in Alexandria in 38 C.E., Philo led an embassy of Jews to the Roman emperor Gaius Caligula, in opposition to a delegation headed by the anti-Jewish Apion, who charged the Jews with being unpatriotic because they did not worship the emperor.[6] This embassy, the subject of an essay by Philo (*Legatio ad Gaium* [*Embassy to Gaius*]), ended in failure, but soon thereafter Caligula was assassinated.

Philo's works may be classified into three groups:

1) Twenty-five scriptural essays and homilies based on specific verses and topics of the Pentateuch, especially the Book of Genesis. The most important of these essays is *Legum Allegoriae (Allegories of the Laws)*, an allegorical exposition of chapters 2 and 3 of Genesis, and *De Specialibus Legibus* (*On the Special Laws*), which is his exposition of various laws in the Pentateuch, especially the Ten Commandments.

2) General philosophical and religious essays. The most important of these are *Quod Omnis Probus Liber Sit (That Every Good Man Is Free)*, in which he proves the Stoic paradox that only the wise man is free; *De Aeternitate Mundi (On the Eternity of the World)*, in which he proves that the world is uncreated and indestructible; and *De Providentia (On Providence)*, in which he argues that God is providential in his concern for the world.

3) Essays on contemporary subjects. These include *De Vita Contemplativa (On the Contemplative Life)*, in which he praises the ascetic Jewish sect of the Therapeutae; *Hypothetica (Apology for the Jews)*, a fragmentary work that has a number of parallels with Josephus's essay *Against Apion* (here Philo answers the charges of critics of Judaism through a defense of the Torah); *In Flaccum (Against Flaccus)*, in which he describes the maladministration of Egypt by the Roman governor Flaccus; and *Legatio ad Gaium*, which, as we have noted above, deals with Philo's unsuccessful embassy to the Roman emperor Gaius Caligula.

As to Philo's reliability as a historian, E. Mary Smallwood has argued that Philo has greater reliability than Josephus when they discuss the same events, despite the fact that Philo is primarily a philosopher and a theologian rather than a historian.[7] This is particularly true where Philo is closer in time to the events, as, for example, when he discusses the procuratorship of Pontius Pilate.

older than he, had been married three times, was the mother of two children and was reputed to have had an incestuous relationship with her brother).[140] Eventually, however, apparently bowing to popular pressure, Titus sent her from Rome, "against her will and his own."[141]

During the reign of Claudius's successor, Nero (54–68 C.E.), a Jewish actor, Aliturus, was a special favorite at court.[142] Nero's wife, Poppea Sabina, was a "Godfearer" (see p. 39).[143]

The economic background

Egypt was by far the most important Roman province because it functioned as a granary, the chief source of food for the Roman army as well as for the masses of Rome itself. Naturally, Alexandria was the chief outlet for the Egyptian grain export. Within two generations of its founding by Alexander the Great in 332 B.C.E., Alexandria displaced Athens as the leading commercial and cultural center of the Mediterranean. As noted above, Alexandria in the first century also included the largest Jewish community in the world, with an estimated Jewish population of 180,000.[144] It was, in effect, the New York City of its day, with Jews constituting 30 to 40 percent of the population; they lived in all five sections of the city, although they were concentrated particularly in two of them.

In his description of the devastation wrought by the pogrom of 38 C.E., Philo gives us a valuable picture of the economic life of the Jews: "The tradespeople had lost their stocks; and no one, husbandman, shipman, merchant, artisan, was allowed to practice his usual business."[145] Under the Ptolemies, the economy had been, in effect, a kind of state socialism very closely controlled by the ruler; after 31 B.C.E., when the Romans won control of Egypt, the path was opened for individual initiative. Apparently, the Jews took full advantage of this opportunity.

The reference to the craftsmen in the passage quoted above is further elaborated by a famous passage in the Talmud,[146] which states that the seating in the great synagogue in Alexandria was by occupation—specifically goldsmiths, silversmiths, blacksmiths, metalworkers and weavers. Thus, when a poor man entered the synagogue he recognized the members of his craft and on applying for employment obtained a livelihood for himself and his family.

Alexandrian Jewish artisans had a reputation for great skill; the rabbinic sages sent to Alexandria for specialists in baking, as well as in preparing incense.[147] In addition, the doors for one of the gates of the Temple court were prepared by Alexandrian craftsmen.[148] Craftsmen from Alexandria were even imported to repair a cymbal and a bronze mortar in the sanctuary of the Temple.[149]

The great majority of Jews who came to Egypt from Palestine had been farmers; it is not surprising therefore that many continued that occupation in Egypt as well.

Under the Ptolemies, many Jews served in the army. In four cases,[150] they reached the rank of commander-in-chief. Under the Romans, however, we hear of no Jewish soldiers, nor were there Jewish tax collectors, policemen or bureaucrats, as there had been under the Ptolemies. We hear of only one Jew who attained high rank, a governor of Egypt; and he was an apostate.[151] Perhaps Jews were not trusted with such positions because of the revolutionary movements that surfaced in Palestine early in the first century.

The religious background

Within two generations of the founding of the city of Alexandria in 332 B.C.E., Greek displaced Hebrew and Aramaic as the language of the city's Jews. This is clear from inscriptions and from their readiness to adopt the translation of the Pentateuch from Hebrew into Greek (the Septuagint). Even the overwhelming majority of names of Jews preserved in papyri are Greek.

Nevertheless, the masses of the Jews remained true to their Jewish religious practices. Philo affirms this when he states that although all people are tenacious of their own customs, the Jewish nation is particularly so.[152]

Philo records the generosity with which the Alexandrian Jews, presumably of all classes, contributed to the Temple in Jerusalem.[153] Josephus also confirms the loyalty with which Jews throughout the world contributed to the Temple.[154] The Mishnah tells us that Egyptian Jews gave relief funds to the poor of Judea during the sabbatical year through the poorman's tithe.[155]

The Jews of Rome also had a reputation for piety. At the end of the first century B.C.E., Horace pokes fun at their readiness to accept everything on faith as if it were proverbial: "Let the Jew Apella believe it!"[156] He likewise alludes to the strictness with which the Jews observe the Sabbath: "Today is the thirtieth, a Sabbath. Would you affront the circumcised Jews?"[157] Horace's contemporaries, the poets Tibullus[158] and Ovid,[159] likewise refer to Sabbath observance by Jews. The notion that the Jews fasted on the Sabbath, found in several pagan writers,[160] may have arisen from a statement of Strabo that confused the Jewish abstinence from work on that day with abstinence from food.[161]

On the other hand, a number of sources indicate that Egyptian Jews may not have been so intensely religious.[162] We have no reference to any academies in Egypt for the study of the written or Oral Torah parallel to those in Palestine. In contrast to Palestine, where we hear that Rabbi Joshua ben Gamla established a system of universal elementary education,[163] we hear nothing of such education in Egypt. Philo speaks only of Sabbath schools intended for adults, where the four cardinal virtues, so prominent in Greek culture, were taught.[164]

Despite the proximity of Egypt to Palestine, we hear of few rabbis going to Egypt and few Egyptian Jews going to Palestine. Even Philo, wealthy as he was, made a pilgrimage to Jerusalem only once, so far as we know.[165]

In apparent violation of the Torah (Deuteronomy 12:13–14), the high priest Onias, after fleeing from Palestine, erected in Leontopolis in Egypt a replica of the Jerusalem Temple at which sacrifices were offered.[166] This temple was closed down on orders from Vespasian in 73 C.E., because of suspicions that it was a center of Jewish revolutionary activity.[167] Philo speaks of "Yom Kippur Jews," that is, "those who never act religiously in the rest of their life," but who are zealously pious on that day.[168] He also attacks intermarriage as leading to the abandonment of the worship of God.[169]

There are still other indications of assimilation in Egypt. For example, a Jewish inscription dating from the first century[170] speaks of the shadowy region of Lethe and the house of Hades; such terms are not merely poetic terms for death—they had significance in contemporaneous Greek religion. And, despite the clear prohibition in the Bible against interest on loans to Jews (Exodus 22:25; Deuteronomy 23:20), several papyri recording loans between Jews, including two dated to 10 B.C.E., specify interest.[171] Another papyrus, dating to 13 B.C.E., is a deed of divorce dissolving the marriage of a Jewish couple;[172] it is drawn up in the usual form of Greco-Egyptian divorces as known from other papyri and gives full equality to the wife in language at complete variance with both the Bible and the Talmud, where the husband alone is permitted to initiate a divorce.

According to the Talmud, Alexandria had a *beth din* (a Jewish religious court).[173] Various papyri, however, indicate the Jews relied instead on gentile courts; this was true in rural as well as urban Egypt. Here we have a clear violation of the talmudic declaration by Rabbi Tarfon, in the generation after the destruction of the Temple, forbidding one Jew to summon another before a gentile court, even when its law is the same as Jewish law.[174]

Philo himself is at variance with Jewish law, as set forth by the Palestinian rabbis, when he declares, for example, that unmarried daughters who have no fixed dowries share equally in the inheritance with the sons.[175]

We must say something about the position of women in the Diaspora. Again, our evidence is meager. Philo, who was the head of the Alexandrian Jewish community, has an extremely derogatory view of women, if we may judge from his comment that the reason Moses commanded the Israelites to take a perfect male sheep rather than a female is that the female is nothing more than an imperfect male.[176] Again, we may take note of contempt for women in his comment on Genesis 25:5–6: "The sons of the women and those of inferior descent are certain to be called female and unvirile, for which reason they are little admired as great ones."[177] Furthermore, we may note his sharp attack on women's wiles in his explanation of why the Essenes do not marry, namely that "a wife is a selfish creature, excessively jealous and an adept at beguiling the morals of her husband and seducing him by her continued impostures."[178]

The success of Jewish proselytism

And yet, a kind of spiritual transfusion was taking place in this period. Side by side with defections, there were apparently numerous additions to the Jewish fold.[179] Philo's remark that Jews comprise half of the human race,[180] even though an exaggeration, must allude to their extraordinary success in proselytism. Indeed, he condemns those who do not convert as "enemies of the Jewish nation and of every place."[181] He significantly ascribes to a non-Jew, Petronius, the view that the Jews gladly receive proselytes of other races no less than they welcome their own countrymen.[182]

Josephus also remarks on the gracious welcome extended by Jews to all who wish to adopt their laws.[183] He states that many Greeks (speaking of Greeks throughout the Mediterranean world) agreed to adopt the laws of Judaism; some remained faithful, while others reverted to their previous way of life.[184] In particular, he refutes the charge of the renowned first-century B.C.E. rhetorician Apollonius Molon that the Jews refused admission to "persons with preconceived ideas about God."[185] In a sweeping comment on the success of the proselytizing movement, Josephus declares that "the masses have long since shown a keen desire to adopt our religious observances; and there is not one city, Greek or barbarian, ... to which our customs have not spread."[186]

The zeal with which the Jews sought proselytes in the first century and the enthusiasm, in turn, with which the proselytes practiced their newly acquired Judaism, had apparently become proverbial, as we may discern from Jesus' pronouncement (Matthew 23:15): "Woe to you, scribes and Pharisees, hypocrites, for you traverse sea and land to make a single proselyte, and when he becomes a proselyte, you make him twice as much a child of Gehenna as yourselves."[187] Though the verse may be an exaggeration, it must have some element of truth in order to be credible. If Matthew was living in Antioch[188] where, as Josephus tells us, the Jews had been constantly attracting multitudes of Greeks to their religious ceremonies,[189] the verse reflects a real situation.

Moreover, a number of Greek and Latin writers allude to the eagerness of the Jews to receive proselytes. At the end of the first century B.C.E., Horace refers to the zeal of Jewish missionary activity as if it were well known: "We are much more numerous, and like the Jews we shall force you to join our throng."[190] Horace is, of course, a satirist; but his satire would fall flat if there were no basis for his obvious exaggeration.

In the middle of the first century C.E., the philosopher Seneca, one of the emperor Nero's chief advisers, writes caustically: "The customs of this accursed race [the Jews] have gained such influence that they are now received throughout the world. The vanquished have given laws to their victors."[191]

At the beginning of the second century C.E., Tacitus bitterly remarks that "the worst ones among other peoples, renouncing their ancestral religions, always kept sending (*congerebant*) tribute and contributing to Jerusalem, thereby increasing the wealth of the Jews."[192] The use of the imperfect tense, *congerebant*, indicates that the contributions were continuous and repeated.

A similar hostility is seen in Juvenal, Tacitus's contemporary, who, after deriding those who sympathize with Judaism by observing the Sabbath and avoiding pork, denounces their children who worship clouds and a heavenly divinity, undergo circumcision and observe all the laws of the Pentateuch. Like Tacitus, Juvenal denounces such converts as renegades from the Roman tradition.[193]

One somewhat speculative theory to explain the widespread success of Jewish proselytism suggests that the Jews absorbed the far-flung Phoenician settlements, which seem to have disappeared in the first century. When the Phoenician mother-cities of Tyre and Sidon on the Syrian coast and the chief daughter-city Carthage in North Africa lost their independence, the Phoenician settlements throughout the world were, in effect, an orphaned diaspora. Their people may have been attracted to Judaism because of the parallel with the kindred Jewish Diaspora. Scholars have long been puzzled by the disappearance of the Phoenicians in the first century; Nahum Slouschz has suggested that Phoenician owners of Jewish slaves may have been exposed to Jewish customs and ideas and may easily have passed over into Jewry, since they had practiced circumcision for ages.[194] Consistent with this theory is the statement of Rav in the third century that "From Tyre to Carthage they know Israel and their Father in Heaven."[195]

The inhabitants of Syria, speaking a kindred language (Aramaic), were similarly attracted to Judaism. Thus, on the eve of the Jewish revolt against Rome, the inhabitants of Damascus, according to Josephus, were fired with a determination to kill the Jews but were afraid of their own wives, "who, with few exceptions, had all become converts to the Jewish religion; and so their efforts were mainly directed to keeping the secret from them [their wives]."[196] That women, in particular, were attracted to Judaism may be due largely to the fact that they did not have to undergo circumcision, a major operation for an adult male; but it may also be due to the relatively more elevated and respected position of women in the Jewish community.

The most remarkable success of the proselytizing movement during this period took place in Adiabene in Mesopotamia in the early part of the first century.[197] According to Josephus, whose lengthy account is confirmed, in large part, in rabbinic sources,[198] a certain Jewish merchant named Ananias visited the Adiabenian king's wives and taught them to worship God after the manner of the Jews. Significantly, it is the women upon whom the emissary had his greatest impact. Through these women, Ananias was brought to the attention of the heir to the throne, Izates; Izates, too, was won over to Jewish practices, though without actually converting.[199] After becoming king, Izates was determined to become a proselyte, but his mother Helena—who in the meantime had converted to Judaism—and the Jewish merchant Ananias urged him not to, as his subjects would not tolerate the rule of a Jew. Another Jew, named Eleazar, however, urged him to undergo circumcision. Izates, together with his older brother Monobazus and his kinsmen, were circumcised.[200] The piety of the Adiabenian converts is stressed by both Josephus[201] and the Talmud.[202] Josephus also notes that the kinsmen of Monobazus, who succeeded his brother, distinguished themselves for valor on behalf of the Jews in their great war against Rome.[203]

Apparently proselytism was very much in evidence in Rome also. Caecilius of Calacte, the most important rhetorician and literary critic of the Augustan Age next to Dionysius of Halicarnassus, was a convert to Judaism.[204] As early as 139 B.C.E., the *praetor peregrinus* (the Roman magistrate in charge of administering justice to foreigners) banished the Jews from Rome "because they attempted to transmit their sacred rites to the Romans."[205] In 19 C.E. we are told that, because of the deception practiced by some Jewish embezzlers on a noble Roman lady who had become a proselyte, the emperor Tiberius ordered the entire Jewish community to leave.[206] (It is hard to believe that Tiberius, who was so careful to adhere to the letter of the law, would have expelled all the Jews without due process; apparently the expulsion order was the work of his adviser, Sejanus.[207] In any case, the expulsion, if it occurred at all, must have been brief, since we find the Jews back again within a short time after Sejanus was dismissed.) In the reign of Domitian (95 C.E.), Flavius Clemens (a cousin of the emperor) and his wife (the emperor's niece) were charged, together with many others, with having "drifted" into the practices of the Jews.

All this is strong evidence of the success of Jewish missionary activity in Rome.

One of the great puzzles of the massive proselytizing movement is how to explain its existence when we do not know the name of a single Jewish missionary (except Paul).[208]

Perhaps the Septuagint, the earliest translation of the Pentateuch—from Hebrew to Greek—played an important role. The first-century pseudo-Longinus, the most celebrated literary critic after Aristotle, not only paraphrases parts of the first chapter of Genesis (specifically 1:3 and 1:9–10), but cites it as an example of the most sublime style.[209] The fact that this passage refers to the "lawgiver of the Jews" without bothering to identify him by name would seem to indicate that the author expected his readers to know that the reference is to Moses.

In addition to proselytes, we hear of some people who adopted some Jewish practices without actually converting to Judaism.*[210] Philo refers to the widespread observance of the Sabbath and of the Day of Atonement (Yom Kippur) among non-Jews.[211] Eleven passages in Acts (10:2,22,35, 13:16,26,43,50, 16:14, 17:4,17, 18:7) referring to "fearers of God" and "reverencers of God" are usually regarded as alluding to this group. Josephus probably refers to them when he remarks that many Jewish customs have found their way to the cities; he declares that the masses have been greatly attracted to Jewish observances, and that there is no city where the Jewish Sabbath—as well as the fasts, the lighting of lamps and the dietary laws—is not observed.[212] The fact that Josephus singles out specific observances shows that he is referring not to proselytes but to "sympathizers."

Additional evidence includes the name "Sambathion," apparently given to children born on the Sabbath, which appears in a number of Egyptian papyri[213]—five of them dating from the first century. The name apparently was popular among adherents of a sect of Sabbath observers, since their kinsmen seem to be non-Jewish and the papyri were found in villages that, so far as we know, were not Jewish. It is striking that no other Hebrew name was ever borrowed by non-Jews. The most likely explanation for the choice of name is that the parents were Sabbath observers.

Suetonius tells of a Sabbath observer, the grammarian Diogenes, who, in the first century, used to lecture every Sabbath in Rhodes.[214] The Roman satirist Petronius, in the middle of the first century, sarcastically distinguishes between those who worship the "pig-god [presumably those who observe the dietary laws] and clamor in the ears of high heaven,"[215] on the one hand, and those who are circumcised and who observe the Sabbath according to the law, on the other. The distinction is between sympathizers and full Jews. Epictetus, the Greek Stoic philosopher of the latter part of the first century, asks, "Why do you act the part of a Jew when you are a Greek?" He then adds: "Whenever we see a man halting between two faiths we are in the habit of saying, 'He is not a Jew, he is only acting the part.' But when he adopts the attitude of mind of the man who has been baptized and has made his choice, then he both is a Jew in fact and is called one."[216] The fact that Epictetus uses the word "whenever" and that he cites this as an example to illustrate a point in a popular exposition of philosophy would seem to indicate that he is describing a frequent occurrence, one which is actually proverbial. He is clearly pointing to a distinction between the part-Jew and the full Jew.

*See Louis H. Feldman, "The Omnipresence of the God-Fearers," *BAR*, September/October 1986.

Archaeological discoveries provide the final bit of evidence. In 1976 two Greek inscriptions were found at Aphrodisias in Asia Minor, dating apparently from the third century.*[217] One lists donors with clearly Jewish names; at the end is the phrase "and those who are Godfearers (*theosebeis*)"; this is followed by a list of clearly Greek or Greco-Roman names. A second inscription lists a number of donors who are Jews (as we can tell from their names), followed by the names of two proselytes and two "Godfearers." One of the inscriptions mentions a *patella*, which may refer to a soup kitchen or to some kind of dish for distributing food, to which the donors on the list may have contributed. Indeed, for those who were poverty-stricken, the food may have been one of the attractions to Judaism, or at any rate to the synagogue.

Some scholars argue that these Godfearers are merely gentiles who befriended the Jews.† The existence of a distinct class of sympathizers in the third century seems, however, to be confirmed by a passage in the Jerusalem Talmud,[218] which quotes a third-century Palestinian rabbi as saying that in the time of the Messiah only gentiles who had nothing to do with the Jews during their bitter past would *not* be permitted to convert to Judaism, but that those "Heaven-fearers" (*yirei shamayim*) who shared the tribulations of Israel would be accepted as full proselytes, with the emperor Antoninus at their head.

This evidence of course relates to the third century, not the first century. But since we find a similar term, "Godfearer," in Acts, it seems most reasonable to conclude that a class of Godfearers existed in the first century also. This seems confirmed by a passage in Juvenal (c. 55–c. 140 C.E.) where he differentiates true proselytes from sympathizers (he uses the term *metuentem*, "fearer") who observe the Sabbath; the latter are not yet full-fledged Jews.[219]

The cultural background

As we have noted, within two generations after the founding of Alexandria, Hebrew and Aramaic virtually disappear from the papyri and are replaced by Greek. We may guess that the translation of the Pentateuch from Hebrew into Greek, generally dated about 270 B.C.E., was undertaken at least as much for the sake of the Jewish community as for the sake of Ptolemy II Philadelphus's request to have it in his library (the reason given in the Letter of Aristeas).‡ The Jews of Alexandria annually celebrated the date of the completion of

*For an overview of the site of Aphrodisias in southwest Turkey, and a significant redating of its donors' inscription to the mid-to-late fourth century C.E., see Angelos Chaniotis, "Godfearers in the City of Love," *BAR*, May/June 2010.

†A. Thomas Kraabel and Robert S. MacLennan, "The God-Fearers: A Literary and Theological Invention," *BAR*, September/October 1986.

‡Leonard J. Greenspoon, "Mission to Alexandria," *BR*, August 1989.

this translation (the Septuagint) as a holiday and regarded it as perfect.[220]

The greatest representative of Alexandrian Jewry, Philo, possessed little or no knowledge of Hebrew, which he regarded as a "barbarian" (that is, foreign) language.[221] If he had known Hebrew he would surely not have claimed that the Greek of the Septuagint corresponded verbatim with the original.[222] If he had known Hebrew he would surely not have commented on the significance of the addition of the Greek letter *rho* to Sarai's name (*Sara* in the Septuagint) to form Sarah (*Sarra*);[223] instead we would expect him to comment on the substitution of the Hebrew letter *heh* for the Hebrew letter *yod* (*Sarai* to *Sarah*).

Philo mentions a wide range of Greek writers, especially the epic and dramatic poets; he shows an intimate acquaintance with the techniques of the Greek rhetorical schools;[224] and he exhibits an extraordinary knowledge of the theory and practice of music.[225] On the other hand, he says nothing about his Jewish education, nor does he mention any rabbis by name, though the great Hillel and Shammai were his contemporaries in Palestine. When he describes Moses' education, he tells us that Moses learned arithmetic, geometry and music from Egyptian teachers, while he studied the rest of the seven liberal arts with teachers imported from Greece[226]—but he tells us nothing about Moses' Jewish education. Clearly, for Philo, the liberal arts, rather than the Torah, are the stepping stones to the highest study, which he declares to be philosophy,[227] since it is through philosophy that man, mortal though he may be, is rendered immortal.[228]

Jews, or at least those of the upper classes who could afford it, were apparently eager to enter their children in Greek *gymnasia*, which were dedicated to various pagan deities whose busts adorned them. The athletic contests in which the students participated took place at pagan religious festivals. Philo himself avidly watched boxing,[229] wrestling[230] and racing;[231] indeed, much of the imagery in his works is taken from athletics. For alumni, the *gymnasium* was a social center, the equivalent of a modern country club. It must have been a tremendous blow for these wealthy and ambitious Jews when the emperor Claudius in his rescript of 41 C.E. expelled the Jews from the games presided over by the *gymnasi-archs*, which, in effect, meant exclusion from the *gymnasia*.[232]

The Palestinian rabbis forbade attendance at theaters because of their association with idol worship[233]—the plays were performed only at festivals of the gods. And yet Philo remarks that he has often been to the theater.[234]

We know of one Jewish playwright, named Ezekiel, who apparently lived in the first century B.C.E. and who wrote a tragedy called *The Exodus*, dealing with Moses and the Exodus from Egypt, with the intention of showing that Jews also had heroic subjects for tragedy and that they could present them in the best style of Euripides, the favorite playwright of the era. Unfortunately, only fragments of Ezekiel's tragedy survive. However, as Howard Jacobson has shown,[235] Ezekiel's text may best be understood in a number of places by comparing it with extant midrashic sources, and, indeed, midrashic exegesis may be found, to some extent, in the Septuagint itself.

Undoubtedly, the most important and most influential cultural achievement of the Hellenistic Jews was the philosophy of Philo, who, largely through the efforts of the late Harry Wolfson,[236] is now regarded as a major philosopher in the Western tradition. Philo was the first in a long series of thinkers—Jewish, Christian and Muslim—who attempted to synthesize faith and reason. Thus, the history of Christian philosophy begins not with a Christian but with a Jew, Philo, an older contemporary of Paul. The Church itself preserved the numerous treatises of Philo still extant; on the other hand, Philo is not cited by a single Jewish writer (except briefly by Josephus) until the 16th century.

Scholars have long debated whether Philo is a Greek in Jewish clothing or a Jew in Greek clothing. Using a kind of literary psychoanalysis, Wolfson concludes that Philonic Judaism is really a derivative of Pharisaic Judaism.[237] However, the very fact that Philo asks how the Greek philosophers could have arrived at the truth without direct revelation[238] implies that the Greeks did have the truth. Philo's twofold answer is that either the Greeks borrowed from the Bible or that philosophy itself was a divine gift to the Greeks to enable them to discover by reason and by the senses what the Jews had learned through revelation.

Because Socrates and Plato were his ideals, Philo converts Moses into an anti-Sophist Socrates-like figure whose speech impediment is transformed into a disdain for sophistic rhetoric.[239] Philo's cosmological proof for the existence of God is derived from Plato's *Timaeus*. With the help of Plato, Philo resolves the seeming discrepancy between the first two chapters of Genesis in their accounts of creation.[240] The first chapter, Philo tells us, describes the creation of Platonic universals, forms or ideas; the second chapter describes the creation of particulars. (In the Greek—the only version of the Bible Philo knew—Genesis 1:2 says that the earth was "unseen"; from this, Philo deduced, in accordance with Plato, that prior to the visible world there existed an invisible world.) Platonic philosophy can also be seen in Philo's explanation of why God did not give the Torah to Abraham: Because Abraham actually observed a higher form of law, of which the *Nomos* (the Septuagint's translation of the word Torah) was only a copy.[241] Here Philo paves the way for the Christian view (cf. Galatians 3:19) that the Torah is inferior to the higher law built into nature, which, according to most Christian theologians, was reaffirmed by Christianity when it abrogated the inferior law.

Philo was obviously disturbed by the thought that God, who is perfect form, should have created lowly matter. To explain this, Philo postulates the intervention of a mediator, the *Logos*, a term he inherited from the pre-Socratic philosophers. He terms this *Logos* "the idea of ideas,"[242] "the first-begotten son of the uncreated Father" and a "second God,"[243] "the man of God."[244] Concepts like these paved the way for the notion of the Godman, as well as the intermediary between God and man reflected in Christian theology.

Philo is original, however, in enunciating the doctrine that God is unknowable in his essence, as well as unnameable and ineffable, and in his insistence on an individual Providence who can suspend the laws of nature, rather than, as with the Stoics, a universal Providence who is himself subject to the unchanging laws of nature. He is likewise original in postulating a great chain of being held together by the *Logos*.[245]

Although Philo speaks disparagingly of the Greek mysteries as humbug and buffoonery[246] (perhaps, we may guess, because they were attracting Jews in sizable numbers in Alexandria), he clearly sees in Judaism elements of a superior mystery cult. He was obviously influenced by non-Jewish ideas (contrary to Wolfson's view).

In a rare autobiographical comment, Philo tells us he himself was initiated into the Greater Mysteries of Judaism.[247] He distinguishes between the Greater and Lesser Mysteries; he refers to Moses as one who had been instructed in all the mysteries of his priestly duties;[248] plainly, Philo is adopting terminology from the Eleusinian Mysteries of Demeter and Persephone. When he talks of a "corybantic frenzy," he evokes the image of the Corybantes, the companions of the earth goddess Cybele, who followed her with wild dances and music.[249] His casual use of the mystic oxymoron "sober intoxication"[250] betokens a borrowing from the spirit of the mystery cults, as does his repeated use of the mystic *enthousiasmos* ("having God within one").[251]

In his attitude toward marriage, Philo adopted an ascetic stance hardly consistent with the mainstream of Judaism. In a passage recalling Paul's "better to marry than to burn" (1 Corinthians 7:9), he says that the institution of marriage was merely a means for perpetuating the human race.[252] Elsewhere he remarks that Moses participated in it merely for the lawful begetting of children.[253] Many passages show how much he prized everlasting virginity.[254] His high praise for such ascetic groups as the Essenes[255] and the Therapeutae (a Jewish sect in Egypt with many similarities to the Essenes)[256] confirms this attitude.

The "what-if's" of history

In the first century C.E., Judaism was at a high point both in numbers and in influence, in Palestine as well as in the Diaspora. Were it not for the disastrous results of the revolts against Roman rule—66–70 C.E. in Judea, 115–117 C.E. in Cyrene and elsewhere, and 132–135 C.E. in Palestine—and for the rise of one of its versions called Christianity, Judaism might well have conquered the world. On the other hand, there were many "Judaisms" during this period. Who could have predicted which would have prevailed?

TWO

The Life of Jesus

E.P. SANDERS

WHAT CAME TO BE KNOWN AS CHRISTIANITY, A NEW RELIGION THAT would spread throughout the world, began in a very modest way, among the followers of Jesus of Nazareth, a Jewish prophet, teacher and healer. Jesus lived from approximately 4 B.C.E. to 30 C.E. He came to be regarded as the Messiah by his followers—the anointed one whom many Jews expected to come and to restore Israel. "Anointed" *is meshiah* in Hebrew and *christos* in Greek, whence the English words "messiah," "Christ" and "Christianity." At an early date, within about 15 years of Jesus' death, some Greek-speaking Christians began to use the title "anointed" as if it were a proper name, and thus Jesus became "Jesus Christ" or "Christ Jesus." Christians have regarded him as the inaugurator of a new era. By the sixth century after his birth, they had begun to date events either B.C. ("Before Christ") or A.D., *Anno Domini* ("in the year of our Lord"). It is now customary in many circles to use the abbreviations B.C.E. and C.E., "Before the Common Era" and "Common Era," since these allow non-Christians to employ the dates of the Christian division of time. Thus 4 B.C.E. is the same year as 4 B.C., but put in terms acceptable to all.

That Jesus was born before the beginning of the era that starts with his birth is one of the minor curiosities of history. In the sixth century, Dionysius Exiguus, a Scythian monk who was resident in Rome, introduced a calendar based on the division before Christ and after Christ, but he miscalculated the year of the death of Herod the Great, putting it four years too late. Since Jesus was born near the time of Herod's death, his birth was also misdated by four years. When subsequent research established the correct year of Herod's death, the calendar was not revised: Year 1 was kept where Dionysius had placed it, and both Herod's death and Jesus' birth were dated to 4 B.C.E.

The story of Jesus is found in the four canonical Gospels in the New Testament. These books were written anonymously, but in the second century Christians began to attribute them to four men: Matthew and John (Jesus' followers) and Mark and Luke (early Christians, but not direct disciples of Jesus).[1] Early Christians wrote many other accounts of Jesus, some of which survive as the apocryphal gospels ("hidden" or "secret" noncanonical gospels). Historians have repeatedly studied these in the hope of finding solid information about Jesus, but without much success. The Gospel of Thomas, which is known from a manuscript found at Nag Hammadi in Upper Egypt, has interesting versions of some of the sayings of Jesus that are also in the canonical Gospels, and it is possible that in a few cases its version is earlier than the one in the New Testament. In general, however, our knowledge of Jesus is limited to the information in the New Testament.[2]

A few non-Christian authors who wrote in the first or second century mention Jesus, but only as the originator of a movement that came to their attention. They add no new information to that given in the Gospels.[3]

Although the canonical Gospels contain almost the only worthwhile information about Jesus, they are by no means straightforward histories or biographies in the modern sense. The material in them was passed on orally for some years, being modified in the process. Further, the authors of the Gospels were more interested in theological truth than in bare historical accuracy, and their theological concerns sometimes shaped the material.

Even if the Gospels were academic histories, full of well-researched information, we would still be faced with problems in describing the life of Jesus. They do not provide us with a simple, consistent portrait of him. Moreover, there are large gaps—things we would like to know about which the Gospels say little or nothing. They tell us virtually nothing, for example, about Jesus' appearance and upbringing, only the name of his village and the names of his parents.

On the other hand, if we are content with a broad outline, we do know a lot about his life and teaching. Let us begin by considering the kind of man he was.

The Jesus who exercises the greatest hold on the public imagination is the Jesus of the Sermon on the Mount (Matthew 5–7). This is the Jesus who blessed the poor in spirit and the meek, who told his followers to "turn the other cheek" and to pray for their persecutors. This portrait of Jesus has served to bolster social and ecclesiastical reform. It supports criticism of those who are preoccupied by worldly concerns, and it helps shape the conscience of countless individuals who are moved by Jesus' example to examine themselves and moderate their behavior.

But we can also find numerous other miniportraits in the Gospels. Around the turn of the present century, Christianity was surprised and shocked by the discovery of the eschatological Jesus, the wild-eyed proclaimer that the end (in Greek, *eschaton*) was near, who predicted that:

> The sun will be darkened, and the moon will not give its light, and the stars will be falling from heaven, and the powers in the heavens will be shaken. And then they will see the Son of Man coming in clouds with great power and glory. And then he will send out the angels, and gather his elect from the four winds ..."
>
> (Mark 13:24–27 and parallels)

This Jesus also promised that some of his hearers would not die before the kingdom of God arrived (Mark 9:1).

We can also find a portrait of Jesus as a kind of revolutionary: "Do not think that I have come to bring peace on earth; I have not come to bring peace, but a sword" (Matthew 10:34). Perhaps this is the Jesus who was executed by Rome for claiming to be "king of the Jews" (Matthew 27:11,29,37).

There is, of course, more than one side to anyone's character. We should not be surprised that this is true of Jesus. Nevertheless, competition among these and other portraits does leave the reader wondering: What was the essence of the man? Where was the center?

Scholars have been writing answers to that question for 200 years. Only toward the end of the 18th century did scholars begin to apply the critical method of historical research to the Gospels. Even today, there is some reluctance among many Christian scholars to use this methodology as vigorously when studying the Gospels as they do when studying other material. Most scholars who deal with the Gospels have a *belief about* Jesus that is not subject to historical scrutiny. One of the consequences is that Jesus usually gets a very good press. Put crudely, people tend to project their own ideals—whatever they happen to be—onto him.

In the end, Jesus remains a more shadowy figure than his greatest apostle, Paul. In Paul's case, we have some of his own letters. There is no mistaking the driving force, the cut and thrust of his mind. We would like to get as close to Jesus as to Paul. It is a disappointment that it cannot be done, since we do not have equally good sources.

The problem of sources

Naturally, in reconstructing the life of Jesus, in searching for his essence, scholars look for the most reliable material. For several decades they have progressively reduced the range of the literature in which he is sought. The earliest source to be excluded was the Gospel of John. This was done partly because the other three Gospels—Matthew, Mark and Luke—line up against John, and the scholar is frequently forced to choose one or the other. This is especially the case in studying the teaching of Jesus, as we shall see below.

Matthew, Mark and Luke are called the Synoptic Gospels because they can be studied in a synopsis. This does not refer to a précis (although that is the common meaning of the word now), but to a book in which similar accounts can be viewed together (*synoptē* in Greek means "see together"). This is done by arranging Matthew, Mark and Luke in parallel columns.[4] Here is one example, Jesus' prediction of his arrest. Although the texts are parallel, there are numerous variations in detail.

Matthew 17:22–23	**Mark 9:30–31**	**Luke 9:43b–44**
As they were gathering in Galilee,	They went on from there and passed through Galilee.	But while they were all marveling at everything he did,
Jesus said to them, "The Son of Man is to be delivered into the hands of	And he would not have any one know it; for he was teaching his disciples, saying to them, "The Son of Man will be delivered into the hands of	he said to his disciples, "Let these words sink into your ears; for the Son of Man is to be delivered into the hands of men."
men, and they will kill him, and he will be raised on the third day."	men, and they will kill him; and when he is killed, after three days he will rise."	

A study of all the Gospel parallels makes it obvious that these three Gospels, the Synoptics, relate very closely to one another.* They tell basically the same story, according to the same outline, placing the same events at the

*For a useful summary, see David E. Aune, "Synoptic Gospels: Matthew, Mark and Luke," *BR*, December 1990.

same point in the outline, often using identical wording. There are exceptions to these rules, but the most striking single feature of the Synoptics is their similarity. They are especially close together when they give the same teaching material. As in the example above, the Synoptics vary more in describing the setting of Jesus' teaching than in the teaching itself.

John's gospel, on the other hand, cannot be fitted into the synoptic scheme in any way. The outline of events is different, and there is little agreement between John and the Synoptics with regard to content.

Moreover, the differences between John and the Synoptics are not such that the accounts are complementary; rather, the accounts are contradictory to a very great degree. We may consider some examples: According to the Synoptics, during Jesus' public career he went to Jerusalem for Passover once; according to John, twice. In the Synoptics, Jesus "cleanses" the Temple at the end of his ministry; in John at the beginning. The synoptic Jesus is an exorcist (for example, Mark 3:22–27); the Johannine Jesus performs no exorcisms.

There are even more striking differences between John and the Synoptics. In the Synoptics, Jesus declines to say who he is; he even refuses to give "a sign," and he rebukes those who seek one (Mark 8:11–12 and parallels; cf. Mark 8:29f.). In John, on the other hand, Jesus talks almost exclusively about himself, and he provides several specific signs. (Note the prominence of the "I am" sayings in John, e.g., 6:35–51, 8:12, 10:7. For "signs," see John 2:11, 4:54, for example.) The Jesus of the Synoptics preaches the kingdom of God, while the Johannine Jesus discourses about himself.

Moreover, the style and manner of speech are entirely different. In the Synoptics, Jesus speaks in short, pithy sentences, parables, similes and metaphors. In John, Jesus offers long allegorical monologues. For example, we may compare the synoptic parable on sheep (Matthew 18:12–13) with the Johannine allegorical discourse on sheep (John 10:1–18). Matthew's parable is short, only two verses:

> If a man has a hundred sheep, and one of them has gone astray, does he not leave the ninety-nine on the hills and go in search of the one that went astray? And if he finds it, truly, I say to you, he rejoices over it more than over the ninety-nine that never went astray.

Thus in Matthew, Jesus uses the story to describe an aspect of God and his kingdom: the inclusion of the lost; a single point is made by telling a short, illustrative story. John, on the other hand, places in Jesus' mouth a long, allegorical monologue; on the surface it is about sheep, but beneath the surface it is about the person and work of Christ, including his death and resurrection (John 10:18). In John's long monologue, we are intended to understand Jesus as being both the shepherd and the door to [God's] fold—which does not make sense, even in the allegorical terms of the parable.

These and other factors resulted in a still-held scholarly consensus: The historical Jesus is to be sought in the Synoptics, not in John. The Johannine Jesus is the Christ of faith. That is not to say that John is "fiction"; somewhere behind John's gospel there are traditions. The author probably knew one or more of the Synoptics; he may have had independent access to other information about Jesus. Some parts of John's narrative (as distinct from the discourses) are intrinsically more probable than the synoptic account. Since Jesus was a law-abiding Jew, and since the Bible commands attendance at the pilgrimage festivals (Passover, Shavu'ot, Sukkot), Jesus probably did go to Jerusalem for more than one festival. (In John, Jesus goes four times, twice for Passover [John 2:13, 12:1] and twice for other festivals [John 5:1, 7:10]. In the Synoptics, he makes only one pilgrimage [Mark 11:11 and parallels]). John's view of Jesus' trial before two of the chief priests is also intrinsically more probable than the synoptic trial scene (see below). Despite these and similar points in favor of John, the overall portrait of the Synoptics must be preferred.

As we shall see, the Synoptics' description of Jesus makes sense in context, while it would be impossible to explain early Christian eschatology if the historical Jesus were like the Johannine Christ. John is better read as a series of meditations on the theological significance of Jesus' coming that the author chose to write in the first person, as if Jesus had said them.

Since the middle of the 19th century, John has been mostly ignored in the search for the historical Jesus. But even the Synoptic Gospels pose difficulties for historical research. As we noted above, they are not biographies or histories in the modern sense. The most important point to consider is the nature of the material they contain.

The problems of context

The Synoptic Gospels are composed of independent compositional units with very little context. We probably owe such context as there is to the Evangelists. We may think of each unit as a snapshot, with the individual snapshots arranged and introduced by the Evangelists (or Christian preachers and teachers before them).

If we want to explain what someone was like—not to give a few random facts about him or her, but to get to the heart of the matter—we aim for *intention, cause and effect* and an *understanding of the circumstances.* "Abraham Lincoln *wanted* all along to free the slaves; he waited until relatively late in the war *because of* tactical considerations." Such a statement requires that we know the sequence of events and that we have enough knowledge of what Mr. Lincoln *thought*—in addition to what he *did*—to allow us to weave desire, external action and the force of circumstances into a coherent whole. How can we do this with Jesus, since we have (1) snapshots that (2) have been transmitted for a generation or so in a language other than Jesus' own and in a variety of contexts? (Jesus spoke Aramaic; the Gospels are in Greek.) Unfortunately, we cannot know as much about Jesus as about Paul (or Lincoln or Churchill). On the other hand, we do not remain entirely in the dark, as we shall see.

That what we have are isolated incidents, quite probably rearranged and reset in unoriginal contexts, is easily shown: The settings of individual passages sometimes vary from gospel to gospel. We must assume that, during the period of oral transmission, Christian teachers exercised this kind of freedom. That is, the material was used, not embalmed; when used, it had to meet a current issue, and thus the context changed. If this were not so, the material would not have sustained the early Christian communities.

The Evangelists not only arranged the material, they added new introductions and conclusions. We may consider a few examples. Both Matthew and Luke include Jesus' lament over Jerusalem, and they have virtually identical wording in a passage that in Greek is just over 50 words long. Thus they used the same tradition, not a generally remembered Aramaic saying of Jesus that was passed down and translated in various ways. The lament contains this prediction: "You will not see me again until you say, 'Blessed is he who comes in the name of the Lord.'" Luke places this passage early (Luke 13:34–35), and it is fulfilled in Luke 19:38, when the crowd cries out, as Jesus enters Jerusalem, "Blessed is he who comes in the name of the Lord." In Matthew, however, the prediction that people will not see Jesus again until they make the appropriate proclamation comes *after* his entry into Jerusalem: The entry into Jerusalem is in Matthew 21:9, the prediction in Matthew 23:37–39. This means that, when the Gospel of Matthew closes, the prediction is still unfulfilled, and the saying, "You will not see me until ...," points forward to the post-resurrection return of the Lord. Thus we must ask: Did Jesus predict his triumphal entry into Jerusalem (Luke) or his own return after his death (Matthew)?

The setting or immediate context of an individual unit is also frequently different from gospel to gospel. An example is the parable of the lost sheep quoted above. A shepherd leaves 99 safe sheep to search for the one that is lost. In Matthew's setting, Jesus tells the parable to the disciples; the meaning is that they should act accordingly (Matthew 18:12–14) and seek the lost. In Luke, the parable is directed against the Pharisees; it defends Jesus' own action in mingling with "tax collectors and sinners" (Luke 15:3–6).

Sometimes scholars reach a consensus in favor of one arrangement or setting, but sometimes there is no consensus. In the two examples I have given, most scholars now would favor Matthew's setting for the saying "You will not see me again." Jesus probably had in mind the future kingdom rather than his next trip to Jerusalem. On the other hand, most scholars accept Luke's setting for the parable of the lost sheep and take it to be a rebuke to the Pharisees for not seeking the lost. Occasionally someone is bold enough to doubt both settings. The correct decision is not self-evident. The answer depends on an overall view of Jesus, and it requires a reconstruction of the larger context of his life and work. Yet since the larger context is provided by other passages that were transmitted by the very same sources, it is difficult to avoid circular argument.

The problem is even more difficult. Not all the material goes back to the historical Jesus. Besides being arranged and set in new contexts, much of it was revised and some was even created. To illustrate how this occurred, we may consider a passage in one of Paul's letters. Paul wrote that he besought the Lord in prayer that his "thorn in the flesh" be removed. The Lord replied, "My grace is sufficient for you, for my power is made perfect in weakness" (2 Corinthians 12:8–9). From Paul's letter, we know that the Lord who spoke this saying was not the historical Jesus, but either the risen Lord or God himself, speaking through the Spirit. If Paul had used the saying in a sermon, however, and it was then quoted and used in different contexts, it would be unlikely that everyone would maintain the nice distinction between the historical Jesus and the Lord who answers prayer.

Christians believed that the Lord still spoke to them, and that sometimes the Holy Spirit spoke through Christian prophets. Paul and other Christians held that they knew the mind of God and that they spoke "in words not taught by human wisdom but taught by the Spirit" (1 Corinthians 2:9–13). Since "the Lord is the Spirit" (2 Corinthians 3:17), words that were "taught by the Spirit" were often attributed to Jesus (whom the Christians called "Lord") when the Gospels were composed. From the point of view of the first Christians, why not? The same Lord spoke. Yet the result was that they created sayings that were then placed in the mouth of the historical Jesus.

A second source of newly created material was the Jewish scriptures, which the Christians accepted as their own. Christians believed that Jesus had fulfilled the biblical prophecies, and this view led them sometimes to draw on those prophecies for information about him. An example is Matthew's statement that, when Jesus entered Jerusalem shortly before his death, he sat on both an ass and a colt. Matthew derived this "information" from the scripture that he thought Jesus fulfilled:

> Rejoice greatly, O daughter of Zion!
> Shout aloud, O daughter of Jerusalem!
> Lo, your king comes to you;
> triumphant and victorious is he,
> humble and riding on an ass,
> on a colt the foal of an ass.
>
> (Zechariah 9:9, cited in Matthew 21:5)

Hebrew poetry makes extensive use of parallelism, and in this case "a colt the foal of an ass" is a parallel that defines "an ass" in the previous line. Matthew, studying the scripture, decided that Jesus had fulfilled this prophecy in a very literal way, by riding on both an ass and a colt.

So there are two problems: unknown context and uncertain contents. If we knew enough about the overall thrust of Jesus' life and work—the context of his own life—we could better control the contents, since some things would fit in the context and some would not. Or if we had a completely reliable list of things Jesus said and did, we could search them to try to determine what context they fit best.

Scholars have addressed both problems, context and content. Drawing partly on general knowledge of the period and partly on more particular knowledge of what happened before and after Jesus' life, they have studied the context in which he worked. To a fair degree these efforts have been successful. Recent studies of religious, social and political currents in Palestine have clarified the general context of Jesus' life (see previous chapter). Judaism is now much better understood than it was before World War II. The discovery of the Dead Sea Scrolls has provided new information. Rabbinic literature—in its present form compiled 200 years or more after Jesus' death—was once considered to represent "first-century Judaism." Jewish society is no longer viewed as having been dominated by the rabbis, and this permits a more realistic assessment of the role of charismatic teachers and healers. Good progress has also been made in the chronological stratification of rabbinic literature, with the result that we can now confidently assign some of it to the period before 70 C.E.[5] This material is useful for our purposes.

The criteria of content

The contents of the synoptic material itself remain difficult. A lot of careful academic effort has gone into establishing criteria of authenticity to test the sayings.[6] Paradoxically, the more the criteria have been refined the less certain we are about which sayings are authentic. In the early days of sifting the sayings, scholars tended to apply the criteria of authenticity mechanically: If saying *x* is contrary to later Christian opinion, Jesus really said it, since a Christian author would not have invented something with which he disagreed. We do not always know what a later Christian author would or would not have invented, and consequently the criteria themselves are subject to doubt. The result of nearly five decades of study is that we know less than we used to think we knew.

Nevertheless, some things are securely known. No one doubts most of the "framework" of the story of Jesus:[7]

- He was born about 4 B.C.E., near the end of Herod's reign.
- He grew into manhood in Nazareth, a Galilean village.
- He was baptized by John the Baptist.
- He called disciples.
- He taught in the towns, villages and open areas (apparently not cities) of Galilee.
- He preached "the kingdom of God."
- About 30 C.E. he went to Jerusalem for Passover.
- He created a disturbance in the Temple area.
- He had a final meal with his disciples.
- He was arrested and interrogated by Jewish authorities, specifically the high priest.
- He was executed on the orders of the Roman procurator, Pontius Pilate.
- His disciples at first fled; they saw him (in what sense is not certain) after his death; as a consequence, they came to believe that he would return to found the kingdom. They formed a community to await his return and sought to win others to believe in him as God's Messiah.

The context of Jesus' career and the framework of his ministry

Jesus' public ministry was bracketed by the preaching of John the Baptist, at its beginning, and the missionary activity of the early Church, after his death and resurrection.

We may be confident that Jesus was baptized by John because of the way the Gospels handle the subject. They all have the Baptist predict that he will be succeeded by one who is greater than he (Matthew 3:11; Mark 1:7; Luke 3:16; John 1:26–27), and Matthew and John both have him explicitly acknowledge Jesus (Matthew 3:14; John 1:29–31,36). The Baptist was widely regarded as a prophet—probably more widely than Jesus.[8] The early Christians were no doubt embarrassed that Jesus began his work by accepting John's baptism. The Christian insistence that Jesus' baptism did not imply his subordination to John shows that he was in fact baptized by him. The authors of the Gospels would not have invented a story which they found embarrassing. John's explicit acknowledgment that Jesus was his greater successor is probably a bit of early Christian apologetics. More likely to be authentic is John's question to Jesus from prison, "Are you he who is to come?" (Matthew 11:3).

From this we learn that Jesus began his mission by accepting baptism at the hands of a man who expected God to establish his kingdom in the immediate future.

Paul, whose letters are our best evidence for early Christian preaching, expected the same thing. He had told his gentile converts in Thessalonica that they would still be alive when the Lord returned. When some of them died, the survivors wondered about the fate of those who were gone. In answer, Paul promised that the dead converts would not lose out. Quoting a "word of the Lord," Paul predicts that when the Lord returns the "dead in Christ" will rise and that both the dead and the living Christians will be caught up "in the clouds to meet the Lord in the air" (1 Thessalonians 4:13–18). Later, when Paul is in prison, he begins to think that he might not live to see the day (Philippians 1:22f.), but he still expects the imminent return of the Lord and the establishment of his "commonwealth" (Philippians 3:20ff.; Romans 13:11–14). This was not a point of contention between Paul and the Jerusalem apostles: Early Christians in general thought that the day was at hand.

Jesus, too, no doubt had this expectation. Since John the Baptist had it before him and Paul, his apostle, had it after him, it would be very difficult to leapfrog over Jesus' own conviction, especially since sayings very much like 1 Thessalonians 4:13–18 are attributed to him: "Truly, I say to you, there are some standing here who will not taste death before they see that the kingdom of God has come with power" (Mark 9:1; see further Matthew 16:27–28, 24:31). Precisely what Jesus thought about the kingdom is less certain. This depends on close exegesis of sayings in the Gospels, which may have been modified or even invented. That Jesus held some sort of expectation about the arrival of "the kingdom" is secure. Nuance and precision, however, can be postulated with less certainty.

This is one of the points that proves that the synoptic Jesus is closer to the historical Jesus than is the Johannine Christ. The synoptic sayings just cited are very close to what Paul thought that Jesus had said, and there are no comparable sayings in John.

The role of the disciples

The next part of the secure framework of Jesus' life is that he called disciples. Both the Gospels and Paul (quoting an earlier tradition) specify that there were 12 special followers (1 Corinthians 15:5; Matthew 10:1–4; Mark 3:13–19; Luke 6:12–16; John 6:67–71). The Synoptics, however, name a total of 13, 11 of them in common (Luke disagrees with Matthew and Mark about the name of the 12th, thus providing a 13th name). John's gospel names another disciple, Nathanael (John 1:45–51), who is not mentioned in the Synoptics. The early Christians seem to have had 12 as a firm number, but they were not certain who should be included. It is probable that Jesus himself spoke of "the twelve," though he was not necessarily followed all the time by precisely 12, nor by precisely the same people. If this is right, the value of the number was symbolic: "The twelve" represented the 12 tribes of Israel. Jesus promised the disciples that "in the new world, when the Son of Man shall sit on his glorious throne, you who have followed me will also sit on twelve thrones, judging the twelve tribes of Israel" (Matthew 19:28). This has the effect of "enthroning" Judas, who was one of the 12 on everyone's reckoning, despite the fact that Judas betrayed Jesus. The early Church, knowing of Judas's betrayal, would not have invented a promise from Jesus that would give Judas a place in the new age, and thus we may accept the saying as authentic.

The use of 12 as a symbolic number and the explicit reference to the 12 tribes points to a very concrete expectation: that the 12 tribes of Israel would be restored. Centuries earlier the Assyrians had scattered ten of the tribes. Obviously it would take an act of God to get them all back together. Numerous Jewish authors hoped that this would happen. Ben Sirach (c. 200 B.C.E.) looked to God to "gather all the tribes of Jacob" and "to give them their inheritance, as at the beginning."[9] The sect associated with the Dead Sea Scrolls (probably a branch of the Essene party) expected the reassembly of the 12 tribes.[10] This same expectation appears in the pseudepigraphical Psalms of Solomon (11, 17:28–31,50) and elsewhere. The tradition was continued in early Christianity (Revelation 21:12).

Jesus himself was a Bible-believing Jew, and like many others he thought that God would honor his promises to the patriarchs and restore the 12 tribes in the last days—just as God had previously wrought miracles on behalf of Israel.

Apparently the disciples thought that they would play an important role in the kingdom that God would establish. In the passage quoted above (Matthew 19:28), Jesus promised to enthrone them in the role of judges. In another passage the disciples debate among themselves about who is greatest.

Jesus rebukes them by saying that those who wish to be first should be last (Mark 9:33–35). More significantly, James and John (who, with Peter, were leading disciples) ask if they could sit at Jesus' right and left in his "glory" (Mark 10:35–45). It seems that there was some dispute among disciples about who would have the leading places in the kingdom.

The destruction of the Temple

The other concrete expectation we can attribute to Jesus is the hope for a renewed Temple. This is reflected in an act and in two sayings. Jesus went to the Temple, where he overturned the tables of the money changers and the stalls of those who sold pigeons (Mark 11:15). When challenged, he justified his action by saying that the Temple, which should be "a house of prayer for all the nations [gentiles]" (quoting Isaiah 56:7), had been turned into "a den of robbers" (Mark 11:17; quoting Jeremiah 7:11).

Later, Jesus predicts that "there will not be left here [in the Temple] one stone upon another, that will not be thrown down" (Matthew 24:1–2; Mark 13:1–2; Luke 21:5–6). According to Mark, this prediction was made privately, to one disciple, while according to Matthew the disciples in general heard it.

After Jesus is arrested, witnesses at his trial before the high priest accuse him of making a different statement about the fate of the Temple: "We heard him say, 'I will destroy this Temple that is made with hands, and in three days I will build another, not made with hands'" (Mark 14:58; Matthew 26:61 lacks the phrases "made with hands" and "not made with hands"). The Gospels maintain that this testimony was false (Matthew 26:59–60; Mark 14:56–59). Nevertheless, when Jesus is on the cross, passersby taunt him by saying "Aha! You who would destroy the Temple and build it in three days, save yourself ..." (Matthew 27:40; Mark 15:29–30).

Thus we have an action at the Temple accompanied by a saying in favor of gentiles; a prediction that not one stone would be left on another; and "false testimony" that Jesus threatened to destroy the Temple. It is difficult to see how these traditions fit together—if they do fit together. Why would Jesus both prepare the Temple for gentile use and predict its destruction? Did he both *threaten* to destroy the Temple and *predict* that it would be destroyed? We begin with the prediction and the threat and consider first the probable early Christian view of them.

By the time the Gospels were written, Christianity had spent several decades making its way in the Roman world. The dominant thrust of the movement was toward acceptance of Roman rule. The Christians' kingdom, they said reassuringly, was not of this world (John 18:36); they posed no threat to Rome, civilization and good order (all of which were more-or-less synonymous). In fact, Christianity was potentially revolutionary, both politically and socially. In some parts of Christianity there was fierce hatred for Rome. In the following passage, "Babylon" is a code word for Rome:

> Fallen, fallen is Babylon the Great! It has become a dwelling place of demons, a haunt of every foul spirit.
>
> (Revelation 18:2)

Christian leaders and spokesmen spent considerable effort trying to convince the rest of society that they posed no threat. On the whole, they were successful. The author of Luke and Acts (both were written by the same man) was especially concerned with this problem. Acts is filled with stories designed to show that Jews made trouble, but the early Christian apostles were completely law-abiding and were always found to be so when tried by a Roman official (e.g., Acts 18:12–27). Not surprisingly, then, the Gospel of Luke does not contain either of the two passages in which Jesus is accused of threatening the Temple. The accusation was known to the author of Luke from his source, or sources (Mark and Matthew), but he simply deleted it.

One way to test the Gospel material for reliability is to ask whether or not it is "against the grain" of the authors or of early Christianity. If it is, it is probably reliable, since an author would not invent a passage that was "against the grain." With regard to the Temple, all three Synoptics want the reader to believe that Jesus *predicted* the destruction of the Temple but did not *threaten* it. We should suspect that in reality it was the other way around: Whatever he did and said with regard to the Temple, it could easily have been taken as a threat of its destruction. We may put this another way: If originally the traditions about Jesus contained a mere prediction of destruction, why would the Christian Church convert the prediction into a threat and then attribute it to false witnesses? The answer is that it would not have done so. The passages in Mark and Matthew about a threat to destroy the Temple are probably there because the accusation was actually made, either at Jesus' trial or when he was on the cross, or both. The Gospels defend him: that was false testimony; Jesus merely predicted, he did not threaten. By the time the Gospels were written, the prediction had been fulfilled: The Temple was destroyed in 70 C.E. A prediction that was fulfilled increased the stature of the prophet.

We can understand why the tradition would have moved from some sort of threatening word or deed to the accusation of making a threat, and then to the Christian reply that the accusers were false witnesses and that Jesus merely predicted. It is difficult, however, to understand the reverse development: A simple prediction, made privately to one or more of his disciples, that had no public consequences would not have resulted in the presence of the threat theme in the Gospels. The authors would have preferred that the threat disappeared entirely. In Luke it does disappear, while in Matthew and Mark it is called "false testimony." It is probable that Jesus really was accused of threatening to destroy the Temple, and Christianity had to answer the accusation.

We may conclude that the accusation that Jesus threatened the Temple is earlier than the claim that he only predicted its destruction. Two reservations must be lodged. First, we cannot hope to know "what Jesus really said." It is possible that he merely predicted and that his words were taken to constitute a threat.

The second reservation is that Jesus did not think, nor could his accusers have thought, that he and his followers could pull down the stones of the Temple or do any serious damage to it. Herod's Temple was enormous, and the stones were monumental. Many of these stones still stand where Herod's workmen laid them. When the high priest and his council heard that Jesus threatened the Temple, they would not have taken it to be a boast of military and engineering skill. However he worded his threat, he would have meant that God would destroy the Temple. The leaders of Jerusalem were not physically afraid of Jesus and his few followers, nor would they have believed that he knew what God would do. They were probably anxious lest his prediction of coming upheaval and the intervention of God should touch off riots.

Overthrowing the tables of the money changers

We now turn from what he said about the Temple's destruction to what he did: overthrowing the tables of money changers and the seats of dove sellers. Biblical law required that sacrifices be offered for numerous reasons and that they be unblemished. This necessitated an inspection of the animal or bird to be sacrificed, an inspection that was carried out by high-ranking priests. At the time of pilgrimage festivals—Jesus was there at Passover—the Temple was full of people wishing to offer sacrifices, and the problem of inspecting the large number of sacrificial victims on the spot would have been considerable. Most offerings were of birds; the solution to the problem was to inspect a lot of doves or pigeons in advance and offer them for sale.* Presumably the Temple and its dealers turned a profit on this, but there is no reason for thinking that it was exorbitant.

The Bible also required that adult males give to the Temple each year

* See Boaz Zissu, "This Place Is for the Birds," *BAR*, May/June 2009.

the Temple tax of one-half shekel, or two drachmas. The Temple demanded that this tax be paid in a standard and reliable coinage, and so pilgrims would need to change their money. Again, there are no accusations of unreasonable charges. In this case, the evidence is against it. Although the Temple tax could be paid at the Temple, it could also be paid in one's own community. If pilgrims found the fees of the money changers too high, news would spread, money would be changed elsewhere and the Temple money changers would be out of business.

What was Jesus doing when he upset the tables and stalls of these worthy citizens who were helping pilgrims to fulfill their biblical obligations? The action of turning over tables and seats was symbolic. The space in which people exchanged money and bought sacrificial birds was large, and just before Passover it would have been crowded. Jesus' action did not seriously disrupt the Temple's business. What did he intend to symbolize? According to the Gospels, he was "cleansing" the Temple for suitable worship. The quotation from Jeremiah in Mark 11:17 (the Temple had become a "den of robbers") gives the tone to the whole: Either the charges were unfair, or the entirety of the trade was wrong and should be removed. A supplementary explanation is based on the quotation from Isaiah, "a house of prayer for all peoples [i.e., gentiles]." This leads to the view that Jesus wanted to break down the barriers built into Temple practice that separated Jew from gentile. Jesus' attack on money changers and dove sellers was really an attack on the cult itself, or on the Temple's separation of people into a hierarchy of purity—priests, Levites, laymen, women and gentiles, in descending order.

Although these views are readily derived from the Gospels, we must look on them with doubt. It is most unlikely that Jesus attacked sacrificial practice or purity distinctions, and very improbable that he sought gentile equality in the Temple. After his death and resurrection, the disciples worshiped in the Temple. They knew nothing of gentile equality. Paul's letters indicate that full commonality between Jews and gentiles developed in Christian circles outside of Palestine (although Acts assigns this dramatic innovation to a series of visions seen by Peter [Acts 10]). In any case, the earliest Church did not attribute to Jesus the idea that there was to be no separation of Jew from gentile. The quotation from Isaiah in Mark 11:17 probably reflects a desire on the part of second-generation gentile churches to ground their own practice in a statement by Jesus himself.

What about the authenticity of the phrase from Jeremiah, "den of robbers" (also Mark 11:17)? This does not suggest that Jesus wanted to overturn the cult, only to purify it of dishonesty. Many scholars, however, delete it from the earliest tradition, and I am inclined to do so as well. The phrase could have been lifted from Jeremiah by anyone. Putting it on Jesus' lips allowed the Christians to depict him as a moral reformer against abuse in high places.

It is probable, then, that we owe both of the quotations in Mark 11:17 ("house of prayer for gentiles"; "den of robbers") to the later Church. If we delete this verse entirely, Jesus' action in the Temple takes on a different coloration. The symbolic action of overturning seats and tables, in and of itself, points at least as readily to destruction as to cleansing. Had Jesus wished to announce symbolically a coming destruction, there is little else that he could have done. A hammer and a carpenter's chisel could have taken out a small hunk of wall, but turning over some tables would have been more public and obvious. This interpretation has the advantage of making sense of both the action and the saying about the Temple's destruction. It is reasonable to think that what he did and what he said ("not one stone left on another") go together. The most likely explanation of this complex of material is that Jesus expected the kingdom to come in the immediate future, at which time the Temple would be destroyed and then rebuilt or transformed. It remains possible, however, that he thought only that the current Temple practice should be reformed for the new age.

To sum up thus far, we have placed Jesus and his message securely in a context of eschatological expectation. He, no less than John the Baptist, Peter and Paul, looked for the arrival of the kingdom in some decisive or final sense. The evidence that has been examined points not to the end of the world, but to a new world, one with leaders (himself and the 12) and a restored or rebuilt Temple.

We should pause to clarify the important term "eschatology." Many people today think that when ancient Jews thought about the end time (*eschaton* in Greek) they had in mind the last moment before the physical dissolution of the universe. Jewish eschatology, however, usually looked forward to a new world in the sense of a new order. Peace and justice will prevail, the lion will lie down with the lamb, life will be easy and food abundant. Jesus and his followers probably shared this general view. Paul thought that Christ, when he returned, would reign for a while before turning the kingdom over to God (1 Corinthians 15:23–28).

The best evidence for Jesus' expectation consists of (1) the saying that the disciples will judge the 12 tribes; (2) the disciples' debates about who will be greatest; (3) Jesus' promise to drink wine with his followers in the kingdom (Mark 14:25); and (4) the material that shows that he expected a renewed or new Temple. All this material is at least basically authentic, and it converges on the same point: the future establishment of the kingdom of God as a new order on earth. "Eschatological expectation" in some sense or other is certain; "new order" is less certain but still highly probable.

Sayings about the kingdom

The word "kingdom" has a diversity of meaning in the Gospels, a diversity that probably goes back to Jesus himself. We may distinguish five sometimes overlapping meanings:

1) The kingdom is a transcendent reality that people enter one by one. Here the kingdom is a sovereignty, or reign, that individuals may accept; acceptance guarantees admission:

> Unless you turn and become as children, you shall not enter into the kingdom of heaven.
>
> (Mark 10:15)

> It is hard for the rich to enter the kingdom of heaven.
>
> (Mark 10:23)

> Not everyone who says to me, "Lord, Lord," will enter into the kingdom of heaven, but the one who does the will of my Father in heaven.
>
> (Matthew 7:21)

2) The kingdom is a future reality that will come, but how it will come and what it will be like are not specified:

> Thy kingdom come!
>
> (Matthew 6:10, in the Lord's Prayer)

3)The kingdom will be established by God's angels, or by the Son of Man, and its arrival will be accompanied by cosmic signs.

Many of the passages that reflect this view do not actually contain the word "kingdom," but the establishment of God's rule is the subject. How the end-time figure came to be called the Son of Man is not clear. Even murkier is Jesus' own view of the relationship between himself and the Son of Man—assuming that he actually predicted the coming of the Son of Man. These are two of the principal passages:

> Whoever is ashamed of me and my words in this adulterous and

> sinful generation, also the Son of Man will be ashamed of him when he comes in the glory of his Father with the holy angels ... There are some standing here who will not taste death before they see that the kingdom of God has come with power.
>
> (Mark 8:38–9:1 and parallels)

> But in those days, after that tribulation, the sun will be darkened, and the moon will not give its light, and the stars will be falling from heaven, and the powers in the heavens will be shaken. And then they will see the Son of Man coming in clouds with great power and glory. And then he will send out the angels, and gather his elect from the four winds, from the ends of the earth to the ends of heaven.
>
> (Mark 13:24–27 and parallels)

4) The kingdom will be a new order on earth.

Several passages already discussed belong in this category: Matthew 19:28 (the disciples judge the tribes of Israel); Mark 9:33–35 (Who is greatest?); Mark 10:35–45 (Who will sit at Jesus' right hand?). There is one further passage that is difficult to assess. According to Matthew 16:18–19, Jesus told Peter that he was "Rock," and that on this rock he would build his church. The saying continues, promising that what Peter binds or looses on earth is bound or loosed in heaven, a promise that is made to the disciples in general in Matthew 18:18.

All scholars agree that Jesus did not foresee an institutional Church with a professional priesthood that would have authority to absolve sins. If that is what the saying means, it is so anachronistic that it cannot be authentic. On the other hand, the nickname "Rock" shows that something authentic lies behind the passage. The name of the disciple whom we call Peter was actually Simon son of Jonas (Matthew 16:17). Paul, however, called him not Simon, but either Cephas (1 Corinthians 1:12, 3:22, 9:5, 15:5; Galatians 1:18, 2:9,11,14) or Peter (Galatians 2:7–8). "Cephas" is the Aramaic word for "rock," while "Peter" is the corresponding Greek word. In other words, Simon son of Jonas went by the nickname "Rock" in both languages. The Gospels were written in Greek for readers of Greek in the second and third generations after Jesus. The synoptic authors felt no need to refer to Simon's Aramaic nickname: He was "Simon" (Mark 1:16 and elsewhere), "Simon called Peter" (Matthew 4:18, 10:2) or simply "Peter" (Mark 5:37 and elsewhere). Paul, however, had met the man in Jerusalem and knew by what name he actually went: Cephas, which Paul turned into Greek (Peter) in only one passage.

The importance of this is that the meaning of Simon's Aramaic nickname was preserved in Greek. It is as if the popular Munich beer were called "Lion's Brew" in the English-speaking world, except by people who had been to Munich and who knew some German, who called it "Löwenbräu." If the brewer wanted to emphasize the "lion-ness" of the beer, he would change its name from country to country: in English it would be "Lion's Brew," in French "Bière de lion," in Hebrew "bîrah shel 'arî" and so forth. In fact, this is not what the brewer has done. What matters to the brewer and the advertising agencies is that it be identified as *German*: its lion-ness is not important. The case of Simon's name, however, fits the hypothetical situation in which Löwenbräu becomes "Lion's Brew." What mattered was the *meaning* of Simon's nickname, "Rock."

From this we should infer that Jesus really did give Simon the name "Rock" or "Rocky" and that the meaning of the nickname was significant. Presumably it did not refer to craggy features, and probably not to strong nerves and emotional stability. Jesus made use of symbols, as we saw in discussing "the twelve." It is a reasonable hypothesis that "rock" was symbolic. If so, "foundation stone" or "cornerstone," as suggested by Matthew 16:18, is a reasonable translation.[11]

Foundation or cornerstone of what? Matthew proposes "church," certainly meaning thereby the Christian Church that he knew (cf. Matthew 18:17). This is the anachronistic part of the saying, which we cannot attribute to Jesus. Jesus could well have thought of Peter as the symbolic cornerstone of the eschatological people of God, including both the reassembled 12 tribes and the gentiles (for gentiles, see Matthew 8:11).

I have spent this many lines on a difficult passage for a reason. This is one of the numerous sayings in the Synoptics that will never yield secure results. We first establish the Aramaic word that Jesus said, and this can be done with certainty. But what did it mean? Did Jesus actually name Simon "Rock" after a messianic confession (so the setting in Matthew)? Was the name symbolic? If so, of what? We may infer here, suggest there, sometimes guess.

Although certainty eludes us, I suspect that the name "Rock" fits some way or other into Jesus' expectation that there would be a new order in which he and his disciples would have the major roles. Beyond this we cannot reasonably go.

5) The kingdom is present in Jesus' words and deeds.

Being asked by the Pharisees when the kingdom of God was

> coming, he answered them, "The kingdom of God is not coming with signs to be observed; nor will they say, 'Lo, here it is!' or 'There!' for behold, the kingdom of God is in the midst of you."
>
> (Luke 17:20–21)

> Now when John [the Baptist] heard in prison about the deeds of the Christ, he sent word by his disciples and said to him [Jesus], "Are you he who is to come, or shall we look for another?" And Jesus answered them, "Go and tell John what you hear and see: the blind receive their sight and the lame walk, lepers are cleansed and the deaf hear, and the dead are raised up, and the poor have good news preached to them. And blessed is he who takes no offense at me."
>
> (Matthew 11:2–6)

Some said that Jesus "casts out demons by Beelzebul, the prince of demons." In his reply Jesus said, among other things,

> If I cast out demons by Beelzebul, by whom do your sons cast them out? Therefore they shall be your judges. But if it is by the finger of God that I cast out demons, then the kingdom of God has come upon you.
>
> (Luke 11:15–20; parallel to Matthew 12:24–28)

These passages have convinced a majority of New Testament scholars that Jesus taught that the kingdom was "somehow" present in his teaching and healing. Although this view is passionately held by many, the evidence for it is not very good. The first passage, "the kingdom ... is in the midst of you" (Luke 17:21), may also be translated "the kingdom ... is within you." Apart from the question of authenticity, the passage does not attribute the presence of the kingdom to Jesus' words and deeds. It is, rather, a denial that the kingdom will be seen in any one place, so that one can point to it. In other words, the kingdom is omnipresent, not a penumbra around Jesus.

Nor does the second passage (Matthew 11:2–6) claim that "the kingdom" is present in Jesus' words and deeds. It is an answer to the question, "Are you the one who is to come?" not "Is the kingdom present wherever you are?" Jesus certainly thought that he was "the one": If his disciples would be the judges of Israel, he presumably would have a higher rank. He may very well have offered his healings and teaching as "signs" to John the Baptist (though to others he said that he would give no signs [Mark 8:11–12]). We noted above that the question of the Baptist is more likely to be authentic than his explicit acknowledgment of Jesus. It does not, however, show that Jesus thought that the kingdom was present, but rather that in his own view *something crucial* was happening in his ministry.

The third passage (Luke 11:20; parallel to Matthew 12:28) states that the kingdom has come upon "you" if Jesus' claim is true, namely that he casts out demons by the power of God, rather than by black magic. Luke does not identify "you," but according to Matthew, Jesus' saying is addressed to Pharisees; in any case, it is directed to people who doubted that he acted by the power of God. What does it mean that the kingdom has "come upon" his opponents? Perhaps that they have run into its power and condemned themselves by not accepting Jesus? In this case, the saying would recall Mark 8:38: "For whoever is ashamed of me and of my words in this adulterous and sinful generation, of him will the Son of Man also be ashamed, when he comes in the glory of his Father with the holy angels." This saying makes crucial one's response to Jesus in the present, but puts the kingdom (the glory of his Father) in the future.

The proponents of the view that these passages show that Jesus thought that the kingdom was present are pushed into saying "present in some sense." But in what sense? It was not present in the sense that God's enemies were defeated. Tiberius, Pilate, Antipas and Caiaphas still ruled. God's will was not yet done "on earth as it is in heaven" (Matthew 6:10).

Admittedly, there is nothing inherently impossible about Jesus having thought that the kingdom was in some way present, while in another way future. Paul could say that the kingdom of God is found where there is "righteousness and peace and joy in the Holy Spirit" (Romans 14:17). The Lord, however, did not yet reign as king; his enemies were not yet defeated. Only after he defeated them would he hand over the kingdom to God the Father (1 Corinthians 15:24–28). By analogy, Jesus could have said that the kingdom of God exists wherever people accept it and live accordingly, but that it would fully come only in the future. He could have thought that the kingdom of God was proleptically (that is, anticipating a future state as though it already existed) and selectively present whenever people encountered him, or that it was omnipresent but unseen. The problem is that the passages about the kingdom do not prove that he thought this. We may accept that he thought that his own work was crucial, and that response to him would determine what happened to the individual when the kingdom arrived; yet it appears that he did not use "kingdom" to refer to the present situation of confrontation and acceptance or rejection. This remains only an intriguing possibility.

What conclusions may we draw about the meaning of the "kingdom of God" as Jesus understood it? The material we have examined neither excludes nor proves any particular meaning beyond doubt. They can all be harmonized: Jesus could have thought that in his own work the kingdom was present by anticipation; that it would come in the future; that it would be marked with cosmic signs and the appearance of the Son of Man with angels; that he and his disciples would have the most prominent places in it; that individual commitment would determine who would enter it when it arrived; *and* that people could enter it in the present time, in the sense of accepting God's reign in their lives and living in accord with his Spirit.

If, however, we ask what is certain, we must answer only that he believed that the moment of decisive change was near and that God was about to establish a new order on earth. This view of the kingdom has sayings in its favor, as do other views. What moves the expectation of a new order from being a mere possibility to a higher status, a meaning that we may confidently attribute to Jesus, is that this is what John the Baptist thought and this is what Jesus' followers thought after his death. Jesus must fit his context; his followers could not have misunderstood him entirely.

Jesus' distinct teaching about the kingdom

This is not to say, however, that Jesus thought only what is common to John the Baptist and Paul. One can make distinctions. The descriptions of John the Baptist, both in the Gospels and in Josephus,[12] indicate that he called all Israel to repent and to live righteously. By contrast, Jesus seems not to have been primarily a preacher of repentance, and the Gospels do not attribute to him a call for *national* repentance. John issued a general appeal for repentance, but Jesus conducted a more personal ministry. John sounds like Billy Graham, but Jesus does not. Many of Jesus' most striking sayings are directed not to crowds, but to a few interlocutors or followers.

It was very much "with the grain" of the Christian movement for Jesus to preach repentance. Both Matthew and Mark summarize Jesus' message as being similar to John's: "The time is fulfilled, and the kingdom of God is at hand; repent, and believe in the gospel" (Mark 1:15; cf. Matthew 4:17), but they give no particular occasion on which he called on "the crowds" to repent. The absence of particular events is especially striking in view of the preference of both authors. Presumably they would have included more passages about repentance if they had them. Luke has several passages on repentance, but the majority of these are best viewed as Luke's own creations. In none of the

Gospels do we hear anything of a mass response in which people renounced their sins (as in the case of John the Baptist), craved God's forgiveness and turned over a new leaf. I am not arguing that Jesus was opposed to general repentance, but rather that his particular message was not that of the mass revivalist.

The thrust of Jesus' ministry—its distinctive character—was that the kingdom would include even sinners if they accepted *him*—not if they reformed. Accepting him may have implied reform, but his message was more the promise of inclusion, especially of sinners, than the requirement of general repentance.

The Gospels several times mention Jesus' association with "toll collectors and sinners" (e.g., Matthew 11:19). We may consider the meaning of each term. In Galilee, toll collectors worked for Herod's son, Antipas. He paid tribute to Rome, but his toll collectors did not directly serve a foreign power. Nevertheless, people assumed that, as a class, the collectors abused their positions by overcharging. In Jesus' view, even they were to be included in the kingdom.

"Sinners" was not a term for ordinary people who, in the normal course of life, sometimes transgressed. The word, rather, represents the Aramaic or Hebrew word that would better be translated as "the wicked"—those who were generally regarded as being beyond God's mercy. People who transgressed and made atonement were not wicked. In the Psalms and subsequent Jewish literature the term is reserved for those who did not attempt to live in accord with God's law. It is these with whom Jesus associated and whom he included in the coming kingdom of God.

Jesus' critics, rather than Jesus himself, used the term "wicked" of some of his followers. Jesus called them by more revealing terms, such as "the lost" (Matthew 10:6, 15:24) and "the poor" (Matthew 11:5; paralleled by Luke 4:18).[13] It is intrinsically likely that Jesus' followers were on the whole from the lower socio-economic orders. Those who were well placed in the present kingdom were less likely to look for another than were the poor. In the ancient world, large numbers of people had little stake in the social order, and it was they who could be mobilized by charismatic leaders. The crowds who followed Jesus, hoping for healings, probably consisted largely of such people.

On the other hand, some of the leading disciples seem to have been fishermen who owned their own boats (Mark 1:16–20) and toll collectors, who were not financially impoverished. Luke indicates that some of Jesus' supporters were women of means (Luke 8:2–3).

Thus "poor," and probably other terms such as "meek" (Matthew 5:5)

DUBY TAL & MONI HARAMATI/ALBATROSS

Sepphoris. *Located only 4 miles from Jesus' hometown of Nazareth, the city of Sepphoris was an important Galilean administrative center during the Roman period. By at least the second century C.E., if not earlier, Sepphoris had many elements of a proper Roman city, including this 4,000-seat theater. Archaeologists continue to debate, however, whether the Sepphoris that Jesus knew was already a thoroughly Hellenized city, or a Galilean town that had largely retained its Jewish character. While some archaeologists have dated the theater to the early first century C.E., for example, others insist that it was built more than a century later.*

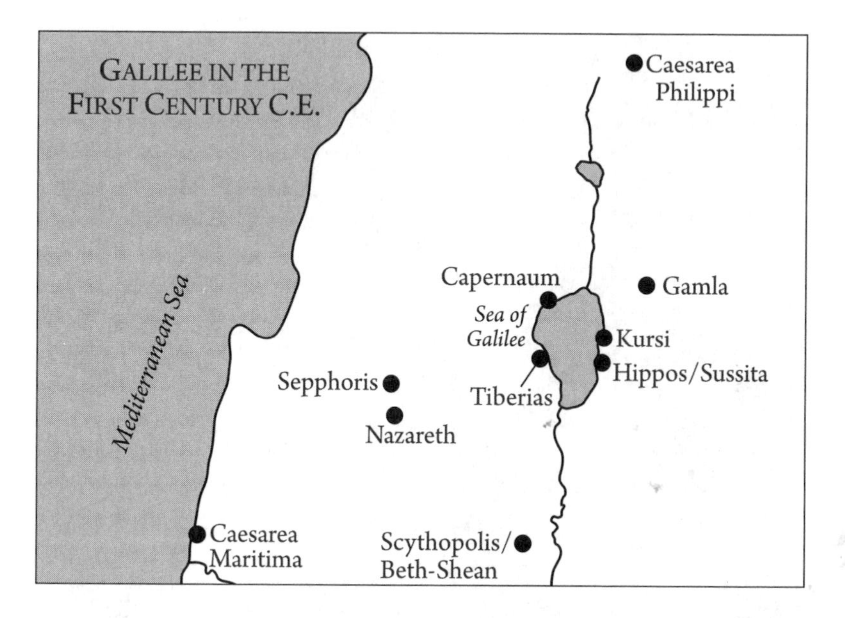

and "lowly of heart" (Matthew 11:29), may be partially accurate and partially misleading if taken as a socio-economic description of those whom Jesus especially sought. On the one hand, he did not seek out the prosperous burghers and the aristocratic priests. The major cities of the Galilee (Tiberias, Sepphoris and Scythopolis) are not mentioned in the Gospels, and Jesus may never have gone to one of them.* In the towns and villages where he did go he would not have met the elite. The crowds he attracted consisted mostly of the economically poor. Yet on the other hand, at least some of his followers were economically above the level of day laborers, and the one group of "sinners" that is identified, the toll collectors, was not financially poor.

Perhaps it is a mistake to try to identify too closely the people to whom he directed his message. We certainly cannot correlate his offer of the kingdom to the sinners with a socio-economic group. The overwhelming impression of the teaching attributed to him is that it was *inclusive.* He proclaimed the kingdom, and he included even sinners in it. We can now say that he did not go to the cities; this may not have been policy on his part, a rejection of urbanism. Perhaps he simply spoke to those who were at hand, the villagers of his native Galilee.[†14]

The inclusive character of his teaching comes out best in the parables that

*But Jesus may well have visited the site of Sepphoris, located just 4 miles from Nazareth. See Mark Chancey and Eric M. Meyers, "How Jewish Was Sepphoris in Jesus' Time?" *BAR*, July/August 2000.

†See Mark Chancey, "How Jewish Was Jesus' Galilee?" *BAR*, July/August 2007.

describe the kingdom as standing the expected order on its head. Laborers who work a short period of time are rewarded as much as those who work all day (Matthew 20:1–16); the lost sheep that is found causes *more* rejoicing than the 99 that did not stray (Matthew 18:12–13; parallel to Luke 15:4–7); the prodigal who returns is feasted, not the obedient and faithful son (Luke 15:25–32). In a word, "many that are first will be last, and the last first" (Mark 10:31, cf. 9:35; Luke 22:26).

Behavior of Jesus' followers

What did Jesus expect his followers to do? The usual problems of authenticity are especially severe in the area of ethics, but there are two even greater difficulties. One is the audience: Did he give ethical admonitions to the populace in general (that is, to all those who would listen), or only to the relatively few who actually *followed* him? The second problem is the relationship of ethical instruction to his expectation that the kingdom would soon come: Did he envisage a very short period during which exceptional moral standards should be maintained?

We turn first to the Sermon on the Mount (Matthew 5–7), the most famous collection of teachings attributed to Jesus. The admonitions of this sermon have three characteristics: They are pacifist, they are perfectionist and they are interiorized. "Interiorization" is seen most clearly in two of the so-called antitheses: Murder and adultery can be committed in the heart (Matthew 5:22,27–30).

Perfection is a main theme. The disciples are to observe every commandment in the Law and prophets and to leave none out (Matthew 5:17–19); to be more righteous than the scribes and Pharisees (Matthew 5:20); to be perfect as God is perfect, loving enemies as well as friends (Matthew 5:44,48). Perfection is implied in many of the individual commands, such as not to take oaths (the perfectly upright do not need to back up their statements); to fast without appearing to do so (avoiding calling attention to oneself); not to pile up wealth (Matthew 5:34–37, 6:16–18, 6:19–21).

Pacifism is one of the hallmarks of the perfect: They pray for their persecutors and are blessed when they are persecuted (Matthew 5:11,44); they "turn the other cheek," give to their legal adversaries more than their suit demands and, if coerced into labor, do more than is required (Matthew 5:39–42).

The admonitions of the Sermon on the Mount are hothouse ethics: They require a special environment and do not do well in the everyday world. The hothouse could be a small sect that partially withdraws from the world, to which members make long-term commitments. They are to grit their teeth, take any manner of abuse and do without all but the bare necessities, knowing that at the end of this life they will gain the eternal kingdom. Or the sect could be eschatological, made up of people living from hand to mouth while they wait for the end of the age. This requires less organization and discipline than the previous possibility and is inherently less stable.

Albert Schweitzer proposed that Jesus taught "interim ethics," that is, ethics valid only for the short period before the arrival of the kingdom, which Jesus expected (according to Schweitzer) within a very few months.[15] Schweitzer's view has generally been rejected, usually because it seems to make Jesus' teaching irrelevant to the ongoing world. There is another objection. Apart from the petition in the Lord's Prayer, "Thy kingdom come" (Matthew 6:10), there is not a whiff of eschatology in the Sermon on the Mount. There is a threat of individual destruction at the end (Matthew 7:24–27), but nothing about the *arrival* of the kingdom or about a looming decisive change.

The perfection required by the Sermon on the Mount is not short-term, buoyed by the expectation of the end, nor is it pneumatological, based on participation in the Spirit of God. Pharisaic daily practice is the model (Matthew 5:20). The differences between Pharisaism and the sermon are interiorization and perfection. One grinds it out, hoping for reward from God (Matthew 6:4,6,18).

Is this the teaching of Jesus? Certain details suggest that it is not. The legal perfection required in Matthew 5:17–20 is counter to the theme that Jesus was not overly strict with regard to the law, as we shall see below. The sermon's requirement to fast is curious in view of the complaint against Jesus that his disciples did not fast (Mark 2:18–22). The ascetic tone is quite different from Jesus' reputation as one who ate and drank, and who associated with toll gatherers and sinners (Matthew 11:19). Toll gatherers, heroes of other passages, are outsiders according to the sermon (Matthew 5:46).

The conflict of individual passages does not, however, constitute irreconcilable contradiction. We must remember the occasional character of Jesus' teaching and also the fact that we can never know whether or not we have the original context—even if we do not doubt the saying itself. He could have said one thing on one occasion but another in different circumstances.

The problem of the Sermon on the Mount

There is a more fundamental problem with the Sermon on the Mount. Considered as a unit, it does not seem to catch the spirit of Jesus' teaching. He expected the kingdom to come in a climactic sense in the near future. If this is correct, the Sermon on the Mount must be seen as striking the wrong note. Expectation of the end of the present order is such a strong factor that it would color everything. Jesus probably taught a perfectionist ethic, but we should view it in the context of eschatological expectation rather than strict intracommunity discipline and practice.

The best evidence for perfectionism is the prohibition of divorce or remarriage. Paul attributes a saying on divorce to Jesus (1 Corinthians 7:10ff.), as do four passages in the Gospels. A short form of the prohibition appears in Matthew 5:31–32 (parallel to Luke 16:18) and a long form in Mark 10:2–12 (parallel to Matthew 19:3–9). Paul's version and the short form in the Synoptics basically prohibit remarriage after divorce, though Matthew's version assumes that divorce makes the woman commit adultery because she will have no means of support unless she remarries. Thus Matthew's short form is tantamount to a prohibition of divorce. The long form, on the other hand, forbids divorce on the basis of biblical interpretation: God originally "made them male and female"; and the Bible states that, when he marries, a man leaves his father and mother and becomes "one flesh" with his wife. "So they are no longer two but one flesh. What therefore God has joined together, let not man put asunder" (Mark 10:6–9; parallel to Matthew 19:6).

This, the best attested of all Jesus' teachings, perfectly illustrates how uncertain we are of precisely what he said. Was it "no remarriage after divorce" (Luke and Paul)?; "no divorce because it requires remarriage, which is adultery" (Matthew's short form)?; or "no divorce because it is contrary to God's intention when he created humans" (the long form)? All the versions are stricter than biblical and common Jewish law, which allowed a man to divorce his wife and permitted both parties to remarry. While we cannot know which of these strict views was Jesus' own, we should nevertheless point out that the long form is probably eschatological. Many people who expected a new order thought that it would be a reestablishment of the original order of creation. The two biblical passages quoted in the long form, "male and female he created them" and "the two become one flesh," are from Genesis (1:27, 2:24), and thus they were read as referring to the state of paradise. The long form of the passage on divorce, by referring back to the time of creation, implicitly points forward to the new age and requires Jesus' followers to start living as if the new age has arrived.

Once we accept one perfectionist teaching, shall we accept them all? Or should we doubt that the "winebibber and glutton, the friend of toll collectors and sinners" required a superhuman perfection of his followers? What counts against the perfectionism of the Sermon on the Mount is its hothouse and noneschatological character. The impression of a small group, striving heroically to be more righteous than the Pharisees, is too communitarian to correspond to the historical circumstances of Jesus and his movement. Perfectionism requires either intense eschatological expectation or a small, disciplined community, or both (as in the sect associated with the Dead Sea Scrolls). The Sermon on the Mount offers us instead the perfectionism of a disciplined community without eschatology. It is unlikely that this kind of perfectionism corresponds to Jesus' movement during his own lifetime, which had the reverse characteristics: eschatology, not a stable, closed society.

Authenticity of individual sayings

This judgment does not decide which individual sayings within the sermon are authentic. These have to be studied one by one. We shall consider a few examples.

The numerous admonitions not to be self-seeking fit well into Jesus' own lifetime. The long passage in Matthew (6:25–34) on not being anxious about material possessions is a case in point. For example:

> Look at the birds of the air: They neither sow nor reap nor gather into barns ... Consider the lilies of the field, how they grow; they neither toil nor spin ... If God so clothes the grass of the field, which today is alive and tomorrow is thrown into the oven, will he not much more clothe you, O men of little faith?
>
> (Matthew 6:26–30)

Jesus and his closest followers did leave their homes, families and possessions, at least for a short period (according to 1 Corinthians 9:5, Peter traveled with his wife), and these verses fit that context. But Jesus was not a 1960s hippie, he was a first-century proclaimer of the kingdom of God. What fueled this passage (assuming that it is his) and the action based on it was eschatological expectation, not childish irresponsibility.

In early Christian literature we can see the Church struggling with this aspect of Jesus' eschatological ethic. Paul urged his converts to "deal with the world as though they had no dealings with it"; the basis for this was the belief that it was "passing away" (1 Corinthians 7:31). Yet this did not mean that they should quit their jobs and beg on the street. Paul had to admonish the Thessalonian Christians to live quietly, mind their own affairs and work with their hands, so that they would be "dependent on nobody" (1 Thessalonians 4:11–12). According to Acts, the members of the early Christian community in Jerusalem sold their possessions and lived in common (Acts 4:32–37). Using capital for daily expenses had the result that we should expect: The funds were soon exhausted. Paul spent a considerable portion of his career taking up a collection for Jerusalem from his hard-working gentile converts. (On the collection, see Galatians 2:10; 2 Corinthians 8–9; Romans 15:25–27.)

From these difficulties over money and work in the early Church, we may infer that the admonition to give up one's possessions and family does go back to Jesus' own teaching, especially his call to follow him (see Mark 8:34–37, 10:29–30; Matthew 10:37–39). It is probable that Jesus did not expect, or even want, many to "follow" him in this way. He proclaimed the good news of the coming kingdom to more people than he directly called into discipleship.[16] He almost certainly thought of surrender of home, property and family as being for a short period only, until the kingdom arrived. In the Sermon on the Mount the admonition to "give to the one who begs from you" (Matthew 5:42) and the implied admonition to live like the lilies of the field are probably authentic sayings, but they have been separated from their original eschatological context. We do not see, on the basis of these chapters, how the Christian community could give practical effect to these sayings. From Acts and Paul we learn more: Share until the money and food run out, then appeal for aid.

Thus in the Sermon on the Mount we have sayings that, individually judged, may be deemed authentic (as well as some that are unauthentic), but which have been transferred from their original context. Originally, they probably applied to a small number of followers for what Jesus thought would be a short period of time.

If we generalize on the basis of this analysis, we shall conclude that Jesus probably did expect "perfection" of his immediate followers: They gave up everything for his sake and the sake of the kingdom. It is, however, doubtful that this was his message to the crowds. Even Matthew 5:1 depicts the Sermon on the Mount as being directed to the disciples, not the multitude. In Luke's parallel (the Sermon on the Plain), Jesus heals many in the crowd, but he delivers the sermon to his disciples (Luke 6:19ff.). We further note that in many of the other crowd scenes there is little or no teaching, and no perfectionist teaching at all (Mark 2:4, 3:9,20, 4:1–9).

In short, Jesus proclaimed the kingdom to all who would hear; he called only a few to a special life of discipleship. To oversimplify only slightly: Parables of the kingdom were directed to the crowds, perfectionist ethics to the disciples.

Jesus told the crowds that God loves the lost and that they would be in the kingdom. What did he expect *them* to do? Presumably to act accordingly. If God treated them with mercy and tolerance, they should treat others in the same way. If Jesus gave them detailed instructions, we do not have them. He seems to have worked on the basis of a principle that was formulated some decades later:

> In this is love, not that we loved God but that he loved us ... Beloved, if God so loved us, we also ought to love one another.
>
> (1 John 4:10–11)

"Love" is the central word in the "two greatest" commandments that Jesus selected from the Hebrew Bible: Love God, and love your neighbor (Mark 12:28–34, quoting Deuteronomy 6:4ff.; Leviticus 19:18). He could summarize the entire scripture using only the second of these commandments:

> So whatever you wish that others would do to you, do so to them; for this is the law and the Prophets.
>
> (Matthew 7:12)

This is not, however, ethical instruction, since it is not sufficiently detailed to determine individual decisions, especially when there are competing claims on one's love. But the main element of Jesus' teaching was the all-encompassing love of God that motivates and inspires those who receive it. We may, after all, find the heart of his ethical teaching in the Sermon on the Mount: "Love your enemies ... so that you may be children of your Father who is in heaven" (Matthew 5:44–45). Human perfection is based on God's love of all, both the good and the evil.

The law

Several stories in the Gospels concern Jesus' relationship to the Jewish law.[17] These passages create the impression that Jesus was lax about observance of the law, but on closer examination we shall see that there are no clear instances of actual transgression. Most of the legal debates concern the Sabbath. In some cases, he was questioned for healing on the Sabbath (Mark 3:1–6; Luke 13:10–17, 14:1–6). According to one passage, he defended his disciples for plucking grain on the Sabbath (Mark 2:23–28). He is depicted as debating hand washing and vows of gifts to the Temple (Mark 7:1–13). One saying seems to be directed against the food laws: "There is nothing outside a person which by going in can defile; but the things that come out are what defile" (Mark 7:14–19). He discussed which are the greatest commandments (Mark 12:28–34). In a section of the Sermon on the Mount called the antitheses, he appears to set his own teaching over against the law (Matthew 5:21–47). We shall begin with the last section.

The format of the antitheses is this: an opening statement, "you have heard that it was said ..." (or "it was said"); followed by a biblical quotation; and then a response, "but I say to you ..." Many scholars have understood "but I say to you" as antithetical to the biblical passage and thus as showing that Jesus opposed the Mosaic law. We saw above that one of these passages, the saying on divorce, is doubtless authentic, at least with regard to general contents:

> It was also said [in the law], "Whoever divorces his wife, let him give her a certificate of divorce." But I say to you that every one who divorces his wife ... makes her an adulteress ...
>
> (Matthew 5:31–32)

Many scholars think that here Jesus sets his own authority directly against the law. This is, however, incorrect. The antitheses are not actually antithetical to the law;[18] they are rather interpretations of the law, as the terminology indicates. In traditional Jewish legal debate, the verb "to say" means "to interpret." "Concerning this we say" in the Dead Sea Scrolls means "this is our interpretation." In rabbinic literature, "Rabbi X says" is used in the same way. The terminology in the antitheses does not imply that Jesus directly opposed the law of Moses.

In the prohibition of divorce, Jesus' view is stricter than that of the law, but it is not against the law. If one never divorces, one will not transgress the Mosaic stipulations (Deuteronomy 24:1–4).

A second example is the saying on murder and anger:

> You have heard that it was said to the men of old, "You shall not kill ..." But I say to you that every one who is angry with his brother shall be liable to judgment ...
>
> (Matthew 5:21ff.)

Here "You shall not be angry" is, according to David Daube, "the revelation of a fuller meaning [of the commandment] for a new age. The second statement unfolds rather than sweeps away the first."[19] Jesus is the interpreter of the law, not its opponent. This was certainly the understanding of the earliest known student of these sayings, the person who put together the Sermon on the Mount, where the antitheses are not against the law, but rather exemplify the preceding passage: "I have not come to abolish [the Law and the prophets] but to fulfill them" (Matthew 5:17)—fulfill them by going beyond them in some instances.

Going beyond the law may imply a kind of criticism of it: It is not rigorous enough, or it is not adequate for the new age. We have already noted this point in discussing the pericope on divorce, and it may be accepted as true of Jesus' teaching to his close followers.

Did he at any point actually oppose the law? The only passage that says this is Mark 7:19, "He declared all foods clean." This is Mark's interpretation of the saying that it is not what goes in that defiles, but what comes out. The Mosaic law explicitly forbids the consumption of some foods (Leviticus 11; Deuteronomy 14). If Jesus said, and literally meant, "what goes in does not defile," he opposed the law. It is, however, more likely that this is an example of hyperbolic antithesis, a well-known device for making a rhetorical point, frequently used in the Bible and subsequent Jewish literature. Hyperbolic antithesis uses "not ... but" in an exaggerated way to mean "less ... more." When Moses told the Israelites that their murmurings were *not* against Aaron and himself *but* against the Lord, they had just been complaining to *him* (Exodus 16:2–8). The sentence means, "Your murmurings directed against us are in reality, and more importantly, against the Lord, since we do his will." When the author of the Letter of Aristeas wrote that Jews "honor God" "*not* with gifts or sacrifices *but* with purity of heart and of devout disposition,"[20] he did not mean that sacrifices were not brought, nor that he was against them (he approved of sacrifices[21]), but rather that what matters most is what they symbolize. Similarly Mark 9:37, "Whoever receives me, receives *not* me *but* the one who sent me," means "receiving me is tantamount to receiving God."[22] "*Not* what goes in *but* what comes out" in Mark 7:15, then, could well mean, "What comes out—the wickedness of a person's heart—is what really matters," leaving the food laws as such untouched. If this interpretation is correct, there is no conflict with the law.

There is a very good reason for doubting that Mark's comment ("he declared all foods clean") correctly describes Jesus' view. The first generation of Christians did not know that Jesus had "canceled" the food laws. According to Acts 10, Peter was first told in a repeated vision that all foods are clean. He found this so hard to accept that, after seeing the vision three times, he was still "inwardly perplexed" (Acts 10:17). In view of this ignorance, we must conclude that Jesus did not command his disciples to ignore the food laws. The saying is either unauthentic or hyperbolic. In either case, Mark's interpretation does not give Jesus' own view.

The other passages on the law do not even represent Jesus as opposing it. In Mark 2:23–28, he justifies a minor transgression on the part of his disciples by arguing that the Sabbath was made for humans, not humans for the Sabbath; therefore, since they had no food, they were justified in plucking grain. In Luke 13:10–17, he justifies healing a woman on the Sabbath by laying his hands on her, again arguing that human need overrides the Sabbath law. Most Jews agreed with this principle, though there were disagreements about when to apply it, some holding that life must be at risk. In any case, the justification of minor transgressions by means of legal argument shows basic respect for the law. A person who defends minor transgression does not oppose the law itself.

The controversies over hand washing and the use of the word *korban* ("given to God") in vowing goods to the Temple do not touch the Written Law, but are (as Mark 7:3 correctly notes) only against the traditions of the scribes and Pharisees.

We must also note that the settings of many of these passages are contrived and appear unreal. Pharisees did not really post themselves around Galilean cornfields on the Sabbath hoping to catch a transgressor (Mark 2:23–24), nor did scribes and Pharisees make special trips from Jerusalem to Galilee to check on the state of people's hands when they ate (Mark 7:1). Further, in both cases it is the *disciples* who were criticized, not Jesus himself; he only springs to their defense. The likeliest explanation of these passages, as Rudolf Bultmann proposed long ago, is that the settings derive from the post-resurrection Christian Church, sections of which had stopped observing the Sabbath and food laws.[23] They utilized sayings in new contexts to defend their own departure from the law. Jesus may have said, "the Sabbath is made for humans, not humans for the Sabbath," but only the Marcan context makes it a justification for transgressing the law.

Finally, while in some few instances Jesus is represented as a kind of legal expert—most notably in the antitheses—this was by no means his primary role. Jesus was a charismatic teacher and healer, not a legal teacher.[24] The contrast between a charismatic, individualistic and populist teacher and a legal expert should be emphasized. Jesus is sometimes called "rabbi" in the Gospels (Mark 9:5, 14:45) or "teacher" (Matthew 8:19, 12:38), and often he is said to "teach" (Mark 1:21, 2:13). Consequently modern scholars sometimes write about Jesus the Rabbi. In such books he is thought of as sitting down with his listeners, opening the Bible (or recalling a passage from memory), laying out competing interpretations and offering his own. Jewish "parties" or "schools" disagreed about interpretation of the law, and Jesus is often seen in this context: He studied the law, adopted distinctive legal positions and schooled disciples.

Following this model, one would expect the primary topic of his teaching to be the law. But the whole model is, I think, wrong. If Jesus' teaching had been of this sort, we should have more material like the antitheses, where he is depicted as taking up a biblical passage and offering his interpretation of it.

The great bulk of his teaching, however, is about the kingdom, and the characteristic style is the parable or brief saying. The focus is on what God is like (he includes the lost and is surprisingly merciful) and on what the kingdom *will be* like (values will be reversed; those who are last will be first). Outside the antitheses, there is virtually no *legal* exegesis.

We misconceive Jesus if we think of him primarily as a teacher of the law—a rabbi in that sense. Rather, he preached the kingdom and God's love of the lost; he expected the end to come soon; he urged some to give up everything and follow him; he taught love of the neighbor. His message did not have primarily to do with how the law should be obeyed.

Miracles

We can better understand the kind of man Jesus was, and how he attracted crowds and followers, if we focus on his miracles. People flocked to him seeking to be healed (see, for example, the summary in Mark 1:32–34).

Neither he nor others thought that his miracles showed that he was a supernatural being. They were evidence, rather, that he had the Spirit of God. Some doubted even that. His opponents charged that he cast out demons with the help of the Prince of Demons (Mark 3:22). He replied, in effect, that it was the Spirit of God that empowered him (Matthew 12:28).

The miracles attributed to Jesus are not significantly different from those attributed to pagan deities, especially the Greek god Asclepius, and to other miracle workers. We glimpse this even within the Gospels. When the Pharisees accused him of casting out demons by the Prince of Demons, Jesus asked, "By whom do your sons cast them out?" (Matthew 12:27), thus acknowledging that the "sons" of the Pharisees—that is, members of the Pharisaic party—could also exorcise. In another instance, someone who was not a follower of Jesus was nevertheless casting out demons in his name (Mark 9:38–41). This probably shows the consciousness of the early Christians that they had competition.

Jesus and his followers, like most other ancients, believed in spiritual powers, some demonic, and they attributed many illnesses, as well as antisocial behavior, to them (see, for example, Mark 5:1–13, where Jesus sent the evil spirits that inhabited a demoniac into 2,000 swine, which rushed into the Sea of Galilee and drowned*). They also believed that God sent sickness and death as punishment for sins; this is reflected in the story of Jesus healing a man by telling him that his sins were forgiven (Mark 2:1–12; parallel to Matthew 9:1–8).

*This miracle has traditionally been commemorated at the site of Kursi on the eastern shore of the Galilee. See Vasilios Tzaferis, "A Pilgrimage to the Site of the Swine Miracle," *BAR*, March/April 1989.

TODD BOLEN/BIBLEPLACES.COM

The Pool of Siloam. *In 2004, the stepped remains of the ancient Siloam Pool, long thought to be located elsewhere, were uncovered in the City of David. It was here that, according to the New Testament, Jesus restored sight to the blind man (John 9:1–11). The pool, dated to the late Second Temple Period (first century B.C.E.–first century C.E.), probably served as a* miqveh, *a Jewish ritual bath.*

Jesus' followers, and possibly Jesus himself, besides seeing the miracles as proof that he had the Spirit of God, saw in them the fulfillment of prophecy. When John the Baptist sent a message to Jesus, asking, "Are you he who is to come?" Jesus appealed to the miracles:

> Go and tell John what you hear and see: The blind receive their sight and the lame walk, lepers are cleansed and the deaf hear, and the dead are raised up, and the poor have good news preached to them.
>
> (Matthew 11:4–5)

This answer draws on both Isaiah 35:5ff. and 61:1. There is a very good possibility that this reply is authentic. We noted above that the later Christian Church, which held that from the outset John had recognized Jesus as "the one who is to come," would probably not have invented a question by John on that point. If the question is authentic, the answer may well be also. Jesus responds that his miracles fulfill prophecy and show that he is "the one who is to come." The precise definition of "the one," however, is left open.

©ERICH LESSING

Basilica at Kursi. *This late fifth- or early sixth-century basilica and monastery overlooking the Sea of Galilee was built on the traditional site of the swine miracle. The story of Jesus casting demons from a man into a herd of pigs is mentioned with variations in the three Synoptic Gospels (Mark 5:1–20; Luke 8:26–39; Matthew 8:28–34). Covering 4 acres, the monastery complex was constructed as a hospice for pilgrims as well as a community for monks.*

Conflict and death

During his ministry, at least according to the account in the Synoptics, Jesus made only one trip from Galilee to Jerusalem; within a week of entering the city he was dead. The trip moved him not only from one geographical region to another, but also from one political sphere to another. Galilee was ruled by Antipas, one of Herod's sons. Although he reigned at Rome's pleasure, he was Jewish. He had his own troops and his own system of justice. When Jesus entered Judea, he moved into a Roman province, in which a Roman held full military and legal authority.

In Jesus' day the Roman prefect was Pontius Pilate. Pilate, like other Roman administrators, used local leaders to handle day-to-day affairs. In Jerusalem, the high priest, surrounded by a council of other aristocrats, governed.[25] He had at his disposal a very large armed police force. The high priest was the man in the middle. If he failed to control the local population and Roman troops had to be used, more blood would be shed than if he maintained order. The Roman troops hardly loved the Jewish population, and we may be sure that the Jews were not fond of them. It was the high priest and his guards who kept the two sides apart, by maintaining order and suppressing unrest.

Jesus came to Jerusalem at Passover time—one of the three pilgrimage festivals of the Jewish year, and the most popular. Jews came from far and near to worship and to eat the Paschal lamb in or near the Holy City. Tents were set up in a substantial area outside the city walls;[26] inside the streets were packed. Passover commemorated the Exodus from Egypt, the time of Israel's liberation from bondage. Thus it was charged with political significance, and many doubtless felt anger and resentment at the Romans, whom they saw as the current equivalent of Pharaoh. The bondage of Israel was light, as bondage goes, but still it was not freedom. Since trouble was likelier to break out at a pilgrimage festival than at any other time,[27] it was the custom of the prefect to come to Jerusalem from Caesarea, bringing extra troops.[28]

The scene changes in another sense. The scribes and Pharisees, so prominent in the story until now, almost vanish. In Mark, after Jesus enters Jerusalem, Pharisees are mentioned only in 12:13 (parallel to Matthew 22:15–22), where they join with others to question Jesus about paying taxes to Caesar. In Luke, they are numbered among the multitude watching Jesus enter, and they offer him advice (Luke 19:39). Pharisees also appear in Matthew 22:34,41, but not in a strongly hostile sense. They are denounced in Matthew 23, and they go with the chief priests to see Pilate in Matthew 27:62, to ask that Jesus' tomb be guarded. Even in Matthew, however, they are not the main adversaries. That role is played by the chief priests.

Jesus' last week

There are five major events in the story of Jesus' last week.

1) He entered Jerusalem on a donkey; people welcomed him by shouting:

> Hosanna! Blessed is he who comes in the name of the Lord! Blessed is the kingdom of our father David that is coming.
>
> (Mark 11:9–10)

According to Matthew and Luke, they explicitly called him "king" or "son of David" (Matthew 21:9; Luke 19:38).

2) He went to the Temple, where he turned over the tables of money changers and the seats of those who sold pigeons (Mark 11:15–19).

3) He shared a last supper with his disciples, saying that he would not drink wine again "until that day when I drink it new in the kingdom of God" (Mark 14:22–25).

4) The high priest's guards arrested him and took him before the high priest and his council. Witnesses accused him of having threatened to destroy the Temple, but he was not convicted. He admitted to the high priest, however, that he was both "Christ" (in Hebrew, *meshiah*) and "Son of God," and he was convicted of blasphemy (Mark 14:43–64).

5) His captors sent him to Pilate, who interrogated him and then ordered that he be crucified for claiming to be "king of the Jews" (Mark 15:1–5,15,18,26).

There are two principal questions: "Why was he arrested?" and "On what charge was he executed?" The second question, which leads to the discussion of Christology (the Christian doctrine of who Jesus was), has drawn a great deal of attention. The first, however, the motive for his arrest, is historically more illuminating. The formal charge against him could have been trumped up, but there must have been some explanation for his arrest.

Some light is shed on the topic by the account of his arrest. Jesus and his disciples shared what would be their last supper, apparently on Passover evening (Matthew 26:17–29; Mark 14:12–25; Luke 22:7–20). After the meal, probably around midnight, he went to Gethsemane (usually placed on the Mount of Olives, a hill east of the Temple) to pray. After some time, but still well before dawn, he was arrested. Matthew gives what is doubtless the right explanation of the time of the arrest: The high priest ordered that it not be "during the feast, lest there be a tumult among the people" (Matthew 26:5). The secret arrest indicates that Jesus had become a public figure during Passover week, and that action against him might lead to upheaval.

Two previous events posed this threat: Jesus' entry into the city and his attack on money changers and bird sellers in the Temple. If the entry into Jerusalem, with people shouting about the kingdom of David, really took place and really involved a lot of people, it is surprising that Jesus was not arrested earlier. There are two possible explanations: (1) The demonstration was extremely small, and was limited to the outskirts of Jerusalem and attracted little attention; (2) The high priest's security forces did not know where to find Jesus. It is likely that both of these are true. A large demonstration almost certainly would have attracted armed intervention. Even a small following, inspired by enthusiasm for the coming kingdom, would have alarmed the high priest. But he may not have known where to find the troublemaker and how to arrest him quietly. Later, one of Jesus' disciples, Judas, betrayed him (Mark 14:10ff., 14:43–46), but earlier in the week Jesus was probably lost in the crowds.

The second incriminating action was Jesus' turning over seats and tables in the Temple area. This, too, was probably a small demonstration. The story does not mention the disciples, who may not even have been present. Had Jesus run rampant, upsetting tables and chairs over the whole area, the Temple guards would have intervened.

That both these incidents figured in the authorities' concern is evident from later events. When Jesus was taken before the high priest and his council, the first charge against him was that he had threatened the Temple. Pilate executed him on the charge of claiming to be "king of the Jews," which reflects his entry into Jerusalem. These charges may have been exaggerated; possibly he did not say "I will destroy the Temple" and "I am the king of the Jews." But, when one considers his teaching about the "kingdom," his view that accepting him was important for future membership in it and the shouts of his followers when he entered Jerusalem, the charge that he claimed to be king is perfectly understandable. Similarly, his statement about the coming destruction of the Temple, coupled with his act of physical violence, could be construed as a threat to destroy it.

Caiaphas and Pilate knew that Jesus did not have an army that could defeat the Temple guards and the Roman troops, much less the larger forces available in Syria. Had the high priest and the prefect suspected a real *putsch,* Jesus' disciples would have been rounded up as well. What they feared was an uprising—the fear of all colonial powers. Especially in Jerusalem at Passover, talk about David's kingdom and a new or renewed Temple could inspire the populace to think that redemption was at hand. They might rise to strike a blow to hasten it, as they in fact did some 30 years later.

Jesus' arrest reveals that he was regarded as potentially dangerous. Why was he not merely flogged as a warning and released? Josephus tells of another

Jesus, the son of Ananias, about 30 years later. At the Feast of Tabernacles (Sukkot), in a period that was otherwise peaceful, Jesus son of Ananias went to the Temple, where he cried,

> A voice from the east, a voice from the west, a voice from the four winds; a voice against Jerusalem and the sanctuary, a voice against the bridegroom and the bride, a voice against all the people.[29]

This prediction of destruction—that it was such is clear from the reference to the bridegroom and the bride, taken from Jeremiah 7:34—led to his being interrogated and flogged, first by the Jewish authorities, then by the Romans. He answered questions by "unceasingly reiterat[ing] his dirge over the city," and was finally released as a maniac. He kept up his cries for seven years, especially at the festivals, but otherwise not addressing the populace. Finally, a stone from a Roman catapult killed him.[30]

Our Jesus' offense was worse than that of Jesus son of Ananias. Jesus of Nazareth had a following, perhaps not very large, but nevertheless a following. He had taught about "the kingdom" for some time. He had taken physical action in the Temple. He was not a madman. Thus he was potentially dangerous. Conceivably he could have talked his way out of execution had he promised to take his disciples, return to Galilee and keep his mouth shut. He seems not to have tried.

The trial of Jesus

In Matthew and Mark there are two hearings before Jewish authorities, but only one in Luke (Matthew 26:57–75, 27:1–2; Mark 14:53–72, 15:1; Luke 22:54–71). It is very likely that the long trial scene of Matthew and Mark is simply an expansion of the short one. In this case, the original report was simply that the chief priests and others consulted about Jesus, bound him and turned him over to Pilate.

It is the longer scene, however, that has always attracted attention. According to Mark's version, witnesses testified that Jesus had threatened the Temple, but they did not agree (presumably on details), and so the charge failed. The high priest then asked Jesus, "Are you the Christ, the Son of the Blessed?" Jesus admitted that he was, but immediately predicted that the Son of Man would come on clouds of glory. The high priest cried, "Blasphemy," and the council condemned Jesus (Mark 14:53–72).[31]

In a Jewish context, it is difficult to construe either "Son of the Blessed [that is, God]" or "Christ" as blasphemy. Neither denigrates God. On the other hand, "Christ" and "Son of God" became the two favorite Christian titles for Jesus, and some Christians understood them in a way that Jews might have regarded as blasphemous. That is, the combination "Christ," "Son of God" and "blasphemy" fits the post-resurrection Church better than the lifetime of Jesus. The "false" charge that he threatened the Temple, on the other hand, is very close to what the Gospels tell us he did. If the trial scene is in any way accurate, it is more likely that the charge about the Temple was the telling one. Jesus was taunted with that accusation while on the cross (Mark 15:29ff.), not with claiming to be the Son of God. The authors of the Gospels, in a period when the Church was making its way in the Roman Empire, did not want Jesus to appear as a rabble-rouser or as someone who threatened peace and good order. They toned down the threat to the Temple to a mere prediction (Mark 13:2 and parallels) and said that the accusation that he threatened it was false. His physical act against it they interpreted as "cleansing," as if the Temple personnel were corrupt ("a den of robbers," Mark 11:17). They preferred that he die for professing the Christology of the Church.

As we saw above, it is probable that we should reverse their preference: He was executed because he posed a threat to public order, not because he applied to himself the titles "Christ" and "Son of God."

Our understanding of how it was that Jesus came to die does not, however, depend on a reconstruction of Mark 14:55–65. It is more instructive to focus on the main movement of events: Jesus' entry into Jerusalem, his demonstration against the Temple, his stealthy arrest by the high priest's guards, his crucifixion and the taunts about the Temple. One can understand the sequence of events without entering into the details of the trial scene.

The attack on the Temple seems to have been crucial in persuading Caiaphas and Pilate that Jesus should die. It confirmed his potential to make trouble, and it showed that he might use physical violence, even if of a very minor kind.

Since Jesus' action in the Temple had such drastic consequences, we need to return to the question of why he did it. We have seen that it was a symbolic gesture, as were some of his other deeds. If we consider them as a group, we may be able to better understand Jesus' intention.

As did many prophets before him, Jesus communicated by symbolic acts as well as by words. He called 12 disciples, apparently to represent the coming restoration of the 12 tribes of Israel. He ate with sinners, in order to indicate that they would be included in the kingdom. He entered Jerusalem on a donkey, perhaps to remind his followers of Zechariah 9:9 (cited at Matthew 21:5: "Your king is coming to you, humble, and mounted on an ass"). When he overturned tables and stalls in the Temple area, he was probably also acting symbolically, perhaps indicating that the Temple would be renewed.

His last meal with the disciples seems also to have been a symbol, one that pointed toward the coming kingdom, which would be like a banquet. (On the kingdom as banquet, see also the parables in Matthew 22:1–14 and Luke 14:15–24.)

Since the other symbolic acts reflect Jesus' expectation of a coming kingdom, it is probable that his demonstration in the Temple was intended in the same way. By both word and deed he proclaimed that the kingdom would come, that Israel would be restored, that the Temple would be rebuilt (or renewed), that he and his disciples would be leading figures in the kingdom and that people previously regarded as "last" (sinners and toll gatherers) would become the "first."

These expectations, however, were not fulfilled, at least not in any obvious way. What did happen was a surprise.

When Jesus was executed, his disciples, reasonably thinking that they would be next, hid. Some of his women followers—who were safer than the men and possibly braver—cared for his body. When they returned to the tomb a day and a half later (he died and was buried on Friday; they returned Sunday morning), they found that the tomb was empty. Jesus appeared to them and then later to the disciples in Galilee. The result of this was that they gathered in Jerusalem to wait for his return, which they expected soon. That is, they did not give up his idea that the kingdom would come; they now expected him to return from heaven to establish it. The movement grew and spread geographically. Twenty-five or more years later, Paul—a convert, not an original disciple—still expected Jesus to return within his own lifetime. But the Lord tarried.

The "delay" led to creative and stimulating theological reflection, seen for example in the Gospel of John. Meanwhile, the man behind it all became remote. The synoptic material was by no means immune from this same kind of development. The consequence is that it takes patient spadework to dig through the layers of Christian devotion and to recover the historical core. Historical reconstruction is never absolutely certain, and in the case of Jesus it is often highly uncertain. Despite this, we have a good idea of the main lines of his ministry and his message.

The risen Lord

A discussion of the resurrection is not, strictly speaking, part of the story of "the historical Jesus," but part of the aftermath of his life. A few words about the different resurrection accounts may nevertheless be useful. According to Matthew and Mark, the disciples went to Galilee and saw Jesus there; according to Luke they did not leave the environs of Jerusalem. The story of

COURTESY ANDRÉ LEMAIRE

COURTESY ANDRÉ LEMAIRE

The James Ossuary. *This simple, 20-inch-long limestone ossuary, or bone box, from first-century C.E. Jerusalem bears a short Aramaic inscription reading "James, son of Joseph, brother of Jesus." If the box did indeed belong to Jesus' brother James, as some have argued, it would be the first archaeological evidence of Jesus ever found. The inscription has been declared a modern forgery by a committee of the Israel Antiquities Authority, but many leading paleographers continue to assert its authenticity.*

Jesus' ascension into heaven is slightly different in Luke 24:50–53 and Acts 1:6–11, though written by the same author. Equally striking are the differences between the stories of Jesus' appearances. In Matthew he appears only twice, once to Mary Magdalene and the other Mary (Matthew 28:1–10), once to the surviving 11 disciples (Matthew 28:16–20)—11 because Judas had committed suicide. In Luke, however, he does not appear to the women (see Luke 24:8–11), but comes first to two unnamed disciples (Luke 24:13–35) and then to all the disciples, before whom he ate (Luke 24:36–49). According to Acts, he was with the disciples for 40 days, appearing off and on (Acts 1:3ff.).

The earliest evidence, however, is not in the Gospels, but in one of Paul's letters. He offers, as part of what had been "handed down" to him, a list of appearances of the risen Lord: He appeared first to Cephas (Peter), then to the 12 (not the 11!), then to more than 500, then to James (Jesus' brother), then to "all the apostles" (apparently not just the 12), then to Paul himself (1 Corinthians 15:3–8).

Before commenting on the problems raised by these divergent accounts, let us first consider what the risen Jesus was like. According to Luke, he was not immediately recognizable; the first two disciples to whom he appeared walked and talked with him for some time without knowing who he was; he was made known "in the breaking of the bread," when they ate together (Luke 24:35). Although he could appear and disappear, he was not a ghost. Luke is very insistent about that. The risen Lord could be touched, and he could eat (Luke 24:39–43).*

When Paul was engaged in a debate with his Corinthian converts about whether or not dead Christians will be raised, body and all, he tried to describe what the coming resurrection will be like. His answer is presumably based on his own firsthand experience when he saw the risen Lord ("Have I not seen Jesus our Lord?" [1 Corinthians 9:1]; God "reveal[ed] his Son to me" [Galatians 1:16]). In the resurrection, Paul explained, each individual will have a body, but it will be transformed: not a physical body, but a spiritual body. One fact is clear: Flesh and blood cannot inherit the kingdom of God; in the resurrection, there will be no flesh and blood. This is directly applied to Jesus: "Just as we have borne the image of the man of dust, we shall also bear the image of the man of heaven" (1 Corinthians 15:42–50). Paul repeated: Everyone will be changed; when they are like the "man of heaven," they will no longer have their perishable bodies, but rather imperishable ones (1 Corinthians 15:51–54).

In the first century, people knew about two experiences similar to resurrection. Luke and Paul both intend to exclude the possibility that the risen Jesus was either a resuscitated corpse or a ghost. A ghost then was what a ghost is now, or what a ghost was to Shakespeare:[32] a phantasm, especially one that appears late at night.[33] Sophisticated ancients, like their modern counterparts, dismissed ghosts as creatures of dreams, figments of the imagination.

*See "Jesus of History vs. Jesus of Tradition: BAR Interviews Sean Freyne," *BAR*, November/December 2010, p. 47.

The less sophisticated, naturally, were credulous. Both Paul and Luke opposed the idea that the risen Lord was a ghost, Luke explicitly ("a ghost has not flesh and bones as you see that I have," Luke 24:39), Paul by implication: What is raised is a *body.* Yet they equally oppose the idea that Jesus was a resuscitated corpse. These were more common then than now, because embalming is now so widespread. It is, however, possible for a person to be dead to all appearances, and later to "regain" life. There are several such stories in ancient literature, some in the Bible and some elsewhere.[34] Paul and Luke, however, deny that the risen Lord was simply resuscitated. In Paul's view, he had been transformed, changed from a "physical" or "natural" body to a "spiritual body." Luke thought that he had flesh and could eat, but also that he had been changed. He was not obviously recognizable to people who saw him, and he could appear and disappear.

Both authors were trying to describe—Paul at firsthand, Luke at second or third hand—an experience that does not fit a known category. What they deny is much clearer than what they affirm.

Faced with accounts of this nature—sharply diverging stories of where and to whom Jesus appeared, lack of agreement and clarity on what he was like (except agreement on negatives)—we cannot reconstruct what really happened. We can, however, make some very general comments.

One is that the authors of the Gospels wanted to give *narrative stories* about the resurrection. They were probably not too worried about agreement or consistency. This may readily and convincingly be illustrated. In Acts there are three accounts of the Lord's appearance to Paul and the immediate aftermath, which differ at various points (Acts 9:1–30, 22:3–21, 26:12–20). For example, in one story (Acts 22:17–21), after the Lord first appeared to Paul, Paul went first to Damascus and then to Jerusalem, where Jesus again appeared to him. It was at this second appearance that the Lord commissioned Paul to be apostle to the gentiles. In Acts 9, however, the statement that the Lord appointed Paul to go to the gentiles comes in Damascus (Acts 9:15). The author of Luke-Acts was not stupid; he doubtless knew that his stories varied. He could have told the same story in the same way, but that would not have been as interesting a narrative. Like many other authors, both ancient and modern, he disliked repetition; like other ancient authors, he would change events in order to avoid it.

Luke, like the other Gospel writers, wanted to tell stories in narrative form. They did not care about "accuracy"[35] in the way that we do. This makes it difficult to peer behind their accounts and describe what really happened.

Much about the historical Jesus will remain a mystery. Nothing is more mysterious than the stories of his resurrection, which attempt to portray an experience that the authors could not themselves comprehend. But we should remember that we know a lot, if we are content with a broad outline. We know that Jesus started under John the Baptist, that he had disciples, that he expected the kingdom, that he went from Galilee to Jerusalem, that he did something hostile against the Temple, that he was tried and crucified. Finally we know that after his death his followers experienced what they described as the "resurrection": the appearance of a living person who had actually died. They believed this, and within a few decades many of them would have given their lives for their belief.

THREE

The Spread of Christianity from Jerusalem to Rome: 30–70 C.E.[1]

JAMES D.G. DUNN

WHAT THE MOVEMENT THAT SPRANG FROM JESUS OF NAZARETH should be called is not entirely clear. The term "Christianity" did not appear before the second decade of the second century.[2] The term "Christians" was probably first coined in the late 30s or early 40s C.E. by the Roman authorities in Syrian Antioch, the Latin term *Christiani* being used to refer to the followers of Christ, "Christ-partisans."[3] Here already "Christ" was being heard by the Roman authorities as a person's name, the Greek translation of the Hebrew "messiah" having already lost its significance as a title. In Judea, where the movement first emerged, however, it was probably regarded as a "sect" or "party" within Second Temple Judaism, the "sect of the Nazarenes,"[4] similar to the "sect" of the Sadducees and the "sect of the Pharisees."[5] "Nazarenes" has continued to be used of Syrian Christians in the Middle East to this day. The lack of a consistent early identifying title for the movement is indicated by an alternative referent—"the Way,"[6] indicating a distinctive lifestyle (way of living) and conduct. From a later perspective perhaps the most accurate sociological description of earliest or embryonic Christianity would be "a Jewish messianic sect."

Sources for a history of the beginnings of Christianity

The sources for this earliest phase of Christianity are almost entirely the Christian writings that make up the New Testament.[7] Apart from them we have only a few references to the first generation Christians (30–70 C.E.) in Jewish and Greco-Roman authors. The Jewish historian Josephus, writing in the 90s C.E., refers to the execution of James, "the brother of Jesus, the so-called Christ" in Jerusalem in 62 C.E.[8] But he says nothing more about any movement behind James. The Roman historian Tacitus, writing early in the second century, gives quite a full description of the persecution of Christians in Rome when the emperor Nero condemned them as responsible for the disastrous fire of Rome in 64 C.E.[9] And his younger contemporary, Suetonius, in his *Lives of the Caesars*, makes brief reference to the same persecution by Nero;[10] but he also provides the earlier information that in 49 C.E. Jews were expelled from Rome because they "were constantly causing disturbances at the instigation of Chrestus."[11] Most infer that Suetonius had misheard "Christus" as "Chrestus" (their pronunciation would have been very similar); also that he had misunderstood a report of unrest within the Roman Jewish community, over early Christian claims that Jesus was the Messiah, as trouble caused by Christ himself. This reference to expulsion of Jews from Rome by Emperor Claudius seems to fit well with a similar reference in Acts 18:2 ("Claudius had commanded

ANCIENT ART & ARCHITECTURE COLLECTION LTD/ALAMY

Roman Emperor Nero. *Nero (54–68 C.E.) came to power on the death of his adoptive father, Claudius. Noted for his vanity and extravagance, Nero was suspected of causing the great fire of Rome in 64 C.E. to create space to build a grandiose new capital. Nero accused the Christians of the arson to divert attention from his own actions. Instead, his persecution of the unpopular sect created sympathy for them and more unpopularity for himself. By tradition, the apostle Paul was executed in Rome during Nero's reign.*

all the Jews to leave Rome"). And since there is no reference in the New Testament to the death of James, the brother of Jesus, or to the Nero persecution, this last detail is the only point at which non-Christian references to Christianity's beginnings can be dovetailed with the account drawn from the New Testament.

The Christian sources include, invaluably, letters written during the period under consideration (30–70 C.E.). These are predominantly the letters of Paul, the missionary most responsible for taking the gospel message about Jesus beyond the boundaries of Palestine and Judaism, that is, to the cities of the gentiles.

Of the 13 letters attributed to Paul,[12] most scholars are convinced that Ephesians, 1 and 2 Timothy and Titus were written pseudonymously after Paul's death by close disciples seeking to represent how Paul would have responded to the developing situations one to three decades later.[13] Opinion is almost equally divided in regard to 2 Thessalonians and Colossians.

There is similar disagreement over the order in which Paul wrote his letters. A likely order is 1 Thessalonians, 2 Thessalonians, Galatians, 1 Corinthians, 2 Corinthians, Romans, Philemon, Colossians and Philippians. But in scholarly discussion on the subject, Galatians is sometimes considered to have been written much closer to Romans. And the "prison epistles"—Philemon, Colossians and Philippians—are assigned either to an inferred imprisonment in Ephesus (in the mid-50s C.E.) or to Paul's (final) imprisonment in Rome (60–62 C.E.).

Another area of disagreement is whether the letters that have been preserved in the New Testament were written as single epistles dictated by Paul. A strong minority opinion maintains that 2 Corinthians and Philippians in particular were composite works composed using several smaller letters or parts of letters.[14]

Nevertheless, despite these continuing disagreements and the historical uncertainties they raise, the fact that we have letters dictated by Paul, one of the principal figures from this period (30–70 C.E.), is quite unusual for ancient history and of inestimable value. Their value is severalfold:

- They give a clear indication of the ground covered by Paul (particularly his mission around the Aegean) and of his success in winning gentile converts and in founding Christian assemblies (churches) in important cities.
- They "take the lid" off some of these churches and give amazingly clear insight into the character of these churches (particularly at Corinth).

- They indicate the tensions within the early Christian mission, as other missionaries attempted to "improve" on Paul's mission (Galatians, 2 Corinthians, Philippians).
- The letters, particularly Romans, spell out Paul's understanding of the key message of Christianity (Paul's theology) and demonstrate the depth of his pastoral concern (e.g., 1 Thessalonians, 1 Corinthians, Philemon).

It is possible that the letter of James, usually ascribed to James brother of Jesus, should also be dated before 70 C.E., though it is as or more likely that the letter consists of the sort of teaching James gave when he was leader of the Jerusalem assemblies and may well have delivered to Christians and Jews making pilgrimage to Jerusalem. The letter to the Hebrews is also sometimes dated prior to 70, because it seems to assume the continuation of the cult in the Jerusalem Temple (destroyed in 70). But early rabbinic tradition through the second century (transcribed in the Mishnah about 200 C.E.) also made the same assumption. The other letters in the New Testament, as well as the Revelation of John, are almost universally dated after 70 and so do not serve as a source for our period (30–70 C.E.).

With the New Testament Gospels the situation is slightly more complex. This is not because any of them can be confidently dated before 70. The Gospel of Mark may have been written toward the climax of the Jewish revolt (about 68–69 C.E.), but it is equally likely to have been written shortly after 70. In the opinion of a wide consensus of specialists, the other three Gospels are to be dated in the final quarter of the first century.

All four Gospels, however, are clearly drawing on earlier traditions about Jesus. The way these traditions were formulated prior to their being written down in the Gospels can tell us much about the priorities and concerns of those who developed them and, to some extent, about the churches that prized them. This was an important insight which emerged in the 1920s when the priority of gospel scholarship moved from a debate about which Gospel was earliest (source criticism) to a debate about the content and forms of the traditions on which the gospel writers drew (form criticism). In addition, recent interest in the earlier oral traditions about Jesus has strengthened the view of the Gospels as sources not only for the period in which they were written, but also for the life of Jesus and the period between his death and the first written Gospels.

The importance here is at least threefold:

- The oral or prewritten-gospel tradition indicates the kind of teaching and priorities for conduct that must have been conveyed to new converts and resonated within worship gatherings of the new sect.

- This tradition indicates a continuing interest in the mission and teaching of Jesus among the first Christians; also that the events and character of Jesus' mission were early on seen as part of the "gospel" (e.g., Mark 1:1, 14:9), preparing the way for the emergence of a new literary form (the gospel genre), where the account of Jesus' mission and teaching climaxed in Jesus' death and resurrection.
- The differing emphases of the Gospels, for example, on the significance of Jesus' miracles and on the Jewish law, indicate the differences and tensions that must have featured in and between many of the new churches during the oral period.

A further question that has arisen with some force in the last 20 years is whether our sources should include other gospel material, particularly the Gospel of Thomas, which was discovered in the 1940s at the site of Nag Hammadi in Egypt.*[15] It is undoubtedly the case that Thomas contains a substantial proportion of tradition known otherwise only through the Gospels of Mark, Matthew and Luke, and some of it may be in forms earlier than the forms used by the New Testament Gospels. So Thomas provides a further source for the sort of teaching given by Jesus that was being used among the first generation of followers of Jesus. On the other hand, the teaching material found in Thomas seems to have been added to a certain understanding of the human condition that cannot be traced back to Jesus and probably reflects a broader spirituality of the eastern Mediterranean region, which subsequently became characterized as "gnostic".[16] As a source, therefore, the Gospel of Thomas probably reflects a mid-second-century development, and though it contains Jesus tradition from the mid-first century, the Gospel itself cannot be described as a source for the first generation of Christianity.

On first impression the most important source for the beginnings of Christianity is the writing known as the Acts of the Apostles, written by the same author who dictated the Gospel of Luke, probably during the 80s C.E.

*Helmut Koester and Stephen J. Patterson, "The Gospel of Thomas," *BR*, April 1990; James Brashler, "Nag Hammadi Codices Shed Light on Early Christian History," *BAR*, January/February 1984. Some of the Thomas material was found in Greek among the Oxyrhynchus papyri, discovered 40 to 50 years earlier, also in Egypt. See Stephen J. Patterson, "The Oxyrhynchus Papyri: The Remarkable Discovery You've Probably Never Heard Of," *BAR*, March/April 2011.

For Acts sets out to tell the story of how Christianity spread from Jerusalem to Rome, starting from Jerusalem and spreading to Samaria and Syria, and thence to Asia Minor, Greece and Macedonia, and finally arriving with Paul in Rome. So, on the face of it, Acts should be our primary source. However there are several problems with this initial assessment. The principal problem is the difficulty of correlating the account of Acts with the information derived from Paul's letters. Since Paul is indisputably the eyewitness, there is a natural tendency to take Paul's version before Luke's. And if Luke is not to be trusted at points where he can be checked, then his whole account is placed into question.

Caught up in the debate on the reliability of Acts is the fact that at several points the narrative switches from third person to first person.[17] The implication seems to be that the author of Acts was actually personally present and involved in the events he narrates. For many, however, the disagreement between Acts and the Pauline letters is so substantial that it becomes impossible to give serious weight to that implication; the author must have been able to draw on some notes from a participant in the particular episodes (usually some travel accounts) or was using some convention where an occasional first person reference was quite acceptable.[18] But a more realistic assessment is that the author did intend his readers/audiences to infer that he had been personally present and thereby would judge his account to be reliable.[19]

Such a judgment would restore Acts as a major source for the history of Christianity "from Jerusalem to Rome," so long as three caveats are heeded.

1) The problem of the differences between Acts and Paul should not be exaggerated. Although Paul provides a firsthand account of his involvements, including the tensions between his mission and the Jerusalem leadership (particularly Peter and James), his account is by no means unbiased—indeed, the opposite is true. For example, in Paul's account of a vital meeting between himself and Barnabas on one side and the Jerusalem leadership on the other, the role of Barnabas is largely marginalized (Galatians 2:1–10). It is quite possible that Luke, perhaps because he knew Paul too well, had a different viewpoint of some episodes and therefore remembered things differently.[20]

2) Luke evidently wanted to present the beginnings of Christianity as largely harmonious and its mission as unified and successful. This is presumably why Luke chose to ignore or draw a veil over most of the rivalry and disputes that Paul's letters so clearly indicate (from Paul's perspective, of course).[21]

3) Finally, Acts should not be judged by the standards of modern historiography. Luke was an ancient historian. And ancient historiography, for example, was not good at estimating the size of large crowds in particular

events. Nor was there any inhibition about reporting speeches as given by the characters in the historical narrative, which were actually formulated by the historian himself as appropriate to the occasion, or based on some knowledge of the occasion, or as rhetorically pleasing to the readers or audience for whom the history was written. Luke might well have written the speeches of his characters with all three motivations, all of the Acts speeches being mini-cameos which, as written, would have taken no more than a few minutes to deliver.

So Acts can be treated as a considerable source, though always to be used with some caution.

The first appearance of Christianity

Christianity owes its beginnings not just to the mission of Jesus but also to two events or series of happenings that came about following Jesus' death.

1) The first was the resurrection of Jesus, or to be more objective, the emergence of the belief that Jesus had been raised from the dead. There is little or no dispute that Jesus was crucified as a messianic pretender by the Roman authorities in Jerusalem, probably in the spring of 30 C.E. His closest disciples must have been shattered by his death, and some of them at least seem to have returned to their native Galilee. But within a few days the belief began to circulate among the disciples that God had raised Jesus from the dead.

This was an astonishing conviction to arise. That great leaders and prophets were translated or exalted to heaven after death was a not uncommon belief. But the first Christians did not seem to be content simply with the comforting thought that God had vindicated the dead Jesus by translating him to heaven. Similarly, belief that the end of the age would bring a general resurrection had established itself in Second Temple Judaism following the outrage felt in Judea at the death of the Judean martyrs during the Maccabean rebellion of the second century B.C.E. (2 Maccabees 7). But in the case of Jesus, his followers believed he had been raised *before* the end of the age. To be more precise, the initial conception seems to have been that with the resurrection of Jesus the general resurrection had *begun*; this very early belief seems still to be echoed in the understanding that Jesus' resurrection was the "first-fruits," that is, the beginning of the harvest of the resurrected (1 Corinthians 15:20,23) and in Paul's reference to Jesus' resurrection as "the resurrection of the dead" (Romans 1:4), not "his resurrection from the dead." Even so it remains an astonishing feature that the disciples were convinced that Jesus had been raised from the dead and that with this event, the end-of-the-age resurrection had begun.

What gave rise to this conviction? Two happenings in particular are important: Jesus was seen alive after his death, and the tomb where he had been laid was found to be empty.

The accounts of the "resurrection appearances" of Jesus are confused and confusing (Matthew 28; Mark 16:7; Luke 24; John 20–21): some in Jerusalem itself, others in Galilee; some giving prominence to women as witnesses, others making no mention of women; some have Jesus appearing on earth, others from heaven. Likewise, the period of the sightings seems to have lasted long enough to allow us to accept Paul's claim to have been granted such an appearance (possibly as much as two years after Jesus' execution) (1 Corinthians 9:1–2, 15:3–8), whereas Luke limits the appearances to 40 days (Acts 1:1–11). Nevertheless, there can be little doubt that during the period following Jesus' death there was a sequence of sightings or appearances of Jesus that were substantial enough to quickly establish the conclusion that God had raised Jesus from the dead. This became the basic claim made in the earliest Christian preaching and was evidently the fundamental and distinguishing creedal conviction of the first Christian groups.[22]

There is more dispute about the veracity of the accounts of Jesus' tomb being found empty, as recorded by all four Gospels. But the earliest conception of resurrection was of the dead body being restored to complete life (2 Maccabees 14:45–46). The same belief is probably indicated also by the Herodian-period practice of gathering in a bone box (ossuary) the deceased's bones after the flesh had decayed,* that is, presumably, to provide a framework for the resurrected body. If that is the case, then the proclamation of Jesus' resurrection very soon after his burial would have been met with incredulity if his burial site was known to have been undisturbed. The fact that Paul distinguishes the body of flesh and blood from the spiritual body of the resurrection (1 Corinthians 15:42–50) has suggested to some that Paul did not know of the empty tomb tradition. But Paul understood the resurrection body as the body of this life transformed into a "spiritual body" (e.g., 1 Corinthians 15:44,52–54; Philippians 3:21); so he presumably also understood Jesus' resurrected body as his dead body similarly transformed. The further fact that there is no indication that a burial site or tomb of Jesus was revered by the first Christians also strengthens the claim that the empty tomb tradition is well grounded in early witness claims.

Despite the astonishing character of the earliest Christian claim that Jesus had been raised, then, the fact of the claim should be recognized as the ground of the earliest Christian confidence that Jesus was indeed Israel's

*See Steven Fine, "Why Bone Boxes?" *BAR*, September/October 2001.

Messiah, that he had been vindicated by God and that this was good news to be broadcast widely. Nor should the claim be lightly discarded or simply dismissed as counterintuitive. There is undoubtedly more to the "big bang" with which Christianity began than the historian can fully fathom.

2) Another event or series of happenings became a compelling and persuasive power within the new movement that helped draw new recruits: the new spiritual vitality and exuberance that the first Christians attributed to the Holy Spirit coming upon and entering their lives and transforming their communities.

Luke recounts the first experience of being "filled" with the Holy Spirit as taking place in Jerusalem on the day of Pentecost, 50 days after the feast of the Passover during which Jesus had been crucified (Acts 2). And it is entirely possible that disciples who had returned to Galilee gathered again in Jerusalem at the first feast after that Passover; at any rate, the initial leadership of the Jerusalem church seems to have been provided entirely by Galileans. But whenever and wherever the first experience of the transforming, empowering Spirit took place, it is clear from several New Testament writings that such experiences quickly became a distinguishing feature of embryonic Christianity.[23] It was evidently the fact that gentile converts were being granted the same Spirit experiences as the first disciples that subsequently convinced the Jerusalem leadership that the gospel should go equally to gentiles as well as to Jews (Acts 11:15–18; Galatians 2:6–9, 3:2–5). And no doubt it was the vitality of spiritual experience enjoyed by the first Christians that made the movement so attractive to spiritual seekers and drew so many into what was to become a new religion.

The first and mother church—Jerusalem

As we shall see, the chronology of Paul's life and mission almost compels the conclusion that he was converted within a very few years (probably two or at most three) of Jesus' death. That leaves at most only about two years for all the events that preceded his conversion, including his own role as a persecutor of the new sect. So even if Luke's chronology leaves several questions unanswered, the emergence of the first Christian community in Jerusalem must be dated to the beginning of the 30s C.E. (Jesus' death most likely to be dated to 30).

From the Acts account (Acts 2–5), as confirmed by Paul's letters, we can derive the following information:

The leadership of the Jerusalem disciples was given first primarily by Peter. Peter had been Jesus' leading disciple, whose leadership had survived the shame of his failure to acknowledge Jesus after Jesus' arrest (Mark 14:66–72

GARO NALBANDIAN

The House of St. Peter. *Beneath the foundations of this octagonal Byzantine* martyrium *church at Capernaum, archaeologists discovered a simple first-century C.E. home. Some scholars believe the dwelling was the home of the apostle Peter which, according to the Gospels, was often visited by Jesus during his Galilean ministry (Matthew 4:14; Mark 1:21,29). The house was located near the synagogue.*

and parallels). The prominence given to Peter in the accounts of the resurrection appearances confirms that his leadership was widely acknowledged (Mark 16:7; John 20:1–10, 21:15–19; 1 Corinthians 15:5). That Peter was the spokesman for the new sect is the consistent theme of Acts 1–5, and is confirmed by the precedence that Paul acknowledges for Peter in Galatians 1:18 and 2:6–10.

Whether "the twelve" (1 Corinthians 15:5) functioned as leaders for any length of time is unclear. The 12 had a huge symbolic role as representing a restored Israel of the 12 tribes (cf. James 1:1; Revelation 7:5–8), a role suggested by the tradition that the place of the traitor Judas was early on filled by a replacement (Acts 1:15–26, and later by Revelation 21:14). But they disappear from view after Acts 6:2, and the memory of who made up the 12 is somewhat confused (Mark 3:16–19 and parallels—Thaddaeus or James son of Alphaeus?), so perhaps their leadership role was overtaken by later developments within the group. Of the 12, the brothers James and John, sons of Zebedee, together with Peter, seem to have formed the closest circle around Jesus during his mission.[24] And the reference to James being targeted for execution by King Herod Agrippa (Acts 12:2) suggests that he had been one of the most prominent members of the new sect. But John, his brother, appears only as a somewhat shadowy companion of Peter (Acts 3:4, 4:13,19, 8:14).

The other figure who seems to have quickly emerged in leadership was James, Jesus' own brother. When he became a disciple of his brother is unclear (especially in view of the tradition in Mark 3:31–35). But the fact that he, too, was acknowledged to have been granted a personal resurrection appearance (1 Corinthians 15:7) must have been a factor (cf. Acts 1:14). In any case James's leading role is clearly acknowledged by Paul in Galatians (1:19, 2:9), where he is listed before Cephas/Peter. Perhaps it was Peter's commitment to mission among his fellow Jews (Galatians 2:7–9) that meant that he was absent from Jerusalem, which allowed James to emerge as the leader there (cf. Acts 9:32–10:48). James is not recalled as active in mission beyond Jerusalem, so it could be simply that as the leader most consistently located in Jerusalem, he came to be regarded as the principal leader.[25] At the same time the obvious fact should not be ignored, that James was known as the brother of Jesus (Galatians 1:19); it would presumably have seemed most sensible to many to regard James as Jesus' successor.

The emergence of James as the principal leader in Jerusalem may indicate something of the character of the Jerusalem community of Jesus believers, particularly their attitude to the Mosaic law and the Jerusalem Temple. For the indications given by Paul are that James was what might be fairly described as a Jewish traditionalist. The clear implication of Galatians 2:12 is that James disapproved of Jewish believers eating with gentile believers (presumably on the basis of Leviticus 20:23–26, designed to maintain Israel's holiness). And the missionaries who sought to undo or improve upon Paul's mission and who described themselves as "Hebrews" (2 Corinthians 11:22; implied also in Philippians 3:5) most probably came from Jerusalem or looked to Jerusalem for validation. Later tradition also recalls James to have been a very devout Jew (James "the Just"),[26] highly regarded by subsequent Jewish Christianity.[27]

From this we may deduce that the assemblies in which James came to prominence (in Jerusalem) maintained traditional Jewish practices. We may say, indeed, that they took it for granted that the Jesus movement was indeed a sect within Judaism dedicated to the renewal of Israel, a sect in which the new covenant promised in Jeremiah had been fulfilled, that is, a new covenant that did not void the law, but rather enabled a deeper devotion to it (Jeremiah

31:31–34).[28] This inference coheres with the testimony of Acts that the new sect and its leaders "spent much time together in the Temple" (Acts 2:46).[29] And from this perspective the note that Peter and John were accustomed to go up into the Temple at the ninth hour, the hour of prayer (Acts 3:1) occasions no surprise. For this was the hour at which the afternoon (*Tamid*) sacrifice was offered.[30] To attend the Temple at just that time was to adhere to and validate the Temple ritual. Twenty-seven years later Luke reports that James urged Paul on the latter's last visit to Jerusalem to take part in a Temple ritual that involved a sin offering and a burnt offering (Acts 21:23–26).[31] Some find the suggestion incredible that Paul would have so compromised his views by thus participating in the Temple cult, and discern a tendency of Luke to portray Paul as Jewishly as possible—though Paul saw himself as quite prepared to compromise in his praxis when the situation demanded some flexibility (1 Corinthians 9:19–23). But at least the episode confirms the strong impression that the Jerusalem believers were traditionalist Jews in the practice of their faith in Messiah Jesus, who did not see any divorce from the law and the Temple as a necessary corollary to their faith.

That such loyalist practices did not protect the leaders of the new sect from litigation and persecution at the hands of the local authorities is clearly indicated by Acts (4:1–22, 5:17–40, 12:1–5) and by the execution of James in 62 C.E. But the central fact remains that a body of Jewish believers in Jesus Messiah maintained a strong presence in Jerusalem at least up to the Jewish revolt against Rome in 66 C.E. That they remained faithful Jews, practitioners of the law and devoted to the Temple throughout that period is the almost unavoidable corollary.

None of this excludes the probability that the new sect was marked by distinctive beliefs, particularly regarding Jesus, and developed distinctive ritual and worship practices that reflected that belief.

Several features marked the earliest Christology of Christianity.

- Jesus was Israel's Messiah. The majority of Judeans had hoped for a military leader who would liberate Israel from Roman domination. For Jesus' followers, however, his crucifixion was not cause to deny his messiahship, but rather pointed to Jewish scriptures that had prophesied a suffering messiah. To demonstrate this was probably one of the main apologetic and evangelistic strategies of the earliest disciple groups in Jerusalem and Judea.[32]
- By his resurrection Jesus had been "appointed Son of God in power." This formulation seems to be a quotation from an early creed (Romans 1:4), and reflects a similar use of Psalm 2:7 ("You are my Son, today I have begotten you") as a way of understanding Jesus' resurrection.[33]
- Not only had Jesus been raised from the dead, but he had also been

exalted to sit at God's right hand. Here another Psalms passage (Psalm 110:1) evidently spoke with force to the first believers as they searched the scriptures to make sense of what they perceived as having happened.[34]

• Acts indicates that as part of the same reflection Jesus was seen to have fulfilled John the Baptist's prediction (Mark 1:8 and parallels) of one to come who would baptize in the Holy Spirit (Acts 1:5, 2:33).

• Expectation of the imminent return of Jesus from heaven seems to have been a major feature of the earliest Christian belief. The assumption that the new movement was experiencing "the last days" is implicit in the understanding of Jesus' resurrection as the beginning ("first-fruits") of the resurrection of the dead. The Spirit poured out, as Jesus' disciples believed, was also a fulfillment of hopes for the age to come.[35] According to Acts 2, the Galilean disciples may indeed have returned to Jerusalem in the hope that Jesus would come back from heaven on the next great feast (Pentecost). Other indications of this eschatological (end time) fervor are the early Aramaic prayer still used in Paul's Greek-speaking churches—*Marana tha*, "Our Lord, come" (1 Corinthians 16:22)—and Paul's own expectation of an imminent return of the Lord Jesus.[36] Some of Jesus' sayings and parables would no doubt have been understood as warning of an imminent return.[37] And although Luke cautions against a too-imminent expectation,[38] he somewhat surprisingly retains the strong note of realized eschatology in Acts 2:17 (Pentecost was the outpouring of the Spirit "in the last days") and the sense of the imminence of Christ's return in Acts 3:19–21.

Such beliefs, it should be noted, were entirely Jewish in character, building on Israel's scriptures and finding in these events fulfillment of Israel's prophetic hopes and expectations. Those who held such beliefs would have been regarded by Jerusalem authorities as odd or as fanatics, but not as unJewish.

The same is probably true of the distinctive practices that probably marked the new sect from the beginning.

• John the Baptist's rite of a once-only baptism seems to have been revived from the first[39]—the New Testament knows of no unbaptized Christian—and, as baptism "in the name of Jesus,"[40] it became at once a rite of entry into the body of his disciples.

• Although the Jerusalem Temple remained an important focus for the first disciples (Was Jesus expected to return to the Temple?—cf. Malachi 3:1), there would probably have been regular worship gatherings in the homes of individual members. Distinctive features would have included prayer to God as "Abba" (Father), reflecting Jesus' own prayer style (Romans 8:15–16; Galatians 4:6–7); the fact that early Greek-speaking congregations retained the Aramaic address assuredly indicates an already prized usage in the Aramaic-speaking assemblies. The *Marana tha* invocation (1 Corinthians 16:22) is another Aramaic formulation carried over into Greek-speaking churches. Nor should it be forgotten that memories of Jesus' mission (the oral Jesus tradition) would have been constantly circulating from the beginning, and that reflection on his teaching (e.g., regarding the Sabbath and the significance of the ritual law) must have provided instruction and encouragement in any controversies in which the first Christians found themselves.

- The house meetings would have included shared meals (what Luke refers to as the "breaking of bread").[41] Table fellowship had been a mark of Jesus' own mission,[42] so it is not surprising that the same practice became a feature of earliest Christian assemblies (e.g., Galatians 2:12; 1 Corinthians 11:20–22). Acts quite naturally takes for granted that such table-fellowship was practiced from the first (Acts 2:46). It remains unclear as to how often and how regularly the meal included the breaking of bread and drinking of wine in memory of Jesus' last supper and death (1 Corinthians 10:16, 11:20–26), but the regular practice of what Paul calls "the Lord's supper [or evening meal]" can certainly be dated to the beginnings of the new sect.
- Acts also reports another distinctive practice of the first Jerusalem believers—the contribution of property to a common fund from which the poor could be helped ("the community of goods") (Acts 2:44–45, 4:34–37). We know of similar practices at that time, among the Pythagoreans, the Essenes and the Therapeutae, an ascetic community near Alexandria.[43] So such a practice might well have commended itself to the first Jerusalem believers, particularly in their state of eschatological enthusiasm. It would be somewhat ironic if the casualness of the practice (selling off goods and possessions as need arose for more funds) was (partly) the cause of the later poverty of the Jerusalem church that moved Paul so deeply (Romans 15:25–27).

In all this can be clearly seen the roots of beliefs and practices that were to become points of increasing tension within first-century Judaism. But in these earliest years the oddities of such a Jewish messianic sect would probably not have caused more than a few ripples within the mainstream of the Judaism of the period—as Acts attempts to demonstrate (Acts 5:33–39). However, the tensions soon became unbearably stressful for some.

The Hellenists and the first outreach beyond Judea

The idyll of Luke's account of the first Jerusalem Christians (Acts 1–5) is rudely disturbed by the abrupt report of complaints made by some about the inadequacy of provision from the common fund.[44] Those complaining are identified as "the Hellenists" (Acts 6:1). Their complaint, directed against "the Hebrews," was that the Hellenist widows were being neglected in the daily distribution of food (from the common fund). Thus begins a sequence in Acts that runs through the following chapters until the end of chapter 11, with 9:1–11:18 as an insertion. There is no explicit confirmation of this information from the rest of the New Testament. Nevertheless, for this period and development, Luke was probably able to draw on good source material, perhaps the church of Antioch's account of its own beginnings.[45]

"Hellenist" denotes one who uses the Greek language, a Greek-speaker. "Hebrew" must denote equivalently a Hebrew- or Aramaic-speaker. Since Greek was quite familiar in Jerusalem, being the *lingua franca* of the Mediterranean world,*[46] it is unlikely that the Hebrews could use only Aramaic. In contrast, it is entirely likely that the Hellenists could function only in Greek. The reference to a synagogue of or for Diaspora Jews in Jerusalem (Acts 6:9) suggests that the prayers and readings in such synagogues must have been in Greek, and may suggest that many of the Hellenists preferred to worship in their synagogues rather than the Temple. A plausible scenario is that the Jerusalem Hellenists were Diaspora Jews who had returned to Jerusalem (in retirement) but who continued to function only in Greek. That young women not long past puberty frequently were married to older men would help explain why there were so many widows among the Jerusalem Hellenists.

The Hellenists Luke refers to had become members (by baptism) of the new Messiah Jesus sect; this strongly suggests that already within a year or so of Christianity's beginnings, the traditions of Jesus had been put into Greek for the benefit of such Hellenists. Probably it was from these Hellenists, according to Luke's report, that seven men were chosen to assist the 12 in remedying the defective distribution (6:3–5). The alignment of some of their number with the Jesus sect presumably caused disquiet among the larger Hellenist community. Luke refers particularly to Stephen as active in promoting and defending the message of Jesus within the Diaspora synagogue community (Acts 6:9). The outcome was an accusation that Stephen was speaking against the Temple and the law of Moses (probably referring particularly to the law governing Temple ritual) (Acts 6:13–14). This would be consistent with the somewhat uncomfortable (for the Jerusalem believers) memory of Jesus warning of the imminent destruction of the Temple (Mark 13:2, 14:58; John 2:19), which Stephen may well have recalled (Acts 6:14).

The speech attributed to Stephen during his trial (Acts 7) is unique in Acts and contains a somewhat unorthodox account of Israel's history.[47] Most strikingly, it climaxes in a denunciation of the Temple, as in effect idolatrous

*See Peter W. van der Horst, "Jewish Funerary Inscriptions—Most Are in Greek," *BAR*, September/October 1992.

(Acts 7:48),[48] which is quite counter to Luke's otherwise consistently positive appraisal of the Temple.[49] The speech, then, is unlikely to be an outright Lukan contrivance, and may well have been drawn from the same source(s) from which Luke derived his information about the Hellenists. At the very least we can see a credible picture emerging of one of the earliest Christians developing Jesus' remembered prediction of the Temple's destruction into a bald denial of any need or continuing function for the Temple. Since the Temple was the focus of Jerusalem's identity and fundamental to its economy and the residents' livelihood, any such criticism of the Temple would have been bound to provoke a violent response. So, again, Luke's portrayal of Stephen's violent lynching is entirely plausible (Acts 7:58–60). That Stephen was the first Christian martyr can be regarded as good history.

According to Acts, the immediate corollary to Stephen's execution was the persecution of the church in Jerusalem. Luke asserts that all (Christians) were driven from Jerusalem except the apostles (Acts 8:2). That seems odd since a decision to act against the Jesus sect that left the sect's leadership unharmed would be a most unusual persecution strategy. A more plausible sequence would be that the Hellenist believers, from whose ranks the attack on the Temple had emanated, would be regarded as equally offensive to the Jewish authorities (and mob) for whom the Temple was absolutely central. The scattering of those persecuted to Damascus, Phoenicia, Cyprus and Antioch (Acts 9:2, 11:19) also suggests that they were Diaspora Jews accustomed to living in non-Jewish cities. The fact that Saul, himself a Diaspora Jew, became the chief persecutor—the point at which Luke's account fits most neatly into Paul's own reminiscence[50]—further suggests that the persecution was essentially intra-Hellenist in character. If the leaders of the new sect also became targets for the persecution, presumably the probable fact that they did not share Stephen's criticism of the Temple meant that they could soon return to Jerusalem to resume their previous roles. At any rate, as already noted, the Jerusalem church remained a conservative Jewish force throughout the first generation of Christianity.

The unexpected consequence of the persecution, in Luke's account, is that those who fled from Jerusalem spoke the word, the good news of Jesus, wherever they went. Perhaps the resurrection appearance to "all the apostles" (1 Corinthians 15:7) took place at this time, since "apostles" is another name for missionaries, and it possibly took such a seeing of the risen Jesus to commission these Hellenists to preach Jesus in the regions and cities to which they fled. At all events, the initial outreach beyond the boundaries of Judea and the Holy Land should almost certainly be credited to the Hellenist believers in Jesus, Diaspora Jews who saw a wider field of opportunity for their evangelistic message.

Acts 8 attributes the first step of outreach to Philip, whose appointment to the Hellenist seven (Acts 6:5), like that of Stephen, betokened his potential as a spokesman for the new sect and its beliefs. Since Samaria was contiguous with Judea (and formed part of greater Judea), and Samaritans were in effect a rival form of Torah religion,* Samaria was an obvious mission target. The success of Philip's Samaritan mission (Acts 8:4–13,25) may be reflected in John 4:35–37; and at any rate we can be fairly confident that the gospel message soon spread and had success in Samaria. Luke's account leaves a number of questions unanswered, but Luke's narrative makes a point of highlighting how important it was in the early expansion that new converts were initiated into the full experience of the Holy Spirit, as demonstrated by the Spirit's visible effects (Acts 8:14–19). Most intriguing is the introduction of the character Simon Magus, whose status as a convert is left unclear (8:20–24), and who subsequently was represented as one of Christianity's most dangerous opponents.†[51]

The principal and most significant breakthrough by the Hellenist missionaries was their successful preaching in Syrian Antioch to Greek-speakers who were not Diaspora Jews, that is to Greek gentiles (Acts 11:20–21). Luke does not make a lot of this development, but it was of major significance as it opened the door to a full and committed mission to non-Jews. Given that the issue of whether such converts should be circumcised did not emerge until some time later (Acts 15; Galatians 2:1–10), it makes most sense to infer that these first gentile converts were not required to be circumcised, that is, they were not treated or regarded as proselytes to Judaism. If circumcision had been required of the first gentile converts, it is inexplicable that such initial practice was not regarded as the decisive precedent, to be cited when the issue arose later. Without such a reference it can be safely assumed that the question of gentile converts being circumcised did not arise in that first breakthrough in Antioch.

This is an astonishing conclusion to have to draw, since circumcision was so fundamental to Jewish identity[52] and such a crucial entry rite into membership of the people of God.[53] The practice of circumcising proselytes was probably near to being universal so that any exceptions would have been noted and acted upon—as evidently Jewish missionaries endeavored to do, correcting Paul's mission in Galatia and Philippi. Was circumcision regarded

*See Reinhard Pummer, "The Samaritans: A Jewish Offshoot or a Pagan Cult?" *BR*, October 1991; Yitzhak Magen, "Bells, Pendants, Snakes & Stones: A Samaritan Temple to the Lord on Mt. Gerizim," *BAR*, November/December 2010.

†David R. Cartlidge, "The Fall and Rise of Simon Magus," *BR*, Fall 2005.

as too much a Jewish identity marker, so that the requirement of circumcision grated too harshly with the openness to gentiles that the Hellenists displayed? Was there a more extensive turning away from the law as the defining feature of those who worshiped the God of Israel and committed themselves to Messiah Jesus? Or was it rather that even more traditionalist Jewish believers were happy to welcome God-fearing gentiles into their midst, in the hope and expectation that in due course they would become full proselytes?

Such questions can only be posed, since we have no way of answering them satisfactorily. But it is likely that the openness of the Hellenists in Antioch to accept (by baptism) gentile believers as members of the new sect (of Judaism) without requiring them to be circumcised was a tipping point in the development of Christianity as something distinct from Judaism. The fact, then, that the term "Christian" for the members of the new movement was coined in Antioch (Acts 11:26) probably has the fuller significance of indicating the emergence of Christianity as such. That a crucial confrontation between Peter and Paul also took place in Antioch (Galatians 2:11–14) is enough to confirm the central significance of Antioch in the development of Christianity.

A number of scholars attribute to the Antioch church much of the development of Christian theology prior to Paul. And certainly much can be attributed to the Hellenists:

- The translation of the traditions about Jesus into Greek.
- The establishment of the Greek translation of the Hebrew Bible (the Septuagint, or LXX) as the early Christians' primary version of the Jewish scripture.
- "Christ" establishing itself as the Greek translation of "Messiah," and *kyrios* as the Greek equivalent to the Aramaic *mar* ("Lord").
- The development of the new sect into the first Jewish missionary movement.[54]
- The beginning of a distancing of the new movement from its Jewish roots (reflected in different understandings of the Temple and circumcision).
- Possibly it is to the Hellenist Christians that we owe the understanding of Jesus' death as a sacrifice for sin (1 Corinthians 15:3), rather than as the sacrifice that established the new covenant (Mark 14:24; 1 Corinthians 11:25)—with the corollary spelt out so bluntly later by Hebrews, that the sin-offering of Christ's death rendered the Temple cult obsolete (Hebrews 8–10).
- Perhaps, too, a different form of ecclesiology can be discerned,

> where elders were not regarded as the inevitably natural leaders,[55] but leadership was more charismatic in character, in which prophets and teachers more naturally came to the fore (Acts 13:1).

It is unclear how much more should be attributed to the Hellenists or to the Antioch church in particular. But certainly they can be regarded as preparing the way for the major contribution of Paul.

The emergence of Paul

Paul is such a gigantic figure in the emergence of Christianity that he deserves and requires special treatment. Apart from anything else, the degree to which the development of Christianity can be tracked around the chronology of Paul's life and mission, even allowing for its uncertainties, means that the events of Paul's life and mission provide the spine of any account of first generation Christianity. The following timeline well illustrates the point, even though it is inevitably provisional, with almost every detail subject to some dispute.

Birth in Tarsus	c. 1 B.C.E.–2 C.E.
Education in Jerusalem	c. 12–26 C.E.
Persecution of Hellenists	31–32 C.E.
Conversion	32 C.E.
Flight from Damascus and first visit to Jerusalem	34/35 C.E.
Missionary of the church of Antioch	34/35–47/48 C.E.
Jerusalem council and incident at Antioch	47–48 C.E.
Mission in Corinth (1 & 2 Thessalonians, Galatians)	49/50–51/52 C.E.
Third visit to Jerusalem and Antioch	51/52 C.E.
Mission in Ephesus (1 & 2 Corinthians)	52/53–55 C.E.
Corinth (Romans)	56/57 C.E.
Final trip to Jerusalem and arrest	57 C.E.
Detention in Jerusalem and Caesarea	57–59 C.E.
Attempt to sail to Rome	59 C.E.
Arrival in Rome	60 C.E.
House arrest in Rome (Philemon, Colossians, Philippians?)	60–62 C.E.
Execution	62 C.E. (?)

Although only Luke attests Paul's birth in Tarsus, Cilicia (Acts 9:11, 21:39, 22:3), there is no reason to doubt the information. When Paul came to Jerusalem, to either begin or complete his higher education, is disputed

(Acts 22:3, 26:4–5). But Paul himself confirms that he was trained as a Pharisee (Philippians 3:5), and only in Jerusalem would such a training be possible or acceptable. This double background explains both Paul's relative facility in Greek (his Bible of choice was the LXX), and the depth of his commitment to Pharisaic interpretation and practice of Judaism (Galatians 1:13–14; Philippians 3:5).

Luke also claims that Paul was a Roman citizen, which is again disputed. But many Jews were granted citizenship, including those enslaved by Pompey and subsequently freed (Philo, *Legatio* 155–157), and probably some of the freedmen (*libertini*) who worshiped in the Jerusalem synagogue of Acts 6:9. And without the appeal to Caesar (Acts 25:14), which was only possible for a Roman citizen, it is difficult to explain why Paul's case was transferred from Judea to Rome.

Paul introduces himself initially as one who violently persecuted the church of God and tried to destroy it (Galatians 1:13), known to the churches in Judea simply as "the persecutor" (Galatians 1:23). As already suggested, Paul's persecution was probably aimed primarily at the Hellenists. But why he pursued them so relentlessly and violently is not clear.

1) Paul would, of course, have rejected the claim that Jesus was Messiah and exalted to heaven; typical Jewish reaction to talk of a crucified messiah is clearly illustrated in 1 Corinthians 1:23 and probably Galatians 3:13. But, as already indicated, the Jerusalem believers were by and large able to continue maintaining Jesus as Messiah in Jerusalem without serious opposition for almost all of the 35 years following Jesus' crucifixion.

2) The Hellenists' presumed support for Stephen, and hence their presumed questioning of the Temple, would extend the opposition of the Jewish mob into action against the Hellenist believers in Jesus. If Paul was a very traditionalist Jew, and a Diaspora Jew horrified by the sort of irreverence that Stephen had displayed toward the Temple, that could go a long way toward explaining the anger implied in the violence of his persecution.

3) The most explicit reason that Paul himself recalls was his "zeal" (Philippians 3:6; Galatians 1:13–14). The term and its cognate "zealot" recall a fundamental Jewish conviction, that God in choosing Israel to be his special people, was a zealous/jealous[56] God who insisted that Israel must remain loyal to Yahweh alone and not follow other gods.[57] Holiness for Israel meant being set apart for God alone, and so also set apart from other nations and their gods. Consequently, the term also evokes the history of Israel's heroes of zeal who fought to maintain that holiness and Israel's set-apartness to God. Most famous was Phinehas whose stern action to prevent the union of an Israelite with a Midianite was seen as an act of zeal that saved Israel

from being consumed by God's jealousy (Numbers 25:6–13). Phinehas was revered for his zeal (Psalm 106:28–31; Sirach 45:23–24) and provided the inspiration for both the Maccabean revolt against Syria in the 160s B.C.E. (1 Maccabees 2:26,54) and subsequently the revolt against Rome led by the Zealots in 66 C.E. The final words of the initiator of the Maccabean revolt was a paean of praise for such zealots and a call to display such zeal (1 Maccabees 2:49–60). This zeal had three characteristic features: (1) defense of Israel's distinctiveness/holiness/set-apartness in face of actions or policies that threatened Israel's unyielding loyalty to its covenant with God; (2) readiness to take preventative action against fellow Jews judged to be imperiling Israel's faithfulness to that covenant; and (3) a willingness to use violence to that end.[58] Against this historical context it becomes clear why Paul attributed his violent persecution of fellow Jews to "zeal." The implication is that Saul (Paul) judged the Hellenists to be as much a threat to Israel's religious integrity and national identity as previous threats that had inspired similar zeal.[59] His zeal was directed primarily to defend and preserve Israel's holiness and set-apartness.

Acts reports that Saul was converted while engaged in his zealous persecution. The event was so important to Luke's account of Christianity's beginnings that he has the story of Paul's conversion told three times (Acts 9:1–19, 22:3–21, 26:4–18). Journeying to Damascus, Saul saw a "heavenly vision" (Acts 26:19), which he experienced as an encounter with Jesus, exalted to heaven, and commissioning him to take the good news of Jesus (thus risen and exalted) to non-Jews.[60] There are sufficient cross-checks in Paul's letters on these details—the location of Paul's conversion (Galatians 1:17), the seeing of Jesus (1 Corinthians 9:1) in heavenly splendor (2 Corinthians 4:4) despite Saul's persecution of the church (1 Corinthians 15:8–9) and his commissioning as apostle to the gentiles (Galatians 1:16; Romans 11:13)—for Luke's account to stand and for Paul's Damascus road conversion to become a classic model of radical conversion. Certainly the complete, 180-degree turn from persecutor to apostle marked a major transition in the history of embryonic Christianity. The confirmation that the good news of Messiah Jesus was also for non-Jews, and Paul's subsequent wholehearted commitment to the gentile mission was probably the single most important factor in the development of Christianity from its seed pod in Second Temple Judaism.

If it is relatively easy to correlate Acts with the Pauline letters so far as Paul's conversion is considered, the picture becomes much less clear as regards the aftermath. Paul refers to spending some time in Arabia, probably the kingdom of Nabatea, south of Damascus and east of the Jordan (Galatians 1:17). Did he throw himself immediately into evangelism, as some infer?

Nabatean Christianity certainly flourished in the period before the Muslim conquest. Or was it a time for reflection and reshaping his whole theology and life-commitment around the new fact of Messiah Jesus being affirmed and exalted by God? Who can tell? What Paul makes clear is that he did not travel to Jerusalem for three years after his conversion (Galatians 1:18). This is where it becomes difficult to match Paul's account with Acts.[61] For Acts 9:19–26 implies that Paul went to Jerusalem after a much shorter time. Indeed, Paul's insistence that he did not go to Jerusalem for three years, and then only spent time with Peter and otherwise saw only James, even affirming it with an oath (Galatians 1:18–20), strongly suggests that he was responding to a different account of his dealings with the Jerusalem apostles—an account that Luke may well have drawn upon (possibly in preference to Paul's)!

What is interesting about Paul's version is the prominence given to Cephas/Peter: Paul spent two weeks getting to know Peter and the two were in close companionship. This both confirms that Peter was regarded as the leading figure in the Jerusalem assembly, and probably indicates an opportunity that Paul took to immerse himself in the traditions about Jesus of which Peter would be regarded as the prime authority. This opportunity for Paul to confirm that the gospel handed on to him in Damascus or in Jerusalem (1 Corinthians 15:3) was in accord with the gospel he received in his encounter with the risen Christ (Galatians 1:11–12) must have been of huge significance for Paul and ensured that there was a clear line of continuity running from Jesus through Peter to Paul. The point is important since the links between Jesus' message and Paul's gospel are mostly implicit, and since the subsequent tensions between Paul and Peter can cloud the extent of their agreement.

The next phase of Paul's career on which we can speak with some confidence is that subsequent to this first visit (as a Christian believer) to Jerusalem, Paul identified himself primarily with the church of Antioch. Acts gives a fuller narrative account—Paul's return to Tarsus before Barnabas brought him to Antioch (Acts 9:30, 11:25–26)—but the extensive missionary work in which Paul tells us he engaged, in the regions of Syria and Cilicia (Galatians 1:21), was most obviously carried out as a missionary sent out by and from Antioch (Acts 13:1–3), and Paul confirms his close association with the church of Antioch (Galatians 2:11–14). Here again it is unclear how to correlate Paul's reference to extensive missionary work in Syria and Cilicia (Galatians 1:21) with the Acts account of a mission (usually known as Paul's "first missionary journey"), under the leadership of Barnabas, to Cyprus, Pamphylia, Pisidia and Lycaonia (Acts 13–14). Possibly Paul limited his reference to churches that he acknowledged to be daughter churches of Antioch. Be that as it may, the fact is that more than half of Paul's active missionary life was evidently spent as a missionary of the church of Antioch. During this period, which extended over about 14 years (Galatians 2:1), Paul's theology would no doubt have absorbed any developments in theology and praxis made by the Hellenists and/or Antioch and would probably have established the shape and character evident in his letters.

The mission to the gentiles

Luke and Paul again give somewhat different accounts of how the mission to non-Jews became acceptable within the Jewish sect of the Nazarenes. Luke attributes the breakthrough to Peter, and in his threefold account of and reference to the episode (Acts 10:1–11:18, 15:7–11) he gives the breakthrough almost as much space and emphasis as his threefold account of Paul's conversion (Acts 9, 22, 26). His account of the conversion of the Roman centurion Cornelius begins with what can fairly be called the conversion of Peter (Acts 10:9–35). In a vision, repeated three times, Peter was informed that God had made clean what Jews had previously regarded as unclean (Acts 10:13–16). From this Peter learned not only that he should no longer regard pork as unclean but that he should not regard any *person* as unclean (Acts 10:28); in every nation those who feared God and did what was right were acceptable to God (Acts 10:35). The significance of this revelation was confirmed when Cornelius and his gentile companions heard Peter's message about Jesus and were granted the Holy Spirit without further ado (Acts 10:44). The evidence of this was evidently irrefutable: Peter had them baptized at once (Acts 10:45–48), and his subsequent report to more traditionalist believers in Jerusalem was fully accepted (Acts 11:15–18).

Paul's account is in terms of the success of his mission (in Syria and Cilicia, or on his first missionary journey). His mission to the uncircumcised had clearly been at God's commission, and its success was proof of the grace given to and through him (Galatians 2:7–9). Sadly, not untypical of Paul, he focuses almost exclusively on his own role; Barnabas is marginalized (Galatians 2:1,9), despite the fact that, if Paul was referring to the mission described in Acts 13–14, Barnabas had initially been the lead partner. The important fact, however, is that the Jerusalem leadership—James, Peter/Cephas and John—accepted that the good news of Jesus was not just for Jews but also for gentiles (Galatians 2:7–9). If a link between Galatians 2:7–9 and Acts 13–14 is justifiable, then it can also be noted that, according to Luke, the gospel was being received by a wide range of gentiles—including no less than a Roman proconsul, Sergius Paulus (Acts 13:7–12), many synagogue devotees, Jews and Godfearers (Acts 13:42–43,48) and less sophisticated provincials (Acts 14:21).

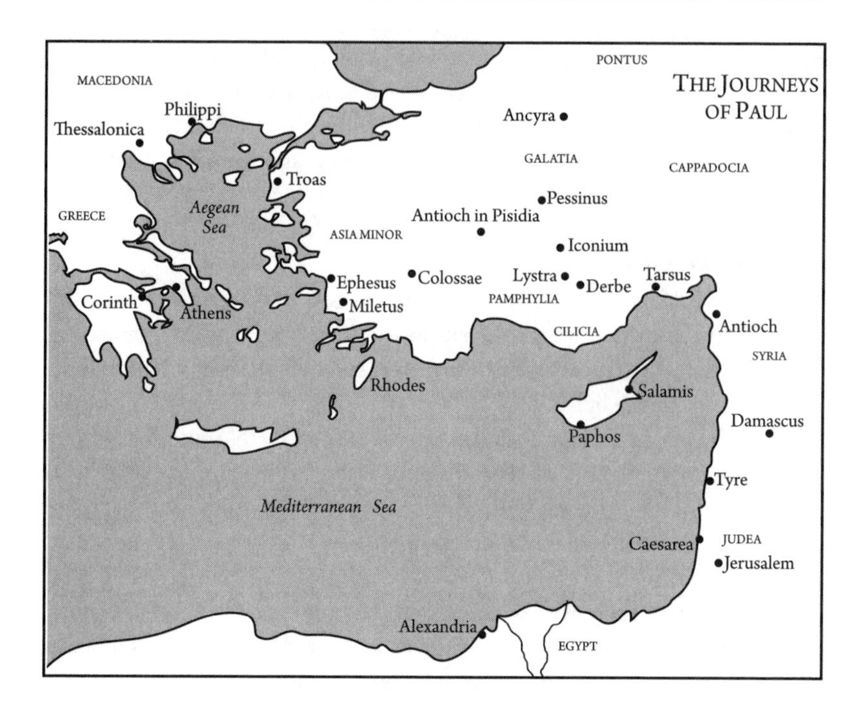

The decisive factors given in both Luke's and Paul's accounts are divine revelation (Acts 10:11–14; Galatians 1:16) and the manifest gift of the Spirit to uncircumcised gentiles.[62] This development in fact was the third fulcrum point on which the earliest history of Christianity turned, the other two being the resurrection of Jesus and the outpouring of the Pentecostal Spirit. All of these points were perceived as divinely ordained and accomplished, irrefutably of God and clearly pointing the way forward. These were the givens, the foundational facts on the basis of which Christianity forged its distinctive identity. Nor should the point be missed that as the resurrection of Jesus indicated and required a fresh reading of ancient scriptures and tradition, so this new realization that the acceptance of the gospel did not require circumcision indicated and required a reevaluation and reprioritizing of laws hitherto regarded as fundamental to Israel's identity.

The matter was not so easily decided and settled. Sooner or later the more traditionalist believers, presumably waking up to the fact that more and more gentiles were being accepted by baptism without being circumcised, began to insist with force that this practice was not (or no longer) acceptable. Was the new sect really going to completely set aside the clear instruction of Genesis 17:9–14, and disown the witness of those who died to maintain that covenant loyalty (1 Maccabees 1:60–61)?

The issue was evidently so important that it required the leaders of the new movement to meet in order to thrash it out. The occasion is usually referred to as the council of Jerusalem, in effect the first Christian council (47 or 48 C.E.). Here again, however, the accounts by Luke (Acts 15) and Paul (Galatians 2:1–10) give different pictures. Since the issue that occasioned each account was evidently the same—whether it was necessary for gentile believers to be circumcised (Acts 15:1–5; Galatians 2:3–6)—it is most likely that the accounts refer to the same event and to the agreement that was reached. Luke again seems to give Jerusalem's version of the discussion, with the decisive contribution made by Peter (Acts 15:7–11), and Paul and Barnabas playing only a supporting role (15:12). In contrast, Paul, as already indicated, focused on his own role and gives the clear impression that it was his testimony to the effectiveness of his (and Barnabas's) mission that won over a somewhat recalcitrant or unwilling Jerusalem leadership (Galatians 2:3–6). Whatever the finer points of detail, it is important once again to note that the Jerusalem leadership and Paul agreed that the new development—gentiles being fully accepted without becoming proselytes—was entirely in accord with God's will. The significance of this needs to be highlighted, as does the fact that James and Peter were full partners in the agreement (Galatians 2:9), since the agreement did not command unanimous assent (Galatians 2:4), and since there were many Jewish believers who subsequently opposed the gentile mission and tried to persuade Paul's converts to be circumcised. However, the agreement reached in Jerusalem raised a flag that could never thereafter be pulled down, and charted a course that Christianity would follow thereafter.

That the agreement was far from secure and only partial soon became evident in what is regularly referred to as the incident at Antioch (Galatians 2:11–14). Paul's sequence of events in Galatians 1–2 most obviously implies that the Antioch incident took place some time after the Jerusalem agreement was sealed with handshakes. The episode indicates Antioch's central role in the developing Christian mission and confirms Paul's association with the city's church. More striking is the fact that Peter/Cephas had also been there for some time. That both the individuals most responsible for the Jewish and the gentile mission (Galatians 2:9) were present for a lengthy period in Antioch strongly suggests the mixed (Jew and gentile) composition of the church. More to the point, as the mother church of the gentile mission, Antioch would have provided a model or precedent for how the fellowship of other mixed churches should express itself.

Initially the pattern was quite liberal: "Peter was accustomed to eating with the gentiles [gentile believers]" (Galatians 2:12), quite likely with some relaxation of the Jewish dietary laws. But when a group came "from James," Peter "separated himself" from the gentiles (Galatians 2:12). Since "the rest of the Jews [Jewish believers]" followed suit, including Barnabas (Galatians 2:13), their reasons for acting so must have been substantial. The most obvious rationale, as already indicated, is to be found in Leviticus 20:23–26, where it is clear that the laws of clean and unclean are seen as expressive of the separation between Israel and other peoples and therefore necessary to ensure Israel's holiness.[63] Paul unkindly maintains that Peter acted as he did (separating himself from the gentile believers), "fearing those of the circumcision" (Galatians 2:12). The reference could be to traditionalist Jewish believers, but may include or refer simply to Jews generally ("the circumcision" as in Galatians 2:9); and the "fear" that Paul attributes to Peter and the others may have been simply a sober recognition, for those tasked to take the gospel to "the circumcision" (the Jews), that such a disregard for a tradition so crucial to the identity of "the circumcision" would render the mission to "the circumcision" much more difficult if not impossible.

Paul was a lone voice in protesting against Peter's *volte face*. He accused Peter of trying to "compel" the gentile believers to "Judaize" (Galatians 2:14), as he had in effect accused "the false brothers" at the Jerusalem consultation of trying to "compel" the gentile Titus to be circumcised (Galatians 2:3–4). A gentile "Judaized" when he began to live like a Jew and observe Jewish customs, even when unwilling to be circumcised.[64] Paul's charge was that by refusing table-fellowship with the gentile believers, except on his own Jewish terms, Peter was in effect compelling the gentiles who wanted to maintain table-fellowship to observe Israel's *kashrut* laws. In Paul's view, to thus insist that gentile believers observe such laws was to make God's acceptance of these believers dependent not only on their faith in Christ but also on their observing such "works of the law" (Galatians 2:16). For Paul, however, it was the essence of the gospel that God's acceptance came into effect only through faith in Jesus Christ, and on that he was unyielding (Galatians 2:5,14).

Paul does not say how the incident ended. And his being the canonical voice, there was a natural tendency for later Christian historians and theologians to assume that Paul's protest was heeded and that Peter and the other Jewish believers returned to their previous practice in table-fellowship with gentile believers. But it is hard to believe that Paul would have remained silent about such a victory. He had made much of the victory he had won in Jerusalem (Galatians 2:6–9), and the issue of table-fellowship was almost as important for the fellowship of the mixed churches that his mission produced (1 Corinthians 8–10; Romans 14:1–15:6). So the impulse to set out his success, given the crucial precedent that it provided, would surely have been irresistible. In contrast, Paul's silence strongly suggests that he did *not* win the day, and probably that the gentile believers accepted the tighter conditions on their table-fellowship with the Jewish believers—though separate house churches is another possibility.

More seriously, it would appear that the incident seriously damaged Paul's relationship with Peter and the Jerusalem leadership, and broke his relationship with the church of Antioch and with Barnabas. At all events, whereas it could be said that Paul's initial mission was carried out as a missionary of the Antioch church (Galatians 1:21; Acts 13–14), his subsequent mission seems to have been much more independent, an independence he was more than ready to assert, as we shall see.

Luke's account is again different. He does not mention the Antioch incident, despite the clearly critical implications for the gentile mission implied in Paul's account. Paul's breach with Barnabas is attributed to different circumstances (Acts 15:36–40). More significantly, Luke's account of the outcome of the Jerusalem conference includes, or rather focuses on, a resolution that would have prevented the incident at Antioch. What is usually known as "the apostolic decree" laid down the terms on which gentile believers could enjoy full participation in the Christian community—in particular, that they eat only kosher food and abstain from anything polluted by contact with idols (and from *porneia*[65]) (Acts 15:20,29).[66]

The difficulty of correlating the diverse accounts of Paul and Luke has been resolved in different ways. One is the hypothesis that the episode referred to by Paul in Galatians 2:1–10 was earlier than the Jerusalem council of Acts 15; and that the council was a response to the incident in Antioch, with the apostolic decree providing the solution. The attraction of this solution is gravely weakened, as already noted, by the similarity of the occasion of both versions (Acts 15:1–5; Galatians 2:3–6), but also by the implausibility of Paul, having been so abandoned by Peter, at the behest of the group from James, and betrayed (as Paul would have seen it) by Barnabas, then going meekly to a council in Jerusalem, with Barnabas in the lead role (Acts 15:12), and agreeing with a resolution that made no reference to the issues raised by the Antioch incident.

The more plausible solution is that the apostolic decree was indeed the solution that emerged from Jerusalem in response to the problems raised in Antioch, and that it was intended for the churches of Antioch, Syria and Cilicia (the daughter churches of Antioch). As in other instances,[67] Luke has compressed the timeline; having cut out the Antioch incident from the timeline, he could fuse the pre-incident and post-incident ends together without misleading his audience to any significant extent.

Paul the apostle

Paul was a Jew who never retreated from or was embarrassed by his Jewish heritage, even when he critiqued his fellow Jews and made light of some of the Jewish law's commandments. He certainly looked back to his earlier life "in Judaism" as one from which he had moved away (Galatians 1:13–14). But he did not hesitate to identify himself as an "Israelite" (Romans 11:1; 2 Corinthians 11:22) and attempted to understand "Israel," "Jew" and "circumcision" in ways that included himself and non-Jews.[68] More noticeable, the signatory phrase by which he most clearly defined himself and the churches that he founded was "in Christ," a phrase that appears 83 times in the Pauline corpus and whose Jewish messianic significance is never wholly lost (e.g., Romans 9:5; cf. Galatians 3:15–29).

Paul insisted most emphatically that he was an *apostle*, that is, he had been granted an appearance by the risen Christ and appointed by him to be his emissary, or apostle. The fact that he insisted on the point so strongly in the opening words of Galatians (Galatians 1:1) suggests that he was reacting against attacks on what he regarded as his apostolic mission—perhaps still smarting over his failure in Antioch and its aftermath. This would explain the care with which Paul records his links with Jerusalem in Galatians 1–2, including his rather jaundiced and dismissive reference to the Jerusalem leadership in Galatians 2:6. It is certainly interesting that thereafter Paul regularly introduced himself in his letters as "apostle of Jesus Christ"[69] and took various opportunities to restate his credentials.[70] It was this vocation that became for Paul an overpowering compulsion to preach the gospel, to bring others to faith in Jesus Christ and to found churches.

Paul seems to have pursued a well-planned strategy: to evangelize across the northern Mediterranean along a semicircle route from Jerusalem to Rome, with the ultimate goal of reaching Spain (Romans 15:18–19,23,28).[71] He also saw his as a pioneering mission, going "where Christ has not been named," and so avoiding the risk of building on another's foundation (Romans 15:20). This, too, may suggest a spirit wounded by criticisms of his earlier mission or a determination to avoid the sort of situation that had cost him so dearly in Antioch. Second Corinthians 10:13–16 certainly seems to be a very distinctive reading of the division of evangelistic labor agreed upon in Jerusalem (Galatians 2:9). Paul understood the agreement as both giving him *carte blanche* in his own field of mission and, by implication, guaranteeing the freedom of his own mission from interference by others. This interpretation gave him some embarrassment in writing to Christians in Rome, since he had not founded the church there (Romans 1:11–15, 15:20–23). But the fact that other missionaries ignored Paul's reading of the Jerusalem agreement and tried to undo or make good his work in Galatia, Corinth and Philippi roused him to anger and fierce response.[72]

Paul's tactics seem to have been well thought out, too. He located his mission in major cities around the Aegean (Philippi, Thessalonica, Corinth and Ephesus). In these cities, he could bank on the fact that Greek would provide the language of communication.[73] Also important, when Paul was in a city, he would more easily find the opportunity to practice his trade as a tentmaker. The latter was important for Paul because he did not want to be dependent on the support of his converts or the patronage of the local elite.[74] As administrative centers, such cities also provided natural centers from which the gospel could spread, as seems to have happened, since Paul was soon able to speak of the many believers and churches that had evidently been won from these centers.[75] In this, he was evidently able to depend on a considerable mission team ("coworkers") whose names pepper the final paragraphs of many of his letters.[76]

In each city Paul usually made a point of preaching the good news of Messiah Jesus in the synagogue, or one of the synagogues. This is certainly what Luke reports.[77] Doubt is often raised on this point, on the assumption that the apostle to the gentiles would have preferred a different setting in which to preach his gospel. But the objection ignores the fact that many gentiles were attracted by Judaism and were willing to "Judaize" to some extent by observing Jewish feasts and attending Sabbath gatherings in the synagogue; they are usually known as "Godfearers," to whom the Jewish writers, Philo and Josephus, and recent inscriptional evidence refer.*[78] Such Godfearers, who had Judaized but held back from becoming proselytes, would likely be the gentiles most open to and attracted by a form of Judaism that did not demand circumcision. The Book of Acts accounts that Paul's preaching won converts from many such gentiles are entirely believable.[79] Acts reports other locations in which Paul sometimes preached and taught—the marketplace (Acts 17:17) and a lecture hall, presumably rented by a supporter (Acts 19:9); but we may infer evangelism carried out both in private homes and at dinner tables to which Paul was invited, and at the work place, where Paul must have spent much of his day,[80] speaking about his faith to passersby and customers.

Although Paul's letters do not contain his evangelistic preaching as such, they provide enough references and allusions to enable us to gain a good idea of the gospel he preached.

*Angelos Chaniotis, "Godfearers in the City of Love," *BAR*, May/June 2010; see also Robert F. Tannenbaum, "Jews and God-fearers in the Holy City of Aphrodite," *BAR*, September/October 1986.

- The Thessalonians turned from idols to the living God (1 Thessalonians 1:9).
- An emphasis on the soon-coming of Jesus from heaven is implicit in 1 Thessalonians 1:10.
- In Corinth Paul determined to preach only Christ crucified (1 Corinthians 1:23, 2:2).
- In Galatians he focuses his gospel on believing in Christ Jesus (Galatians 2:16).
- He assumes that the Roman believers had come to believe that God had raised Jesus from the dead, and to confess "Jesus is Lord" (Romans 10:9).
- His frequent references to his converts' reception of the Holy Spirit imply that his gospel must have included the promise of the Spirit.[81]

The churches that Paul founded were all house churches; there is no evidence of true Christian church buildings before about 200 C.E., although in the early years a sizable apartment in a large private house may well have become a *de facto* church building. (For a detailed discussion, see "The origins and development of early Christian architecture," pp. 311–318.) But while some of the local elites became Christians and could provide such accommodation (e.g., Romans 16:23), the great majority of the first Christians were poor and living at or near subsistence level. In many cases the house churches in cities would be better described as apartment or tenement churches, where only a small group could meet. Alternatively, some groups might well have been able to meet at their workplace. But even larger groups, hosted in the sizable houses of highborn citizens, probably numbered no more than 50 members each.

Such gatherings were familiar in the Greco-Roman world—these included family, neighborhood, regional or occupational associations, as well as religious cult associations.[82] Synagogues were regarded as legally equivalent to such associations, and the first churches were probably initially regarded as a subset of the synagogue and sheltered under the legal permission granted to synagogues. Consequently, in their structure the early churches would probably seem to the curious outsider to be variants of the more familiar voluntary association. The extent to which slaves and women were active in their membership would have been notable but not unparalleled, though the fact that women were among the leaders of the churches would have been more surprising.[83]

The most distinguishing feature of these new cult associations was their foundational belief in Jesus Christ (1 Corinthians 3:11). Paul himself did not hesitate to integrate the early conviction that "Jesus is Lord," as attested by Psalm 110:1, with Israel's traditional belief in one God (Deuteronomy 6:4; 1 Corinthians 8:6) who alone was to be worshiped (Philippians 2:10–11, echoing Isaiah 45:23). Baptism as an initiation rite would also have been distinctive, even though ritual cleansings and purifications were well known as preparatory for initiation into mystery cults; baptism was thought to transfer the baptized into the lordship of the one in whose name it was performed (1 Corinthians 1:12–13). The shared meal was certainly a common factor, focusing attention particularly on the salvific effect of participating in Jesus' death (1 Corinthians 10:16), although the absence of priests, sacrifice and libations would have made it hard for most outsiders to recognize "the Lord's supper" as a religious meal. How the shared meals (1 Corinthians 11:17–34) correlated with worship sessions (1 Corinthians 14) is not clear. And leadership seems to have been both partly spontaneous (1 Corinthians 16:15–18; 1 Thessalonians 5:12) and partly structured (1 Corinthians 12:28; Philippians 1:2), although the early Paul makes no mention of elders.

Paul did not see his role merely as the founder of these churches. He was also deeply exercised about their growth and ongoing life. Paul was not only a missionary; he was also a pastor. And even when he had moved on from a particular church to continue his pioneering missionary activity, his churches filled his concerns and prayers. He even climaxed the frightening list of sufferings he had endured with the note: "And besides other things, I am under daily pressure because of my anxieties for all the churches" (2 Corinthians 11:28). For the most part, it is the problems that arose in or in relation to Paul's churches that caused him to call for an amanuensis to dictate his letters (Romans 16:22; see also Galatians 6:11). Had the communal life of his churches not experienced so many difficulties and crises, not least in their continuing relationship with Paul, we might not have had such a rich sequence of letters and such fascinating insights into the beginnings of Christianity as pioneered by Paul.

Paul's Aegean mission

The ten years following the incident at Antioch were the most significant and fruitful of Paul's mission. During that period he established churches in important cities on the three sides of the Aegean Sea and wrote most of the letters that can be indubitably attributed to him.[84] That is to say, during this period Paul probably established Christianity in major provinces of the Roman Empire (Asia Minor, Macedonia and Achaia), established a character of Christianity that was already breaking through the constraints of a Jewish messianic sect, and wrote documents that contributed immeasurably to the definition and identity of Christianity. That Paul was "the second founder of Christianity" has sometimes been asserted as a criticism of Paul and of the Christianity he preached. But it is nevertheless a well-deserved tribute that can be justly regarded as a fitting encomium.

This period is usually referred to as Paul's second and third missionary journeys. These are misleading descriptions, since they imply that Paul continued to act as a missionary of the church in Antioch, whereas, as already indicated, by then he was almost certainly functioning more independently. The descriptions also fail to recognize that during this period of mission, Paul in effect set up his headquarters first in Corinth (for about two years) and then in Ephesus (for a somewhat longer period).[85]

According to Acts, Paul began this mission by traversing the territory of Galatia. There is a long tradition among commentators that insists that by "Galatia" Paul would not be referring to the towns listed in Acts (Derbe, Lystra, etc.—Acts 16:1–6) but to what is usually denoted as "north Galatia" (the region of Ancyra and Pessinus). However, there were no Roman roads leading north to these cities, there is no other evidence that Paul evangelized so far north in Galatia, and the cities of Antioch, Iconium, Lystra and Derbe would be naturally understood at the time as belonging to the province of Galatia. So there are no real problems about linking Paul's letter to the Galatians with the cities mentioned in Acts 13–14.[86]

The natural route westward, following the Roman roads, would be into Asia Minor, heading for Ephesus, the principal city of Roman Asia. But according to Acts, Paul was pushed (by the Spirit) north and west, then headed across the northeast corner of the Aegean to the Roman colony of Philippi (Acts 16:6–12). His fruitful mission there (Acts 16:13–15,40) is corroborated by the later letter to the Philippians, and its less satisfactory ending (Acts16:16–40) is indicated by 1 Thessalonians 2:2. Following the Via Egnatia, Paul's small team next came to Thessalonica, the capital of Macedonia, where another fruitful mission was cut short (Acts 17:1–10) in circumstances again echoed in 1 Thessalonians (1 Thessalonians 1:6, 2:14–16). Had Paul intended to follow the Via Egnatia directly to Rome? If so, that goal had to be postponed. Acts relates a sequence of movement that ended in Athens (Acts 17:10–15), still a natural target for a strategist like Paul, even though its days of glory were long past. Here, Acts narrates an encounter with other philosophies (Epicureans and Stoics) and a Pauline speech that has parallels with Romans 1, but otherwise is uncharacteristically Pauline (Acts 17:16–31). The Acts account is confirmed to the extent that Paul mentions that he spent some time in Athens (1 Thessalonians 3:1), but there is no other indication that Paul preached in Athens or had any success there (no letter to Athens exists), so any contact he had with Athens must have proved almost entirely ineffective, as Acts 17:32–34 implies.

A more plausible strategic center was the highly cosmopolitan and commercial community of Corinth, a Roman colony and administrative center that straddled both north-south and east-west trade routes. Acts narrates that Paul met there the husband and wife, Aquila and Priscilla, who his letters confirm became most valued members of his mission team.[87] Paul also practiced his trade as a tentmaker during his time in Corinth (Acts 18:3). Here we may note that Paul subsequently vigorously defended his determination to provide for himself rather than to depend on payment for his preaching or on a patron's subsidies for his upkeep (1 Corinthians 9). The account in Acts of a painful breach with the Corinthian synagogue (Acts 18:4–17) is not explicitly corroborated in Paul's letters, but the sequence of events (initial preaching in the synagogue, followed by establishment of effectively separate congregations of Jewish and gentile believers) must have become a regular pattern, since Paul thereafter wrote to several such congregations ("assemblies," "churches").

More significant at the time would have been, according to Luke, the ruling of the well-known proconsul Gallio[88] in favor of the Christians (Acts 18:12–16), since it would have ensured that these new churches could legally continue to shelter under the aegis of Rome's sympathetic policy toward the synagogues of the Jewish Diaspora. That Paul settled in Corinth for a substantial time (Acts 18:11,18) and used Corinth as his headquarters (from which the gospel would have gone out to "the whole of Achaia"—2 Corinthians 1:1) is corroborated by the special place that the Corinthian church had in Paul's affections and pastoral concerns (1 and 2 Corinthians).

The period following the establishment of the church in Corinth is one of the most obscure of Paul's life and mission. Luke records that after a brief visit across the Aegean to Ephesus (Acts 18:18–21), Paul returned to Syria-Palestine, probably visiting Jerusalem (Luke is strangely inexplicit on the point) before returning back to Antioch (Acts 18:22). Such a visit (the fourth indicated by Luke) is hard to square with the very negative attitude toward Jerusalem and emissaries of the mother church expressed in Paul's letters.[89] One possible solution, which has proved quite attractive, is to infer that Luke has mistakenly separated Paul's trip to Jerusalem (Galatians 2:1–10) into two separate trips. But dating the council in Jerusalem (and the Antioch incident) after Paul's Macedonian and Achaian mission is difficult to reconcile with the strong sense of independence with which Paul refers to and defends his mission in Corinth (2 Corinthians 10:12–16). A plausible alternative is that Paul grasped an opportunity to seek reconciliation with the Jerusalem and Antioch leadership; he would hardly have wanted his whole mission to become quite separate from the movement's beginnings in Jerusalem and from the early mission out of Antioch, of which he had been an integral part. If so, the bare mention that Luke makes of the trip may be sufficient to suggest that Paul's irenic approach was effectively rebuffed. It is also notable that it was in the next period of mission that Paul gave a high priority to making a collection among his churches for the poor among the believers in Jerusalem[90]—perhaps his final attempt to heal the breach between Jerusalem and his mission and to reaffirm the agreement between the two missions sealed at the earlier Jerusalem meeting (Galatians 2:7–10).

The next phase evidently focused on Ephesus and the province of Asia. Luke, as usual, gives a very sketchy account of an extensive mission, including another breach with the local synagogue (Acts 19:9), a two-year-long lecture series (Acts 19:9–10) and a notable triumph over magic (Acts 19:19). It would have been good to know what such a lengthy series of lectures covered (Did Paul work out the main lines of argument that he later used in his letter to the Romans?), and Paul is strangely missing from the account of the near riot caused by the silversmiths' protest that the success of the new cult was threatening the great temple of Artemis on which their livelihood depended (Acts 19:23–41). But at least Paul confirms that he spent some time in Ephesus (1 Corinthians 15:32), and his first three letters to Corinth were written from Ephesus (16:8). It is also evident that Paul's evangelism was very successful (Acts 16:9), resulting in the establishment of many "churches of Asia" (Acts 16:19; Romans 16:5), including those in the inland cities of the Lycus valley, founded by Epaphras (Colossians 1:7, 4:11–16). The big unknown is what Paul refers to as a major crisis that brought him near to death (2 Corinthians 1:8–11; cf. 1 Corinthians 15:32). Most infer that this must have included a time in prison, from which Paul was at least able to write the so-called "prison epistles," Philemon and Philippians. Such a traumatic period must have been well known in early church tradition, so Luke's failure to mention it remains a puzzle—along with his failure to make any reference whatsoever to Paul's letter-writing!

Paul's concern for the church at Corinth seems to have dominated his time in Ephesus, so much so that he sought to return there, using Titus as his emissary. His concern was only eased by his meeting some way around the north of the Aegean with Titus, who was able to assure him that reconciliation had been achieved (2 Corinthians 2:12–13, 7:5–16). The time he then spent in Corinth (three months—Acts 20:3) must have been among the happiest of Paul's whole mission. No doubt the time was much occupied in making arrangements needed to gather the collection for Jerusalem, as well as in welcoming and providing hospitality for the representatives of the churches to accompany it, and to ensure the safe travel of both. It was also during this time that Paul composed his letter to the Romans (Romans 16:23), in which it becomes clear that Paul regarded his Aegean mission as completed (15:15–29).

Paul's letters

As already noted, the dating of Paul's letters, particularly Galatians and the prison epistles, is much disputed. But most of what is to be learned from the letters does not depend on their chronological relationship.

1) *1 Thessalonians.* The letter was probably born out of Paul's concern for the small body of believers he had left behind in Thessalonica (1 Thessalonians 2:17, 3:1,5). It can be dated to about 50 or 51 C.E., probably not long after Paul reached Corinth. In this case Timothy had been the go-between (1 Thessalonians 3:2,6–8). The Thessalonian believers had been suffering persecution (1 Thessalonians 1:6, 2:14, 3:4) and Paul wrote to encourage them and to reassure himself that they were not abandoning their faith (1 Thessalonians 1:3,7, 3:2–10). They had evidently been rather successful in their own evangelistic outreach (1 Thessalonians 1:7–9, 4:10).

But there were, however, some pastoral issues that seem to have arisen from Paul's preaching of Jesus' imminent return from heaven (1 Thessalonians 1:10). One may have been an enthusiastic overconfidence that brought them to public attention and caused some of them to think that they no longer needed to work with their hands; Paul counsels them to live quietly and to be self-sufficient (1 Thessalonians 4:9–12). A more serious problem was that some of them were evidently worried that deceased believers among their group would miss out when Jesus returned (1 Thessalonians 4:13–18). Paul reassures them on the point: "The dead in Christ will rise first" (1 Thessalonians 4:16). The keynote regarding Jesus' coming was not imminence so much as unexpectedness and their preparedness (1 Thessalonians 5:1–11).

2) *2 Thessalonians.* Although 2 Thessalonians is regularly assigned to the pseudonymous category (written after Paul's death), the differences in style can easily be exaggerated. The issue addressed in fact takes up one of the main themes of 1 Thessalonians ("the coming of the Lord Jesus Christ" [2 Thessalonians 2:1]), and this different situation and emphasis may simply be evidence that such enthusiasm for an imminent end is mercurial and erratic as it works out. So a date not much later than 1 Thessalonians is quite conceivable. Paul is certainly quick to reaffirm that Christ will come again, not least to avenge their suffering (2 Thessalonians 1:5–10). But now reassurance has

to be given that "the day of the Lord" has not yet come (2 Thessalonians 2:1–2), and will not come until "the man of lawlessness" has appeared, who is currently being restrained (2 Thessalonians 2:3–12). The latter is one of the most enigmatic passages in the New Testament.[91] In the face of both the reassurance and the uncertainty, the exhortation is still stronger: that they should follow Paul's example (2 Thessalonians 3:7–9), working quietly and earning their own bread (2 Thessalonians 3:11–12).

Although Paul continued to look for a soon-coming of Jesus,[92] this belief is not given the same prominence as in the Thessalonian letters. It is quite possible, even likely, then, that his experience of dealing with the eschatological enthusiasm in the church of Thessalonica made Paul much more circumspect on the subject and led him to give more emphasis to what he had simply alluded to in the Thessalonian correspondence.

3) *Galatians.* As already noted, some argue that Galatians should be dated before the Jerusalem council (Acts 15). Others think that the closeness of its theology and theme to that of Romans must mean that the interval between them was very short. It is most likely, however, that Galatians was written early in the Aegean mission, when Paul received word that other missionaries had gone to Galatia and were trying to make good on what they regarded as the shortcomings of Paul's mission (namely, failing to have the Galatian believers circumcised).[93] The most plausible suggestion is that the missionaries came from Jerusalem or Antioch to ensure that churches established by an Antioch mission team remained within the traditionalist circle of influence.[94] In any case, the occasion set the scene for the first major conflict between traditionalist Jewish believers and the gentile mission as pioneered by Paul, and became the occasion for Paul to define the distinctiveness of the gospel over against an understanding of the new movement still determined by reference to the demands of the Torah.

Paul's response was to reassert the authority of his gospel, as revealed to him by Christ (Galatians 1:11–12), and as affirmed at the Jerusalem council (Galatians 2:7–9). The defining factor was that the gospel, as the blessing to the gentiles promised through Abraham (Galatians 3:8), had been fulfilled by the Galatians' reception of the Spirit through faith (Galatians 3:2–5,14). The role of the law was different from that of the Spirit (Galatians 3:21). It was primarily to provide for and instruct, to guard and discipline Israel, until the Christ had come (Galatians 3:19–24). But now that Christ had come, and the Spirit been given to faith in Christ, the law no longer had that determinative role, and the Galatians should not be tempted to put themselves under the law (Galatians 3:25–4:11). The point is rammed home by a piece of tendentious exposition in which Abraham's two sons by different mothers, Ishmael, son of the slave woman Hagar, and Isaac, son of Sarah, are taken to represent respectively the traditionalist Jews and those born of the Spirit. The argument ends with a strong plea not to accept circumcision (Galatians 5:1–11), followed by a rather offensive gibe (Galatians 5:12). We do not know how successful Paul's letter was, but the mention of the Galatian churches in 1 Corinthians 16:1 and the fact that the letter itself has been preserved suggests that, unlike the Antiochenes (Galatians 2:11–16), the Galatians followed Paul's lead.

4) *1 Corinthians.* First Corinthians should properly be entitled 2 Corinthians, since it had a predecessor (1 Corinthians 5:9). It was written from Ephesus in the early 50s C.E. in response to several reports reaching Paul from Corinth (1 Corinthians 1:11, 16:17). These raised a number of problems and indicated that the Corinthians were quite divided on several issues.

The appeal to avoid factionalism runs through the letter, but is most prominent in the opening chapters (1 Corinthians 1–4). The tensions in view here were predominantly because Paul's rhetoric was regarded as inferior (most probably to that of Apollos). Paul responds by contrasting God's wisdom, as evidenced by the cross (1 Corinthians 1:17–25) and the effectiveness of his preaching (1 Corinthians 2:1–4, 12–16), with the wisdom of the world, as evidenced by their fractiousness (1 Corinthians 3:1–4).

A second problem was the clash of value systems: What society deemed as acceptable (consorting with courtesans) and engaging in litigation should not be regarded as acceptable among believers (1 Corinthians 5–6).

A third set of problems related to marriage, particularly as to what each partner owed to the other and whether marriage was advisable if the time was so short (1 Corinthians 7).

A fourth problem area was the clash of rights, particularly the right (presumably of believers from the higher echelons of society) to take part in civic feasts held in temples.[95] Paul was clear that while an idol was "nothing," believers should not participate in temple meals (1 Corinthians 8:1–13, 10:6–22). He illustrated his case by citing his own right (to be supported by those to whom he preached) as a right he refused to claim (1 Corinthians 9); but nevertheless he encouraged the Corinthians to maintain social relations with non-believers (1 Corinthians 10:23–30). A related issue on which Paul had to speak forcefully was the shared evening meal, the Lord's supper, where the social divisions were particularly obvious—the well-to-do eating their meal before the slaves and freedmen could arrive and leaving too little for the late arrivals (1 Corinthians 11:17–22,33–34). This passage contains the only clear record that the Lord's supper (Eucharist) was celebrated in the first generation churches—in the context of a complete meal.

Other problems focused on worship—women praying and prophesying in the assembly (1 Corinthians 11:2–16), and the fundamental importance of spiritual gifts (charisms) and, above all, love (1 Corinthians 13) in the functioning of the church as the body of Christ (1 Corinthians 12–14).

The final issue (and the only theological one, as such) was the question of the resurrection—not the resurrection of Christ, which was firmly grounded in the foundation traditions (1 Corinthians 15:1–11), but the individual believer's hoped-for resurrection after death (1 Corinthians 15:12–19). Here, Paul affirms that each believer will have a resurrection like that of Jesus (1 Corinthians 15:20–23), a bodily resurrection (1 Corinthians 15:35–49), that is, of the spiritual body (1 Corinthians 15:44–50).

5) 2 *Corinthians.* Following from the argument above, 2 Corinthians could be identified as at least 4 Corinthians,[96] though a number of scholars believe that it is actually the amalgamation of several letters.[97] But while such a thesis would explain the disjointedness evident in the letter as it now stands, it is difficult to envisage an editor who felt free enough to cut off beginnings and endings of two or more letters but was editorially inhibited when it came to smoothing out the roughness of the joins.[98] A perhaps more plausible scenario is that the letter was not a finished product, but the composite of a number of drafts composed while Paul moved through Macedonia waiting for Titus to report back. These drafts would have then been hurriedly put together and sent off to prepare for Paul's own trip to Corinth (about 56 C.E.).

Part of the prompting of the letter was the news that, as in Galatia, Paul's mission in Corinth was being challenged by incoming Jewish Christian missionaries (2 Corinthians 11:4,13–23) who had evidently commended themselves to the Corinthians by their eloquence, miracles and willingness to accept the Corinthians' support (2 Corinthians 10:10, 11:6–11, 12:11). Paul's response includes a very personal statement about the crisis he endured in Asia, as well as his defense against the charge that he vacillated over his plans to visit Corinth (2 Corinthians 1:3–2:13). He also evidently felt it necessary to express an apologia for his ministry, contrasting it with that of Moses (2 Corinthians 2:14–4:6) and mounting a moving exposition of its character of suffering as the medium of the gospel (2 Corinthians 4:7–7:4). Two chapters in the collection have the appearance of two letters or two drafts of a letter (2 Corinthians 8–9); here it becomes clear from the "gospel" language Paul uses for the collection that the obligation and enterprise was for Paul wholly integral to his apostolic commission.

The implication from 2 Corinthians 7:5–16 is that, despite the subsequent chapters (10–13), and in whatever form the letter(s) came to Corinth, Paul succeeded in defending himself against the charges leveled against him (2

Corinthians 7:2,12) and restored relations with the Corinthian church to their former warmth and mutual trust.

6) *Philemon.* This is the most personal and intimate of Paul's letters. It was written to one of Paul's well-to-do converts and close coworkers (Philemon) who probably lived in Colossae. Its purpose was to intercede on behalf of one of Philemon's slaves (Onesimus) who had wronged his master in some way. Onesimus had fled from his master, perhaps to seek out Paul, or had somehow come into contact with Paul and been converted by him. The proximity of Colossae to Ephesus makes it plausible that Onesimus had fled to Ephesus and had met Paul there just prior to or even during Paul's crisis period (2 Corinthians 1:8–11). If so, the letter would have been written about 54–55 C.E., though the view that it was written from Rome is equally if not more popular.

The letter gives an insight into the realities of first-century slavery. But its most interesting feature is the pastoral sensitivity and care with which Paul encouraged the offended Philemon to accept or welcome Onesimus back "no longer as a slave, but more than a slave, as a beloved brother" (Philemon 16). Paul appears to be asking Philemon to free Onesimus, but the mixture of gentle pressure and pleading (Philemon 14–16, 19–21) would have allowed Philemon to respond with dignity and generosity in a way that would both maintain and display his honor.

7) *Colossians.* The close parallels between Philemon 23–24 and Colossians 4:10–14 strongly suggest that the two letters were written at about the same time. Paul had never visited Colossae, but the foundation of a church there by one of Paul's mission team, Epaphras (Colossians 1:7, 4:11–16), meant that he could count it as one of his churches. The difference in style from other undisputed Pauline letters is sufficient to convince many that the letter was not written by Paul himself and is therefore pseudonymous. But it is also plausible that the letter was actually composed by its joint author, Timothy (Colossians 1:1), on behalf of both, and Paul was content to add his own handwritten greeting at the end (Colossians 4:18).

News had come from Epaphras (Colossians 1:7–8) that the Colossian believers were embarrassed by followers of an older established "philosophy" and religious system who had passed negative judgment on them and dismissed their beliefs (Colossians 2:8–23). The identity of this older "philosophy" is much disputed. Many think it may have been a kind of early gnosticizing syncretism, indicated, for example, by the letter's references to "wisdom" and "knowledge,"[99] "the elements of the universe" and cosmic powers (Colossians 2:8–15), and talk of the "worship of angels" (Colossians 2:18). But the Jewish character of the claims made for the Colossians (Colossians 1:12, 2:11,13) and of the dismissive judgments directed against them (Colossians 2:16,21) strongly suggests that the criticisms were coming from the synagogue. "The worship of angels" is probably better read as "worship rendered *by* angels," with the implication that the Colossian synagogue believed that they participated in such worship (as at Qumran and in various Jewish apocalypses).

The response contains one of the high-water marks of Paul's Christology (Colossians 1:15–20), what may have been a hymn lauding Jesus in terms drawn from Jewish talk of divine Wisdom (cf. 1 Corinthians 6:8). Colossians 2:9 is as close as Paul comes to a statement of incarnation, and 2:15 is a unique expression of the subsequent Christus Victor theme—Christ on the cross triumphing over the cosmic powers. The paraenesis (exhortation to a way of life) (Colossians 3:1–17) has distinctively Jewish notes (Colossians 3:5). And Colossians 3:18–4:1 is the first example of a Christian *haustafel* (household rule), reflecting a concern that the churches should not be regarded as a threat to the good order of society.

8) *Philippians.* There are more grounds for dating Philippians to Paul's Rome imprisonment (61 or 62 C.E.), but an Ephesian prison date is also very possible, so the letter can be considered here (about 55 C.E.). This is the most friendly letter that we have from Paul, expressed particularly in the opening (Philippians 1:3–11) and in the closing (Philippians 4:10–20). The Philippians had sent him financial support during his imprisonment through Epaphroditus; Paul writes to thank them (Philippians 4:18). Epaphroditus had fallen ill and Paul was sending him back, presumably as bearer of the letter (Philippians 2:25–30). He takes the opportunity to reassure the Philippians that he is still in good heart, despite various discouragements (Philippians 1:12–30), and to offer some encouraging exhortation on personal relations (Philippians 2:1–4, 3:17–4:3). As part of this, he includes another early Christ hymn, portraying Christ as the lordly example that they should follow: He who was in the form of God, who took the form of a slave and submitted to the humiliation of crucifixion, he who in consequence was highly exalted by God and now shares in the worship due to God (Philippians 2:5–11).

The most awkward part of the letter is the abrupt note of sharp denunciation of Jewish missionaries who seem to have intervened in Philippi, as they or a similar group had in Galatia (Philippians 3:2). The following passage is Paul's most powerful statement indicating the transformation in values and goals that his conversion had brought to him (Philippians 3:3–11). What he had previously regarded as most definitive of his identity (as a Jew), he no longer regarded as important. All that mattered now was knowing Christ and his top priority was the relationship with God that Christ brought about. Equally striking is Paul's clear sense that the working out of his new vocation and the process of his salvation were not yet complete (Philippians 3:12–14).

9) *Romans.* If the prison epistles are all dated to Paul's Ephesian imprisonment, then his letter to Rome was his final letter. And even if one or more of the prison epistles should be dated to Paul's imprisonment in Rome, the letter to Rome does mark a climax and peak that towers over all the others. This is because it is the most lengthy and carefully composed of Paul's letters, in which, at the end of his Aegean mission (Romans 15:19,23), Paul set out to explain to the Christians already in Rome[100] his understanding of the gospel to which he had committed himself (Romans 1:16–17). The extensive focus in the letter on Jew-gentile relations, on the law and on Israel indicates that Paul saw in this letter the opportunity to express in detail what had become most important for him as a result of his conversion and mission to the gentiles. In so doing, Paul makes clear that for him the dynamic interaction between Jewish roots and gentile fruit was central to his understanding of both the gospel and of Christianity itself. His hope was that his exposition would persuade the Roman believers to support what he saw as the next stage of his mission—a journey to Spain (Romans 15:23–24,28).

The main body of the letter seems to fall into three parts, each of them charting the course of the same gospel but in different terms and aspects. The first tackles the issue of how a Jewish gospel can extend also to gentiles (Romans 1:18–5:11). Paul has no doubt that humankind has fallen far short of God's creative purpose; his analysis in 1:18–32 uses typical Hellenist Jewish critique of other religions as a general indictment—failure to honor God aright results in idolatry, sexual license and a dysfunctional society. Jewish assumptions that "the Jew" stands in a privileged position by virtue of possessing the law are dismissed (Romans 2:1–3:8), and both Jew and gentile are included in the general indictment (Romans 3:9–20). God's solution is Jesus' atoning death (Romans 3:21–26), which becomes effective through faith in this Jesus, quite apart from anything demanded by the law (Romans 3:27–4:24), and will be fully realized in final salvation (Romans 5:1–11).

The second part focuses on the power of sin and the power of death, forces that, once they entered into human history, cannot be escaped (Romans 5:12–14). God's solution is again in terms of Christ, bringing grace to conquer sin and life to conquer death (Romans 5:15–21). The following three chapters address the continuing problems caused by sin and death for those who believe in Christ (Romans 6). A major complicating factor is that the law (the Jewish dimension of the gospel cannot be sidelined for long) has been used by the power of sin to increase the bondage that sin exercises over the typical person who knows the law (Romans 7). But the gift of the Spirit of

God brings the grace and life in Christ into effect, enabling a fulfillment of what God demands (Romans 8:4), a close personal relationship with God (Romans 8:14–17), promise of conformity with Christ (Romans 8:18–30) and assurance that God's love in Christ will never fail (Romans 8:31–39).

The third retelling of the story of salvation focuses on Israel, God's chosen people (Romans 9:1–5). What constitutes Israel is God's call (Romans 9:6–12), which has both the negative corollary that some are not called (Romans 9:13–23) and the positive corollary that the call can embrace gentiles as well as Jews (Romans 9:24–10:13). The bulk of Israel, by failing to recognize that God's same purpose has been completed in Jesus Christ, has experienced the negative corollary (Romans 10:14–11:10). But Israel's failure has opened the door to the positive corollary of gentiles coming to faith and to participation in the olive tree that is Israel (Romans 11:11–24). The final outcome will be the salvation both of "the full number of the gentiles" and of "all Israel" (Romans 11:25–26). For "the gifts and call of God are irrevocable," and God's purpose is driven primarily by his mercy (Romans 11:26–32).

The remaining chapters re-express Paul's understanding of the church as the charismatic body of Christ (Romans 12:1–8), and provides wise counsel as to how believers should live their lives in the capital city of the world's most ruthless empire (Romans 12:9–13:14). Romans 14:1–15:6 show that the tensions between Jew and gentile believers, the very tensions that had provoked earlier crises and that had caused Paul to formulate his gospel as he had in chapters 1–11, were very real in the Roman congregations. It is clear here that the situation that Paul envisages in Rome was different from that which provoked the crisis (for Paul) in Antioch (Galatians 2:11–16). In Antioch the problem had been that a Jewish majority were in effect insisting that the gentile believers must "Judaize"; for Paul such a policy undermined "the truth of the gospel" (Galatians 2:14). In Rome, however, the problem seems to have been that a gentile majority was riding roughshod over the scruples of the Jewish believers (Romans 14:1,13). Paul was equally insistent that traditionalist Jewish believers should be free to observe their scruples, so long as they did not condemn the more relaxed conduct of others (Romans 14:4–12); the minority's scruples should be fully respected (Romans 14:13–15:6). Here Paul provides further wise pastoral counsel on how such tensions and disagreements should be dealt with in the Christian assembly.

The fact that so many of Paul's letters have been preserved indicates that they were valued by those who received them, probably treasured and used over many gatherings to instruct and prompt both reflection and worship. They were certainly passed to other congregations (cf. Colossians 4:16) and may have been circulated in various groupings. At a very early stage, the letters came to be held in ever-widening regard, a process that eventually resulted in their canonization.

The end of the beginning

The early 60s C.E. saw a series of calamities that might well have resulted in Christianity's disintegration or fragmentation. Most damagingly, the three principal leaders of the first generation, Paul, Peter and James the brother of Jesus, were killed, executed by ruthless foes.

1) Acts gives a full account of Paul's final years, fuller than the description of the first martyr's (Stephen's) death (Acts 6–7) and much fuller than the brief reference to the execution of the apostle James (Acts 12:2). The description runs from Acts 20–28 and is supported by a few occasional references outside Acts that provide confirmation (particularly 1 Clement 5:6–7). But the account's high plausibility is not lost in the obvious delight Luke has in spinning out such a good tale. The outline is straightforward: Paul set his mind to return to Jerusalem, despite the obvious dangers (Acts 20:3,22–24, 21:13–14); we know from Paul's letters that his set purpose was to deliver there the collection made by his churches for the poor among the believers in Jerusalem (Romans 15:25–28), even though he was fearful that he would thereby be running into danger, and the collection might not prove acceptable (Romans 15:31). In Jerusalem these fears were evidently realized, though Luke makes no clear reference to the collection (cf. Acts 24:17). According to Acts, Paul was accused of bringing gentiles into and thus defiling the Temple (Acts 21:28)—possibly as escorts of the substantial collection. The riot that followed resulted in Paul's arrest by the Roman authorities (Acts 21:31–35).

Here Luke's story-telling technique takes over. The following chapters narrate in vivid color and detail how Paul was held in custody, first in Jerusalem* and then for two years in Caesarea, where the Roman governor's headquarters was located. Luke includes two more accounts of Paul's conversion (Acts 22:1–21, 26:1–23), a confirmation of Jewish hostility (Acts 21:35, 22:22, 23:12–15) (even though his message was so essentially Jewish [Acts 23:6, 28:20]), the slowly mounting climax through Roman uncertainty on how to deal with Paul (Acts 24–26) and the drama of the troubled voyage toward Rome that ends in both disaster and triumph (Acts 27:1–28:10). The historical point on which we can have most confidence is that for Paul to have been transported to Rome for trial, he must have appealed to Rome for justice, thereby exercising the right of a Roman citizen (Acts 25:11–12, 26:31–32).

*See Ehud Netzer, "A New Reconstruction of Paul's Prison," *BAR*, January/February 2009.

Luke, however, leaves us with several surprises as he draws his final scenes. For one thing, he alludes to the Christians in Rome who come out to meet Paul (Acts 28:15), but in Rome itself he narrates only Paul's encounter with the city's Jews (Acts 28:17–28). Why so, when we know from Paul's letter to Rome that there were many believers already there? Was it because he wanted to give the impression that Paul brought the gospel to Rome? Just as he had focused Christianity's beginnings in Jerusalem, so Luke maintains a narrow focus on how Christianity came from Jerusalem to Rome.

For another, Luke fades out his story with the picture of Paul in Rome, under house arrest, but at his own expense, and able to continue his preaching to all (presumably Jew as well as gentile) who come to visit him (Acts 28:30–31). Paul's final speech in Miletus had already hinted that Paul would "finish his course and his ministry" in this way (Acts 20:24). And the most plausible outcome is that eventually he was brought to trial and was executed in about 62 C.E., by which time Emperor Nero was becoming increasingly erratic. The Pastoral Epistles presuppose that he was released and engaged in further mission in the Aegean area, but the content and character of these epistles make it likely that they were written after Paul's death. The source of the information they use is unknown and may be only a little more than pious and regretful imagining.

The lasting effect of Paul's mission is indicated by the continuation of many of his churches, as indicated by the letter of Clement some 30 years later (to Corinth) and by the letters of Ignatius some 50 years later (including to Ephesus, other cities of Asia presumably evangelized from Ephesus, and Rome). The success of Paul's Aegean mission endured. And, as already mentioned, the increasing circulation of his letters must have extended his influence ever more widely among the developing churches of the Roman Empire.

2) As for Peter, we have hardly any information or even hints to go on. We know nothing of his missionary work beyond what Luke tells us in Acts 9:32–11:18. In Acts he disappears from view after evading the clutches of Herod Agrippa in Jerusalem (Acts 12:18), apart from his decisive appearance at the Jerusalem council in Acts 15:7–11. Paul, however, confirms that he engaged in a successful mission to his fellow Jews (Galatians 2:7–9; 1 Corinthians 9:5) and there are hints in the Corinthian correspondence that he may have visited the church there (presumably during one of Paul's several absences), although the slogan used in Corinth ("I belong to Cephas/Peter" [1 Corinthians 1:12]) may only indicate a way of expressing antagonism toward or disaffection for Paul. Other passages in the New Testament indicate that Peter was held in high esteem, particularly as shepherd of the flock (John

21:15–17; 1 Peter 5:1–4), and Matthew gives special prominence to his role as the rock (Aramaic *kepha'*) on which the church is to be built (Matthew 16:18–19). These passages must reflect a widely recognized authority and respected ministry during his life. That 1 Peter was sent to "the exiles of the Diaspora in Pontus, Galatia, Cappadocia, Asia and Bithynia" (1 Peter 1:1) indicates the possibility of a wide-ranging ministry to Jews (and gentiles) in Asia Minor, but for that there is no further confirmation.

At all events, Peter seems to have followed Paul in going to Rome, most probably after Paul's execution. One possible supporting fact is that 1 Peter was sent from "the church in Babylon" (1 Peter 5:13), with "Babylon" probably serving as code for Rome. His death is certainly hinted at in John 21:18–19 and 1 Clement 5:3–4. But the only tradition with any claim to credibility is that Peter was one of those who perished in the persecution arbitrarily initiated by Nero following the great fire of Rome in 64 C.E.[101] The horrific persecution authorized by Nero was the first of several savage pogroms directed against the Christians by the Roman authorities and must have devastated the church(es) in Rome, setting back the hitherto steady expansion of the new religious movement by some years. Peter's reputation, however, continued to grow, perhaps most effectively as representing the *via media* between the contrasting visions of Paul and James.

3) The third loss was probably most devastating of all for Christianity's future. James, the brother of Jesus, had established himself as the undisputed leader of the Jesus sect in Jerusalem. Even when Peter was still present in Jerusalem, James had been ranked before him (Galatians 2:9; Acts 15). But with Peter absenting himself more and more from Judea's capital (cf. Acts 12:17), James was evidently left in sole command and was subsequently regarded as the first bishop of Jerusalem. This accords well with Luke's account of Paul's last visit to Jerusalem (Acts 21:18). That James also engaged in mission is suggested by 1 Corinthians 9:5, but he may have seen his role primarily as representing the interests of believing Jews in Judea and further afield. Such indeed is suggested by the opening to the letter of James—"to the twelve tribes in the Diaspora" (James 1:1)—and, as already suggested, the letter itself may well be best explained as a collection of the sort of teaching James had been accustomed to giving to fellow Jews (not just Christians) when they came in pilgrimage to Jerusalem.

The account of James's death (in 62 C.E.) is the most reliable of the three. Josephus, the Jewish historian, narrates how James was a victim of the increasingly internecine politics in the buildup to the Jewish revolt against Rome.[102] That the high priest Ananus was against him and that James was executed by stoning suggests that his beliefs regarding Jesus allowed a charge of blasphemy to be brought against him.[103] The tradition drawn on by Eusebius suggests that James suffered judicial execution for reasons similar to those that proved fatal to Stephen (and indeed to Jesus).[104]

As already noted, all we know about James as leader of the Jerusalem church points to the conclusion that as a believer in Jesus as Messiah, he understood the sect of the Nazarene in more traditionalist Jewish terms than did Peter and particularly Paul. It is certainly significant that the letter attributed to James includes a rejoinder to the sort of argument Paul mounts in Romans 3:27–4:25, a rejoinder that reasserts the more traditional Jewish interpretation of Genesis 15:6 and refutes the sort of antithesis between faith and works that characterized Paul's preaching to gentiles (James 2:18–26). In contrast, the letter attributed to Peter (1 Peter) can be regarded as strongly influenced by Pauline themes (particularly 1 Peter 4:10–11).

The death of James and the destruction of Jerusalem and the Temple that followed eight years later (in 70 C.E.) thus marked the demise of the Jerusalem church, or the departure of the Jerusalem believers from Jerusalem, and the end of Jerusalem's role as the mother church of infant Christianity. This also meant that the traditionalist wing of infant Christianity was virtually cut off, resulting in the loss of a vital dialogue for clarifying the still emerging identity of the new movement. The dialogue was still maintained to a significant extent in Matthew, John, Hebrews and even Acts. But the most strident voice of traditionalist Christian Judaism had been lost and the Jewish Christian sects thereafter could be too easily dismissed as having lost the way. Even with the letter of James retained, the case for maintaining the Jewishness of Christianity was lost largely by default. It was the heirs of Paul and Peter, not James, who were to determine the future of Christianity and to give the faith its definitive identity.

FOUR

Judaism from the Destruction of Jerusalem to the End of the Second Jewish Revolt: 70–135 C.E.[1]

Lee I.A. Levine

JOSEPHUS CONCLUDES BOOK 6 OF HIS *JEWISH WAR* WITH THE anguishing query: "How is it that neither its antiquity, nor its ample wealth, nor its people spread over the whole habitable world, nor yet the great glory of its religious rites, could aught avail to avert its ruin? Thus ended the siege of Jerusalem" (*War* 6.10.442).

Undoubtedly, Jews both in Judea and the Diaspora were traumatized by the destruction of the Jerusalem and its Temple. True enough, a similar catastrophe had occurred centuries earlier in 586 B.C.E. with the destruction of the First Temple, although many exiles had subsequently managed to return to the city and restore their holy site; this was, perhaps, a comforting and encouraging memory for the post-70 generation. The Second Temple had stood for almost 600 years and had served as a pivotal component of Jewish identity and pride as well as international renown; thus, its loss undoubtedly constituted a dramatic and shocking turn of events.[2]

Both Jewish and Christian traditions emphasize the extent of this tragedy, each for its own theological reasons. The destruction of the Temple in later Jewish tradition signaled the beginning of a long and difficult exile, God's punishment for the sins of the people ("Because of our sins we have been exiled from our land"—said during the traditional *Musaf* service for festivals).[3] For Christians, the destruction of the Temple was the Jews' deserved punishment for their refusal to accept Jesus and because of their alleged role in his crucifixion; it was the ultimate sign of God's rejection of the Jews.

Aftermath of the destruction of the Temple

Theological considerations aside, however, the objective reality for Jews following the destruction of 70 C.E. was far more complex. On the one hand, much of Jewish life lay shattered: Jerusalem was totally destroyed, and only the three great towers that had once guarded Herod's palace as well as remnants of the western city wall remained intact (*War* 7.1–2). The Temple had been razed and the city's population massacred or exiled. The high priesthood and Jerusalem's aristocratic class, which had dominated Jewish religious and political life for much of the Second Temple period, all but disappeared. Judea had dared rebel against mighty Rome; having failed, she paid a heavy price.

Many of the Jewish sects that had played an important role in the religious life of first-century Jerusalem apparently disappeared: The Sadducees, associated with the Jerusalem priesthood in the late Second Temple period, lost their base of political and religious authority with the Temple's destruction; the Essene center at Qumran[4] was destroyed by the Romans in 68 C.E.; members of the various pre-70 revolutionary movements (Sicarii, Zealots, followers of John of Gischala and Simon bar Giora) were either killed, taken captive, fled to North Africa or went underground. Only the early Jerusalem church seems to have survived, although having fled the city in 66 C.E. its subsequent history is shrouded in mystery.

The destruction of 70 C.E. led to a radical change in the composition and character of Jewish leadership, a drastic shift in the religious and communal focus of Jewish life, and a relocation of the Jerusalem-centered society of Judea to the Galilee—all of which dramatically altered many fundamental beliefs and practices of Jews, particularly those living in Roman Palestine. By the second and third centuries, Tiberias and Sepphoris had become the urban centers of the Jewish population, replacing Jerusalem, which became a pagan city in 135 C.E. and, several centuries later, a Christian one.*

Later tradition aside, it is easy to overstate the effects of the year 70. Contrary to popular opinion, the exile did not commence in that year—in fact, most Jews were already living in the Diaspora before 70 C.E.—nor did that year signal the loss of Jewish independence. In reality, Judea had been conquered by the Roman general Pompey 130 years earlier, in 63 B.C.E. Although Herod had been granted much autonomy (37–4 B.C.E.), it had already been greatly curtailed following Judea's annexation as a Roman province in 6 C.E.

Moreover, the disruption between the pre-70 and post-70 periods was far from complete. A large degree of continuity was maintained by the ongoing rule of Rome; culturally, economically and socially, Jewish life outside of Jerusalem and its environs was not seriously interrupted between the pre- and post-destruction era, as large parts of the Jewish population were unaffected or only marginally affected by the revolt and its aftermath. Few Jewish communities in the Galilee were destroyed, Jotapata and Gamla† being the major exceptions. The Roman military advance toward Jerusalem had little, if any, effect on the large Jewish settlement in Perea east of the Jordan, on the communities along the coastal plain or even on many areas in Judea itself. Thus, beyond Jerusalem and parts of Judea, the upheavals of the First Jewish Revolt were not all that widespread demographically or economically.

The 60-year period between the First Jewish Revolt against Rome (66–70 C.E.) and the Second Jewish Revolt (the so-called Bar-Kokhba Revolt, 132–135 C.E.), though poorly documented by historically oriented sources, may well be considered one of the most remarkable and complex eras in Jewish history.[5] It constituted a watershed, and what emerged at the end already bore the trappings of a far different Jewish society than before. The period itself was a time of defeat and creativity, of continued confrontation and conflict alongside efforts toward adaptation and adjustment. While major segments of the old guard had been obliterated or marginalized, many Jews refused to abandon hope of some sort of restoration; some may have been actively engaged in planning a military-political option, while others sought a religious and social *modus vivendi* with Rome. As for the rabbis, they slowly began to forge new directions, which in the course of the coming millennium would eventually come to dominate Jewish religious and communal life.

*For the post-70 C.E. history and archaeology of Roman Jerusalem, see Hillel Geva, "Searching for Roman Jerusalem," *BAR*, November/December 1997.

†For the remains at Gamla, see Danny Syon, "Gamla: Portrait of a Rebellion," *BAR*, January/February 1992.

Roman reaction in the wake of the first revolt

Roman reactions to the revolt were mixed. On the one hand, there was no attempt to take wholesale vengeance on the Jews or to prohibit the practice of Judaism, and Rome did not change the name of the province (as happened following the Bar-Kokhba Revolt, when it became Syria-Palestina). The province of Judea was not reduced in size, and its administration continued to function as before. The Roman authorities even moved to correct certain abuses in the system that may have contributed to the unrest in the pre-66 period. Recognizing that the earlier prefects-procurators drawn from the equestrian class* had shown little interest in or talent for dealing with the local inhabitants, often being interested only in their own self-aggrandizement, Rome now determined that the governors of Judea would come from the senatorial class, on the level of an imperial legate of praetorian rank. Alongside this legate, there would also be a procurator in charge of finances. In addition, the auxiliary troops previously drawn from the non-Jewish pagan residents of the province were deemed inadequate for policing Judea. These military units were disbanded and replaced by the Tenth Legion. As part of Vespasian's redeployment of troops in the East, this measure, *inter alia*, was calculated to serve as a deterrent to any future uprisings.

Some have claimed, albeit unconvincingly due to meager evidence, that the legal standing of the Jews in the Roman Empire suffered and that they were henceforth characterized as alien residents (*peregrini dediticii*). Josephus speaks about the confiscation of land and the imposition of a special tax (*War* 7.216-218), but these statements—particularly the former—must be understood as limited in extent and application, referring principally to those who had been directly involved in the hostilities. There is no substantial evidence that the Romans persecuted the Jews in the wake of the revolt.[6]

On the other hand, Rome exercised a heavy hand in suppressing the revolt and tried to eradicate every pocket of Jewish resistance, extending its campaign by four years in order to conquer the last outposts of the rebels—the most famous being Masada. It may not be coincidental that insignia of the Tenth Legion depicted a wild boar, a symbol clearly abhorred by Jews given their strict avoidance of pork. In addition, a new tax (the *Fiscus Judaicus*) was imposed on Jews everywhere in place of the annual contribution to the Temple.† To add insult to injury, these monies were donated to the temple of Jupiter Capitolinus in Rome. Other than this general tax, however, no

*Literally, "horsemen," members of the Roman middle class, second to the nobility, from which horsemen were originally drawn.

†See Schlomo Moussaieff, "The 'New Cleopatra' and the Jewish Tax," *BAR*, January/February 2010.

Judea Capta Coin. *One of a series minted during the reign of the Roman emperor Vespasian to commemorate the fall of Jerusalem in 70 C.E., this coin depicts Judea as a mourning woman and a bound male captive, both shown beneath a palm tree, a common symbol of Judea. The large number of Judea Capta coins in gold, silver and bronze indicate the importance the Romans attached to their victory over the Jews.*

collective punishment was meted out to the Jews. The only act (of omission) one can point to is the apparent Roman refusal to consider rebuilding the Jerusalem Temple in the decades following 70 C.E. Finally, the Romans minted a series of coins known as Judea Capta ("Judea Conquered"), on which a woman representing Judea is depicted in a position of subjection and humiliation, a theme clearly intended to acclaim the Roman victory.*

Rome also tried to deter any future revolutionary thoughts by supporting Josephus's writing of his *Jewish War,* which chronicled the enormity of the conflict and vindicated Rome by placing the blame squarely on irresponsible Jewish fanatics. Josephus downplayed any role that Rome or her governors had in the events leading up to the revolt (compare the somewhat more balanced presentation of these same events in his *Antiquities of the Jews,* written some 20 years later).

Some Jewish responses to 70 C.E.

However we assess the Roman response to Judea's revolt, when all is said and done, the heart of the Second Temple Jewish body politic had been seriously compromised. Both religiously and ethnically, much of the vigor and

*Robert Deutsch, "Roman Coins Boast 'Judaea Capta,'" *BAR,* January/February 2010. Deutsch argues that some of the Roman victory coins even depict one of the captured leaders of the revolt, Simon bar Giora.

confidence of the people had been undermined. Thus, the tragedy of 70 C.E., following an era of dramatic Jewish demographic, religious and social growth, undoubtedly caused serious reverberations throughout the Jewish world. Generally speaking, it may be assumed that those living closest to Jerusalem and the Temple were most affected by the destruction, the Jews in the region of Judea proper more than those in the Galilee, and those in the Galilee more than those living in the Diaspora. In most cases, geographical propinquity likely correlated with a sense of attachment, dependence and loss.

The early Jewish Christian community, specifically those residing in Jerusalem at the beginning of the revolt, fled to Pella, east of the Jordan, at the outbreak of hostilities. The destruction of the Temple ended any desire or possibility for this group to see itself as an integral part of the Jewish people.[7] The subsequent history of the Jewish Christians and their various sects is well nigh impossible to reconstruct, but it would seem that they pursued a religious and communal agenda that differed from the rest of the local Jewish community.

Reactions within the Jewish community to the destruction of Jerusalem and the Temple included the attempts of some revolutionaries to continue their activities in the Diaspora, and some fled to Egypt to pursue their resistance against Rome. Still others doubtless went underground, continuing in one form or another to nurture hopes of a future uprising. Eusebius's statement that Vespasian (69–79 C.E.), and then Domitian (81–96 C.E.), sought to destroy the remnants of the seed of David (*Eccles. Hist.* 3.12,19) has been interpreted as an allusion to continued revolutionary activity. Such elements of dissension may have played a role in the unrest that possibly engulfed Judea in the second decade of the second century, and if indeed it endured, surely contributed to the outbreak of the Second Jewish Revolt in 132 C.E. (see below).

Nevertheless, elements of continuity are likewise in evidence. For instance, until his death in the mid-90s C.E., Agrippa II, the last of the Herodians, continued to govern in the northeastern sector of Roman Judea and southern Syria (Trachonitis, Gaulanitis, Batanẹa, Auranitis), as well as in the eastern Galilee. There is no indication that Agrippa's reign suffered from the effects of the year 70, and just the opposite may have been the case. Coins minted in the mid-80s C.E. with both Greek and Latin legends seem to indicate a flourish of activity in his realm, and the initials *SC* (*Senatus Consultum*, "Resolved by the Roman Senate") on these coins may well reflect increased Roman recognition of his rule. In addition, rabbinic literature preserves a series of discussions between one Agrippa and contemporary rabbis, especially Rabbi Eliezer ben Hyrcanus (late first to early second centuries), in which the former is referred to in a positive light (Mishnah *Sotah* 7:8). It was generally assumed that these references were to Agrippa I, who ruled from 41 to 44 C.E., before the destruction of the Temple. However, if indeed of historical value, it is quite possible that they refer instead to Agrippa II, who may have filled a part of the political and communal vacuum left in the Jewish community owing to the destruction of the Temple and Jerusalem.[8]

Moreover, it appears that a number of works from the late first-century Diaspora almost completely ignore the effects of 70. The Fourth Sybil[9] proclaims, in the name of God, that a series of catastrophes will befall the peoples and cities of Europe and Asia unless they repent, and at the end of days God will raise people from the dead, pronounce judgment and grant new life to the righteous. Surprisingly, however, this work reflects no particular concern with the destruction of the Temple or Jerusalem.

Similarly with regard to the intriguing *Liber Antiquitatum Biblicarum*, erroneously ascribed to Philo of Alexandria.[10] This book covers biblical history from Adam to David, often integrating aggadic* themes and occasionally altering the biblical material in an original fashion. Although dated to the late first century C.E., the author of this work, too, makes no mention of the events of the year 70, which appear to have had no significant impact on his outlook.

In a similar vein, the books written by Josephus several decades after the destruction of the Temple—*Antiquities of the Jews, Against Apion* and *Life*—discuss Jewish history, institutions, ideas and beliefs in the post-destruction period without any discernible reaction to the destruction or to the trauma that it caused. Not only in his writings, but in his personal life as well, Josephus appears to reflect the ability of many Jews, both in Judea and the Diaspora, to adjust to the new circumstances and to restructure their political and religious policies in accord with conditions in the post-70 era.†

Apocalyptic literature of despair and hope

Nevertheless, several apocalyptic books dated to the post-destruction period reflect deep distress and despair, yet they also express hope and comfort in a promising future.[11] For example, the following poetic lament appears in the Syriac apocalypse of 2 Baruch:

> Blessed is he who was not born,

**Aggadot* (singular, *aggadah*) are non-halakhic (legal) expositions of the biblical text or comments and stories relating to more current figures and events.

†For Josephus's personal story and its impact on his writings, see Steven Mason, "Will the Real Josephus Please Stand Up?" *BAR*, September/October 1997.

> or he who was born and died.
> But we, the living, woe to us,
> because we have seen those afflictions of Zion,
> and that which has befallen Jerusalem.
> ...
> You, farmers, sow not again.
> And you, O earth, why do you give the fruit of your harvest?
> Keep within you the sweetness of your sustenance.
> And you, vine, why do you still give your wine?
> For an offering will not be given again from you in Zion,
> and the first fruits will not again be offered.
> And you, heaven, keep your dew within you,
> and do not open the treasuries of rain.
> And you, sun, keep the light of your rays within you.
> And you, moon, extinguish the multitude of your light.
> For why should the light rise again,
> where the light of Zion is darkened?
> And you, bridegrooms, do not enter,
> and do not let the brides adorn themselves.
> And you, wives, do not pray to bear children,
> for the barren will rejoice more.
> And those who have no children will be glad,
> and those who have children will be sad.
> For why do they bear in pain only to bury in grief?
> ...
> You, priests, take the keys of the sanctuary,
> and cast them to the highest heaven,
> and give them to the Lord and say,
> "Guard your house yourself,
> because, behold, we have been found to be false stewards."
>
> (2 Baruch 10:6–18)

But all was not despair; in this same book, Israel was bidden to await the redemption that was not far off:

> And that period is coming that will remain forever; and there is the new world which does not carry back to corruption those who enter into its beginning, and which has no mercy on those who come into torment or those who are living in it, and it does not carry to perdition. For those are the ones who will inherit

> this time of which it is spoken, and to these is the heritage of the promised time. These are they who prepared for themselves treasures of wisdom. And stores of insight are found within them. And they have not withdrawn from mercy and they have preserved the truth of the law. For the coming world will be given to these, but the habitation of the many others will be in the fire.
>
> (2 Baruch 44:12–15)

A similar composition from this period is 4 Ezra,[12] the most widely circulated Jewish apocalypse in antiquity and continuing into the Middle Ages. Ezra, regarded in this work as a second Moses, bemoans Israel's tragic fate in contrast to the prosperity enjoyed by gentiles. In a series of dialogues with an angel, Ezra is assured that wickedness will soon cease, the dead will be resurrected and the approaching end, brought about by God himself, will include the coming of the Messiah, the salvation of the few and the destruction of the many. The book's final sections describe visions related to issues raised in the dialogues—the rebuilding of Zion, the reinstitution of the Temple and its sacrifices, the advent of God who will redeem mankind and the coming of the Messiah that will signal the end of godlessness and the approach of the day of judgment.

Finally, although dating from the third century C.E. and thus perhaps of problematic relevance, the following tradition in the Tosefta* likewise gives expression to this post-destruction distress:

> After the last Temple was destroyed, ascetics who would not eat meat or drink wine increased in Israel. Rabbi Joshua met them, saying, "My sons, why do you not eat meat?"
> They said to him, "Shall we eat meat, for every day a continual burnt-offering [of meat] was offered on the altar, and now it has been discontinued?"
> He said to them, "Then let us not eat it. And then why are you not drinking wine?"
> They said to him, "Shall we drink wine, for every day wine was poured out as a drink-offering on the altar, and now [this practice] has been discontinued?"
> He said to them, "Then let us not drink it." He said to them, "But if this is so, we also should not eat bread, for from it did they bring the Two Loaves and the Show-Bread. We also should not drink water, for they poured out a water-offering on the Festival [of

*A collection of tannaitic rabbinic sources relating to and expanding upon the Mishnah.

> Sukkot]. We also should not eat figs and grapes, for they brought them as First Fruits on the Festival of the Atzeret [Shavu'ot]." They were silent.
>
> (Tosefta *Sotah* 15:11)

Rabbinic traditions for the post-70 era: the period of Yavneh

The overwhelming majority of sources that relate to the time frame of this chapter derive from rabbinic materials. Were one to collect and organize this material from the dozens of rabbinic compositions dating from the third to 12th centuries, a somewhat detailed picture (though still quite incomplete and far from harmonious) would emerge with regard to rabbinic circles, their internal relations, the institutions they cultivated, attitudes and contacts with other Jews and non-Jews, as well as a variety of socio-economic issues. Indeed, most scholars until now have based their descriptions of this era on these sources, and although the resultant narratives might have differed from one another, the basic assumptions were generally very much the same: (1) all, or virtually all, of these sources are historically reliable; (2) the rabbis were the leaders of the Jewish community; and (3) their opinions determined how most Jews thought and acted.

Over the last generation or two, however, such assumptions have come into question.[13] Rather than regarding such traditions as historical facts, they are now often assumed to be later traditions that tell us more about the tradents and editors, and the issues in their respective communities, than about the people and times purportedly described. As a result, skepticism has come to play a central role among many historians in determining the reliability of these descriptions.

This latter scholarly approach is far from new in modern scholarship. Throughout the 19th century and into the 21st, scholars of the Hebrew Bible, the New Testament, Jewish literature from the Second Temple period and classical Greco-Roman literature have been relating to their respective sources in this fashion. However, what often allows for an assumption in favor of historical plausibility is the ability to correlate a particular tradition with evidence appearing in other independent sources. However, in our case, the late first and early second centuries, there is no extra-rabbinic evidence—either Jewish or non-Jewish, literary or archaeological—that might confirm rabbinic accounts of the internal workings of Jewish society. Thus, verification of these traditions is impossible. The chronological proximity of a source to an event described is often regarded as an advantage in sorting out historical "truths," although even then one must remember that there is always a possibility that the report could be tendentious and biased. Josephus, who lived at the same time as many of the events he described, is a striking case in point. Moreover, with regard to rabbinic activities at Yavneh (see below), the most explicit and detailed traditions derive from sources redacted centuries later (e.g., the Jerusalem Talmud, Babylonian Talmud and aggadic *midrashim** from the fifth century and later). When added to the sages' lack of interest in historical inquiry *per se* (in contrast to the *Heilsgeshichte* of their rabbinic forebears), information stemming from much later sources makes the reliability of such data suspect (not to mention that there are many discrepancies between them on marginal and very basic matters). Thus, in attempting to determine what might be the most reliable historical information, we will focus primarily on the earliest corpora of rabbinic literature (i.e., tannaitic material), especially the third-century Mishnah and Tosefta.

Rabbinic traditions trace the presence of some rabbis immediately following the destruction of 70 C.E. to the town of Yavneh (Jamnia in Greek), located between Jaffa and Ashdod. To transpose Theodore Herzl's well-known statement to fit the context of rabbinic tradition: In Yavneh, the rabbinic way was born. Yavneh was reputedly the seat of rabbinic activity in this period, where the foundations of rabbinic culture were established. This, according to the rabbinic narrative, marked the beginning of a process that eventually led to the reconstruction of Rabbinic Judaism.

However, what exactly was accomplished at this time is far from clear, as it is lost in the mists and myths of later traditions. The triumph of rabbinism was far slower and more complex than these traditions would seem to indicate, reaching the degree of authority and influence assumed for Yavneh only many centuries thereafter. Indeed, this may have occurred as late as the ninth century, when both the Babylonian rabbinic institutions and the exilarch, the head of Babylonian Jewry, moved to Baghdad, the capital of the Islamic caliphate, where up to 90 percent of the Jewish people then lived.

The Yavnean era lasted for some 60 years, until the outbreak of the Second Jewish Revolt against Rome (70–132 C.E.),[14] and can be conveniently divided into two stages, each associated with the sage who allegedly headed the Yavnean academy† in successive generations—Rabbi Yoḥanan ben Zakkai and Rabban Gamaliel II.[15]

*Nonhalakhic commentaries of biblical text.

†The term "academy" is often used to describe a rabbinic setting in this and later periods. However, this term implies a formal and institutional framework that evolved only several centuries later in Palestine (and even later in Babylonia). At this juncture (i.e., the Yavnean period), the usual rabbinic setting was a more informal study session associated with a particular sage that might have changed locales as circumstances warranted. However, according to the

The period of Rabbi Yoḥanan ben Zakkai

Yoḥanan ben Zakkai is a most enigmatic figure, as the evidence relating to him is quite limited. His pre-70 activities are only hinted at in much later sources (including an 18-year stint in the Galilee), his reputed escape from Jerusalem during the Roman siege of the city is narrated in four different and often contradictory traditions centuries later, and his stay in Yavneh, for what appears to have been a short time, was low-keyed, with minimal accomplishments, few students, no known institutional framework and no contact with the Roman authorities.[16]

Rabbinic sources report virtually nothing about Yoḥanan's public life in Yavneh. The thrust of his activity, according to these sources, seems to have centered around the issuance of a series of *takkanot* (religious enactments). Tradition speaks of nine such *takkanot*, some already attested in the Mishnah (and therefore arguably of greater historical value) and others recorded in the Babylonian Talmud (arguably of little worth). These *takkanot* are of interest both for what they tell us and for what they omit (Mishnah *Rosh Hashanah* 4:1–4; Mishnah *Sukkah* 3:12; BT *Rosh Hashanah* 31b; BT *Sotah* 40a). Three deal with an attempt to transfer certain minor Temple practices to a post-70 setting (the synagogue?). For example, it is noted that before 70, when Rosh Hashanah fell on the Sabbath, the *shofar* (ram's horn) was blown only in the Temple; Yoḥanan is said to have declared that after 70 the *shofar* could be blown everywhere. Similarly, in the pre-70 period the *lulav* (palm branch) was used only in the Temple for the seven days of the Sukkot festival (i.e., the Feast of Tabernacles), but only for one day in other places; here, too, Yoḥanan declared that the *lulav* could be used everywhere for seven days.

Three other *takkanot* adjusted certain practices that had been in some way associated with the sacrifices in the Jerusalem Temple. In the pre-70 period, testimony for the appearance of the new moon could be given only until the afternoon sacrifice was offered; Yoḥanan declared that such testimony was acceptable throughout the day. Another *takkanah* abolished the requirement from Temple times that a convert set aside a quarter of a shekel in lieu of a sacrifice (BT *Rosh Hashanah* 31b; BT *Keritot* 9a; JT *Shekalim* 8, 4, 51b),[17] and yet another annulled the requirement that the first fruits of a newly planted tree be brought to Jerusalem in the fourth year (BT *Rosh Hashanah* 31b; BT *Bezah* 5a-b).[18]

There is no way of determining the historicity of these *takkanot*. Were they later decisions ascribed anachronistically to Yoḥanan ben Zakkai, or

classical rabbinic narrative, i.e., the Babylonian Talmud, such a full-fledged institution had already existed in Yavneh (and even beforehand).

did he indeed issue them? And if the latter, to whom were they directed—to those closely associated with him, to all rabbis, to all or only some Jewish communities, or to virtually none at all? There is also the question of their effectiveness; did anyone pay attention to these decisions and abide by them? What is striking about these *takkanot* is that they focus on only certain ritual and procedural matters originally connected with the Temple. They are thus quite limited in scope and marginal to Jewish life generally, certainly in the years following the catastrophe of 70 C.E.

For example, none addresses what a Jew is to do given the cessation of sacrifices, how one is to worship God, ask forgiveness or request help; nor do they address modes of Jewish religious behavior such as observance of the festivals or the Sabbath, or how to conduct oneself in prayer now that the Temple cult is nonexistent. Moreover, beyond ritual matters, no *takkanot* deal with social, institutional or economic issues that undoubtedly beset the Jewish community at the time. Nothing relates to the new situation experienced by individuals and communities given the fact that the Temple, its functionaries and institutions (e.g., the judiciary) were no longer operative. These *takkanot,* therefore, may indicate the narrow scope—or should we say the severe limitations—of Yoḥanan's purported activities in Yavneh.

This impression is reinforced by several other considerations. We have no evidence of any contact between Yoḥanan ben Zakkai and Roman officials (in contrast to his successor Rabban Gamaliel II; see below), nor do our sources reflect any kind of recognition of Yoḥanan's position among Jews generally or their communal heads. He is never reported to have visited Jewish communities, and there is no indication that anyone consulted him on halakhic issues (again, in contrast to Gamaliel).

Also striking is the limited number of sages who seem to have joined ben Zakkai in Yavneh. Some may have resented his abandonment of Jerusalem during the Roman siege. Certain circles may have opposed his attempts to realign aspects of Jewish religious practice, opposing his readiness to make adjustments and "compromises" regarding Temple prerogatives and privileges. This was probably true among the surviving Temple priesthood, who very likely resented any attempt to transfer Temple practices to other Jewish frameworks. They might well have preferred preserving the uniqueness of the Temple with regard to various ceremonies, such as the blowing of the *shofar* and the use of the *lulav,* even if this meant a suspension of these rituals in the post-70 era.

Given the fact that later generations considered Rabbi Yoḥanan ben Zakkai the "founder" (or perhaps the re-establisher) of Rabbinic Judaism following the destruction of the Temple, it is no wonder that they attributed to him the values, attitudes and perspectives that had become important to them. Thus, the historicity of such attributions is weak. For example, in a late *midrash*, Yoḥanan is credited with advocating that alternative forms of worship and atonement had to be found in the absence of sacrifice and other Temple-related rituals. When asked, "Now that there are no sacrifices, how can we seek atonement?" Yoḥanan reputedly replied that good deeds (literally, acts of loving-kindness) will atone as sacrifices once did (*Fathers According to Rabbi Nathan* A 4). Moreover, the political, social and religious statements ascribed to him often reflect a position of moderation and accommodation:

> Do not rush to destroy the altars of the gentiles, lest you will have to rebuild them yourselves; do not destroy those of bricks, lest they say to you, "make them of stone"; [nor those] of stone, lest they say to you, "make them of wood."
>
> (*Midrash Tannaim*, ed. Hoffman, I, p. 58; *Fathers According to Rabbi Nathan* B 31)

Elsewhere, Yoḥanan is said to have interpreted the phrase "whole stones" (Deuteronomy 27:6) as referring to "stones that establish peace," which is then applied to humans: "How much the more then should he who establishes peace between man and his fellow-man, between husband and wife, between city and city, between nation and nation, between family and family, between government and government, be protected so that no harm should come to him" (*Mekhilta of Rabbi Ishmael*, ed. Lauterbach, II, p. 290). While it is unclear whether he escaped Jerusalem because he was a pacifist or a political realist, these later traditions associate him with a nonbelligerent stance vis-à-vis the gentiles and an accommodating position within the Jewish community itself. Also with regard to the pre-70 era, he reportedly advocated the abolition of the rite of drinking the "bitter water" (Numbers 5:11–31), a Temple ritual for determining whether a woman was guilty of adultery (Mishnah *Sotah* 9:9; see also Tosefta *Sotah* 14:1–2).

In short, Yoḥanan is viewed by subsequent generations as having striven to avoid extremism in any direction, seeking to combine hope for the future with recognition of the loss sustained in the present while, at the same time, addressing aspects of Jewish life requiring adjustments in light of changing times. Similarly with regard to messianic expectation as recorded in the following: "If you have a plant in your hand and they say to you, 'The Messiah has come,' go and complete the planting and afterwards go out and receive [the Messiah]" (*Fathers According to Rabbi Nathan* B 31).

Thus, little can be ascertained with any degree of confidence about the life and activities of Rabbi Yoḥanan. As noted, given the overall paucity of sources, their late dating, clearly aggadic nature, lack of any sort of corroborating evidence and considering Yoḥanan's "founder" status, we can only conjecture as to the veracity of these sources. When taken together and accepted uncritically, they ostensibly tell us who he was, what he accomplished and what his impact undoubtedly must have been on his contemporaries. However, it is not clear how much is historical and how much is the invention of later tradition; the myth is indeed substantial; unfortunately, there is little possibility to get behind it with any modicum of confidence.

The period of Rabban Gamaliel II

When we turn to Rabban Gamaliel and the second stage at Yavneh (and I am assuming that this sequence of leadership is historically reliable—who would conceivably have invented it and why?), the picture changes significantly. For one, the number and variety of sources increases dramatically, including reports dealing with internal rabbinic affairs as well as external relations with other Jewish communities and the Roman government. Central religious and communal matters noted above as missing from Yoḥanan's agenda now surface under Gamaliel and are to be found in significant numbers from both earlier and later compositions. This may perhaps help us distinguish between varying degrees of probable historical accuracy. Once again there are no external sources with which to compare these rabbinic traditions, and we are thus left entirely at the mercy of the evidence preserved in diverse rabbinic sources.

Before addressing those traditions that may have a relatively greater degree of probability, several general considerations might justify an assumption of their relative trustworthiness. One is the fact that Rabban Gamaliel was in some way the first (or at least the forerunner) of a dynasty of Jewish leaders in late Roman-Byzantine Palestine called the patriarchs (or *nesi'im*).[19] Thus, it is more than likely that some of the functions and activities associated with this dynasty in subsequent generations may have already been part of Gamaliel's agenda, especially if they are explicitly related to him and reflect an earlier and less established stage than what was to be the case in the third and fourth centuries, when patriarchal dominance went all but unchallenged.

Secondly, in several areas (e.g., the development of prayer and holiday observances), the reports noting Gamaliel's activity fit a neat diachronic order, between an earlier stage known from the Second Temple period and a later, more developed one already evidenced with regard to the subsequent generations of rabbis in the second half of the second century C.E. and beyond. In such cases, therefore, any temptation to simply dismiss such evidence as historically worthless should be resisted.

A third and final consideration, perhaps of less weight, is the fact that certain traditions regarding Gamaliel were well known early on and included in the Mishnah, which was composed by Gamaliel's grandson, Rabbi Judah I. If so, the time gap between the activities of the one and the recording of such events by the other is approximately a century. While such sources could certainly be tendentious, and undoubtedly some are, to assume that they are all unfounded and thus fictional seems rather unlikely. Many people in the generation or two after Gamaliel might well have contested any "fabricated" historical memories.

To cite several instances of what should be considered more reliable traditions, at least in their main thrust if not in all details: One such report relates to Gamaliel II's highly regarded ancestry at Yavneh, and here we are aided by non-rabbinic material. In both rabbinic sources and the New Testament, a Gamaliel is named as a leading Pharisee in Jerusalem (Tosefta *Sanhedrin* 2:6; Acts 5:34–39) in the first half of the first century C.E. This earlier Gamaliel, often referred to as "the Elder" (e.g., Tosefta *Shabbat* 13:2), was the father of Rabban Simeon ben Gamaliel, a leader in Jerusalem during the revolt (Josephus, *Life* 38.189–194; Mishnah *Kritot* 1, 7). Thus, these two figures, the Yavnean Gamaliel's father and grandfather respectively, attest, at least in a general way, the prominence of this family in the pre-70 era. Given such a relatively well-documented ancestry, it has often been opined that Gamaliel's pedigree was a key factor in his prominent position at Yavneh, and this is probably correct.

Rome's recognition of Gamaliel II's leadership position at the time, *de facto* if not *de jure*, may also shed some light on this figure.[20] The cluster of sources in this regard is indeed unique with respect to Gamaliel. For example, no other rabbi, patriarchs included, is mentioned as having traveled to Rome as many times as Gamaliel. True, the sources refer to these visits in the context of some halakhic or homiletical matter, but the fact remains that such journeys seem to have taken place, and the need to visit Rome (the destination most often mentioned) may very likely have had some political ramifications (JT *Sanhedrin* 7,10,25d and elsewhere). Yet another enigmatic tradition tells of several Roman officials who visited Gamaliel's academy. The circumstances of this visit are never fully disclosed but, once again, it is attested only with respect to Gamaliel (*Sifre Deuteronomy* 344; BT *Bava Qama* 38a). Finally, the most explicit, yet elliptic, source regarding Gamaliel's contact with Roman officialdom is the account of his trip to Syria "to be granted authority by the Roman governor" (Mishnah *Eduyyot* 7:7). Although the precise nature of that authority is never spelled out, based on its context in the Mishnah it may well have had to do with the right to decide on calendrical issues.[21]

Why Rome may have granted some sort of recognition to Gamaliel is yet another question. Perhaps the Romans were simply following their long-established policy throughout the empire, and in Judea beforehand, of seeking support among the local aristocracies in order to stabilize their rule over conquered provinces. Gamaliel was a logical candidate for the Romans to cultivate given his pedigree and status. If what we are suggesting seems plausible, then some sort of "appointment" by the Romans was probably conferred on Gamaliel around the turn of the second century.*

It is also possible—though admittedly speculative—that recognition of Gamaliel's public standing may have been connected to the death of Agrippa II in the mid-90s C.E. If, as has been suggested, Agrippa served as some sort of liaison between the Jewish community and the Roman government in the decades following the destruction of the Temple, Rome may now have been inclined to look for another such intermediary at this time and found it in the person of Rabban Gamaliel.

According to rabbinic sources, a considerable effort under Gamaliel's auspices was invested in liturgical matters. Such an emphasis is easily understood in light of the fact that in this post-destruction generation, the sages under the activist leadership of Gamaliel indeed addressed such issues. First and foremost was the area of daily and Sabbath worship, specifically with regard to the two central prayers, the *Amidah* (Eighteen Benedictions) and the *Shema'* with its accompanying blessings.[22] In the absence of Temple sacrifices, prayer became the primary conduit for contact with God. On the one hand, reports of liturgical activity at this time are seemingly pervasive since, to the best of our knowledge, regular daily prayer did not exist in the Judean synagogue of the pre-70 era. Only in isolated cases (e.g., the officiating priests in the Jerusalem Temple, at Qumran and perhaps also in Pharisaic circles) is there any evidence of daily prayer in Judea. On the other hand, sages in the generations after Gamaliel were apparently working out the particulars of the general framework attributed to Gamaliel's generation. Thus, given the situation before and after Gamaliel's time, the claim that a basic rabbinic

*It is unlikely that the Flavian dynasty would have accorded such recognition to a Jewish leader, especially during the reign of its last representative, Domitian (81–96 C.E.), who appears to have harbored a decidedly negative attitude toward Jews and Judaism. As previously noted, it was Domitian who reputedly made an attempt to hunt down Jews suspected of being from the Davidic line (*Eccles. Hist.* 3.19), and it was he who supposedly initiated a persecution of supposed converts to Judaism in Rome (E.M. Smallwood, *Jews Under Roman Rule* [Leiden: Brill, 1976], pp. 376–385). Thus, it was probably only after Domitian's death that Rome was willing to consider cultivating a new type of leadership for Judea's Jews.

format for prayers had crystallized at this time appears credible. Furthermore, it is not surprising that later generations viewed some of these intensively debated issues as having engendered a serious conflict between Gamaliel and other sages. The details of these reports are often contradictory in many details and thus far from being historically trustworthy. Nevertheless, they do constitute evidence, however exaggerated and tendentious, that such issues did engage Yavnean sages under Gamaliel's leadership (JT *Berakhot* 4,1,7c-d; BT *Berakhot* 27b–28a).

A second area of liturgical activity focused on holidays, and particularly those whose observance was most seriously affected by the absence of the Temple. One such holiday, Passover, had been intimately connected with the Temple sacrifice, as each household was bidden to participate in the Passover meal following the sacrifice of the Paschal lamb either within the Temple precincts or elsewhere in Jerusalem. But after 70, when such practice was no longer possible, a home observance known as the Passover *seder* was created.[23] The core of this liturgy, beginning with the early report in Mishnah *Pesaḥim* 10 and culminating with the Passover *haggadah* at a much later date, quotes only sages from Yavneh, not the least of whom was Gamaliel.

Another liturgical focus concerned the High Holidays—Rosh Hashanah and Yom Kippur. Before 70, neither Rosh Hashanah nor Yom Kippur had played a major role in the religious practice of Jewish communities. Rosh Hashanah was important largely because it marked the beginning of the seventh month in the Jewish calendar.* The highly significant Yom Kippur ceremonies were confined to the Temple precincts. After 70, however, the sages of Yavneh began to create an entirely new liturgy for what became known as the High Holidays (or in Hebrew, Days of Awe), a process that would continue for many centuries. New themes were introduced—the kingship of God, remembrance, redemption, days of judgment and forgiveness of sins, etc.—and requisite blessings and prayers were formulated. Appropriate scriptural readings were incorporated, along with a special ceremony on Rosh Hashanah for the blowing of the *shofar*. Yom Kippur was institutionalized as a fast day with a day-long synagogue ritual focusing on sin, penitence and forgiveness.

A further issue that required the attention of Gamaliel and the sages of his generation was the calendar, a concern that periodically surfaced from biblical times through the early Middle Ages. With the destruction of Jerusalem, finding a substitute procedure for intercalating Jewish months

*The number seven has special symbolic significance in Jewish tradition (seventh day of creation, seven days a week, seven years to a sabbatical year, etc.).

and years was high on Gamaliel's and the Yavnean sages' agenda, and a wide range of rabbinic sources (some tannaitic and many amoraic) attest to the conflict between them in this era (Mishnah *Rosh Hashanah* 2:8–9). While all these sources are tendentious and inflated, it is quite likely that they refer to a highly charged issue that engaged the Yavnean generation. Moreover, it is also likely that certain details of these reports may reflect historical reality, e.g., who opposed whom and the issues at hand, though probably not the details of these deliberations or their outcome. In any event, by the third and fourth centuries, it was the patriarchal descendants of Gamaliel who were responsible for these matters.

Despite the above-noted flurry of activity, many aspects of the Yavnean era in rabbinic life defy any sort of historical assessment. How did the Jewish community in Judea relate to Gamaliel's leadership and did it change over time? What exactly was his position vis-à-vis the Roman government? Were there periodic, or only sporadic, meetings of the sages in an academy-like framework at Yavneh or did the overriding majority of rabbinic discussions take place in scattered small study circles? Did Gamaliel actually make almost a dozen trips to various communities, as reported, and, if so, why and in what capacity? Furthermore, to what extent were the Yavnean sages involved in the canonization process of the Bible and did some sort of codification of Jewish law take place under their auspices?

Behind all this activity lies the very basic issue regarding the collective role of the Yavnean sages within contemporary Jewish society. Once again, given our exclusive dependence on rabbinic sources, there is no way of verifying their claims of what happened or their overall impression of rabbinic leadership and influence at the time. As noted above, Yoḥanan's standing is completely unknown, and no source even begins to suggest a prominent role for him in the wider Jewish community. Matters were quite different for Gamaliel, but it is still impossible to assess his status and stature in the range of issues noted above. He reportedly made calendrical decisions among the rabbis themselves, but did he also control the calendar of Jewish communities throughout Judea and in the Diaspora? Furthermore, were the prayers generated at Yavneh accepted and adopted in second- and third-century synagogues? When was the early rabbinic proto-*seder* introduced into Jewish homes? Or did all these matters affect only contemporary rabbinic circles or, even then, only some of them?

Despite the reservations raised above regarding the historicity of rabbinic sources for this period, it would seem that many, if not most, rabbis associated with Yavneh were geared politically toward some sort of rapprochement and cooperation with Rome, and religiously toward the implementation of adjustments in ideology and practice deemed necessary for Jewish survival in the post-Temple era. However, a very different sentiment was apparently also operating elsewhere in Judea. In certain circles, Jewish nationalist aspirations were far from squelched by the destruction in 70. Some Jews aspired to eliminate, or at least drastically curtail, Roman rule in Judea and reestablish a Jewish presence in Jerusalem. Whether such sentiments in and of themselves would have ever found expression is a moot point. In fact, it took a drastic decision (perhaps even two; see below) by Rome to ignite a revolt that was apparently supported by a considerable portion of southern Judea's population. A second Jewish rebellion against Rome, also known as the Bar-Kokhba Revolt, was the political and military expression of this explosion.[24]

The Diaspora revolts (115/116–117 C.E.)

Even before the Bar-Kokhba Revolt, a series of major disturbances erupted under Trajan (98–117 C.E.) that affected primarily the Jews of the Diaspora.[25] In 115/116 C.E., Jews in Egypt and Cyrene (on the North African coast in present-day Libya) took advantage of Trajan's absence while on a campaign against the Parthians in the East to attack their Greek neighbors. The devastation in both Greek and Jewish communities was enormous, although caution must be exercised with regard to the penchant of Roman and Christian sources to exaggerate such circumstances. The Egyptian revolt purportedly stretched over large parts of the country, with the Jews gaining the upper hand in the rural areas of Egypt but defeated in Alexandria. The hostilities were severe enough that, as late as 199/200 C.E., an annual festival was celebrated in the Egyptian town of Oxyrhynchus to commemorate the victory over the Jews.[26]

Trajan sent one of his prized generals, Marcius Turbo, to subdue the revolt in Cyrene (Eusebius, *Eccles. Hist.* 4.3), where the hostilities were even more devastating—some 220,000 people were massacred (Dio Cassius, *History of Rome* 68.32). The leader of these Jewish uprisings—called Lukuas by Eusebius and Andreas by Dio—appears to have had royal, if not messianic, aspirations; he claimed the title of king, although the sources in this regard are probably tendentious (Eusebius, *Eccles. Hist.* 4.4; Dio Cassius, *History of Rome* 68.32.1). Archaeological and epigraphical evidence from Cyrene seems to bear out the enormity of this revolt; at least one Hadrianic milestone found there refers to the "Jewish revolt,"[27] and a number of Roman temples in the city of Cyrene seem to have been destroyed or damaged during these hostilities.

Cyprus was another area of conflict. In this rebellion, reputedly led by one Artemion, some 240,000 pagans were reportedly killed, Salamis was destroyed and its Greek inhabitants decimated; as a result, Jews were banned from the island.[28]

Finally, as Trajan advanced southward along the Tigris River, the Jews of Mesopotamia rose in revolt. His general, Lucius Quietus, was sent to quell the rebellion, which resulted in the death of thousands of Jews.[29]

Whether these Diaspora revolts included Judea as well is a much-debated question. Hadrian's biographer notes that there was some kind of uprising in Judea at about this time (Spartiani, *Vita Hadriani* 5.2, in *Scriptores Historia Augustae*), and rabbinic tradition also records the "war" of Quietus (possibly occurring in Judea; Mishnah *Sotah* 9:14; *Seder Olam* 30), named after the general who later became governor of the province. The causes of these revolts—be they religious, nationalistic, messianic, ethnic (i.e., anti-pagan) or perhaps a combination of the above—remain a mystery. There is simply no solid evidence to determine if they were instigated by Jews from Judea or were spontaneous Diaspora uprisings.

The Roman reaction to these revolts was reportedly extremely harsh. Accordingly to Appian (2.90), Trajan "exterminated" the Jewish race in Egypt, while the Jerusalem Talmud states that the blood of the Jews killed in Egypt reached all the way to Cyprus (*Sukkah* 5,1,55b). As a result, Diaspora Jewish life in these provinces was severely affected—land was confiscated, Jewish institutions were abolished and almost all traces of Jewish life disappeared for some time.

The Bar-Kokhba Revolt (132–135 C.E.)

The Bar-Kokhba Revolt was the last attempt by Jews to achieve some sort of independence or political autonomy in antiquity.*[30] Unfortunately, our knowledge of this revolt is woefully limited and fragmentary. In contrast to the two other major Jewish revolts in antiquity—the Maccabean uprising against the Seleucids in 166 or 165 B.C.E. and the First Jewish Revolt against Rome in 66 C.E.—no historical account describes the Bar-Kokhba Revolt, nothing comparable to 1 and 2 Maccabees, which chronicles the Maccabean uprising, or to Josephus's *Jewish War*, which gives an extraordinarily detailed account of the First Jewish Revolt. The only literary evidence that has been preserved are scattered references found in later pagan, Christian and Jewish sources (see below).

Until relatively recently, scholars had assumed that most Jews living in the province of Judea (including the Galilee and the coastal plain) mobilized and actively supported the Bar-Kokhba Revolt. This view is based on highly exaggerated accounts that magnified the suffering, tragedy and loss of lives during the revolt (e.g., JT *Ta'anit* 4,8,68d–69a).

*See Werner Eck, "Hardian's Hard-Won Victory," *BAR*, September/October 2007.

Moreover, the extant literary sources are all critical of Bar-Kokhba and his efforts, each for its own interests. Later rabbinic tradition referred to him as Bar-Kosba (Son of the Lie) and sought to discredit him and demonstrate the futility of armed rebellion. The church fathers also viewed the Bar-Kokhba Revolt as an abortive attempt to restore the Jewish independence that God had taken from the Jews as punishment. Even the Roman historian Dio Cassius seems to have exaggerated the scope of the violence, thereby enhancing the significance of the Roman victory; he speaks of the destruction of some 50 fortifications and 985 villages, and the loss of 585,000 lives (*History of Rome* 69.14.1)!*

More recently, archaeology has been able to provide new evidence. However the coins, papyri, milestones, caves and fortresses dating from this period fall far short of providing a comprehensive or coherent picture. Without ample literary sources to provide a context for these finds, it is difficult to draw firm historical conclusions. Nevertheless, the new archaeological discoveries as well as recent reevaluations of the surviving literature have enabled us to correct, or at least challenge, some of the old assumptions regarding this revolt.

Archaeological discoveries indicate that the hostilities were confined to southern Judea, where almost all remains of the revolt—whether coins, caves for refuge, papyri or fortifications—were found. Most were concentrated in the eastern Judean Desert (near the Dead Sea), in caves located in a series of wadis: Wadi Murabba'at, Nahal Hever, Nahal Se'elim and others.† It appears that the Galilee was not drawn into these battles and remained virtually untouched by the devastation caused by the revolt, thus enabling the region to assume a position of leadership as it absorbed refugees from the southern part of the country in the wake of the hostilities.

Leadership of this revolt was very much unified, in marked contrast to the First Jewish Revolt against Rome, which was characterized by anarchy among the Jewish forces and the lack of any overall planning or direction before or during the revolt. The leadership of Simeon bar Kosba,‡ more popularly known as Bar-Kokhba, is attested not only from the literary sources, but also from archaeological evidence. The coins and papyri (which record both his name and title—*nasi*) recently found in the Judean wilderness reflect the presence of a strong and stable leadership throughout the course of the revolt,

*See Boaz Zissu, "Village Razed, Rebel Beheaded," *BAR*, September/October 2007.

†See Ro'i Porat and Hanan Eshel, "Fleeing the Romans: Judean Refugees Hide in Caves," *BAR*, March/April 2006.

‡His actual name as we now know from letters found in the Judean Desert was Simeon bar Kosba (or Kosiba).

RICHARD NOWITZ

Bar-Kokhba Caves. *When Simeon bar Kosba, known as Bar-Kokhba, led a rebellion against the Romans (132–135 C.E.), his followers fortified caves in the Judean desert as hiding places and supply depots. These were the last strongholds to fall to the Romans.*

ranging from religious and ritual concerns to taxation and military discipline.[31]

The once widely held view that there was a messianic component in Bar-Kokhba's leadership has recently been called into question. While it is true that a statement in JT *Ta'anit* 4,8,68d claims that Rabbi Akiva, a

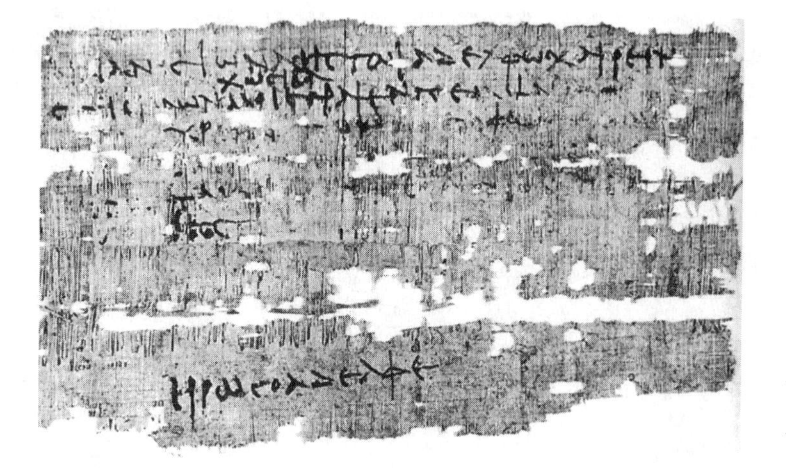

B. LIFSHITZ, *AEGYPTUS*, VOL 42, 1962

Bar-Kokhba Letter in Greek. *Simeon, leader of the Second Jewish Revolt, was also perhaps called Bar-Kokhba, or Son of the Star, an allusion to Numbers 24:17, "A star shall come out of Jacob." Several of Bar-Kokhba's own letters were recovered by Israeli archaeologist Yigael Yadin from caves in the Judean Desert where Bar-Kokhba and his followers had organized and planned their revolt against the Romans. Some of the correspondence found in the Bar-Kokhba caves was written in Greek (above), indicating the use of that language even among nationalist Jews.*

leading figure in Yavnean circles, hailed Bar-Kokhba as the Messiah, it is difficult to assess how widespread this belief was. Even if this report is more or less accurate, it may reflect only the view of Rabbi Akiva and his close circle, and not necessarily that of other sages, much less the people at large, or even those supporting his cause. Indeed, it is not even clear whether Bar-Kokhba viewed himself in messianic terms. It should be remembered that he is referred to on revolt coins minted under his authority as *Nesi Yisrael* ("Leader" or "Head" of Israel), a term having no overt messianic implications.

Moreover, the import of Akiva's role in the uprising may well be exaggerated.[32] It is often overlooked that the above talmudic tradition also records his colleague Yoḥanan ben Torta's immediate disavowal of Akiva's messianic statement: "Akiva, grass will grow on your cheeks [i.e., you will long be dead] and the Son of David will still not have come" (JT *Ta'anit* 4,8,68d). A similar statement by another Yavnean sage against confrontation with Rome is likewise attested (*Genesis Rabbah* 64:10). Finally, the principal thrust of the rabbinic endeavors at Yavneh was to forge, explicitly or implicitly, a *modus vivendi* with Rome that would probably preclude any such military confrontation.

Causes of the Bar-Kokhba Revolt

The causes of the Bar-Kokhba Revolt, for which we have only sparse and contradictory information, has been a frequent subject of discussion. The emperor Hadrian's (117–138 C.E.) fourth-century biographer claims that his decree prohibiting the practice of circumcision was the immediate reason for the outbreak of hostilities (Spartianus, *Vita Hadriani* 14.2, in *Scriptores Historia Augustae*). However, the Roman historian Dio Cassius reports that it was Hadrian's intention to build a new city on the site of Jerusalem, to be called Aelia Capitolina, that triggered the rebellion (Dio Cassius, *History of Rome* 69.12). As the name implies (Aelia after Hadrian's middle name, Aelius; Capitolina after the temple of Jupiter Capitolinus), the city was to be a thoroughly pagan one, devoid of any Jewish association.* The discovery of a coin from Aelia Capitolina, dated to the year 131, strengthens Dio's explanation as it shows that plans for this city were well underway before the onset of conflict.

Opinion is divided whether there was only one basic cause or, alternatively, whether several factors may have contributed to the outbreak of hostilities. While these decrees may well explain its specific timing, a passage by Eusebius, the fourth-century bishop of Caesarea, often ignored owing to the suspicion of his being theologically tendentious, suggests a very different cause. He claims that the revolt was not a sudden eruption of Jewish nationalist and religious fervor, but rather the culmination of decades of discontent and unrest following the destruction of the Second Temple (Eusebius, *Eccles. Hist.* 4.6).[33]

Recent archaeological evidence seems to corroborate this picture of unrest in Judea in the decades before the actual outbreak of the Bar-Kokhba Revolt. The building of roads by the Roman army in the second and third decades of the second century may have had military implications.[34] Moreover, a number of legions, or parts thereof, appeared in Judea during this period, possibly in response to unrest among the local population or in anticipation of a future confrontation. It may be that the reasons behind such Roman moves were related to signs of unrest among Jews, and that this ferment may have helped ignite the tinderbox provided by the decree(s) of the early 130s C.E.

The aims and course of the Bar-Kokhba Revolt

Besides the strong element of protest and resistance against one or more decrees that had led to open rebellion, the coin legends of Bar-Kokhba seem to point to more ambitious aspirations. They speak of the "Freedom

*Hanan Eshel, "Aelia Capitolina: Jerusalem No More," *BAR*, November/December 1997.

Aelia Capitolina Coin. *Minted in c. 131 C.E., this coin depicts a temple to Jupiter, flanked by statues of Juno and Minerva, which the Roman emperor Hadrian may have intended to build—or perhaps did build—on the Temple Mount in Jerusalem. Hadrian's plan to transform Jewish Jerusalem into a Roman city named Aelia Capitolina sparked the Second Jewish Revolt against Rome in 132 C.E. The new Roman name for the city is inscribed on this coin: COL(onia) AEL(ia) KAP(itolina).*

of Jerusalem" and the "Redemption of Israel." What precisely this meant in political terms is not clear. It is hard to imagine that, with the Roman Empire at its zenith, Bar-Kokhba might have aspired to overthrow Roman rule. Perhaps he only sought to repeal the recent decrees and gain some kind of local autonomy. It is equally possible that the leadership of this revolt was so intoxicated by religious dreams of national restoration, and perhaps also by its initial successes, that no effort was made to read the international political and military map with objectivity. In the end, however, we simply do not have enough information to resolve this question with reasonable certainty.

It is also difficult to track the course of the revolt. The outbreak of hostilities clearly caught Rome unprepared, a not infrequent occurrence under the empire. The Jews appear to have won a number of victories in the early stages of the conflict,[35] although they never succeeded in destroying military bases or capturing cities. Based on archaeological evidence, Jewish military activity seems to have been restricted primarily to guerilla tactics in the subterranean caves in Judea where soldiers would hide, venture out and attack the enemy, and then retreat for regrouping. How grave the situation was in terms of Roman interests is difficult to tell, but Hadrian was forced to dispatch one of his most highly regarded generals, Julius Severus, to quash the rebellion. The Romans conquered Judea, leaving the rebels to gather for a last stand at Bethar (a town in the Judean hills, southwest of Jerusalem), which fell to

Bar-Kokhba Revolt Coin. *When Simeon bar Kosba, known as Bar-Kokhba, led the Second Jewish Revolt against Rome in 132 C.E., the insurrectionists minted coins to demonstrate their independence. Over 80 percent of these coins mention Jerusalem, and all symbols on the coins relate to the holy city, showing its importance as the center of national identity. One particular coin depicts the Jerusalem Temple, perhaps with a representation of the Ark of the Covenant, which had been lost since the destruction of the First Temple in 586 B.C.E.*

them in the summer of 135 C.E.

Indeed, the Romans invested great efforts in suppressing the revolt. Large numbers of troops were mobilized and many casualties were incurred; at one point, the most famous of Rome's commanders was appointed to lead the army.*[36] In the aftermath of the revolt, a lavish triumphal celebration was held but, significantly, the emperor Hadrian omitted the customary declaration to the Senate: "The legions and I are in health." All the above point to Rome's formidable attempts to defeat the rebels (Dio Cassius, *History of Rome* 69.14.3).

The collapse of the Bar-Kokhba Revolt spelled the end of active Jewish nationalism in antiquity. Nationalist aspirations had been a significant factor in Jewish history for 300 years, since the successful Maccabean revolt in the second century B.C.E., often finding expression in revolts against the occupying power or attacks on gentile neighbors. With the end of the Bar-Kokhba Revolt, such active Jewish nationalist aspirations were all but eliminated.

The aftermath

Following the suppression of the revolt, the name of the province, Judea,

*Eck, "Hadrian's Hard-Won Victory," *BAR*, September/October 2007.

was changed to Syria-Palestina so as to obliterate any reference to the Jews. Aelia Capitolina was built on the site of Jerusalem and, as noted, bore a decidedly pagan character for the next several centuries, with Jews virtually banned from the city and its environs. Moreover, rabbinic literature reports that for a brief period Jews were forbidden to observe their most traditional and basic practices, including prayer, study, circumcision, holiday observance and more.[37]

Cumulatively, the two major Judean revolts—the First Jewish Revolt against Rome (66–70 C.E.) and the Second Jewish Revolt under Bar-Kokhba (132–135 C.E.)—had far-reaching effects on Jewish life, spiritually, institutionally and psychologically. After almost a thousand years, the center of Jewish life now shifted from Jerusalem and Judea to the Galilee, which assumed a central role in Jewish Palestine for the next 800 years. New political and religious institutions and leadership now emerged, replacing those that had been centered in Jerusalem and had now largely disappeared. The end of the Bar-Kokhba hostilities also witnessed the beginning of a substantial exodus of Jews to the Diaspora. For the first time, we read of sages who took up residence in Babylonia.

Yet, side by side with these traumatic political and military upheavals, rabbinic activities in Yavneh were making strides to lay the groundwork for the renewal of Judaism, what would eventually have a profound effect on the future of Jewish religious life, norms, values and practices. However, as noted, the full impact of this new and innovative direction would be realized on the wider societal level only many centuries later.

ה

FIVE

Christianity from the Destruction of Jerusalem to Constantine: 70–312 C.E.

HAROLD W. ATTRIDGE

THE PERIOD BETWEEN 70 AND 312 C.E. IS BOUND BY TWO SIGNAL events, each of which was recognized by contemporaries as well as by later historians as having special significance. On August 30 in the year 70, Roman legionnaires under the command of the future emperor Titus burned the Temple of Jerusalem to the ground.[1] Almost two and half centuries later, on October 27, 312, at the Milvian Bridge outside the city of Rome, two generals fought a decisive battle for dominion in the western half of the empire. The victor was Constantine, who then entered the "eternal city" where he later erected a statue of himself, the remains of which may still be seen in the Capitoline Museum. In its hand this colossal statue held a cross. Constantine claimed he had "saved and delivered the city from the yoke of the tyrant

Constantine the Great. *The emperor Constantine (306–337 C.E.) brought an end to the Roman persecutions of Christians that were at their height from 303 to 311 C.E. Although he was not baptized until the end of his life, Constantine's support gave the new religion official status. This colossal head was originally part of a massive marble statue that Constantine erected in Rome after his victory at the Milvian Bridge. The head and a few other fragments from the statue are now in Rome's Capitoline Museum.*

TIMOTHY MCCARTHY/ART RESOURCE, NY

under this sign."[2]

The first of these two dates marks the end of an epoch in Jewish history as well as the limit of the first generation of the Jesus movement. At that time the Jesus movement was still a rather loosely knit, often despised, sect composed of Jews and gentiles excited by the anticipated establishment of the reign of God upon earth. The second of these two dates marks a critically important event in the increasingly triumphal advance of the well-organized Christian Church into a position of dominance in ancient Mediterranean society.

Between these two events the Christian movement gradually solidified its internal organization and, after numerous challenges, formalized the structure of its beliefs. In the process it defined itself over against the people of Israel from which it had emerged and over against the larger Hellenistic-Roman society of which it became an increasingly important part.[3]

Evidence for the history of Christianity in the pre-Constantinian period is primarily literary,[4] although there is also some archaeological evidence as we shall see.[5] Christian writers produced a wide range of works—homilies and expositions of scripture; tales of apostles and martyrs to instruct and inspire believers; hymns and poems to celebrate divine actions in Christ and in the Church; polemical tracts against Jews, pagans and other factions within the Christian movement; apologies to deflect criticism and entice outsiders; and eventually more speculative works attempting to make coherent sense of Christian claims. Most of this large literary corpus was preserved by what emerged as the orthodox Church of the fourth century, although chance discoveries of the last century and a half have yielded important evidence, particularly for versions of Christianity that did not succeed. In addition, a fourth-century bishop, Eusebius of Caesarea, composed an *Ecclesiastical History*, giving an account of the period from Jesus to Constantine that remains valuable, both for its overall framework and for the remains of otherwise lost writers that it preserves.[6]

By 70 C.E. Christian communities had formed not only in Israel, but also in many parts of the Mediterranean basin and beyond. As Paul's letters and the Book of Acts reflect, followers of Jesus were certainly present in the land of Israel itself, in Jerusalem and, no doubt, in Galilee. Missionaries from Jerusalem, apparently members of the "Hellenist" faction there, had founded a congregation in Antioch, the third major metropolis of the empire after Rome and Alexandria. Antioch in turn had served as the initial base for Paul's successful missionary activity in Asia Minor, particularly in Ephesus and Greece. Missionaries had already visited Rome and their activity caused such turmoil in the Jewish community that the emperor Claudius expelled Jews in the 40s C.E. According to the tradition in the the Book of Acts (8:26–40), African Christianity was inaugurated by missionary activity of the Jerusalem Hellenists who converted an Ethiopian official. Other missionaries may also have reached Egypt. An "eloquent" Alexandrian named Apollos appears in connection with Paul's missionary activity (Acts 18:24–28; 1 Corinthians 1:12, 3:4–5, 4:6, 16:12); there were undoubtedly other Christians in Alexandria. Paul himself, after his years in Greece and Asia Minor, intended to pursue missionary activity in the Iberian peninsula; at least one early Christian source suggests that he was released from his Roman imprisonment and made the journey to the far west.[7] By 70 C.E., then, there was clearly a Christian presence throughout the Mediterranean, particularly in what were to become several of the major ecclesiastical centers of the subsequent centuries—Alexandria, Antioch and Rome.[8]

In the second century, Christianity continued to expand from the major urban centers of the Greek-speaking portion of the empire into the hinterland of Syria, Asia Minor, Italy and Egypt. In the early second century, Pliny, the Roman governor of Bithynia-Pontus on the southern shore of the Black Sea, reported to the emperor Trajan the extensive presence of Christians in his province.[9] The movement spread farther afield into the Latin West and the Syriac-speaking East. By the third quarter of the century we hear of major communities in Gaul, modern France. At Lyons a group of Christians was martyred and a new bishop, Irenaeus, launched a vigorous literary defense of orthodoxy. At Carthage, the capital of North Africa, a community with a strong sense of its separate identity also produced martyrs and a major literary figure, Tertullian, active in the late second and early third century (190–220 C.E.). In the East, evidence in the late second century surfaces for Christians at the Syrian trading city of Edessa. Christians apparently conducted missionary activity even farther to the east. Eusebius reports that a leading Alexandrian intellectual of the middle of the second century, Pantaenus, traveled to the west coast of India. There he found a group of Christians who traced their origins to the activity of the apostle Bartholomew.[10]

Beginning in the late second century, Christians produced numerous legendary accounts of the missionary activities of the apostles; although often pious fantasy, some historical reminiscences may underlie reports that the apostle Andrew preached among the cannibals on the Black Sea, or that the apostle Thomas introduced a life of holy chastity in Parthia (modern Iran) and the Indus Valley (modern Pakistan).[11] By 312 C.E., when Constantine triumphed at the battle of the Milvian Bridge, Christians had become, if not a majority, then at least a substantial and fairly coherent minority throughout the Roman Empire and beyond.

Development of the institutional Church

Organizing members of what Paul called the "body of Christ" so as to provide mutual aid and to confront an often hostile world was no simple matter. The Christian community soon formalized the ways in which it worshiped. As it did so, a leadership structure evolved in which authority came to be increasingly vested in functionaries of local communities—first in boards of elders, later in individual bishops. These local leaders eventually organized themselves in regional and empire-wide networks, with the bishops of the principal sees playing an increasingly prominent part.

Succeeding generations could find various models of ecclesiastical organization in the history of the first apostolic generation. In Jerusalem a troika of Peter, James and John eventually gave way to a community in which James, the brother of Jesus, played the leading role.[12] Paul's community at Corinth met in the houses of wealthy patrons, such as Chloe (1 Corinthians 1:11) and Phoebe (Romans 16:1); but ecclesiastical functions, such as praying, "prophesying" (or delivering inspiring messages) and speaking in tongues, were gifts of the Spirit that fell on various members of the community, male and female, slave and free. By the end of the century, more stable forms of order began to appear, but variety and experimentation is evident. (For the early history of the structures and spaces of Christian worship, see "The origins and development of early Christian architecture," pp. 311–318.) In the area of Paul's missionary activity, itinerant missionaries were soon replaced by local bodies of elders. The situation is attested in Acts, written by a disciple of Paul in Asia Minor in the late first century.* Before leaving the Aegean area on his final journey to Jerusalem, Paul bids farewell to a leadership cadre of "presbyters" or elders (Acts 20:17). The account of this departure, with its formal farewell, may have served as a legitimation of the organizational structure that emerged after Paul's death.

Paul's disciples addressed the question of organization in a series of pseudepigraphical compositions (i.e., works written in Paul's name)—the Pastoral Epistles, 1 Timothy, 2 Timothy and Titus.[13] These texts portray a hierarchical arrangement consisting of an apostolic figure with regional authority (Timothy and Titus) and, in the local churches, two tiers of elders—bishops and deacons (1 Timothy 3:1–13)—as well as an order of "widows" (1 Timothy 5:1–16). The latter were apparently real widows who both received support from the church and assisted its leaders. The office of bishop remains poorly defined. The designation of the office, *episkopos* ("overseer"), indicates that its holders had some administrative or supervisory duties, but there is no indication that the bishops were yet the sole authorities in their communities.

The Pastoral Epistles reflect some of the social pressures that affected the formation of an ecclesiastical order. The author demands that leaders be men of good standing and repute, solid citizens who have been duly ordained (1 Timothy 4:14). Christianity is no longer an eschatological cult eagerly awaiting the end of time, but a religious philosophy teaching its adherents virtues appropriate to the various states of civilized society. Women, slaves and children no longer learn the equality preached by Paul (Galatians 3:28), but the submissiveness appropriate to their subordinate social roles.[14] The Christian movement is accommodating itself to society; in doing so it loses some of its initial radical character.

The Didache

The *Didache,* a handbook of church order, reflects this development.[15] Claiming to be "The Teaching of the Twelve Apostles to the Gentiles," it depicts the organization of a Christian community in the Syrian region in the late first century and it formed the basis for numerous subsequent works of the same type. According to the *Didache,* community life is to

*Traditionally, both the Gospel of Luke and Book of Acts are attributed to Luke, a physician and gentile convert, who was for a time one of Paul's companions. See Mikeal Parsons, "Who Wrote the Gospel of Luke?" *BR,* April 2001.

be based on ethical instruction (chapters 1–6) about the "two ways": the way of sin leading to death; the way of the decalogue, interpreted through Jesus' teachings, leading to life.[16] The *Didache* also evidences a major concern with the proper celebration of the rituals that formed the focus of Christian community life. The initiatory rite of baptism (chapter 7) was effected by immersion in running water, while the celebrant invoked the names of Father, Son and Spirit, as in Matthew 28:19. The eucharistic meal (chapters 9–10) had a decidedly eschatological tenor, in which the bread signified scattered people restored to unity at the end of time. The instructions for celebrating the Eucharist make no mention of Jesus' death, prominent in Paul's description of the sacred meal (1 Corinthians 11:17–34); obviously, there was room for considerable diversity in Christian ritual at this stage.

The regulations for worship stipulate that the Christian liturgical celebration takes place on the Lord's Day, which is not the traditional Jewish Sabbath, but the first day of the week, the day of Jesus' resurrection. Other evidence from the late first and early second century suggests that Christians had shifted the focus of their sacred time. Reports of liturgical activity in the middle of the second century indicate that the practice of Sunday observance was well entrenched.[17]

Two structures of authority are mentioned in the *Didache*. On the one hand, churches must welcome and support (but also test) itinerant "apostles and prophets" (chapters 11–13). These individuals, reminiscent of Paul and other early wandering teachers, still enjoy pride of place. Alongside them, however, "bishops and deacons" (chapter 15) lead local congregations. These officials are hierarchically distinguished, but not in the rigid way they would be in later years. Men charged with specific functions held both offices, and, as in the Pastoral Epistles, bishops are not yet solitary leaders.

The pattern of leadership in the Christian congregation in Rome is reflected in the Epistle to the Hebrews, an elaborate homily that interprets the death of Christ as a counterpart to the purification ritual conducted by the Israelite high priest on the Day of Atonement. The text was apparently sent to Rome, or to a segment of the Roman community, late in the first century, from an uncertain location, perhaps Antioch or Alexandria.[18] Its concluding admonitions (Hebrews 13:7,17) to obey leaders hint that a rather loose structure of governance led by elders was still in effect.

Both the presbyterial structure and the cultic symbolism are prominent in a late first-century document. First Clement purports to be a letter from the leaders of the church in Rome to the church in Corinth.[19] Tradition attributes the letter to Clement, who is mentioned in later succession lists as the third or fourth bishop of Rome.[20] The attribution may indicate that Clement was the "executive secretary" of the Roman council of elders. The letter indicates that leaders of the Roman church intervened in Corinth to settle a dispute that had resulted in the deposing of some Corinthian leaders. Relying heavily on examples from the Hebrew scriptures and on Paul's epistles to Corinth and Rome, the letter urges reconciliation and obedience to the established structure of authority. As in the Pastorals and the *Didache*, this structure consists of a two-tiered hierarchy: bishops and deacons.[21]

Ignatius of Antioch

A new development in Church organization appears slightly later, in the letters of Ignatius of Antioch.[22] This bishop had run afoul of Roman authorities and, about 115 C.E., was sentenced "to the beasts" in Rome. Escorted there by armed guards, he sent one letter ahead to Rome and six letters back to communities in Asia Minor that had assisted him along his way.[23] Ignatius expresses his ardent desire to follow Christ in suffering and advises well-wishers against any efforts to save him. At times, he polemicizes against Christian factions, perhaps having in mind the situation back in Antioch. Ignatius castigates "Judaizers" who resisted the growing gulf between Jews and Christians,[24] as well as "docetists" who doubted the full reality of Jesus' humanity and claimed that Jesus only "appeared" to be human.[25] Both issues—the relationship to Judaism and the nature of Jesus' humanity—remained troublesome in the second century. In criticizing these factions, Ignatius urged all Christians to cleave to their bishops, since union with God depends on union with the unique head of each community.[26] The urgency of his arguments suggests that leadership by a monarchical bishop was a recent innovation. The institution of the monarchical bishop increasingly became the bulwark of what Ignatius, for the first time, calls "the Catholic Church."[27]

The principle enunciated by Ignatius eventually became the norm. By the end of the second century, most Christian communities were headed by individual bishops. Not everyone agreed that this was a positive development, however. As the formality of ecclesiastical organization increased, rival groups emerged, and various Christian sects contested the overall hierarchical arrangement.

Followers of Marcion and of Valentinus provide examples. Just before the middle of the second century, their followers formed influential communities in Rome. The development of a stronger episcopal office in Rome at this time may have been a response to the threat of Marcionites and Valentinians. More about them later.

The focal point of institutional development, however, was the liturgy. Some sense of how Christians were worshiping in Rome around 150 C.E.

emerges from the apologetic writings of Justin Martyr. He describes baptismal rites and the Sunday assembly, held to read "the memoirs of the Apostles or the writings of the prophets," to hear the homily of the president, to pray and to partake of the eucharistic gifts of bread and wine, which are the flesh and blood of Christ.[28] The overall structure of the Roman Mass was in place.[29]

The episcopacy of Rome

Evidence of the emerging Roman episcopacy comes from Hegesippus, an easterner active in Rome in the latter part of the second century.[30] As part of an effort to combat heresy, Hegesippus traveled around the Christian world collecting traditions and lists of leaders in the principal metropolitan areas. He finally wrote up the results of his investigations in five books of *Memoirs*, giving the "unerring tradition of the apostolic preaching."[31] Fragments of Hegesippus's memoirs survive in Eusebius's *Ecclesiastical History*.[32]

The Quartodecimans and the Easter controversy

The trend toward uniformity in belief and practice, as well as the growing power of the monarchical episcopacy at Rome, are evident in a controversy that erupted in the last years of the second century. The controversy arose because Christians of the Roman province of Asia (i.e., western Asia Minor) had traditionally commemorated Jesus' death and resurrection at the time of Passover, following the Jewish lunar calendar. Because Passover begins on the 14th day of the Hebrew month of Nisan, Christians who observed Easter according to this calendar were dubbed Quartodecimans, or Fourteeners.* On the basis of this chronological reckoning, Easter, celebrated on the third day after the death of Jesus, could fall on any day of the week.[33] Christians in Rome, as well as in other areas of the Church, insisted on celebrating Easter on the Sunday following Passover, thus observing the day of the week on which Christ rose. In the mid-second century, leaders of the churches in Asia and leaders of the churches in Rome had agreed to disagree, but under Victor (189–198 C.E.) attitudes changed. The Roman bishop tried to enforce uniformity by excommunicating those who followed the Quartodeciman tradition of the Asian churches. Victor's initiative failed when other bishops, preferring to preserve ecclesiastical unity, refused to join him. One influential bishop, Irenaeus of Lyons, mediated the dispute in the interests of Church unity. Eusebius reports that, true to his name, he acted "irenically" during the controversy, urging Victor by letter to remain in union with the churches

*See Samuele Bacchiocchi, "How It Came About: From Saturday to Sunday," *BAR*, September/October 1978.

of Asia Minor.[34] The dispute continued to smolder until finally settled by the Council of Nicaea in 325 C.E., which stipulated that Easter was to be celebrated on the Sunday following the full moon after the vernal equinox.[35] Nonetheless, Victor's attempt to enforce uniformity was a forerunner of later claims to widespread jurisdictional authority on the part of the Roman pontiffs.

A reaction against the growing authority of the episcopal structure also appeared in the late second century in the Montanist movement. Around 171 C.E.,[36] in the province of Phrygia (in Asia Minor), a group emerged that styled itself the "new prophecy." A certain Montanus, along with two women, Priscilla and Maximilla, engaged in ecstatic prophecy and proclaimed that the *Parousia* (second coming of Christ) would soon take place in the Phrygian villages of Pepuza and Tymion, which they named Jerusalem.*[37] This prophetic movement revived several features of primitive Christianity—an intense eschatological expectation, and reliance on charismatic gifts working outside the established hierarchy. The Montanists also tended to be ascetics who rejected contemporary society. The movement aroused the ire of the hierarchical establishment.[38] Although condemned by councils and suppressed by church leaders,[39] Montanism and its moral rigor continued to attract followers. These included the North African polemicist Tertullian.

In the early third century, the rivalry generated by growing episcopal power is evident. We are particularly well informed about developments in Rome through the writings of Hippolytus, a prolific author, heresiologist and anti-pope, martyred around 235 C.E. One of the major works attributed to Hippolytus, the *Apostolic Tradition,*[40] deals with the practical questions of organizing ecclesiastical life, giving regulations for liturgical practice and for the installation of various ranks of the hierarchy.

Penance and the forgiveness of sin

At roughly the same time, the early decades of the third century, Christians in Syria produced a similar church order, the *Didascalia,* composed in Greek on the model of the *Didache.*[41] This Syrian work gives instructions about the election and installation of bishops, priests and deacons, liturgical celebrations, the behavior of widows and deaconesses, organized charity and the education of children. On an issue that was to become increasingly controversial during the third century, it takes the position that penance is allowed even for severe sins such as adultery and apostasy, although unrepentant

* For more on Montanism, see also Francesco D'Andria, "Conversion, Crucifixion and Celebration at Hierapolis," *BAR,* July/August 2011.

heretics are to be expelled from the Church.

In Rome, Hippolytus had taken a different position. When one Callistus ascended to the episcopacy, he adopted a lenient disciplinary policy: He was ready to forgive even serious sins, accepted as members of the clergy men who had been married more than once, tolerated socially unacceptable marital or quasi-marital arrangements between highborn women and slaves or freedmen, and allowed a second baptism.[42] Hippolytus found in Callistus's policies neither compassion nor egalitarianism, but only accommodation with evil. He accused Callistus of merely setting up a sectarian school. Hippolytus himself became a rival bishop, continuing in schism under succeeding popes, Urban (222–230 C.E.) and Pontianus (230–235 C.E.). At that point a reconciliation apparently occurred. In 235 C.E. both Hippolytus and Pontianus were exiled by the new emperor, Maximinus Thrax, and they both died in exile. The united community of Rome elected a single new bishop, Anteros (235–236 C.E.), and revered the memory of Hippolytus as a martyr.

At about this time, learned and vigorous bishops in the leading Christian centers attempted—with varying degrees of success—to forge a wide-ranging consensus on issues of doctrine and practice. One of the main issues on which bishops united was the matter of penitential practice that had divided Callistus and Hippolytus. The rigorist position defended by Hippolytus had deep roots in early Christianity. The Evangelists recorded a saying attributed to Jesus excluding forgiveness for the "sin against the Holy Spirit" (Matthew 12:32; Mark 3:29; Luke 12:10; see also Gospel of Thomas 44). For a first-century writer like the author of the Epistle to the Hebrews, certain kinds of post-baptismal sin could not be forgiven (Hebrews 6:4). On the other hand, in the early second century a revelation recorded in a Christian apocalypse written in Rome, the Shepherd of Hermas, allowed for the possibility of a single act of repentance for serious sin—such as adultery—committed after baptism.[43] Not all Christians could accept this innovation, and Tertullian, the North African controversialist of the late second century, derided the "shepherd of the adulterers."

In the mid-third century a series of events occurred that highlighted tensions on this issue. A key figure was Cyprian, the bishop of Carthage. Shortly after Cyprian became bishop, in 248 or 249 C.E., the emperor Decius inaugurated the first empire-wide persecution of Christians. During the persecution, Cyprian led his community from hiding. After the emperor's death, Cyprian confronted the problem of dealing with Christians who, during the persecutions, had sacrificed to the Roman gods or had purchased certificates (*libelli*) indicating that they had done so. Now they wanted to return to communion with the Church. Should this be permitted?

In response to the problem of "the lapsed," several factions emerged. One group favored immediate reconciliation, based upon the forgiveness granted by martyrs or confessors. Cyprian, however, insisted[44] on the necessity of a penitential discipline, supervised by episcopal authority. This position was confirmed by a synod of bishops at Carthage in 251 C.E., the attendance at which shows how widespread the Church was in North Africa.

A more serious challenge came from rigorists who resisted granting any reconciliation to the lapsed. In Rome this faction, in the tradition of Hippolytus, formed a schismatic community headed by a presbyter named Novatian.[45] Bishops throughout the empire were called upon by Pope Cornelius (251–253 C.E.) to take sides in the controversy over the lapsed.[46] Cyprian entered the fray with his *On the Unity of the Church*, insisting that Christians remain in union with their bishops, whose authority was bound up with the promise to Peter in Matthew 16:18.[47] Cyprian even acknowledged a "primacy" to the successor of Peter in Rome, although this was apparently more temporal or honorific than juridical.

Whatever Cyprian thought of the importance of the Roman bishop in the controversy over the lapsed, he sharply differed with Pope Stephen (254–257 C.E.) on another matter. Following the custom in North Africa, Cyprian insisted that persons baptized by schismatics and heretics, such as the Novatianists, needed to be rebaptized if they wanted fellowship with the Catholic Church. Stephen defended the traditional Roman practice that recognized the validity of baptism no matter who administered the sacrament. He sharply rebuked Cyprian and a heated interchange ensued, at which time Cyprian apparently issued a revised version of his tract on unity, downplaying the role of Peter's Roman successor.[48] The controversy ended when both bishops died in 257 C.E., Cyprian as a martyr. Although Stephen's position eventually prevailed, Cyprian's ideal of a pure Church with worthy ministers continued to dominate North Africa and would fuel the bitter Donatist controversy that erupted in the fourth century.

The row between Cyprian and Stephen indicated both the strengths and weaknesses of the developing institutional Church. A vigorous bishop, particularly when acting in consort with other bishops organized in regional councils, could provide effective leadership and act as a strong unifying element for a community in a situation of crisis. Yet forceful bishops, convinced of the righteousness of their cause in a matter under dispute, could readily lead to schism in the universal Church.

Christianity's self-definition: Neither Jew nor Greek

As the Christian movement developed institutionally, it created its own ethos and evolved its own self-understanding. This occurred in varying ways in different regions, but there were several factors with widespread influence.

The roots of the Christian movement were obviously in the Hebrew Bible, and Christians claimed to be the authentic continuation of ancient Israel. This claim naturally led to tension with emergent Rabbinic Judaism.

Christians within the Roman Empire, and even in the Syriac speaking regions to the east, were heirs also of the Hellenic cultural tradition that had been shaping Mediterranean civilization for several centuries. Christians needed to decide how they would relate to that culture, too.

The Gospel of Matthew

The Christian confrontation with the Jewish traditions that developed after the destruction of Jerusalem are evident in those portions of the New Testament produced in the post-war generation, the period, in fact, when most of the Christian movement's sacred documents reached their final form. Within two decades of the destruction of Jerusalem (i.e., by 90 C.E.),[49] Christians, probably in Antioch, produced the Gospel according to Matthew, combining two strands of tradition: (1) Accounts of Jesus' miracles, death and resurrection came from a version of the Gospel according to Mark; (2) Many of Jesus' teachings derived from a collection of sayings, now commonly labeled "Q," known also to Luke.*

The author of Matthew gave a distinctive cast to his compilation, while claiming that Jesus was the anointed Son of God, the agent of salvation for humankind. Jesus played that role as descendant of David, who fulfilled the expectations of Israel's scriptures. The first two chapters clearly express Matthew's perspective. A genealogy (Matthew 1:1–17) traces Jesus' Davidic descent, and legends about his birth and infancy cite scriptural texts as prophecies (Matthew 1:23, 2:6,15,18). This device, found elsewhere in Matthew as well (Matthew 4:14–16, 12:17–20), is similar to the so-called *pesher*† commentaries found among the Dead Sea Scrolls, which also cite scripture as prophecy.[50]

For Matthew, Jesus had not only been predicted by scripture, he was also its definitive interpreter, as a teacher of strict obedience to God's revealed will. Matthean Christians were summoned to follow the written Torah (Matthew

*See Stephen J. Patterson, "Q: The Lost Gospel," *BR*, October 1993.

†*Pesher* means "interpretation." The term is used in Qumran commentaries to introduce the interpretation of a biblical verse.

5:17–20) and the Pharisaic Oral Law, but not the Pharisees' personal example (Matthew 23:2–3). Matthew's observant followers of Jesus had a universal mission, to teach all nations to obey what had been commanded by their risen Lord, now expected as the ultimate and imminent judge of humankind (Matthew 25:31–46). Matthew thus maintains continuity with the faction that had opposed Paul in Antioch half a century earlier over the issue of whether or not to keep *kashrut* laws (determining what foods were kosher) (Galatians 2:11–14).

Matthew's author was concerned with the problems of maintaining a community composed of "weeds" as well as "wheat" (Matthew 13:24–30). He collected into one of Jesus' "discourses" traditional sayings on community life (Matthew 18:1–22), urging, for example, reconciliation among alienated members of the Church (Matthew 18:15–17). Although the precise structure of authority operative in the community is unclear, Matthew certainly revered Peter. Matthew's gospel alone records Jesus' saying about the foundational "rock" of the Church ("You are Peter, and on this rock I will build my church," Matthew 16:18). There may be a connection between that saying and the later emergence in Antioch of a church organization centered on a single powerful bishop.

Luke's gospel and the Acts of the Apostles

Another approach to the problem of continuity with Israel appears in the works traditionally attributed to Luke. Luke's gospel, composed in the late first or early second century,[51] was the first of a two-volume set. Not content to tell Jesus' story, the author of the third Gospel recounted in his Acts of the Apostles the expansion of the Christian movement into the Mediterranean world. These two volumes, the largest component of the New Testament, constitute one of early Christianity's most sophisticated literary products. Luke's skill is particularly apparent in Acts, where vivid narrative alternates with the rhetorical appeals of dramatic speeches.[52]

Like Matthew, Luke's gospel combined two major written sources, a version of Mark and the collection of Jesus' sayings ("Q"). Luke also drew upon other sayings and stories, including a number of Jesus' parables.[53] While Matthew and Mark insisted on Jesus' imminent coming as divinely-appointed judge, Luke portrays him as a peripatetic teacher who, on his way to Jerusalem (Luke 9:51–19:27), instructs his disciples in appropriate conduct and attitudes. Luke suggests that the Way (Acts 9:2) inaugurated by Jesus is continuous with the traditions of ancient Israel. The scriptural allusions of the carefully crafted infancy narratives (Luke 1–2) convey this conviction as effectively as Matthew's citation of prophetic texts in his infancy narrative.[54]

Acts 5:27–42 makes a similar point: The apostles teach in the Temple and Gamaliel, a leading Pharisee, advises the Jewish leaders to take a "wait and see" attitude; if this movement "is of human beings, it will fail, but if it is of God, you will not be able to overthrow it" (Acts 5:38–39).

Despite emphasizing continuity with Judaism, Luke does not presume that Christians are strict observers of the Pharisaic Oral Torah. Where Matthew's Jesus calls for a "higher righteousness" and for "perfection" (Matthew 5:48), Luke's calls for "mercy" (Luke 6:36). Jesus displays the quality in his consolation of grieving women (Luke 23:28) and in his assurance of salvation to the penitent thief (Luke 23:43). In Matthew, Jesus built a fence around the Torah, in effect extending the reach of the commandments in order to avoid the possibility of transgressing them. In Luke, on the other hand, Jesus abstracts from the Torah an ethic of compassion.

Acts 15 recounts an apostolic council held in Jerusalem. At its conclusion, the council decrees that gentiles may become Christians without circumcision, the sign of membership in the covenant community for Jews. In short, gentile Christians need not follow Jewish religious law (*halakhah*) except that they must refrain from idolatry and unchastity and observe minimal dietary restrictions. But that is all. Whatever the historicity of this account,[55] it represents Luke's understanding of some of the practical obligations demanded of the gentile Christians who apparently constituted the bulk of the Gospel's readership.

For Luke, Christianity is a new and universally applicable religious and moral way of life. Acts emphasizes the distinction of Christians from Jews. In the account of Paul's ministry, Jews appear as his major opponents and toward them he directs his most fervent rhetoric (e.g., Acts 22:1–21). The fact that Jews did not accept Paul's proclamation distressed Luke, but he consoled himself by arguing that prophets had foreseen this development (Acts 28:26–27).[56]

Luke's treatment of Israel and the Jews is part of Luke's attempt to help a gentile Christian community understand itself. Luke also does this by correlating Jesus' life with universal history (e.g., dating events with reference to Roman rule—Luke 2:1–2, 3:1–2), thereby laying the groundwork for later Christian periodizing of history. This correlation enables him to show the "fit" between the Christian movement and the Greco-Roman world. The emphasis on its Israelite roots certifies the new movement as part of an ancient and honorable tradition, a claim to be developed by later apologists. On the other hand, distinguishing between Christians and Jews enables Luke to disassociate his community from politically dangerous Jewish nationalist sentiments. In Acts, Roman authorities repeatedly exonerate Christians, the consummate good citizens, from various charges.[57] Acts ends before Paul's execution, which, according to tradition, took place in Rome under Nero. Acts thereby avoids what might have been embarrassing evidence of Rome's negative judgment on Christians.

Luke-Acts formed a basis for Christian self-definition in the second and following centuries. In its vision, Christians—including gentile Christians—were a people chosen by God in the light of his ancient promises to Israel; this new Israel was a people called to a high morality and a compassionate concern for the weak. This universal message would have a powerful and broad appeal.

Pseudo-Pauline Epistles

Other Christians working with a Pauline heritage display analogous approaches to the movement's self-definition. Pseudepigraphical literature in the Pauline tradition flourished during this period in the environment that spawned Luke-Acts. Colossians is attributed to Paul and his co-worker Timothy (Colossians 1:1), but differences in nuance between Colossians and the major Pauline epistles suggest that Paul was not, in fact, its author. Instead, the letter is by an admirer in the succeeding Christian generation, adapting Paul's heritage to new situations.[58] Its portrait of Christ as the "image of God," active in creation and now enthroned over the cosmos, counters a religious movement felt to be problematic. At issue is apparently some mystical practice ("self-abasement and worship of angels, dwelling on visions," Colossians 2:18); perhaps this was derived from some form of speculative Jewish piety, bound up with the liturgical cycle of "festivals, new moons and Sabbaths." Several oblique references (Colossians 2:6–19) criticize this piety and propose as an alternative the ethical observances (Colossians 3:1–4:6) appropriate to those who revere the cosmic Christ. Details of the exhortation exemplify the tendency of Christian texts of this period to emphasize socially accepted moral norms. Wives are to be subject to their husbands, children to their parents, slaves to their masters (Colossians 5:18–22).

Another Paulinist drew on Colossians to compose Ephesians. This text celebrates the mystery of the Church, Christ's body (Ephesians 1:23) or bride (Ephesians 5:32), which had broken down the barriers separating Jew and gentile ("He is our peace, who has made us both one, and has broken down the dividing wall of hostility, by abolishing in his flesh the law of commandments and ordinances," Ephesians 2:14). The intense polemic that characterizes Matthew and John over the separation from the synagogue is not in evidence here.

The Fourth Gospel and the Apocrypha

In the same general period (90–110 C.E.), the Gospel according to John emerged in virtually its final form.[59] Tradition places John in Ephesus.[60] The Gospel may have have been edited there, though on the basis of traditions from Judea and Samaria.

This complex work developed as an elaboration of a source, rather like Mark, recounting the miraculous activity of Jesus. Teachers, reflecting on Jesus' significance, gradually expanded this narrative, composing the lengthy discourses now set on Jesus' lips. The result is what Clement of Alexandria in the late second century called the "spiritual Gospel," an evocative text that presents Jesus as the "Word" (John 1:1), God's definitive revelation. Perhaps in opposition to other speculative Christians who conceived of Jesus in similar terms, including the "docetists" combatted by Ignatius, the Fourth Gospel insists that Jesus is revealed not simply in his teaching, but on the cross: Jesus' death is an act of selfless love (John 15:13), by which he glorifies God and draws all people to him (John 12:28–33).

Tensions that affected Christianity in the late first century are obvious in the Fourth Gospel. John clearly attests the rupture with the synagogue, perhaps caused by the reconstitution of Jewish life under the rabbis at Jamnia (Yavneh) in the post-war period (see pp. 148–149).[61] The text anachronistically portrays people of Jesus' day being expelled from the synagogue for allegiance to Jesus (John 9:34), a scenario that reflects the Christian community's own experience. This experience led in turn to a bitter polemic against the Jews (John 8:44), who became generic symbols of unbelief.

The polemic in Matthew against emerging Rabbinic Judaism and the tensions between Jew and Christian apparent in texts such as Ignatius's letters attest the continuing rivalry between the two communities in Syria. Many Christian communities retained a Jewish identity and observed Torah. That situation would continue throughout the first several centuries. These Christians adapted and lightly reworked numerous apocrypha of the Old Testament, works attributed to figures of the Hebrew scriptures. One of the earliest is the Martyrdom or Ascension of Isaiah, which recounts the execution of Isaiah by being sawn apart.[62] Before his death he utters a prophecy,[63] describing the crucifixion of the "Beloved One" and giving a warning appropriate to Christians in the early second century, a warning against "many who will love office ... elders and shepherds who wrong their sheep."[64] This portion of the work is probably a Christian interpolation into an older Jewish legend. Similarly, the Testaments of the Twelve Patriarchs probably had a Jewish prehistory, although in its current form it is replete with Christian allusions. For example, the Testament of Benjamin 9:3 prophesies that "the unique prophet ... will enter the Temple, and there the Lord will be abused and will be raised up on the wood." Most of the contents of the Testaments consist of ethical exhortations delivered by the sons of Jacob before death. Yet within these exhortations are allusions to Christian messianic beliefs. Thus the Testament of Simeon 6:7 offers a blessing "because God has taken a body, eats with human beings and saves human beings."[65]

Some Jewish Christian groups traced their lineage to the Jerusalem Christians gathered around James, the brother of Jesus. Their tradition maintained that, after James's martyrdom around 64 C.E.,[66] the community in Jerusalem fled to the city of Pella in Transjordan. Whatever the report's historical value,[67] there did emerge in the Syrian area Christians who venerated the memory of James and observed the Torah as he had. Their works include recently discovered First and Second Apocalypse of James, probably dating from the second century, containing accounts of James's martyrdom at the hands of the Jerusalem authorities.[68]

Some traditions about Jesus preserved in Jewish Christian communities attained written form in the early second century. Later sources mention the Gospel of the Nazarenes, the Gospel of the Ebionites and the Gospel of the Hebrews. Like the Jewish Christian communities that produced them,[69] these texts have vanished, with the exception of a few fragments.[70] Another Jewish Christian document, the Book of Elchasai, was a collection of sayings that claim to have been revealed to a prophetic figure of the same name. The work refers to the third year of Trajan (101 C.E.), so it was probably composed just at the turn of the century.[71] The fragmentary remains suggest that this group, like the Matthean Christians, maintained strong eschatological interests, along with a rejection of the Temple and its sacrificial rituals. The Elchasaites would continue to be active at least into the third century,[72] when a prominent religious reformer, Mani, emerged from the sect. Mani's Jewish Christian background has been amply confirmed in a recently discovered Greek biography, known as the Cologne Mani Codex, dating to the third century, the decipherment of which began in 1969.*[73] Mani eventually created a religious movement that attempted to synthesize the major religions of the Greco-Roman and Persian worlds. Manichaeism became a major competitor for Christianity in the fourth century. Eusebius's comments that it was a "deadly poison" come from the land of the Persians;[74] he doubtless expresses a widespread Christian attitude.

*John C. Reeves, "Adam Meets the Evil Archon," *BR*, August 2001.

INSTITUTE FOR ANTIQUITY AND CHRISTIANITY, CLAREMONT, CALIFORNIA

Nag Hammadi. *The fourth-century Nag Hammadi codices were discovered in 1945 at the base of the rugged cliffs of Jabal al-Tarif near the Nile River in Upper Egypt. The Nag Hammadi library consists of 13 codices, or books, written in Coptic, the language of Christian Egypt, although most are translations of earlier Greek writings. The preserved manuscripts contain 52 separate tractates, or essays, that reflect the views of the Gnostics, a Christian group declared heretics by orthodox Christian authorities.*

The Gospel of Thomas

Another early gospel that incorporates some Jewish Christian traditions—known as the Gospel of Thomas—has survived. This work is a collection of 114 sayings of Jesus, only some of which have parallels in the canonical Gospels.* The text was previously known from Greek papyrus fragments, the earliest dating to 200 C.E. A translation into Coptic, the language of Christian Egypt, was discovered at Nag Hammadi in Upper Egypt in 1945.[75] Although the Gospel of Thomas grew over time, a substantial portion was probably assembled in written form by the early decades of the second century.[76]

The Gospel of Thomas (Saying 1) presents the "living Jesus" as a source of divine wisdom, whose sayings conceal mysterious teaching. It invites meditation and reflection on the nature and destiny of the self, as

*Helmut Koester and Stephen J. Patterson, "The Gospel of Thomas," *BR*, April 1990.

The Gospel of Thomas. *The Gnostic Gospel of Thomas, a complete copy of which was found among the Nag Hammadi codices, is a collection of 114 sayings of Jesus known to have existed in written form as early as 200 C.E. Some have parallels in the canonical Gospels, but many do not. The book presents the "living Jesus" as a source of divine wisdom (gnosis is Greek for "knowledge") and invites meditation on the nature and destiny of the self. The sayings include proverbs, parables, aphorisms, prophetic sayings and community rules.*

INSTITUTE FOR ANTIQUITY AND CHRISTIANITY, CLAREMONT, CALIFORNIA

well as renunciation of the world. It thus gives evidence of an ascetical strain that will consistently characterize Syrian Christianity. The attribution to Didymus Judas Thomas, traditionally venerated in the east Syrian city of Edessa, suggests an association with the East.[77] The Gospel of Thomas eventually attracted Christians with Gnostic predilections, who added touches reflecting their approach to religious questions. (For more on the Gnostics and their beliefs, see pp. 189–191 below.) Nonetheless, among its ancient traditions are Jewish Christian elements including a reverence for "James the Just ... for whose sake heaven and earth have come to exist,"[78] as well as sayings of Jesus paralleled in the fragmentary Jewish Christian gospels.

Epistle to the Hebrews

In other parts of the Christian world the polemics between Christian and Jewish groups continued. The notion that Christianity had superseded the Israelite cultic tradition is a presupposition of the Epistle to the Hebrews, apparently written to Rome late in the first century, from an uncertain location, perhaps Antioch or Alexandria. The Epistle to the Hebrews, not really a letter but a homily urging increased commitment to the Christian community, draws heavily on cultic images associated with the sacrificial rituals of the Day of Atonement and its solemn sprinkling of blood in the inner portion of the Temple (e.g., Hebrews 9:11–14).[79] Its portrait of Jesus, unique in the New Testament, depicts a heavenly high priest whose sacrificial death inaugurated the new covenant promised in Jeremiah 31. This portrait combines features of Jewish apocalyptic literature with language at home in the Platonic philosophical tradition. Hebrews intimates that in the life of covenant fidelity Christians have access to ultimate reality. Despite its heavy use of cultic symbolism, it pays little attention to any actual Christian rituals.

The situation in Egypt may be reflected in the Epistle of Barnabas, which, incidentally, was cited as authoritative scripture by Clement of Alexandria at the end of the second century, although it ultimately failed to be included in the canon of scripture.[80] Its prominence in Alexandria and its allegorical approach to scripture suggest that it was composed there. It was certainly written after the destruction of the Temple in 70 C.E., and probably before the end of the Bar-Kokhba Revolt in 135 C.E.[81] The text is concerned primarily with the Christian interpretation of the Old Testament. As in the Epistle to the Hebrews, institutions of ancient Israel, such as the Temple and the sacrificial system, are seen as symbolic types of Christianity, the true continuation of Israel.

The works of Justin Martyr mark a new stage in the Christian debate with Judaism. Justin was an apologist or defender of the faith active in Rome from the 40s through the 70s of the second century C.E.[82] According to his own stylized account,[83] as a youth he engaged in a quest for truth and sampled various philosophical options. Though attracted by Platonism, he finally rejected all philosophical solutions to life's questions in favor of Christian revelation. In Rome, Justin established himself as a Christian teacher and engaged in controversy against enemies inside and outside the Church. Justin's *Dialogue with Trypho* is a record of a dispute with a Jewish sage. It reflects the continuing problems the Christian community had with the other heirs of Israel's religious traditions. The work is largely a discussion of biblical interpretation in which Justin argues for the Christian reading of the Hebrew scriptures as Messianic prophecy fulfilled in Jesus.[84] Justin here illustrates the insistence of mid-century "orthodox" Christianity on grounding Christian claims in Israel's holy scriptures.

Christians in Egypt engaged in similar polemics. The third-century church father Origen reports on a *Dialogue Between Jason and Papiscus,* in which Jason was portrayed as a Christian, and Papiscus as a Jew of Alexandria who finally acknowledges Christ and requests baptism.[85]

Christians in Syria and Egypt also adapted Jewish Pseudepigrapha by inserting obvious Christian glosses in the texts. This process can be seen in the fragmentary narrative Jannes and Jambres,[86] and in the Christian layers of the Sibylline Oracles, verse prophecies attributed to the pagan prophetess that Egyptian Jews had long used.[87]

Even more intense polemics against Jews surface in the writing of Melito, a late second-century bishop of Sardis in Asia Minor. Archaeological excavation of an opulent synagogue from several centuries later suggests that there had long been a strong Jewish community in Sardis, the ancient capital of Lydia.* Melito's homily *On the Passover* was discovered in 1932 on an Egyptian papyrus purchased by the Chester Beatty Library in Dublin. It is a piece of florid rhetoric that interprets the Passover as symbolic of the Passion of Jesus, and bitterly denounces Jews as responsible for Jesus' death.

Emergence of Christian orthodoxy

By the time of the destruction of the Temple, Christian beliefs were already considerably developed. Although Christians may have disagreed about the precise nature of the salvation of which Jesus was the agent, they generally agreed that God worked through Jesus in a special way. They celebrated this saving event in story and song, conferring on the resurrected and exalted Jesus ever greater titles of honor. In New Testament documents composed in the last quarter of the first century, considerable diversity remains in both the titles and functions attributed to Jesus. Matthew thinks of Jesus as the Son of David, but also the Son of God, whose special birth designates him as the eschatological agent of judgment (Matthew 25:31–46). Luke, like Paul in Romans 1:3, describes Jesus installed, by virtue of his resurrection, as the eschatological Messiah, destined to come as final liberator and judge (Acts 2:32–36, 3:20).

Early doctrinal controversy

Neither Matthew nor Luke, however, regard Jesus as somehow one with God from all eternity. Precisely that affirmation is made by the author of the Fourth Gospel (John 1:1–2, 10:30, 14:11) and the Epistle to the Hebrews (1:3, 7:3, 13:8).

These affirmations about Jesus were rooted in Israelite traditions, particularly in speculation about Wisdom (Proverbs 8:22–32; Wisdom of Solomon 7:22–8:1) or an angel as intermediary between God and humankind.[88] The first steps in attributing divine status to Jesus involved equating him with such heavenly intermediaries. Regarding Jesus as one with God soon posed a new set of theoretical problems for Christian thinkers. First of all, affirming that

*John S. Crawford, "Multiculturalism at Sardis," *BAR*, September/October 1996.

Jesus is divine challenged traditional monotheism. What is the relationship between this divine being and the God known through Israel's scriptures? This affirmation also raised questions about the nature of the man Jesus. Was he human as other men are or did his divinity compromise his humanity in some way? These two fundamental questions, and several related questions, generated controversy through the pre-Constantinian period and on to the era of the great councils of the fourth and fifth centuries.

Some New Testament documents provide evidence of early doctrinal controversies. The Fourth Gospel highlights a "Beloved Disciple," an anonymous figure whom later tradition will identify as John the son of Zebedee. Whoever he may have been, this hero of the Johannine community is viewed as superior to Peter,[89] the latter perhaps symbolizing the "mainline" churches of the day. Yet an appendix (John 21) recognizes Peter's status and, by implication, the authority of the churches that revered him. What originally distinguished Johannine and Petrine Christians may have been certain doctrinal issues. John's gospel, for instance, minimizes expectations of Jesus' imminent coming and emphasizes instead his abiding presence (John 15:4–8). The Gospel's insistence that Jesus is one with God from "the beginning" (John 1:1-3, 10:30) may also have been distinctive.

Continued friction among Christians regarding such issues is also evident in the so-called Johannine epistles, letters related to the Fourth Gospel but probably not by its major author.*[90] First John criticizes "secessionists" who departed in a dispute over the fleshly (i.e., human) character of Christ and the reality of sin.[91] Similar issues are at stake in 2 John. Third John 9–10 reflects personal antipathy among Christian leaders. Some of this animosity may have stemmed from the development of hierarchical authority (one Diotrephes is opposed because he "loves first place").

Marcion and the Christian canon

A major rival to the emerging "mainline church" of the second century was Marcion, a native of Asia Minor, whose teaching and organizational ability had far-reaching influence. Marcionite churches continued in existence down through the fifth century in the Syriac East, while heresiologists (experts on heresies) from Justin[92] through Clement of Alexandria,[93] Irenaeus,[94] Tertullian[95] and the fifth-century Ephraem of Syria[96] found it necessary to refute Marcion's theology. Unfortunately, Marcion's own writings have not

*The Johannine epistles are attributed to the author of the Fourth Gospel but are probably from a different hand. The relationship of the Gospel and epistles is much debated. Part of the problem lies in the fact that the Gospel is not the product of a single author.

survived. We know them only from the differing portraits of his critics.[97] This has resulted in various assessments of his career and the character of his thought.[98]

A successful merchant who had been raised in a Christian home, Marcion came to Rome late in Hadrian's reign (137–138 C.E.) and made a substantial donation of 200,000 sesterces to the church. In 144 C.E. he was expelled from the community, but he continued his religious activity and founded an enduring ecclesiastical organization. Marcion composed at least two influential works. One was an edition of what he considered authoritative scripture, consisting of a version of Luke and the Pauline epistles.[99] The second was his *Contradictions*, where Marcion laid out differences between the Hebrew scriptures and his own New Testament, and then articulated his controversial theology. At the core of Marcion's theology was a distinction between the God of goodness revealed by Jesus and an inferior God of justice, operative in creation and in Israel's history. Jesus was the agent sent to bring souls back to the true God.

Marcion's rejection of the Hebrew Bible contributed to the emergence of another major Christian institution—scripture as we know it. The fact that Marcion had radically limited authoritative Christian writing to Luke and the Pauline corpus was one factor that forced the Christian community to define its more encompassing canon of scripture, including both Old and New Testament.[100] Some of the history of New Testament canonization is revealed in the Muratorian Canon that lists the contents of the New Testament acknowledged as authoritative at Rome around 185 C.E.[101] It mentions the Gospels, Acts and the Epistles of Paul, including the Pastorals, but not Hebrews. In addition, Jude, Revelation and one epistle of Peter appear, along with the Wisdom of Solomon. The list excludes apocryphal letters of Paul to the Laodiceans and the Alexandrians as well as the "recently composed" Shepherd of Hermas. Although, at this time, the contents of the New Testament are not yet fixed, as they would be in the fourth century, the outlines are clear. Apocryphal works such as the Gospel of the Ebionites and the legends about the miraculous infancy of Jesus,[102] in circulation in some form at this time, might serve for edification, but they were not to be accepted as authoritative scripture.

Gnosticism—A challenge to mainstream Christianity

Another challenge to mainstream Christianity, as radical as that of the Marcionites, was Gnosticism, which emerged with clarity in the second century. *Gnostic* means "one who knows." It is often loosely applied to various speculative or syncretistic movements. The precise delineation of the phenomenon and its development remain matters of debate.[103]

Church fathers, who were familiar primarily with Christian Gnostics, assumed that the phenomenon was a Christian heresy,[104] ultimately deriving from the Simon Magus mentioned in Acts 8:9–24.*[105] Despite the prominence of second-century Christian Gnostics, it is unlikely that the movement originated simply as a revision of Christianity.

In 1945 peasants working near Nag Hammadi in upper Egypt discovered a collection of more than 50 tractates, many of them Gnostic.† Most were composed in Greek in the first centuries C.E. and then translated into Coptic, the language of Christian Egypt, by the fourth century. The Nag Hammadi codices contain such Coptic translations finally copied in the mid-fourth century. These codices have shed significant new light on the phenomenon of Gnosticism both within and outside Christianity.[106]

Among fringe elements of Judaism, perhaps in Syria-Palestine or in Egypt in the late first and early second century, certain individuals claimed a distinctive form of knowledge. This "knowledge," or *gnosis,* found expression in a myth about the transcendent, spiritual world that was combined with a symbolic interpretation of the creation stories in Genesis. Although details vary, Gnostic texts regularly posit a primordial deity, utterly transcendent and unknowable. From that primal source flowed a series of emanations, one of whom was Lady Wisdom described in traditional Jewish sources.[107] This divine entity, for a reason variously defined, fell from the fullness of the godhead and produced worlds made up of soul and matter. Over these now reigned a creator god who constantly struggled to control the spirit imprisoned within matter by Lady Wisdom's fall. Gnostics read the creation stories of Genesis as a record of the hostility of the "jealous" creator. This hostility is manifest, for example, when the creator prohibits Adam and Eve from eating from the tree of knowledge. Gnostics wanted to escape from the prison over which this creator god ruled. The first step was to attain awareness (*gnosis*) about the true origin and identity of the self. Such knowledge made final reintegration into the world of spirit possible.[108]

Whether the myth and the doctrine it spawned were originally created by Christians or Jewish heretics is unclear. In any event, its massive rejection of the God of the Old Testament appealed to gentile Christians radically disaffected from Jewish traditions or stung by Jewish repudiation of their message.[109]

*David R. Cartlidge, "The Fall and Rise of Simon Magus," *BR,* Fall 2005.
†James Brashler, "Nag Hammadi Codices Shed New Light on Early Christian History," *BAR,* January/February 1984.

Christian Gnostics were especially active in Alexandria in Hadrian's reign (117–138 C.E.). One Carpocrates inaugurated a sect that apparently drew libertine consequences from the Gnostic denigration of the material world. In Carpocrates's view, if only spirit was important, then what was done in the body hardly mattered.[110] On the other hand, one Basilides, a philosophically inclined teacher, combined Gnostic myth with more conventional Stoic ethics.[111]

Valentinus and his disciples

Another Alexandrian named Valentinus went to Rome and planted there the most influential Christian Gnostic school of the second century. Although he shared the popular Platonism of his day,[112] Valentinus was also influenced by the speculative currents that characterized Alexandrian intellectuals. He was active in Rome in the 140s and 150s C.E.[113] and, according to Tertullian,[114] even became a candidate for "bishop" in the Roman community.

As with Marcion, Valentinus's writings have perished, with the exception of a few tantalizing fragments and possibly one longer tractate.[115] The fragments suggest that he taught a docetic Christology that disparaged the reality of Jesus' humanity. Valentinus may have been the author of a strikingly original work found in the Nag Hammadi library, the Gospel of Truth.[116] This work is not a narrative gospel but a meditative homily, obviously the work of a sensitive literary artist. Its poetic imagery depicts a wretched human condition, sunk in ignorance and subject to Error. At the coming of revealing Truth, embodied in Jesus, people experience an awakening from sleep and become united with their divine source.

The influence of Valentinus extended through several prominent disciples, active both in Italy and the East. One of these followers, Ptolemy, produced disciples who encountered Irenaeus in Gaul in the 180s C.E. and stimulated his heresiological work. Ptolemy once wrote an epistle to a laywoman, Flora, expounding the principles of Valentinian interpretation of scripture; like other Valentinians, he did not reject the Old Testament, as had Marcion, but claimed that it derived either from human traditions or from beings inimical to the one transcendent God. Ptolemy thereby discovered different levels of meaning and truth in the text.[117]

Valentinus's disciples like Ptolemy developed certain doctrinal positions that may have been only implicit in the work of Valentinus himself. One distinctive claim was that there were three types of people: (1) pneumatics or "spiritual" folk, who had full possession of the truth, i.e., Valentinians; (2) psychics or "soulful" folk, who had limited insight and were devoted to the God of creation, i.e., ordinary Christians; and (3) hylic or "material" folk, who were outside the ecclesiastical community altogether.

Because Valentinians insisted on the importance of divine grace in the process of restoring human beings to their transcendent source, they were read by their opponents as denying free will. They also developed a complicated theory that held that the inner workings of the godhead were composed of eight bipolar entities. These entities constituted abstract, spiritual principles dimly imaged in the ordinary world. It was the Gnostic's destiny to rejoin them in the Pleroma or fullness of deity.

The Valentinians' general denigration of the created order led to severe criticism by "orthodox" theologians. Nonetheless, Valentinian communities continued down into the fourth century.[118]

Response to the Gnostic challenge

Other writers inspired by "Gnostic" theologies continued within Christian circles to challenge the emerging hierarchical Church and its practices. Among the more interesting examples are the Gospel of Mary, a report of a dialogue between Jesus and his disciples after the resurrection in which Mary Magdalene interprets the teaching of Jesus.* Her right to do so, challenged by Peter, is defended by another apostle. The whole dialogue reflects continuing debates over the role of women in the leadership of the Christian movement.[119]

A different protest surfaces in the recently discovered Gospel of Judas.†[120] The text incorporates elements of the standard "Gnostic" explanation of the world and the place of humankind in it. In addition, it incorporates a vision seen by Judas, in which his apostolic colleagues are equated with the priests of the Jerusalem Temple. The equation is not flattering and connects the liturgical Church and its hierarchical leadership with a rejected institution.

The Gnostic challenge called forth a varied response. In Alexandria, the major hotbed of Gnosticism, the course of the debate is difficult to trace. Christian Pseudepigrapha apparently played a role in the anti-Gnostic struggle. For example, the Epistula Apostolorum, an anti-Gnostic encyclical attributed to the 12 apostles, utilizes, in addition to canonical texts, second-century works such as the Apocalypse of Peter, the Epistle of Barnabas and the Shepherd of Hermas.[121] The Epistula Apostolorum purports to record the apostles' reminiscences of Jesus' activity during his life as well as a post-resurrection dialogue between Jesus and his disciples. This dialogue describes

*See Robert J. Miller, "The Gospels That Didn't Make the Cut," *BR*, August 1993.
†For a review of this discovery, see Birger A. Pearson, "Judas Iscariot Among the Gnostics," *BAR*, May/June 2008.

BIBLIOTECA APOSTOLICA VATICANA

Early Copy of 2 Peter. *This third- or fourth-century papyrus manuscript written in Greek is the earliest known copy of 2 Peter. Originally composed in the second century by an author claiming to be the apostle Peter, the Second Epistle of Peter was likely intended to counter Gnostic strands in the early Christian movement. The letter was widely adopted as part of the New Testament canon by the fourth century.*

in detail the process of the incarnation, predicts the second coming in the "hundred and fiftieth year," emphasizes the reality of the resurrection and judgment on sinners. Its polemical aims are clear, for the reminiscences are said to be composed to counter the teachings of false epistles of Simon (Magus) and Cerinthus, often regarded as the earliest Gnostics.

At least one of the works eventually included in the canon of the New Testament may have been composed as part of the debate with Gnosticism that developed in Alexandrian circles in the mid-second century. The clearly pseudepigraphical 2 Peter appeals to Peter's authority as an eyewitness of Jesus to condemn dangerous "false teachers," who made questionable use of Paul's letters. In response, 2 Peter insists on a hierarchy of religious values in which knowledge (*gnosis*) and ascetical practice are subordinated to love (2 Peter 1:4–7). This text, unlike the Gnostics, affirms traditional eschatological hopes (2 Peter 3:8).

The Second Epistle of Clement was also composed around the mid-second century, perhaps in Alexandria.[122] The work is not an epistle, nor does it have any explicit reference to Clement. It is a hortatory treatise, calling for repentance, a life of virtue and loyalty to the Church. It strongly defends the reality of Jesus' incarnation and bodily resurrection, doctrines called into question by some Gnostics. The text illustrates the process of theological polemic that took place in the second century. It contains traditional sayings of Jesus, some of which are not found in the canonical Gospels.

A principal adversary of Marcion and the Gnostics was Justin Martyr, whose *Dialogue with Trypho* has already been mentioned. He also wrote a treatise on heresies, criticizing the Marcionites and perhaps the Valentinians as well.[123] Unfortunately, the work has not survived. What has survived, in his *First* and *Second Apologies*, is Justin's Christological reflection on Christ as the Word (*Logos*) or Reason of God.

Justin's notion of Christ as the *Logos* may owe something to John's gospel, although he never explicitly cites it. Justin may also have been influenced by Hellenistic Jewish speculation, like that of the first-century Alexandrian Jewish philosopher Philo.[124] The concept of the *Logos* enabled Justin to make several moves as he wrestled with the fundamental theological issues raised by belief in Christ. On the one hand, he could rationalize the Christian affirmation of the deity of Jesus. Taking his cue from Stoic theories of language, he could affirm that the Son was the outward expression (the *logos prophorikos*) of the thought (the *logos endiathetos*) of the Father.[125] The concept of the *Logos* also enabled Justin to explain the continuity of Christianity with the entire history of humankind. Again relying on a Stoic notion—rational principles "sown" like a seed (*logos spermatikos*) in all matter, a sort of DNA code that makes development and growth possible—Justin argues that the Son is a principle of rationality "sown" throughout human history but "brought to fruition" with the incarnation.[126] In these notions we see the beginnings of a speculative theology, that is, a systematic attempt to restate the meaning of Christian faith in a new set of categories.

Rise of asceticism in Syrian Christianity

Gnosticism was not the only problematic development in the second century. The Syrian East in the later years of the second century was home to a version of Christianity that pursued asceticism to extremes that were sometimes viewed with suspicion elsewhere. Around 177 C.E., Tatian, a pupil of Justin, who left Rome for his native Syria after his master's execution, composed a strident apologetic work called the *Oration Against the Greeks*, bidding a less than fond farewell to Greek culture.[127] Tatian also composed a harmony of the four Gospels, the *Diatessaron*, that remained extremely influential in the Syriac-speaking world, where it was widely used at least until the fourth century.[128] Unfortunately the work has perished apart from a small Greek fragment and traces that survive in later gospel harmonies both East and West.[129]

Heresiologists claim that Tatian professed a doctrine similar to that of Valentinus.[130] Yet what was objectionable, especially for later orthodoxy, was not so much his doctrine but the lifestyle he espoused—that is, a radically ascetical form of Christianity known as Encratism that even forbade marriage.[131]

Another example of the Encratism for which Tatian stood is *The Book of Thomas the Athlete* (Thomas is an "athlete" or "contender" because of his struggle for mastery over passion), a document found in the Nag Hammadi codices. This text vigorously condemns the "blazing fire" of sexuality and provides further evidence of the extreme views on sexual matters popular in Syria at this time.[132] It urges disciples to escape the bond of desire that "has fettered them with its chains and bound all their limbs with the bondage of lust." The asceticism of early Syrian Christianity continues in the Acts of Thomas, which advocates strict sexual continence.[133]

Another element of eastern Christianity rejected Paul and gentile Christianity. An anonymous Christian novel composed in the Syrian East in the early third century purports to recount experiences of the bishop with Peter on the latter's journey to Rome. The work, which survives only in fourth-century editions, the *Pseudo-Clementine Homilies* and the *Recognitions*, constitutes one of the most vivid documents of Jewish Christianity of the period.[134] Peter here proclaims a Christ who is the "true prophet" (*Homilies* 1.19.4); Peter's great adversary, Simon Magus, becomes a transparent cypher for Paul, who preaches a false gospel (*Homilies* 2.17.4).

Irenaeus and ecclesiastical orthodoxy

A comprehensive vision of Christian doctrine emerges toward the end of the second century in the work of Bishop Irenaeus of Lyons, in Gaul, who assumed the leadership of the community after a major persecution in 177 C.E.[135] Although Lyons was a provincial city, Irenaeus played a significant role in the empire-wide network of Christian leaders. He composed, among several other works,[136] a treatise *Against the Heresies,*[137] in which he sets the Valentinian Gnostic movement in a larger context and catalogues numerous Gnostic groups and their literary products. Irenaeus goes on to offer a thorough critique of Gnostic theology, articulating the principles on which ecclesiastical orthodoxy was being based. The first was scripture. Although Irenaeus does not have a complete list of the books that eventually became the canonical New Testament,[138] he insists on the importance of the four Gospels as the heart of the collection. His arguments for four—no more, no less—are highly artificial. For example, he associates the four Gospels with the four figures of Ezekiel's visions (lion, calf, man, eagle).[139]

A scriptural canon was important in defining what was orthodox, since it excluded appeals to secret traditions or apocryphal gospels. Yet, for Irenaeus, scripture by itself was not sufficient, because the text could be interpreted in many ways. What guaranteed correct interpretation was the ecclesiastical structure, consisting of a succession of bishops reaching back to the apostles.[140] The hierarchical organization supervised the liturgical tradition, where the ordinary Christian experienced the process of the formation of orthodoxy. Especially important was the baptismal liturgy; there the initiand would be asked a series of questions about God, Jesus, the Spirit, the Church and the Christian's hope for the future.[141] This question and response procedure eventuated in the "rules of the faith," or summaries of belief, to which Irenaeus alludes and which formed the basis for most formal creeds.[142]

For Irenaeus, scripture, structures founded on the apostles and formal statements of belief or creeds were the pillars of orthodoxy. According to Irenaeus, they taught that God acted in human history through Jesus, who "recapitulated" or restored God's original intention for humankind.[143] Through the incarnation of the Son of God, it was possible for humans to be in communion with God and share divine incorruptibility.[144]

Rome as the center of theological debate

Rome became increasingly significant as a center of Christian theological debate in the late second and early third centuries. At the heart of these debates was the problem posed for traditional monotheism by the claim that Jesus is the Son of God. Some Christian teachers—labeled "dynamic monarchians"—rejected the pagan charge that Christians believed in two gods.[145] They explained their faith by affirming that Jesus was a human being on whom the power (*dynamis* in Greek) of God had descended at his baptism. He was thus an "adopted" Son of God, and their position is occasionally known as "adoptionism." Christians of this monarchian persuasion apparently established an independent community and elected as their bishop a presbyter named Natalius, whom they paid 150 denarii a month. In him we find the first recorded instances of an "anti-pope" and an ecclesiastical salary.[146]

Another Christian teacher named Noetus, originally from Smyrna in Asia Minor, then active in Rome, preserved the unity or "monarchy" of God by denying any real distinction between the Father and Christ. The divine element in Jesus was simply a "mode" of the one God.[147] Sabellius, who also taught this doctrine, was excommunicated from the Roman congregation under Pope Callistus (217–222 C.E.).[148] Teachers like Noetus and Sabellius were derisively dubbed Patripassionists, since they seemed to affirm that in Jesus' crucifixion, God the Father had suffered and died. Theologians concerned with the Trinity in the third century constantly took as a starting point a denial of this position, regularly known as Modalism or Sabellianism.

Clement of Alexandria

Theologians in the Greek East continued to wrestle with the legacy of Gnosticism. The most prominent was Clement of Alexandria, who headed the catechetical school (where new Christians received basic instruction in the faith) of the Egyptian metropolis in the last decade of the second century. Early in the third century, a persecution of Christians erupted and Clement left Egypt for Cappadocia, where his pupil Alexander was bishop. Clement died there in approximately 215 C.E.

With Clement, "orthodox" Alexandrian Christianity finally achieves forceful literary expression. Clement's major surviving works constitute a trilogy devoted to the explanation of the principles that governed his educational program. The first, the *Exhortation to the Greeks,*[149] uses a form familiar to Greek philosophy, the "protreptic discourse," a discourse that is designed to encourage the audience to "convert" to the author's school. The form is as significant as the content. Clement, like other major Alexandrian teachers, was committed to the appropriation of philosophy for the service of Christianity. The *Exhortation,* like second-century apologies, appealed to the presence of the divine *Logos* (or Reason) active throughout history and finally incarnated in Jesus.

Clement's second important treatise continues to play with this notion. The *Paedagogus* ("The Tutor")[150] discusses the role of the divine *Logos* in bringing people to moral and spiritual perfection, doing, that is, what Clement and other Christian educators considered their own task.

The eight rambling books of Clement's *Stromateis* conclude his trilogy.[151] The title may be translated "Carpets" or "Miscellanies" and resembles other learned but loosely structured works of the period. Here Clement delicately threads his way between the ecclesiastical factions of Alexandria. He defends the use of Greek philosophy by Christian theologians against the simpler believers who rejected such sophistication as dangerous to the faith. Faith, however, remains supreme, and philosophy only prepares for it. Through his insistence on faith, Clement resists the exaltation of knowledge by Gnostics who have only "falsely called knowledge." True *gnosis* is to be found among Christians who cultivate the virtues of faith and charity. Clement not only rejects the theoretical claims of the Gnostics, but also some of their extreme ascetical practices. Thus, he defends the importance of marriage against an ideal of celibacy. He insists that marriage aims not only at procreation, but at the welfare of the married couple.

Heresiological works of Tertullian

Another eloquent spokesman for the faith and a trenchant polemicist was the North African Tertullian.[152] Born around 170 C.E., he engaged in his vigorous literary activity between 196 and 212 C.E. His earliest writings, which appeared around 196 C.E., include apologies that defend Christians and denounce pagan immorality. Like Justin, he wrote a treatise *Against the Jews*, indicating that the rivalries between Christian and Jewish communities extended to North Africa. Like Irenaeus, he composed heresiological works. *On the Prescription of Heretics*, written in 203 C.E., uses legal conceits to argue that heretics have no basis on which to argue for their doctrine. More positively, Tertullian, like Irenaeus, argues that the credal "rule of faith" and the "apostolic succession" guarantee orthodoxy.[153] His later *Against the Valentinians* and *Against Marcion* (written between 206 and 208 C.E.) focus on the major heresies of the second century, although the former is more satire than argument.

In refuting his opponents, Tertullian engages in serious theological analysis. In *Against Hermogenes* he treats the doctrine of creation, defending the position that God created from nothing. In *On the Soul* he argues that the soul is corporeal and created with the body; hence, it does not preexist, nor does it transmigrate, as Platonists and some Gnostics held. In *On the Flesh of Christ* he insists on the reality of the incarnation and rejects docetic notions of a purely spiritual body of Jesus. In *On the Resurrection of the Dead* he defends the analogous position about the believer's resurrected body against those who, like the Gnostics, denied or severely qualified belief in a corporeal resurrection.[154] In *Against Praxeas*, he argues against the monarchian position, popular in Rome in the early third century, that denied any substantial distinction between Father and Son in the godhead.[155] Tertullian's response to the monarchian position, which insisted on the unity of "nature" but distinction of "persons" within the Trinity, provided categories that would later define orthodox theology.

Origen

By far the most significant Christian intellectual of the third century was Clement's successor, Origen (c. 185–253 C.E.).[156] Born in Alexandria, he became an ardent enthusiast for the faith. The story is told that he tried to follow his father Leonidas to martyrdom in the persecution of 203 C.E., but was prevented when his mother hid his clothes. The earnest youth would not appear naked and so escaped martyrdom. Since his father's property had been confiscated, Origen supported himself by teaching, while he practiced a life of rigorous asceticism. According to one account, Origen went so far as to take Matthew 19:12 literally and castrated himself.[157] Shortly after his father's death he assumed responsibility for the catechetical school at Alexandria, which he headed until 230 C.E. He rapidly acquired a reputation for theological acumen and was even called upon to resolve controversies outside Egypt. His travels brought him to Palestine, Arabia, Antioch, Rome and even an audience with the emperor's mother.[158]

Demetrius, bishop of Alexandria, objected to the fact that Origen, a layman, had preached before Palestinian bishops. In 231 C.E., however, two of those bishops—Alexander of Jerusalem and Theoctistus of Caesarea—ordained him. This led to a definitive break with Demetrius, who excommunicated him. Origen left Alexandria, where the school was taken over by his assistant, and future bishop, Heraclas. Thereafter, Origen was headquartered in Caesarea, where he conducted a school for theological studies. He continued to travel as a theological consultant. Origen appears not only as a master of theological reasoning, but also an individual with pastoral sensitivity. He finally died at Tyre in 253 or 254 C.E. as a result of tortures inflicted during the persecution of the emperor Decius.

Origen's literary output was astonishing for its range and depth. As a Christian apologist, he composed a lengthy refutation of the philosopher Celsus.[159] As a biblical scholar, he produced an enormous reference work, the *Hexapla,* which compared six versions of the text of the Old Testament in parallel columns. He was also concerned with issues of interpretation and composed numerous homilies and commentaries, including treatments of John and Romans.[160] As a pastoral theologian, he wrote tracts *On Prayer,* and an *Exhortation to Martyrdom.*[161] As a systematician, he produced *On First Principles;*[162] this text presents a comprehensive vision of the drama of salvation, of the process of devolution from and return to God.

Origen was convinced that all rational beings, angels as well as human beings, are endowed by their Creator with freedom of choice. This helps explain the human condition. By a free act of will some angels refused to serve God and "fell." This position contrasts with the Gnostic understanding of a fall within the godhead itself. The doctrine also helps to explain the union of humanity and divinity in Christ; Jesus' soul, which, like all human souls, preexisted his birth, freely chose from all eternity to contemplate the eternal Reason (*Logos*) that is the Son of God. Finally, because all rational creatures are endowed with free will, it is possible even for some of the worst fallen angels to choose God in the end, an optimistic notion that scandalized many of Origen's critics.

While Origen was interested in theological speculation, he was above all concerned with the interpretation of scripture, the source of revealed wisdom. According to Origen, scripture can have a variety of senses.[163]

Origen's legacy had enormous influence. His principles of interpreting scripture were assumed by most Greek patristic authors. His complex doctrinal position, however, had a more checkered afterlife. Origen's understanding of the second person of the Trinity—the *Logos* or Son—contained elements that could easily be appropriated by rival theologies of the next century. He insisted that the Son was eternally generated by the Father.[164] Theologians such as Athanasius of Alexandria, the great fourth-century defender of orthodoxy, would also insist on this point. Yet, like most theologians who used the notion of the *Logos*, Origen maintained that the Son was in some sense subordinate to the Father.[165] This position, carried to its extreme, would mark the Arian side of fourth-century debates (see pp. 290–293).[166]

Dionysius, a pupil of Origen and bishop of Alexandria (248–265 C.E.), played a leading role in ecclesiastical affairs in the third century. He headed the Alexandrian catechetical school after Origen's successor, Heraclas, had become bishop, then succeeded him in that episcopal post. The extant fragments of his works, preserved primarily by another Origenist, Eusebius, attest both the intellectual and pastoral skills he had learned from Origen.

While Dionysius illustrates the continuing influence of Origen's sophisticated theological program in Alexandria, other factors were at work in the hinterland. Late in the third century certain individuals in Egypt committed to an ascetical lifestyle, which had long been popular in various Christian communities, began a process of "withdrawal" (*anachoresis*) from society and thus became the first "anchorites" or solitary monks. The paradigm for such people is often said to be Antony, whose biography was written by Athanasius, the fourth-century patriarch of Alexandria.[167] The situation was more complex than the heroic literary portrait suggests, but that a new style of Christian asceticism began to develop in Egypt in the late third century is clear.[168]

The last years of the third century saw the emergence of critics of Origen, such as Methodius, bishop of Olympus, an erudite scholar and literary artist. His *Symposium* (or *Banquet*) mimicked Plato's classic dialogue on love, but celebrated the Christian ideal of chastity.[169] In other works, he refutes elements of Origen's thought, his notions of the preexistence of the soul and the spiritual character of the resurrected body.[170] Methodius met the fate that was denied Origen and perished as a martyr in 311 C.E.

Confrontation with Rome

For a movement that was to dominate the Roman Empire, Christianity began inauspiciously—with the execution of its founder as a Roman criminal. That shady past, along with the rejection by Christians of significant elements of Greco-Roman religion, produced suspicions and hostilities that were not easily overcome. We have already seen in the work of some of the later authors of the New Testament, particularly Luke-Acts and the deutero-Pauline epistles, a concern to reach some accommodation with society. Not all Christians in Asia Minor in the late first century approved of such tactics.

The Book of Revelation (or the Apocalypse) seethes with vehement hostility toward Rome.[171] Drawing on the rich symbolic language of Jewish prophetic and apocalyptic literature[172] and on Hellenistic myth, John the seer*[173] creates a tapestry of vivid images. The work's surrealistic tableaux delivers a message of warning and of consolation for Christian churches in the Roman province of Asia in the last decade of the first century. John urges Christians to resist the threats of the "great beast from the sea" (Revelation 13:1–10)—a symbol of Roman imperial might, and the blandishments of "the beast from the land" (Revelation 13:11–18)—a symbol of local magnates who supported Roman power. The seer assures his readers that, despite trials and tribulations, they may be confident of ultimate victory, because the evil at work in Roman oppression has already been overcome. The "blood of the lamb" (Revelation 12:11) has conquered the transcendent source of evil and has inaugurated God's earthly reign. The fact that oppression continues means that mopping up operations are still underway, but Christians can anticipate the imminent realization of the divine kingdom (Revelation 19:11–22:5).

Interpretation of Revelation's imagery occasioned debate throughout antiquity. Eventually, teachers such as Origen, Eusebius and Augustine understood the thousand-year-long (millennial) kingdom of the saints (Revelation 20:4–6) to be a symbol for the Church itself. Yet many, including Justin and Irenaeus, took the promised kingdom literally.†

Revelation lavishes special concern on those who suffer and die for their testimony to Jesus. Ignatius of Antioch, if he knew the work, would certainly have approved. The actual number of people who had suffered by the time of composition is unclear. Revelation mentions at least one individual by name—Antipas (Revelation 2:13). Other Christians in Asia Minor followed in his footsteps.

Correspondence between the emperor Trajan and Pliny, the Roman governor of Bithynia, provides an interesting picture of Roman policies

*The author of the Book of Revelation, who claimed experience of an ecstatic vision (Revelation 1:10) is clearly named John (Revelation 1:4,9). He makes no claim to be John the son of Zebedee. His style and theological perspective are quite different from that of the Fourth Gospel. See "Who Was John?" sidebar to "Ephesus: Key to a Vision in Revelation," *BAR*, May/June 1993.

†On whether the Book of Revelation was intended literally, see Adela Yarbro Collins, Biblical Views, "Is Hershel Doomed to the Lake of Fire?" *BAR*, January/February 2011.

toward Christian martyrs.[174] Upon assuming his position as governor around 110 C.E., Pliny was confronted with the problem of people who had been denounced as Christians. He investigated the matter and found the Christians to be harmless. They gather, he reported, once a week and "sing hymns to Christ as to a God."* Nonetheless, when some Christians proved stubborn in their adherence to what Pliny considered a vile superstition, he ordered them executed. He then wrote to Trajan to review his actions. Trajan approved, although he discouraged Pliny from accepting anonymous accusations or from actively searching out Christians. Hadrian later confirmed the essentials of Trajan's policy.[175] There were oddities in the official policy, as later apologists pointed out.[176] The mere fact of being a Christian, a member of an unauthorized association, was itself a crime, whether or not Christians performed any of the acts of which they were often accused. Yet imperial policy at this period was not to search actively for members of the group. Until the middle of the third century, persecution of Christians was generally occasioned by local factors and not the imperial government.[177]

Christian apologists,[178] beginning in Hadrian's reign, defended the faith. A certain Quadratus addressed a defense to Hadrian when he visited Athens in 124 C.E. From it a small fragment survives, emphasizing the reality of Jesus' miracles.[179] Another early apologist, Aristides, defended Christianity as the true heir of Jewish monotheism and its strict morality.[180]

Justin Martyr as Christian apologist

Justin Martyr, whom we have already encountered as a polemicist and heresiologist, plays an important role as a spokesman for Christians at Rome in the mid-second century. In 156 C.E., the aged bishop of Smyrna, Polycarp, was martyred.[181] A graphic account of his martyrdom survives.[182] Justin's two apologies[183] may have responded to this event.

Justin, like many second-century apologists, refutes anti-Christian slanders; on the offensive, he attacks traditional Greco-Roman religion as superstitious and defends the rationality of his own faith. The stereotypical slanders against Christians were obvious misperceptions or malicious distortions. According to their critics,[184] Christians partook of "Thyestian" banquets, named for the mythical figure who ate his own children. Christians also reportedly engaged in incestuous "Oedipal" sexual practices, named for the tragic figure who married his mother.[185] The charges of cannibalistic feasts

*For an example of an early house church where such gatherings would have taken place, see Vassilios Tzaferis, "Inscribed 'To God Jesus Christ': Early Christian Prayer Hall Found in Megiddo Prison," *BAR*, March/April 2007.

were no doubt occasioned by reports of Christians "eating the flesh" of Jesus and "drinking his blood." The charges of sexual misconduct arose from their practice of having "love feasts"—nocturnal meals in which men and women mingled and exchanged "sacred kisses" with their "brothers and sisters." Justin and later apologists ridiculed such charges and asserted the lofty morality of the Christian community, while condemning the immorality of pagan life.[186] When Christianity was charged with being an innovation, Justin and his fellow apologists further argued that Christian faith was the authentic continuation of Israel. They turned the tables on their critics and, following the polemics of Hellenistic Jews, argued that Greek culture was derivative: Plato learned all he knew from the Torah![187] Finally, against the charge that Christians were irrational, Justin boldly claimed that they were the followers of Reason (the *Logos*) incarnate.

Justin's apologies aimed to prevent the persecution of Christians but in that they were unsuccessful. Justin himself was denounced by Crescens, a rival Cynic philosopher. As a result, Justin was hauled before the city prefect, tried and executed along with several companions around 165 C.E. The account of the trial has been preserved as one of the first "Acts" of the Christian martyrs.[188]

Early Christian martyrs

It is probably in Justin's later years that Roman Christians established memorials to the apostles Peter and Paul who had been martyred in Rome. One of these "trophies," as a third-century Roman presbyter called them,[189] has been uncovered under St. Peter's basilica in the Vatican. Despite speculation that it marks Peter's actual grave, it is no more than a memorial of the area where he was believed to have died.*[190] It is, however, testimony to the solidarity that second-century Roman Christians felt with the martyrs of the first generation.

The martyrdoms of Polycarp and Justin were not part of a systematic campaign against Christians; neither were they totally isolated incidents. In both East and West, the reign of the emperor Marcus Aurelius (161–180 C.E.) witnessed considerable hostility toward Christians. Occasional acts of persecution, with the involvement of imperial authorities, were supported by the attitude of educated pagans who continued to treat Christianity with disdain or revulsion. The satirist Lucian ridiculed Christians, and viewed them as religious fanatics typified by one Peregrinus Proteus, who committed

*See Julie Skurdenis, "Destinations: City of the Dead," *Archaeology Odyssey*, March/April 2001; Jack Finegan, "The Death and Burial of St. Peter," *BAR*, December 1976.

SCALA/ART RESOURCE, NY

High Altar of St. Peter's Basilica. *Based on the Gospel of Matthew's account of Jesus saying, "You are Peter, and on this rock I will build my church" (Matthew 16:18), the Roman Church perceived the martyred disciple Simon Peter as the precursor of the authority of the bishops. Peter was revered by first-century Christians for his leadership and martyrdom. Around 165 C.E., the Roman Christians established a memorial to him that was uncovered in the early 1940s beneath the high altar of St. Peter's basilica in Rome (pictured). It is probably not the site of Peter's actual grave, but rather the area where he was believed to have died.*

a spectacular suicide by immolating himself at the Olympic games in 165 C.E.[191]

In the winter of 174–175 C.E., while Marcus was subduing the Quadi and other Danubian tribes, Avidius Cassius, one of his leading generals and legate of the East, led an unsuccessful revolt. After this revolt was suppressed, several Christian apologists appeared, eager to show their loyalty to Rome and its emperor and at the same time to refute the slanders that enemies continued to raise. One Apolinaris of Hierapolis in Phrygia is remembered for claiming that a fortuitous thunderstorm that saved Marcus's legions in his northern campaigns was the result of the prayers of Christian soldiers.[192] The message is clear: Christians are no danger to Rome; they are instead the cause of its security.

Sardis, the ancient capital of Lydia, was the home of Bishop Melito, who had traveled to Palestine to inquire about the works rightly included in the canon of the Old Testament.[193] Melito also composed apologies, only fragments of which survive. Among these, however, appear sentiments frequently echoed in subsequent apologies: that the Christian "philosophy" arose providentially under Augustus, that it grew with the empire and that only emperors generally recognized to be wicked had persecuted the Church.[194] Melito's approach was probably designed to appeal to the storied "clemency" of the philosophical emperor, Marcus Aurelius.

Another apologist, Athenagoras of Athens, addressed his *Embassy* to Marcus and Commodus, Marcus's son and co-regent in his last years. Like all the apologists, Athenagoras exalts the lofty morality of Christians. His work also displays an openness to Greek philosophy, especially Platonism, and to Greek literature, which he mined to support Christian doctrine. All of this is not surprising in a university town like Athens.

Another outpost of Christianity produced a crop of martyrs late in the reign of Marcus. In 177 C.E. persecution erupted at Lugdunum, modern Lyons, on the Rhone River. Surviving Christians sent an account of the affair to churches in Asia; that dramatic record was preserved by Eusebius.[195] Christians at Lyons were subject not simply to mob violence or random denunciation. Local Roman officials now engaged in active prosecution of the illicit religion. Many Christians were arrested and tortured, including the bishop Pothinus. Those who remained faithful, called "noble athletes," experienced a variety of grisly tortures, which the account records in detail.

Near the beginning of the reign of the emperor Commodus (180–192 C.E.), a Christian community surfaces in North Africa. As at Lyons, the evidence again involves persecution. Christians from the village of Scillium near the provincial capital of Carthage were brought before the governor, Vigellius Saturninus, on July 17, 180, and executed when they refused to take an oath by the emperor's "Genius."[196] The deaths of these Scillitan martyrs mark the first skirmish in a long battle between the native church and the imperial government in North Africa.

Tertullian, inspired by the courage of such martyrs, wrote numerous tracts on particular aspects of appropriate Christian behavior. Should Christians attend games and shows (*On the Spectacles*)? Should Christians engage in professions that involve intimate contact with pagan cults, such as the teaching of rhetoric or the military (*On Idolatry*)? What should Christian women wear (*On Women's Dress, On the Veiling of Virgins*)? What are appropriate marital practices for Christians (*On Monogamy*)? In these and similar works, Tertullian showed himself a puritan, with an ideal of the Church as an undefiled community, radically distinct from its depraved environment.

In the early third century (202 C.E.), two young women, a 22-year-old nursing mother named Vibia Perpetua and her personal slave Felicitas, vehemently rejected the family and society that had nurtured them; they became Christians. As a result, they were imprisoned, tortured and killed. The account of their imprisonment, torture and death, written soon after their execution, is a gem of martyrological literature.[197] Their exemplary testimony to the faith served as a model for Christians in the following century.

The martyrs, incidentally, were by no means all orthodox Christians. For example, Perpetua and Felicitas, who died so bravely for the faith, were probably adherents of Montanism.

Tensions between Christians and imperial authorities mounted in the third century. The tolerant Severan dynasty that had ruled the empire from 193–235 C.E. was followed by a half century of military rulers, none of whom enjoyed a long or peaceful reign. Not all were inimical to Christianity, and Eusebius transmits a report, probably erroneous, that at least one, Philip "the Arab" (244–249 C.E.), was a Christian.[198] At mid-third century, however, hostile attitudes toward Christians prevailed, and for most of the 250s C.E. there was considerable pressure on the Church.

Philip's successor, Decius, concerned to halt the disintegration of traditional Roman society, launched the first empire-wide persecution of those who refused to show allegiance to Rome and its traditions by sacrificing to her gods. Some Christians refused and were martyred, including Fabian, bishop of Rome. Others, including leading bishops, such as Cyprian in North Africa and Gregory Thaumaturgos in Pontus, went into hiding. Some Christians did not sacrifice, but purchased documents (*libelli*) certifying that they had done so.[199] On the other hand, many Christians simply complied with the law.

Decius fell in battle with the Goths south of the Danube in 251 C.E., inaugurating two years of a power struggle. When Valerian emerged victorious in 253 C.E., the persecution temporarily ceased, but was rekindled in 257 C.E. as the emperor, desiring a unified empire under divine protection, prepared for a new Persian campaign. This phase of persecution cost the lives of Pope Sixtus in Rome and Cyprian in Carthage.

After Valerian fell captive to the Persians in 260 C.E., his son Gallienus reversed his father's policy and allowed Christians to go about their business.[200]

With the accession of Diocletian (284–305 C.E.) to the throne, the period of political turmoil that marked the mid-third century ended. Diocletian initiated sweeping reforms in imperial administration. The most important was the institution of the tetrarchy: The empire was divided into two halves, each of which was ruled by a senior emperor, the Augustus, assisted by a junior emperor, the Caesar. In the East, Diocletian was aided by Galerius; in the West, Maximian was assisted by Constantius. This cumbersome arrangement brought stability to the realm and breathing space for recuperation. During most of Diocletian's tenure, the Christian movement continued to enjoy peace. Christians were tolerated and their churches flourished. The persecution that erupted in February of 303 was, for this reason, all the more shocking.[201] The abrupt change in imperial attitudes was especially advocated by Diocletian's associate Galerius who revered Roman tradition and perhaps saw the policy as a way of gaining political leverage against Constantius and his son. Galerius, who became eastern Augustus when Diocletian abdicated on May 1, 305, continued in his war against the Church until shortly before his death, when, in April 311, he issued an edict reversing the policy of persecution.

Constantine—defender of the Christian faith

From 303 to 311 C.E., however, the persecution raged, at least in the East, and a long series of martyrs paid with their lives for their adhesion to the faith. Conditions were better in the West under Constantius, first the Caesar, then after 305 C.E., the Augustus. After his death in 306 C.E., a new political figure, even more favorable to Christians, emerged. Constantine, the son of Constantius, was raised at Diocletian's court. Constantine had served in Galerius's army and seemed to be destined for the purple, but was threatened by the maneuvers of Galerius. When Galerius and Constantius became Augusti, Galerius arranged the appointment of Caesars closely allied to him. At an opportune moment in 305 C.E., Constantine left the eastern court and rejoined his father in Britain. There the legions proclaimed him emperor—on July 25, 306. At that point, he controlled Britain, Gaul and Spain. With his western legions behind him, Constantine was accepted by Galerius as a Caesar, but Constantine's ambitions aimed higher. Shortly after Constantine's acclamation, Maxentius, the son of the former western Augustus, revolted and gained control over Italy and North Africa. Maxentius emulated Constantine and ended persecution in his domains in the winter of 306–307 C.E. Rivalry between Maxentius and Constantine continued until Constantine invaded Italy and was successful in a final confrontation that took place at the Milvian Bridge, a few miles north of Rome, on October 28, 312.

Before the battle, Constantine, claiming to have seen a vision, ordered his troops to affix a new symbol to their equipment, the *labarum*, which prominently featured the *chi-rho* monogram of Christ.[202] Constantine thus entered Rome and took control of the western empire, as the defender of the Christian faith.

In the East, Licinius, successor of Galerius, ruled in an unstable alliance with the eastern Caesar, Maximinus Daia, who briefly renewed the persecution of Christians in 312 C.E. Constantine and Licinius met at Milan in January 313 C.E., to formalize their relationship as Augusti. They agreed on the formal conclusion of persecution of Christians, extending throughout the empire the conditions that prevailed in the West. Once Licinius had defeated Maximinus (on May 1, 313) he sent to all eastern provincial governors copies of the decisions that he and Constantine had reached. This rescript has come to be known as the Edict of Milan.[203]

The rise of Constantine marked a major change in the relationship of the Church and the imperial government. Persecution was now a thing of the past. The Christian community was not simply tolerated but was protected. In 324 C.E. Constantine defeated Licinius. Henceforth, Constantine was in sole control of the empire; the relationship between the Church and the imperial government solidified further. That process, however, will be discussed in a subsequent chapter.

Eusebius of Caesarea, a major source of Christian history

In the early years of Diocletian (280–290 C.E.), Eusebius, our major source for the period and future bishop of Caesarea, was a theological student at Caesarea.[204] There he studied under the Origenist scholar Pamphilus. In the peaceful years before the great persecution, Eusebius began the apologetic writing that was to occupy him for most of his adult life. His major project at this time was an ambitious one, inspired perhaps by Origen's massive biblical study, the *Hexapla*. Eusebius was interested, however, not in philology but in history. In his *Chronicle*, he attempted to synthesize into tabular form the dates of all known historical kingdoms.[205]

Eusebius's *Chronicle* served as the basis for his major work, which was to undergo several revisions during his lifetime, the *Ecclesiastical History*. This began as a triumphal statement about the progression of Christianity until the time of Diocletian. The first seven books were probably completed in the early fourth century.[206] Eusebius later added to his history a version of his account of the great persecution, *The Martyrs of Palestine*.[207] Ultimately his *Ecclesiastical History* celebrated the triumph of Constantine over his enemies, including Licinius in 324 C.E. Eusebius, as bishop of Caesarea, continued to admire the emperor and celebrate his combination of the Church and the empire until they both died in the late 330s C.E.

Upon Constantine's victory, Eusebius hymned what he viewed as the dawn of a new age, when:

> All things were filled with light, and men, formerly downcast, looked at each other with smiling countenances and beaming eyes; with dancing and hymns in city and country alike they gave honor first of all to God the universal King, for this they had been instructed to do, and then to the pious Emperor with his sons beloved of God; old ills were forgotten and oblivion cast on every deed of impiety; present good things were enjoyed, with the further hope of those which were yet for to come.[208]

How far his hopes were realized will be the subject of Chapter VIII.

SIX

Judaism to the Mishnah: 135–220 C.E.

SHAYE J.D. COHEN

THE PERIOD COVERED BY THIS CHAPTER—FROM THE END OF THE Bar-Kosba* (or Bar-Kokhba) Revolt against Rome in 135 C.E. to the publication of the Mishnah by Rabbi Judah the Patriarch in about 200 or 220 C.E.—was the time of the *Pax Romana* ("The Roman Peace"). It included the reigns of the "good emperors"—Antoninus Pius, from 138 to 161 C.E., and Marcus Aurelius, from 161 to 180 C.E. In the words of Edward Gibbon in his classic *Decline and Fall of the Roman Empire,* this was "the period in the history of the world during which the condition of the human race was most happy and prosperous."[1] What was good for the rest of the world, however, was not necessarily good for the Jews—as some of the aftermath of the revolt of 132–135 C.E. illustrates.

Unfortunately, our information about the Jewish history of this period is both scanty and one-sided. Practically all the literary evidence is rabbinic—which means we hear much about the rabbis and their concerns, but little about non-rabbinic and Diaspora Jews, and virtually nothing about "political" events. In short, our sources do not allow us to write a complete history of the Jews and Judaism of the second and early third centuries.

*In various documents discovered in the Judean desert, Simeon writes his name "Simeon bar KSBA." The name was probably pronounced either "Kosba" or "Kosiba."

The effects of the war of 132–135 C.E.

With the fall of Bar-Kosba (or Bar-Kokhba) at Bethar in 135 C.E., the last Jewish revolt against Rome ended. The severity of this war and the intensity of the persecution that accompanied and followed it are subjects of scholarly debate. But even if the conflict was more a rebellion than a war and even if the persecution was not as ruthless or systematic as it has sometimes been portrayed, nevertheless the conflict clearly was a serious one that had serious consequences in both the long and short terms.

De-Judaization of Judea and Jerusalem

To punish the Jews for initiating yet another military action against the state—the third in 70 years—the Romans decided to de-Judaize their country. Jerusalem became a pagan city—renamed Aelia Capitolina.* According to various Christian sources, Jews were prohibited from entering the city, except on the 9th of Av, the national fast day commemorating the destruction of both the First (or Solomonic) Temple (destroyed by the Babylonians in 587/586 B.C.E.) and the Second Temple (destroyed by the Romans in 70 C.E.). Jews were permitted to enter the city only to lament these destructions.[2] This Christian tradition is not confirmed by Jewish sources and may well be an exaggeration, but the facts were bad enough. Perhaps a modest Jewish community was reestablished in Jerusalem in the latter part of the second century, but its presence could not change the fact that Jerusalem was no longer a Jewish city.[3]

The Romans also changed the official name of the country from Judea to Palestina. No longer was Israel the land of the Jews; it was the land of the Philistines, of which "Palestina" is the Greek equivalent.

This legal and administrative change reflected a demographic change as well. The Jewish population of the district of Judea (the area around Jerusalem) was severely diminished by the war (whether by death, capture or flight), and the Jewish population continued to decline (with occasional contrary growth spurts) in subsequent centuries. Few details are available, but the impression of decline is unmistakable.†[4] The center of Jewish life moved from Judea to the towns and villages in Galilee that had survived the war unscathed. Perhaps there was a modest revival of the Jewish population in Judea at the end of the second century and later,[5] but the overall trend is clear.

*See Hanan Eshel, "Aelia Capitolina: Jerusalem No More," *BAR*, November/December 1997.
†For representative archaeological evidence, see Boaz Zissu, "Village Razed, Rebel Beheaded: How Hadrian Suppressed the Second Jewish Revolt at Horvat 'Ethri," *BAR*, September/October 2007.

The weakening of the center

With the emergence of Galilee as a major center of Jewish life, the rabbinic leaders also moved there. From Judean towns and villages, and even from larger settlements like Yavneh and Lydda, they migrated north. Indeed, the first rabbinic literary works were redacted (that is, compiled and edited) in Galilee, not Judea.

Although in the short term the shift was from Judea to Galilee, in the long term the decline of Judea meant the decline of the entire land of Israel as the center of Jewish life (again, with occasional contrary growth spurts).

Even in the period preceding 70 C.E., when the Temple still stood and the high priest still officiated in all his splendor, the central Jewish authority in Jerusalem had no real control over the Jewish communities of the Diaspora. With the developments that began in 70 C.E. and continued thereafter—the destruction of the Temple, the dissolution of the authority of the priesthood, the transformation of Jerusalem into a pagan city, the cessation of Jewish pilgrimage to the central shrine and the decline of the Jewish population of the country—the communities of the Diaspora acquired ever greater opportunities to develop as centers of Jewish life in their own right.

According to a story preserved in the Talmudim,* Rabbi Hananiah, the nephew of Rabbi Joshua, fled to Babylonia after the Bar-Kosba Revolt and there attempted to intercalate the calendar.[6] Control of the calendar was of immense importance in Jewish life because calendar intercalation determined the days on which all religious observances, including those mandated in the holy scriptures, were observed. Calendar control thus involved the ultimate political authority in Judaism. During the Second Temple period (which ended in 70 C.E.), this authority was very probably vested in the high priest. In the period after 70 C.E., the rabbis arrogated this authority to themselves. In the story that appears in the Talmudim, Rabbi Hananiah, an emigré Judean scholar, tried to assert the supremacy of Babylonian Jewry by asserting its right (i.e., his own right while in Babylonia) to intercalate the calendar. His attempt was unsuccessful because it was several centuries too early. This authority remained for some time with the rabbis in the land of Israel (in Hebrew, *Eretz Yisrael*). But by the tenth century, Babylonia became the center of Jewish life, a position that would be inherited in turn by various North African and European Jewish communities, and the control of the calendar inexorably moved to Babylonia.[7] If Jerusalem had continued to exist as the

*Plural of Talmud. The Talmudim are two massive commentaries on the Mishnah, one written in the land of Israel between about 220 and 400 C.E., usually if erroneously called the "Jerusalem Talmud," and the other written in Babylonia between about 220 and 600 C.E., known as the Babylonian Talmud.

center of Jewish life and the seat of Jewish political authority, would these developments have taken place? Probably not, and even if they had, surely the configuration of authority would have been far different.

Impact on theology and practice

Many scholars have suggested that the defeat of 135 C.E. had a major impact on Jewish theology and practice. The evidence, however, comes almost exclusively from the Talmudim and assumes that the Talmudim reliably quote the opinions of rabbis who lived in the second century, long before the Talmudim were written. (The Talmud of the land of Israel [also known as the *Yerushalmi*, or Jerusalem Talmud, and as the Palestinian Talmud] was completed about 400 C.E. or somewhat earlier. The Babylonian Talmud [the *Bavli*], which would come to exercise greater authority in the history of Judaism, was completed about 600 C.E. or later.) Nevertheless, the talmudic evidence for theological change makes sense in the context of the post-Bar-Kosba period. We will consider a number of these post-Bar-Kosba theological developments.

- With the defeat of Bar-Kosba, who may have had messianic pretensions (or, at least, who may have been looked on as a messiah by some of his followers), the belief that eschatological deliverance was imminent was replaced by more realistic expectations. The Messiah would come, the wicked Roman Empire would be destroyed and the righteous would be vindicated—all this would surely happen, but it would happen later rather than sooner.
- Precisely when the Jews began to realize that their Temple would not be rebuilt anytime soon is a matter of debate, but the process clearly begins after 135 C.E. In the fourth century, under the emperor Julian, the Jews almost regained their Temple, but the initiative for that remarkable episode came from the emperor, not from the Jews.* In order to discomfit the Christians, Julian, the last pagan emperor of Rome, promised the Jews that he would rebuild their Temple. He died in battle, however, before the plan could be realized.
- With the defeat of Bar-Kosba, the Jews came to realize that the rebuilding of the Temple and the reassertion of their national independence were to be the work not of humanity but of God, and certainly not the work of a pagan king (like Julian—or even Cyrus, the Persian ruler who in the sixth century B.C.E. permitted the Jews to return from the Babylonian Exile and rebuild their Temple, the Second Temple). The Jews were to await the appointed

*Jeffrey Brodd, "Julian the Apostate and His Plan to Rebuild the Jerusalem Temple," *BR*, October 1995.

hour of their deliverance, which would be hastened not by military or political action but by study and living a life of Torah.

• In the Second Temple period, many Jews believed that the end time (the *eschaton*) would be accompanied by the appearance of not one but two messiahs. For example, texts among the Dead Sea Scrolls speak of "the messiahs of Aaron and Israel."[8] One passage in the Babylonian Talmud also reflects a belief in two messiahs, the messiah of the tribe of Judah and the messiah of the tribe of Ephraim.[9] What is striking about this talmudic passage, however, is that the messiah of Ephraim is a *failed* messiah.* He fights the gentiles in order to prepare the way for the messiah who is the son of David; but the messiah of Ephraim is killed in the process. This peculiar belief in a messiah who is killed while fulfilling his assigned task is probably a reflection not of Christian theology but of the disappointment felt after the defeat of 135 C.E. Bar-Kosba, the messiah of the tribe of Ephraim, was killed fighting the gentiles, but he prepared the way for the messiah of the tribe of Judah—sometime in the distant future—who will complete the process of initiating the *eschaton*.[10]

• Paradoxically, the decline of the Jewish character of Judea (and ultimately of the entire land of Israel) after the defeat of Bar-Kosba led to a kind of sanctification of the land. After 135 C.E., the rabbis living in the land of Israel began to speak of the special qualities of the land and the importance of dwelling there:

> The settlement of the land of Israel is equivalent to all the other commandments in the Torah ... Anyone who leaves the land [of Israel] at a time of peace and emigrates, is reckoned like an idolater ... Jews dwelling outside the land of Israel are idolaters.[11]

Such sentiments are absent from the traditions that rabbinic literature ascribes to the rabbinic masters before 135 C.E., but become more and more common in the generations after that date.[12] Rabbis who lived in Babylonia, on the other hand, clearly had a different view of the value of settling in the land of Israel—they obviously valued it less highly than rabbis living there—but even among the sages in Israel, the ideological and metaphysical importance of the land began to rise only when its importance in reality began to fall.

• The Jewish attitude toward martyrdom also changed after the Bar-Kosba

*New light on the doctrine of the dying messiah is perhaps cast by a mysterious and poorly preserved document that has only recently come to light. See Israel Knohl, "The Messiah Son of Joseph," *BAR*, September/October 2008.

defeat. The new attitude that emerged had an enormous impact on the responses of medieval Jewry toward Christian and Islamic persecutions.

To appreciate this change in attitude, we must go back to the successful Jewish revolt against the Seleucids in 167–164 B.C.E., which led to an independent Jewish state under the Hasmonean dynasty. That revolt featured both martyrs and martyrologies.[13] The first-century C.E. Jewish historian Josephus boasts that the Jews, unlike the Greeks, are ready, if necessary, to die for their laws and their sacred books, and Josephus is not alone in describing the martyr in glowing terms.[14] The Bar-Kosba war, too, had its share of martyrs.[15] This enthusiastic endorsement of martyrdom was tempered by rabbinic legislation in the wake of the Bar-Kosba Revolt. According to one opinion, martyrdom was justified only if a Jew was being compelled to commit murder, idolatry or fornication; other prohibitions could be violated in order to save one's life. According to another opinion, martyrdom was justified only if a Jew was being compelled to violate Jewish law *in public*; in such circumstances death was preferable to the violation of any commandment, even the most trivial.[16] This debate, which in effect limited the precise conditions under which martyrdom was permitted or required, would echo and re-echo throughout Jewish society of medieval Europe and the Levant, as the Jews deliberated their responses to Christian and Islamic persecutions.

• As we learned in the previous chapter, Hadrian's edict against circumcision was one of the major causes of the outbreak of the Bar-Kosba Revolt in 132 C.E. According to rabbinic accounts, during and after the war some Jews underwent an operation called epispasm to disguise their circumcision.[17] (This operation had also been practiced by some Jews under the influence of Hellenism in the second century B.C.E.) In an effort to halt such operations in the future, the rabbis after 135 C.E. ordained that *peri'ah* (the slitting of the inner lining of the foreskin) be part of the circumcision ritual, because the procedure renders epispasm extremely difficult. The ruling has had a continuing effect: To this day Jewish ritual circumcision includes *peri'ah.*[18]

• The end of the Bar-Kosba Revolt also marks the end of more than three centuries of Jewish militancy. During the period from the Maccabees (160s B.C.E.) to Bar-Kosba (132–135 C.E.), the Jews in both the land of Israel and the Diaspora mounted a number of military campaigns against the state, sometimes successful, sometimes not. Each of these campaigns had its own unique causes and circumstances, but what they had in common was their exceptional character. When the Jews were exiled to Babylonia in the first decades of the sixth century B.C.E., the prophet Jeremiah counseled them to:

> Build houses and live in them ... take wives and beget sons and

> daughters ... seek the welfare of the city to which [God] has exiled you and pray to the Lord in its behalf; for in its prosperity you shall prosper.
>
> (Jeremiah 29:4–7)

The Jews of Babylonia followed the prophet's advice, even after they returned to the land of Israel. The Jews had learned to live under foreign dominion, without their own national sovereignty. This tradition was broken by the Maccabees when they rebelled against the Seleucid king Antiochus IV and reestablished national sovereignty—until Rome imposed its rule in 63 B.C.E. Then came the disastrous defeats of 66–70 C.E., 115–117 C.E. and 132–135 C.E. Finally, the Jews once again realized the wisdom of a Jeremianic political stance. In the centuries after 135 C.E., the Jews both in the land of Israel and in the Diaspora occasionally became restive and rioted against the state, but they no longer mounted any large-scale or sustained military action. Not until the 20th century would Jews again resort to arms in order to control their own political destiny in their ancestral land. The defeat of Bar-Kosba was the defeat of Jewish militancy for the next 1,800 years.

The Jews and the state: 135–220 C.E.

Although the Jews were defeated in the war of 132–135 C.E., their struggle was not without accomplishments—for example, repeal of the prohibition against circumcision. The Roman emperor Antoninus Pius rescinded Hadrian's edict[19] and thenceforth the Jews were permitted to circumcise their sons without any interference from the state. Only the circumcision of slaves and proselytes would continue to be an issue well into Christian times.

The Romans must have recognized quickly that it was in their own interest to restore peace as soon as possible to the region; accordingly, they did not adopt punitive measures against the Jews. True, Judea was renamed *Palestina* (Palestine) and lost its Jewish character, and Jerusalem became a pagan city renamed Aelia Capitolina; perhaps the head-tax on Jews was increased (thus paralleling the institution of the *Fiscus Judaicus* after 70 C.E.).[20] But the Romans made no attempt to uproot Judaism from other parts of the land of Israel or to abolish Jewish privileges. The persecutions were over.

Nor is there any evidence that the Jews of the Diaspora were molested in the aftermath of the revolt. They continued living as before. Although the three emperors who followed the revolt (Antoninus Pius [138–161 C.E.], Marcus Aurelius [161–180 C.E.] and Commodus [180–192 C.E.]) were not particularly friendly to the Jews—indeed, Aurelius is reported to have had a decided antipathy toward them[21]—peace nevertheless reigned.

In intellectual circles, Judaism was not only tolerated, but even respected to a degree not documented previously. Galen, the second-century Greek physician, and Celsus, the second-century philosopher, wrote substantive critiques of Judaism as a philosophical system. Neither writer was attracted to Judaism, but each took its truth claims seriously.[22] Their contemporary, Numenius of Apamea, the Neoplatonist, went even further; for him Judaism and Greek philosophy were a fundamental unity, different expressions of the same truths. "For what is Plato but Moses speaking in Attic Greek?" is a remark attributed to Numenius.[23] Whether this new-found respect for Judaism was a consequence of the war of 132–135 C.E. or of the growing prominence of Christianity or of internal developments in the polytheisms of the late Roman Empire or of some combination of these is not clear. What is clear is that Judaism's status in the empire did not suffer as a result of the war.

Unfortunately, we have no reliable evidence documenting the Jewish adjustment to the new Roman peace. According to a story that appears in the Babylonian Talmud and other collections, Rabbi Eleazar ben Simeon, a figure of approximately this period, was appointed a tax collector by the Roman government and in that capacity supervised the execution of several people "who were worthy of being executed." The story recounts how a fellow rabbi criticized him for such behavior. If the story is true, it shows that some Jews in the land of Israel were willing to cooperate, even collaborate, with the Romans in the wake of the war of 132–135 C.E.[24] But is the story true? And, if it is true, was Rabbi Eleazar's action exceptional or typical? We do not know and we have no way of finding out. It is unfortunate for us that the Mishnah and other early rabbinic works (the tannaitic literature [See "Tannaim and Amoriam," p. 235]) were not interested in contemporary history and politics. These works have other (and, from their perspective, far more important) items on their agenda. But the best argument that the Jews in the land of Israel were able to reestablish a *modus vivendi* with the Romans is the argument from silence: There is no evidence for continued military conflict, resistance or persecution.[25]

The Severan dynasty: 193–235 C.E.

Following Marcus Aurelius, Commodus reigned as emperor from 180 to 192 C.E. His reign ended in strife and civil war. In 193 C.E., Septimius Severus, an energetic and competent soldier but an outsider in the world of imperial politics, declared himself emperor, thus inaugurating the Severan dynasty, which lasted until 235 C.E. Severus was of Punic stock, from the province of Africa (modern-day Libya and Tunisia). He was succeeded by his son Caracalla (211–217 C.E.). Our sources are ambiguous and even somewhat contradictory regarding the relations of Severus and Caracalla with the Jews. According to the *Life of Septimius Severus,* on his way to Alexandria in 195 C.E. Severus "conferred numerous rights upon the communities of Palestina" and "forbade conversion to Judaism under heavy penalties and enacted a similar law in regard to the Christians."[26] Whether the recipients of his generosity were Jewish or pagan communities (or both) is not stated. Many historians, however, doubt the authenticity of this prohibition against Jewish conversion, because neither it nor the companion prohibition of conversion to Christianity is attested anywhere else.[27]

When Severus visited Roman Palestina later in 195 C.E., the Jews of Kasyoun (in Upper Galilee) erected a Greek inscription "for the well-being of our masters, the emperors and Caesars, L. Septimius Severus ... and M. Aurelius Antoninus ..."[28] (Marcus Aurelius Antoninus was Caracalla's official name.) The cold face of the stone does not reveal the emotions or motives of the Jews who erected it: Were they terrified at the approach of an emperor whose presence did not bode well for the Jewish community, or were they delighted to receive an emperor whom they regarded as their friend and for whose safety and success they entertained only the fondest hopes? Severus had just spent the previous two years suppressing a rival claimant to the purple, a man who had apparently received substantial support from some segments of the Palestinian population (including some Jews?); perhaps the inscription was meant to reassure Severus of the loyalty of the Jews. In any event, the inscription is exceptional: Of the thousands of Jewish inscriptions that have been discovered in the land of Israel, whether Greek, Hebrew or Aramaic, it is the only one dedicated to the welfare of a reigning monarch. The feelings that motivated it must have been exceptional, too. Unfortunately, we do not know what those exceptional feelings were.

In 197 C.E. there was a "Jewish and Samaritan war"—at least according to the church father Jerome (c. 342–420 C.E.).[29] On its face, this passage could refer to a war between the Jews and the Samaritans or a war by Rome against the Jews and Samaritans. A passage in the *Life of Septimius Severus* may suggest the latter interpretation; the passage states that Severus "gave permission for his son (Caracalla) to celebrate a triumph; for the senate had decreed to him a triumph over Judea because of the successes achieved by Severus in Syria."[30] On the other hand, a triumph in or over Judea was not necessarily a triumph over the Jews, since the Jewish character of Judea severely declined in the second century, as we have already seen. If these passages demonstrate anything, they emphasize the paucity of historical data in the sources available to us, as well as their ambiguity. They help explain why it is so difficult to write a Jewish history of this period.

Aside from the questionable prohibition against conversion to Judaism, Severus and Caracalla enacted another significant law affecting Jews, the historicity of which is not in doubt. The new law permitted Jews to hold municipal offices, but also imposed on the Jews "liturgies such as should not transgress their religion."[31] "Liturgies" is a technical term for municipal or provincial offices that entailed substantial financial liabilities and were filled compulsorily. Thus this law granted the Jews a boon, but at a price: Jews could now achieve rank and power in their cities, but they could also be appointed to undesirable posts with financial liabilities from which they had previously been exempted. This law can be labeled neither pro-Jewish nor anti-Jewish; nevertheless, in operation it meant that urban Jews of both the land of Israel and the Diaspora could not escape the financial crisis of the empire in the third century.[32]

The evidence we have surveyed thus far concerning the relationship of the Jews to the state under the Severans is ambiguous. Some of it seems to imply either tension or at least no love lost between the Jews and the Severans. In contrast, Jerome (who flourished at the end of the fourth century and the beginning of the fifth) gives us a somewhat different view. In his commentary on Daniel 11:34 (the verse is "Now when they shall stumble they shall be helped with a little help"), Jerome writes that "Some of the Hebrews [i.e., Jews] understand these things as applying to the princes Severus [i.e., Septimius Severus] and Antoninus [i.e., Caracalla], who esteemed the Jews very highly."[33] According to this interpretation of the biblical verse, after the Jews "stumbled," that is, after the wars of 66–70 and 132–135 C.E., they were "helped with a little help" by the Severans. The identity of the Jews who proposed this interpretation is unknown, but they clearly remembered Severus and Caracalla favorably.

Perhaps this interpretation of Daniel originated among Jews who were admirers or supporters of the patriarchal house. As I shall discuss below, the office of the Jewish patriarchate attained new prominence and importance at the end of the second century and beginning of the third century C.E. This was the period of Rabbi Judah the Patriarch (Judah ha-Nasi, in Hebrew; he is also known as Judah the Prince), who seems to have enjoyed excellent relations with the Roman government and who, as evidence of his power, edited the Mishnah, the authoritative rabbinic legal text that left an indelible imprint on the character of Judaism from his time to ours. According to Jewish tradition, Rabbi Judah was of such outstanding significance that he is often referred to simply as "Rabbi." For admirers of Rabbi Judah, for students of the Mishnah and for supporters of rabbinic political power, the period of Severus and Caracalla was indeed "good for the Jews." Those, however, who opposed the patriarch,[34] who objected to his creation of the Mishnah[35] and who competed with the rabbis for political power[36] may have entertained a somewhat different view of these Roman emperors. In any case, the Severans supported Rabbi Judah for reasons of their own,[37] believing that he would promote peace and stability in the land and further Roman interests. There is no reason to think that they were disappointed in their choice.

Position of non-rabbinic Jews

The bulk of our evidence for the history of Jews and Judaism in the second century C.E. is provided by rabbinic literature; unfortunately, this literature does not represent all Jews or all varieties of Judaism. Rabbinic literature, beginning with the Mishnah, presents a decidedly partisan view of the world. Before we examine that view and the sources that document it, we should look at the life and culture of non-rabbinic Jews—those who lived in the Diaspora, those who lived in the urban areas of the land of Israel, the *'amme ha'aretz* (the people of the land) living in the Land of Israel and, lastly, the "heretics."

The Jews of the Diaspora

The Jewish communities of Alexandria in Egypt and in Cyprus and Cyrene were devastated in the revolt of 115–117 C.E. Other Jewish communities of the Roman Diaspora, however, remained vigorous throughout the second century. These included especially the community in Rome and numerous Jewish communities in Asia Minor (western Turkey). That Rome had a large and varied Jewish population is demonstrated by the Jewish catacombs,*[38] the underground burial chambers used by the community. The inscriptions in the catacombs reveal a community with at least 11 synagogues (or congregations), each with its own officers and leaders, a vigorous population and a robust Jewish identity. Other cities on the Italian peninsula (notably Ostia and Venosa) also had a Jewish presence, as archaeological remains (including a synagogue at Ostia) and inscriptions attest. But obviously these Jewish communities could not compete in importance with the one in Rome.

In Asia Minor Jewish communities also flourished. In the late second century, the Jewish community of Sardis, as archaeological excavations have shown, gained control of a large building that had been owned by the municipality and that fronted on the *agora* (the main city square). The Jews promptly converted this magnificent building into a synagogue.† This synagogue

*Letizia Pitigliani, "A Rare Look at the Jewish Catacombs of Rome," *BAR*, May/June 1980.
†John S. Crawford, "Multiculturalism at Sardis," *BAR*, September/October 1996.

HERSHEL SHANKS

Jewish Catacombs of Rome. *Jewish symbols and inscriptions, including this depiction of a menorah, adorn the catacombs used by Rome's Jewish community in the early centuries of the common era. The catacomb inscriptions document the existence of at least 11 different synagogues, proving that there was a robust and vibrant Jewish presence in imperial Rome.*

© ARCHAEOLOGICAL EXPLORATION OF SARDIS/HARVARD UNIVERSITY

Sardis Synagogue. *This large synagogue at the site of Sardis in modern-day Turkey was originally a Roman municipal building constructed next to the city's* agora, *or main square. Sardis's wealthy Jewish community acquired the more than 100-yard-long building in the late second century and converted it into an opulent synagogue that could hold 1,000 people. At the far left is the peristyle atrium that served as an entrance. Flanking the doorway into the large hall are two niches, one for Torah scrolls and the other for a menorah. Pillar bases parallel the walls. On the right by the semicircular apse is a large table that was probably used for the Torah scroll during public readings.*

ZEV RADOVAN/WWW.BIBLELANDPICTURES.COM

Sardis Synagogue. *The supports of the massive table showing eagles grasping a tied bundle of rods are in secondary use in the synagogue. They were originally part of a Roman monument.*

Sardis Synagogue. *This doorway flanked by two niches is the main entrance to the atrium. Fragments of mosaic decorations can be seen on the floor and walls.*

Sardis Synagogue. *This stylized marble carving found in the synagogue at Sardis represents a menorah with a* lulav *(palm branch) on the left,* shofar *(ram's horn) on the right and a rolled-up Torah scroll seen from the end. Similar plaques have been found at synagogues across Asia Minor, including Priene on the Ionian coast and, more recently, Andriake, the port city of ancient Myra on the Lycian coast.*

was longer than a football field and opulent even by modern standards. It obviously reflects a Jewish community that was both wealthy and influential.[39] At nearby Aphrodisias, a monolithic donors' inscription records the support that a Jewish charitable organization received from "the righteous gentiles" (Godfearers) of the city.* These gentiles included nine members of the city council, a fact that shows that this Jewish community also was well-connected, secure and thriving.[40] The exact date of the inscription is uncertain (many scholars now date it to the Byzantine period), but we may assume that other communities, too, whether in Asia Minor or elsewhere and whether in the second century or the third, enjoyed a peaceful and happy existence in their Diaspora setting.[41]

The linguistic barrier between Diaspora Jews and the rabbis of Israel

Although our evidence is meager, nothing in it suggests that the Jews of the Roman Diaspora looked to the rabbis of the land of Israel for guidance and support. Nor is there any indication that they practiced a rabbinic form of Judaism. Inscriptional remains of Diaspora Jewry contain virtually no references to rabbis; nor do other archaeological remains indicate the presence of Rabbinic Judaism.†[42]

The Jews of the Roman Diaspora spoke Greek; their knowledge of Hebrew ranged from meager to nonexistent. In the first century C.E., Philo, the most literate and learned Jew produced by the Roman Diaspora, studied the Torah in Greek, thought about it in Greek and wrote about in Greek. As far as is known, the Diaspora Jews were no more fluent in Hebrew in the second and third centuries than they had been in the first. The rabbis, however, made no effort to translate their teachings into Greek and had no interest in Greco-Jewish literature. Josephus, Philo and all the other extant works of Greco-Jewish literature were preserved by the Church, not by Rabbinic Judaism. The languages of Rabbinic Judaism were Hebrew and Aramaic. Diaspora Jews knew little if anything of either of these two languages, so they could not have been part of the world of the rabbis. Perhaps a few rabbis of the second and third centuries knew enough Greek to speak to the local governor or other

*See Louis H. Feldman, "The Omnipresence of the God-Fearers," *BAR*, September/October 1986; Robert Tannenbaum, "Jews and God-Fearers in the Holy City of Aphrodite," *BAR*, September/October 1986; and Robert S. MacLennan and A. Thomas Kraabel, "The God-Fearers: A Literary and Theological Invention," *BAR*, September/October 1986. For a more recent treatment, see Angelos Chaniotis, "Godfearers in the City of Love," *BAR*, May/June 2010.

†Doron Mendels, "Why Paul Went West: The Differences Between the Jewish Diasporas," *BAR*, January/February 2011.

COURTESY ANGELOS CHANIOTIS

Aphrodisias Inscription. *This 9-foot-tall marble pillar was probably used in the synagogue of Aphrodisias in Asia Minor. Two of its faces are inscribed in Greek with the names of at least 120 donors who commissioned the memorial. Among the donors are many Jews, but also a surprising number who identify themselves as* theosebeis, *or "Godfearers," gentiles who were sympathetic to Judaism, identified with the synagogue and probably observed some, if not all, Jewish religious practices. While some scholars date the pillar to c. 200 C.E., recent studies suggest it was erected several hundred years later, probably in the mid-to-late fourth century.*

high-ranking officials, but there is no indication that such knowledge was widespread or was deemed useful for communication with the Jews of the Diaspora.

Furthermore, there is no evidence that the rabbis of the land of Israel in either the second or the third century ever made an effort to reach out to the Jews of the Diaspora. Rabbinic literature is filled with stories about the travels of the rabbis of the second century, especially of the pre-Bar-Kosba period. These stories have not yet been systematically collected and evaluated, but whatever historicity they may have, they do not demonstrate that the rabbis of whatever period—whether the actors or the storytellers—were interested in spreading their message and hegemony to the Jews of the Diaspora. There is a persistent tradition in rabbinic literature that a convert to Judaism named Aquila revised the Greek translation of the Torah (the Septuagint, abbreviated LXX) under the supervision of Rabbi Eliezer and Rabbi Joshua, but the historicity of this claim is hard to establish.[43] In any case, there is no clear evidence before the sixth century that the Greek translation of Aquila was actually used by Diaspora Jewry.[44]

Thus, there was a serious linguistic barrier between the Jews of the Roman Diaspora and the rabbis in the land of Israel, and there was little interest or ability on the part of these rabbis (at least in the second and third centuries) to become involved in the religious life of Diaspora Jewry. Diaspora Jews attended their synagogues; prayed and read the Torah; observed the Sabbath, holidays and food laws; believed in the one God who created heaven and earth and chose Israel to be his people; obeyed (or did not obey) their traditional authority figures—all, however, without the help of the lettered elite that was emerging in the land of Israel.

The Jewish Diaspora in Babylonia was Aramaic-speaking, and therefore could communicate far more easily with the rabbis of the land of Israel than could the Greek-speaking Jews of the Roman Diaspora. Various rabbis of the second century were reported to be of Babylonian extraction, and various rabbis were said to have traveled to Babylonia from the land of Israel, but Babylonia was not yet in the rabbinic orbit in the second century C.E. Although the Babylonian Talmud reveals a great deal about the religious and social life of Babylonian Jewry in the third to fifth centuries C.E., it tells us almost nothing about life in the second century. We may assume that the Jews of Babylonia, like their co-religionists in the Roman Diaspora, continued to observe their traditional practices without the help of the rabbis from the land of Israel.[45]

The urban Jews of the land of Israel

Like the Jews of the Roman Diaspora, the Jews of the coastal cities of the land of Israel lived in a gentile, Greek-speaking environment. In the middle of the third century, many rabbis began to make their home in these cosmopolitan and mercantile centers, notably Caesarea, but in the second century they did not. There were Jews in these cities in the second century—one Jew even became the *agoranomos* (market inspector) of the city of Joppa[46]—but not rabbis. In the immediate post-135 C.E. period, the rabbinate was primarily a rural phenomenon, located in the small towns and villages of Galilee and Judea.[47] In the fourth century, the Greek-speaking Jews of the coastal cities recited even the *Shema'* (the fundamental declaration of faith in the Lord as the "One God") in Greek in their synagogues,[48] and we may presume that they did so in the second century as well. They were not part of rabbinic society.

The 'amme ha'aretz *of the land of Israel*

Even in the rural heartland of the land of Israel, not everyone was a follower of the rabbis. Many Jews were *'amme ha'aretz*, "people of the land" (singular, *'am ha'aretz*), Jews who could not be trusted to observe properly the laws of purity and tithing. Many rabbinic texts contrast the *'am ha'aretz* with the *ne'eman*, someone who is "trustworthy," that is, someone who is presumed to observe properly the laws of tithes, and with the *haber*, or "associate," someone who is presumed to observe properly the laws of purity. Here is the Mishnah's formulation:

> *A*. He that undertakes to become trustworthy [*ne'eman*] must tithe what he eats, what he sells and what he buys; and he may not be the guest of an *'am ha'aretz*.
> *B*. Rabbi Judah says: Even he that is the guest of an *'am ha'aretz* may still be reckoned trustworthy ...
> *C*. He that undertakes to become an associate [*haber*] may not sell to an *'am ha'aretz* [foodstuff that is] wet or dry, or buy from him [foodstuff that is] wet; and he may not be the guest of an *'am ha'aretz* ...
> *D*. Rabbi Judah says: Nor may he rear small cattle, or be profuse in vows or levity, or become impure through contact with the dead, but shall minister in the house of study.[49]

In this passage, the *'am ha'aretz* is presumed to observe the laws of purity and tithing either unsatisfactorily or not at all; therefore, the trustworthy and the associate must absent themselves from his table (paragraphs *A* and *C*). The laws of purity and tithing center on food, which is very susceptible to impurity. Therefore these laws (unlike, for example, the laws regarding Sabbath observance) erect clear social barriers between those who observe them and those who do not.* The emphasis on the laws of tithing and purity as social markers is probably a vestige from the sectarian past of at least one strand of Rabbinic Judaism; sects encourage separation from the society around them and use the concepts of purity and impurity to define who is in the group and who is out. The table fellowship that is reserved exclusively for members of the group is clearly reflected in paragraphs *A* and *C* of this mishnah. The *'am ha'aretz* is clearly out.

The modifications advanced by Rabbi Judah (not to be confused with

*The laws of purity and tithing are distinct from the laws of *kashrut*. The laws of *kashrut* derive from Leviticus 11 and Deuteronomy 14:1–21; the laws of purity derive from Leviticus 12–15 and Numbers 19; the laws of tithing derive from Numbers 18:8–32 (and various other passages).

Rabbi Judah the Patriarch, who will be discussed below) in paragraphs *B* and *D* suggest that in his time (the middle of the second century C.E.) the old structure was breaking down. Rabbi Judah allows the trustworthy to sup with an *'am ha'aretz*. His definition of an associate does not require separation from the *'am ha'aretz*; it does not even center on the laws of purity. According to Rabbi Judah, the distinguishing characteristic of the associate is his readiness to follow rabbinic norms and serve the rabbis, not his abstention from contact with the *'amme ha'aretz*.[50] In Rabbi Judah's terms, an *'am ha'aretz* is simply someone who does not follow rabbinic piety, i.e., a non-rabbinic Jew. Rabbi Judah's redefinition of the *'am ha'aretz* in paragraphs *B* and *D* of the quoted mishnah reflects an effort to break down, or at least to soften, the sectarian and separatist aspects of the more restrictive definition in paragraphs *A* and *C*.

The social reality lurking behind these rules and this debate is obscure. Did all rabbinic Jews properly observe these laws? If not, what was the relationship between those who did and those who did not? What percentage of the population did the *'amme ha'aretz* constitute? What was their social status? What and who brought about the de-emphasis of the sectarian and separatist elements in the definition of *'am ha'aretz*? Unfortunately, we cannot answer these important questions.

But the rabbinic legislation on the *'am ha'aretz* shows that the rabbis were well aware that there were Jews "out there" who did not attend upon the rabbis' every word and who did not follow a rabbinic way of life. Elsewhere, too, the rabbis reveal their awareness of such Jews. Everyday a rabbinic Jew was supposed to thank the Lord for not creating him "a gentile, an 'outsider' [*bur*] or a woman," three categories of people who could not experience rabbinic piety.[51] When Rabbi Akiva remembered what he had done in his youth before becoming a rabbi, he said, "I thank you, Lord my God, that you have placed my lot among those who sit in the house of study (*beth ha-midrash*) and you have not placed my lot among those who sit on the corners [?] in the marketplace."[52]

Since these Jews did not look to the rabbis for leadership—and were in turn spurned by the rabbis[53]—to whom did they turn for religious guidance? Still again, the answer is not clear. What is clear, however, is that these Jews, like the non-rabbinic Jews of the Diaspora and the Greek cities, were neither "sectarian" nor "deviant." The rabbis had to admit that the *'amme ha'aretz* did observe many of the commandments, notably the prohibition against eating food grown during the sabbatical years. They also observed the Sabbath.[54] We may presume that they observed the explicit commandments of the Torah and continued to practice Judaism as they had always done.

The place of prayer

We may presume, too, that private and public prayer was part of the traditional piety of the *'amme ha'aretz*. Little is known of the synagogue in the second and early third centuries C.E. A few synagogues are attested archaeologically for the Second Temple period, and numerous synagogues are attested archaeologically for the late third century and onwards, but not a single synagogue is attested archaeologically for the period from the Bar-Kokhba Revolt to the redaction of the Mishnah (c. 235 C.E.). Perhaps in the wake of the destruction of the Temple, the Jews hesitated to erect buildings that might seem to be replacements for that which was irreplaceable. In the absence of buildings built specifically for prayer and Torah study, public prayer probably took place in generic public buildings, in town squares or in any open and accessible place.[55]

In Jewish circles known to the author of the Gospel of Matthew, the Pharisees took the best seats (or "the seats in front") in synagogues, that is, public assemblies (Matthew 23:6), but the rabbinic texts that took shape during the second century seldom claim rabbinic leadership of public prayer. In fact, the Mishnah and related documents show remarkably little interest in public prayer or in the gatherings (the synagogues) in which this prayer took place. The simplest explanation for this phenomenon is that the synagogue was not a rabbinic institution. The rabbis neither created nor supervised the institution of public prayer, and it would be some time before the rabbis would become communal authorities in matters of liturgy and liturgical practice. The Jews, many of them *'amme ha'aretz*, who frequented public prayer assemblies in the second century C.E. had no need for rabbinic leadership. They had neither time for, nor interest in, the demands of the rabbis whom, we may conjecture, they regarded as eccentric at best, fanatic at worst. The feeling was mutual; "sitting in the assemblies [alternative translation: synagogues] of the *'amme ha'aretz* drives a man from this world" was a rabbinic saying.[56]

"Heretics"

Just as the rabbis used the term "gentiles" (*goyim*) to refer to all non-Jews, whatever their ethnic origin, theological belief or ritual practice, so too the rabbis used a single term "heretics" (*minim*) to designate a wide variety of Jews whose theology or practices the rabbis found offensive. The Mishnah refers in a few passages to these heretics and their heresy (*minut*), and later documents supply numerous additional references.[57] Rabbinic texts also refer to "apostates" (*meshumadim* or *mumarim*). The rabbis sometimes label a specific practice or belief as "the way of outsiders" or "the way of the Amorites" and other similar expressions.[58] Thus the rabbis of the second century seem to have known not only *'amme ha'aretz*, the great unwashed, but also heretics and apostates; the former rejected beliefs or practices that the rabbis, at least, regarded as normative, while the latter removed themselves from the social control of the Jewish community.

The precise identity of these deviant Jews (deviant, that is, from the perspective of the rabbis) and their non-normative ways (non-normative, that is, from the perspective of the rabbis) is an intriguing question that has aroused much speculation. Many scholars have suggested that Christian Jews (that is, ethnic Jews who accepted the divinity or messiahship of Jesus and modified their Judaism accordingly) were the likeliest target of these rabbinic polemics, but the question is open.

More important than the precise identity of the *minim* is the fact that the rabbis paid so little attention to them. The rabbis in the Mishnah and later documents did not formulate creeds and dogmas that would serve as touchstones to distinguish between the true and the false. Nor did they create social mechanisms and institutions that would allow them to exclude those whom they did not like. Perhaps the rabbis were not interested in doing any of these things because no one would have listened to them even if they had, but it is striking that the rabbis went about their work all but oblivious to the varieties of Judaism around them. Christian writers of the second century were interested in normative self-definition, and wrote numerous treatises against both heretics and Jews, but the rabbis of the period were interested neither in heresy nor in Christianity. We may be sure that heretics and Christian Jews were out there in the second century, but the rabbis paid them little attention.[59]

Rabbinic Judaism

Having discussed categories of non-rabbinic Jews, let us turn to Rabbinic Judaism.

The rabbis, or sages, emerged as a distinctive group in the decades after the destruction of the Temple in 70 C.E., as we have seen in a previous chapter. But only at the end of the second century and the beginning of the third century did the rabbis begin to find a place for themselves in Jewish society at large in the land of Israel. This change was the work of Rabbi Judah the Patriarch (c. 175–220 C.E.).

The leader of the rabbis was the patriarch (this was his title in Greek and Latin; in Hebrew the title is *nasi*).[60] The clearest expressions of his authority were his right (1) to appoint (or ordain) judges in the rabbinic judicial system, and (2) to supervise the intercalation of the calendar. The first patriarch about whom we have any reliable information is Rabban Gamaliel, one of the dominant figures of the Yavnean period after the First Jewish Revolt.* But it was only in Rabbi Judah's time that the patriarch became more than just the first among equals. Rabbi Judah was the first patriarch to develop rules of etiquette governing behavior at his court, to amass substantial personal wealth and to claim (or, perhaps more accurately, to allow others to claim on his behalf) descent from the royal house of King David.

One rabbinic tradition has Rabbi Gamaliel, the patriarch of Yavneh and Rabbi Judah's grandfather, "receive authorization" from a Roman governor in Syria. But there is not a single rabbinic tradition bringing Rabbi Simeon ben Gamaliel, Rabbi Judah's father and predecessor, into contact with a Roman official; perhaps the Romans suspected the rabbis generally, or the patriarchal house specifically, of supporting the Bar-Kokhba Revolt of 132–135 C.E., and the two sides kept their distance. In stark contrast, numerous rabbinic traditions report that Rabbi Judah was befriended by a Roman official—Antoninus, sometimes called King Antoninus. The legendary character of many of these traditions is obvious, but some of them may well have a historical core. Even if the identity of this Antoninus is uncertain (if indeed he was an emperor he may have been the emperor Caracalla, i.e., Marcus Aurelius Antoninus, but it is more likely that Antoninus was some local Roman official),[61] the stories show that Rabbi Judah enjoyed some measure of recognition from the Roman government and, as a result, gained benefits both for himself and for the Jewish community.

Rabbi Judah ha-Nasi

Rabbi Judah's tenure as patriarch also had a major impact on the development of the rabbinate. The tension between the rabbis and non-rabbinic Jews did not disappear, but as a result of the work of Rabbi Judah, the rabbis became much more involved in the society around them and aspired not only to religious virtuosity but also to communal leadership. Here are several examples of the ways by which Rabbi Judah sought to bring the rabbis into Jewish society at large.

• He greatly enhanced the power of the patriarchate and thereby the power of the rabbinate. Rabbi Judah was asked by the people of Simonias (in Galilee) to appoint for them a man who would "deliver sermons; serve as judge, deacon (*hazzan*) and scribe (or teacher of children, *sofer*); teach us (rabbinic tradition); and fulfill all our desires"—quite a request! Rabbi Judah also sent Rabbi Romanus to check the family purity of the Jews in a certain distant place.[62] No such traditions are recorded for any of the previous

*On Rabban Gamaliel and his influence, see pp. 153–158.

patriarchs.[63] It was only from the time of Rabbi Judah the Patriarch and afterward that rabbis became communal functionaries under the authority of the patriarch.

• The two major rabbinic institutions in antiquity were the school and the judicial court (not the synagogue). Most rabbinic schools in antiquity, in both the land of Israel and Babylonia, were disciple circles (a master attended by his faithful students) rather than academies (perpetual institutions with a corporate identity). These disciple circles were small and reached only small numbers of people; they were not intended to promote Rabbinic Judaism among the broad reaches of the population.[64]

Interaction between rabbis and plain Jews took place primarily not in schools but in courts. A study of all the legal cases reported in tannaitic literature (principally the Mishnah and its supplement, the Tosefta) reveals that the scope of authority of the rabbinic judges in the second century was rather narrow. They were consulted most often in cases dealing with the laws of purity and marriage law. In these areas the rabbis were apparently acknowledged as experts, but in other areas—civil law, the laws of *kashrut* (dietary laws), the laws of the Sabbath and the practices of the synagogue—the rabbis were rarely consulted, either because people had other authority figures to whom to turn or because the people simply followed traditional pre-rabbinic precedents. However, the legal cases in which Rabbi Judah the Patriarch and later rabbis became involved show a somewhat different topic profile. Here marriage law, civil law, the laws of *kashrut* and the laws of the Sabbath all figure prominently. This demonstrates that the scope of rabbinic jurisdiction expanded significantly during Rabbi Judah's tenure, and that the rabbis were becoming more involved in the lives of the general population.[65]

• In the period before Rabbi Judah, the rabbis had been well-to-do, had associated with the well-to-do and had interested themselves in questions that were important to the landed classes. Perhaps some of the sages were poor, but their poverty has been rendered invisible in tannaitic literature.[66] Those rabbis about whose economic status anything is known seem to have been landowners. They even shared the eternal prejudice of landowners against shepherds and goatherds, whom the rabbis regarded as inveterate thieves and contumacious liars.[67] Although traditions in the later Talmudim refer to the poverty of some second-century rabbis, who allegedly were employed in menial occupations, these traditions receive no confirmation from the Mishnah itself, or from the rest of tannaitic literature. They are probably retrojections, or throwbacks, from the conditions of later times. The rabbis of the second century encouraged Jews to support the poor, tried to regulate the collection and disbursement of charity and perhaps even served as charity agents themselves, but they never say that charity should be given to needy rabbis and never report that poor students actually received any charity.[68]

By contrast, in the period of Rabbi Judah the Patriarch we observe the beginnings of tension between the well-to-do and some rabbis. Rabbis are appointed to salaried posts; these are not wealthy, landed people. In Rabbi Judah's tenure, a "poor tithe" is distributed for the first time to needy students. During Rabbi Judah's tenure and afterwards, as the patriarchate enlarged its power, the rabbinic movement expanded its social horizons in order to find ways to include the poor among its numbers. The links between the rabbis and the people were becoming closer.[69]

• Before Rabbi Judah, the rabbinate had been primarily a rural phenomenon in Judea and especially in Galilee. Most of the legal cases presented to the *tannaim* originated in rural settlements, not in cities. Rabbinic traditions consistently place the rabbis of the second century, both before and after the war of 132–135 C.E., in rural towns and villages. The urbanization of the rabbinic movement is also the work of Rabbi Judah. When Rabbi Judah moved the seat of the patriarchate from Beth Shearim to Sepphoris (both in Lower Galilee), the rabbinic movement was headquartered in a city for the first time since its early days in Yavneh and Lydda (in the generation immediately after 70 C.E.). Rabbi Judah attempted to establish the ritual purity of the cities of the land of Israel and to free their inhabitants from the requirement of giving the priestly tithes. Both reforms were clearly intended to facilitate the entrance of rabbis and rabbinic Jews into the cities. Probably not by coincidence, Roman Palestina entered a new phase of urbanization during Rabbi Judah's tenure.[70]

Rabbi Judah's crowning achievement, however, was the Mishnah, the foundation document of rabbinic literature.

The organization of the Mishnah

The Mishnah is a large work, some 800 to 1,000 pages in English translation.[71] It consists of laws, debates on legal questions and brief narratives on legal subjects. Strangely enough, it contains few citations or explanations of scripture. Moreover, with the exception of an atypical tractate called *Avot* (Fathers, often titled The Sayings of the Fathers), the Mishnah contains very little homiletical or ethical material. Nor does it contain explicit theology or eschatology. In short, the Mishnah is a book of laws.

It is divided into six orders, or divisions, which are in turn subdivided into 63 tractates. Each tractate is in turn divided into chapters, and each chapter into individual pericopes or sections, each of which is often called, simply, a mishnah.

Tannaim and Amoraim

The rabbis who lived in the generations before about 220 C.E. when the Mishnah was completed are known as *tannaim*, "teachers" (singular, *tanna*). Most of the *tannaim* lived between about 80 and 200 C.E. The rabbinic works that contain the sayings of, and stories about, the *tannaim*, and that do not cite any named authority who lived after about 220 C.E., constitute tannaitic literature. The first and most important of these works is the Mishnah (literally, "repetition" or "instruction"), described on pages 234–236; other works in this category are the Tosefta, a supplement to the Mishnah, and a set of commentaries on Exodus through Deuteronomy (the *Mekhilta*, the *Sifra* and the *Sifre*).

Although they contain many sayings of, and stories about, the *tannaim*, the two Talmudim are not tannaitic works, because they cite numerous authorities who lived after the *tannaim*. These authorities, who lived from about 220 to 500 C.E., are known collectively as *amoraim* (singular, *amora*), and therefore the two Talmudim and various related works are said to constitute amoraic literature.

Each of the orders is devoted to some overarching theme or set of issues, and each of the tractates in turn addresses an aspect of the theme. The first order, *Zera'im*, or "Seeds," concerns the obligations incumbent upon an Israelite before he—for the Mishnah the paradigm of normality is the free Israelite male—may partake of the bounty brought forth from the earth. The earth is the Lord's, and the Israelite, in return for tenancy on the Lord's domain, must either recite benedictions or separate some of the produce for the poor or for the priest or for the Levite, or present some of it at the Temple. The second order, *Mo'ed*, or "Appointed Times," concerns Holy Times, the sacred times of the year and their rituals, especially the rituals that were enacted in the Temple (even though it had been destroyed long before). The third order, *Nashim*, or "Women," concerns marriage law and the authority of a husband to cancel his wife's oaths. The fourth order, *Nezikin*, or "Damages," is devoted to interpersonal relations: civil law, torts, contracts, bailments, the authority of the judiciary, relations between Jews and gentiles and relations between one Jew and another (here appears the anomalous tractate *Avot*). The fifth order, *Kodashim*, or "Holy Things," concerns the sacrificial cult, the structure of the Temple, the misuse of animals and objects dedicated to the cult and the slaughter of non-sacrificial animals. The sixth order, *Tohorot*, or "Purities," concerns the purity system: sources of impurity, the means by which impurity is transferred, objects susceptible to impurity and modes of purification.

This large and complex work is highly edited and stylized, suggesting the existence not only of a strong editor but also of a sustained period of peace and stability (from after the revolt of 132–135 C.E. to about 220 C.E.). The Mishnah demonstrates a passion for classifying things, for numbering the resulting categories and for exploring the precise contours of the boundary that separates one category from another. The Mishnah also shows a passion for stating abstract principles and demonstrating how the principles are to be applied with different results in different cases.[72] But for all its abstraction and formal precision, the Mishnah is not a collection of Aristotelian treatises. It is highly digressive and often links one pericope to the next by verbal association or some other literary criterion. Most important, the Mishnah is not arranged logically. It has no beginning or end; it has only middle. The closest thing to an introduction to the work is tucked away in the fourth order in the opening chapters of the tractate *Avot*; there we learn that the authority assumed by the Mishnah can be traced back to Moses at Sinai. For the rest, however, the Mishnah starts where it wants and ends where it wants; it treats in great detail fragments of themes, but seldom treats an entire theme.

Thus, for example, the very first mishnah addresses the question "From what time in the evening may the *Shema'* be recited?" (*Berakhot* 1:1). But how do we know that this prayer is to be recited in the evening at all? And by whom? And why? All these questions are logically anterior to the question posed by the mishnah, but the mishnah ignores them completely.

The Mishnah as a book of laws, not a law book

The Mishnah is, as I said, a book of laws; yet it is not a law book. Unlike most law books, it contains numerous disputes and divergent opinions without giving any obvious indication which opinion is the one to be followed. Unlike most law books, it often omits the penalty for infractions of its rules or the manner in which a wrong is to be righted. Unlike most law books, it describes institutions (the Temple, the Sanhedrin) and authorities (the high priest) and rituals (the sacrificial cult) that no longer existed when the book was written. Unlike most law books, it all but ignores the institutions (the synagogue) and authorities (the Roman government, the municipal governments in Roman Palestina, the rabbis themselves[73]) and rituals (public prayer, public and private study of Torah[74]) that did exist when the book was written. The

Mishnah thus is not a law book.[75]

If not a law book, what is it and why was it written? The answer remains elusive. The Talmudim, which are in effect commentaries on the Mishnah, state on several occasions that the Mishnah was edited or arranged by Rabbi Judah the Patriarch.[76] Modern scholars generally accept this claim, even though the Mishnah itself nowhere advances such a claim.

Why did Rabbi Judah edit the Mishnah? The publication of the Mishnah was an integral part of his program to extend the power of the patriarchate. By superseding previous legal collections and incorporating them into a single Mishnah, Rabbi Judah asserted his authority over the rabbinic movement, the intended audience of the new book: From now on all rabbinic study would focus on one collection only—*his*.

Yet the Mishnah is more than an implicit assertion of power by the patriarch. It is the core document of Rabbinic Judaism, forming the foundation for virtually all rabbinic literature that would follow it, from the third century C.E. to our day. Although the Mishnah has become a "classic," safely located within the confines of the sacred traditions of Rabbinic Judaism, the Mishnah was (and to some extent still is) a radical work.

The Mishnah is radical in that it is the first Jewish work, whether biblical or post-biblical, whether in Hebrew or Greek or Aramaic, whether from the land of Israel or from the Diaspora, to attribute conflicting legal opinions to named individuals who, despite their differences, belong to the same group. The legal materials in the Hebrew Bible are not uniform, to be sure. The Holiness Code (Leviticus 19–20 and related passages), the Covenant Code (Exodus 21–24), the priestly laws, the laws of Deuteronomy, etc., are products of different schools and different philosophies, and those differences are often manifest in legal contradictions. But the editor of the Torah combined these codes anyway, without even hinting to the reader that the collections do not always agree, thus allowing later Jews to pretend (or rather, to *insist*) that the collections always do agree. But the Mishnah allows no such pretense.

The very first mishnah opens with a question ("From what time in the evening may the *Shema'* be recited?") which leads to a second question ("Until what time in the evening may the *Shema'* be recited?") that receives three different answers, each one ascribed to a different authority. The Mishnah not only tolerates legal disputes, it relishes them. Legal dispute is the core of Mishnaic discourse. And the disputes are open-ended: The Mishnah does not contain any explicit rules by which the winning position can be determined.[77] Whether these disputes are entirely rhetorical (in other words, the Mishnah is the record of a debating society) or whether they mirror real diversity in practice is not clear: If the latter, the social mechanisms that held this disputatious and fractious group together must have been remarkable, but they too are unclear.[78]

The Mishnah is radical in another respect, too. With few exceptions it does not attach its legal rulings to scripture. In the opening chapter of tractate *Avot,* we are told of a chain of tradition that links Moses at Mount Sinai to the rabbis of the Mishnah, specifically the patriarchal house of Rabbi Judah. *Avot* thus asserts that rabbinic authority derives from Moses and God. But the Mishnah itself is not interested in proving this assertion. In the Mishnah, rabbis debate numerous points of law but seldom cite the biblical authority that would substantiate their positions. Many of their rulings probably were derived from a close reading of the laws of the Torah, but the Mishnah obscures this fact by omitting the scriptural source.

As a result, it is impossible to tell from the Mishnah whether a given ruling is derived from scripture or not. Nor does the Mishnah reveal whether a given ruling is ancient or modern, traditional or innovative. The authority for the Mishnah's statements is entirely internal to the Mishnah itself: anonymous sages as well as named sages speak, and the reader is supposed to respect their words. By ignoring all external sources of authority, including scripture, the Mishnah implicitly presents itself as a source of authority, endorsing the right of its human authors to debate and legislate. (Presumably such a view would also enhance the power of the patriarch to legislate.)

This radical and unsettling thesis was rejected by virtually all of the Mishnah's commentators, beginning with the Talmudim and the tannaitic commentaries on the Torah.[79] These works attempt to demonstrate that the Mishnah—not just the Mishnah in general or in theory, but the specific rulings of the Mishnah, one-by-one—derives from scripture: Law must be subordinate to revelation, and must somehow be derived from the Torah of Moses. In this conception the only innovation allowed is the innovation that claims to be traditional, that claims to be the working out of what had been revealed to Moses long before. Thus in one sense the Mishnah lost; its implicit defense of the autonomy of human reason was rejected. But in another and much larger sense the Mishnah won; it gave rabbinic learning a secure base on which to build for the future.

SEVEN

The World of the Talmud: From the Mishnah to the Arab Conquest

Isaiah M. Gafni

TO SOME EXTENT, THE FOUR CENTURIES OF JEWISH HISTORY surveyed in this chapter—from the completion of the Mishnah (c. 220 C.E.) to the Arab conquest of the East (early seventh century)—represent a continuation of the post-Bar-Kokhba period. No longer do we encounter major political or military opposition to the empires that ruled over those lands where the vast majority of Jews lived—whether in Palestine or the Diaspora. While the yearning for messianic redemption will continue to assert itself at certain major junctures, beginning in the latter part of the Mishnaic period (135–220 C.E.) this messianism finds expression in a far more spiritualized way, rather than being centered around another Bar-Kokhba-like Jewish military figure. Indeed, these messianic passions will henceforth arise primarily as a Jewish reaction to events totally beyond the control of the Jewish community itself—whether it be the pagan-Christian clash in the days of the Roman emperor Julian (361–363 C.E.) that almost led to the restoration of Jewish Jerusalem, or the three-way struggle for control over the land of Israel (Byzantium-Persia-Arabia) that paved the way for the Muslim conquest.

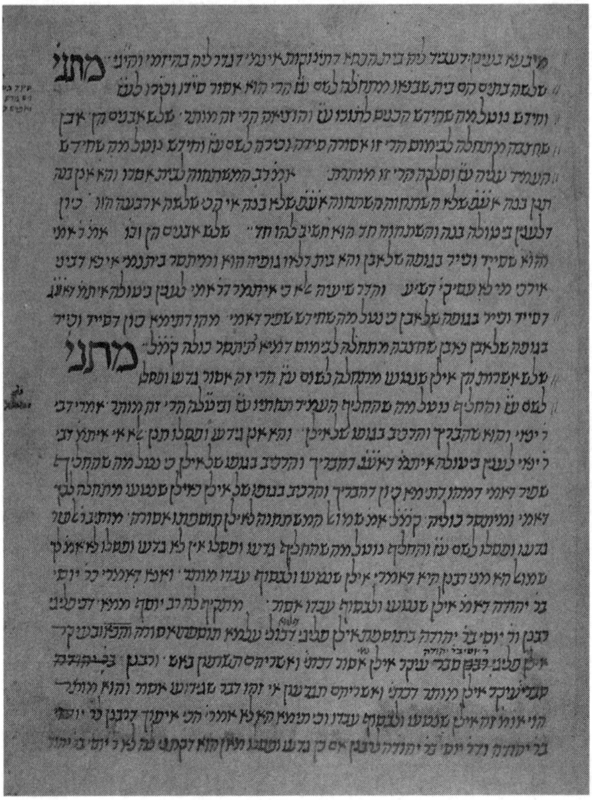

COURTESY OF THE LIBRARY OF THE JEWISH THEOLOGICAL SEMINARY

A Page from the Talmud. *The Talmud (Hebrew for "instruction") is an authoritative collection of rabbinic commentary that includes the Mishnah (a collection of Jewish laws compiled by the patriarch Judah ha-Nasi at the beginning of the third century C.E.) and Gemara (an elaboration and commentary on the Mishnah). Here we see part of the tractate* Avodah Zarah, *copied in Spain in 1290 C.E.*

More radical in its ultimate consequences is the slow but constant shift in the delicate relationship between the Jewish center in Palestine and the emerging Jewish community of Babylonia.[1] While the unchallenged status of the Mishnah as the definitive compilation of Jewish law still suggests a preeminent role for Jewish leadership in Palestine, the redaction of the Mishnah itself served as a watershed in Jewish communal life. The universal acceptance of the Mishnah as the definitive statement of Oral Law represents the last stage of an unchallenged Palestinian dominance over the process of legal development within Rabbinic Judaism. The subsequent parallel emergence of the two monumental corpora of rabbinic discussions and interpretation of the Mishnah, namely the Palestinian Talmud (also known as the

Yerushalmi or Jerusalem Talmud, JT) and the Babylonian Talmud (BT)—with the ultimate superior status attached to the latter—is only the most obvious of a growing number of signs pointing to changes on a worldwide scale that reshaped the face of the Jewish community.

At the beginning of the third century, the Jews were still the predominant ethnic community in the land of Israel,[2] notwithstanding the fact that Hadrian had already attempted to blur this reality by changing the name of the Roman province from Judea to Syria-Palestina.[3] If there was another major community for the Jews of Palestine to contend with at this early stage, it was still probably the Samaritans[4] and not the fledgling Christian community, which had yet to multiply in the land of Israel at the same swift pace apparent in the rest of the Roman Empire. Even by the year 325, one year after all of the eastern Roman Empire came under the rule of the first Christian emperor, it is still evident that the vast majority of Christians in Palestine continued to reside primarily in the Greek cities of the land, and had a long way to go before emerging as a major demographic force.[5] Within one century, however, these proportions may slowly have begun to reverse themselves; but the extent of this shift is still hotly debated by scholars. Some estimates maintain that by the end of the fourth and the early fifth centuries, the Jews comprised barely one-third of the total population, while the Christian community gradually emerged as a dominant demographic factor. Propounders of this claim go on to argue that by the sixth century, the Christian community of Palestine had grown to become the overwhelming majority among the inhabitants of the land.[6] Other recent studies tend to temper this conclusion, suggesting that Jews maintained their demographic edge well into the Byzantine period.[7]

Whatever the degree of this new demographic reality, it naturally influenced the nature of Jewish-Christian confrontation and polemics, at least as reflected in the writings of the religious leaders of both groups. Beginning in the third century, the rabbinic attitude toward Christianity was no longer seen as addressing an internal Jewish social and religious schism that must be resolved through a reappraisal or redefinition of what was legitimately "Jewish."[8] What emerged now, and remained a constant factor in the Palestinian rabbinic literature of the talmudic era, was a confrontational attitude toward Christianity as a distinct religion, which nevertheless required the attention of the rabbis in light of its growing strength and influence in the land of Israel as well as throughout the empire.[9] Care should be taken, nevertheless, not to go to the other extreme and overstress this attention to Christianity on the part of the rabbis, a trend that seems to have taken hold in some recent scholarship.[10]

By the fourth century the rabbis, like most Jews, were aware of the fact that "the Kingdom [Rome] had become a heresy (*minut*)," [11] and this dramatically affected the status of the Jews. With the Church now able to assert a major degree of authority over the empire's administration, the Jews in Palestine and the empire at large found themselves—for the first time—at the mercy of their religious rival. While the official status of Judaism as a legitimate religion did not change overnight, it was only a matter of time before the antagonism and hostility between the two groups erupted on various levels: legislation, religious decrees aimed at separating the Christian masses from all Jewish influence, even physical clashes.

Beyond all this, the third century served as yet another turning point—one in the realignment of Jewish leadership. After centuries of almost total absence from the historical scene, save for isolated first-century anecdotes recorded primarily by Josephus,[12] the Jewish community beyond the Euphrates River resurfaced, ultimately laying claim to a growing degree of independence, if not outright hegemony, regarding all aspects of Jewish communal life dependent on rabbinic leadership. This reemergence coincided dramatically with the political changing of the guard in Persia. After hundreds of years of Parthian Arsacid rule, the Jews (as well as others) found themselves not only under the rule of a new Persian dynasty founded by the Sassanians (c. 224 C.E.), but also in the midst of a major religious revival of the Zoroastrian church and a political radicalization that led to the outbreak of new hostilities between Persia and Rome. And thus, while scholars argue, not without some justification, the merits of designating the period of Jewish history beginning in the third century C.E. as the "talmudic era,"[13] the fact is that the new literary development that followed the compilation of the Mishnah dovetails precisely with major political and religious developments that reshaped for all time the history of all the peoples of the Near East, and to a very large degree that of the Jewish people among them.

The Jews of Palestine in the late Roman period: 220–324 C.E.

The first years of the post-Mishnaic period in Palestine coincided with the reign of the last of the Severan emperors, Alexander Severus (222–235 C.E.). Following his death, the Roman Empire sank into 50 years of political chaos and economic crisis. Emperors rose to power only to be assassinated within a few months, or a year or two at most; rampant inflation rendered Roman coins worthless; ultimately, the *principate* system of government that had existed for over two centuries collapsed, thus requiring a total restructuring of imperial administration.[14] (This was carried out by Diocletian in the final decades of the third century.) The Jewish nation was just one of many passengers on this storm-tossed ship. The vicissitudes of Roman rule in the third century were surely felt in Palestine as in the rest of the empire, although some recent scholarship has suggested that Palestine may have been spared some of the harsher elements of this decline, with some even positing demographic growth during this period.[15]

Jewish life under the Severan dynasty has been described by some historians as the high point of Roman-Jewish relations,[16] which date back to the initial contacts between the two nations during the early stages of the Hasmonean uprising. Moreover, while the pact between Rome and Judah Maccabee was essentially nothing more than a declaration resulting from common political aims and interests, the favorable relationship between the Jews and the empire under the Severans was far more striking. Not only did it yield practical advantages for the Jewish side, but it evolved a mere two generations after the terrible devastation wrought by Roman legions upon the land and people of Israel during the Second Jewish Revolt.[17]

The growth of the patriarchate[18]

The most obvious result of the improved relations with Rome was the enhanced status of the patriarchate in the days of Judah ha-Nasi (frequently translated as "Judah the Prince"; c. 180–220 C.E.), the redactor of the Mishnah (see the previous chapter). Judah's unique position, combining political power with rabbinic authority, did not go unnoticed by the rabbis ("From the days of Moses until Rabbi [Judah] we have not found Torah and [political] greatness in one place [i.e., in one person]"),[19] and while the spiritual and halakhic power wielded by subsequent patriarchs may have wavered, the political role of the patriarch remained a constant factor in Jewish life until the abolition of the office in the early fifth century. While our knowledge of the patriarchs in the fourth and fifth centuries derives exclusively from non-Jewish sources, the third-century patriarchate is well documented in rabbinic literature, and thus we enjoy certain insights into the nature of Jewish communal leadership of this period in Palestine that tend to become somewhat obscured in later centuries.

The patriarch was the Jewish representative before imperial authorities.[20] Simultaneously, he provided a unifying factor within the Jewish community. Rabbinic as well as non-Jewish sources attest to the fact that messengers (*apostoli*) were dispatched to Diaspora communities for purposes of collecting funds as well as supervising local communal authorities.[21] It was this role, together with the fact that the patriarchs claimed Davidic lineage, that ultimately rendered the office a major target of ecclesiastical pressure.

As we proceed into the third century, a number of changes in the nature of the office emerge, as well as in the expressed attitudes of the rabbis toward the various patriarchs. One major departure from the days of Judah is the physical removal of the court of the patriarch from Sepphoris to Tiberias (c. 250 C.E.). This move of the focal point of Jewish leadership appears to have taken place in two stages, and is indicative of a major development within the rabbinic class. Following the death of Judah we can clearly discern a decentralization of the all-embracing powers maintained by the patriarch.[22] Under Judah, for instance, ordination of rabbis was the sole prerogative of the *nasi*, or patriarch; afterward this authority was divided between the office of the patriarch and the rabbis.[23] The wish to assert their independence as a distinct class may have induced the rabbis, following Judah's death, to remove their central academy from Sepphoris to Tiberias. Apparently, only later, during the days of Judah's grandson Judah II (c. 250 C.E.), did the patriarch's court move to Tiberias.[24] While this move rendered Tiberias the main center of Jewish Palestine for the next few centuries,* it also suggests a heightened degree of tension in the relationship between the patriarchs and the rabbinic class.[25] In fact, numerous sources raise serious questions surrounding the propriety of patriarchal behavior during the third century, in particular regarding the ordination—"for money"—of unqualified judges.[26] Rabbinic criticism of the patriarchs sometimes alludes to other examples of improper behavior, especially their heavy-handedness in the collection of various taxes from an already overburdened population.[27]

From a purely historiographical perspective, it must be stated that we have only one side of the story—that of the rabbinic class as reflected primarily in the Talmud and Midrash,[28] and we can only speculate on what response the patriarchs might have made to these attacks. Nevertheless, the weakening of the central power structure within the Jewish community should not surprise us, for, as we have seen, it coincided precisely with the collapse of central Roman authority throughout the empire.

New forms of taxation

Social tensions were of course linked to the difficult economic situation. With Roman currency in essence rendered worthless, it was now meaningless to exact taxes in fixed sums. Rabbinic literature introduces us to a whole new system of painful taxation: forced labor (*angaria*) in the service of the Roman administration; billeting of soldiers and Roman officials (*akhsania*), which frequently created various religious problems; supplying food and clothing to the army (*annona*); and a host of other levies.[29] The well-known phenomenon of *anachoresis*, whereby members of a municipal council, individuals or even

*See Strata, "Digging Up Ancient Tiberias," *BAR*, July/August 2004.

COURTESY ISRAEL ANTIQUITIES AUTHORITY

Beth-Midrash Lintel. *By the third century C.E., Jewish rabbis were becoming more involved in the spiritual needs and concerns of their local communities. Some opened* beth-midrashim *(or academies) for the study of the Mishnah, the earliest collection of rabbinic laws. According to its Hebrew inscription, this decorated stone lintel found in the village of Dabbura in the Golan once adorned such an academy. It reads: "This is the* beth-midrash *of Rabbi Eliezer ha-Kappar [a rabbi frequently cited in the Mishnah]."*

whole communities simply abandoned their homes and fled to avoid taxation, is vividly documented in rabbinic literature.[30] Appointment to the municipal council took on a new and ominous significance, for members of the *boule* (council) were responsible for the full payment of local tax assessments, even if this meant paying it out of personal funds. Thus we understand Rabbi Yoḥanan's warning to the potential appointee to the council: "If you have been named to the *boule,* let the Jordan become thy neighbor [i.e., take flight across the Jordan]."[31]

The economic situation notwithstanding, the multifaceted spiritual activity of the rabbinic class seems to have flourished during the third century. Indeed, the most outstanding authority of the second half of the third century, Rabbi Yoḥanan bar Napha (d. 279 C.E.), may be considered the supreme Palestinian sage of the entire talmudic era.[32] His influence as head of the Tiberian academy transcended the boundaries of Palestine. Even in the Babylonian Talmud, almost every page bears his name or reflects one of his traditions. Together with his colleague Resh Laqish (talmudic tradition also makes him a brother-in-law as well), as well as a host of other sages—many of whom were recent arrivals from Babylonia—the rabbinic movement of third-century Palestine seems to have played a major role in transforming the rabbis from a somewhat elitist and remote group of scholars into an influential, community-oriented class of social leaders. Whether this was the result of the creation and spread of permanent academies in numerous urban centers (called *beth-midrashim*),[33] or possibly a consequence of the economic plight of the time that served as a great equalizer, contributing to the removal of social barriers, is unclear. Other factors, such as a growing need for intellectual leadership capable of fending off confrontation with the growing Christian community may also have played a role, but what is clear is that the rabbis now assumed a heightened degree of communal responsibility, primarily on a local scale, but sometimes as national figures as well.[34] To be sure, not all scholars have embraced this rabbino-centric portrayal of Jewish society, and the degree to which the rabbis actually enjoyed widespread influence among the general Jewish population of Palestine is still one of the most fiercely-debated issues of Jewish history in the first centuries of the common era.[35]

The role of the sages in Jewish-Christian confrontations

One of the roles played by certain sages in the land of Israel was as disputants in the growing debate between Jews and Christians.[36] Sometimes the dispute was carried on by the dispensation of responses to hypothetical questions before purely Jewish audiences, most likely in the synagogue. But live confrontations also occurred, probably in major cosmopolitan centers such as Caesarea. It is not by chance that one of the major figures involved in these disputes was Rabbi Abbahu of Caesarea. One need not tax the imagination to uncover the targets of some of Abbahu's statements,[37] frequently based on an exegetical interpretation of scripture:

> Rabbi Abbahu said: If a man says to you: "I am God"—he lies; "I am the son of man"—in the end he will regret it. "I will rise up to heaven"—he says this but will not do it.[38]
>
> Rabbi Abbahu said: A parable of a mortal king: he reigns and has a father or a son or a brother. Said the Holy One Blessed be He: I am not like that. "I am first" (Isaiah 44:6)—I have no father. "I am last"—I have no son. "And beside me there is no God"—I have no brother.[39]

The implications of these confrontations and the need of Palestinian sages to be well versed in Bible and biblical exegesis for just such occasions may help to explain an important literary phenomenon as well. The rabbis of Palestine were responsible not only for the formation of the Palestinian Talmud, but also for the birth of a different literary genre—aggadic *midrash* (see below, pp. 273–274). These works reflect the broad spectrum of social and spiritual activity in third- and fourth-century Palestine. Oddly enough, no equivalent midrashic corpus was produced by the sages of Babylonia. This fact has led to much speculation. One solution may be supplied by Rabbi Abbahu himself: In the course of explaining to his apparently Christian co-residents of Caesarea why he, Abbahu, was well versed in the Bible while his Babylonian colleague Rav Safra was not, the Palestinian sage replied: "We [in the land of Israel] live among you, hence we take it upon ourselves to learn."[40]

The nature of the debates between Christian figures such as Origen (and later Eusebius) and the rabbis of the day can be seen most clearly by comparing the contemporaneous writings of the two groups regarding the very same scriptures. Such a comparison makes it clear that each side was well aware of the attacks launched against it by its adversary. Indeed, the comparison makes one wonder whether the two disputants were not in fact arguing face-to-face "before a live audience."[41]

These debates—and other contacts between certain sages and their non-Jewish counterparts—assume not only a familiarity with the adversary's theological claims, but also a shared knowledge of language, folklore and popular culture. It is not by chance that of all the sages it was Rabbi Abbahu who claimed it was permissible to teach one's daughter Greek "for it is an ornament on her";[42] nor should we be surprised that this sage was capable of repeating riddles based on knowledge of the Greek language and the numerical values of the Greek letters of the alphabet.[43] Rabbinic familiarity with "Greek wisdom" has been amply discussed in modern scholarship.[44] The brilliant studies of Saul Lieberman[45] have shown that although there is no explicit citation in rabbinic works to specific Greek literature, and although no Greek philosopher is discussed by name, it is clear that knowledge of Greco-Roman ideas, phrases and parables—as well as grammatical and rhetorical systems—infiltrated not only rabbinic literary work, but even religiously motivated deliberations.[46] We assume that these Greco-Roman elements were transmitted through a variety of intermediaries, most probably in oral rather than written form. Thus, the rabbis had no trouble comparing the stages of the Jew's daily *Amidah* prayer (as well as the praises of Moses, David and Solomon) with the structure and sequence found in the presentations of Roman rhetors.[47] Nor did Resh Laqish think it improper to compare the activity of the public preacher in the synagogue with that of the Greek mime in the theater.[48]

Obviously, these Greek influences were more pronounced among certain social strata within the Jewish population of Roman Palestine. Geographical proximity to large urban centers also played a role in determining the degree and intensity of such influences. While the use of Hebrew may have receded somewhat following the Bar-Kokhba uprising, it appears that many Jews in the land were bilingual, with Aramaic and Hebrew serving as their primary languages. But this situation was not uniform throughout the land. The number of Greek synagogue inscriptions found in Galilee, for instance, greatly exceeds those found in the synagogues of Judea and southern Palestine,[49] where Aramaic (and Hebrew) inscriptions were the norm rather than the exception. For our purposes, it is important to note that these Greek influences seem to have intensified in the third and fourth centuries as opposed to their prevalence in Mishnaic times. It is a good guess that *amoraim* (the sages of the Talmud) knew more Greek than *tannaim* (the sages of the Mishnah). The post-talmudic Jewish population became even more familiar with aspects of Greek-pagan culture than their predecessors.[50]

Transition to the Roman-Byzantine era

The 50 years of Roman anarchy came to an end with the reign of Diocletian (284–305 C.E.), but in a larger sense Diocletian's rule represents a period of transition from the late Roman period to the Roman-Byzantine era. While the religious upheaval brought about by Constantine affected Palestine only from the year 324, many of the administrative practices of Roman rule in the Byzantine period had their roots in the reforms introduced by Diocletian.[51] It was he who finally realized that the very size of the Roman dominion would ultimately be its undoing, and thus he decided to divide the empire into East and West. This division did not become permanent until the end of the fourth century, but its very inception had an impact on the administrative framework in which the residents of Palestine found themselves. Added to the basic geographical division was the innovative system of imperial rule known as the tetrarchy: Each of the two sections of the empire was ruled by an Augustus, under whom served a Caesar, who was designated as his eventual heir. The empire was thereby in effect divided into four sections, or prefectures, and these in turn were divided into dioceses. Palestine would henceforth be part of the prefecture of the East, with the seat of the governor of the prefecture (*praefectus praetorio*) situated in Constantinople.

The diocese in which Palestine was included was also called Oriens. Among its other provinces were Arabia and Egypt. This subdivision was designed not only to create a more efficient administration, but also to weaken the military power of any local governor. Interestingly, while the tendency under Diocletian was to limit the size of the provinces, the boundaries of Palestine in fact grew; major territories were added to the province in the south—the Negev and central and southern Sinai—at the expense of the province of Arabia. However, within the next century the province of Palestine would be divided twice. In 358 C.E. Palestine was split into two provinces, with much of its southern territory as well as parts of southern Transjordan becoming Palestina Salutaris, with its capital first in Haluza in the Negev and then in Petra. The capital of the northern province of Palestine remained at Caesarea, but in 409 C.E. this province was itself split in two: Palestina Prima comprising the central portion of the land (Judea, Samaria, the coast and parts of Transjordan), with the capital remaining at Caesarea;

and Palestina Secunda comprising the Jezreel Valley, the Galilee, portions of the Golan and northern Transjordan. The capital of Palestina Secunda was Scythopolis (Beth-Shean). It is this province that was home to the greater portion of the Jewish population in the land of Israel.

Diocletian's fiscal and administrative reforms were favorably received by the Jews of Palestine. Moreover, under his rule, the Jews apparently maintained the status of a *religio licita* (permitted religion): "When King Diocletian came up here[52] he decreed and proclaimed: 'All the nations will pour libations save for the Jews.'"[53] This passage is particularly noteworthy, in that it contrasts sharply with the steps taken by Diocletian against the Christian community in the final years of his reign.

The third century in general introduced some of the harshest persecution of Christians, particularly in the days of Decius (249–251 C.E.). Although Diocletian seems to have tolerated Christian communities during the earlier years of his reign, events took a sharp turn for the worse in the year 303, possibly at the urging of the Caesar Galerius. That year saw the beginning of what may have been the severest persecution of Christians in all of the late Roman Empire, lasting until the year 311. From an edict requiring the burning of all scriptures and the dismantling of churches, events quickly turned to the torture and execution of Christians.* Eusebius, bishop of Caesarea, was eyewitness to these events in Palestine and in other portions of the eastern empire. He recorded them vividly in his *Ecclesiastical History*, as well as in a special treatise on the Palestinian martyrs. For those acquainted with the Jewish martyrdom stories depicting events of 200 years earlier, during the Bar-Kokhba uprising, Eusebius's descriptions are strikingly similar, even to the system of torture employed by the Romans.[54]

One can only wonder how Jews in Palestine reacted to the punishment of Christian martyrs by descendants of the very same rulers who had used the same modes of torture against the generation of Rabbi Akiva and his colleagues. If Saul Lieberman, in his famous study on "The Martyrs of Caesarea," is correct, there is testimony in rabbinic literature to a degree of respect and admiration expressed by the rabbis for these martyrs, displayed just a few years before the "kingdom would become a heresy,"[55] and Jews suddenly found themselves subject to Christian rule.

*For a particularly brutal but little-known form of torture, see Mohammad Najjar and Thomas Levy, "Condemned to the Mines: Copper Production and Christian Persecution," *BAR*, forthcoming.

The Jews under early Roman-Christian rule: 324–361 C.E.

Constantine's victory over his last major opponent, Licinius, on September 18, 324, at Chrysopolis near Chalcedon, effected not only a reunification of the Roman empire under one ruler, but for the first time placed the land of Israel, as well as the Jews of the entire empire, under Christian domination. The social and legal status of the Jews underwent a steady redefinition in Roman eyes.[56] While it would be mistaken to suggest that Judaism was immediately rendered illegitimate and subjected to outright persecution,[57] it clearly found itself the target of a series of declarations issuing from ecclesiastical as well as legal sources. Indeed, it is in the various decrees of the Church councils of the fourth century, on the one hand, and the laws promulgated by Constantine and his successors, on the other, that one notes the dual nature of the steps now taken to define the role of Jews within society. Already in the decisions of the pre-Constantinian Church council at Elvira, Spain (306 C.E.), one senses the efforts of the Church authorities to isolate the Jews and remove any influence they might still possess over the growing numbers of adherents to Christianity. The thrust of these decisions, the long list of decrees that followed in the various eastern councils, was to create as great a distance as possible between the old Israel and the followers of the Church.

At Elvira, for instance, special attention was given to the prevention of intermarriage between Jews and Christian women, as well as any sort of concubinage wherein a Christian male might have relations with a Jewish (or pagan) woman. Accepting any sort of Jewish hospitality was forbidden. Jews were even prohibited from blessing the fields of a Christian.[58]

It was in the land of Israel in Palestine, however, that the Church authorities felt the greatest need to separate Jews from Christians. Not only were Jews far more numerous in this part of the empire, but they apparently still wielded influence over the religious behavior of certain Christian communities.

The most obvious and sensitive example of ongoing ties between the two religious groups was related to the celebration of Easter and its undeniable ties to the Jewish feast of Passover. Different Christian groups celebrated Easter on different days, many of them in conjunction with the Jewish Passover.* For these groups, the intolerable reality was that the Jewish leadership in Tiberias (the patriarch and the Sanhedrin), by virtue of its ongoing intercalation of the Jewish calendar, in effect determined when Christians celebrated Easter. The agenda of the Council of Nicaea (325 C.E.) therefore included, possibly at the request of Constantine himself, not only issues of theological

*See Samuele Bacchiocchi, "How It Came About: From Saturday to Sunday," *BAR*, September/October 1978.

differences within the Church, but also the need to establish a new system for determining the date of Easter. As stated by Eusebius, "It seemed very unworthy of this most sacred feast, that we should keep it following the custom of the Jews."[59]

Various other Christian councils forbade any participation of Christians in Jewish worship or attendance at Jewish synagogues. One intriguing decree explicitly forbade Christians to tend the lamps in Jewish synagogues on certain holidays, apparently alluding to a practice whereby non-Jews performed certain services forbidden to Jews themselves.[60]

Parallel to this new ecclesiastical demarcation between Jews and Christians, Constantine's victory also brought in its wake new legislation intended to define the status of the Jews. In certain instances a degree of continuity was maintained under Constantine,[61] but this could not overcome the basic fact that in embracing Christianity the empire would be left with no choice but to redefine the legal status of its Jewish subjects. Thus, while the state continued to recognize Judaism as a *religio licita,* it nevertheless created the impression that Jews would not be encouraged to play a major role in society.

Protection was granted to Jews who abandoned their religion; the legislation to this effect under Constantine suggests that the process of conversion from Judaism did not go uncontested by the Jewish community:

> We want the Jews, their principals and their patriarchs informed, that if anyone ... dare attack by stoning or by other kind of fury one escaping from their deadly sect and raising his eyes to God's cult, which as we have learned is being done now, he [the attacker] shall be delivered immediately to the flames and burnt with all his associates.[62]

Roman legislation also made it more difficult for Jews to own gentile slaves.[63] In this way, a religious scruple (lest the Jew convert the slave) had a major economic impact. It has even been suggested that this prohibition led the rabbis to rethink Jewish law regarding the conversion of gentile slaves, with the aim of circumventing the new legislation.[64]

Other Roman laws enacted during the first decades of Christian rule seem to have steered a middle path. Thus, while Jews were now required in principle to participate in curial liturgies (compulsory functions imposed on local council members), certain exemptions were granted to leaders of the community "in order to leave them something of the ancient custom as a solace."[65] In the late fourth and fifth centuries, however, the situation became progressively worse, although variations evolved in different parts of the empire: Legislation in the West followed a more rigid approach in its attitude toward the Jewish community than in the East, where possibly out of deference to the far greater concentration of Jews in that part of the empire, a more moderate policy was embraced.[66]

It is unclear whether the legal status of the city of Jerusalem was redefined, or whether the Jews were again—as in the days of Hadrian—denied access to the city, both as pilgrims and as residents.[67] However, it is clear that the character of the city changed. Christian pilgrims began to flock to the Holy Land in general and to Jerusalem in particular. One of the most prominent of these pilgrims, Helena, mother of Constantine, established several churches in the city. If indeed Jews were forced to reside beyond the confines of the city, it is possible that this regulation took effect in 335 C.E., coinciding with the consecration of the Church of the Holy Sepulchre.[68] But the large concentrations of Jews in other parts of the land, most particularly in the Galilee, prevented a similarly swift introduction of Christianity and its symbols into those regions.

Testifying to this Jewish communal vitality is the unique story of the Jewish apostate Joseph. At first a high official in the court of the Tiberian patriarch, Joseph clandestinely embraced Christianity but was ultimately discovered and removed from the Jewish community. As a friend (*comes*) of the emperor, however, Joseph was granted permission to establish churches "in the cities and villages of the Jews, where *heretofore* no man could erect churches, for they [the Jews] do not have [living] among them either a pagan or a Samaritan or a Christian [but only Jews]."[69] Joseph's attempts to build churches in the Galilee proved unsuccessful; in the end he removed himself to Beth-Shean, where, as a somewhat bitter old man, he managed to tell his story to Epiphanius.[70]

Clashes between Romans and Jews; the Gallus revolt

The determination of the Galilean Jews to assert themselves came to the fore again in the middle of the fourth century, in the so-called Gallus revolt.[71] Following the death of Constantine in 337 C.E., the empire was divided among his three sons, with the East, including Palestine, falling to Constantius. After a series of civil wars, by the middle of the century Constantius was the sole ruler of Rome. While he was off in the West, however, delivering the decisive blow to his opponent Magnentius, events in the East once again led to a Jewish uprising in Palestine, albeit of limited proportions. Before leaving for the West, Constantius had appointed his cousin, Gallus, to the rank of Caesar.

If we are to believe the Roman historian Ammianus Marcellinus, Gallus was ill-equipped for the job, and his ineptness soon became apparent. The pagan historian Aurelius Victor relates that "at that time a revolt of the Jews, who nefariously raised Patricius to the royal power, was suppressed."[72] To this brief report, which leaves vague not only the question of Patricius's identity but also the causes of the revolt, a number of Christian historians add some details. Jerome relates that the Romans, in suppressing the revolt, destroyed not only Sepphoris, but also Tiberias, Lydda and "many other fortresses."[73] This report, with certain variations, is repeated in the writings of other Church historians.[74] Interestingly, while mention is made of a Jewish slaughter of Roman soldiers as well as of "gentiles, Hellenes and Samaritans," no mention is made of any attack on the Christian community. If such an event had occurred, it would surely not have gone unnoticed by Christian historians. We may therefore conclude that religious tension between the two communities was not the cause of the uprising. Furthermore, we would expect a Christian reaction, if "Patricius" were in fact a Jewish pretender to the throne, thereby suggesting messianic overtones. Since this was not the case, it seems likely that the Gallus revolt of 351–352 C.E. was the result of some local disturbances in the eastern part of the empire, when various local commanders appear to have tried to capitalize on the absence of Constantius and the presence of an ill-equipped Caesar, Gallus, to assume positions of power.

Rabbinic sources, as well as archaeological evidence, suggest that various clashes occurred at this time between Roman forces and Jewish civilians. Some Jewish towns may have been destroyed, the most important of which was Beth Shearim.[75] But the disturbances seem to have been local in nature, probably in reaction to certain isolated injustices rather than the result of a new quest for national independence. It is difficult to point to any lasting result of the Gallus uprising.

The Jews and Julian: 361–363 C.E.

Gallus was executed by order of Constantius in 354 C.E. One year later, Constantius appointed his younger stepbrother, Julian, as Caesar of the western provinces of the empire: Spain, Gaul and Britain. To everyone's surprise the young Caesar, who until then had been occupied with intellectual rather than administrative endeavors, proved an overwhelming success in defeating the various invading tribes in Gaul and in restoring a measure of tranquility to the western provinces. Slowly Julian gained the enthusiastic support of the legions under his command. By the year 360, word reached Julian's legions of Constantius's plans to invade Sassanian Persia. Julian's legions thereupon revolted and declared Julian the new Augustus. Constantius's sudden death in 361 C.E. saved Rome from a civil war; the empire was

RICHARD NOWITZ

The Necropolis of Beth Shearim. *Three limestone arches frame the entrance to catacomb 14 at Beth Shearim, a complex of 26 catacombs cut into a limestone hill in the Galilee. Judah ha-Nasi, called Judah the Prince or simply "Rabbi," was buried here in the third century C.E.; indeed the cemetery became the final resting place for pious Jews from all over the Diaspora as well as Palestine. In the fourth century, Roman armies destroyed the city of Beth Shearim and use of the necropolis came to an end.*

ZEV RADOVAN/WWW.BIBLELANDPICTURES.COM

Inside the Catacombs of Beth Shearim. *A menorah is carved in relief above the head of a man dressed in a Roman tunic. Among the tomb carvings are numerous Jewish symbols such as the menorah as well as pagan motifs of eagles, bulls' heads and garlands.*

united under the rule of Julian, a 30-year-old descendant of Constantine who suddenly declared his total opposition to Christianity and the marriage of Church and empire that had begun to evolve just a few decades earlier.[76]

Julian did not abandon plans for a Roman invasion of Persia, and in 362 C.E., after having made his way to the East, he spent some nine months at Antioch preparing for a military campaign. Here the young emperor issued a startling declaration, which must have caught Jews as well as Christians totally off guard—he offered to restore the Jewish Temple in Jerusalem!

Julian had already made public, in late 361 C.E., his wish to abandon Christianity and restore pagan religion to its rightful position in the empire; to this end he had declared a renewed religious tolerance throughout the empire. Julian restored the status of pagan temples to their pre-Constantinian position and reintroduced pagan ceremonies into the military. He even went so far as to remove all Christian clerics from their positions as teachers of literature. His justification for this is interesting: How could anyone teach a literature replete with allusions to Greek deities while concurrently denying the very existence of the entire Greek pantheon? The true aim of the decree was not lost on his contemporaries, for in fact it was intended as a means of removing all Christian influence from the educational institutions of the empire.

Only in this larger context can we understand Julian's turning to the leaders of the Jewish community with an offer to restore the Jewish Temple in Jerusalem. Julian, it must be remembered, was only one link in the chain of Neoplatonic philosophers who—beginning with the likes of Celsus in the second century, Plotinus and Porphyry in the third century and Julian's own (albeit indirect) mentor Iamblichus in the fourth century[77]—either championed a revival of Hellenistic philosophy and religion, or went further and, like Celsus, considered Christianity something of a barbarian superstition, which now threatened the very existence of the empire. The mystic element of Neoplatonic thinking led directly to an appreciation of sacrifices and temple worship; thus Julian (along with his spiritual predecessors) attacked Christians for abandoning sacrificial worship. This attack on Christianity did not really need the Jews for support. Recent scholarship suggests that, although the Jewish phenomenon of sacrificial worship in the Temple was introduced into this essentially pagan-Christian conflict, Jews themselves were not really an integral or active part in the confrontation.[78] Yet the Jews could not have totally ignored these developments. The paucity of our sources relating to their reaction is probably due more to the nature of extant Jewish literature from the period than a total ignorance of, or indifference to, the events surrounding them.[79]

In any event, during his stay at Antioch in 362 C.E., Julian apparently invited a Jewish delegation to meet with him and inquired why they did not resume sacrificial worship in their accustomed manner. This question, as well as the reported reply (i.e., that they were forbidden to perform these rituals outside the Temple of Jerusalem), smacks of a degree of innocence or poetic license that may be attributed to Christian sources for the story.[80] Nevertheless, as a result of this meeting Julian promised to restore the Jewish Temple. Two letters written by the emperor himself attest to the nature of his promise. Only one of the letters has survived in its entirety, and much has been written surrounding its authenticity,[81] which today is accepted by the broad majority of scholars. The critical portion of the letter reads:

> To the Community of the Jews:
> In times past, by far the most burdensome thing in the yoke of your slavery has been the fact that you were subjected to unauthorized ordinances and had to contribute an untold amount of money to the accounts of the treasury. Of this I used to see many instances with my own eyes, and I have learned of more, by finding the records which are preserved against you. Moreover, when a tax was about to be levied on you again I prevented it ...
>
> And since I wish that you should prosper yet more, I have admonished my brother Iulus [Hillel], your most venerable patriarch, that the levy which is said to exist among you should be prohibited, and that no one is any longer to have the power to oppress the masses of your people by such exactions; so that everywhere, during my reign, you may have security of mind, and in the enjoyment of peace may offer more fervid prayers for my reign to the Most High God, The Creator, who has deigned to crown me with his own immaculate right hand. For it is natural that men who are distracted by any anxiety should be hampered in spirit, and should not have so much confidence in raising their hands to pray; but that those who are in all respects free from care should rejoice with their whole hearts and offer their suppliant prayers on behalf of my imperial office to Mighty God, even to him who is able to direct my reign to the noblest ends, according to my purpose. This you ought to do, in order that, when I have successfully concluded the war with Persia, I may rebuild by my own efforts the sacred city of Jerusalem, which for so many years you have longed to see inhabited, and may bring settlers there, and, together with you, may glorify the most High God.[82]

To understand the reasoning behind this letter and its promise to rebuild

Jewish Jerusalem and the Temple, one need go no further than Julian's major literary attack on Christianity, *Against the Galileans.*[83] Julian's admiration for Jewish ritual is manifest in that work, as is his disdain for the Christians who, while professing to have inherited Israel, have in fact abandoned the loftiest components of that religion, only to have preserved the one unacceptable tenet of biblical Judaism, which is the claim that God is an exclusive deity, jealous of all other gods:

> For envy and jealousy do not even draw near the most virtuous of *men*; they are all the more remote from angels and gods ... Like leeches, you have sucked the worst blood from that source [i.e., the Jews] and left the purer.[84]

Julian's claim, then, is that in fact biblical Judaism is praiseworthy; Christianity, on the other hand, has ignored the positive elements of Judaism:

> Why is it, I repeat, that after deserting us [pagans] you do not accept the law of the Jews or abide by the sayings of Moses? No doubt some sharp-sighted person will answer, "The Jews, too, do not sacrifice." But I will convict him of being terribly dull-sighted, for in the first place I reply that neither do you also observe any of the other customs observed by the Jews; and secondly, that the Jews do sacrifice in their own houses, and even to this day everything that they eat is consecrated ... but since they have been deprived of their temple, or as they are accustomed to call it, their holy place, they are prevented from offering the first fruits of the sacrifice to God.[85]

This argument, of course, serves as the theoretical underpinning for providing the Jews with precisely what they are now lacking. In Julian's eyes a natural coalition ought to exist between pagans and Jews, with Christians being the odd man out:

> I wished to show that the Jews agree with the gentiles [pagans] [in that the Jews, too, would sacrifice if their Temple were restored], except that they believe in only one God. That is indeed peculiar to them and strange to us [pagans]; since all the rest we have in a manner in common with them—temples, sanctuaries, altars, purifications and certain precepts. For as to these we differ from one another not at all or in trivial matters ...[86]

Needless to say, Julian was well aware of the fact that by restoring the Jews to Jerusalem he would also be destroying the Christian argument that

ZEV RADOVAN/WWW.BIBLELANDPICTURES.COM

Isaiah Inscription from the Temple Mount. *When the Roman emperor Julian, called "The Apostate," sought to reduce the power of the Christian Church in 363 C.E., he allowed Jews to return to Jerusalem with hopes of rebuilding the Temple. These hopes were quickly dashed with Julian's unexpected death that same year. Archaeologist Benjamin Mazar believed that this inscription, which quotes Isaiah 66:14 ("You shall see, and your heart shall rejoice"), was carved near the Temple Mount during that year when Jews expected the Temple to be rebuilt. Subsequent study, however, has shown the inscription to be an epitaph from a burial dating to the 11th century.*

placed so much importance on the destruction of the city (Matthew 24:2; Mark 13:2; Luke 21:6) and the removal of the Jews from it.[87] Subsequent Christian authors who described the events caught the message perfectly, and Sozomen, for instance, was absolutely correct when he claimed that Julian "thought to grieve the Christians by favoring the Jews."[88]

The whole affair ended as abruptly as it began. Although the Roman historian Ammianus Marcellinus relates that the building of the Temple was undertaken,[89] some of the archaeological discoveries, including an inscription quoting the prophet Isaiah (66:14), found at the excavations of the Temple Mount, and that were at first interpreted as a reflection of messianic expectations deriving from Julian's enterprise, have since been discounted, dating centuries later and having no connection whatsoever to the affair.[90] Julian's death in 363 C.E. during the campaign against Persia—legend attributes the fatal spear to one of his own Christian soldiers—put an end to any hopes the Jews may have entertained for rebuilding their Temple.[91]

Julian's death to the abolition of the patriarchate: 363–c. 425 C.E.

Julian's immediate successors did not retaliate with any anti-pagan or anti-Jewish reaction. Following Jovian's brief rule (February 364), the empire was again divided, this time between brothers—Valens in the East and Valentinian in the West. These rulers continued to grant a degree of tolerance to the Hellenistic religions, and Judaism benefited from this moderation. As an Arian Christian, Valens had enough on his hands just maintaining his position versus the growing orthodox majority within the Church; this probably explains why he was careful not to arouse opposition among the other minorities in the East, including the Jews.

The two brothers promulgated the first law by Christian emperors relating to the status of the synagogue. The law exempted the synagogue from the forced imposition of *hospitium*, i.e., the requirement to lodge either soldiers or officials.[92]

In another, later law the brothers extended the exemptions of "the elders and others occupied in the rite of that religion [Judaism]" from serving in the curial liturgies.[93] The Jewish officials mentioned in this law, we are told, are "subject to the rule of the Illustrious Patriarchs." This point is important. From a variety of sources—all of them non-Jewish—it appears that the Palestinian patriarchs of the late fourth century were a potent force in the Jewish community, both in Palestine and in the Diaspora communities.[94]

This situation soon came under attack by various leaders of the Church. Beginning with Theodosius I (383–408 C.E.), both the synagogues and the patriarchal leadership were subjected to a variety of pressures. Legislation took a decidedly negative turn. Outspoken attacks came from prominent personalities in the Church; these verbal attacks soon led to physical attacks on Jewish synagogues.

The synagogue as a focus of attack

Why did the synagogue become a prime target in the late fourth century? First, because more than any other institution, the synagogue was the focal point of Jewish communal life.[95] Here the Jew not only prayed, but was also the recipient of a varied Jewish education: On any given Sabbath, he (and she) would hear a reading of the scriptures (from the Prophets as well as from the

Five Books of Moses), together with a translation (*targum*) that was frequently not just a verbatim rendition of the texts into the local Aramaic vernacular, but also an enhancement of the text intended to enrich the message of the scriptures.[96] To this was added a sermon (*derasha*) that probably served as the major vehicle for the transmission of rabbinic oral tradition, encompassing legal as well as moral guidance for the masses. So the synagogue provided the most immediate source of spiritual enrichment to the common Jew.

But to all this was added, at least in the minds of certain Church authorities, the knowledge that gentiles, too, whether Christians or those with leanings in that direction, might also be attracted to the activities in the synagogue. Thus the need to restrict the institution by rendering it unattractive in the minds of the masses. At the same time, Church leaders sought legislative steps to prevent the synagogue from continuing to flourish.

In 386 C.E. John Chrysostom, presbyter at Antioch (later bishop of Constantinople), delivered the first of a series of sermons against the Jews. While his words may be an extreme example, they reflect the growing distrust and even fear of the powers of the synagogue:

> A place where a prostitute offers her wares is a house of prostitution. But the synagogue is not only a house of prostitution and a theater, it is also a hideout for thieves and a den of wild animals.[97]

Chrysostom knew that Christians sometimes frequented synagogues*:

> When they see you, who worship the Christ who was crucified by them, observing Jewish customs and reverencing Jewish ways, how can they not think that everything done by them is the best? How can they not think that our ways are not worth anything when you, who confess to be a Christian and to follow the Christian way, run to those who degrade these same practices?[98]

Two years after Chrysostom delivered this sermon, a Christian mob, led by the local bishop, destroyed the Jewish synagogue at Callinicum on the Euphrates. The emperor Theodosius demanded that the offenders be punished and the synagogue rebuilt, but Ambrosius, bishop of Milan, convinced him to rescind this decree.[99]

Subsequent Roman legislation makes it clear that this was not an isolated case. A law issued in 393 C.E., defending the synagogues, referred to the

*This was certainly the case in ancient Aphrodisias in southwestern Anatolia where Jews, some Christians and people who identified themselves as "Godfearers" all attended synagogue together. See Angelos Chaniotis, "Godfearers in the City of Love," *BAR*, May/June 2010.

"excesses of those persons who, in the name of the Christian religion, presume to commit unlawful acts and to despoil the synagogues."[100] Such warnings continued into the early fifth century, but by then they were joined with threatening statements intended to project a more "even-handed" approach:

> No one shall be destroyed for being a Jew ... their synagogues and habitations shall not be indiscriminately burnt up, nor damaged without any reason ... But just as we wish to provide in this law for all the Jews, we order that this warning, too, should be given, lest the Jews, perchance insolent and elated by their security, commit something rash against the reverence of the Christian cult.[101]

Another law, issued in 423 C.E., prohibited the indiscriminate seizure or burning of a synagogue, but also stated that if the structure was dedicated to the Church, "they [the Jews] shall be given in exchange new places."[102] This could well be interpreted as encouraging the confiscation of synagogues; indeed, so as not to leave any doubt as to the ultimate intentions of the legislators, the law concluded by proclaiming: "No synagogue shall be constructed from now on, and the old ones shall remain in their state."[103]

The archaeological evidence of synagogues in Palestine during the Byzantine period makes it evident that these laws were frequently more symbolic than practical. Not only did Jews continue to build synagogues in the land, but they felt no qualms at incorporating into those structures elements obviously borrowed from the scores of churches that were now part of the Palestinian scene. These contacts were preserved "in the detailed construction, ornamentation, furnishing, stone-carving and mosaics of [the] respective houses of worship in the Byzantine period."[104]

The decline of the patriarchate

The office of patriarch did not fare as well. By the late fourth century, the patriarchs found themselves under growing pressure, again obviously coming from ecclesiastical circles. Church leaders attempted to influence the emperors to limit the powers of the Jewish leaders. Given the fact that the patriarchs provided a convenient link between the Jewish community and the Roman administration, it was not in the latter's interests to limit the influence of the patriarchs.

In 396 C.E. a law was issued that prohibited public insults to the patriarchs: "If someone shall dare make in public an insulting mention of the Illustrious Patriarchs, he shall be subjected to a vindicatory sentence."[105] Three years later, however, a series of attacks on the Jewish leader began. He was referred to in one law as the "despoiler of the Jews"; he was warned, as were his messengers, to desist from gathering funds from the Jewish communities to be sent to the patriarch.[106] Chrysostom referred to the patriarchs as "merchants" or "traders," stressing their greed.[107]

At least in the East, these anti-Jewish laws met with considerable opposition, probably from the Jews themselves. Their efforts were initially successful. In a law promulgated in February 404, the privileges of the patriarch were reinstated.[108] A few months later, another law renewed permission to send funds to the patriarch.

This, however, was the last law that gave unqualified support to the office of the patriarch. With the ascension to the throne of Theodosius II (408–450 C.E.) pressure against the patriarch began to mount. In 415 C.E., a number of new restrictions were imposed on the Jewish community: New synagogues were prohibited. The patriarch was encouraged to destroy synagogues in places that had been deserted, provided this would not cause a disturbance. Patriarchs and Jews in general were prohibited from converting non-Jews. Any Christian slave belonging to the patriarch was to be transferred to the Church. This detailed law was, in effect, a direct attack on the patriarch, beginning with a personal reference—"Since Gamaliel supposed that he could transgress the law with impunity"—and proceeding to demote Gamaliel to a lower rank than he had hitherto enjoyed.[109]

This was not simply another attempt to weaken the unity of the Jewish community. Much more was involved. The patriarchs still claimed Davidic lineage. Although the messianic implications of this pedigree played no practical role in Jewish life, it did reflect Jewish commitment to the claim that the House of David still had a prophetic role to play in history's unfolding drama. Beyond this, a blow to the patriarchate was interpreted as a major step toward the ultimate dissolution of the Jewish community.

We do not know precisely what led to the final abolition of the patriarchate. A law in 429 C.E. stipulates that the Primates of the Jews, whether in the provinces of Palestine or in the other provinces, must transfer to the imperial treasury those funds that they have received "since the cessation of the patriarchs."[110] True, this law makes no direct mention of an imperial act that had eliminated the office of patriarch, but it is difficult to suppose that a lack of legitimate heirs brought an end to an office that had existed for centuries and had played such a crucial role in Jewish history since shortly after the destruction of the Second Temple.[111] Accordingly, many scholars believe that sometime between 418 and 429 C.E. some event sufficiently aroused the imperial administration that it forcibly brought an end to the office of patriarch. Yaron Dan notes that according to one source a rebellion broke out in Palestine in 418 C.E. and was put down by the Goth *comes* Plinta, who was later appointed consul.[112] If the Jews were believed to have played a role in this rebellion, this might have served as a pretext for the abolition of the patriarchate.

The law of 429 C.E. quoted above points to the existence of two Sanhedrins in Palestine. This, too, may have been the result of a Roman attempt to decentralize Jewish communal life and thereby weaken it.

Nevertheless, the Palestinian Jewish community was not significantly devastated by the cessation of the patriarchate. To be sure, some archaeologists have recently posited a general demographic decline and crisis of Jewish settlement in the eastern Galilee, extending from the mid-third to the late fourth century C.E., and have seen this as a logical backdrop not only for the abolition of the patriarchate but for the "completion" of the Jerusalem Talmud as well.[113] Be that as it may, other institutions of Jewish leadership in Tiberias continued to exercise influence not only over the Jews of Palestine, but, in certain cases, in the Diaspora as well.[114]

The final two centuries of Byzantine rule in Palestine: 425–614 C.E.

The effects of the last two centuries of Roman-Christian rule in Palestine on the Jewish community are enigmatic, and even somewhat surprising. All signs should have pointed to the slow demise of the Jewish community's vitality: Central leadership in the form of the patriarchate had been abolished; beginning with Theodosius II, the legal status of the Jews came under renewed pressure; demographically, the Jews of Palestine were clearly outnumbered by their Christian counterparts. And yet an apparently active and vital Jewish community continued to exist in the Holy Land.[115]

Synagogue building and restoration continued at full steam.* Many of the synagogue structures that can be securely dated by means of inscriptions were either constructed or restored precisely at this time. The mosaic floor at Beth Alpha was produced during the reign of "King Justinus" according to the Aramaic inscription at the entrance to the main hall, almost certainly referring to the reign of the emperor Justin I (518–527 C.E.). The mosaic in the synagogue of Gaza was laid in 508 C.E.† What is possibly the most interesting synagogue dedicatory inscription was found on the lintel from what must have been the entrance to the synagogue at Kfar Naburaya: "In the year 494 to the destruction [of the Second Temple, i.e., in 564 C.E.], the house was built under the leadership of Hanina ben Liezer and Luliana (Julian)

*See Steven Fine, "Did the Synagogue Replace the Temple?" *BR*, April 1996.
†See Connie Kestenbaum Green, "King David's Head from Gaza Synagogue Restored," *BAR*, March/April 1994.

bar Judan."[116] Other impressive dated synagogue inscriptions come from Rehov, Ein Gedi and elsewhere. Clearly this was not a period of decline in the building and refurbishing of Palestinian synagogues.[117] Indeed, recent excavations—and the re-examination of earlier ones—have led some archaelogists to propose a later date (fifth and sixth centuries) even for those synagogues that had previously been dated to the third century.[118]

All sorts of reasons have been proposed to explain the continued viability of the Jewish community in what should have been a period of decline. In purely economic terms, the late Byzantine period in Palestine was a prosperous one.[119] Christian pilgrims in ever-growing numbers continued to make their way to the Holy Land, not only spending money while there but frequently bringing with them donations for a variety of religious institutions, primarily churches and monasteries.[120] Moreover, the religious inclinations of some of these pilgrims were at times quite friendly toward the Jews. For example, Eudocia, the wife of Theodosius II, visited Palestine in 438 C.E. During her stay[121] she evinced much sympathy for the Jewish community. She may even have revoked the prohibition against Jews residing in Jerusalem, much to the consternation of Church leaders, such as Barsauma of Nisibis, who visited Palestine at the time.[122] According to Barsauma's biography, as a result of the empress's benevolence, the Jewish leadership issued the following proclamation to their people:

> To the Great Nation of the Jews, from the Priests and Leaders in Galilee, Peace: Know you that the end of the dispersion of our people has arrived and the day of the ingathering of our tribes is upon us. For the Kings of Rome have decreed that our city of Jerusalem shall be restored to us. Hurry then to come to Jerusalem for the feast of Sukkoth, for our Kingdom is destined to arise in Jerusalem.[123]

While the authenticity of this letter, in precisely this version, is not above suspicion, there is no reason to doubt Eudocia's generosity, nor the existence of a certain degree of messianic fervor among the Jews.

This proclamation also indicates that a recognized Jewish leadership existed in Galilee even after the abolition of the patriarchate. Testimony to this leadership appeared again in the sixth century. Then its influence extended beyond the borders of Palestine, reaching as far as southern Arabia. Numerous Christian-Byzantine authors attest to the fact that the tribe of the Himyarites in southern Arabia—modern Yemen—adopted Judaism in no small measure as a result of the activities of Jews sent from Tiberias. In the sixth century, the Himyarite Jews, in cooperation with Jews from Palestine, came to the aid of the local king, Dhu-Nuwas, who had also converted to Judaism and was resisting Ethiopian efforts to dominate the area. Southern Arabia was critical because it controlled important trade routes to the east. The Jewish leadership in Tiberias apparently felt it could alleviate its own plight under Byzantine rule by using the Himyarites as leverage.[124] The Christian author, Simon of Beth Arsham, describes how "these Jews of Tiberias send priests every year and all the time and arouse disputes with the Christians of Himyar"; Simon clearly understood the intentions of the Jews. He therefore warned them that "if they do not cease, their synagogues will be burnt and they themselves will be molested in all places where the Crucified one is reigning."[125] The allusion to priests in Arabia is all the more meaningful in light of a discovery made in 1970 in a mosque some ten miles east of the Yemenite capital of Sana'a. There, on a portion of a column, Dr. Walter Miller discovered a list of the 24 priestly orders (*mishmarot*), similar to the lists that existed in Palestinian synagogues at the time.[126]

The nature of the Jewish leadership in Tiberias is far from clear. One medieval source claims that a descendant from a different branch of the House of David appeared in the city approximately 100 years after the end of the patriarchate. This ninth-century Babylonian chronicle, known as *Seder Olam Zuta*, was apparently produced to support the ongoing claim to Davidic lineage on the part of the Babylonian Jewish exilarchs (*rashei golah*).[127] The source describes a Jewish uprising against the Persian Sassanian monarchy approximately during the years 495–502 C.E. The leader of the insurrection, the exilarch Mar Zutra, was ultimately executed by the Persians, but his son Mar Zutra managed to flee to Palestine, where he was appointed *resh pirka* (head of the academy [?]) and/or *resh sanhedrin* (head of the Sanhedrin) in Tiberias.[128] It is not clear whether these titles refer to two distinct offices and thus designate stages in Mar Zutra's Palestinian career,[129] or whether they are synonymous phrases. In either case, the source seems to suggest that Tiberias in the early sixth century did not suffer a void in the leadership structure of the Jewish community.

The fact that the community continued to be led, or at least taught, on a regular basis, primarily in the synagogue, by a circle of spiritual leaders is evident from a law introduced by the emperor Justinian in 553 C.E. Preserved in the Greek *Novellae*,[130] the law deals ostensibly with the language to be used by Jews in the synagogue, specifically when reading the scriptures. In effect the law permitted the Jews to use Hebrew, Greek or any other language, although when reading the Bible in Greek they were encouraged to use the Septuagint version, but were also permitted the Greek translation of Aquila. Regarding the oral Jewish tradition, the law took a harsher tone, however:

"What they call *deuterosis*, on the other hand, we prohibit entirely, for it is not included among the holy books."[131] Scholars are divided as to the precise meaning of the outlawed material. Some translate it as "Mishnah,"[132] but it is unclear what connection there was between the Mishnah and synagogue activity. *Deuterosis* may therefore be a general reference to the rabbinic oral tradition, which indeed was seen as tradition *secondary* to the written Bible. The intention here seems quite obvious: It is the corpus of rabbinic tradition in its entirety, legal as well as homiletical, that could never be accepted by the Church; "It was not handed down from above by the prophets, but it is an invention of men in their chatter, exclusively of earthly origin and having in it nothing of the divine."[133] This is but a thinly veiled attack on the leadership of the Palestinian sages and their representatives, who were still, it appears, a potent force on the Jewish scene even in the middle of the sixth century.

Jews and Judaism in the Mediterranean Diaspora

Until now we have focused on the Jewish situation in Roman Palestine for which we possess a unique blend of literary and physical evidence. This is not the case with the various Diaspora concentrations of Jews in late antiquity. Here we are confronted by a totally different situation. The Jews of the Persian east (commonly referred to as Babylonia) produced a monumental literary composition (the Babylonian Talmud) but left behind almost no archaeological evidence that might be used to describe their communal frameworks. Conversely, the Greek- and Latin-speaking Jewish communities of the late Roman period, from Syria and Asia Minor in the east to Rome and Spain in the west, are known to us firsthand almost exclusively from their impressive archaeological heritage, composed primarily of the remains of ancient synagogues, cemeteries and short inscriptions and graffiti.[134] In striking contrast to the Jews of both Roman-period Palestine and Persian Babylonia, the Jews of the vast Mediterranean Diaspora have provided us with virtually no literary texts.[135]

Historians are thus left with a dubious choice. Some have attempted to describe the nature of the Judaism(s) that characterized the Mediterranean Diaspora community on the basis of arguments from silence. Others have proposed imaginative—but at times highly speculative—interpretations of the archaeological evidence. More specifically, scholars have raised the question of how "rabbinic" these communities were, i.e., to what degree did the rabbinic traditions developed in Roman Palestine (and Babylonia) determine the religious practices and beliefs of Jews throughout the Roman Empire? Since no references to identifiable rabbis or their teachings have been found among the archaeological or epigraphic remains of the Mediterranean

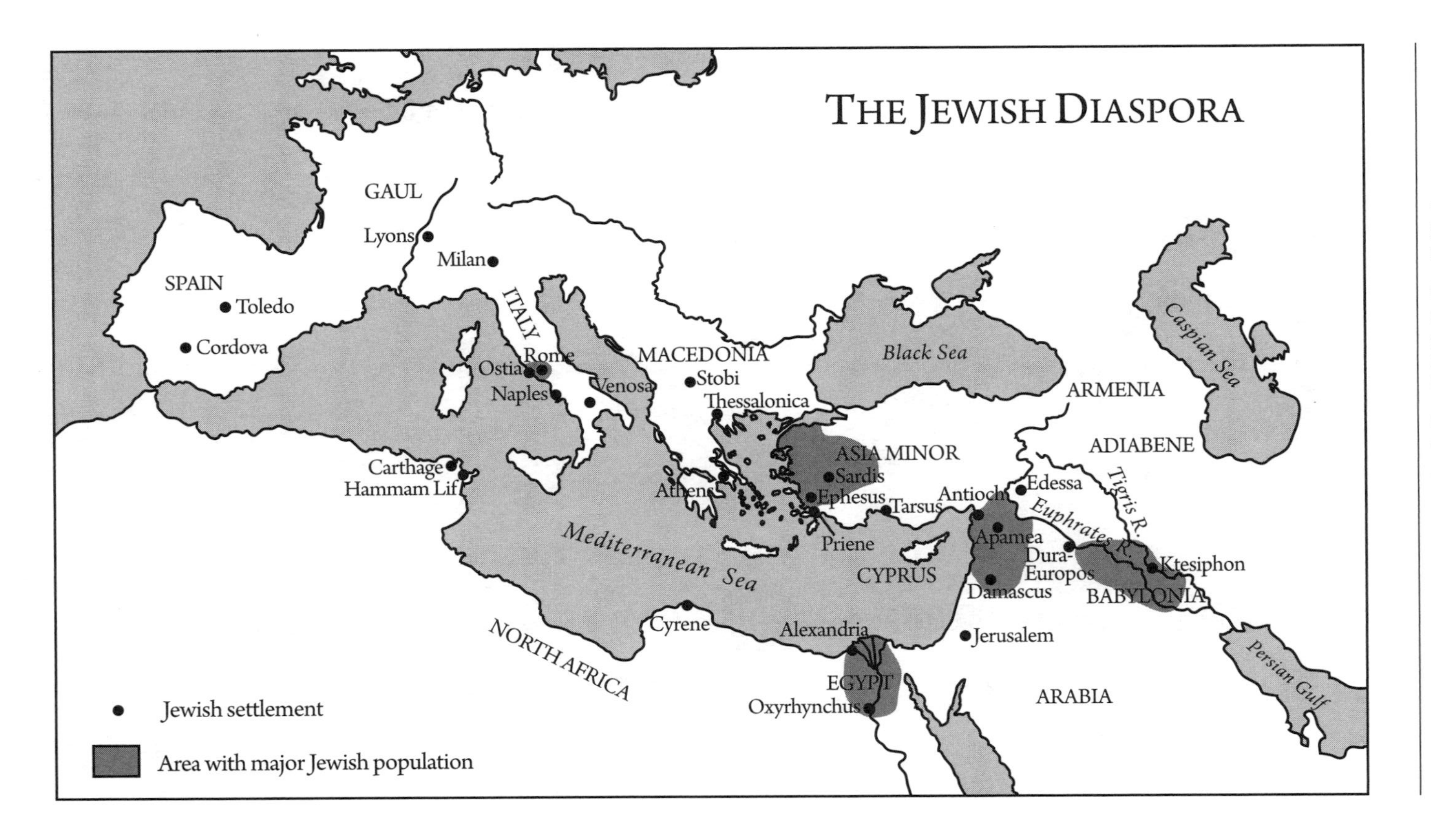
THE JEWISH DIASPORA
GAUL
Lyons
Milan
SPAIN
Toledo
Cordova
ITALY
Rome
Ostia
Naples
Venosa
MACEDONIA
Stobi
Thessalonica
Black Sea
Caspian Sea
ARMENIA
ADIABENE
ASIA MINOR
Sardis
Ephesus
Tarsus
Antioch
Edessa
Tigris R.
Euphrates R.
Carthage
Hammam Lif
Athens
Priene
Mediterranean Sea
Apamea
Dura-Europos
Ktesiphon
CYPRUS
Damascus
BABYLONIA
Cyrene
Alexandria
Jerusalem
NORTH AFRICA
EGYPT
Oxyrhynchus
ARABIA
Persian Gulf
Jewish settlement
Area with major Jewish population

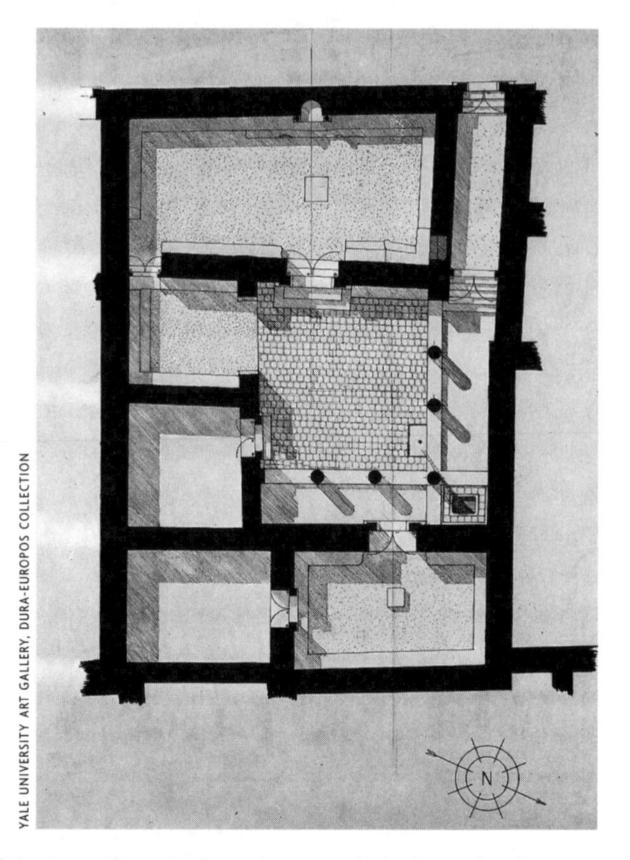

YALE UNIVERSITY ART GALLERY, DURA-EUROPOS COLLECTION

Plan of the Dura-Europos Synagogue. *In the 1930s, archaeologists uncovered this ancient synagogue at the site of Dura-Europos in modern Syria. Although the building originally functioned as a private residence, it was transformed into a synagogue in the early third century and was remodeled and expanded several times, apparently to accommodate Dura's growing and vibrant Jewish community. The ceiling and walls of the synagogue's main hall were lavishly decorated with extensive and colorful paintings of stories from the Hebrew Bible, including the drowning of the Egyptians in the Red Sea and the binding of Isaac (see Plate 4). The synagogue was destroyed in 256 C.E.*

Diaspora, should we assume that an alternative system, or systems, of Jewish behavior was normative among these populations?

One major approach in addressing this question has been to carefully examine the evidence of ancient synagogues in the Greek- and Latin-speaking Diaspora.

Over the years, the remains of approximately 13 synagogues from late antiquity have been discovered. These have all been conveniently described in Lee I. Levine's monumental work *The Ancient Synagogue*,[136] and span the empire from sites such as Dura-Europos and Apamea in the east (Syria), through Sardis and Priene in Asia Minor, to Stobi in Macedonia, Ostia in Italy and Hammam Lif in North Africa. References to some synagogue officials, as well as the names of the synagogues, can also be found in the Jewish funerary inscriptions of the catacombs of Rome.[137]

What is striking is that scholars, on the basis of this evidence, have drawn radically different and, at times, diametrically opposed conclusions as to the nature of the Judaism embraced by these communities. Thomas Kraabel and others, for example, have cited the diverse elements found in these synagogues as proof of different forms of Judaism in these communities. Others have come to the opposite conclusion, based on how much these Diaspora synagogues seem to have in common.[138] This same evidence is also frequently cited to prove just how different Diaspora Judaism was from the Judaism practiced in Palestine. Thus, for example, Kraabel has claimed that "the popularity of the permanent Torah shrine in the Diaspora" may provide "an indication that devotion to the written scriptures ... may have begun earlier and been felt more deeply in the Diaspora than in Palestine."[139] Levine, on the other hand, citing the very same synagogue evidence, concludes that "Diaspora Judaism was not radically different from Palestinian Judaism, at least as far as the synagogue is concerned."[140]

Other scholars have used the archaeological remains from the Mediterranean Diaspora as evidence for the lack of Palestinian rabbinic influence in these communities. While this may—or may not—be the case, the lack of references to specific rabbis in the catacombs beneath Rome, or the use of the Greek title *sophodidaskalos* to designate a teacher of wisdom (or wise teacher) in a mosaic at Sardis, hardly informs our understanding of the nature of intellectual activity and religious practice in these communities, and certainly does not warrant, in the latter case, a conclusion that "Sardis was well removed from the rabbinic sphere of influence."[141] A far more prudent observation has been made by Jonathan Price: "The most predominant evidence for 'Diaspora Judaism' is archaeological and epigraphical, two media which by their nature would not reveal much detail about religious belief, much less retain many traces of rabbinic influence."[142]

That we have no literary expression of the Judaism embraced and practiced by these Diaspora communities has justifiably led some scholars not only to ask why rabbinic literature did not make its way to the western communities, but also to posit an alternative mode of Jewish religious expression. Some suggest that a language barrier precluded the Hebrew and Aramaic rabbinic corpus from being embraced by the Greek- and Latin-speaking communities of the west. If the western Diaspora nevertheless maintained a Jewish character, the argument goes, it must have relied on a different Judaic corpus, namely the Septuagint (the Hebrew scripture translated into Greek), and was far removed from the norms of Jewish liturgy and festival commemoration (e.g., Passover with the Haggadah) as practiced by their brethren in the east.*[143]

Here, again, we encounter a hypothetical "other" form of Judaism, based not so much on concrete evidence but rather on a paucity of information on what *did* exist. Granted we do not possess evidence that would suggest Hebrew or Aramaic was significantly used by the mass of Jews in the Roman west, but the unfortunate reality is that this very same community did not leave behind a meaningful literary heritage in Greek or Latin either.[144] As noted by scholars, most of the epigraphic (and even archaeological) evidence we do possess tells us far more about *Jews* of the Diaspora (e.g., their communal titles and roles, professions and favorite symbols) than about the *Judaism* they practiced. Even the long list of "Godfearers" in the Aphrodisias inscription, now dated to the fourth or even fifth century C.E.,[145] probably tells us more about the religious proclivities of non-Jews than about the Judaism practiced by the local Jewish community.†[146]

As for language, it is certainly true that most Jews expressed themselves in Greek and Latin (78 percent of the Roman catacomb inscriptions, for example, are written in Greek, while 21 percent are in Latin). Within the Diaspora communities, however, even the presence of only a handful of persons with a working knowledge of Hebrew or Aramaic—a presence evidenced in at least some communities[147]—would have enabled a measure of Palestinian rabbinic influence to have made its way into their midst. Whether this was the case or not, we simply cannot know. Rabbinic literature describes various sages making their way from Palestine to Rome and to other portions of the Mediterranean Diaspora, but there is absolutely no confirmation of these visits in any external source, either literary or epigraphic.

In sum, our knowledge of Judaism throughout much of the Mediterranean Diaspora remains limited. Greater clarity will begin to emerge only as we approach the early Middle Ages.

The literary achievement in Palestine: Talmud and Midrash

The sages of Palestine in the post-Mishnaic period were not only an influential spiritual factor in their own day; they also left behind an impressive literary heritage.

*See Doron Mendels, "Why Paul Went West," *BAR*, January/February 2011.

†See Chaniotis, "Godfearers in the City of Love," *BAR*, May/June 2010.

Elements of continuity as well as innovation are to be found in the works of the Palestinian *amoraim.* But a word of caution and qualification must precede any discussion of this corpus, or corpora, of rabbinic literature. We commonly refer to the sages of the third and fourth centuries (and in Babylonia, the fifth century as well) as *amoraim,* and to the talmudic works they produced as amoraic literature (see "Tannaim and Amoraim," p. 235). This is, however, correct only in the sense that the books we are about to examine contain the statements, ideas and homiletics of those rabbis. The final redaction of almost all of these works came later, sometimes decades or even a century or two after the amoraic period. In some cases—including books that provided much of the source material for this chapter—they underwent a final redaction process hundreds of years after the deaths of the people whose statements and deeds they recount. This is a result of the unique process of transmission and preservation of rabbinic material, which in many cases was not put into writing in a formal sense until the early Middle Ages.[148] Thus, for instance, we speak of books such as *Genesis Rabbah* or *Leviticus Rabbah* as amoraic *midrashim,* but this is only true in regard to the persons whose statements are quoted therein. In these two cases the final literary redaction probably did not take place until more than a century or two following the talmudic period, i.e., in the fifth to seventh centuries.[149] Other *midrashim* make obvious references to the period after the Islamic conquests. *Numbers Rabbah,* for example, was probably not finally edited until the 12th century! So we must be careful how we use this material, especially as a source for the history of the talmudic era.

The amoraic literature of Palestine differs markedly from the literature of the earlier, Mishnaic period. While the Talmudim of both Palestine and Babylonia are, in a sense, discussions and elaborations of the Mishnah text, and as such are a direct continuation of earlier rabbinic endeavors, the nature of these deliberations as recorded is totally different from the presentation of the Mishnah. The corpus of law in the Mishnah evolved, at some time following its redaction, into the definitive code of Jewish law, to be studied in fine detail. But its structure is that of a legal code, organized topically and systematically, and with very little non-legal material or digression from the main theme of each tractate. Not so the Talmudim. While constantly building on the Mishnah, the Talmudim nevertheless provide the student with a much more fluid and elaborate text. The highly associative or suggestive nature of talmudic discussion enables it not only to digress, but also to introduce into supposedly legal discussions lengthy non-halakhic material: legend, folklore and popular wisdom. In a sense, one feels far more "in the real academy" when studying Talmud as opposed to Mishnah. The doubts and misgivings of named rabbis appear alongside absolute *halakhah*. Sometimes we are witness to lengthy deliberations that precede the final formulation of a legal statement.

Differences between Palestinian and Babylonian Talmudim

Within this framework scholars have searched for signs peculiar to the Palestinian Talmud, as opposed to that of the Babylonian.[150] It is assumed, to begin, that a major chronological difference exists. Whereas the last generation of Babylonian *amoraim* referred to in the Babylonian Talmud belong to the late fifth century (the last Babylonian sage, Ravina, died in 500 C.E.), the names and events mentioned in the Palestinian Talmud suggest a work whose development ceased approximately 120–130 years earlier.[151]

But beyond this difference is one of style as well. The discussion of the same Mishnah passage is almost always more concise in the Palestinian Talmud, which frequently does not contain a detailed analysis of each and every word in the Mishnah, as is common in the Babylonian Talmud. Thus the Babylonian Talmud frequently suggests an emendation of the Mishnah text, or at least of our understanding of that text.[152] The question is whether these discrepancies between the Talmudim are attributable to varying styles and systems of study, redactional processes[153] or to the historical contexts in which the two works underwent the final stages of their respective redactions.[154] Some scholars would attribute the brevity, and sometimes even abruptness, of the Palestinian Talmud to the difficult political situation that pressed upon the Jews of Palestine during the Byzantine period.[155] While this might not be the only solution, it is clear that the different cultural contexts as well as political and social conditions under which the two works were composed all played some role in determining not only the language of the two Talmudim (Palestinian Aramaic with a major dose of Greek in the Palestinian Talmud; Babylonian Aramaic and numerous Persian loanwords in the Babylonian Talmud), but also diverging attitudes toward a number of the main issues of the day.

One enlightening example relates to the attitude of the two Talmudim to the gentile governments under whose rule the two major Jewish communities found themselves. The underlying perception of many Palestinian sages, already evident in the Mishnah[156] and later even more so in the Palestinian Talmud, is that Roman rule in Palestine is not only evil but in fact illegitimate, at least within the boundaries of the land of Israel—thus encouraging, for instance, anyone who might wish to refrain from paying taxes to do so by any means at their disposal. The accepted attitude in the Babylonian Talmud, on the other hand, is that "the law of the kingdom is law" (*dina de-malkhuta dina*), with all the concomitant requirements to remain a law-abiding citizen.[157]

GARO NALBANDIAN

Plate 1. Ossuary Inscribed "Joseph bar Caiapha." *The inscription on this limestone ossuary, or bone box, may refer to Caiaphas, the high priest who presided over the trial of Jesus and was present when Peter and John, arrested for preaching in Solomon's Portico of the Temple, spoke before the Sanhedrin (Acts 4:6). The name is scratched on a side of the box in Aramaic, the common language of the time.*

ISRAEL MUSEUM/P. LANYI

Plate 2. Heelbone of a Crucified Man. *A nail still pierces the heel of a man crucified in Jerusalem within decades of Jesus' death. The bone was found in an ossuary in a tomb. The point of the nail is curled, probably from hitting a knot in the wood when it was driven into the cross.*

DAVID HARRIS

Plate 3. Hadrian. *The Roman emperor Hadrian (ruled 117–138 C.E.) may have triggered the Second Jewish Revolt against Rome (132–135 C.E.), sometimes called the Bar-Kokhba Revolt, when he announced his intention to build a new Roman city to be called Aelia Capitolina on the ruins of Jerusalem. When the revolt was crushed, Jerusalem was renamed in this way and Judea was renamed Syria-Palestina. Thousands of inhabitants were sold into slavery. The practice of Judaism was restricted and Jews were forbidden to enter Jerusalem. This statue of the emperor was discovered by an American tourist in 1976 near Tell Shalem in Israel.*

DEPARTMENT OF ANTIQUITIES AND MUSEUMS, SYRIA

Plate 4. Synagogue at Dura-Europos. *Located on the Euphrates, Dura-Europos was destroyed in 256 C.E. Completed five or ten years before that, the highly decorated synagogue reflects a sea change from the Hellenistic period when paintings were rare. Above the Torah niche are a menorah,* etrog, lulav, *the Temple of Jerusalem and the binding of Isaac. Above a ram and a tree, Abraham holds a knife, Isaac lies on the altar and Sarah stands in a tent. All face the hand of God to the left of the tent.*

TODD BOLEN/BIBLEPLACES.COM

Plate 5. Mar Saba. *For 1,500 years monks have lived at Mar Saba in the Judean desert east of Jerusalem. One of the oldest occupied monasteries in the world, Mar Saba is still home to a small number of Greek Orthodox monks. The first monastery was built in 482 C.E. by the hermit St. Sabas (439–532 C.E.) as a place of worship for the many other anchorites who lived in caves in the surrounding cliffs. St. Sabas's mummified body is housed in the domed church. Destroyed and rebuilt over the centuries, Mar Saba's current structure was constructed in 1840.*

SCALA/ART RESOURCE, NY

Plate 6. Catacomb of Priscilla. *Jesus was called the Good Shepherd both by himself (John 10:11) and his followers (Hebrews 13:20). This fresco is an example of the art used by early Christians to decorate the catacombs used from the second through the fourth centuries C.E. for burials and perhaps as meeting places. Some 600 miles of catacombs lie beneath the streets of Rome.*

HERSHEL SHANKS

Plate 7. Ostia Synagogue. *The city of Ostia, which served as the port of Rome, had a large Jewish community. The city's synagogue was built in the first century, although the restored remains seen at the site today date to the fourth century. The photograph shows the Torah shrine on the right and a four-columned gateway to the synagogue. The synagogues at Ostia, Sardis and Priene attest to the widespread prosperity and vigor of Jewish life in the Diaspora during the Roman period.*

DAVID HARRIS

Plate 8. Mosaic of Loaves and Fishes. *This fifth-century floor mosaic in the Church of the Multiplication at Tabgha on the Sea of Galilee commemorates the "Feeding of the Five Thousand." In a story recounted in slightly different forms in all four Gospels (Matthew 14:13–21; Mark 6:30–44; Luke 9:10–17; John 6:1–15), Jesus, using a boy's offering of five barley loaves and two fish, fed a hungry crowd of thousands. By tradition, this isolated area not far from Capernaum and Magdala was the site of the miracle.*

COURTESY ZEEV WEISS, THE SEPPHORIS EXCAVATIONS/PHOTO BY GABI LARON

Plate 9. Sepphoris Zodiac Mosaic. *Four steeds pull a chariot bearing the sun god Helios, represented by a disk with rays emanating from it. The depiction appears, surprisingly, as part of an elaborate mosaic floor uncovered in an ancient synagogue at Sepphoris, in the Galilee. In the mosaic, Helios is surrounded by the 12 signs of the zodiac. Sepphoris was not unique; Helios (usually shown with very human features) and the zodiac appear in several Galilean synagogues from about 400 to 500 C.E.*

JOINT SEPPHORIS PROJECT, DUKE UNIVERSITY

Plate 10. Mona Lisa of the Galilee. *This richly colored mosaic portrait of an unnamed woman was discovered among the ruins of the Roman city of Sepphoris in the Galilee. The enchanting tilt of her head and near-smile earned her the nickname "Mona Lisa of the Galilee." The portrait is part of a much larger early-third-century mosaic carpet depicting scenes from the life of Dionysus, the Greek god of wine. The prevalence of such graven images suggests that by the third century, this traditionally Jewish town located just 4 miles from Jesus' hometown of Nazareth was also thoroughly Hellenized.*

SCALA/ART RESOURCE, NY

Plate 11. The Apse Mosaic in the Basilica of St. Pudenziana in Rome. *This mosaic, dating to about 400 C.E., depicts an enthroned Christ, dressed as divine ruler, teaching to his 12 apostles who are all seated before him. In the background of the scene are the major churches and landmarks of Byzantine Jerusalem, dominated by an ornate cross perched atop the hill of Golgotha. Emerging out of the heavens above the scene are four winged beasts, symbolic representations of the four Evangelists. Crafted at a time when Christians were looking to suppress Jewish traditions and worship, the mosaic, according to some scholars, represents an overt attempt to claim Jerusalem as a Christian city.*

In addition, the manner in which the Mishnah was studied in the two Jewish centers may also have determined the differences between the finished products.[158] Neither of the Talmudim contains discussions attached to all six orders of the Mishnah. This may be a consequence of different curricula in the academies of the two centers.[159] Moreover, some scholars have suggested that not all portions of each of the Talmudim emanate from a single center in their respective land. Saul Lieberman attempted to prove that certain tractates of the Palestinian Talmud were redacted in Caesarea rather than in Tiberias, where the bulk of the work seems to have been edited,[160] but this claim has been questioned by others.[161]

The aggadic midrashim

As noted above, in Palestine a second genre of rabbinic literature emerged alongside the Talmud, namely the amoraic *midrashim.* These works are frequently referred to as aggadic because their contents address primarily the vast and varied world of Jewish thought, morality and biblical exegesis, rather than legal material. When all is said and done, the only really acceptable definition for *aggadah* is anything (and everything) that is not *halakhah.*

The aggadic material in the *midrashim* finds its genesis in a number of contexts. Discussions relating to the patriarchs of Israel and the ancient heroes of the nation could easily have developed out of constant rabbinic involvement in biblical exegesis. This, we have already seen, might have played a social role in the synagogue, as well as a purely academic one in the rabbinic circles of the third and fourth centuries in Palestine. Even when the rabbis dealt with post-biblical persons or events, up to and including the events of their own generation, this was not done out of any critical need or intellectual desire to preserve "history" as we conceive of it. Rather, the past played a role only if it could be used to support some moral or ethical motive whose relevance was above time or place. Rabbinic history, then, is subservient to a higher goal, and we must never lose sight of this when using rabbinic *aggadah* for the purpose of deriving historical realities.[162] Thus, for example, the sages were not all that interested in ascertaining *what* happened during the Bar-Kokhba war (or any other major catastrophe), in the manner of a Cassius Dio, but rather strove to disclose the improper behavior on the part of the Jewish people that led to the calamity. In the words of the Palestinian sages themselves:

> If you wish to know Him who decreed and [as a result] the world was created, study *aggadah.* For through this [*aggadah*] you know Him ... and attach yourself to His ways.[163]

Two distinct types of aggadic *midrash* survived. One would appear to be the product of the *beth-midrash* (academy). It is learned, and—most important—follows the scriptures, word for word. We can regard these *midrashim* as commentaries on the Bible; indeed, they are frequently referred to as exegetical *midrashim.* One of the most prominent of these is *Genesis Rabbah,* which, together with *Lamentations Rabbah,* is possibly the best example of an exegetical *midrash* redacted not long after the end of the amoraic period.

The second genre, while obviously having undergone a literary redaction, nevertheless impresses us as being closer to the sermons that might have been delivered in synagogues on any given Sabbath or holiday.[164] Rather than explaining each biblical verse, these works focus on a major issue or theme, usually linked in the opening of the discussion to a scriptural passage. This passage is then linked, during the course of the discussion, with many other passages from all over the Bible, interspersing these references with stories and parables, many from everyday life. Slowly, the *midrash* weaves a case on any given issue, until finally returning, in a most acrobatic fashion at times, to the scriptural passage with which the discussion opened. Such *midrashim* are often referred to as homiletical *midrashim.* One of the best and earliest examples of this genre is *Leviticus Rabbah.* Some of the most beautiful specimens of rabbinic teaching can be found in these *midrashim* and, if nothing else, they make it abundantly clear why the emperor Justinian would consider the propounders of this kind of *deuterosis* to be the truly influential teachers of the Jewish community.[165]

Halakhic and liturgical literature

The post-talmudic era (fifth to seventh centuries) in Byzantine Palestine does not mark a regression in the literary output of the country's spiritual leaders. Rather, we begin to encounter new literary genres in two specific categories of spiritual endeavor: *halakhah* and liturgy.

Discoveries in the Cairo Genizah now make it apparent that the late Byzantine period saw the emergence of a unique type of halakhic literature: collections of halakhic rules on particular issues of religious law, such as the laws of ritual slaughtering, blessings, formulas for documents and the like.[166] Compilations of halakhic decisions apparently became quite popular during the late Byzantine period. Known as books of *ma'asim,* these compilations supply us with a unique collection of sources on daily life in late Byzantine Palestine, touching on a variety of economic, social and religious issues.[167]

Alongside these halakhic works, the Byzantine period appears to represent the first major historical context for the appearance of the unique liturgical poems known as *piyyutim* (singular, *piyyut*). The first renowned *paytanim* (authors of *piyyutim*), such as Yosi ben Yosi and Yannai, made their appearance at this time. *Piyyutim*, which accompanied the regular prayers in the synagogue, frequently address the issues and hopes of the time. They are a unique expression not only of a renewed yearning for redemption, but also of a return on a popular level to the use of the Hebrew language throughout the land of Israel.

Late Byzantine rule in Palestine; the Persian invasion and Arab conquest of the Holy Land

The first four decades of the seventh century—more precisely 614–638 C.E.—were tumultuous years in the history of Palestine. In that brief span the rule over the land changed hands at least three times, messianic hopes were raised, cruelly dashed, raised once again—and similarly crushed a second time. In this short time, two monotheistic religions—Judaism and Christianity—and a fledgling third religion—Islam—all focused their spiritual and political attentions on this small territory. In Palestine, the two great empires of the Near East clashed once again, the culmination of 400 years of strife between Rome and Sassanian Persia. Each enjoyed astounding victories and suffered terrible defeats. The ultimate consequence of these clashes was the complete exhaustion of both sides, opening the way for relatively easy conquests by a third party, conquests that determined the dominant character of this part of the world for the next 1,300 years.

Over the centuries, the confrontation between Rome and Persia had amounted to something of a standoff. Persia ruled as far west as the Euphrates, Rome got as far as the Near East. The unfortunate buffer states—Armenia, Mesopotamia, Syria and Palestine—served as battlefields when one side or the other tried to gain an advantage. By the late sixth century a *modus vivendi* had emerged between the two empires. Correspondence between the Byzantine emperor Mauricius (582–602 C.E.) and the Persian king Chosroes II (590–628 C.E.) points to their shared interest in achieving stabilization, if only as a means of freeing their respective armies to fight on other fronts. An "eternal" pact was signed between the two, which almost reflects their self-perception as the bearers of a shared role to preserve peace. Interestingly, this idea found its way into Jewish sources as well, such as the midrashic statement that "God did not divide the world among two nations and two kingdoms, except for the purpose of watching over Israel."[168]

The pact itself remained in effect for about ten years. The situation became destabilized, however, when the Roman army rebelled, placing one of its own, a man named Phocas, at the helm. Phocas proceeded to engineer the death of the emperor Mauricius (602 C.E.). This in turn freed the Persian king Chosroes to go to war against Byzantium. In the spring of 604 C.E. the Persian king took the border city of Edessa. A year later (605 C.E.) the Persian army defeated a Byzantine force in Mesopotamia. The following year (606 C.E.) the Persian forces conquered Byzantine Armenia. By 607 C.E. Roman fortresses along the Euphrates began to collapse, and Persian raids reached territory in Syria, Phoenicia and even Palestine. This pressure led to the assassination of Phocas (on October 5, 610). He was succeeded by Heraclius, the son of the Roman governor of Africa. At first, Heraclius fared no better at stopping the Persian forces. Antioch and then all of Syria fell. With the fall of Damascus in 613 C.E., the road to Jerusalem was open.

It is not hard to imagine how these events were interpreted by the Jews of Palestine. For years, and indeed for centuries, Jewish eyes always turned eastward when they considered how the Holy Land might be wrested from Rome.[169] In the second century, one noted Palestinian sage, Rabbi Shimon ben Yohai, was recorded as saying: "If you see a Persian horse tied to graves in *Eretz Yisrael*, wait for the feet of the King, the Messiah."[170] A contemporary, Rabbi Judah ben Illai, stated outright: "Rome is destined to fall to Persia."[171] And now, Jews were apparently taking a more than passive interest in the events. According to some reports, Jews aided the Persian advance near Antioch, and even served as soldiers in the Persian army.[172]

To what extent the Jews of Palestine were actually willing to aid the Persians is not entirely clear. But at least in Christian eyes there was no doubt as to where the Jews stood: Sabeos, the Armenian historian of the late seventh century, stated:

> All of Palestine surrendered willingly to the Persian king; in particular the remnants of the Hebrew nation rose up against the Christians and out of national zeal perpetrated great crimes and evil deeds against the Aryan community. They united with, and acted in total conjunction with, the Persians.[173]

According to another source, attributed to a Jewish convert named Jacob (c. 640 C.E.), the leader of the Jews of Tiberias had prophesied that in eight years the Messiah would appear and restore the kingdom of Israel.[174] Such messianic expectations are also reflected in a unique new literary genre commonly referred to as *midreshei ge'ullah,* that is, *midrashim* of redemption.[175] The fact that the Persian kingdom was poised to usher in this messianic age made it even easier for Jews to identify these events with the biblical return to Zion following the Babylonian Exile 12 centuries earlier. That the current Persian king's name, Chosroes, was similar to Cyrus didn't hurt either.

The rise and fall of Jewish fortunes under the Persians

It was this ferment that greeted the Persians as they entered Palestine. In the early summer of 614 C.E., the Persians entered Jerusalem and for three days conducted a mass slaughter of the local population.* This was followed by a respite, during which those in hiding were encouraged by the captors to come out. Here our sources are divided as to what befell Christian captives, and in particular what role was played by the local Jewish population. Some have claimed that the Jews were proclaimed rulers of the city, invested with full powers of government. This of course played into the hands of those who then blamed the Jews for the systematic destruction of all the churches in the city. Pent-up hostility between the two religious communities so impressed our sources that it is difficult to form any clear picture of what actually happened.[176] One anonymous source has the Jews informing the Persians of an enormous treasure of gold and silver under the Church of the Holy Sepulchre. The aim was clear in the eyes of the reporter: a Jewish attempt to have the church destroyed.

At the same time, a Jewish source, one of the *midreshei ge'ulah* known as *Sefer Zerubavel*, describes a process of Jewish Temple restoration: sacrifices, building a tabernacle on the Temple Mount, prayers at the gate of the Temple Mount and the like.[177] But that same source goes on to describe what appears to have been a change of heart by the Persians. It is possible that after their initial successes in Palestine, the Persians realized that the Jewish population in the land, as well as in Jerusalem, was by now a small minority, and decided to come to terms with the far more powerful Christian community. As a result the Jews appear to have lost any control they may have initially enjoyed in Jerusalem, and Sabeos now quotes Modestus, the leader of the local Christian community:

> They [the Jews] that dared to fight and destroy this true site, the mercy of God led to their banishment from His holy city. Those who hoped to become its citizens heard themselves banished ... they were not deemed worthy to see ... the holy grave ... nor the gloriously renewed Golgotha. For others witnessed the return of their glory ...[178]

Jewish sources allude to a messianic figure named Nehemiah ben Hushiel (or ben Joseph) who appears to have resisted this change in Persian policy,

*Ronny Reich, "'God Knows Their Names': Mass Christian Grave Revealed in Jersualem," *BAR*, March/April 1996; more recently, see Strata, "Persians Massacre Jerusalem Christians," *BAR*, November/December 2010.

but, we are told, the king of Persia "went up against Nehemiah and all Israel ... and he pierced Nehemiah through and they exiled Israel into the desert and there was woe in Israel like never before."[179]

Whatever messianic hopes the Jews had as a result of the Persian conquest were soon dashed. Indeed, they realized that among the three powers converging on Palestine and Jerusalem, only the Persians were devoid of any religious motivation. Thus, the Persians were the only force likely to grant the Jews autonomous existence in their land. As Michael Avi-Yonah analyzed it:

> The deception, which the Jews suffered in their alliance with the Persians, marks therefore the real end of the political history of Judaism in Palestine.[180]

The defeat of the Persians

Persian fortunes, however, also began to suffer. The Byzantine empire under Heraclius launched a major counterattack. By 627 C.E. this offensive reached almost to Nineveh, where the Persians were again defeated. Their capital, Ktesiphon, soon came under attack. Chosroes was then deposed and murdered; his son died before he could strike a deal with the besiegers. Finally the Persian general Shar-baraz made a deal with Heraclius: Heraclius would recognize Shar-baraz as the Persian monarch in exchange for a Persian retreat from Mesopotamia, Egypt, Syria and Palestine; in addition, the remains of the Holy Cross—which the Persian army had seized—would be restored. On March 21, 629, Heraclius entered Jerusalem in a splendid procession; the return of the cross was regarded as a miracle.

It was the last great moment of glory in Byzantine Jerusalem. Within five years (634 C.E.) the Arabs attacked Gaza. Four years later Jerusalem was in Arab hands; the city surrendered in the spring of 638 C.E.

The appearance of yet a third force on the horizon could only have rekindled desperate Jewish hopes. Testimony to this is obviously reflected in the following *midrash*:

> The year when the King Messiah will be revealed, all the nations of the world will be at strife with one another. The King of Persia will arouse the King of Arabia. And the King of Arabia will go to Edom [Rome] to take counsel with them. And the King of Persia will again lay the whole world waste. And all the nations of the world will clamor and be frightened ... and Israel will clamor and be frightened and say "to where shall we go and to where shall we turn." And He says to them: My sons, do not fear ... the time of

> your redemption has arrived.[181]

The events of this time found equally dramatic expression in *piyyutim.* One of the most beautiful and touching of these liturgical poems, written to be recited on the 9th of Av (commemorating the destruction of both the First and Second Temples), was apparently read during the year that the Arabs concluded their conquest of the Holy Land:

> On that day when the Messiah, the scion of David, comes to a people pressed, these signs will be seen in the world ...
> And the King of the West and the King of the East each other will pulverize ...
> And the King of the West will establish his soldiers in the Land ...
> And from the land of Yoktan [Arabia] a King shall appear and his camps in the land will be strengthened ...

The poet goes on to describe how Israel will first be cleansed of its sins and then, realizing it is on the verge of the messianic era, gather in Jerusalem where the Messiah will proclaim himself:

> And the Priests on their orders will stand;
> And the Levites on their platforms will be raised;
> And He will declare: I have returned to Jerusalem in mercy.[182]

Beyond the Euphrates: The Jews of Babylonia

The sages of the Babylonian Talmud list the successive births and deaths of prominent rabbis:

> When Rabbi Akiva died, Rabbi [Judah the Patriarch] was born, when Rabbi died Rav Judah [ben Yehezkel] was born ... This teaches that a righteous man does not depart from the world until [another] righteous man like himself is created, as it is written: "The sun riseth, the sun goeth down" [Ecclesiastes 1:5].[183]

One can only wonder whether in the backs of their minds the Babylonian sages did not interpret this theme as part of the larger history of Israel as well. For as the Jews of Palestine began their slow decline, the Jewish community of Babylonia was about to embark on its own great chapter in Jewish history, beginning in the third century C.E. down to the end of the geonic[184] period in the 11th century.

Jews had reached Babylon even before the destruction of the First Temple, as a result of the earlier Babylonian conquest of Jerusalem in 597 B.C.E. Their numbers substantially increased after the Babylonian destruction of Jerusalem in 586 B.C.E. that led to a second wave of captivity, thereby creating the Babylonian Exile. But in one of those inexplicable twists of history, we lose track of the Babylonian community almost immediately, save for bits and pieces of isolated information in the later books of the Bible, and scraps of archaeological evidence.*[185] During the latter part of the sixth century B.C.E., a minority of Jews returned from the Babylonian Exile following permission granted by the Persian monarch Cyrus the Great.† But until the Roman destruction of the Second Temple in 70 C.E., we need to be, and are, constantly reminded that Jews are still in Babylonia, indeed in numbers "so great that no one knows their precise number."[186] But the fact remains that for approximately 1,000 years, the Jews of Babylonia were isolated from the mainstream of Jewish history—or at least from that history for which we have any substantial documentation. This paucity of documentation includes literary sources similar to the writings of Josephus, as well as archaeological evidence, especially when we compare the relative wealth of Jewish inscriptions from the Hellenistic-Roman world with that of the east.

Yet we know the Jews of Babylonia were numerous and powerful, for Jews in the Hellenistic-Roman world repeatedly took into consideration the powerful potential support of their brethren in Babylonia before embarking on any major uprising, usually against the Romans.[187]

Every now and then a Babylonian Jew pierced the wall of silence and made his way onto the stage of Jewish history, in Palestine or elsewhere in the Greco-Roman world. One of the best-known examples is Hillel the Babylonian, who made his way to Jerusalem, probably during the reign of Herod (37–4 B.C.E.), and ultimately became the founding father of a school of proto-rabbinic teaching. But these are exceptions; the truth is that until after the Bar-Kokhba Revolt (132–135 C.E.) the Jewish community in Babylonia does not appear to have left any major impression on the life or the leaders of Palestinian Jewry.[188]

This began to change, however, in the third century C.E. Ultimately the rabbis of Babylonia themselves cited, in retrospect, the return from Palestine of one of their own scholars, Rav (Abba), to Babylonia in 219 C.E.,[189] as the beginning of a new era in the relative status of the two great Jewish communities: "We have made ourselves [or, consider ourselves] in Babylonia like *Eretz Yisrael* ... from when Rav went down to Babylonia."[190] While this may seem

*For a discussion of the exiles in Babylon and a discussion of the Exile's significance, see André Lemaire, "The Universal God," *BAR*, November/December 2005.

†Lisbeth S. Fried, "Cyrus the Messiah," *BR*, October 2003; see also Aaron Demsky, "Who Returned First: Ezra or Nehemiah?" *BR*, April 1996.

to telescope a long drawn-out process into one identifiable event, the fact is that the date and event cited in that statement indeed point precisely to the early third century, when Jewish Babylonia's star began to rise.

Why was Babylonian Jewry unique? To begin, this was not only one of the largest concentrations of Jews in the world, but the one major community that did not find itself within the framework of the Hellenistic and Roman world. As such, it was impervious to the impact of the pervasive and assimilatory nature of Hellenistic culture. Although Greek influence certainly existed during the Seleucid rule throughout much of Iran, and continued to thrive even under their Parthian successors, it would be mistaken to ascribe a policy of active Hellenization aimed at the various ethnic groups that populated the region.[191] In practice, these communities seem to have enjoyed a major degree not only of semi-political self-rule, but of cultural autonomy as well.

As we proceed into the third century C.E., we hear for the first time that the Jews of Babylonia have at their head an exilarch (*resh galuta*, "head of the Diaspora") with claims to Davidic lineage. To be sure, there is absolutely no mention of this position before the late second or early third century (and these early allusions are also doubtful), and it was only in geonic times that apologists for one of the branches of the exilarchate would find it necessary to invent genealogical tables to prove the Jewish leader's pedigree.[192] But the exilarchate was undoubtedly a potent force throughout the talmudic period in Babylonia—the period that began as the Sassanian dynasty assumed the local throne from their predecessors, the Arsacids, in c. 224 C.E. Change of regime, coupled with an initial perceived repression by the founding monarch of the new dynasty,[193] made the need for Jewish representation at the royal court critical, and it is not by chance that the exilarchate ultimately established its presence in Mahoza, which as Be-Ardashir (previously Ktesiphon/Seleucia) was also the royal capital city. Interestingly, the bishop of that same city was also the official representative (*catholicos*) of Persian Christianity, and recent scholarship has shown that a comparison of the offices of Jewish and Christian leadership provides us with significant insights into our understanding of the behavior of Sassanian authorities toward the various minorities.[194] It is far from certain to what extent the exilarchs played a major role in the economic and social life of the Jewish community at large,[195] but their diplomatic activity, as well as their interaction with certain rabbinic circles, appears to have contributed to the pride and self-image of the broader community.

The exilarchate did not rule the Babylonian Jewish community single-handedly. Alongside this office, a new framework of leadership gradually appeared, namely the rabbis of Babylonia.

Much has been written about the stages of development of rabbinic leadership, as well as the degree to which the Jewish "man in the street" was actually affected by rabbinic influence.[196] Moreover, it has become increasingly evident in recent years that rabbis and commoners alike were not removed from the Persian environment, and that social surroundings and even legal precepts had a profound impact on the Jewish world and the deliberations of the talmudic sages.[197] As for any formal Babylonian rabbinic organization, it seems evident that rabbinic academies (*yeshivot*) did not spring up overnight in third-century Babylonia;[198] such institutions usually undergo protracted periods of development before assuming roles of recognized communal leadership, and it is possible that here, too, the final version of the academy emerges only as we head into the late-talmudic and post-talmudic periods.[199] A marked difference, however, characterizes the emergence of Babylonian rabbinic leadership, as compared to its Palestinian counterpart. The Palestinian patriarchs began their history as "rabbis," that is, central figures within the religious circles that disseminated religious teaching; but gradually they accreted political power. In Jewish Babylonia, as we have seen, the exilarch ruled, exercising political power within the community by virtue of his Davidic lineage. The Babylonian rabbis confined their concerns to moral and religious responsibilities, ever careful not to overstep their position and thereby offend the exilarch.[200]

If the rabbis of Babylonia were prudent in their relations with the exilarch, they were even more cautious in defining and publicly stating their attitude toward the government. As we have already noted, it is in Babylonia that we encounter the well-formulated principle that "the law of the government is law." Even when the revitalized Zoroastrian religious establishment took extreme steps to ensure that the major tenets of its religion not be debased,[201] these steps were not construed by the local Jewish community as persecutions. In fact, the Zoroastrian-Sassanian religious establishment avoided any sort of forced missionary activity that might impinge on Jewish behavior.[202]

In the fourth century it was the local Christian community whose loyalties were suspect. While that community might naturally be suspected of allying itself with the Roman-Christian empire, the Jews were clearly beyond such suspicion; it was assumed that they—if anyone—surely hated Rome, the destroyer of the Jewish Temple. Indeed, as we have seen, the rabbis of Babylonia even suggested that in the future Persia would defeat Rome. After all, Achaemenid Persia not only defeated the destroyers of the First Temple (Babylonia) but also encouraged, under Cyrus, the building of the Second Temple. Rome, on the other hand, destroyed the Second Temple, and so "Is it not reasonable that Rome fall to Persia?"[203]

Although not all Babylonian Jews were enamored with the new Sassanian regime, the *modus vivendi* that emerged was the decisive factor in the subsequent success of Babylonian Jewry. Here, not surprisingly, we can observe a kind of reversal of roles between the Jewish community and the Christian Church. In the first half of the fourth century, Aphraates, the bishop of Mar Mattai (near Mosul), told his Christian flock not to heed the scoffing of the apparently more secure Jewish community:

> The impure say that this church has no God ... for if it had a God why doesn't He fight their battle ... and even the Jews scoff at us and lord it over our people.[204]

The bishop knew of Jews who had succeeded in converting Christians; he delivered sermons against this danger.

While conversion to Judaism does not seem to have been a major issue in Jewish Babylonia, it is true that there was little fear of Christianity among the local Jewish community. The rabbis of Babylonia evinced little insecurity regarding the viability of their community. In time, this self-assurance of the Babylonian Jewish community affected relations between Babylonian Jewry and Jewish Palestine. The Babylonian Jews came to regard themselves as the "purest" of the Jewish communities in terms of their pedigree, even when compared with Palestine.[205] By the late third century, rabbinic authorities in Babylonia advised their disciples against "going up" to Palestine.[206] For many Jews—at the time and subsequently—Babylonia served as the prototype of the successful Diaspora, a place where one ought to remain until the ultimate redemption and deliverance. This obviously did not sit well with the Jewish leaders in Palestine. But Babylonian local patriotism continued to thrive. By the post-talmudic era we encounter Babylonian apologists who suggest that their land is the real land of Torah, rather than Palestine.[207]

Babylonian Jewry thus shaped Jewish life and religious behavior at a critical stage in the development of Judaism. The Babylonian Talmud ultimately attained overriding authority, in striking contrast to its Palestinian counterpart. For centuries it remained the central and most universally studied religious text among those Jews who devoted their lives to the study of "Torah." Moreover, the Babylonian *geonim* succeeded in spreading Babylonian tradition and legal decisions throughout much of the Jewish Diaspora. All this was true notwithstanding the central role filled by the land of Israel in Jewish thought, as well as in so many other spheres of Jewish religious behavior.

EIGHT

The Religion of the Empire: Christianity from Constantine to the Arab Conquest[1]

DENNIS E. GROH

THE BREATHTAKING RISE AND DEVELOPMENT OF CHRISTIANITY before the fourth century was equaled and even surpassed in the years 312 to 640 C.E. Constantine became the sole ruler of the Roman Empire in 324 C.E.—just 13 years after the last systematic imperial persecution of the Christian churches in the East. From Constantine to the end of antiquity, with the exception of the brief reign of Julian (361–363 C.E.), the empire would be continuously ruled by Christians.

Until the conversion of the emperors, Christianity had no true political center for its ambitions and no comprehensive agenda for the public ordering of its life. The continuous succession of Christian emperors provided the necessity, the machinery and the financing for the creation of a Christian empire. Thus the ecclesiastics who had portaged through the turbulent persecutions of 303 to 311 C.E. found themselves suddenly sailing on a great new public lake.[2]

The prestige of legitimacy and the largess of rich donors now showered upon the bishops of the Church who, for the first time in Christian history, became powerful figures in society. These centuries gave to Western history, as articulated by both imperial and ecclesiastical spokespersons, the dream of an entirely Christian world—ruled by Christian princes, decorated with a newly developing Christian art and architecture and held together by unanimity of doctrine.

In fact, when we look closely, we see that these centuries were also characterized by an enormous diversity in all areas—differences in language, doctrine, wealth and lifestyles.[3] But for all the diversity and difference, we nevertheless see a gradual confluence of this new public religion with much older Mediterranean customs and traditions. By the sixth century C.E., there is a clearly recognizable commonality in pottery, mosaic styles, small artifacts, public works and roads. This is especially true of urban culture. If you missed the name on your way in, you would be hard put to know exactly in what city you were.

In this sense, civilization meant standardization—uniform weights, measures, etc. By the sixth century, there existed an integral culture across the Mediterranean that can properly be called Byzantine. As we move into the welter of detail and dissent that forms the inevitable subject of history, it is good to remember that a Byzantine Christian civilization, centered in Constantinople, is being born that will endure and grow for at least the next 1,000 years, long after the Islamic conquest removes the old eastern provinces from Roman rule.

Constantine becomes sole ruler in the East

Until recently, the question of when Constantine became a Christian, or even whether he was ever a Christian, was open to debate. The question has now been largely settled by the authentication of a sermon he preached sometime in the years 317–324 C.E.[4] In that sermon, Constantine publicly declared the Christian God to be his sponsor and the author of all his exploits:

> When people commend my services, which owe their origin to the inspiration of Heaven, do they not clearly establish the truth that God is the cause of the exploits I have performed? ... and surely all persons know that the holy service in which these hands have been employed has originated in pure and genuine faith toward God ... Hence, it becomes all pious persons to render thanks to the Savior of all, first for our own individual security, and then for the happy posture of public affairs: at the same time entreating the

> favor of Christ with holy prayers and constant supplications, that he would continue to us our present blessings.[5]

In 324 C.E., Constantine defeated and killed his pagan rival Licinius and took possession of the East; he could then drop all pretense of interest in other religions and, he hoped, take his rightful place among the "saints" of the Christian Church.[6]

Immediately after Licinius's defeat, Constantine began laying out a new capital for himself, which later writers would call "the new Rome," but which we know familiarly as Constantinople (Constantine's city).[7] Constantine included Christian churches within the very plan of the new city—without running afoul of vested pagan interests of the old Roman Senate, as he might have if he had built his city in the West.

Like so many aristocrats of the East in the fourth century, Constantine was not baptized until his deathbed, fearing that during his lifetime the judicial and military duties imposed on officeholders might require him to break one or more of the commandments. At his death in 337 C.E., he was buried in Constantinople in the Church of the Holy Apostles, where he had erected six coffins, symbolizing the apostles, on either side of his resting place.[8]

The new Christian mind of the East

The world that Constantine's sons inherited was a far different world than their father had entered as a young soldier. Constantine had attributed the fortunes of his house to the Christian Church and its prosperity. He had been no friend of other religions; but, although he fulminated against other faiths, he did not actually persecute them.[9]

We can see this tone of distaste for other religions in his legislation regarding the Jews. Constantine's relation to the Jews, as judged by his legislation, conforms to that of his predecessors.[10] Jews continued to exercise their full civil rights, even serving on municipal councils. Jews since Hadrian's day (c. 135 C.E.) had been prohibited from visiting Jerusalem. Constantine both lifted this prohibition and allowed Jews to mourn the loss of the Temple annually.[11] What is new in his legislation regarding the Jews is the nasty tone of the language about Judaism,[12] in keeping with Constantine's distaste for non-Christian religions: It is described as a "deadly sect," "a nefarious sect":

> It is our will that Jews and their elders and patriarchs shall be informed that if, after the issuance of this law, any of them should dare to assail with stones or with any other kind of madness—a thing which We have learned is now being done—any person

> who has fled their feral [deadly] sect and has resorted to the worship of God, such assailant shall be immediately delivered to the flames and burned, with all his accomplices. Moreover, if any person from the people should betake himself to their nefarious sect and should join their assemblies, he shall sustain with them the deserved punishment.[13]

As we can see from the above law, Constantine wished to protect converts to his new faith, which he considered to alone practice the true "worship of God." But he and his successors had "adopted" a religion that had grown teeth even before his advent in the East. The early Christian emperors were under continuous pressure from Christian bishops in the East to silence all other cults. The roots for this lay, we now know, in the Christian reaction to the last great persecution of the Church by the emperor Diocletian and successors in the years 303 to 311 C.E. The details of that persecution need not detain us, but the results of it sealed the fate of all other religions in the East. Christians who had been willing to consider coexistence with pagans found the pagan state turning on them in the worst persecution of Christians to date. They adopted a "never again" attitude toward paganism and, when the opportunity arose, sought to make Christianity the only legally permitted religion.

The writings of Eusebius of Caesarea, one of the most influential bishops of the East, allow us to trace the progress of this new hardline policy toward non-Christians. Early in his writing career, Eusebius seemed to think of Christianity as the true religion, but not the only religion that should exist in the Roman Empire. By late in Constantine's reign, Eusebius became convinced that other religions should be suppressed; and by the time of Constantine's death, Eusebius was demanding that the new emperors eliminate all other religions.[14]

A long campaign was beginning that would culminate in Christianity's being recognized as the official religion of the Roman Empire. By 392 C.E. edicts were issued closing all temples and ending sacrifices at pagan shrines.[15] Thus in the reign of Theodosius 1 (379–395 C.E.), Christianity became the official religion of the empire. Theodosius himself was raised suddenly to the throne as co-emperor by the emperor Gratian (375–383 C.E.), who needed his help in ruling the eastern portion of the empire. Historians have suggested this sudden, almost miraculous, elevation contributed to Theodosius's commitment to Christianity. Moreover, as a result of an illness early in his reign, Theodosius was baptized. Unlike his predecessor who had been baptized only at the end of their lives, Theodosius sat on the throne as a baptized Christian.[16] Early in his reign he issued a famous edict (*Cunctos Populos*)

© ERICH LESSING

Theodosius I. *Roman emperor of the East from 379 to 395 C.E., Theodosius I was a vigorous champion of orthodox Christianity, making it the official religion of the empire. Although he deprived dissenters and heretics of civil rights and outlawed marriages between Christians and Jews, Theodosius protected most Jewish legal rights and tried by law to protect synagogues from hostile Christians.*

bringing all peoples under the orthodox (or "catholic") view of the Trinity, thus identifying Christian imperial orthodoxy with Roman citizenship.[17] It was Theodosius who empowered Christian consensus on the doctrine of the Trinity at the Council of Constantinople in 381 C.E. (see below) and followed his commitment to orthodoxy by laws depriving dissenters and heretics of civil rights.[18]

The Christian empire had found its rallying cry and a most memorable way to identify its partisans: as followers of the triune god.[19] At the very end of antiquity, the inscribed copper plates over the eastern and western gates of the great Islamic shrine of the Dome of the Rock in Jerusalem recognized, in a kind of off-handed compliment, the ideological power of the new unifying Christian doctrine forged in these earlier centuries:

> The Unity of God and the Prophecy of Mohammad are True.
>
> *and*
>
> The Sonship of Jesus and the Trinity are False.[20]

Yet Theodosius, with the exception of laws restricting Jewish ownership of Christian slaves and prohibiting intermarriage between Jews and Christians, was careful to protect the previous legal rights of Jews and to try to control by law hostile Christians who on occasion sought to destroy or despoil synagogues.[21]

The fourth century also saw the gradual conversion of the upper classes to Christianity. Frequently upper-class women converted first; the men followed, often pushed by the women or lured by the promise of imperial preferment. Both men and women found the transition easier because of the gradual assimilation into the new faith of many of the old Roman traditions.[22]

The persecution of 303–311 C.E. left another signal mark: People were cautious in giving unreserved praise to any Christian, even an emperor. In that persecution, Christians had witnessed betrayal by many prominent Christian officials, even bishops. (Eusebius does not give us the name of his predecessor as bishop in the see of Caesarea, probably because his predecessor abandoned Christianity in the face of the persecutions.[23]) Thus Constantine came to an East where Christians were preoccupied with the problem of people who seemed to be solid and secure Christians and yet might turn and fall away from their baptismal vows, backsliding into pagan idolatry.[24] Only after Constantine died, still safely a Christian, could Eusebius pull out all the stops in praising the Christian emperor. This he did in his panegyric *Life of Constantine*.[25] The care with which he ties Constantine's "happy" life to his loyalty to the Christian God shows Eusebius's anxiety that the sons might not follow their father's religious example.

Thus, despite the privileges showered on the Christian Church by the emperors, Christians retained an ambivalent attitude toward living emperors. That ambivalence was further accentuated when Julian (361–363 C.E.) came to the throne and, throwing off his Christian background, in fact attempted an actual, though brief, reestablishment of paganism.[26]

The Arian controversy and the Council of Nicaea

In 324 and 325 C.E., when Constantine, fresh from his triumph over his rival, rushed into the arms of the Christian bishops, he found himself embroiled in an enormous doctrinal controversy among Christians in the East, a controversy that dogged his last years and preoccupied his successors for the next half century: the Arian controversy.*

Even before his arrival in the East after his victory over Licinius, Constantine sent his ecclesiastical troubleshooter, Hosius, bishop of Cordova, to make contact with the Christians of the East. Hosius found not a peaceful people awaiting the triumphant approach of their first imperial co-religionist, but a Church rocked by controversy over questions involving the nature of Christ and Christ's relation to God the Father.

The terms "East" and "West" are somewhat confusing in Roman studies. The western portion of the empire was comprised of the territory on both sides of the Mediterranean north and west of the Adriatic Sea, an area in which most people spoke Latin. East and south of the Adriatic on both

*For an overview, see Dennis E. Groh, "The Arian Controversy—How It Divided Early Christianity," *BR*, February 1994.

sides of the Mediterranean, Greek was the spoken language. In 293 C.E., the emperor Diocletian formalized the division of the empire into western and eastern provinces, though the rule was considered to be one. Constantine's uniting of the *imperium* did not, however, affect those signal linguistic and geographical distinctions. Thus the later emperors of the fourth and fifth centuries were assigned certain "spheres" of their rule corresponding to this subdivision of the empire into East and West.

The Arian controversy began in the great eastern city of Alexandria, Egypt in 318 C.E. when a presbyter named Arius challenged Bishop Alexander's teaching on the nature of Christ. After briefly hesitating, Alexander took disciplinary steps against Arius, who in turn appealed to the powerful bishop of Nicomedia, Eusebius. (Don't confuse Eusebius of Nicomedia with the church historian, Eusebius of Caesarea. Although both originally may have supported Arius, their courses diverged after the Council of Nicaea.) Eusebius of Nicomedia owed his power and prominence not to his writing ability (only one letter survives from his hand),[27] but to his position as bishop of Nicomedia, then the imperial capital of the East, and to the fact that he was a member of the patrician class.[28] He belonged by birth to imperial circles, followed Constantine to Constantinople, and baptized him just before Constantine's death in 337 C.E. Despite the rule enacted by the Council of Nicaea in 325 C.E. prohibiting bishops from changing their sees, Eusebius became the bishop of that new city in 338 C.E. under Constantius.[29] Eusebius of Nicomedia was influential not only as an adviser to Constantine but also to Constantine's sons, thus guaranteeing that the Arian case would have a more than sympathetic hearing at the imperial court. The settlement of the controversy would have to await the formation of a true consensus of eastern bishops and a change of imperial sentiments.

The controversy soon spread to Caesarea, where Eusebius of Caesarea also seems to have supported Arius.[30] In Antioch, a council to elect a new bishop took up the Arian controversy under the urging of Hosius.[31] The Council of Antioch in February 325 wrote a statement of faith (condemning Arianism)[32] and seems to have placed the church historian Eusebius of Caesarea in disrepute for his support of Arian views.

By now the matter had grown both so serious and so divisive that it became apparent to Constantine that it could only be settled by calling a full council of the eastern bishops. They met in May of 325 at the town of Nicaea in Bithynia (in the northwest of modern Turkey) near Constantine's palace. The exact number of bishops in attendance is not properly recorded, nor is the progress of the three-month-long discussions. The results of the Council of Nicaea, however, have been normative for Christians—both East and West—to the present day. A creed was produced at this first ecumenical (universal) council that Hosius and Constantine hoped would unify Christians of the East in their doctrinal thinking about Christ's relation to God the Father.[33] They failed.

What was at stake at the Council of Nicaea that made this early Christian discussion so universally important and so potentially explosive?

Bishop Alexander of Alexandria, whose views Arius opposed, had maintained a doctrine of the eternal and essential sonship of Christ. For the Alexandrian bishops, it was inconceivable that Christ was not eternally the Son of God who possessed all the natural properties of the Father.[34] When Alexandrian bishops like Alexander and his successor Athanasius (328–373 C.E.) read about Christ's sonship in the scriptures, they saw a natural and biological kind of sonship, which differed from the adoptive sonship conferred on believers who were being redeemed by God (cf. John 1:12; Galatians 4:5–7).[35]

When the Arians read the same Bible, they focused on the similarity of Christ's sonship to ours. Thus they saw Christ's life as the perfectible model of our redemption—an adopted and obedient redeemer, created by God to increase in wisdom, stature and favor (grace) (Luke 2:52). Thus the Arians stressed the changeable (improvable) nature of Christ as redeemer.[36]

This view horrified the Alexandrian bishops. If Christ could change for the better, he could also change for the worse, thus jeopardizing human salvation. Church people who had witnessed the backsliding of lifelong Christians during the persecutions of 303–311 C.E. could not pin human salvation to so shaky a model as a changeable redeemer.

A secular age that had seen too much change in the crises of the third century could not abide much change of any kind.

During the reigns of Constantine and his successors, farmers were bound to the land by imperial legislation in order to end dramatic shifts in the agricultural tax base. Constantine set a new stable value for the gold coin, the *solidus* (which held against inflation and devaluation for the next seven centuries). Frontier armies and borders were rearranged to regularize their lines. Another imperial fiat prevented transfer from one governmental agency to another; this applied to civil bureaucrats of all ranks, because the lucrative Palatine ministries tended to clump and glut with warm bodies, while the less remunerative (but also important) desks went begging—all this in an effort to bring order and stability to a too-changing world.[37]

It should be no surprise then that the bishops who came to the Council of Nicaea in 325 C.E. condemned Arianism and voted in favor of a creed that conceived of Christ's relationship to God in stable, unchanging, essentialist terms:

> One Lord Jesus Christ, the Son of God, begotten from the Father as only-begotten, that is from the substance of the Father, God from God, light from light.

Nor should it surprise us that they rejected anyone who claimed that Christ was "of another hypostasis or a creature, or *mutable or subject to change*" (emphasis added).[38]

The doctrine of **homoousios** *as one substance*

What was surprising was that all but two bishops signed a creed that contained a non-scriptural term for the first time in Christian history—*homoousios*, of the same substance. Christ was said to be "of the same substance" with the Father.

Although previously Eusebius of Caesarea had been accused of Arianism, he voted against it at the Council of Nicaea. Eusebius wrote home to his church in Caesarea Maritima in Palestine to explain why he voted for the term *homoousios*. Eusebius writes:

> "*Homoousios* with the Father" indicates that the Son of God bears no resemblance to originated creatures but that he is alike in every way only to the Father.[39]

Constantine, who had called the synod, assured the bishops that the term did not imply anything heretical, such as that God had a substance that could be divided between Father and Son. If we accept Eusebius's explanation for endorsing this bizarre and unforeseen turn of events, the council, lost in the luster of unprecedented imperial attention, thought they were simply using a term that made unequivocally clear that *Christ was more like God than he was like us*.

After concluding some additional business, the bishops were free to celebrate the 20th anniversary of Constantine's reign as his special guests. Later in the century, some Arians admitted they signed the Creed of Nicaea to please Constantine; they dismissed their action with these words:

> The soul is none the worse for a little ink.[40]

But a time bomb had been planted at the heart of the Christian proclamation. Constantine's unity was both illusory and dangerous, as the next 50 years of church history show.

The aftermath of Nicaea

When Constantine died in 337 C.E., he was succeeded by his three sons,

Constantius (337–361 C.E.), Constans (337–350 C.E.) and Constantine II (337–340 C.E.), whose separate spheres of rule divided the Constantinian political unity. War between Constans and Constantine II in 340 C.E. resulted in the death of the latter; Constans, the western emperor, was killed in battle by a usurper named Magnentius in 350 C.E. Thus Constantius inherited his father's eastern empire and ruled it for 24 years. He also inherited the influence of Eusebius of Nicomedia, now bishop of Constantinople, who had moved in as a key adviser to Constantine the Great immediately after Nicaea. The court was now under Arian influence. Until his death in 340/341 C.E., Eusebius of Nicomedia maneuvered to remove and reverse the Creed of Nicaea and to remove its supporters. Foremost among his enemies was Athanasius of Alexandria, who succeeded to the bishopric there in 328 C.E.

Of all the people at Nicaea, Athanasius (present as Bishop Alexander's secretary) was the clearest in his anti-Arian insistence that Christ was the eternal Son of God, the very Word of the Father, an essential offshoot of God's deity. As the first bishop of Egypt who spoke the native language, Coptic, Athanasius was able in his 45-year reign as bishop of Alexandria to marshal the people of Egypt and the monks of the desert (see below) behind his adherence to the Nicene cause, as he interpreted it. Exiled five times for his opposition to the Arians and for his failure to reestablish communion with them, Athanasius proved himself a master politician.[41] On one of his exiles, in 339 C.E., he fled to Rome where he won the support of the bishop of Rome, Pope Julius (337–352 C.E.)—though he weakened his standing among eastern theologians because of his support in Rome of a too-radical Nicene supporter, Marcellus of Ancyra.[42]

Two interrelated factors prevented an early resolution of the Arian crisis. First, the active interest of Constantius and subsequent emperors meant that any theological discussion in a synod or council was followed by imperial fiat enforcing, as a matter of law, the decisions of that council on churches of the East. Thus, in an attempt to find that uniformity of doctrine that the rapidly "Christianizing" empire required, a huge number of councils were held from 325 to 381 C.E. But each synod tended to reproduce the current theological sentiments of the reigning emperor.[43] Not until Theodosius I (379–395 C.E.) did an emperor with Nicene sentiments reign long enough to call a council that would genuinely enforce the anti-Arian doctrinal settlement of Nicaea.

Second, the conversion of the emperors to Christianity created a central forum for Christians to discuss issues face to face. No such ecumenical forum had existed in the days before Nicaea; thus Christians could no longer take doctrinal agreement for granted. Forced to talk with each other, they had to come to grips with the vast variety of beliefs that Christians actually held.

Thus the East was divided into a variety of doctrinal positions. Though the majority of Christian bishops were not Arian in their sympathies, they could not agree on terminology to express their view of the relation between God and Christ.

Urban unrest, always a danger in late antiquity (c. 300–640 C.E.), added to the inflammatory atmosphere. Forced councils, depositions and deportations of disgruntled Church leaders, with new bishops imposed on local populaces, all this reflected the high degree of imperial meddling in ecclesiastical affairs. For example, in 356 C.E., a radical Arian, George of Cappadocia, was imposed by Constantius on the Christians of Alexandria in place of their beloved bishop Athanasius, who was radically anti-Arian. At Constantius's death in 361 C.E., the citizens of Alexandria rose up and murdered the usurping bishop.[44]

The doctrinal breakthrough came when Athanasius began to talk with the theologians of Asia Minor—especially Basil of Caesarea (c. 330–379 C.E.), his younger brother Gregory of Nyssa (c. 335–395 C.E.) and their close friend Gregory of Nazianzus (c. 330–390 C.E.)—who were respected by a large number of anti-Arian bishops of the East.[45] It was these theologians of Asia Minor, principally Cappadocians, who were able to bring two kinds of theological language back together. Theologians of the previous centuries had spoken of the redeemer in scriptural terms that emphasized his obedience to God's will. They had also described him as "divine by nature." The Arian controversy had broken this theological language into two camps—Nicene supporters who emphasized Christ's divinity by nature and Arians who emphasized Christ's willing obedience. The Cappadocians were able to use both ontological and volitional language in such a way as to satisfy the wider East's desire for a redeemer both divine by nature and obedient to his Father's will.[46]

The doctrine of the Trinity

The Cappadocians also effected a major advance in the doctrine of the Trinity, building on the work of the anti-Arian Athanasius. Earlier thinkers had located the point of mediation between God and the world in the doctrine of the preexistent *Logos* (Word) of God, which they identified with the preexistent Christ (cf. John 1:1–3). But Athanasius in his numerous writings had laid stress on the incarnation of the very Word of God as the meeting point between God and creatures. The Cappadocians more clearly shifted that point of mediation to the incarnate one (i.e., the divine made flesh)[47] (cf. John 1:14), thus producing a connection between God and the world that focused attention on salvation rather than on cosmology. This new focus on the incarnation and away from the preexistent *Logos* took Christian theology into a distinctive arena where neither pagan philosophers nor philosophically-inclined Jews could participate.

Basil's work stressed the essential divinity of the Holy Spirit;[48] he thus completed Christian thinking about the doctrine of the Trinity, and helped to pave the way for the Council of Constantinople in 381 C.E. This council produced a creed affirming the essential natural unity of Father and Son, applying the term *homoousios* (of the same substance) to the Son, while at the same time speaking of the Spirit's "proceeding" from the Father.[49]

The canon of the New Testament and the Christian Bible

The importance of the exegesis of scripture, especially the New Testament, in the Arian controversy invites a brief comment on the canon of the New Testament. The term "canon" (measure, rule) refers to those books of the New Testament that are authoritative as *scripture* for Christians. Such canonical books were not the only beneficial or even "inspired" writings that could be employed by Christians for devotional or ecclesiastical purposes; but they were the books by which the *inspiration* and *orthodoxy* of other writings were to be "measured," or judged.

The last generation of Protestant scholars (especially) maintained that the canon of the New Testament was largely identified by the beginning of the third century C.E.[50] That contention was based primarily on a misdating of a famous list of New Testament books (called the Canon Muratori) to the end of the second century, instead of the late fourth century where it properly belongs.[51] Thus, although "Paul" and the Gospels plus some other books of our present New Testament had long been accepted as canonical, it was not until the fourth century that a Christian writer gave us a list of New Testament books that exactly matches ours. The list is contained in Athanasius of Alexandria's Easter Letter of 367 C.E.[52] By the early fifth century, the Council of Carthage (419 C.E.) adopted the list of New Testament books used by the West.[53]

It is probably no accident that the fourth century, in which our modern New Testament canon was selected, is the very century that witnessed the translation from Greek into the native Coptic language of numerous second- and third-century gospels, epistles and treatises, like the newly discovered Gospel of Judas.*[54] It is only now that we can see and recover the welter of alternate and diverse varieties of Christianity lost to history's awareness,

*For a summary of the Gospel of Judas, see Birger A. Pearson, "Judas Iscariot Among the Gnostics," *BAR*, May/June 2008. For reviews of the apocryphal and Gnostic gospels, see Charles W. Hedrick, "The 34 Gospels: Diversity and Division Among the Earliest Christians," *BR*, June 2002; and Robert J. Miller, "The Gospels That Didn't Make the Cut," *BR*, August 1993.

SCALA/ART RESOURCE, NY

Four Books for Four Gospels. *Even though the books of the New Testament had largely been canonized by the fourth century C.E., they were not collected into a single volume until centuries later. Instead, the books were kept as separate codices, as depicted in this fifth-century mosaic from the Mausoleum Placidia in Ravenna. The mosaic shows an open cabinet containing the four Gospels, each separate and identified with its Latin name.*

except for occasional notices left to us by the victorious writers of "orthodox" Christianity.[55] In a sense, then, "orthodox" means "victorious," though the great theologians would eventually give formulaic precision to the term.

We also have to realize that there was no widespread availability of a single volume in antiquity that corresponds to our one-volume modern Bible. The codex had certainly come into widespread use by the early fifth century, and the ancients did possess single volumes of books of the Bible instead of the scrolls used previously. These codices, however, usually contained *only* single books or collections of books of our present Bible—primarily the four Gospels,[56] the Psalms or Paul—not our entire Bible. As such, it is no wonder that one of the greatest Christian theologians and scriptural exegetes of antiquity, Augustine of Hippo Regius (see below), never held an entire Bible in his hand at one time.[57]

Christian social life in the fourth century

The great theologians who participated in the councils of the fourth century were functionaries of a Christian Church whose social composition and obligations had been transformed along the lines of the wider society, a society in which 80 percent of the available and useful land was already owned by fewer than 5 percent of the total population. If one could characterize this transformation in a single line, it would follow Ramsay MacMullan's dictum about the later empire: "Fewer have more."[58] In the closing years of the third century, a wave of prosperity had settled on selected provinces of the eastern Mediterranean, especially Egypt, Syria and Palestine.[59]

The new prosperity was accompanied by the rise of a class of people determined to garner this new wealth for themselves and their families and to wield for their own benefit the power that flowed from such wealth. Fourth-century texts call these people *potentiores*, the "more powerful ones." This focus on power was entirely appropriate in differentiating them from their second- and third-century forebears, who were termed *honestiores*, the "more honorable ones."[60]

We can sense their power and smell their greed in countless early Christian sermons denouncing abuses of wealth and counseling mercy for the poor. At the end of the fourth century, for example, John Chrysostom (354–407 C.E.), priest of Antioch and later bishop of Constantinople, repeatedly warns against the risks of attachment to money and power:

> He who loves money harbors countless suspicions of others, and there are many who are ready to accuse him of wrongdoing, many who envy, slander and plot against him because they have been wronged ... Moreover even those more powerful than he, because they are resentful and indignant at his treatment of inferiors, yet envious of him too, are likewise hostile and hate him.[61]

Thus the *potentiores* called forth Christian invective and also evoked one of the most characteristic fourth-century sins and fears—envy.[62] Envy was aroused—and wallowed in—by this class particularly because of its determination to enjoy wealth and power publicly at the expense, and to the detriment, of the wider community.[63] Nowhere is the *potentior* class's ostentation more apparent than in the private "palaces" they built in towns and cities. Their large houses ramble across whole city quarters, encroaching on both neighbors' and public space, significantly and contemptuously changing plans of quarters and even streets.

The private houses of Ostia, seaport of Rome, spread out across former apartment houses, reusing earlier walls.[64] The so-called House of the Hunt at Bulla Regia in North Africa [modern Tunisia], completed before 350 C.E., covered several lots from an earlier period. Its walls moved out toward the public street when a repaving operation was underway, apparently with the connivance of local officials.[65] The house contained a basilica (or reception hall) where the *dominus* (or lord) received the homage of dependents and clients.[66]

Such homage paid to the great landowners is depicted in the House of Julius mosaic from Carthage, in which tenants bring first fruits of the land to the *potentiores* who own the large rural estates.[67] Houses ten times larger than the insulae (or blocks) of the central city were built in the North African town of Timgad.[68] Frequently, the great urban house owners would take over portions of the public street, squeezing down traffic patterns.

When the *potentiores* left home, they took symbols of their importance with them in the very clothes and ornamentation they wore. The plain toga of the earlier empire gave way to long tunics of fine linen with banded insignias of rank or to gaily colored silk robes.[69] When some of these people converted to Christianity they may have changed the patterns of their clothing, but not the quality. Wealthy Christians sometimes had depictions from the life of Christ or the Gospels woven into their tunics. The dour fourth-century bishop Asterius of Amaseia in Turkey dryly quipped, "When they come out in public dressed in this fashion, they appear like painted walls to those they meet."[70]

To light their way when they went out at night, they carried clay lanterns that held ceramic lamps with molded figures of praying saints or other cult figures.[71] By the fifth century, their fine tableware was decorated with stamped representations of crosses and saints, churned out in large quantities by pottery factories in Carthage and Asia Minor, whose affordability to distant eastern provincials was made possible by including the wares in consignments of already state-subsidized shipping cargos.[72] Even when the *potentiores* came to church, they were seated in the front of the basilica. The rest of the congregation tended to arrange itself by class, with the poor toward the rear.[73] Those who had run afoul of Church law, the penitents, were in a special section at the very rear.[74]

On the other side of this great social watershed lay the *tenuiores*—the millions of ordinary citizens, the urban and rural poor, whose numbers and desperation begin to blur even so firm a Roman boundary as the one between slave and free.[75] By the end of the fourth century, the plight of the poor had worsened to the point where contemporary and later Christians revived an old classical and biblical distinction between the "indigent" poor and the "improvable" poor,[76] so that Christian largess could be properly distributed where it would do the most good.

The fourth-century discovery of "the poor"

Fourth-century texts register a new discovery and sense of obligation for the poor. For the first time in human history, the literary sources of the ruling class, outside of the biblical record, begin to describe and speak about the "faceless poor" of antiquity—homeless and unbefriended, unprotected from rain and weather; huddling against the walls of the bathhouse to warm themselves in Amaseia; gathering in the porticos of the churches in Ancyra (Cappadocia) to keep out of the rain; sheltering under the colonnades of the street in Scythopolis (Beth-Shean in Palestine); and presenting themselves in grave need at the gates of every city.[77]

The bishops of the Church undertook the care of the lifelong helpless or "indigent" poor. In fact, Peter Brown has recently argued that it was the Christian bishops of the fourth century who actually "invented" the poor for late antiquity. Prior to that time, "poor" referred not so much to the nameless and faceless masses of the indigent, or even to the improvable poor, but only to one's fellow "citizens" who might at any moment slip into real poverty. Civic gifts and their recipients were confined to "fellow citizens"; and distributions of largess were given in equal amounts to every citizen, not just the "poor." The long-held Jewish and biblical notion of justice and support for the widow, the orphan and the poor, now enters mainstream Roman society for the first time, introduced and championed by the Christian bishops who came to be regarded as the special protectors of the poor.[78]

In this way, the newly created virtue of supporting crowds of poor and dispossessed gave rise to a new kind of building in the cities of late antiquity, the *xenodocheion*. This establishment, which appears around mid-century on both the ground and in literary sources, was something of a cross between a hospice for the poor, a hospital and an orphanage.[79]

Newly discovered rural prosperity in late antiquity

Based on evidence drawn from literary sources, it has traditionally been thought that in the second half of the fourth century, rural villagers, especially in Palestine, tended to be squeezed out by high taxes and wealthy neighbors, further swelling the ranks of the poor.[80] Although the true state of rural life is often difficult to gauge, both because of the paucity of inscriptions and variation from province to province, archaeological fieldwork during the past decade has provided a new and much more vibrant picture of village life in the East.

The surveys of French archaeologists working in various regions of northern Syria have revealed nearly four dozen villages dating from the late third to mid-sixth centuries C.E. The sustained agricultural wealth of these sizable villages, represented archaeologically by numerous buildings, rooms and installations, allows us to see for the first time the emergence of a broadly-based middle class taking its place between the richest and the poorest inhabitants of the empire.[81] The agricultural expansion and steady growth of population evidenced in Syria also found in the villages and countryside of Israel's northern Negev, and may also be found in future studies of Asia Minor. Thus when the Arabs entered the lands of the empire from the east in the seventh century, they would have found a land that had already reached its capacity to support the local population.[82]

Voluntary poverty and spiritual power

Such a vast redistribution of wealth and power in the social order had its correlates in the spiritual realm. Here, too, "fewer have more" power.[83] By the fourth century, religious leaders emerged whose claim to special intimacy with the divine buttressed their gift of special spiritual powers that they wielded on behalf of the divine. Constantine was one of those new fourth-century "friends of God." The increasing importance of the Christian bishops, as we have already seen in the councils of the Church, was also part of this general movement toward identifying spiritual *potentiores* who could mediate between heaven and earth and, especially, between human neighbors and groups caught in the morass of secular conflict.[84]

The rise to prominence of an entirely new group of Christian spiritual powers, who were themselves voluntary imitators of the poor, should be seen in this light: the Christian monks. The origins of the monastic movement are shrouded in obscurity. In the closing decades of the third century, a new kind of ascetic hero and heroine appeared in the deserts of Egypt. The first name associated with this new practice of departing the local congregations in towns and villages for the solitary life of prayer and fasting in the desert is St. Antony (c. 270–356 C.E.). But Antony had predecessors inasmuch as he learned this way of life from a long-practicing ascetic in a neighboring village.[85] Antony was a *monachos*, a solitary, or monk. The earliest appearance of the term in this sense occurs in an early fourth-century papyrus from Egypt, in which an anonymous monk is making peace between contending neighbors.[86] That power to reconcile contending parties, to resolve complicated political and theological disputes, to predict the future and to wield other powers ascribed to Christian solitaries depended on the degree to which ascetics had cut all social bonds with the community and had "died" to themselves that they might live only to God.

Thus Antony moved by stages deeper and deeper into the desert where he could carry on warfare with the demons and emerge victorious in virtue.

Throughout the fourth century, monks filled the Egyptian and Syrian deserts—and crowds of townspeople followed them to seek their spiritual help and intercession with God.[87]

The hermit-figure, surrounded often unwillingly by his entourage, reflects a deep Roman commitment to life in the human community. The solitaries could not completely shake this off. A former soldier named Pachomius, converted by the kindness of Christian villagers, ultimately founded a community of monks in the Thebaid (Upper Egypt), south of Antony's hermitage. An angel appeared to Pachomius while he was still a solitary and told him, according to a fifth-century account, that he had "done well those things which pertain to your own affairs" but urged him on to found a community of monks.[88] This he did. Each monk had his own cell, but the monks were housed together behind a wall with a gatekeeper, assembling for the saying of a few psalms.

This communal (cenobitic) style of monasticism was the type that many Christian aristocrats preferred, especially in provinces like Cappadocia in Turkey. There the Cappadocian fathers (Basil of Caesarea, Gregory of Nyssa and Gregory of Nazianzus) would practice "withdrawal" from the world into a small community gathered on their rural estates. The old Mediterranean love of one's friends was wedded with a Christian principle. As Basil of Caesarea, whom we have already met in discussions on the Trinity, put it: "If you always live alone, whose feet will you wash?"[89] While the solitary remained the highest ideal for many Christians of the East, communal asceticism tended to lure educated or wealthy Christians.

The power of this new communal monasticism can be seen in the radical transformation that occurred in the Judean desert. At the height of the monastic movement in the sixth century, this arid, inhospitable region was festooned with numerous monasteries and up to 3,000 monks.*[90] In addition, the movements of the pious persons who came to seek the favor of various monks and to pray at their shrines have left traces along the numerous footpaths that once crisscrossed the desert.[91] Hospices were attached to most of the larger monastic compounds to house these travelers and included provisions for both rich and poor, though only one hospice has actually been found.[92]

Beginning in the fourth century, travelers who came as pilgrims to the holy shrines were starting to become Christian fixtures of late antiquity, despite the objections of theologians like Gregory of Nyssa, who was discussed above in

*See Yizhar Hirschfeld, "Spirituality in the Desert: Judean Wilderness Monasteries," *BAR*, September/October 1995.

ZEV RADOVAN/WWW.BIBLELANDPICTURES.COM

St. George's Monastery. *Clinging to the cliffs overlooking the ravine of Wadi Qelt, this monastery in the Judean hills between Jerusalem and Jericho was established in the late sixth century by St. George of Coziba. (The current monastic complex, however, dates only to 1880.) By the last centuries of the Byzantine period, scores of monasteries had been built in the Judean desert to accommodate the thousands of Christian monks who had withdrawn to the desert for worship and reflection.*

connection with the Trinitarian controversy. By the fifth century, pilgrimage was a full-blown religious practice of pious Christians, as pilgrims flocked to the shrines of both local holy men and those of the Holy Land.[93]

Such asceticism set hearts to moving, as well as feet: It called the rich to a life of poverty. The greatest miracle in that age of "getting and spending" was the presence of thousands of ascetic "voluntary poor," who simply withdrew from public and family life and gave their money to the poor. Such a stunning *anachoresis* (withdrawal)[94] from wealth allowed a special freedom to aristocrats, and, above all, to aristocratic women. Women like the patrician Melania the Elder could exert enormous power and influence *as women*, uncontrolled by the otherwise obligatory male guardianship of patriarchal society.[95]

> A woman of more elevated rank, she loftily cast herself down to a humble way of life, so that as a strong member of the weak sex she might censure indolent men, so that as a rich person appropriating poverty, and as a noble person adopting humility, she might confound people of both sexes.[96]

Among these holy persons were not only prominent women, but also the first prominent black ascetic, the great St. Moses, whose sayings are preserved among the *Sayings of the Desert Fathers*.[97]

The West in the age of Augustine

On Constantine's death, the empire was again divided into East and West. Although the West was linked in many ways to Constantinople, it was basically quite independent of the East—and far less prosperous. While wars in the western half of the empire between factions backing usurping emperors in 350–353 C.E. and 383–387 C.E. disrupted daily life,[98] the pattern of village life continued, even evincing some prosperity, especially in Britain and the region of Trier,[99] though trade between the continent and the eastern Mediterranean was generally down in the late fourth century.[100]

The major factor in the West's beginning to go its own way was the presence on its frontiers of the Germanic barbarian tribes seeking entry into the western provinces.[101]

In the second century, the barbarian was seen as a noble figure. Unspoiled and uncorrupted by civilization, the barbarian was considered "wise," the possessor of a certain "natural" wisdom. Second-century Christian apologists often describe their own Christian sentiments as "the philosophy of the barbarians."[102] By the fourth century, however, the barbarian had become a threat to civilization. In late antiquity, texts refer to such a one as a "wild beast."[103]

The most notable of late antiquity's barbarians, the Visigoths, were converted to a heretical Arian brand of Christianity sometime around 382–395 C.E.[104] Now twice damned—both as barbarians and as heretics—they migrated from their temporary home in Dacia (Romania) to Italy. In 410 C.E. they sacked the city of Rome. Although it had long since ceased to be the imperial capital of the West (the capital was at Ravenna, where the marshes of the city protected it from the barbarians), the sack of Rome was, nevertheless, an enormous blow to Christians of the West. In the works of the two greatest eastern church historians, Socrates Scholasticus and Sozomen, only a brief paragraph or two is devoted to the sack of Rome;[105] but St. Augustine's *City of God* consists of 22 books occasioned by the destruction of Rome at the hands of the Visigoths.

The Visigoths continued on their western migration, finally settling in Spain and establishing a kingdom there. But the disruptions caused by the migrations of a number of such tribes on numerous frontiers isolated Gaul (France) and brought an end to the Roman cities of eastern Britain, which threw off Roman control between 408 to 410 C.E. in despair of receiving help from the empire. The Britons themselves succumbed to the invasion of the Saxons in 428 C.E.[106] In 596 C.E., the pope sent a number of missionaries, including one Augustine (St. Augustine of Canterbury), to Britain, which helped ensure that medieval Britain would not only be Christian, but Roman-rite. Similar contacts were maintained with Gaul.

Augustine of Hippo

In the closing decades of the fourth century, North Africa was also rapidly Christianized. In 354 C.E. Aurelius Augustinus (St. Augustine of Hippo) was born into the crossfire between Christianity and paganism. Augustine's mother, Monica, was a devout and relentless Christian; his father, Patricius, a genial pagan. We know a great deal about Augustine's home life, education and early career from his *Confessions,* written between 397 and 401/403 C.E. By that time he had become the middle-aged bishop of Hippo Regius (modern Annaba in Algeria), where he served until his death in 430 C.E.[107] Augustine's heart was a battleground for his parents until, in 387 C.E., he converted to Christianity. Both parents agreed, however, that he should have the best education possible. As a professor of rhetoric (speech and literature), he eventually found himself in the imperial capital of Milan. It was a fateful move for the young man, for there he encountered the preaching of Bishop Ambrose of Milan. The mid-life Augustine would trace God's providential hand in all this:

> All unknowing, I was led to him by you, so that through him I might be led, while fully knowing it, to you [God].[108]

As he would later tell the story, Augustine spent his first three decades running for the prizes of honor and glory and from his mother's faith and her God. Neither the low literary style of the Christian scriptures nor Christianity's high moral claims on his sexuality interested him.[109] Influenced by the high standards of the ascetic movement, Christians of Augustine's circle thought of the conversion to Christianity as a simultaneous conversion to the most rigorous kind of asceticism—namely, sexual continence. A man both as warm and as sexually active as Augustine could not bear to walk such a celibate path.

As a young searcher after truth, Augustine had fallen in with the Manicheans, an underground pagan sect favored by a powerful circle of western aristocrats. Attracted by the promise of scientific knowledge, he remained a Manichean long after his disappointment with its doctrine because of the boost to his career that its aristocratic connections provided.[110] Ambrose of Milan's preaching steadied Augustine's resolve to leave the Manicheans and started him on his odyssey toward an intellectual Christianity heavily tinged with late Platonism.[111] It was, as for so many people of his day, a simultaneous adult conversion to sexual continence.

Returning to his native North Africa after his mother's death, Augustine became a priest and then bishop of the large city of Hippo Regius. A changed man, the Augustine of the *Confessions* was on the verge of making most of the great intellectual discoveries of his life, especially those concerning the nature of grace in Christian life.

As a late convert to Christianity, he hoped to make up for lost time and to achieve—through study, prayer and contemplation—that vision of God reserved to those perfected in grace. By the time of the *Confessions* (401/403 C.E.), he realized that perfection in this bodily life remains an impossibility.[112] The middle-aged bishop, bruised in the conflict-ridden world of pastoral ministry, deepened in his understanding of the scriptures and more aware of himself, now portrayed the Christian life as a pilgrimage, a lifelong journey that awaits the resurrection for completion and final healing. In words echoing St. Paul, who was a decisive influence, he wrote: "Yet with us it is still by faith and not yet by sight."[113]

The Donatist controversy

Augustine needed all the faith he could muster in dealing with his large seaport town and the surrounding countryside. Not only were the churches of North Africa filled with scores of new converts driven to the Church by imperial decrees ending paganism (Augustine called these pagan converts *ficti*—"fakes"),[114] the Church itself in North Africa was divided into two major wings—Catholic and Donatist. When Augustine became the Catholic bishop of Hippo Regius he inherited the leadership of only a minority of the Christian populace.[115] The more popular church was the Donatist church, which traced its roots to a schism in 311 C.E. in the aftermath of the last persecution.[116] The Donatist church, which regarded itself as the "pure church," held sway in the countryside and in the towns.[117] Claiming descent from bishops who had not abandoned Christianity in the great persecutions of 303–311 C.E. and rejecting cooperation with the Roman state, especially the Christian emperors who had persecuted their founders, the Donatist "saints" formed a separatist church uncorrupted by the sinful contagion of their Catholic neighbors. They even practiced rebaptism (sometimes forcibly) upon unwary Catholics who crossed their path.

For a Catholic like Augustine, who was in the process of tracing human descent from sinful Adam, not saintly martyrs, the Donatists posed a grave theological difficulty. Augustine and his circle of Latin-speaking bishops were classicists, far removed from the rude Berber-speaking peasantry who were led by Donatists opposed to Roman values.[118] Beginning in 393 C.E., Augustine began attacking the Donatists in pamphlets, discussions and sermons.[119] By 405 C.E. he persuaded the western emperor Honorius (395–423 C.E.), whose capital was at Ravenna, to outlaw Donatism.[120] In 411 C.E. a great council was convened at Carthage where the imperial commissioner, after hearing the debates, ruled against the Donatists. A law was soon enacted prescribing severe penalties for adherence to the sect. This drove many Donatists underground[121] where, like so many of the old Roman religions,[122] Donatism survived to the Muslim conquest in the seventh century.

When the pagans did surface in Augustine's Africa, as when they rioted against the bishop and church of the town of Calama near Hippo, Augustine and the courts were quick to pounce.[123]

Augustine now turned his attention to a new controversy. A young British ascetic named Pelagius, who had been teaching the epistles of St. Paul to Christian aristocrats in Rome,[124] arrived in Hippo Regius in 411 C.E. while Augustine was attending the council on Donatism. Pelagius paid a visit to Augustine, but was unable to see him.[125] Pelagius and Augustine had heard about each other, but not favorably. When Pelagius had heard a famous passage of the *Confessions,* he had thrown a fit.[126] Augustine had there begged God to "Give what you command, and command what you will."[127] It was exactly the kind of theology that Pelagius and his party feared would undercut their belief that adults could turn to good works and break the ties with the sinful habits of the old life. To see God as the sole supplier of the power to do good works seemed to counter the moral injunctions of the New Testament and the old classical belief in the perfectibility of human nature.[128]

By 412 C.E. Augustine had moved even further along the road toward ascribing the power to do good solely to God. Death and the continuing struggle with sexuality that all Christians underwent (even celibates) had convinced Augustine of the incurable frailty of Adam's descendants.[129]

Hereditary sin

This vast divergence on so momentous a subject exploded in 412 C.E. when Augustine fired off an anti-Pelagian tract, *On the Merits and Remission of Sins and on the Baptism of Infants,* in which he championed the taint of Adam's sin in infants (1.13, 68), denied that persons can fulfill the commandments (2.23), attacked the perfection of the favorite Pelagian biblical saint, Job (2.17) and reiterated his belief that none can be perfect in this life (2.2). Augustine even insisted that free will must be ascribed to the grace of God (2.7).

Augustine had begun to discover the involuntary dimension, what Freud would call the Unconscious, in human beings. In Augustine's view there is a flaw (*vitiam*) at the core of the self that sets our conscious desire to do good against our actual ability to perform the good (cf. Romans 7:21–23). This flaw inevitably results in failure to fulfill God's commandments unless God's grace intervenes and assists the self.[130]

Many people beside the Pelagians smelled something very new in this interpretation of St. Paul and its harsh new doctrine of hereditary sin. Augustine was—and continues to be—relentlessly criticized for breaking with classical Christianity on the doctrine of perfection.[131] But his continuous tracts against the Pelagians carried the day and convinced the Church that this was what it had always taught. Thus the doctrine of original sin, the obligatory baptism of all Christians and the necessity of grace for the performance of the good entered the West's theology.[132]

Augustine's The City of God

From 413 to 426/427 C.E., Augustine turned his attention to the problem that had set Pelagius, like so many other Christians of the day, in motion—the sack of Rome. Pagans pointed to the event as proof that Rome's apostasy from the old religion had caused its fall.[133] *The City of God* was Augustine's response. The work reflected the maturation of a thinker who encompassed the entire sweep of biblical and Roman history within his theological agenda. For Augustine, all humanity has been divided into two great "cities" or "societies"—the city of God and the human or earthly city (the city of the devil). Late in the work, Augustine gives his definition of a city, or society or people, a distinctly Christian definition:

> [A] people is an assemblage of reasonable beings bound together by a common agreement as to the objects of their love; then, in order to discover the character of any people, we have only to observe what they love.[134]

The primary characteristic of the earthly city is its love of dominating others. *The City of God* (15.7; cf. 14.13) thus chooses *superbia* as the earthly city's chief sin. The primary characteristic of the city of God is its love of God and its subjugation to God's will; thus its primary virtue is humility.[135]

Here on earth the city of God shares turf with the damned and the unjust. The great Roman state, so praised by other writers for its benefits to humanity, is reduced to a utilitarian role: At its best it can only cooperate with the Church in helping humanity. The Church itself is but a mixed body of saints and sinners. But in life after the resurrection, the city of God will rise unmixed from the mists of human history that make sinner and saint unrecognizable from the outside. That great eschatological city shimmers over Book 22 of *The City of God,* a holy communal pyramid drawing Christians to the end of history:

> But, now, who can imagine, let alone describe, the ranks upon ranks of rewarded saints, to be graded, undoubtedly according to their variously merited honor and glory. Yet there will be no envy of the lower for the higher, as there is no envy of angel for archangel—for this is one of the great blessednesses of this blessed city. The less rewarded will be linked in perfect peace with the more highly favored, but lower could no more long for higher than a finger ... could want to be an eye. The less endowed will have the high endowment of longing for nothing loftier than their lower gifts.[136]

In that passage Augustine foresees the healing of so many of Rome's political problems—the demise of the struggle for glory and honor, two of the most crucial concepts in the Roman political vocabulary,[137] and the healing of that most characteristic sin of late antiquity—envy.[138] The passage also highlights the hierarchical thinking that subjugates individual interests to a community and a community to a single head—whether bishop, pope or abbot. When St. Benedict, the founder of the Benedictine monastic order, wrote his *Rule* sometime in the 530s C.E. in Italy, he embodied in the western monastic system the ranking of the community in humble submission to a single ruler, the abbot. It is through such a monastic community on earth, living in love by submission to the *Rule,* that monks will arrive at that greatest of late antique Christian paradoxes: the height of humility.[139]

Book 22 of *The City of God* also heralds the triumph of the cult of the saints. Their healings and other miraculous events testify to that greatest of miracles, the resurrection (the sheer number of these miracles almost swamps the book). These miracles make common cause with the rise of elaborate ceremonies in the West venerating local saints and describing the benefits derived from such observance at their shrines.[140]

The West at the end of antiquity

As Augustine lay dying in August of 430, Hippo Regius was being besieged by Vandal barbarians. Africa was thereafter detached from the empire for the next 100 years.

Christians in the old imperial city of Rome, left to find their own way with the new barbarians, turned to the bishops of Rome as their guides and protectors. The church at Rome had long enjoyed a unique position in the West. It was the only church in the West that could claim apostolic foundation (e.g., St. Peter) and that was located in the imperial capital. The bishop of Rome had, by the third century, used the title "pope" (*pappa*), but bishops of the major cities of the empire (e.g., Carthage, Antioch, Alexandria) were also so styled. During the Arian controversy (318–381 C.E.), various bishops of Rome had served as the theological voice of the West; but in the Donatist controversy the bishop of Rome had played an important role as the final ecclesiastical court of appeal for the West. As imperial power waned in the fifth century, a new political sovereignty, buttressed by a heightened religiosity, emerges in the Roman episcopate.

During the reign of Pope Leo I (440–461 C.E.), we see the shape of the new papacy. The power and voice of the great apostolic martyr Peter, who watches over people everywhere, but especially over those who hold his see, energized Leo's papacy.[141] Over a century later, Pope Gregory the Great (590–604 C.E.) put the matter charmingly. Telling the story of an appearance of St. Peter to a deacon of a church in the city of Palestrina east of Rome, Gregory says:

> With this vision, the blessed Apostle wished to assure his followers that he was watching over them constantly and would always see to it that what they did out of veneration for him would be repaid with an eternal reward.[142]

The western popes' stress on Petrine authority gave further muscle to their arguments with the bishops of Constantinople. Tensions between western and eastern Christians increased. When Pope Leo wrote his famous *Tome to Flavian* (see below) to help clarify an eastern Christological controversy, the bishops at the Council of Chalcedon in 451 C.E. accepted it as orthodox, but not solely because it came from Peter's successor; rather because "it *agrees with* the confession of the great Peter and is a common pillar against those who think wrongly."[143]

Western bishops struggled to maintain their authority in the cities, but the major event in the eventual Christian continuity of the West was the conversion of the Franks to "orthodox" rather than Arian Christianity at the end of the fifth or beginning of the sixth century.[144] Especially in Gaul, the orthodox bishops were members of the old Roman aristocracy and their followers were devoutly Catholic (= Nicene). To be ruled not only by barbarians, but heretical Arian barbarians was untenable politically. The conversion of the Franks helped ease the difficulty of Arian (heretical) barbarians ruling a Catholic populace. Traces of the unseemly hatred of the

Catholics for such Arian rulers and for the Jews, who made common cause with them, appear in the sixth-century *Life of St. Caesarius of Arles.*[145]

The origins and development of early Christian architecture

Before we consider some of the great Christian church buildings of late antiquity, we need to pause for a moment and take a brief detour through the development of Christian architecture in earlier centuries. From what we can see in the New Testament, early Christians met in a house owned by a Christian. The New Testament term "church" (*ecclesia*) refers to the people, sometimes worshiping as a "household" and sometimes gathering for worship simply in a house or other private structure (e.g., a warehouse or apartment), owned by a Christian believer. Thus, Aquila and Priscilla in Rome, whom Paul designates as "heads of the churches," were the owners of domestic structures in which the congregations held meetings.[146]

In fact, across the empire throughout early Christianity, Christians met primarily in houses occupied by other Christians in which no structural changes were made to signal that the space used for worship differed in any way from the standard domestic spaces available for daily activity or living. Thus, it seems clear that church architecture developed far more slowly than the congregations themselves.

We do know that by the beginning of the third century C.E., we get the first traces of adjustments to Christian domestic rooms to indicate that more permanent places for assembly and worship had begun to develop. Beneath present churches in Rome, like Santi Giovanni e Paolo and San Crisogono, scholars have seen changes of earlier domestic structures as indications of permanent appurtenances, signaling a specially designated liturgical space not devoted to simple daily living. The theory has been that the "tituli" churches in Rome were founded upon previous Christian-owned domestic spaces that were eventually given over to congregations for worship (hence, the use of the legal term *titulus,* indicating ownership "titled" to the named Christian). Thus was born a *domus ecclesiae* ("house of the church"), to be distinguished from an ordinary domestic space that was only temporarily converted for worship.[147]

While it is often assumed that there was continuity of Christian usage as these domestic spaces began to be transformed in the late second and third centuries, such continuity is not actually provable, however probable it might be.[148] Even the famous house of St. Peter in Capernaum, which shows

Megiddo House Church. *This intricately patterned mosaic decorates the floor of an early place of Christian worship found near the site of Tel Megiddo in northern Israel. Two fish facing in opposite directions—a common Christian symbol—are enclosed within a medallion circumscribed by an octagon (top). Surrounding the octagon are squares, rhombuses and triangles, many infilled with elaborate geometric patterns. Built near the headquarters of the Roman Sixth Legion, this* domus ecclesiae *served the spiritual needs of Christian soldiers, as evidenced by several memorial inscriptions in the mosaic. The one pictured here (bottom), written in Greek, was dedicated by "the God-loving Akeptous" to "God Jesus Christ."*

a continuity of Christian graffiti from the second to the early third century,* does not provide us with indisputable evidence of the architectural transition from *domus* to *domus ecclesiae*.[149] We must wait until the third decade of the third century for the first clear example of such a *domus ecclesiae*. In fact, two examples from the first half of the third century have been identified and excavated—the earlier one at the ancient and venerable site of Megiddo in Palestine, and a slightly later one at the Roman fort of Dura-Europos on the Syrian frontier.

The *domus ecclesiae* at Megiddo, dated to around 230 C.E., was found in the southwest corner of a large domestic building used by Roman legionnairies near the outskirts of a nearby Jewish village. Here, a large renovated hall (measuring 16 by 32 feet) with traces of supports for a eucharistic table was uncovered, along with several mosaic floors adorned with Christian symbols and inscriptions.† The excavators suggest that the area functioned as a "prayer hall." In addition, it should be noted that the reconfigured structure highlights the sacramental importance of the eucharist for Christian communal worship. This is emphasized by both the table supports that were found and the content of the mosaic inscriptions. The renovated hall at Megiddo, therefore, is the first clear, stratigraphically dated example of a *domus* that was converted into a *domus ecclesiae*.[150]

Then, by the middle of the third century, we have a full house church at Dura-Europos, located in a discreet house just a few feet away from the town synagogue.‡[151] There one can see a previously constructed house (measuring nearly 200 square feet) entirely taken over and reused as a building for Christian worship sometime between 232/233 C.E. and 256 C.E. Into one side of the house, a large assembly hall (42 by 17 feet) was constructed with a podium (or *bema*) adjoining the east interior wall.

In a room across the newly tiled courtyard, a canopied baptistery was constructed. The canopy's underside was painted blue and decorated with stars. Painted scenes of the woman at the well (John 4), various New Testament miracles and the battle between David and Goliath leave little doubt that this was a Christian congregation that renovated and used the original *domus*.[152]

By the end of the third century, there must have been many Christian buildings designated and set aside for Christian worship. We know, for

*James F. Strange and Hershel Shanks, "Has the House Where Jesus Stayed in Capernaum Been Found?" *BAR*, November/December 1982.

†Vassilios Tzaferis, "Inscribed 'To God Jesus Christ'," *BAR*, March/April 2007.

‡See Stephen Goranson, "7 vs 8: The Battle Over the Holy Day at Dura-Europos," *BR*, August 1996.

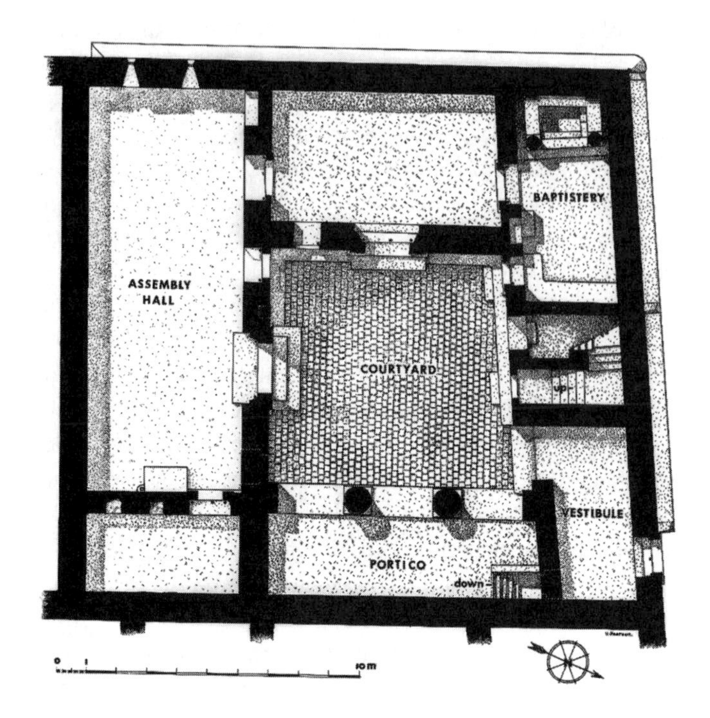

Plan of House Church from Dura-Europos. *Contemporaneously with the house turned into a synagogue (plan on p. 268), a two-story dwelling at Dura was converted into a house of Christian worship (or* domus ecclesiae*). It included a central paved courtyard, large assembly hall, a raised platform (possibly for a eucharist table) and a baptistery. The walls of the baptistery were decorated with frescoes illustrating scenes from the Bible such as Adam and Eve, the woman at the well (John 4) and the battle between David and Goliath.*

example, that the persecutions of Diocletian commence at Nicomedia with the destruction of a church building, while numerous literary sources attest the existence of Christian church buildings around the empire.[153]

Archaeologists are still debating the identification and precise dating of pre-Constantinian church buildings. In contrast, church buildings from the latter third and early fourth centuries appear to have been specifically built as large halls dedicated to worship and assembly, though some of these halls grew out of adaptations of previously existing house churches. L. Michael White has named this new type of structure an *aula ecclesiae*, or "hall of the church."[154] Thus, even well known pre-Constantinian churches, such as the so-called "double basilica" at Aquileia on the Adriatic in Italy, and an earlier version of the church of Julianos in Syria, may now be considered as versions of these large assembly hall churches known as *aulae*.[155]

Although it is now possible to distinguish three types of church buildings in the pre-Constantinian period—the household meeting place, the *domus ecclesiae* and the *aula ecclesiae*—it is important to note that each type was constructed and used throughout the early centuries, depending on local conditions and tastes. The ascension of the Roman emperor Constantine the Great (312–337 C.E.), however, brought a new kind of Christian monumental architecture that would epitomize church buildings until the end of antiquity—namely, the Christian basilica.*

In all the major cities where Constantine's influence prevailed, large, easily identifiable Christian basilicas were built, beginning with the church of St. John in Laterano in Rome (c. 314–316 C.E.). The basilica style was characterized by a long rectangular room with supporting colonnades, creating a two-story central nave flanked by one-story side aisles. The nave was entered from the west and culminated in an open apse at the church's eastern end. The basilica's long-room plan and its colonnaded, two-story interior lit by clerestory windows were ideal for the processional character of early Christian liturgies.[156] While theories abound as to how the basilical plan came to be adapted for Christian use,[157] it seems clear, based on current research, that the Christian basilica did not derive from architectural developments in Jewish synagogues, which developed along a different architectural path.[158]

Finally, the basilica's large interior spaces allowed early Christian artists to employ new forms of decorative art, particularly interior wall mosaics that were used to decorate apses and the spaces beneath and beside the clerestory windows (see below). These innovative mosaic adornments constitute one of Christianity's greatest artistic contributions to the religious architecture of late antiquity.

While the cities declined and governments shifted, the building of churches continued as other structures were falling into ruins. In Rome, for example, the beautiful Church of Santa Maria Maggiore was built in the fifth century with a triumphal arch adorned with mosaics proclaiming the divinity of Christ in accordance with the doctrine adopted at the Synod of Ephesus in 431 C.E.[159]

In the first quarter of the same century, the apse of the *titulus* church in Rome, Santa Pudenziana, was outfitted with a polychrome mosaic of Christ seated on a throne, dressed as a divine ruler, between representations of the 12 apostles dressed as his counselors (see Plate 11). The development of the depiction of Christ in this church supports the orthodox (anti-Arian)

*For an overview of some early Christian basilicas, see Yoram Tsafrir, "Ancient Churches in the Holy Land," *BAR*, September/October 1993.

© ERICH LESSING

Tomb of Theodoric. *King of the Ostrogoths, Theodoric (493–526 C.E.) invaded Italy in 489 C.E., defeating the barbarian ruler Odoacer and leading to a long period of prosperity. Although a follower of the Arian sect, Theodoric established a policy of religious tolerance. When he established his capital at Ravenna, he built several impressive structures, including this massive and imposing domed mausoleum. Emulating the tombs of earlier emperors, Theodoric outfitted his two-storied tower tomb with an astonishing 300-ton marble dome carved from a single block of stone.*

Christian Church's program establishing the divinity of Christ through the use of the large-scale apse mosaic.*[160]

However, it is equally important to notice that in this mosaic, Christ sits enthroned directly in front of a representation of the mount of Golgotha, topped by a bejeweled cross. In his hand, he holds a scroll that reads *dominus ecclesiae* ("Lord of the Church").[161] This implies to the viewer that he is also the Lord of Jerusalem, for the depiction enshrines Jerusalem—and Christ's lordship over the Holy City—on a monument located at the very heart of the city of Rome. Thus, the mosaic becomes a benchmark of the struggle to detach the city of Jerusalem from the Jews and their Temple and claim its sanctity as a Christian city at the very time Christians were earnestly battling to claim Jerusalem as their own—namely, the early years of the fifth century.[162]

In the splendid group of monuments found at Ravenna, the last Roman imperial capital of the West, we can see the glitter of this new ecclesiastical age: The mausoleum of Empress Galla Placidia (d. 450 C.E.), built in the shape of a cross, was both a shrine to the martyr St. Lawrence and an imperial tomb. The entire upper zone is covered with shimmering mosaics, pointing

*For depictions of Christ in early Christian mosaics, see Robin M. Jensen, "The Two Faces of Jesus: How the Early Church Pictured the Divine," *BR*, October 2002.

SCALA/ART RESOURCE, NY

SCALA/ART RESOURCE, NY

Justinian and Theodora. *These stunning mosaics from the sixth-century Church of San Vitale in Ravenna depict the emperor Justinian (c. 527–565 C.E.) and his wife Theodora who together presided over a brilliant period of the late Roman Empire. In addition to significant military victories, Justinian oversaw several major building projects, including the construction of the magnificent Hagia Sophia in Constantinople (p. 324) and the Nea Church in Jerusalem (p. 327).*

toward that upper world that saints achieved and to which emperors aspired.[163]

In 476 C.E., the last Roman emperor, ironically named Romulus, was pensioned off by Odoacer, the Visigoth master of the palace. To Renaissance scholars, this marked a great tragedy; for to them it symbolized the end of Rome. In fact, the barbarian rulers carried on many of the old imperial traditions, adapted to the new Christian world. When the Ostrogoth king Theodoric (493–526 C.E.) died, he was buried at Ravenna in a round tomb, just as earlier Roman emperors had been.*[164]

The Catholics also built a new baptistery at Ravenna when the town passed to the eastern empire after 540 C.E. Because Arians did not baptize in the name of the Trinity,[165] the Arian baptistery would not suffice for the Catholics of the sixth century, and it was transformed into an oratory, or chapel.[166] A similar Catholic transformation occurred with the basilica of San Apollinare Nuovo, built as Theodoric's palace church; the mosaics of Theodoric and his court were covered up and replaced with mosaic curtains; a procession of virgins and saints leading to Christ and Mary enthroned as

*Harry Rand, "The Mystery of Theoderic's Tomb Solved!" *Archaeology Odyssey*, November/December 2003.

Byzantine rulers was created above the side aisles of the nave.[167]

The apex of mosaic art in Ravenna is the beautiful Byzantine Church of San Vitale. In a mosaic of extraordinary quality, the great Byzantine emperor Justinian (527–565 C.E.), here depicted in his sixties, and his empress Theodora stare out at the high altar in regal and liturgical attentiveness from this last great work of imperial western antiquity, a church never seen by him in a city he never visited.[168] This is perhaps also the last time in antiquity that a Roman emperor could look out over an entire Mediterranean world ruled by him.[169]

The East to the Council of Chalcedon: 451 C.E.

The triumphant formulation of the doctrine of the Trinity by Basil and his party at the Council of Constantinople (381 C.E.) left a large problem unresolved: How does one describe the incarnation of Jesus Christ if the historical Jesus shares in the eternal deity of God? One solution was proposed by Apollinaris of Laodicea, who substituted the Word of God (the *Logos*) for the human mind of Jesus. Fearful that if the Savior had a human mind, he would be unable to resist the power of sinful flesh, Apollinaris substituted the unconquerable *Logos* to ensure Christ's victory over sin.[170] Apollinaris was condemned at the Council of Constantinople on the mere say-so of Basil of Caesarea.[171] But this condemnation did not deal with a whole school of Christological thinking that emphasized Christ's single divine nature even after the incarnation. That school included the great bishops of Alexandria.

The doctrinal situation was complicated by the presence of an opposing school of thought represented by another great apostolic see, Antioch.[172] If the Alexandrians tended to emphasize the monophysite (one nature) dimensions of the incarnation, the Antiochenes stressed the dual nature of Christ—both divine and human—and the voluntary (rather than natural or divinely-brought-about) character of Jesus' work. Moreover, the Antiochenes tended toward a more contextual and historical style of biblical exegesis, which made much of the human temptation and sufferings of Christ.[173] They bitterly opposed the Monophysite teachings of the Alexandrians. In a later attempt to win over the Monophysites, the emperor Justinian had the great Antiochene exegete, Theodore of Mopsuestia, posthumously condemned in the *Three Chapters Edict* (553/554 C.E.).[174]

The Nestorian controversy

In 428 C.E., Theodore's pupil, Nestorius, became bishop of Constantinople. Nestorius criticized the use of the term *theotokos* ("mother of God") as applied to Mary. "I cannot term him God who was two and three months old," said Nestorius.[175] Nestorius's attempt to placate his enemies by calling Mary *christotokos*, the "mother of Christ," fell on deaf ears.

The dynamic and irascible bishop Cyril of Alexandria (412–444 C.E.) immediately took exception to Nestorius's new formulation. At the heart of Cyril's theology was the birth of the divine Word:

> We do not say that the flesh was changed into the nature of Godhead, nor that the ineffable nature of the Word of God was transformed into the nature of flesh, for he is unchangeable and unalterable, always remaining the same according to the scriptures. But when seen as a babe and wrapped in swaddling clothes, even when still in the bosom of the Virgin who bore him, he filled all creation as God, and was enthroned with him who begot him.[176]

Despite the fact that the best historian of the century, Socrates Scholasticus, did not consider Nestorius's views heretical,[177] his work was condemned by the Synod of Ephesus (431 C.E.) and the Council of Chalcedon (451 C.E.); Cyril's position was approved by both.

Nestorius's condemnation and subsequent exile provided only a momentary breathing spell in a long and complicated advance toward the formation of Christian dogma regarding the person of the incarnate Christ. The period from Ephesus to Chalcedon is checkered with theologians and councils attempting to settle the issue.[178]

In 451 C.E. a great council was assembled at Chalcedon to resolve the matter. The emperors Marcian and Pulcheria instructed the fearful bishops to write a creed that would definitively end the controversy.[179] We do not have a copy of the first draft that the bishops produced,[180] but their final *Definition of Faith* justified all their fears. Far from producing unity in the Church, the final *Definition* offended theologians of both the Antiochene and the Alexandrian schools. The creed established the duality of Christ's unmixed and unconfused natures—the presence of both the divine and human in the redeemer. The key phrase—"in Two Natures"—that underscored this was borrowed, not from the then-current eastern discussion, but from the *Tome to Flavian* of Pope Leo of Rome written in 449 C.E. to Flavian, bishop of Constantinople. That Christ was "acknowledged in Two Natures" seemed a sellout of the Antiochene or Nestorian position to the Monophysites. On the other hand, the connection of the term *theotokos* with Christ's humanity, rather than his deity, infuriated the Antiochenes as a sellout to the Alexandrians.[181]

The bishops also reiterated Canon 3 of the Council of Constantinople, which raised Constantinople to primacy in the East,[182] over apostolic sees like Alexandria and Antioch. This further deepened the schisms within the Church.[183]

The Monophysite Christians then split off from the Church to go their own way in the East.[184] Later attempts by the emperor Justinian to win them back failed.[185] A hundred years after Chalcedon, dozens of Monophysite bishops were consecrated as a new church formed across the East from Asia Minor to Mesopotamia.[186] Nestorian Christians also remained outside the Chalcedonian settlement. Traces of their churches and monuments may be seen all the way east to China.[187]

Church and society in the later eastern empire to the Islamic conquest

The first half of the fifth century was a golden time of church construction in the East, especially in Palestine. The empress Eudocia, following the earlier example of Constantine and his family, inaugurated a great building program in Jerusalem.[188] That program had a darker side—the claiming of Mount Zion, abandoned since the second century, as Christian territory. The fight was on to determine whether Jerusalem was to be a Christian or a Jewish city.[189]

Recent studies of legislation against the Jews indicate a more lenient attitude toward Jews in the Roman Empire than had been previously thought from a reading of the church fathers alone.[190] Yet the Jews certainly experienced diminished civil rights, such as the prohibition of intermarriage between Jews and Christians,[191] a ban on building new synagogues (never enforced) and the elimination of the Jewish patriarchate in 425 C.E.[192] Especially nasty rhetoric comes from Christian pens in the first half of the fifth century concerning Jewish-Christian relations in Syria, Constantinople, Crete and Alexandria.[193]

In early fifth-century Antioch, John Chrysostom's sermons against the Jews focused on Christians in Antioch who were observing the Jewish law and tying Christianity to Sabbath attendance at synagogues and to other Jewish observances, such as ritual bathing.[194] As Robert Wilken has shown, Chrysostom's rhetoric against Jewish practices by Christians was tied to the issue of which religion—Judaism or Christianity—was the true religion: "If the Jewish rites are holy and venerable, our way of life must be false."[195] The attempt of the apostate emperor Julian (361–363 C.E.) to rebuild the Temple at Jerusalem, cut short by his early death, had affected Christian thinking deeply.* The fact that the Temple was in ruins had been used by apologists

*Jeffrey Brod, "Julian the Apostate and His Plan to Rebuild the Jerusalem Temple," *BR*, October 1995.

for centuries to prove that the old Israel was disinherited and Israel's mantle had passed to the Christian Church. By the early fifth century, as the empire moved toward the suppression of all other religions besides Judaism and Christianity, Christian writers had determined to lay final claim to Israel's inheritance.

This desire to deny Judaism's claim to the Old Testament and to the land of the Bible lies behind the huge number of polemical and outrageously negative references to Jews and Judaism in Bishop Cyril of Alexandria's writings (412–442 C.E.).[196] Cyril's virulent anti-Semitism, and the anti-Judaism of Christian theologians of his day, seems to have been inflamed by fears of Judaism's legitimate claim to be the continuation of the biblical Israel.[197]

The vibrant Jewish synagogue life of the fourth and fifth centuries, both in Israel and in Diaspora cities like Alexandria, Antioch and Apamea (in Syria), testifies to the prosperity of late Judaism.[198] The seriousness with which Christian authors and Christian emperors regarded Judaism also reflects the powerful place held by Jews in both the fear and esteem of this rapidly developing Christian empire.

Yet, for all the respect, points of genuine contact and positive interchange between Christians and Jews do seem to have diminished in the Byzantine period. For example, in earlier centuries, Jews and Christians had engaged in dialogue on scriptural texts and various exegetical points common to the two faiths.[199] By the fifth century, Jews and Christians followed parallel, but not often intersecting, paths in their exegesis. Newer studies indicate that Christian knowledge of the rabbis and the Jewish world in this period was less than previously supposed, although a great deal of work still needs to be done in this area before any firm conclusions are drawn.

In the Holy Land itself, pagans were persecuted—and taken over—far more than Jews. For example, Emperor Justin I (518–527 C.E.) transformed the temple of Hadrian at Caesarea into a church;[200] his nephew and successor, Justinian, promoted the Christian academy at Gaza and at the same time prohibited (in 529 C.E.) anyone who was not a Christian from teaching classical philosophy.[201] Nevertheless, Jews living in the Holy Land, if not persecuted, certainly felt "crowded" by a new Christian populace that now constituted the overwhelming majority of the population while the Jewish populace had declined.[202]

The growing Christian presence in the Holy Land

As we saw earlier, Christian pilgrimage to the Holy Land steadily grew during the fourth and fifth centuries. Numerous western Christians like Jerome, the translator of the Bible into Latin, came to settle there.[203] The Negev was

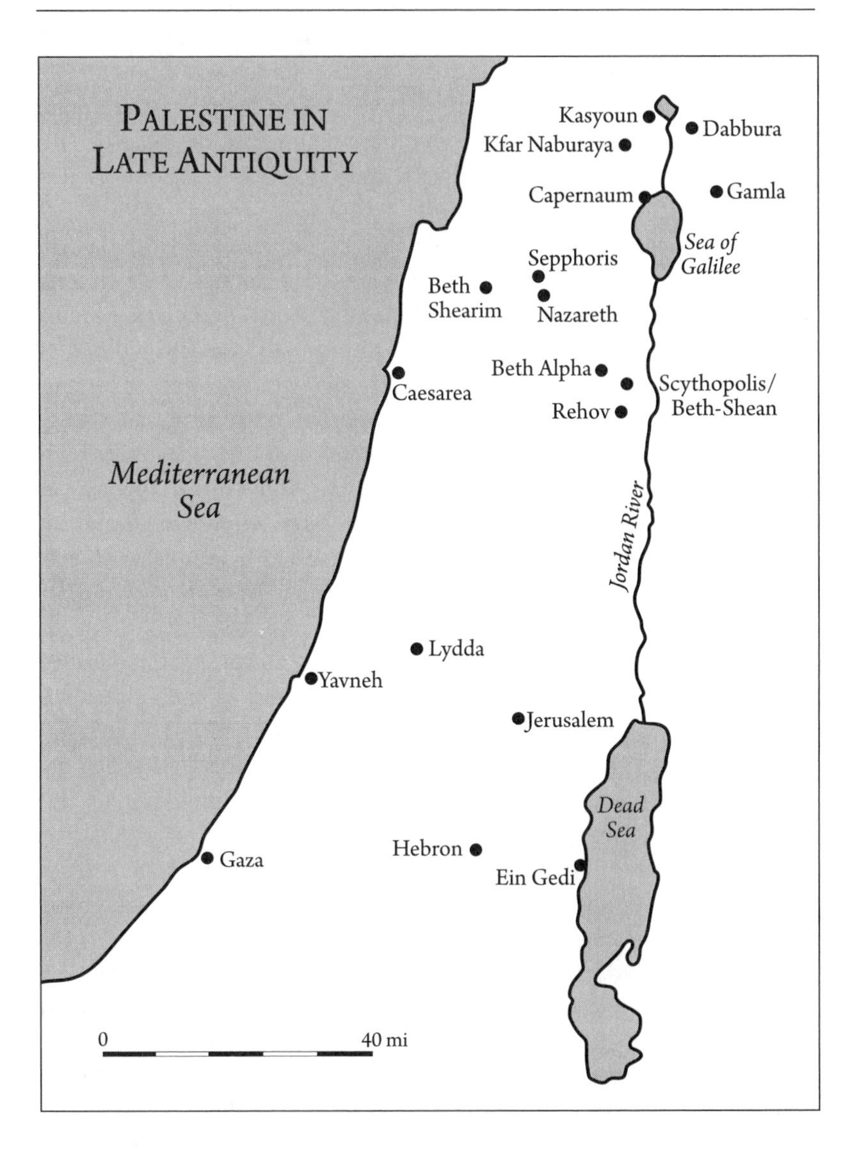

Christianized at a time when there was a great burst in agricultural technology that made this possible.[204] Entire Christian villages, festooned with multiple churches, sprang up.[205] The explosion in size of these large Byzantine villages[206] served the needs of both the new Christian empire and the Christian pilgrims en route to and from Jerusalem. Whereas the dominant setting for growth and settlement in the West was the rural fortified farm or villa, in the eastern empire the village filled this role.[207]

In some sections of the country, even traditional Jewish "turf" like

ZEV RADOVAN/WWW.BIBLELANDPICTURES.COM

Cross-Shaped Baptistery. *This baptistery next to an early Byzantine church at Subeita (Shivta) in the central Negev is made from a single block of stone. Steps are carved in the east and west arms of the cross. The initiate descended into the water by one set of steps and "died to sin" (Romans 6:2–3), then emerged by the other set of steps, symbolizing a new life.*

the Galilee was often encroached upon by Christians in the Byzantine period. From a fourth-century narrative, we learn of the attempt of Count Joseph of Tiberias, a converted Jew, to place church buildings in Sepphoris, Tiberias, Nazareth and Capernaum; this proved to be merely a straw in the wind.[208] By the mid-fifth century, the city of Sepphoris (Diocaesarea), a traditional Jewish stronghold,* had a Christian bishop in attendance at the Council of Chalcedon (451 C.E.), as well as bishops who attended the Jerusalem synods in 518 and 536 C.E.[209] A church shrine was raised over the House of St. Peter in Capernaum. A basilica was placed over the site of the Annunciation at Nazareth.[210] Even at Hebron, a Jewish settlement area in the Byzantine period,[211] a Christian church was erected.[212] Around the Sea of Galilee, pilgrimage churches arose to serve Christians who traveled to venerate Christ's miracles at places like Tabgha and Kursi.[†213]

The invention of the pendative (a triangularly shaped part of a sphere placed at the cornering of walls) by architects of Justinian's day enabled a round dome to be placed on a square building. This provided Byzantine ecclesiastical architecture with a new form. The round dome was pioneered

*Mark Chancey and Eric M. Meyers, "How Jewish Was Sepphoris in Jesus' Time?" *BAR*, July/August 2000.

†Ulrich Hübner, "The Rediscovered Byzantine Church of Tabgha," *BAR*, May/June 1984; Vassilios Tzaferis, "A Pilgrimage to the Site of the Swine Miracle," *BAR*, March/April 1989.

Hagia Sophia. *One of the world's architectural marvels, Hagia Sophia in Constantinople was built by the emperor Justinian in the sixth century to be the chief basilica of the imperial capital. Its majestic central dome, which rises to a height of 180 feet and is more than 100 feet in diameter, is supported by pendentives that distribute the dome's weight to the central walls of the basilica. After the Ottoman Turks captured Constantinople in 1453 (renaming the city Istanbul), the church was converted into a mosque and four minarets were added. Since 1935, it has been a museum.*

in the Church of St. Irene and perfected in Hagia Sophia, both in Constantinople.[214] In Jerusalem, Justinian had a round dome placed over the basilical church at Siloam.[215]

Archaeological excavations in Jerusalem reveal how extensive Justinian's building program was. Literary sources had preserved references to a huge church called the Nea that Justinian had constructed in Jerusalem. The Madaba mosaic map of Jerusalem had actually depicted such a large basilical structure. The Madaba map also detailed a long, porticoed street thought to be the *cardo maximus* of Byzantine Jerusalem. Nahman Avigad's excavations in Jerusalem have exposed the few remains of the Nea Church, as well as a long stretch of the southern cardo with its portico for shops and

GARO NALBANDIAN

Madaba Map of Jerusalem. *This sixth-century mosaic depiction of Jerusalem found in 1884 in a church in Madaba, Jordan gives a colorful schematic rendering of the most significant sites in Byzantine Jerusalem. Inside the towering Damascus Gate, shown on the left side of the map, is an oval-shaped forum with a lofty Roman column that probably once supported a statue. Centrally located along Jerusalem's colonnaded main thoroughfare, the* cardo maximus, *is the Church of the Holy Sepulchre. It is beautifully depicted as a basilica, behind which is the domed rotunda that stood over Jesus' tomb. At the far end of the map and opening directly onto the cardo is the Nea Church.*

stores running along the line of Jewish Quarter Street in modern Jerusalem.* The Nea Church was securely identified by an inscription found in a huge vaulted cistern attributing the work to Justinian and dating its construction to 549/550 C.E.[216]

Such a huge Christian building complex in the heart of Byzantine Jerusalem indicates the degree to which the emperor at Constantinople regarded Jerusalem as a Christian city. This notion of Jerusalem as a Christian city and the Holy Land as a Christian place also had a wide following among

*For the cardo excavations, see Suzanne F. Singer, "The Ancient Cardo Is Discovered in Jerusalem," *BAR*, December 1976; and "Is the Jerusalem Cardo Roman After All?" *BAR*, December 1977. For the Nea Church, see Joan Taylor, "The Nea Church: Were the Temple Treasures Hidden Here?" *BAR*, January/February 2008.

HERSHEL SHANKS

The Cardo. *The principal street of Roman and Byzantine Jerusalem, the cardo was a 40-foot-wide thoroughfare running north-south through the city. The well-paved street was flanked by 10-foot-wide covered colonnades lined with shops and stalls.*

both clergy and laity. Imperial donations to found churches in the Holy Land did leave their mark on the landscape, but the burgeoning of new churches across Palestine was overwhelmingly due to clerical and lay donors, not merely to imperial donations.[217]

Prosperous Jews of Palestine responded both passively and actively to this new Christian presence. Passively, they stopped doing some things they had practiced for centuries, such as ossuary burial (secondary reburial of desiccated bones in boxes called ossuaries, about a year after death). The Jews abandoned this practice because it had been taken over by Christians.[218] On the active side, the Jews built a beautiful new synagogue at Capernaum, dated now to about 370 C.E.* This white limestone synagogue can be interpreted as a restatement of the Jewish community's solidarity in the face of Christian encroachment at the House of St. Peter, just a few yards away.[219] That Greek-speaking Jews still claimed the classical tradition for themselves, not surrendering it to Christians, can be seen in the floor of the fifth-century House of Leontius, a Jew of Beth-Shean, with its scenes from the Odyssey and quotation from Homer.[220]

*See Strange and Shanks, "Has the House Where Jesus Stayed in Capernaum Been Found," *BAR*, November/December 1982.

ISRAEL EXPLORATION SOCIETY

Foundations of the Nea Church. *The Nea Church, completed in 549/550 C.E., was one of the most impressive structures of Byzantine Jerusalem. Built on such an immense scale that it had to be supported by massive barrel vaults (left), the sixth-century church surpassed even the size and grandeur of the Church of the Holy Sepulchre. A Greek inscription (below) found on one of the vaults praises the emperor Justinian for carrying out the project, but also mentions Constantinus, the abbot of the church's monastery, who supervised the work. The inscription was carefully framed by a* tabula ansata *with its flanking triangular handles.*

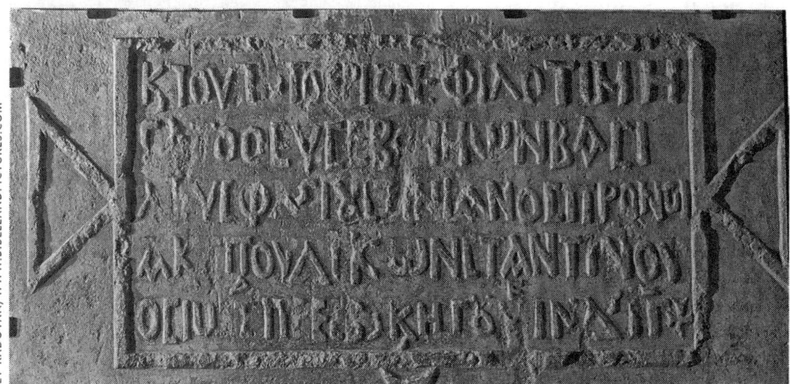

ZEV RADOVAN/WWW.BIBLELANDPICTURES.COM

Disease and the "unofficial religion" of the late empire

Far below and slightly beyond the control of the sublime theologians and powerful bishops and ecclesiastics of our period, another figure flits in and around the sources, both literary and material—the "healer." For all the focus on "power" that our historical narratives evoke, whose trajectories we have been tracing since Constantine's ascent to the throne, a different and more personal preoccupation predominates life at the ground level: disease and its consequences give the role of the healer and "objects that cure" emotional and numerical superiority to the ever-present politics of the day. In the precisely technical world of the amulet or magical tablet, those invocations that seek cure from disease far outnumber those that promise power over, or revenge upon, one's enemies.[221]

Every city or village had its professional healer to call upon when disease or illness struck an individual or an area. Healers came from all religious persuasions and were often used serially by people—if the Christian healer failed them, there was ever a fine Jewish or Hellenic one just around the corner to be consulted next.[222] No period in the ancient world since the days of Herodotus, nine centuries before, was so much in need of its healers.

In the years 541–543, bubonic plague makes its first appearance in Roman history, sweeping relentless and unforgiving across the entire empire. Outbreaks of a new pandemic disease on a scale never before seen in antiquity began in July 541 just east of Alexandria in the city of Pelusium and spread from there around the Mediterranean. There were at least five outbreaks of the disease that swept across the Roman Empire before 600 C.E.; and historians can still find remnants of such a pandemic in the West as late as the mid-eighth century C.E.[223] Historians have counted up to 18 outbreaks at various places, or one outbreak every 11.6 years for the next 200 years[224]; but whether these outbreaks were manifestations of a single pandemic disease or separate occurrences of a variety of plagues is still being debated.[225]

Both typhus and malaria were active in late antiquity and mimic the symptoms of bubonic plague in their early stages, as do numerous other diseases. But for the five outbreaks that began appearing in the 540s C.E., including the first, or the so-called "Justinian Plague" (541–543 C.E.), our Greek, Syriac and Latin sources clearly and precisely describe diseases that are manifestations of the oldest strain of bubonic plague.[226] What is more, forensic science has identified the bacteria responsible for spreading the plagues of these centuries.[227]

The results at the ground level must have been devastating if so famous and well-cared-for a figure as the emperor Justinian could succumb to an early version of the plague (though his strength and level of care did allow him to survive).[228] In fact, all of the literary sources that give extended descriptions of the plague describe massive numbers of dead in both cities and the countryside and the elimination of whole populations. In these accounts, the number of victims ranges from the hundreds to the hundreds of thousands.[229]

But here, the archaeological evidence and the clear testimony of the literary sources part company. The kinds of mass graves that testify to such numbers of dead simply have not yet been found, though a couple of unpublished communal graves are now being studied.[230] Nor have the accounts of massive depopulations of the countryside matched the booming demographics of the sixth and early seventh centuries. Some historians, however, have tried to argue that the effects of the pandemic can be seen in some urban centers where they perceive a downturn in civic construction.[231]

More important for this discussion is the way "disease" and "divine punishment for sins" are joined at the hip in both Judaism and Christianity. Pandemics thus become a profoundly religious phenomenon; and the search for God's forgiveness, mercy, protection and healing from disease allows us to identify an unofficial religion operating alongside the religion of the councils and the empire. As with the archaeological evidence for mass burials, however, there is little evidence for liturgies and services aimed at medicinal forgiveness, as we might expect.[232] But perhaps we are looking in the wrong places; some evidence may be found in the period's ubiquitous magical amulets and tablets that were intended to ward off or cure disease. The use of such amulets seems to have cut across all levels of society and all religious persuasions.*[233]

The end of antiquity in the East

By the second half of the sixth century, the Christian imperial dream of a unified and doctrinally homogenous Roman Empire had foundered on its own rejection of the very pluralism that had lifted the Romans upon the shoulders of so many disparate regions, languages and peoples. Both outside the boundaries of the empire, and within its borders, there were clear signs that the great theo-political experiment was about to slip away, and Roman control of the eastern Mediterranean's cities and villages was about to vanish.

In Palestine, the continuous pressure from the Christian populace and the occasional destruction of synagogues drove the Jewish population into the arms of their old enemies, the Samaritans. Together they made common cause and rioted at Caesarea in 556 C.E. and commenced an unsuccessful revolt in 573 C.E.[234] A few decades later, when the Persians invaded the eastern empire (613–619 C.E.), many Jews collaborated with them in hope of deliverance from Christian oppression.[235]

By the time the Byzantine emperor Heraclius recovered the Holy Land from the Persians in 628 C.E., a number of churches had been destroyed. Indeed, the city economy of the wider eastern Mediterranean region had been disrupted to the point that the Christian communities would never fully recover their numbers and churches in the few decades left before the Muslim conquest.[236] Yet life continued as usual in most places right up to and beyond

*For a similar use of incantation bowls among Babylonian Jews of the period, see Hershel Shanks, "Magic Incantation Bowls: Charms to Curse, to Cure and to Celebrate," *BAR*, January/February 2007.

the Muslim conquests of 634–640 C.E. Both churches and synagogues were built and used throughout the seventh and even the eighth centuries and beyond under Muslim rule.[237]

Yet how profound a change it must have been for Christians, steeped in the "heady brew" of Byzantine triumphalist Christianity, to be forced not only to "share turf," but also their very churches, with the new Muslim religionists of the East.*[238] Cut off from their roots, which now lay to the West in what remained of the eastern empire, and surrounded by encouragements to convert to Islam, it is no wonder that Christian communities continued to decline in numbers under Islam.[239]

Thus, the end of Judeo-Christian antiquity is measured not so much by destruction as by a disruption—of trade and allegiance. With the Islamic conquest, trade with the West ceased; people relied on local products and then turned their allegiance and purchasing power toward the East. On sites across Palestine, ceramic products from North Africa and Asia Minor[240] were replaced by local wares.[241] Byzantine coinage gave way to transitional Latin/Arabic coins minted in Damascus.[242] A great watershed in the history of Mediterranean civilization had been crossed. From the sixth century B.C.E. to the early seventh century C.E., Palestine had traded and faced toward the west.[243] When the sun rose again over Palestine in the seventh and eighth centuries, all the people of the East—Christians, Jews, Samaritans, Muslims—faced east toward a new medieval world.

*For an example of a *martyrium* church that was at least partially converted into a mosque and jointly used by both Muslims and Christians, see Hershel Shanks, "Where Mary Rested: Rediscovering the Kathisma," *BAR*, November/December 2006.

ט

NINE

Christians and Jews in the First Six Centuries

JAMES H. CHARLESWORTH

DURING THE FIRST SIX CENTURIES OF THE COMMON ERA, BOTH JEWS and Christians shaped a clear and formative self-definition. This self-understanding enabled Jews and Christians to explain to themselves and to others who they were and why they were that way. For Jews as well as Christians, the process of self-identification was slow and often costly. Precious lives were sometimes lost—including those of Jesus, Paul, Akiva and Bar-Kokhba. Creative traditions were sometimes sacrificed—since neither rabbinic texts nor the New Testament preserve all the creative traditions that were regnant earlier in Second Temple Judaism.

Were all these sacrifices of lives and literary creativity necessary? Did survival require them? Should Jews and Christians today, along with secularists, not boldly face the shocking possibility that each survives only by sacrificing part of what is cherished? The Danish philosopher Søren Kierkegaard, for example, asserted that much was sacrificed in the transference from Jesus to Peter, and that all was abandoned when the erstwhile purity became contaminated with enthronement as "the Holy Roman Empire."[1]

As a Christian, I must confess that this "elevation" of Christianity as "the Holy Roman Empire" is in many ways less attractive than the Jewish world of thought that led to the enthronement of Moses in Ezekiel the Tragedian and the elevation of Enoch in 1 Enoch. Why did each "religion" (or better, each social unit known from rabbinic texts and the New Testament) feel the need to eliminate some old traditions and to focus on new formulas? Why was delimiting self-definition, and excluding others (e.g., the minim or the Arians) so important? And why did Judaism and Christianity, which in the first century C.E. often could not be distinguished, become so different from each other?

Despite the opinions of some 19th- and early-20th-century scholars, Jews and Christians did not develop in isolation from one another. Early Judaism is misrepresented if it ignores or minimizes the roles of the Righteous Teacher (the mysterious figure behind the Dead Sea Scrolls), Hillel (who is too often relegated to rabbinic texts) or Jesus and his Jewish followers. Similarly, rabbinic works are miscast if they are portrayed without reference to a growing social problem: the Christians who increasingly cast disdain on the nation that produced Jesus. These insights and perceptions define a new perspective on early Judaism and early Christianity. This perspective will focus the present discussion.

The age of variety and standardization: 167 B.C.E.–70 C.E.

In Judaism, two overarching trends can be discerned during the period from 167 B.C.E. to 70 C.E.: variety and, at the same time, standardization.

In 167 B.C.E. the desecration of the Temple by Antiochus IV Epiphanes led to the famous Maccabean revolt. Sacrifices in the Jerusalem Temple were restored in 164 B.C.E. through the victories of Judas Maccabee. His exploits are still celebrated, notably by Jews in the festival of Hanukkah and by Christians in Handel's opera, "Judas Maccabaeus." In modern Israel, Handel's famous "conqu'ring hero" has become a Hanukkah song.

Sometime between 152 and 140 B.C.E., however, the Zadokites, the descendants of Aaron and the legitimate high priests, were expelled from the Temple (1 Maccabees 10–14) or abandoned a corrupt priesthood ("Some Precepts of the Torah" [MMT, or *Miqsat Ma'aseh ha-Torah*] among the Dead Sea Scrolls), to be superseded by the Maccabees and the Hasmoneans. Many of these Zadokite priests—along with some Levites—withdrew to the wilderness of Judea and settled at what is now called Qumran. There, west of the Dead Sea, they founded a community that preserved old "apocryphal" writings, like the earliest books of Enoch and other Pseudepigrapha. It was these priests who wrote the sectarian Dead Sea Scrolls. Using the rhetoric of the ancient world, but in a unique and powerful way, they castigated the officiating priests in the Jerusalem Temple as prostitutes and fornicators.

Their writings revealed how much Jewish thought was dependent not

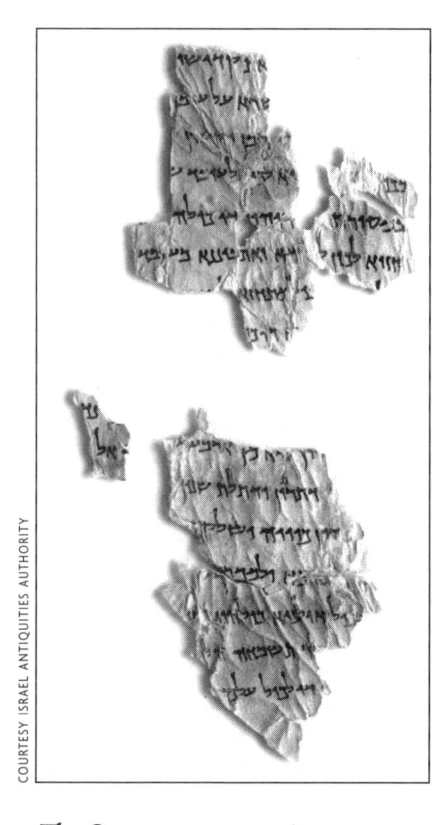

COURTESY ISRAEL ANTIQUITIES AUTHORITY

Fragments of Enoch Found Among the Dead Sea Scrolls. *The apocalyptic Book of Enoch is quoted in the New Testament Epistle of Jude (Jude 14–15) that was written around 100 C.E. The Enoch fragments among the Dead Sea Scrolls are in Aramaic.*

only on ancient sacred writings, like Isaiah, but also on the creative and challenging new thoughts from other cultures, especially Persian metaphysics. For example, their hymnbook (the Thanksgiving Hymns, or *Hodayot*) shows the mixing of the concepts of Eden (from the Hebrew scriptures) and paradise (from the Old Persian *pairidaêza*). This pre-Christian hymnbook also emphasizes that salvation is possible only by God's grace (a concept once attributed to the creative genius of Paul).

The Qumran community

The Qumran community was united and led by a charismatic and prophetic man called the "Righteous Teacher." He (or his followers) claimed that all the mysteries of the prophets were disclosed to the Teacher, and to him alone.[2] A similar prophetic claim was later attributed to Jesus by the Evangelists, and probably by Jews who lived before 70 C.E. (see Luke 4:16–22; Mark 1:22,27; Matthew 7:29; John 7:46). According to the Talmudim, the Jewish sage Akiva hailed the warrior Bar-Kokhba as "the Messiah."[3]

Adapting and mixing ideas from Jewish scriptures and from cultures to the east, the Righteous Teacher probably thought of himself as the "gardener" who was commissioned by God to plant "the shoot for the eternal planting,"[4] which was for God's glory. He or his followers developed the belief that they were living at "the end of days," and that God would soon send two messiahs, a priestly messiah and a kingly messiah. Their community was like an antechamber of heaven. The angels were present in their worship services. It was possible, they fervently believed, for a Qumran covenanter to move beyond the limitations of the human and to approximate angelic status. The

Qumranites believed they were "the most holy of Holy Ones" because they lived in "the Holy House" in which "the Holy Spirit" dwelt. Thus, their *Yaḥad*, or community, functioned like the Temple.

The Qumran covenanters were anti-Hasmonean. That dynasty, established after the Maccabean revolt, declined distressingly. It began with a commitment to the "Lord God" and devolved to the nadir in which a self-professed "king," who had been dishonored in the Temple, would later crucify hundreds of fellow Jews. That is, the Hasmonean "king" Alexander Jannaeus (103–76 B.C.E.). He was pelted with citrons in the Temple during the feast of Tabernacles by his Jewish subjects.[5] At one point, he crucified 800 Jews and murdered their wives and children before their eyes. What did this "king" do as the Jews were dying on crosses? He feasted and frolicked with his concubines.[6]

The demise of the Hasmonean dynasty was accompanied by major divisions within Judaism. The most important groups or sects were the Essenes (some of whom were responsible for the Dead Sea Scrolls), the Pharisees, the Sadducees, the Samaritans, the Baptist groups and the Enoch groups. Tragically, Roman forces were introduced into Palestine. In 63 B.C.E. Pompey and his troops were actually invited into Palestine because of a civil war between Hasmonean rivals for the throne. The Jewish hatred of Pompey is attested in the Psalms of Solomon. In the following quotation, most scholars agree that "his insolence" is a reference to Pompey, the gentile who trampled Jerusalem (Psalms of Solomon 2:18):

> And I did not wait long until God showed me his insolence
> pierced on the mountains of Egypt,
> more despised than the smallest thing on earth and sea.
> (Psalms of Solomon 2:26)

In 40 B.C.E., following the nomination of Marc Antony, the Romans declared Herod to be king. He murdered his way to actual enthronement in 37 B.C.E. He befriended Antony and then Octavian (Caesar Augustus) after the great non-battle at Actium in 31 B.C.E. When Herod died in 4 B.C.E. he had proved himself not only the greatest builder ancient Israel ever knew, but also a ruler who (by overtaxation) had enslaved and robbed many Jews, turning them from landlords into tenant farmers under heathen landlords.

Jewish factionalism and Hellenistic rhetoric

The two centuries before 70 C.E. witnessed terrible factionalism among the Jews. The authors of the Psalms of Solomon called other Jews "sinners." Pharisees and Essenes also castigated other Jews, often using the vilest polemics. Sometime before 63 B.C.E. the Jewish miracle worker from Galilee, Honi, was stoned outside Jerusalem by fellow Jews. He could not be persuaded by them to curse other Jews.

According to the Gospels, Jesus of Nazareth called many Pharisees hypocrites and sinners. He was opposed by some leaders in the Jerusalem sacerdotal aristocracy. Some of these leading priests may well have turned Jesus over to the Romans; but it was Roman soldiers who crucified him. Sometime around 33 C.E., Stephen, a brilliant but tactless follower of Jesus from the Diaspora, was stoned by other Jews. Around 44 C.E., James the son of Zebedee was beheaded by Herod's grandson Agrippa I (Acts 12:2). James, Jesus' brother, was killed by some misguided Jews in 62 C.E.[7]

This Jewish factionalism was a reflex of the Hellenistic age. The polemics of the Hellenistic world are filled with incendiary rhetoric. Dio of Prusa called the sophists "ignorant ones," "liars" and "flatterers." Colotes, an Epicurean, branded some philosophers "prostitutes." Romans castigated Christians for being fornicators and cannibals. Such was the rhetoric and the *topoi* of the ancient world in which the two powerful survivors of Second Temple Judaism—rabbinic Jews and Christians—shared a birth crucible.

This rhetoric within Hellenistic life and the contextualizing of Jewish fratricidal polemics, unfortunately, was forgotten when the Hebrew and Christian canons were closed. In the Talmudim, Jesus is branded as a sorcerer or a demonized miracle worker. Matthew's portrayal of the Pharisees as "hypocrites" was taken as reliable, even God's description. This misrepresentation was costly since the Pharisees were the only other surviving branch of early Judaism.[8] What had been an internecine debate among Jews became early forms of anti-Judaism and eventually anti-Semitism. A paradigmatic and deadly shift occurs when what had been Jews saying priestly Jews were responsible for Jesus' death transforms into gentiles claiming Jews killed "God." Such hatred brews genocide and betrays the truly Jewish man called Jesus who stands out in history for his excessive emphasis on love.

During the second to sixth centuries, Jesus is misrepresented by Christians who eventually saluted him as "God" despite the Nicene Creed that proclaimed him fully God and fully man. Jesus is portrayed as anti-Pharisaic (yet the Christian canon indicates that many Pharisees admired him, cf. Luke 11:37, 13:31). Most costly for millennia of Jews and Christians was Matthew's addition that Jesus' death would be on future generations of Jews (Matthew 27:24–26), and John's blaming of Jesus' death on the *Ioudaioi*, which was misinterpreted to mean "Jews" (as if there were a monolithic Judaism and Jesus was not a Jew). The Greek term sometimes means "Judean leaders" (John 11:54).

Only in the last few decades has it become obvious that a monolithic or orthodox Judaism did not exist in Second Temple Judaism (c. 300 B.C.E. to 70 C.E.), and that the period from the first century to the sixth was a time in which "Judaism" and "Christianity" each developed a coherent self-definition. Attempts to reconstruct the history of Judaism and Christianity without warning about these age-old misrepresentations do violence to history. Moreover, it also perpetuates an atmosphere of fear that separates Jews and Christians, the twin sisters of early Judaism, and undermines any form of historiography that must be practiced by Jews and Christians working together, as in this book.

While Jesus, in many sayings, felt his mission was only "to the lost sheep of the house of Israel" (Matthew 10:5–6), Peter and then Paul perceived that Jesus' Palestinian movement had a world mission. While Paul believed that the Torah embodied God's law,[9] he argued for abandoning the efficaciousness of the Jewish dietary laws, rules of exclusion, the rite of circumcision and the observance of festivals. In so doing he removed most of the barriers separating Jews from gentiles, and made it far easier to enter the new religion. His emotional apocalyptic claims and soteriology (a theology of salvation that offered free and full forgiveness) won many converts to Christianity. The earlier believers in Jesus' messiahship and divinity offered a heady wine: They offered resurrection after death to a blessed immortal existence.

The First Jewish Revolt of 66 C.E.—which was squelched by two future emperors (Vespasian and Titus)—effectively ended in 70 C.E. with the burning of Jerusalem and the destruction of the Temple. This, in effect, marked the end of the history of ancient Israel. Large numbers of Palestinian Jews were killed or sold into slavery. Some were paraded through the Roman Forum, and then forced to build the Colosseum.* Various legends relate that in the mid-60s (perhaps sometime between 62 and 66 C.E.) Peter and Paul were martyred in Rome by Nero. Inscriptions in Hebrew have been found in Pompeii and Herculaneum and in slave quarters that were destroyed in 79 C.E.; now we have further evidence that Jews captured in the Great Revolt appeared as slaves in Italy shortly after the destruction of Jerusalem in 70 C.E.[†10]

Before the destruction of the Temple, Palestinian Jews enjoyed a rich and creative vitality. They were stimulated by surrounding cultures, especially the Greeks, Persians, Egyptians and Romans. The essence of Judaism,

*Louis H. Feldman, "Financing the Colosseum," *BAR*, July/August 2001.

†For additional evidence that Jews may have been living in Pompeii, see Hershel Shanks, "The Destruction of Pompeii—God's Revenge?" *BAR*, July/August 2010; and Theodore H. Feder, "Solomon, Socrates and Aristotle," *BAR*, September/October 2008.

monotheism, was threatened by deifications—or better, angelifications—of Adam, Enoch, Jacob and Moses. But angelolatry was not feared as much as idolatry, which was polemicized against by many Jewish authors in Second Temple Judaism.

The concept of paradise that emerged during this period (250 to 63 B.C.E.) was a mixture of Persian and Edenic (i.e., Hebrew) traditions; these were enriched by Plato's concept of the real world and myths about the Isles of the Blessed Ones. Many Palestinian Jews came to believe that the good life was not to be found in the Holy Land or in "This Age"; it was transferred to another place and to a future time. The "Age to Come" promised all answers; in that future age God's promises would be fulfilled.

Standardization of the texts and canon of scripture

While these varied thoughts were developing, another phenomenon, appreciably antithetical to it, was progressing. It was the process of standardization. Scribes were defining the contents and textual forms of scripture. Because of biblical books found in Hebrew fragments among the Dead Sea Scrolls, we now know about some appreciably different versions of some biblical books—especially Jeremiah and 1 and 2 Samuel. Before 70 C.E., the Hebrew texts of these books were not standardized into the versions known today. The standardization of the biblical text was a gradual process, which probably began sometime in the first century C.E., was "institutionalized" after 70 C.E. and basically concluded in the second century C.E.

Standardization also progressed in the Hebrew script itself. It moved from archaic scripts to Hasmonean forms and finally to the Herodian form in the first century B.C.E. That evolved script is so similar to today's Hebrew script that children in Israel can easily read it.

Finally, like content, text and script, the canon of scripture was being standardized. The number of books to be labeled "scripture" was defined and reduced. Many of these standardizations were settled by the first century C.E. Jews for centuries after the first century, however, debated the canonicity of Ben Sirach, which was eventually excluded, and the Book of Esther, which was included in the canon.

Liturgy, too, began to take the forms known to Jews and Christians today. The Psalter was obviously the hymnbook of the Second Temple. We now have two early versions of the Aaronic blessing preserved in tiny silver scrolls from about 600 B.C.E., found in a burial cave west of the walls of Jerusalem.* These

*See Gabriel Barkay, "The Riches of Ketef Hinnom," *BAR*, July/August/September/October 2009.

PHOTOGRAPH BY BRUCE AND KENNETH ZUCKERMAN, WEST SEMITIC RESEARCH, WITH THE COLLABORATION OF ANDREW VAUGHN, ASOR
COURTESY ISRAEL ANTIQUITIES AUTHORITY

Ancient Priestly Blessing. *This inch-and-a-half tall silver plaque discovered in a sixth-century B.C.E. Jerusalem tomb contains the oldest-known reference to a passage from the Bible: the priestly blessing in Numbers 6:24–26, which beseeches the Lord to bless the children of Israel. The plaque's blessing—"May YHWH bless you and keep you, May YHWH make his face shine upon you"—are still uttered by both Jews and Christians today.*

early versions became standardized in the priestly blessing we know from Numbers 6:24–26. This very form continues to be said in synagogues and churches throughout the world.

The *Amidah* prayer (especially the 18 benedictions said during the weekdays) took a standardized shape similar to the prayer said today in synagogues—even though later rabbis cautioned that spontaneous prayer is more desirable.[11] It is startling for many Christians to realize that the synagogal prayers recited by Jesus and his earliest followers are said today only by Jews in their synagogues and homes. Jesus and his followers also affirmed the widely recited credo from Deuteronomy 6:4, the *Shema'*. During the pre-70 period, the followers of Hillel and Jesus shared the same scriptures and liturgies.

The languages of scripture

During this process of standardization, the sacred language of the Jews moved from exclusively Hebrew to Hebrew and Aramaic. Then for many Jews both in the Levant and the western Diaspora it included some Greek scriptures (the Septuagint and the so-called Apocrypha that were composed in Greek). Finally, with rabbinic literature, especially in the eastern Diaspora, the religious language of the Jews moved back to Hebrew and Aramaic.

The earliest Christians may have written some traditions of and about Jesus in Aramaic, but the earliest extant records are only in Greek. This remained the language for the composition of the New Testament and many apocryphal books. Beginning with Tertullian (c. 160–220 C.E.), who also wrote in Greek, the language of Rome, Latin, became the major vehicle for discussing the essence of Christianity. It was in Latin that St. Augustine (354–430 C.E.) composed his famous and influential tomes.

Christian scholars in the East composed their works in Syriac (a form of Aramaic), from perhaps the late first century C.E. until after the Arab conquest of the seventh century. Syriac Christianity almost always developed alongside Jewish centers. Many brilliant eastern Christian scholars, notably Ephraem Syrus (c. 306–363 C.E.), knew and preserved early Jewish writings. In the East, both Jews and Christians were free from the politics of the Roman Church. They were driven together by a sea of "paganism," and were united by shared scriptures and a Semitic language.

Discussing the process of standardization has moved us beyond the historical period of the age of variety and standardization (167 B.C.E. to 70 C.E.). The year 70 marks the end of a singularly important period in Jewish and Christian history and the beginning of another age in history.

The age of centralization: 70–132 C.E.

If variety and standardization characterized the period from 167 B.C.E. to 70 C.E., the period between the two Jewish revolts—from 70 to 132 C.E.—was marked by centralization.

A pupil of Hillel named Yoḥanan ben Zakkai, according to legend, miraculously escaped from Jerusalem during the siege of 70 because he told the Roman general Vespasian that he was about to become emperor. This rabbi established the first rabbinic academy at a place called Yavneh (Jamnia) in the fertile coastal plain (where once the Philistines lived).

At Yavneh about 84 C.E. two major decisions were made: First, Judaism would be shaped primarily by the remembered insights of Hillel (and to an increasingly lesser degree by Shammai); second, the Jewish canon, which had been developing for centuries, was closed, except for some decisions regarding "the Writings" (especially Ben Sirach and Esther). These early Jews were not only the People of the Book; they also gave the Book to the People.

The Gospels—Mark, then Matthew, Luke and John—were composed between 69 and 100 C.E. In them the blame for Jesus' crucifixion was shifted progressively from Pontius Pilate and the Romans to the Jewish high priest

Caiaphas and "the Jews." Unfortunately, later generations of Christians forgot the social context of these charges. The setting was the factionalism within Judaism and the struggle for self-identification by Christians and Jews, both relatively marginalized people in the early Roman Empire.

The Gospel of Matthew was composed by a "school" that included some well-trained Jews; some of them were skilled in rabbinic methodology. John was produced by a school in which there were many Jews; some of them appear to be Samaritans and Essenes. Some Johannine Jews were apparently expelled from synagogues where they wished to continue to worship (the Greek word *aposunagogos* ["expelled from the synagogue"] appears only in John).

Minim is the rabbinic term for "heretics." It is unclear when a curse on the *minim* was added to the daily *Amidah* prayer recited in synagogues. While minim never clearly denotes Christians in the Talmudim, some Jews influenced by Yavneh may have considered Jews who professed Jesus as Christ to be outside their acceptable boundaries, that is, *minim* (but certainly not apostates).

Between the two Jewish revolts against Rome (66–70 C.E. and 132–135/136 C.E.) some of the major Jewish apocalypses were composed. These included, probably in this order, 4 Ezra, 2 Enoch, 2 Baruch and the Apocalypse of Abraham. These apocalypses are contemporaneous with the canonical Gospels, which also contain some deeply apocalyptic sections, like Mark 13 (and 8:38), Matthew 24–25, some sections of Luke (9, 12, 17, 19, 21) and some old traditions in John (cf. 5:29, 14:26, 15:21, 16:2).

Under the influence of the school of Hillel and the fear of further rebellion (as well as the attempt to define itself over against Christianity), post-70 Jews—especially after 135/136 C.E.—attempted to eliminate the apocalyptic elements from rabbinic traditions. Christianity, on the other hand, would be sustained by apocalypsology (apocalyptically focused reflection), especially by the two most important dimensions of Jewish apocalyptic thought: the concept of the resurrection of the body after death (at the end time), and the dawning of a new and glorious age. When rabbinic Jews chose to stress *halakhot* (rules for living) and to eliminate apocalyptic perspectives and, at the same time, ecclesiastical Christians embraced them and deified Jesus Christ, Judaism and Christianity followed different forks on the road to self-definition.

The contributions of Philo, Paul and Josephus

The first century C.E. was clearly the most important of the first six centuries for both Judaism and Christianity. No focus on this century with a view of the different paths to be followed by Jews and Christians would be complete without mentioning three significant Jews—Philo, Paul and Josephus. Each provides important data regarding customs, festivals, historical events (especially the relations between Judaism and Rome) and the evolving and dynamic world of early Judaism. To include them together now safeguards us from perceiving 70 C.E. as an absolute barrier.

The great bookends to first-century Judaism are Philo (c. 20 B.C.E.–50 C.E.) and Josephus (c. 37–100 C.E.). Paul is the creatively controversial thinker in the middle.

Paul was possibly martyred in Rome and Josephus died in Rome; much earlier (in 39 C.E.) Philo joined an embassy from Alexandria to Rome. Each Jew was a prolific and fertile writer.

Philo makes no mention of Jesus, his contemporary in Palestine. Paul followed Jesus as cosmic "Lord." In a controversial passage, Josephus probably mentions Jesus, perhaps with respect, although he is included among those who were stirring up the Jews in Galilee and Judea.*[12]

Philo of Alexandria developed an allegorical interpretation of Torah, the source of truth, by which he was able to collect syncretistically what he considered the perspicacious insights of non-Jews, especially Greeks like Plato. Philo stressed the importance of Jewish customs, such as observance of the Sabbath and circumcision. At least once he made the mandatory pilgrimage to the Holy City, Jerusalem.

Paul (Saul of Tarsus) was born a Roman citizen and a Pharisee. He moved to Jerusalem, persecuted Jesus' followers and eventually joined the Palestinian Jesus Movement sometime in the mid-30s C.E. He zealously traveled westward from Palestine to proclaim the "good news." It was from God; it focused on Jesus Christ, the crucified Messiah and resurrected Lord through whom God had saved all (male and female, slave and free, rich and poor).

Paul's thought is complex, nonsystematic and at times frustratingly contradictory. It was shaped by the contingencies and needs of local churches. We have some of Paul's letters, but we can only infer the issues and questions that evoked them. His letters perplex most exegetes. His thought nevertheless remains theocentric, as well as deeply shaped by Jewish apocalyptic eschatology. He may have studied in Jerusalem under the great Gamaliel (Acts 22:3); he certainly continued to be indebted to Pharisaic Judaism of an apocalyptic strain. In ways difficult to comprehend in light of his conviction that salvation is solely through faith in Jesus, he claimed both that God has by no means forsaken his covenant with the Jews and that eventually "all Jews" will be saved (Romans 9–11).

*See John P. Meier, "The Testimonium: Evidence for Jesus Outside the Bible," *BR*, June 1991.

According to his autobiography (*Life*), Josephus became a member of the Pharisaic party, and was awarded Roman citizenship by the emperor Vespasian. Josephus's historical works—*The Jewish War* (c. 77–78 C.E.) and *Antiquities of the Jews* (c. 94 C.E.)—are replete with invaluable information about Jewish life, the topography of the land, Jewish groups, sects and movements, and the descriptions of cities and villages. He provides data, sometimes tendentious, for understanding the social and intellectual forces that led to the First Jewish Revolt against Rome (66–70 C.E.).

Josephus's works are a mixture of truth and distortion. His topographical descriptions are often amazingly accurate, as anyone can attest standing east of Gamla and reading his narrative composed in Rome. His descriptions of the war are often confirmed by related research, although he distorts the position of Zealots and messianic movements, essentially blaming their hotheadedness as much as the corrupt Roman procurators for the ill-conceived revolt. His praise for the grandeur of the Temple is not nearly so exaggerated as once thought. The Temple was a stupendous wonder; archaeologists have uncovered a stone that weighs well over 570 tons.* Josephus's depiction of Jewish thought is slanted, but not distorted; he wanted to persuade the Romans of the beauty of Jewish customs and thought and couched Jewish concepts in Greek terms. After all, his livelihood and honoraria came from the Flavian emperors near whom he lived in Rome when he composed the *The Jewish War*.

The apocryphal gospels

In early Christianity we see the beginnings of the glorification of Jesus' mother, Mary. In Matthew and Luke she is hailed as the virgin who gave birth to the long-awaited Messiah, Jesus. In one of the earliest so-called apocryphal gospels, the Birth of Mary (also called the Infancy Gospel of James), she is portrayed as the fairest virgin in the Temple. In this work, her virginal nature, after giving birth to Jesus, is confirmed by a physical examination conducted by Salome. With this new tradition, "the virgin birth" shifts from a concept symbolizing Jesus' divinity to a gynecological examination.

Numerous apocryphal gospels were composed before 150 C.E., including the Jewish Christian gospels of the Hebrews, the Ebionites and the Nazarenes. The so-called Gospel of Judas was not written by Jesus' disciple and sheds no light on the historical Judas; but it is an important Christian apocryphal work and informs us of the struggles for survival of the early Christians as they

*See especially Murray Stein, "How Herod Moved Gigantic Blocks to Construct Temple Mount," *BAR*, May/June 1981.

sought to define their scriptures and obtain a coherent self-understanding.*

For understanding Jesus' sayings, the most important of the apocryphal gospels is the Gospel of Thomas.† Although it contains some teachings that were later considered heretical, this document provides a record of the transmission of Jesus' sayings that is intermittently independent of the canonical Gospels. It is conceivable that in some passages the Gospel of Thomas preserves Jesus' words more accurately than the canonical Gospels. The Gospel of Thomas is also closely linked with Judaism; for example, Peter says to Jesus: "You are like a righteous angel [*enouangelos endikaios*]" (Saying 13), which comports well with Jewish angelology.

During the years 100 to about 150 C.E., the latest documents in the New Testament were also completed. At this same time apocryphal works like 2 Baruch, the Apocalypse of Abraham, the Odes of Solomon and 3 and 4 Baruch were being composed. Ignatius (died 111 C.E.) was writing his letters, Polycarp (69–155 C.E.) and Papias (flourished c. 140 C.E.) were preserving early traditions, and at least 13 versions of the Mishnah were taking shape for Rabbi Judah ha-Nasi later to edit. At the same time, Plutarch (46–125 C.E.) was composing his *Parallel Lives*, the Stoic Epictetus (60–117 C.E.) was completing his *Discourses*, and a little later, Marcus Aurelius (121–180 C.E.) completed his Stoic *Meditations*. Galen (130–200 C.E.) would publish the first medical work since Hippocrates (c. 469–399 B.C.E.), despite the appearance of the *De Re Medicina* of Aulus Cornelius Celsus (25 B.C.E.–50 C.E.). The devotees of Asclepius developed legends that portrayed him as the great physician who died and was raised again from the dead. The worshipers of Mithra considered him the "all-conquering sun god." The priests in the imperial cult hailed certain emperors as "gods"; all in the Roman Empire had to agree publicly or face the "invisible might" of Rome. Christianity and Judaism were struggling for existence against daunting odds.

Before the fourth century, it is misleading to refer to Christian "heresy," because there was no dominant orthodoxy before this time. It is also misleading to use (without quotation marks to warn the reader) the terms "apocryphal" and "canonical" because the New Testament canon was not closed until the fourth century, at the earliest.

The most dangerous theological tendency during the first six centuries—one which still threatens Christian theology today—was Docetism. Docetism claims that Jesus only seemed (Greek, *dokeo*) to be human, but was actually a being of celestial substance. Docetism explains away Jesus' suffering: only

*See Birger A. Pearson, "Judas Iscariot Among the Gnostics," *BAR*, May/June 2008.
†Helmut Koester and Stephen J. Patterson, "The Gospel of Thomas," *BR*, April 1990.

the human apparition suffered, while God remained removed from the world of suffering.

The Docetists opposed the Johannine school. The author of 2 John wrote: "Deceivers [are those] who will not acknowledge the coming of Jesus Christ in the flesh [*en sarki*]" (2 John 7). Yet Docetism was advocated in the second-century Acts of John, in which the apostle John, weeping in Gethsemane over Jesus' crucifixion below him to the west, is told by a celestial Jesus, who saunters up to him, that what is happening down there is only illusory. According to another passage in the Acts of John, John fails to see Jesus' footprints in the sands as they walk together: Jesus was not a human. Fortunately, "the Great Church" did not include such distortions of the man called Jesus, son of Joseph (John 6:42).

In the period from 70 to 150 C.E., Christianity and Judaism became centralized. Jesus' teachings, as remembered by those who proclaimed him, were collected into the first Gospels. After about 85 C.E., Paul's letters were collected and read in Christian services as if they were part of scripture (2 Peter 3:16), and all the New Testament documents were composed. Judaism moved toward Rabbinic Judaism with emphasis on the themes (especially the *halakhah* [rules for living in the present world]) found in the Mishnah, which was taking shape during this period. Christians claimed that all problems were solved by faith in Jesus Christ, their risen Lord. Jews stressed that all answers were revealed in the Torah (see 2 Baruch, Akiva and the early portions of the Mishnah).

The beginnings of concentrated canonization and codification: 70–200 C.E.

The period from the First Jewish Revolt (66–70 C.E.) to the Mishnah (c. 200–225 C.E.) can be described as the beginnings of concentrated canonization for Christianity and Judaism, even though the origins of the process antedate the year 70 by centuries. After the Roman burning of the Temple, the need for some order after the chaos of the revolt was necessary. A coherent collection of scriptures was demanded for daily guidance, since some sects like the Samaritans had scriptural texts that offended some Jews, and some groups, like those behind 1 Enoch, the Temple Scroll and Some Precepts of the Torah (MMT) threatened the types of Judaism that were regnant in Jerusalem.

Before considering how Judaism may have been codifying its scriptures, we must discuss the revolt of 132–135/136 C.E. Events are impossible to reconstruct confidently. Whether the greatest rabbi of the time, Akiva (c. 50–132 C.E.), actually declared that Simeon bar Kosba, the leader of the revolt, was none other than Bar-Kokhba, the "Son of the Star," the Messiah, is a moot question. Nevertheless the revolt clearly had its messianic aspects. Christians did not join the forces of Bar Kosba, but they should not be criticized for this apparent lack of loyalty. According to later rabbinic judgment, Bar Kosba was a false messiah.

The schism between Judaism and Christianity had widened; that is clear. But it is inaccurate to objectify it and say, as is claimed in so many books, that Judaism and Christianity separated completely after 132 C.E. (see the judicious insights in Chapter VIII). Such a reconstruction fails to note that Christians continued, at least in some places, to frequent synagogues despite the protestations of John Chrysostom (c. 347–407 C.E.) and Ephraem Syrus. Origen and Jerome knew at least some Hebrew (and were presumably taught by Jews). Christians shared with Jews a major portion of their scriptures: the Hebrew Bible or "the Old Testament." And almost all of the recent section—the New Testament—was written within early Judaism by Jews.

The first moves toward a canonical New Testament occurred in the second century. Irenaeus (c. 130–200 C.E.), for example, claimed that there must be only four gospels as there are four winds. He may have been reacting to Tatian, who compiled the first harmony of the Gospels around 175 C.E. Irenaeus's odd claim indicates that in some major centers of Christianity only four gospels were considered authentic and "canonical."

The need for "Christians" to define "Christianity" is apparent from the situation in Rome about the middle of the second century. Several of the movement's leaders were there, and all were claiming to be Christians. Justin Martyr (c. 100–165 C.E.) was an erudite and highly influential scholar who admired the Greeks and was the first Christian to attempt to reconcile reason and faith. Tatian, who became a Christian between 150 and 165 C.E. in Rome, was Justin's student, but he hated the Greeks (see *Address to the Greeks,* especially chapter 26). Valentinus, who was in Rome from c. 136 to 165 C.E., was one of the founders of Gnosticism as a philosophical system. Rhodo (second century), a student of Tatian, was an anti-Gnostic apologist. Marcion (died c. 160 C.E.) seems to have compiled the first "canon," and threatened the coherence of Christianity; his money was returned to him by Roman Christians and he was banished from their midst. Christians were trying to find out what "Christianity" meant and did not mean.

The "orthodox" Justin claimed that God's covenant with the Jews was no longer valid and that gentiles had replaced Jews. Marcion argued that the canon should be expunged of everything "Jewish," and contended that the God of law of the Old Covenant had nothing in common with the God of love revealed in Jesus the Christ. Both Justin and Marcion had rejected

Paul's solution (cf. Romans 9–11). It is significant, however, that Paul's letters were included in the canon and the works of Justin and Marcion were not. Christianity clearly needed normative self-definition (see Chapter V), and some decisions, as we have seen, fortunately protected the new religion from being totally separate from Judaism.

At this time and in this same process, Judaism was ahead of Christianity. After the two great revolts, the Zealots vanished, as did the numerous "sects." The revolts had revealed the dangers of baseless dreams and false messiahs. The academy was transplanted to Yavneh in Judea, and then to Usha in the Galilee and finally to Tiberias also in the Galilee.

The first attempts to codify the Mishnah (Hebrew, "instruction") had already begun. The leaders in this process were the heirs of a single group, the Pharisees. No longer was power divided between opposing camps (i.e., the Hillelites and the Shammaites). The followers of Hillel had triumphed, and a unified concept had emerged. Deviants were excluded from synagogue services. The canon was virtually closed at Usha (c. 140 C.E.), with the exclusion of Ben Sirach and the inclusion of Esther. Within post-135/136 C.E. Judaism, messianism and apocalypticism were largely excised or at least greatly diminished.

The process was completed by a descendant of Hillel, Rabbi Judah the Prince (also known as Judah ha-Nasi; c. 135–220 C.E.) around 200 C.E., when he gave the Mishnah its final, well-known form. This collection of Jewish Oral Law defined the proper conduct of the faithful in their daily lives, explaining even minutiae so that the boundaries for acceptable conduct would be prescribed. The Mishnah, the basis for the Talmudim, focused Judaism. Its powers for self-definition derived from the claim that both the Written and Oral Law were divinely delivered to Moses at Sinai and from him to God's elect.

From the Christian perspective, what was lacking in Judaism was "a gospel," that is, a proclamation of God's good news to all about Jesus. He was the One Promised. And he had brought a coherent dream for the future. Apocalyptic Christianity embodies the dream of the One resurrected by God.

In Judaism, messianism, apocalypticism and belief in another world were never completely expunged by the rabbis, however. Hence, we hear the continuing volcanic explosions in Judaism that echo from 3 Enoch, the *Hekalot* literature, the Zohar and the pseudo-messiah Sabbatai Sevi (17th century). Dreams never vanished; they produced the complex forces that created in 1948 the dream of a Jewish state in the land promised to Abraham and his descendants.

The age of differing scriptures: 200–313 C.E.

Between 200 and 313 C.E., Judaism and Christianity followed different—but intertwined—courses. Each added something very different to their shared scriptures—the Hebrew scriptures (or Old Testament). During this period the rabbis completed scripture with the Mishnah, then the Tosefta; much later in the fifth century they completed scripture with the Talmudim. Christian scholars completed scripture with the 27 writings in the New Testament that had circulated as independent scrolls but by the second century were circulating in collections that had some, but not all, of the books. The shared allegiance to the "Old Testament" is remarkable, even if Christians were by this time dependent on the Greek translation, the Septuagint (which Akiva wished to replace and so supported Aquila's Greek translation).

A growing disdain for "the outside books" was shared by many Jews and Christians. Such was the unfortunate cost of self-definition based on a closed canon of scripture.

Codex Sinaiticus. *Discovered in the 19th century in St. Catherine's Monastery at the foot of Mount Sinai, the Codex Sinaiticus is a fourth-century C.E. copy of the Septuagint, the earliest translation of the Hebrew scriptures—from Hebrew into Greek. It is written in an uncial script, a curved form of capital letters.*

The third century also saw the flowering of Gnosticism. Its beginnings can be traced to the pre-Christian era in Platonic, Jewish and Persian emphases on *gnosis* ("knowledge") as the key to salvation; it reached the stage of a philosophical system during the middle of the second century C.E., especially in the work of Valentinus. The Gnostics thought that salvation was possible only for those who had fallen from a primordial stage of purity and who, through introspective personal "knowledge," could ascend again individually to the heavenly realm, often with the help of a descending godlike figure.

In 1945 near the town of Nag Hammadi in Egypt, a Gnostic library was recovered; in it were preserved Coptic treatises that preserved Gnostic works.* One of them, the Apocalypse of Adam, may be a Gnostic reworking of an earlier Jewish work that mirrors the baptist groups of the first century C.E. The Gospels, Josephus and the Sibylline Oracles preserve traditions that indicate charismatic figures were baptizing Jews; these baptizers congregated beside the Jordan River.

Gnosticism was deeply influenced by many writings. Various Gnostic compositions are deeply indebted to Christianity (especially the Gospel of John), to the Neoplatonists (especially Plotinus [205–270 C.E.]) and to Jewish apocalypticism (especially the Jewish compositions in the Enoch and Adam cycles).

Gnosticism proved to be a major threat to Christianity. Most scholars of the Church were forced to refute it. The most influential scholar in Rome, Hippolytus (c. 170–236 C.E.), directed his famous *Refutation of All Heresies* against Gnosticism. Clement of Alexandria (c. 150–215 C.E.) agreed with the Gnostics that *gnosis* was the key to salvation, but he defined it as "illumination," which presupposed the "faith" of the apostolic scriptures and the continuing revelation to the Church. For Clement, ignorance—not sin—was the fundamental evil.

His protégé was none other than the genius who was called Origen (c. 185–254 C.E.). He was so committed to his beliefs that he yearned (unsuccessfully) for martyrdom[13] and castrated himself because of a literal, and false, interpretation of Matthew 19:12 (it speaks of those "who have made themselves eunuchs for the sake of the kingdom of heaven"). Exiled by the bishop of Alexandria because of alleged improper ordination by bishops in Caesarea Maritima, he fled back to Caesarea where he founded a school in 231 C.E. that would become renowned for, among other things, its immense library, which rivaled the one in Alexandria (both libraries have been lost).

*James Brashler, "Nag Hammadi Codices Shed New Light on Early Christian History," *BAR*, January/February 1984.

In my judgment, Origen is the first biblical scholar. His most valuable work is the *Hexapla,* which places in six (sometimes nine) columns the text of the Old Testament according to six (or more) versions, beginning with the Hebrew. He was seeking to obtain the accurate text and meaning. His method of studying scripture was literal, moral and especially allegorical. Although his thought is sometimes contradictory and some of his major works are not preserved (at least in the original), he believed that God is one and transcendent.

Like many early scholars of the Church, Origen could not comprehend the relation between Father, Son and Holy Spirit. Some of Origen's thoughts are mysterious; in some ways he was a mystic.

In the first two centuries, Christians appropriated Jewish scriptures, especially the Septuagint, without re-editing them. Beginning in the second and third centuries, however, they felt compelled to re-edit what was being borrowed, namely the Testaments of the Twelve Patriarchs, which was used to teach morality; the Martyrdom or Ascension of Isaiah, which was expanded to clarify the descent of Christ into this world; the Testament of Adam, which was augmented to clarify time and the cosmos; and the Hellenistic Synagogal Hymns, which was interpolated so that the creative powers of Christ—not Wisdom—could be chanted in the churches (earlier Christ was identified with Wisdom; see Matthew 11:19 and the Odes of Solomon). All these redactions, interpolations and expansions served the needs of the self-defining Christian community. After such editorial work, which delimited the possibilities for speculation, only a Christian could use them; they reflected a Christian perspective.

Other "Christian" thinkers were veering off in wild directions. Montanus (late second century) claimed that the heavenly Jerusalem would descend to earth near Pepuza in Phrygia. Manes (c. 215–275 C.E.), a dualist, contended that portions of light and darkness that had been imprisoned in human brains by Satan were released only by messengers: the biblical prophets, Jesus, Buddha and—of course—Manes, who was rewarded for such weird thoughts by being flayed alive by the head of the Persian empire.

The Cologne Mani Codex[14] contains excerpts from numerous Jewish apocalypses otherwise unknown; they seem to be authentic and another indication of Judaism's continuing influence on almost all aspects of Christianity. Bardsanes (154–222 C.E.), the father of Syriac hymnbooks, affirmed that Christ's body was a phantom (cf. Acts of John) but denied a future resurrection. These wild offshoots resulted from a volatile mixture of mysticism and apocalyticism. Before the fourth century, Christianity was like a puppy that knows no boundaries. This condition could not continue. It had to be outgrown.

The age of councils: 313–451 C.E.

The first century was obviously the most important of the first six, since origins dictate the spirit of a movement. Next in importance was the fourth century, since in it the mentality of Christianity was clarified. Three dates in the fourth century are especially significant: 313, 325 and 367 C.E.

In 313 C.E. Constantine the Great (c. 288–337 C.E.) declared all religions free from Roman persecution (see Chapter VIII). This edict (the misnamed Edict of Milan) did not elevate Christianity; it signaled Christianity's triumph over persecution, which was severe, as is well known in clichés about lions and Christians. Only on his death was Constantine himself baptized as a "Christian." Before his time, it was not clear what constituted Christianity. After his century, Christians would be so clear about "orthodoxy" that far too frequently the Semitic spirit that impregnated earliest Christianity waned.

In 325 C.E. at Nicaea, Constantine summoned the leaders of the Church. He ordered them to define the essence of Christianity, not because he was interested in theology, but because he needed ecclesiastical unity. As with Yavneh (Jamnia), there are no records of what actually took place. The most famous scholar in attendance was Eusebius (c. 260–340 C.E.), the father of Church history. At Nicaea, the major issue was Christology. Scholars debated the precise relationship between Father and Son. In response to the challenge of the brilliant Arius, Eusebius submitted a creed that when enriched by the word "of one substance" (Greek, *homoousios*) was judged to be "orthodox." The creed finally adopted, however, was another one (see p. 296); it is the popular "Nicene Creed" said frequently today in all churches claiming to be "catholic" and "apostolic." Arius's perception that Father and Son were not absolutely identical was rejected by the Nicene decision. Henceforth, orthodox Christians would confess that God and Jesus shared one substance (*homoousios*). Christians were making bold decisions as they sought to define themselves and their beliefs. With exceptional claims, inspired rhetoric and the media of the Holy Roman Empire, Christianity solidified its own self-definition and success.[15]

Here we see another major break with Judaism; Jews could not remain within Judaism and believe that Jesus is God or that Jesus and God shared one substance. Many followers of Origen preferred the term *homoiousion*, "of like substance"; it provided the possibility for some distinction between Jesus and God. But in any discussion of Jesus' substance we move from the world of Judaism in which Christianity originated to a different level of discourse. Never in Jewish apocalypticism, for example, is Adam, Enoch or Moses considered of one substance—or even of like substance—with God. Rather, in some sectarian texts they are enthroned and elevated to angelic status.

We may ask whether these Christian debates forced too much to be defined too precisely. Has the supra-categorical dimension and ineffable-ness of God been sacrificed by the need to think in Greek logical and philosophical categories? Did the success and popularity—and the unity—of Christianity (in the West) demand such logical precision?

In 367 C.E. Athanasius (c. 296–373 C.E.), an influential opponent of Arianism, wrote a festal letter that listed, for the first time, the 27 books of the New Testament and in the order known today. Yet, after 367 C.E., and until about the sixth century, some Christians still considered unacceptable or uninspired numerous books that Athanasius had included in the New Testament; they are Hebrews, 2 Peter, Jude and Revelation.

Canonization was a process. It was not tied to a particular council. It resulted from four centuries of experience. Moreover, the contents of the canon continued to be debated in the Greek Orthodox Church, the Ethiopian Church and the Syrian Church long after the fourth century. Even in the fourth-century West, the canon was not universally accepted as closed.[16]

The date of Athanasius's list, 367 C.E., is important. From that date, we can talk about the existence of a canonical list of the books in the New Testament. And that list is the same one that is used today by Roman Catholics and Protestants.

Relations between churches and synagogues in Palestine

During the fourth and fifth centuries, despite what is taught today in some universities and claimed in numerous publications, Christians did relate with Jews (as Chapter VIII demonstrates). Some Christians attended synagogue services. John Chrysostom (c. 347–407 C.E.), who referred to the Jews as "wretched and miserable," was forced to admit that "many" of the members of his church who claimed to accept his teachings did "attend their [Jewish] festivals, and even share in their celebrations and join in their fasts."[17] The synagogue, he said, is "a house of prostitution" and "a dwelling place of demons," yet some Christians "go to these places as though they were sacred shrines."[18] He calls such a Christian "a jackass" and perpetuates the foul myth that the Jews crucified Jesus. John Chrysostom misinterpreted the New Testament writings, especially John and Revelation; but his writings are still revered throughout much of Christendom.

Fortunately, abundant evidence indicates a positive relation among Jews and Christians. With the legalization of Christianity in the fourth century, Constantine initiated massive building programs in Palestine. Some of his monumental buildings are still visible today beneath the Church of the Holy

DAVID HARRIS

***Anastasis* of the Church of the Holy Sepulchre.** *Supposedly the site of Jesus' burial and resurrection (*anastasis *means "raising up" in Greek), this ornate construction in the Church of the Holy Sepulchre in Jerusalem includes remains of the original fourth-century structure that stood over the tomb. Beginning with the reign of Constantine (306–337 C.E.), the Byzantine kings built monumental churches like the Church of the Holy Sepulchre to commemorate and protect Christianity's most significant holy sites.*

Sepulchre in Jerusalem and the Church of the Annunciation in Nazareth.* Yet, in the fourth and fifth centuries, impressive synagogues were also built

*See Yoram Tsafrir, "Ancient Churches in the Holy Land," *BAR*, September/October 1993.

ZEV RADOVAN/WWW.BIBLELANDPICTURES.COM

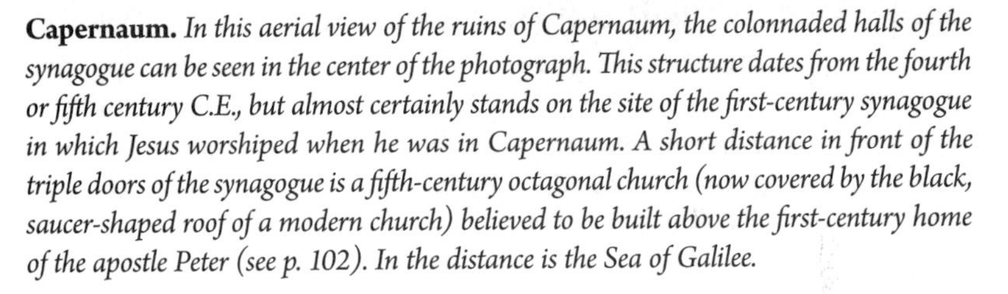

Capernaum. *In this aerial view of the ruins of Capernaum, the colonnaded halls of the synagogue can be seen in the center of the photograph. This structure dates from the fourth or fifth century C.E., but almost certainly stands on the site of the first-century synagogue in which Jesus worshiped when he was in Capernaum. A short distance in front of the triple doors of the synagogue is a fifth-century octagonal church (now covered by the black, saucer-shaped roof of a modern church) believed to be built above the first-century home of the apostle Peter (see p. 102). In the distance is the Sea of Galilee.*

in Palestine.* In Galilee, especially in Capernaum, these synagogues stood in close proximity to the churches. Sometimes the new synagogue was built above an older one so that the church was built near a synagogue. Sometimes the synagogue is later and so was built near a church. Obviously, Jews and Christians often chose to worship close to each other.

Additional evidence of a positive relation is found in the life and work of Jerome (c. 342–420 C.E.). He probably learned Hebrew from Jews. He was devoted to the Hebrew scriptures and translated the Hebrew Bible (Old Testament) and the Greek New Testament into Latin. His work assisted in the process of Christian self-definition; now Christians in the West had one accepted text of scripture. His translation, the Vulgate, encompassed in one volume the Hebrew scriptures and the New Testament.

Jerome's famous contemporary was Augustine (354–430 C.E.). This fertile and influential thinker argued that God is the creator of all, that

*See Steven Fine, "Did the Synagogue Replace the Temple?" *BR*, April 1996.

creation is essentially good and that evil is to be explained as the absence of some good. He experienced God's grace in a profound way. He set for the next millennium a paradigm for thought: "the City of God" versus "the city of the world." His vision was of the final triumph of the City of God. He was certainly influenced by the Hebrew scriptures, especially the visions in Isaiah; he may well have been indirectly influenced by early Jewish apocalyptic thinkers (cf. 4 Ezra).

The year 451 is important for three reasons. It was the year of the fourth ecumenical council, held at Chalcedon. Only seven councils are universally considered ecumenical, that is, producing judgments on doctrine and discipline that are binding for all Christians. These seven were held at Nicaea (325 C.E.), Constantinople (381 C.E.), Ephesus (431 C.E.), Chalcedon (451 C.E.), Constantinople II (553 C.E.), Constantinople III (680–681 C.E.) and Nicaea II (787 C.E.). The ecumenical councils were all held in one small section of the civilized world (Asia Minor). They reflect the fact that by the fourth century, Christianity was such a powerful institution that the only means of defining itself was the rigid bureaucracy of a council. At Chalcedon the focus of attention was not so much on defining and closing the canon of scripture, as many assume, but, as at Nicaea in 325 C.E., the real question was the precise relation between Jesus Christ and God and the nature of Jesus as Christ. The council sought to clarify the limits of speculation within acceptable Christian theology.

The year 451 is also important because it is probably the year Nestorius died. Nestorius's own theology is difficult to ascertain, because his thought was so altered by the Nestorians. It is evident that he rejected the title *Theotokos* ("God-bearer") for Mary, because he could not accept the idea that she was the bearer of God. Nestorius rejected any title or concept that would undermine the full humanity of Jesus. Nestorius was declared a heretic and exiled in 436 C.E. to Upper Egypt. The growing devotion to Mary would lead beyond *Theotokos* to *Dei Genitrix* ("Mother of God"). This trend was more typical of the West than the East. One can imagine that in some ways Nestorius felt Christianity was drifting too far away from its own mother, Jesus' Judaism.

The eastern bishops who supported Nestorius broke free from the councils and established the Nestorian Church. Centered in Persia, this Syriac-speaking Church became powerful, controlling the great school (really a university) at Nisibis. The Nestorians actually occupied the largest part of the civilized world. Before the Arab conquest in the seventh century, the Nestorians were powerful and influential from Cyprus to eastern China, and from southern Russia to the Malabar Coast of India.

Finally, the year 451 is important because that was the year of the Battle of Troyes (Battle of Châlons). Attila the Hun, after overrunning Europe and entering France, was defeated at Troyes. Europe nearly became a part of Asia. After his defeat at Troyes, Attila retreated to Italy were he suddenly died. The Huns, now without leadership, disappeared from history, but the West would take centuries to recover. The feudal ages were not far off.

The age of final institutionalization: 451–571 C.E.

The last half of the fifth century and all of the sixth century saw the institutionalization of Christianity. In short, Christianity solidified its position. Paganism was branded and banished. Christianity triumphed as the Holy Roman Empire. By the fifth century, Rome had established herself as the head of the Church, the place of the pope ("father," from Greek *papas*, through Latin *papa*). One reason was the universal recognition that Peter and Paul had been martyred and were buried in "the eternal city." In 385 C.E. the pope was accorded power to issue decisions without a council. Pope Gelasius I (492–496 C.E.) declared Rome's superiority over all other churches, including Constantinople.

In the sixth century the erudite monk (or abbot) Dionysius Exiguus (c. 470–544 C.E.) compiled the first collection of canon law. Pope John I asked him to clarify the dates for Easter. Influenced by the claim of Hippolytus (170–236 C.E.) that Jesus was born on 25 December, he subsequently categorized ecclesiastical chronology and the "Christian Era" (using *Anno Domini*, "in the year of the [birth of our] Lord," which influenced over a millennium of Westerners). Unfortunately, he incorrectly calculated the year for the birth of Jesus, working from the supposed date of the founding of the city, Rome. Today the Western world follows his dates, but that requires us to place the date of Jesus' birth before 4 B.C.E.

The Roman emperor Justinian I (527–565 C.E.) sought to unify West and East through his legal code and his energetic building campaigns. Among his best-known buildings are Hagia Sophia in Constantinople and the fortress-monastery at the foot of Mount Sinai (St. Catherine's Monastery). The constricting force of "orthodoxy" led him in 529 C.E. to close the philosophical schools in Athens. The influence of Aristotle would continue, eventually influencing many, including St. Thomas Aquinas.

Something else was also happening, as previously intimated. Christians whose ancestors in the faith had been fed to the beasts were now vengefully placarding Jews as "Christ killers."

Before 600 C.E. four important bodies of law affecting Jews had been promulgated: (1) Constantine's laws (315 C.E.) compromised the full equality of Jews as citizens; (2) Constantius's laws (399 C.E.) forbade a Christian woman to marry a Jew; (3) Theodosius II's laws (439 C.E.) closed leading government offices to Jews; and, finally, (4) Justinian's laws (531 C.E.) prohibited Jews from testifying against Christians. A dark light peered into the future; it is no wonder Jews would suffer so much from the Middle Ages to the Shoah (the Holocaust).

These injustices, however, were shared by almost all non-Christians. The historian Max I. Dimont has perceptively argued that these laws must be grasped in terms of the pre-sixth-century world. In *Jews, God and History* he offers this sane advice:

> These laws had two purposes: to protect the infant religion from the competition of other religions, and to protect key posts for co-religionists. When Jews are singled out by historians as the only victims of these laws, we are given a false picture of their intent.[19]

How, then, did anti-Judaism evolve? When one forgets the social context of the documents in the New Testament, one may see its beginnings in the anti-Judaic passages in the New Testament, especially in the Gospels of Matthew and John as well as in the Revelation of John. As early as the second century, Melito of Sardis (died c. 190 C.E.) defended the unity of the two Christian Testaments by denouncing "law" and elevating "gospel." Melito used his obvious poetic genius vehemently to denounce the Jews:

> He who hung the earth is hanging; ... he who fastened the universe has been fastened to a tree; ... the King of Israel has been put to death by an Israelite right hand.[20]

No wonder that, hundreds of years later, at Easter time, the great pogroms would erupt all over the Western world. Melito's thoughts were anathema to the essential Christian preaching as it developed in the early years; but his ideas would become explosive in later centuries in the hands of those with absolute power and in need of a myth for hatred.

Might it now be possible to ponder to what degree the persecution of "Jews" was at least somewhat linked with Jewish claims to be exclusively "God's chosen people," and with the charge that Mary, Jesus' mother, had conceived Jesus through sex with a Roman soldier named Panthera?[21] Some Jews obviously thought that Jesus was a demonic magician.[22] Some Jews claimed that the disciples had stolen Jesus' corpse (cf. Matthew 27:22–26), denying the resurrection. Understandably, by these polemics some Jews explained away Christian claims regarding the virgin birth, Jesus' miracles and the resurrection.

By the sixth century, Judaism and Christianity had parted; while sibling rivalry would degenerate into fratricide, Christianity can never break its umbilical cord with Jesus' Judaism. Christians believe that Jesus was a Jew, taught the coming of God's rule and was raised from the dead by God. These concepts were created in Second Temple Judaism and are fundamentally Jewish; they were codified in gospels that were composed by Jews.

In the first six centuries, Rabbinic Judaism was developing in ways distinct from Christianity. After Rabbi Judah's compilation of the Mishnah (c. 200–220 C.E.), rabbinic writings continued to appear. These included the Tosefta (a post-Mishnaic work of uncertain date), but most importantly the massive volumes of the Talmudim, first in Palestine (c. 400 C.E.) and then in Babylonia (c. 500–600 C.E.). These writings complete the Torah and are considered scripture. Together they are reputed to contain the Written and Oral Law delivered by God to Moses at Sinai. These writings, and the Targumim (translations of the Hebrew Bible into Aramaic), preserve very old traditions, but they are edited in line with the needs and perspectives of these later centuries. Cumulatively, Judaism succeeded in defining itself so that it could survive outside the land of Israel and without the Temple.

According to the Christian perception, the development of orthodoxy and the decisions of the councils were always by the guidance of a being separate from God and called "the Holy Spirit." Neither this concept, nor the title, is found in the Hebrew scriptures; there we find multiple references to God's holiness" (cf. "your holy spirit" in Psalm 51:11). "The Holy Spirit" does appear, although infrequently, in Jewish apocryphal works[23] and in the Mishnah.[24] It is also frequently found in the Dead Sea Scrolls.[25] Jesus probably knew the term "the Holy Spirit," and his followers certainly developed and emphasized this Jewish title for a divine person. Jesus, or at least his followers, probably inherited the concept of the Holy Spirit from the Essenes.[26]

Rabbinic thought is appreciably different. Although far from presenting a unified concept, many sages stressed the idea that the Holy Spirit left Israel with the cessation of prophecy.[27] It was impossible, therefore, to proclaim that Hillel was blessed by the presence of the Holy Spirit.[28] What could be and was claimed, however, was that he alone of his generation was worthy of receiving the Holy Spirit.[29] Since Judaism and Christianity evolved with significant knowledge of the other, the rabbis may have been subtly rejecting the triumphant Christian claim that Jesus (Hillel's contemporary) had received "the Holy Spirit" and that Christians alone were guided by the Holy Spirit.

In 571 C.E., the prophet Mohammad was born. He succeeded in giving the Arabs a book of revelations—like the ones cherished by Jews and Christians—that would unite and strengthen them. A new age would begin, but it is beyond the scope of this book.

The history of Christianity has been written, with few exceptions, by historians trained only in Greek and Latin, who myopically focused solely on the records of the triumphant western majority. The result is a tendency toward theological triumphalism, Western parochialism and an anti-Jewishness that shreds, if it does not cut, the umbilical cord of Christianity. These historians fail to perceive that Christianity's road to self-definition was shaped in a social and often polemically reactionary arena that included Judaism.

Notes

I. Palestinian and Diaspora Judaism in the First Century

[1] See particularly, Virgil's *Aeneid*, esp. 8.678–681 and 714–728. Virgil's Fourth Eclogue, Horace, *Odes* 1.2.

[2] On Herod as messiah, see Epiphanius, *Panarion* 1.1, 20.1. On Herod's strong-arm measures and popularity, see *War* 1.204–205; *Antiquities* 14.159–160.

[3] *Antiquities* 15.96–103.

[4] *War* 2.1–3; *Antiquities* 17.188.

[5] *War* 2.111–117; *Antiquities* 17.342–355.

[6] Because in antiquity there was no separation of church and state, Tiberius Julius Alexander, as governor of Egypt from 66 to 69 C.E. (*War* 2.309) participated in pagan religious ceremonies, as we see, for example, in an inscription (Wilhelmus Dittenberger, *Orientis Graeci Inscriptiones Selectae* [New York: G. Olms, 1986]), p. 663. It is significant, as John M.G. Barclay (*Jews in the Mediterranean Diaspora* [Edinburgh: T&T Clark, 1996], p. 106) points out, that Roman historians never mention his Jewish origins, so far removed was he from them.

[7] The fact that Pontius Pilate served as procurator for such a long time would indicate that he had the confidence of the Roman emperor. Hence, he was hardly under the thumb of the Jewish high priest in determining the punishment to be meted out to Jesus.

[8] Tacitus, *Histories* 5.10.1.

[9] *Antiquities* 19.236–247.

[10] *Antiquities* 19.341.

[11] See Josef Meyshan, "The Coinage of Agrippa the First," *IEJ* 4 (1954), p. 187, note 2. Wolf Wirgin (*Herod Agrippa I. King of the Jews* [Leeds, UK: Leeds University Oriental Society, 1968]) suggests that Agrippa regarded himself as the Messiah; but this seems unlikely since Josephus would hardly have praised him if that were so, inasmuch as a messiah, by definition, would have been a rebel against the ruling power of Rome. On Agrippa, see the definitive work by Daniel R. Schwartz, *Agrippa I: The Last King of Judaea* (Tübingen: Mohr Siebeck, 1990). Schwartz, pp. 138–139, convincingly concludes that it is most unlikely that Agrippa was engaged in an anti-Roman conspiracy, since Agrippa made no attempt to hide the visiting kings from Marsus, the Roman governor of Syria. Rather, there is good reason to believe that Marsus was jealous of Agrippa.

[12] Mishnah *Sotah* 7:8. The Mishnah refers to King Agrippa without differentiating between Agrippa I and Agrippa II. After weighing the evidence at great length, Schwartz (*Agrippa I* [see endnote 11]

pp. 157–171), finds little support for the widely-held view that the image of Agrippa, whether I or II, was positive in rabbinic literature.

[13] *Antiquities* 19.330–331.

[14] See Uriel Rappaport, "The Relations Between Jews and Non-Jews and the Great War Against Rome," *Tarbiz* 47 (1977–1978), pp. 1–14 (in Hebrew).

[15] *Antiquities* 18.6.

[16] See Shimon Applebaum, "Josephus and the Economic Causes of the Jewish War," pp. 237–264, and Heinz Kreissig, "A Marxist View of Josephus' Account of the Jewish War," pp. 265–277, as well as comments on these two essays by Louis H. Feldman, "Introduction," pp. 37–41, all in *Josephus, the Bible, and History*, eds. Feldman and Gohei Hata (Detroit: Wayne State University, 1989). For a critical survey of the bibliography on Josephus as a historian of the Jewish war, ibid., pp. 385–393.

[17] *Antiquities* 20.181.

[18] Peter A. Brunt ("Josephus on Social Conflicts in Roman Judaea," *Klio* 59 [1977], pp. 149–153) argues that the revolt was directed almost as much against native landlords and usurers as against the Romans. Martin Goodman ("The First Jewish Revolt: Social Conflict and the Problem of Debt," *JJS* 33 [1982], pp. 417–427) concludes that the main cause was the rotting away from within of Judean society due to social imbalance resulting from excessive wealth attracted to the city during the *Pax Romana*. Consequently, both the small, independent farmers and the craftsmen and urban plebs of Jerusalem fell heavily into debt and turned to banditry. Richard A. Horsley ("Josephus and the Bandits," *JSJ* 10 [1979], pp. 37–63, and "Ancient Jewish Banditry and the Revolt against Rome, A.D. 66–70," *CBQ* 43 [1981], pp. 409–432) emphasizes social banditry as a major cause of the revolt.

[19] *War* 2.427. See also Louis H. Feldman, "Conversion to Judaism in Classical Antiquity," *HUCA* 74 (2003), p. 138, who suspects that the round number 15,000 may well be exaggerated, but that the number 204 is plausible. He follows Julius Beloch (*Die Bevölkerung der Griechisch-Römischen Welt* [Leipzig: Duncker and Humblot, 1886], pp. 242–243), in suggesting that perhaps each of the 204 towns had 2,000 inhabitants, thus giving a total for Galilee of approximately 400,000 inhabitants.

[20] *Life* 235; cf. Magen Broshi, "The Population of Western Palestine in the Roman-Byzantine Period," *BASOR* 236 (1979), p. 1.

[21] *War* 3.43.

[22] *War* 6.420.

[23] *War* 2.295. See the excellent discussion by Martin Goodman, *The Ruling Class of Judaea: The Origins of the Jewish Revolt Against Rome A.D. 66–70* (Cambridge: Cambridge University Press, 1987), pp. 170–172.

[24] *War* 2.305–308.

[25] *War* 6.425.

[26] *War* 2.169–174; *Antiquities* 18.55–59.

[27] *Antiquities* 18.121–122.

[28] *War* 2.184–203; *Antiquities* 18.261–309.

[29] R.J. Coggins ("The Samaritans in Josephus," in *Josephus, Judaism, and Christianity*, eds. Louis H. Feldman and Gohei Hata [Detroit: Wayne State University, 1987], pp. 257–273) stresses both the hostility and the ambiguity in Josephus's attitude toward the sect. On the other hand, Rita Egged (*Josephus Flavius und die Samaritaner: eine terminologische Untersuchung zur Identitätsklärung der Samaritaner* [Göttingen: Vandenhoeck and Ruprecht, 1986]) concludes that there is no ground for asserting that Josephus was anti-Samaritan, but that he failed to differentiate among the terms for Samaritans, and suggests that it was his assistants who had confused the terms. We may respond, however, that the major references to the Samaritans are in *Antiquities*, and that it is in *War*, as we learn from Josephus himself (*Apion* 1.50), that he had assistants.

[30] See Clemens Thoma, "The High Priesthood in the Judgment of Josephus," in *Josephus, the Bible, and History* (see endnote 16), pp. 196–215.

[31] *War* 4.153–157.

[32] For a critical bibliography of the messianic background of the Jewish war, see Louis H. Feldman, *Josephus and Modern Scholarship (1937–1980)* (Berlin: de Gruyter, 1984), pp. 489–491.

[33] Suetonius, *Vespasian* 4.5.

[34] Tacitus, *Histories* 5.13.2.

[35] *War* 6.312.

[36] *War* 6.423–425.

[37] *Antiquities* 20.97–98; cf. Acts 5:36.

[38] Salo W. Baron, "Population," *EJ*, vol. 13, col. 869; and *A Social and Religious History of the Jews*, 2nd ed. (New York: Columbia University Press, 1952), vol. 1, p. 170, and esp. pp. 370–372, n. 7.

[39] For a critical bibliography on Josephus's views concerning the Temple, see Feldman, *Josephus and Modern Scholarship* (see endnote 32), pp. 438–448.

[40] *Apion* 2.165.

[41] *Antiquities* 20.251.

[42] *Antiquities* 20.180–181.

[43] See Hugo Mantel, *Studies in the History of the Sanhedrin* (Cambridge, MA: Harvard University Press, 1961). For other views, see Feldman, *Josephus and Modern Scholarship* (see endnote 32), pp. 463–467.

[44] Mishnah *Sanhedrin* 1:5.

[45] Tosefta *Sanhedrin* 3:4.

[46] See Hugo Mantel, "Sanhedrin," *EJ*, vol. 14, col. 837.

[47] Mishnah *Hagigah* 2:2.

[48] *Antiquities* 20.200.

[49] Josephus, however, mentions only one Sadducean high priest, Ananus the Younger, in connection with the condemnation of James, the brother of Jesus; *Antiquities* 20.199.

[50] See Mantel, "Sanhedrin" (see endnote 46), col. 838.

[51] So Haim Cohn, *The Trial and Death of Jesus* (New York: Harper & Row, 1971).

[52] *War* 2.285–289, in Caesarea; *Antiquities* 19.305, in Dora; *Life* 280, in Tiberias.

[53] JT *Megillah* 3:1.

[54] BT *Ketubbot* 105a.

[55] Mishnah *Sotah* 7:7–8; *Yoma* 7:1.

[56] The Theodotus inscription is generally dated to the first century C.E. It refers to an earlier synagogue official who was Theodotus's grandfather. See Hershel Shanks, *Judaism in Stone: The Archaeology of Ancient Synagogues* (New York: Harper & Row, 1979), pp. 18–20.

[57] See Shmuel Safrai ("The Synagogue and Its Worship," in *The World History of the Jewish People*, vol. 8: *Society and Religion in the Second Temple Period*, First Series, eds. Michael Avi-Yonah and Zvi Baras [Jerusalem: Massada, 1977], pp. 65–98, 338–345), who surveys the sources: the beginnings of the synagogue and its spread in the late Second Temple period; the names of the synagogues in Palestine and in the Diaspora; the character of the synagogue and its form of divine worship; assemblies on Sabbaths, festivals and weekdays; prayer, Torah reading and sermons; the conduct of the synagogue and its officials; the location and structure of the synagogue; and various uses of the synagogue. See also Bernadette Brooten, *Women Leaders in the Ancient Synagogue* (Chico, CA: Scholars Press, 1982). Heather A. McKay, *Sabbath and Synagogue: The Question of Sabbath Worship in Ancient Judaism* (Leiden: Brill, 1994) argues that the synagogue was a place where men gathered but that there is no evidence that they gathered for purposes of worship; however, the fact that Josephus (*Life* 277, 280) refers to a synagogue as a *proseuche*, "prayer-house," where people were engaged in prayer (295) is a clear indication that it served as a house of prayer. Furthermore, Agatharchides in the second century B.C.E. says that the Jews have a custom of abstaining from work on every seventh day and that on those occasions they pray with outstretched arms in the temples (*hierosis*) until evening. The fact that Agatharchides refers to "temples" in the plural indicates that he is not referring to the Temple and must refer to holy places.

[58] Baruch Lifshitz, *Donateurs et fondateurs dans les synagogues juives* (Paris: Gabalda, 1967), pp. 70–71.

[59] Elias J. Bickerman, *The Jews in the Greek Age* (Cambridge, MA: Harvard University Press, 1988), p. 139.

[60] *Sifrei Deuteronomy* 357.

[61] BT *Shabbat* 31a.

[62] BT *Sukkah* 28a.

[63] *War* 7.399.

[64] *Antiquities* 4.219.

[65] See Cheryl Anne Brown, *No Longer Be Silent: First Century Portraits of Biblical Women: Studies in Pseudo-Philo's Biblical Antiquities and Josephus' Jewish Antiquities* (Louisville: Westminster/John Knox Press, 1992).

[66] For a critical bibliography on the Jewish sects, see Feldman, *Josephus and Modern Scholarship* (see endnote 32), pp. 542–672.

[67] JT *Sanhedrin* 10.6.29c.

[68] *Antiquities* 13.171–173.

[69] *Antiquities* 18.23–25.

[70] Philo, *De Vita Contemplativa* 8.64–11.90.

[71] See also Epiphanius, *Panarion* 20.1.

[72] Mishnah *Demai* 2:2–3.

[73] The *'amme ha'aretz* did not give the prescribed tithes, did not observe the laws of purity and were neglectful of the laws of prayer. So great was the antagonism between them and the learned Pharisees that, in an anonymous statement, their wives are called vermin, and to their daughters was applied the verse (Deuteronomy 27:21): "Cursed be he that lieth with any manner of beast" (BT *Pesahim* 49b). Rabbi Akiva (ibid.), referring to his youthful days in the middle of the first century, notes the bitter antagonism which the *'amme ha'aretz,* in turn, felt toward scholars: "When I was an *'amme ha'aretz* I said: 'I would that I had a scholar, and I would maul him like an ass.'"

Perhaps the nonobservance of the *'amme ha'aretz* has been exaggerated: See Mishnah *Tevul Yom* 4:5; *Tohorot* 8:5; *Hagigah* 3:4–5. See also Chapter VI, Cohen, pp. 228–229.

[74] This will help to explain why the Essenes, who are described at such length in *War* (2.120–161), get so much less space in the discussion of sects in *Antiquities. War* was written somewhere between 79 and 81 C.E., shortly after the destruction of the Temple; by the time that *Antiquities* was written, in the year 93 C.E., the memory of the Essenes had faded.

[75] See Günther Baumbach, "The Sadducees in Josephus," in *Josephus, the Bible, and History* (see endnote 16), pp. 173–195.

[76] *Antiquities* 18.17.

[77] Cf. Acts 5:17: "The high priest stood up and those that were with him (which is the sect of the Sadducees)." It seems strange that Josephus says nothing at all (except for the fact that one high priest, Ananus [*Antiquities* 20.199] belonged to the Sadducees) about the connection of the Sadducees with the high priesthood and the Temple. The explanation may be that Josephus, as a priest himself, felt embarrassed by the predominance of priests in the ranks of the Sadducees and hence played down this relationship. Victor Eppstein ("The Historicity of the Gospel Account of the Cleansing of the Temple," *ZNW* 55 [1964], pp. 42–58), stressing the fact that only one high priest is specifically mentioned by Josephus, concludes that the Temple was not the headquarters of the Sadducees and that they were not, in fact, the party of the sacerdotal establishment. But to some degree this is an *argumentum ex silentio,* since Josephus's comments about the Sadducees are extremely brief.

[78] *Antiquities* 18.17.

[79] Mishnah *Avot* 3:2.

[80] *Antiquities* 20.201–203.

[81] *Antiquities* 18.23.

[82] It may seem surprising that Josephus mentions this distinction only once (*Antiquities* 13.297–298), whereas to the rabbis this is the major point of difference between the Pharisees and the Sadducees. The explanation may be that Josephus is writing primarily for a non-Jewish audience, as we can see from the proem to *Antiquities* (1.10), where he cites as the precedent for his work the translation of the Torah into Greek (the Septuagint) for King Ptolemy II Philadelphus; and gentiles would appreciate a distinction based on the attitude toward fate, since this was so central a point of argument between the two leading philosophical schools of the time, the Epicureans and the Stoics. Secondarily, the nonacceptance of the Oral Torah may not have been such a major difference, since we hear that the Sadducees had their own oral law in the form of a *sefer gezerata* (book of decrees) (*Megillath Ta'anith* 4). Jesus, we may note, denounces the Pharisees and the Sadducees together (Matthew 16:6–12); but we may suggest that perhaps Jesus agreed with the Sadducees in not washing his hands before eating (Luke 11:37ff.), a requirement according to the Oral Torah. When Jesus is rebuked by the Pharisees for not censuring his disciples, who ate without washing their hands,

he replies, "Hypocrites, you give up what God has commanded, and hold fast to what men have handed down" (Mark 7:9), an allusion, it would seem, to the Oral Torah, which was transmitted orally from generation to generation.

Of course, the question of why we never hear of the excommunication of the Sadducees presupposes that the Pharisees, prior to 70 C.E., were in an authoritative position to set the boundaries of the Jewish community. To be sure, E.P. Sanders (*Judaism: Practice & Belief 63 BCE–66 CE* [London: SCM, 1992], esp. pp. 458–490) argues that the Pharisees governed neither directly nor indirectly; but as Steve Mason (*Flavius Josephus on the Pharisees: A Composition-Critical Study* [Leiden: Brill, 1991]) has convincingly shown, there is ample evidence in Josephus's writings that the Pharisees enjoyed the steady and eager support of the ordinary people. This is all the more convincing inasmuch as Josephus himself actually disdained the Pharisees. Though some have disputed the later rabbinic claim that the Pharisees dominated the ritual of the Jerusalem Temple, texts from the Dead Sea Scrolls indicate that the views assigned to the Pharisees in a number of mishnaic disputes are precisely those that were practiced in the Jerusalem Temple. See Lawrence H. Schiffman, *From Text to Tradition: A History of Second Temple and Rabbinic Judaism* (Hoboken, NJ: Ktav, 1991), p. 107, and his "New Light on the Pharisees—Insights from the Dead Sea Scrolls," *BR*, June 1992, pp. 30–35, 54.

[83] *Antiquities* 18.17.

[84] See William R. Farmer, *Maccabees, Zealots, and Josephus: An Inquiry into Jewish Nationalism in the Greco-Roman Period* (New York: Columbia University Press, 1956). Farmer argues that Josephus deliberately omitted the connection because he was descended from the Hasmoneans, the family of the Maccabees, who had been allies of Rome, and hence praised them, whereas he bitterly opposed the revolutionaries. Of course, there is a major difference between the Maccabees and the Zealots; namely, that the former revolted, at least initially, because of the suppression of the Jewish religion, whereas the latter sought political liberty, which, to be sure, they viewed in religious terms as the *sine qua non* for Judaism.

[85] *War* 7.259–274.

[86] The relationship of the Sicarii and the Zealots has been much debated. In a sharply worded article, Morton Smith ("Zealots and Sicarii: Their Origins and Relation," *HTR* 64 [1971], pp. 1–19) insists that the Sicarii must be distinguished from the Zealots in date of origin, locale, leadership and philosophy. We may suggest, however, that the fact that the name "Sicarii" is Latin while the name "Zealots" is of Greek origin is an indication that the names were given to these groups by their opponents. Moreover, the fact that the names "Sicarii" and "Zealots" do not occur in *Antiquities* and that the strange name "Fourth Philosophy" does not occur in *War*, even in the enumeration of the five revolutionary groups (*War* 7.259–274), may be an indication that the latter is a term for an umbrella organization that embraced the various revolutionary groups. Indeed, Menahem Stern ("Zealots," *EJ* Yearbook 1973, pp. 135–152) persuasively concludes that only a hypothesis connecting the Fourth Philosophy, the Sicarii and the Zealots can explain the significance that Josephus assigns to the first.

[87] See Valentin Nikiprowetzky, "Josephus and the Revolutionary Parties," in *Josephus, the Bible, and History* (see endnote 16), pp. 216–236.

[88] *War* 2.434.

[89] *War* 2.444.

[90] *War* 7.29.

[91] *Antiquities* 18.63–64.

[92] For a discussion of this issue at length, see Louis H. Feldman, "The Testimonium Flavianum: The State of the Question," in *Christological Perspectives*, eds. Robert F. Berkey and Sarah A. Edwards (New York: Pilgrim, 1982), pp. 179–199, 288–293. See also John P. Meier, *A Marginal Jew: Rethinking the Historical Jesus*, vol. 1: *The Roots of the Problem and the Person* (New York: Doubleday, 1991), pp. 56–88.

[93] *War* 2.235–236, 253; *Antiquities* 20.121, 161.

[94] Midrash, *Song of Songs Rabbah* 2:18.

[95] See Lawrence H. Schiffman, "The Significance of the Scrolls," *BR*, October 1990, pp. 18–27.

[96] See Frederick E. Greenspahn ("Why Prophecy Ceased," *JBL* 108 [1989], pp. 37–49), who concludes that the claim that prophecy had ceased was made by the rabbis in order to remove a real threat to their authority. On the cessation of prophecy, see Louis H. Feldman, "Prophets

and Prophecy in Josephus" and Lester L. Grabbe, "Thus Spake the Prophet Josephus ...: The Jewish Historian on Prophets and Prophecy," in *Prophets, Prophecy, and Prophetic Texts in Second Temple Judaism*, eds. Michael H. Floyd and Robert D. Haak (New York: T&T Clark, 2006), pp. 222–227, 240–247. Feldman cites Josephus (*Apion* 1.41), who speaks of the failure of the exact succession of the prophets in the reign of Artaxerxes (465–424 B.C.E.). Grabbe insists that prophecy did not cease then but continued, as we see in references to John Hyrcanus (*War* 1.68–69; *Antiquities* 13.299) and to Josephus himself. The rabbis (Mishnah *Soṭah* 9:12, t. *Soṭah* 13:2, *Soṭah* 48b, *Yoma* 9b, *Sanhedrin* 11a) record a tradition that after the later prophets (Haggai, Zechariah, and Malachi) died, the Holy Spirit of prophecy departed from Israel, after which they availed themselves of the *bat kol* (a voice descending from heaven to offer guidance in human affairs but clearly a lower level than prophecy). Josephus (*War* 3.399–408) made a prediction that Vespasian would become emperor but he never refers to this as a prophecy. He is similarly careful to refer to Balaam as a seer (*mantis*) but not as a prophet. To be sure, Josephus (*Antiquities* 1.240) refers to Cleodemus, a non-Jewish historian dating somewhere between 200 B.C.E. and 50 B.C.E, as a prophet, but he is here quoting Alexander Polyhistor, who presumably did not have Josephus's qualms about applying the term "prophet." As to Hyrcanus's prophecy, it is a prophecy in the loose sense of a prediction like a *bat kol* but not prophecy as it applies to the "former prophets" of the Hebrew Bible.

[97] See Louis H. Feldman, "Prolegomenon" to M.R. James, *The Biblical Antiquities of Philo* (New York: Ktav, 1971), esp. pp. xxxviii–xlv.

[98] See, in particular, Martin Hengel, *Judaism and Hellenism: Studies in Their Encounter in Palestine During the Early Hellenistic Period*, 2 vols. (Philadelphia: Fortress Press, 1974). I have challenged this view in "Hengel's *Judaism and Hellenism in Retrospect*," *JBL* 96 (1977), pp. 371–382; "How Much Hellenism in Jewish Palestine?" *HUCA* 57 (1986), pp. 83–111; *Jew and Gentile in the Ancient World* (Princeton, NJ: Princeton University Press, 1993), pp. 3–44; and "How Much Hellenism in the Land of Israel?" *JSJ* 33 (2002), pp. 290–313.

[99] *Apion* 1.60.

[100] On the low level of Greek among Palestinian Jews, see Jan N. Sevenster, *Do You Know Greek? How Much Greek Could the First Century Jewish Christians Have Known?* (Leiden: Brill, 1969), pp. 65–71; Joseph A. Fitzmyer, "The Languages of Palestine in the First Century," *CBQ* 30 (1972), pp. 501–531.

[101] *Antiquities* 20.263–264.

[102] *War* 5.361.

[103] *Life* 65–67.

[104] Erwin R. Goodenough, *Jewish Symbols in the Greco-Roman Period*, 13 vols. (Princeton, NJ: Princeton University Press, 1953–1968). See Morton Smith, "Goodenough's *Jewish Symbols* in Retrospect," *JBL* 86 (1967), p. 60.

[105] See Victor Tcherikover, "The Greek Towns of Palestine," in *Hellenistic Civilization and the Jews*, ed. Tcherikover (Philadelphia: JPS, 1959), pp. 90–116.

[106] *Life* 235.

[107] *War* 3.43.

[108] Cf. Eric M. Meyers, "Galilean Regionalism as a Factor in Historical Reconstruction," *BASOR* 220–221 (1976), p. 97.

[109] *Life* 40.

[110] On Hellenizations in Josephus, see Louis H. Feldman, "Hellenizations in Josephus' Account of Man's Decline," in *Religions in Antiquity: Essays in Memory of Erwin Ramsdell Goodenough*, ed. Jacob Neusner, Studies in the History of Religions 14 (Leiden: Brill, 1968), pp. 336–353; "Abraham the Philosopher in Josephus," *TAPA* 99 (1968), pp. 143–156; "Hellenizations in Josephus' Version of Esther," *TAPA* 101 (1970), pp. 143–170; "Josephus as an Apologist to the Greco-Roman World: His Portrait of Solomon," in *Aspects of Religious Propaganda in Judaism and Early Christianity*, ed. Elisabeth Schüssler Fiorenza (Notre Dame, IN: University of Notre Dame, 1976), pp. 69–98; "Josephus' Portrait of Saul," *HUCA* 53 (1982), pp. 45–99; "Abraham the General in Josephus," in *Nourished with Peace: Studies in Hellenistic Judaism in Memory of Samuel Sandmel*, eds. Frederick E. Greenspahn, Earle Hilgert and Burton L. Mack (Chico, CA: Scholars Press, 1984), pp. 43–49; "Josephus as a Biblical Interpreter: The 'Aqedah," *JQR* 75 (1984–1985), pp. 212–252; "Josephus' Portrait of Deborah," in *Hellenica et*

Judaica: Hommage à Valentin Nikiprowetzky, eds. André Caquot, M. Hadas-Lebel and J. Riaud (Paris: Editions Peeters, 1986), pp. 115–128; "Hellenizations in Josephus' Jewish Antiquities: The Portrait of Abraham," in *Josephus, Judaism, and Christianity* (see endnote 29), pp. 133–153; "Use, Authority, and Exegesis of Mikra in the Writings of Josephus," in *Mikra: Text, Translation, Reading and Interpretation of the Hebrew Bible in Ancient Judaism and Early Christianity*, eds. Martin Jan Mulder and Harry Sysling, sec. 2, vol. 1 (Assen, Netherlands: Van Gorcum, 1988), pp. 455–518; "Josephus' Portrait of Noah and Its Parallels in Philo, Pseudo-Philo's Biblical Antiquities, and Rabbinic Midrashim," *PAAJR* 55 (1988), pp. 31–57; "Josephus' Version of Samson," *JSJ* 19 (1988), pp. 171–214; "Josephus' Portrait of David," *HUCA* 60 (1989), pp. 129–174; "Josephus' Portrait of Jacob," *JQR* 79 (1988–1989), pp. 101–151; "Josephus' Jewish Antiquities and Pseudo-Philo's Biblical Antiquities," in *Josephus, the Bible, and History* (see endnote 16), pp. 59–80; "Josephus' Portrait of Joshua," *HTR* 82 (1989), pp. 351–376; "Josephus' Interpretation of Jonah," *AJSR* 17 (1992), pp. 1–29.

[111] *Apion* 1.50. Henry St. John Thackeray (*Josephus the Man and the Historian* [New York: Jewish Institute of Religion, 1929], pp. 107–118), on the basis of a close study of Josephus's vocabulary and style, theorized that in books 15 and 16 of *Antiquities* Josephus utilized an assistant who had a particular love of Greek poetry, especially Sophocles, and that in books 17–19 he had an assistant who was particularly fond of Thucydides. In response to this "higher" criticism of Josephus, however, we may note that Sophoclean and Thucydidean traces are to be found throughout *War* and *Antiquities*. Moreover, the presence of many similar phrases in other Greek works of the period, notably in Dionysius of Halicarnassus, shows that they are characteristic of first-century Greek rather than that they are the work of a special assistant.

[112] *War* 1.3.

[113] *Antiquities* 1.5.

[114] See *Genesis Rabbah* 68.20.

[115] Baron, *Social and Religious History* (see endnote 38), vol. 1, p. 170.

[116] *Antiquities* 18.314–371.

[117] *Antiquities* 18.376.

[118] *Antiquities* 12.119; *Apion* 2.39.

[119] *War* 7.45.

[120] Ibid.

[121] *War* 2.477–478.

[122] *War* 2.479.

[123] *War* 7.100–111.

[124] Cicero, *Pro Flacco* 28.68.

[125] See, for example, *Antiquities* 14.213, 244–246. On the vertical alliance of the Jews with governments in antiquity, see Louis H. Feldman, "Anti-Semitism in the Ancient World," in *History and Hate: The Dimensions of Anti-Semitism, ed. David Berger* (Philadelphia: JPS, 1986), pp. 16–21. Horst R. Moehring ("The 'Acta Pro Judaeis' in the Antiquities of Flavius Josephus: A Study in Hellenistic and Modern Apologetic Historiography," in *Christianity, Judaism and Other Greco-Roman Cults: Studies for Morton Smith at Sixty*, part 3: *Judaism Before 70*, ed. Jacob Neusner [Leiden: Brill, 1975], pp. 124–158) contends that the documents quoted by Josephus were forged, and that since the fire of 69 C.E. destroyed about 3,000 documents in the Roman archives, no one was in a position to challenge him. We may reply that even if the documents in Rome had been burned, it is hard to believe that there were no copies in the cities of Asia Minor affected by them or that people were not still alive who had an oral tradition as to their contents.

[126] *Antiquities* 16.163.

[127] *Antiquities* 14.188.

[128] Philo, *In Flaccum* 7.47.

[129] This is the conclusion of Aryeh Kasher, *The Jews in Hellenistic and Roman Egypt: The Struggle for Equal Rights* (Tübingen: Mohr Siebeck, 1985). This conclusion is challenged, however, by Constantine Zuckerman, "Hellenistic Politeumata and the Jews: A Reconsideration," *Scripta Classica Israelica* 8–9 (1985–1988), pp. 171–185. For a discussion of the scholarly literature on the subject, see Feldman, *Josephus and Modern Scholarship* (see endnote 32), pp. 331–338.

[130] On this riot and its aftermath, see Philo, *In Flaccum*, passim, and *Legatio ad Gaium* 18.122, 19.131–20.132.

[131] *Antiquities* 18.257–260.

[132] Victor Tcherikover, *Corpus Papyrorum Judaicarum* (Cambridge, MA: Harvard University Press, 1957), Prolegomena, vol. 1, p. 67.

[133] *Antiquities* 19.280–285.

[134] *War* 2.487–498.

[135] *War* 2.497.

[136] Cicero, *Pro Flacco* 28.66.

[137] Suetonius, *Julius Caesar* 84.5.

[138] Philo, *Legatio ad Gaium* 23.158.

[139] *Antiquities* 18.143–168. There is good reason to doubt the statement of Suetonius (*Claudius* 25.4) that Claudius expelled from Rome the Jews who persisted in rioting at the instigation of Chrestus. Most scholars think that the reference is to Christos, that is Jesus, and to a Christian group in Rome. But Dio Cassius (*Roman History* 60.6.6) specifically says that Claudius did not expel the Jews; and Josephus and Tacitus, who have detailed accounts of this period, do not mention it at all. See Harry J. Leon, *The Jews of Ancient Rome* (Philadelphia: JPS, 1960), pp. 23–27.

[140] Suetonius, *Titus* 7.1.

[141] Ibid.

[142] *Life* 16.

[143] *Antiquities* 20.195.

[144] See Diana Delia, "The Population of Roman Alexandria," *TAPA* 118 (1988), pp. 287–288, who bases this estimate on a passage in the *Acta Alexandrinorum*.

[145] Philo, *In Flaccum* 57.

[146] BT *Sukkah* 51b.

[147] BT *Yoma* 38a.

[148] Ibid.

[149] BT *Arakhin* 10b.

[150] Onias and Dositheus (*Apion* 2.49); Helkias and Ananias (*Antiquities* 13.349).

[151] *Antiquities* 20.100.

[152] Philo, *Legatio ad Gaium* 31.210.

[153] Philo, *Legatio ad Gaium* 216.

[154] *Antiquities* 14.110.

[155] Mishnah *Yadayim* 4.3.

[156] Horace, *Satires* 1.5.100.

[157] Horace, *Satires* 1.9.69–70.

[158] Tibullus, *Works* 1.3.18.

[159] Ovid, *Ars Amatoria* 1.76,415–416.

[160] For example, Suetonius, *Octavius Augustus* 76.2.

[161] Strabo, *Geography* 16.2.40.763.

[162] See Louis H. Feldman, "The Orthodoxy of the Jews of Hellenistic Egypt," *JSS* 22 (1960), pp. 212–237.

[163] BT *Bava Batra* 21a.

[164] Philo, *De Specialibus Legibus* 2.15.62.

[165] Philo, *De Providentia* 2.64.

[166] *War* 7.420–436; *Antiquities* 12.387–388, 13.62–73, 20.236.

[167] *War* 7.421. The temple at Leontopolis is also mentioned in the Mishnah (*Menahot* 13:10) and in the Gemara (*Avodah Zarah* 52b, *Megillah* 10a), but the extant works of Philo make no mention of it, either because of its unimportance or because Philo remained loyal to the Jerusalem Temple.

[168] Philo, *De Specialibus Legibus* 1.35.186.

[169] Philo, *De Specialibus Legibus* 3.5.29.

[170] Jean B. Frey, *Corpus Inscriptionum Iudaicarum*, (Città del Vaticano, 1952), vol. 2, no. 1530.

[171] Ibid., nos. 148, 149.

[172] Ibid., no. 144, pp. 10–12.

[173] BT *Ketubbot* 25a.

[174] BT *Gittin* 88b.

[175] Philo, *De Specialibus Legibus* 2.25.125.

[176] Philo, *Quaestiones in Exodum* 1.7 on Exodus 12:5.

[177] Philo, *Quaestiones in Genesin* 4.148 on Genesis 25:5–6.

[178] Philo, *Hypothetica* 11.14–17.

[179] On Jewish proselytism, see Louis H. Feldman, "Proselytism and Syncretism," in *World History of the Jewish People*, First Series: *The Diaspora in the Hellenistic-Roman World*, eds. Menahem Stern

and Zvi Baras (Jerusalem: Am Oved, 1984), pp. 188–207, 340–345, 378–380 (in Hebrew), and "Jewish Proselytism," in *Eusebius, Judaism, and Christianity*, eds. Harold W. Attridge and Gohei Hata (Detroit: Wayne State University Press, 1992).

[180] Philo, *De Vita Mosis* 2.5.27.

[181] Philo, *De Virtutibus* 41.226.

[182] Philo, *Legatio ad Gaium* 31.211.

[183] *Apion* 2.210.

[184] *Apion* 2.123.

[185] *Apion* 2.258.

[186] *Apion* 2.282.

[187] For the many theories as to the interpretation of this verse, see Bernard J. Bamberger, *Proselytism in the Talmudic Period* (Cincinnati: Hebrew Union College, 1939), pp. 267–273.

[188] For the evidence, see Jack Dean Kingsbury, "Matthew, the Gospel According to," in *Harper's Bible Dictionary*, ed. Paul J. Achtemeier (San Francisco: Harper & Row, 1985), p. 613.

[189] *War* 7.45.

[190] Horace, *Satires* 1.4.142–143. John Nolland ("Proselytism or Politics in Horace, *Satires* I, 4, 138–143," *Vigiliae Christianae* 33 [1979], pp. 347–355) argues that Horace is here referring not to proselyting activities but to political influence, such as Cicero imputes to the Jews (*Pro Flacco* 28.66); but his skepticism is based on his unwillingness to believe that Horace has in mind the kind of forced acceptance of Judaism that was imposed on the Idumeans in the Maccabean period. In any case, the passage in Horace speaks clearly of forcing others, that is, non-Jews, to join the Jews in their activities. There is nothing in the passage in Cicero that speaks of Jews seeking to get non-Jews to join them as a pressure group.

[191] Mentioned in Augustine, *City of God* 6.11.

[192] Tacitus, *Histories* 5.5.1.

[193] Juvenal, *Satires* 14.96–106.

[194] Nahum Slouschz, *Hébraeo-Phéniciens et Judéo-Berbères: Introduction à l'histoire des juifs et du judaisme en Afrique* (Paris: Leroux, 1908) and his Travels in North Africa (Philadelphia: JPS, 1927).

[195] BT *Menahot* 110a.

[196] *War* 2.559–561.

[197] See Lawrence H. Schiffman, "The Conversion of the Royal House of Adiabene in Josephus and Rabbinic Sources," in *Josephus, Judaism, and Christianity* (see endnote 29), pp. 293–312. For a critical survey of the bibliography on the conversion, see Feldman, *Josephus and Modern Scholarship* (see endnote 32), pp. 730–732.

[198] See esp., *Genesis Rabbah* on Genesis 46:10.

[199] *Antiquities* 20.35.

[200] See Jacob Neusner, "The Conversion of Adiabene to Judaism," *JBL* 83 (1964), pp. 60–66.

[201] *Antiquities* 20.49–53.

[202] Mishnah *Nazir* 3:6 and *Yoma* 3:10; BT *Sukkah* 2b.

[203] *War* 2.520.

[204] See Leon, *Jews of Ancient Rome* (see endnote 139), p. 15.

[205] Valerius Maximus, *Facta et Dicta Memoribilia* 1.3.3.

[206] *Antiquities* 18.81–84; cf. Tacitus, *Annals* 2.85; Suetonius, *Tiberius* 36; Dio Cassius, *Roman History* 57.18.5a.

[207] Ernest L. Abel ("Were the Jews Banished from Rome in 19 A.D.?" *REJ* 127 [1968], pp. 383–386) argues that only the proselytes were driven out, since it would have been contrary to existing law, which Tiberius strictly obeyed, to banish any citizen without a trial. This seems likely since the Roman writer Tacitus, who was most hostile to the Jews, speaks of 4,200 Jewish freedmen being sent to Sardinia (*Annals* 2.85.4); and Suetonius, who is likewise hostile to them, is careful to mention the proselytes as included in the expulsion (*Tiberius* 36). Cassius Dio (57.18.5a) clearly states that Tiberius banished the Jews because they were converting many of the natives to their ways. Margaret H. Williams, "The Expulsion of the Jews from Rome in A.D. 19," *Latomus* 48 (1989), pp. 765–784, concludes that Dio is speaking of the immigration of a group of Jews who were causing trouble through their proselyting activities; but in none of the five sources for this event, including the notoriously anti-Jewish Tacitus (*Annals* 2.85.4), is this given as the reason.

[208] On the question of how such ideas might have been disseminated, see Louis H. Feldman, "Pro-Jewish Intimations in Anti-Jewish Remarks Cited in Josephus' *Against Apion*," *JQR* 78 (1987–1988), pp. 187–251.

[209] Pseudo-Longinus, *On the Sublime* 9.9. George P. Goold ("A Greek Professorial Circle at Rome," *TAPA* 92 [1961], pp. 168–192) suggests that pseudo-Longinus belonged to the same circle that produced Philo and that he is in some sense a Jew.

[210] See Louis H. Feldman, "Jewish 'Sympathizers' in Classical Literature and Inscriptions," *TAPA* 81 (1950), pp. 200–208.

[211] Philo, *De Vita Mosis* 2.4.21–23.

[212] *Apion* 2.282.

[213] See Tcherikover, *Corpus Papyrorum Judaicarum* (see endnote 132), vol. 3, pp. 43–87.

[214] Suetonius, *Tiberius* 32.2.

[215] Petronius, fragment 37, Ernout.

[216] Epictetus, mentioned in Arrian, *Dissertations* 2.19–21.

[217] Published by Joyce Reynolds and Robert Tannenbaum, *Jews and God-Fearers at Aphrodisias: Greek Inscriptions with Commentary*, Cambridge Philological Society suppl. 12 (Cambridge, MA: Cambridge Philological Society, 1987). See also, Louis H. Feldman, "Proselytes and 'Sympathizers' in the Light of the New Inscriptions from Aphrodisias," *REJ* 148 (1989), pp. 265–305.

[218] JT *Megillah* 3.2.74a.

[219] Juvenal, *Satires* 14.96–99.

[220] Philo, *De Vita Mosis* 2.7.40–41.

[221] Philo, *De Confusione Linguarum* 38.190. Occasionally, to be sure, Philo has etymologies of proper names which would seem to indicate a knowledge of Hebrew. But, as David Rokeah has demonstrated ("A New Onomasticon Fragment from Oxyrhynchus and Philo's Etymologies," *JTS* 19 [1968], pp. 70–82), Philo may well have derived such information from an onomasticon of Hebrew names similar to the one found at Oxyrhynchus.

[222] Philo, *De Vita Mosis* 2.7.38.

[223] Philo, *De Mutatione Nominum* 11.77–80; *Quaestiones in Genesin* 3.53.

[224] See Alan Mendelson, *Secular Education in Philo of Alexandria* (Cincinnati: Hebrew Union College, 1982).

[225] See Louis H. Feldman, "Philo's View on Music," *JJML* 9 (1986–1987), pp. 36–54.

[226] Philo, *De Vita Mosis* 1.5.21–23.

[227] Philo, *De Sacrificiis Abelis et Caini* 10.43–44; *De Congressu Quaerendae Eruditionis Gratia* 14.77–78.

[228] Philo, *De Opificio Mundi* 25.77.

[229] Philo, *De Cherubim* 24.80–81.

[230] Philo, *Quod Omnis Probus Liber Sit* 5.26.

[231] Philo, fragment, cited in Eusebius, *Praeparatio Evangelica* 8.14.58.

[232] London Papyrus 1912, lines 92–95. See Louis H. Feldman, "The Orthodoxy of the Jews in Hellenistic Egypt," *JSS* 22 (1960), pp. 223–226.

[233] BT *Avodah Zarah* 18b.

[234] Philo, *De Ebrietate* 43.177.

[235] Howard Jacobson, *The Exagoge of Ezekiel* (Cambridge: Cambridge University Press, 1983), pp. 20–23.

[236] Harry A. Wolfson, *Philo: Foundations of Religious Philosophy in Judaism, Christianity, and Islam* (Cambridge, MA: Harvard University Press, 1947), vol. 2, pp. 439–460.

[237] See Louis H. Feldman, *Studies in Judaica: Scholarship on Philo and Josephus (1937–1962)* (New York: Yeshiva University, 1963), pp. 6–8, for a critical appraisal of Harry A. Wolfson's work and for references to major reviews of his work. On Philo's orthodoxy and orthopraxy, see Alan Mendelson, *Philo's Jewish Identity* (Atlanta: Scholars Press, 1988).

[238] Philo, *Quis Rerum Divinarum Heres* 43.214; *Quod Omnis Probus Liber Sit* 8.57.

[239] Philo, *Quod Deterius Potiori Insidiari Soleat* 12.38–39.

[240] Philo, *De Opificio Mundi* 44.129–130.

[241] Philo, *De Abrahamo* 46.275.

[242] Philo, *De Migratione Abrahami* 18.103.

[243] Philo, *De Posteritate Caini* 18.63.

[244] Philo, *De Confusione Linguarum* 11.41.

[245] Philo, *De Fuga et Inventione* 20.112; *Quis Rerum Divinarum Heres* 20.188.

[246] Philo, *De Specialibus Legibus* 1.59.319.

[247] Philo, *De Cherubim* 14.49.

[248] Ibid.

[249] Philo, *De Migratione Abrahami* 7.35.

[250] Philo, *De Opificio Mundi* 23.71.

[251] Philo, *De Confusione Linguarum* 31.159.

[252] Philo, *Quod Deterius Potiori Insidiari Soleat* 27.102.

[253] Philo, *De Vita Mosis* 1.6.28.

[254] Philo, *De Fuga et Inventione* 9.50.

[255] Philo, *Quod Omnis Probus Liber Sit* 12.75–13.91; *Hypothetica* 11.1–18.

[256] Philo, *De Vita Contemplativa* in its entirety.

The Rabbinic Sources

Pages 10–11

[1] See list in Emil Schürer, *The History of the Jewish People in the Age of Jesus Christ (175 B.C.–A.D. 135)*, rev. Geza Vermes and Fergus Millar (Edinburgh: T & T Clark, 1973), vol. 1, pp. 74–75.

[2] Jacob Neusner, *Judaism: The Evidence of the Mishnah* (Chicago: University of Chicago Press, 1981).

[3] See Eliezer Berkovits, "Talmud, Babylonian," and Louis I. Rabinowitz, "Talmud, Jerusalem," *EJ*, vol. 15, cols. 755–768 and 772–779, respectively.

[4] See Moshe D. Herr, "Midrash," *EJ*, vol. 11, cols. 1507–1514.

[5] See, in particular, Bernard J. Bamberger ("The Dating of Aggadic Materials," *JBL* 68 [1949], pp. 115–123), who notes, for example, that inasmuch as the second-century Rabbi Meir (*Megillah* 13a) states, as does the Septuagint (Esther 2:7), that Mordecai had married Esther, it is more likely that the translators were acquainted with this ancient tradition than that Rabbi Meir consulted the Septuagint.

[6] For Josephus's knowledge of midrashic tradition, see Salomo Rappaport, *Agada und Exegese bei Flavius Josephus* (Vienna: Alexander Kohut Memorial Foundation, 1930), and Louis H. Feldman, various articles on Josephus, notably "Josephus' Version of Samson," *JSJ* 19 (1988), pp. 171–214.

[7] Jay Braverman (*Jerome's Commentary on Daniel: A Study of Comparative Jewish and Christian Interpretations of the Hebrew Bible* [Washington, DC: CBA, 1978]) notes 16 such Jewish midrashic traditions in Jerome's commentary on Daniel, only four of which have definite parallels in extant rabbinic literature.

[8] Shaye J.D. Cohen, "Parallel Historical Tradition in Josephus and Rabbinic Literature," in *Proceedings of Ninth World Congress of Jewish Studies, Jerusalem, Aug. 4–12, 1985, Div. B, vol. 1: The History of the Jewish People (From the Second Temple Period until the Middle Ages)* (Jerusalem: World Union of Jewish Studies, 1986), pp. 7–14. In view of the distrust that Cohen (*Josephus in Galilee and Rome: His Vita and Development as a Historian* [Leiden: Brill, 1979], pp. 38–39) has for Josephus's paraphrase of the Bible, as well as for his account of the Jewish war, his general preference for Josephus in episodes that parallel the rabbinic accounts seems surprising.

[9] BT *Megillah* 15a.

[10] See Shraga Abramson, ed., *Abodah Zarah* (New York: JTSem, 1957), pp. xiv–xv.

Who Was Josephus?

Pages 26–27

[1] For critical bibliographies of scholarship on Josephus, see Louis H. Feldman, *Josephus and Modern Scholarship (1937–1980)* (Berlin: de Gruyter, 1984); "Flavius Josephus Revisited: The Man, His Writings, and His Significance," *ANRW* 2.21.2 (1984), pp. 763–862; "A Selective Critical Bibliography of Josephus," in *Josephus, the Bible, and History*, eds. Feldman and Gohei Hata (Detroit: Wayne State University, 1989), pp. 330–448. Per Bilde, *Flavius Josephus between Jerusalem and Rome: His Life, His Works, and Their Importance*, JSP

Suppl., series 2 (Sheffield, UK: Sheffield Academic Press, 1988).

[2] *Life* 2.

[3] *Life* 9.

[4] *Life* 10–12. See Steve Mason (*Flavius Josephus on the Pharisees: A Composition-Critical Study* [Leiden: Brill, 1991], pp. 342–356), against the commonly held view that Josephus actually underwent a conversion to Pharisaism, has argued convincingly that Josephus was not and never claimed to be a Pharisee and that he actually disdained the Pharisees.

[5] *Life* 13–16.

[6] *Life* 28–29; *War* 2.562–568.

[7] *War* 3.392.

[8] BT *Gittin* 56a.

[9] *Life* 423. For a critical survey of the literature dealing with Josephus's life, see Feldman, "Selective Critical Bibliography" (see endnote 1), pp. 340–344.

[10] Seth Schwartz ("The Composition and Publication of Josephus' Bellum Iudaicum Book 7," *HTR* 79 [1986], pp. 373–385) argues persuasively that parts of Book 7 were composed as late as the early part of Trajan's reign (c. 100 C.E.).

[11] *War* 1.3.

[12] *Apion* 1.50.

[13] For a critical bibliography dealing with Josephus's works, see Feldman, "Selective Critical Bibliography" (see endnote 1), pp. 393–400.

[14] See the essays by individual scholars in *Josephus, Judaism, and Christianity*, eds. Louis H. Feldman and Gohei Hata (Detroit: Wayne State University, 1987), and *Josephus, the Bible, and History* (see endnote 1), esp. my comments on those essays in my introductions, pp. 23–67 and 17–49, respectively.

Who Was Philo?

Pages 30–31

[1] For the evidence, see Jacques Schwartz, "Note sur la famille de Philon d'Alexandrie," *Annuaire de l'Institut de Philologie et d'Histoire Orientales de l'Université Libre de Bruxelles* 13 (1953; Mélanges Isidore Levy), pp. 591–602.

[2] See Alan Mendelson, *Secular Education in Philo of Alexandria* (Cincinnati: Hebrew Union College, 1982), and Louis H. Feldman, "Philo's Views on Music," *JJML* 9 (1986–1987), pp. 36–54.

[3] See Joshua Amir, "Explanations of Hebrew Names in Philo," *Tarbiz* 31 (1962), p. 297 (in Hebrew), and David Rokeah, "A New Onomasticon Fragment from Oxyrhynchus and Philo's Etymologies," *JTS* 19 (1968), pp. 70–82.

[4] Philo, *De Specialibus Legibus* 2.15.62.

[5] Philo, *De Migratione Abrahami* 16.89.

[6] *Antiquities* 18.257–260.

[7] E. Mary Smallwood, "Philo and Josephus as Historians of the Same Events," in *Josephus, Judaism, and Christianity*, eds. Louis H. Feldman and Gohei Hata (Detroit: Wayne State University, 1987), pp. 114–129. For the view that Philo has an apologetic bias and that Josephus's account is simpler and more convincing, see Daniel R. Schwartz, "Josephus and Philo on Pontius Pilate," *Jerusalem Cathedra* 3 (1983), pp. 26–45.

II. The Life of Jesus

[1] On the names of the Gospels, see E.P. Sanders and Margaret Davies, *Studying the Synoptic Gospels* (Philadelphia: Trinity Press International, 1989), pp. 5–16.

[2] On the extra-canonical traditions, see Helmut Koester, *Ancient Christian Gospels* (Harrisburg, PA: Trinity Press International, 1990); Christopher Tuckett, *Nag Hammadi Gospel Traditions: Synoptic Tradition in the Nag Hammadi Library* (Edinburgh: T & T Clark, 1986). On the Gospel of Thomas, see Risto Uro, *Thomas: Seeking the Historical Context*

of the Gospel of Thomas (London/New York: T & T Clark, 2003).

[3] See W.D. Davies, *Invitation to the New Testament* (Garden City, NY: Doubleday, 1966), pp. 63–71; Gerd Theissen and Annette Merz, *The Historical Jesus: A Comprehensive Guide* (Minneapolis: Fortress Press, 1998), pp. 63–89.

[4] There are numerous synopses available for study in both Greek and English. A good English synopsis is Robert Funk, *New Gospel Parallels: The Gospel of Mark*, 2 vols., rev. ed., Foundations and Facets Reference Series (Sonoma, CA: Polebridge Press, 1990); see also *Synopsis of the Four Gospels*, ed. Kurt Aland (Stuttgart: Deutsche Bibelgesellschaft, 1985) and Burton H. Throckmorton, Jr., *Gospel Parallels: A Comparison of the Synoptic Gospels* (Nashville: Thomas Nelson, 1993). For introductions to the study of the Synoptic Problem, see Sanders and Davies, *Studying the Synoptic Gospels* (see endnote 1); and Mark Goodacre, *The Synoptic Problem: A Way Through the Maze* (London/New York: T & T Clark, 2001).

[5] See, for example, Jacob Neusner, *Rabbinic Traditions About the Pharisees Before 70*, 3 vols. (Leiden: Brill, 1971); *A History of Mishnaic Law*, 41 vols. (Leiden: Brill, 1974–1982); and David Instone-Brewer, *Traditions of the Rabbis in the Era of the New Testament*, vol. 1: Prayer and Agriculture (Grand Rapids, MI: Eerdmans, 2004); more volumes forthcoming.

[6] For a list of secondary literature on criteria of authenticity, see E.P. Sanders, *Jesus and Judaism* (Philadelphia: Fortress Press, 1985), p. 357, note 28. See also Sanders and Davies, *Studying the Synoptic Gospels* (see endnote 1), pp. 301–334; John P. Meier, *A Marginal Jew: Rethinking the Historical Jesus: vol. 1, The Roots of the Problem and the Person* (Garden City, NY: Doubleday, 1991), pp. 167–195; Gerd Theissen and Dagmar Winter, *The Quest for the Plausible Jesus: The Question of Criteria* (Louisville: Westminster/John Knox Press, 2002); and Dale Allison, *Jesus of Nazareth: Millenarian Prophet* (Minneapolis: Fortress Press, 1998), chapter 1.

[7] Sanders, *Jesus and Judaism* (see endnote 6); see also E.P. Sanders, *The Historical Figure of Jesus* (London: Allen Lane, 1993).

[8] John's greater prominence is indicated in part by Jesus' appeal to his reputation in Mark 11:27–33 and parallels. Josephus also comments on John's great influence on the populace (*Antiquities* 18.116–119). See further Robert L. Webb, "John the Baptist and His Relationship to Jesus," in *Studying the Historical Jesus: Evaluations of the State of Current Research*, eds. Bruce Chilton and Craig A. Evans, NTTS 19 (Leiden: Brill, 1994), pp. 179–230.

[9] Apocrypha: Wisdom of Ben Sira [Sirach], or Ecclesiasticus, 36:11, cf. 48:10.

[10] Dead Sea Scrolls: The War Scroll (1QM) 2.2ff.; The Temple Scroll (11QTemplea) 18.14–16, 57.5ff.

[11] See Ben F. Meyer, *The Aims of Jesus* (Philadelphia/London: Trinity Press International/SCM, 1979), pp. 185–197.

[12] *Antiquities* 18.117.

[13] See Joachim Jeremias, *The Proclamation of Jesus*, Eng. trans. (London: SCM, 1971), pp. 108–113.

[14] The Gospels attribute a few miracles to Jesus while he is en route to or near gentile cities (Mark 5:1, 7:24,31), but they depict no activities *in* these cities. The authors of the Gospels all believed fervently in a mission to gentiles, and they work in references to gentile territory, but they cannot actually describe Jesus as working within gentile cities. More likely to be authentic is Jesus' limitation of his mission, and that of his disciples during his lifetime, to "the lost sheep of the house of Israel" (Matthew 10:6–7, 15:24).

[15] Albert Schweitzer, *The Quest of the Historical Jesus*, 3rd ed., trans. W. Montgomery (New York: Macmillan, 1956), pp. 354–357.

[16] Martin Hengel, *The Charismatic Leader and His Followers*, trans. J.C.G. Greig (Edinburgh: T & T Clark; New York: Crossroad, 1981), pp. 50–63.

[17] See E.P. Sanders, *Jewish Law from Jesus to the Mishnah* (Philadelphia: Trinity Press International, 1990), pp. 1–96.

[18] David Daube, *The New Testament and Rabbinic Judaism* (London: Athlone Press, 1956; reprinted New York, 1973), pp. 55–62; W.D. Davies, *The Setting of the Sermon on the Mount* (Cambridge: Cambridge University Press, 1964), pp. 101–103.

[19] Daube, *New Testament and Rabbinic Judaism* (see endnote 18), p. 60.

[20] Letter of Aristeas 234.

[21] Letter of Aristeas 170–171.

[22] See Andre B. DuToit, "Hyperbolical Contrasts: A Neglected Aspect of Paul's Style," in *A South African Perspective on the New Testament*, eds. J.H. Petzer and P.J. Martin (Leiden: Brill, 1986), pp. 178–186.

[23] Rudolf Bultmann, *The History of the Synoptic Tradition* (San Francisco: Harper & Row, 1963).

[24] Geza Vermes, *Jesus the Jew: A Historian's Reading of the Gospels* (Philadelphia: Fortress Press, 1981); Hengel, *The Charismatic Leader* (see endnote 16); Ellis Rivkin, *What Crucified Jesus? The Political Execution of a Charismatic* (Nashville: Abingdon, 1984); Sanders, *Jesus and Judaism* (see endnote 6), pp. 237–241.

[25] On Jewish self-government and the "Sanhedrin," see E.P. Sanders, *Judaism: Practice and Belief, 63 BCE–66 CE* (Philadelphia: Trinity Press International, 1992), chapter 21; James McLaren, *Power and Politics in Palestine: The Jews and the Governing of Their Land, 100 BC–AD 70*, JSNT Supplement 63 (Sheffield, UK: Sheffield Academic Press, 1991).

[26] *Antiquities* 17.217.

[27] *War* 1.88; *Antiquities* 17.213–218; *War* 2.224–227; see also Matthew 26:5; parallel to Mark 14:2.

[28] *Antiquities* 20.107.

[29] *War* 6.300–301.

[30] *War* 6.302–309.

[31] Matthew has an interesting variant: After the high priest asks, "Are you the Christ, the Son of God?" Jesus replies, "You have said so, but I tell you that you will see the Son of Man ..." (Matthew 26:63–64). It is not certain whether "you have said so" means yes or no.

[32] In *Macbeth*, Banquo's ghost and the ghostly dagger, "a dagger of the mind"; in *Hamlet*, his father's ghost.

[33] See, for example, Plutarch, *Brutus* 36.

[34] 1 Kings 17:8–14; 2 Kings 4:18–36; Mark 5:21–43 (parallel to Matthew 9:18–26; Luke 8:40–56); Luke 7:11–17; Acts 9:36–43; John 11:5–44. See also Philostratus, *Life of Apollonius of Tyana* 4.45; Pliny, *Natural History* 26.13; Apuleius, *Florida* 19.

[35] They had their own views of accuracy: See Sanders and Davies, *Studying the Synoptic Gospels* (see endnote 1), pp. 36–38.

III. The Spread of Christianity

[1] This chapter is in effect a summary of my *Christianity in the Making, Vol. 2: Beginning from Jerusalem* (Grand Rapids, MI: Eerdmans, 2009). For other treatments, see Martin Hengel and Anna Maria Schwemer, *Paul Between Damascus and Antioch* (London: SCM, 1997); Rainer Riesner, *Paul's Early Period: Chronology, Mission Strategy, Theology* (Grand Rapids, MI: Eerdmans, 1998); Christopher Rowland, *Christian Origins: An Account of the Setting and Character of the Most Important Messianic Sect of Judaism*, 2nd ed. (London: SPCK, 2002); A.J.M. Wedderburn, *A History of the First Christians* (London: T & T Clark, 2004); and Paul Barnett, *The Birth of Christianity: The First Twenty Years* (Grand Rapids, MI: Eerdmans, 2005).

[2] Ignatius, *Magnesians* 10:1–3; *Romans* 3:3; *Philadelphians* 6:1.

[3] Acts 11:26, 26:28; 1 Peter 4:16.

[4] Acts 24:5, also 24:14, 28:22.

[5] Acts 5:17, 15:5, 26:5. The Jewish historian Josephus used the same term for the Sadducees, Pharisees and Essenes (*War* 2.119–166; *Antiquities* 18.11–25).

[6] Acts 9:2, 19:9,23, 22:4, 24:14,22.

[7] Among the most useful introductions to the New Testament writings are Udo Schnelle, *The History and Theology of the New Testament Writings*, trans. M. Eugene Boring (London: SCM, 1998) and Raymond E. Brown, *An Introduction to the New Testament* (New York: Doubleday, 1997).

[8] *Antiquities* 20.200.

[9] *Annals* 15.44.

[10] *Nero* 16.2.

[11] *Divus Claudius* 25.4.

[12] The belief that Paul was also responsible for Hebrews was quite strongly held in the patristic period (it is still attributed to Paul in the King James Version), but it now has no support.

[13] Pseudonymity carries the connotation of immoral practice, a deliberate attempt to deceive recipients or audiences to whom the letters were read. But in the ancient world concepts of copyright were hardly known or observed, and the practice of disciples honoring their teacher by writing in their teacher's name was well known and regarded as entirely acceptable. See further Norbert Brox, *Falsche Verfasserangaben: Zur Erklärung der frühchristlichen Pseudepigrapha*, Stuttgarter Bibelstudien 79 (Stuttgart: Katholisches Bibelwerk, 1975), pp. 72–74.

[14] Regarding 2 Corinthians, see Günther Bornkamm, "Die Vorgeschichte des sogenannten Zweiten Korintherbriefes," *Geschichte und Glaube: Gesammelte Aufsätze* Band IV (München: Kaiser, 1971), pp. 162–194; regarding Philippians, see, for example, Helmut Koester, *Introduction to the New Testament*, 2 vols. (Berlin: de Gruyter, 1982), pp. 132–134.

[15] For further discussion, see April D. DeConick, *The Original Gospel of Thomas in Translation*, LNTS 287 (London: T & T Clark, 2006).

[16] See James D.G. Dunn, "The Earliest Interpreters of the Jesus Tradition: A Study in Early Hermeneutics," in the festschrift for Anthony C. Thiselton, ed. S.E. Porter (Grand Rapids, MI: Eerdmans, 2011).

[17] Acts 16:10–17, 20:5–15, 21:8–18, 27:1–28:16.

[18] See, for example, Richard I. Pervo, *Acts: A Commentary*, Hermeneia (Minneapolis: Fortress Press, 2009).

[19] See particularly Claus-Jürgen Thornton, *Der Zeuge des Zeugen: Lukas als Historiker der Paulusreisen*, WUNT 56 (Tübingen: Mohr Siebeck, 1991).

[20] See James D.G. Dunn, "Luke's Jerusalem Perspective," in *Reading Acts Today* (Festschrift for L. Alexander), ed. Steve Walton (London: Continuum, 2011).

[21] Luke gives no hint of the confrontation between Paul and Peter in Antioch (Galatians 2:11–16) or of the challenges to Paul's mission, probably from Jewish Christian missionaries, in Galatia, Corinth and Philippi.

[22] See, for example, Werner Kramer, *Christ, Lord, Son of God* (London: SCM, 1966).

[23] See Acts 8:17–19, 19:5–7; Romans 5:5, 8:9–27; 1 Corinthians 12:13; Galatians 3:2–5; Hebrews 2:4; John 7:37–39.

[24] Mark 1:29, 3:16–17, 5:37, 9:2, 13:3, 14:33.

[25] Later addressed as "James, the lord and the bishop of bishops, who rules Jerusalem, the holy church of the Hebrews" in the pseudo-Clementine Epistle of Clement to James (*Ante-Nicene Fathers* 8.218).

[26] Hegesippus in Eusebius, *Eccles. Hist.* 2.23.3–9; Epiphanius, *Panarion* 78.14.1–6.

[27] See pseudo-Clementine, *Recognitions* 1:17,72, 4:35; *Homilies* 1:20, 11:35.

[28] The motif of the "new covenant" runs through the New Testament literature (particularly Luke 22:20; 1 Corinthians 11:25; 2 Corinthians 3:6; Hebrews 8:8, 9:5).

[29] See also Luke 24:53; Acts 3:11, 4:1, 5:12,20–21,42.

[30] *Antiquities* 14.65—a male lamb was sacrificed twice each day. Prayer at the time of sacrifice was a common practice.

[31] The rules regarding the Nazirite vow; see Numbers 6:13–17.

[32] Acts 3:18, 17:3; see also Luke 24:26–27,46. As indicated particularly by Acts 8:32–33 and 1 Peter 2:22–25, Isaiah 53 played a prominent role.

[33] Particularly Acts 13:33; Hebrews 1:5, 5:5.

[34] Psalm 110:1 is one of the most frequently quoted scriptures in the New Testament—Mark 12:36 and parallels, 14:62 and parallels; Acts 2:34–35; Romans 8:34; 1 Corinthians 15:25; Ephesians 1:20; Colossians 3:1; Hebrews 1:3,13, 8:1, 12:2; 1 Peter 3:22.

[35] See Isaiah 32:15, 44:3; Joel 2:28–29.

[36] 1 Thessalonians 1:10; 4:15; 1 Corinthians 7:29; 15:51; Romans 13:11–12; Philippians 4:5.

[37] Particularly Mark 13:28–37/Matthew 24:32–44.

[38] Luke 19:11; There is no note of imminence in Acts 10:42 and 17:31.

[39] The "great commission" in Matthew 28:19 is almost certainly formulated in later terms (baptism "in the name of the Father and of the Son and of the Holy Spirit"), but may nevertheless indicate a conviction that the practice of baptism as the mark

of entry into discipleship was authorized by the risen Christ.

[40] Acts 2:38, 8:16, 10:48, 19:5; 1 Corinthians 1:13–15.

[41] Acts 2:42,46; 20:7,11.

[42] See Mark 2:16; Matthew 11:19/Luke 7:34; Luke 15:2.

[43] 1QS 6:19–22; Philo, *Hypothetica* 11:4–12; *Vita Contemplativa* 16.

[44] Perhaps Luke intended to echo or parallel the complaints made within the Israelite assembly following their miraculous delivery from Egypt (Exodus 16:1–12).

[45] See further Dunn, *Christianity in the Making* (see endnote 1), pp. 242–245.

[46] More than a third of the ossuary inscriptions found in Jerusalem dating to this period are written in Greek. See Martin Hengel, *The "Hellenization" of Judaea in the First Century After Christ* (London: SCM, 1989), pp. 9–11.

[47] Particularly the burial of the patriarchs in Shechem (Samaria) rather than Hebron, as recorded in Israel's official history (Acts 7:16; cf. Genesis 49:30–31, 50:13).

[48] "Made with hands" was the term that characterized Israel's dismissal of idols (Leviticus 26:1,30; Isaiah 2:18, 10:11; Daniel 5:4,23).

[49] Luke 1:8–23, 2:22–38,41,50, 24:53; Acts 2:46, 3:1, 5:42.

[50] Acts 8:3, 9:1–2, 22:4–5, 26:9–11; Galatians 1:13–14,23; Philippians 3:6.

[51] For Simon Magus, see R.F. Stoops, "Simon (person)," in *Anchor Bible Dictionary,* ed. David N. Freedman (New York: Doubleday, 1992), vol. 6, pp. 29–31.

[52] It is Paul who refers to Jews as "the circumcision"—not "the circumcised" (Romans 2:26, 3:30; Galatians 2:7; Colossians 3:11).

[53] Genesis 17:9–14; 1 Maccabees 1:14–15,60–61, 2:46; *Antiquities* 13:257–258, 318.

[54] Second Temple Judaism was not noted for a concern to evangelize non-Jews; see particularly Scot McKnight, *A Light Among the Gentiles: Jewish Missionary Activity in the Second Temple Period* (Minneapolis: Fortress Press, 1991), and Martin Goodman, *Mission and Conversion: Proselytizing in the Religious History of the Roman Empire* (Oxford: Clarendon, 1994).

[55] Acts 11:30, 15:2,4,6,22–23, perhaps following the model of synagogue organization.

[56] The Hebrew *qn'* can be translated equally as "zeal" or as "jealousy."

[57] Exodus 20:5, 34:14; Deuteronomy 4:23–24, 5:8–9, 6:14–15, 32:21.

[58] See E. Reuter, *Theological Dictionary of the Old Testament*, vol. 13, p. 49: "In the human domain *qn'* refers primarily to a violent emotion aroused by fear of losing a person or object."

[59] As well as Phinehas, others would probably come to mind, like Simeon and Levi who "abhorred the pollution of their blood" (Genesis 34; Judith 9:2–4), and Elijah who resolutely confronted the prophets of Baal (1 Kings 18; Sirach 48:2–3; 1 Maccabees 2:58).

[60] The commissioning is attached to all three versions of Saul's conversion, though whether it should be attached to a particular point in the episode is unclear (Acts 9:15–16, 22:10,15,17–21, 26:16–18).

[61] Though his dramatic escape from Damascus (Acts 9:25) is confirmed by 2 Corinthians 11:32–33.

[62] Acts 10:44–48, 11:15–18. Paul speaks in terms of "grace" in Galatians 2:7–9, but from Galatians 3:2–5,14 it is clear that he saw the gift of the Spirit as the decisive expression of that grace.

[63] Note the reference to "gentile sinners" (Galatians 2:15), a phrase probably quoted from the protest that the James group lodged with Peter over his eating with gentiles.

[64] Esther 8:17 (LXX); *War* 2.454, 463.

[65] *Porneia* was defined not just as adultery or fornication, but rather as any kind of sexual license. Abstaining from this mode of conduct was more demanding in permissive Hellenistic society; a link between idolatry and sexual license was taken for granted (e.g., Jeremiah 3:6–8; Ezekiel 16:15–46; Wisdom 14:12; Revelation 2:14,20).

[66] See, for example, A.J.M. Wedderburn, "The 'Apostolic Decree': Tradition and Redaction,"

Novum Testamentum 35 (1993), pp. 362–389; R.J. Bauckham, "James and the Jerusalem Church," in *The Book of Acts in Its Palestinian Setting*, ed. Bauckham (Grand Rapids, MI: Eerdmans, 1995), pp. 450–480.

[67] As well as the compression of the timeline of resurrection appearances, Luke also reports that Paul appointed elders in his churches (Acts 14:23), even though elders never appear in the undisputed letters of Paul (only in 1 Timothy 5:1,2,17,19; Titus 1:5).

[68] Romans 2:28–29, 9:24, 11:13–24; Philippians 3:3.

[69] 1 Corinthians 1:1; 2 Corinthians 1:1; Romans 1:1; Colossians 1:1. The fact that 1 and 2 Thessalonians do not begin in the same way may suggest that they were written before Paul felt his apostolic status to be questioned and his gospel challenged.

[70] Romans 1:5, 11:13, 15:16; 1 Corinthians 3:5–15, 9:1–2,16; 15:8–11; 2 Corinthians 5:20; Galatians 1:12.

[71] Several have suggested that Paul may have drawn inspiration from Isaiah 66:19–20.

[72] Galatians 1:6–9, 5:7–12; 2 Corinthians 11:12–15; Philippians 3:2.

[73] According to Acts 14:8–18, the use of the local Lycaonian language proved to be a very confusing factor.

[74] 1 Thessalonians 2:9–10; 1 Corinthians 9:12.

[75] Romans 15:26; 2 Corinthians 1:1, 8:1; 1 Thessalonians 1:7–8, 4:10.

[76] A list of more than 50 individuals, many of them women, can easily be compiled. See Dunn, *Christianity in the Making* (see endnote 1), §29.6.

[77] Acts 13:14, 14:1, 16:13, 17:1,10,17, 18:4,19, 19:8, 28:17,23.

[78] Irina Levinskaya, *The Book of Acts in Its Diaspora Setting* (Grand Rapids, MI: Eerdmans, 1996), chapters 4–7, especially the review of the epigraphic evidence in chapter 4; Bernd Wander, *Gottesfürchtige und Sympathisanten: Studien zum heidnischen Umfeld von Diasporasynagogen*, WUNT 104 (Tübingen: Mohr Siebeck, 1998).

[79] Acts 14:43,48, 14:1,27, 16:14, 17:4,12, 18:4,8, 19:8–10.

[80] See particularly Ronald F. Hock, *The Social Context of Paul's Ministry: Tentmaking and Apostleship* (Philadelphia: Fortress Press, 1980).

[81] Romans 8:15; 1 Corinthians 2:12, 12:13; 2 Corinthians 1:21–22, 3:3; Galatians 3:2–3, 4:6; 1 Thessalonians 1:6, 4:8.

[82] Philip A. Harland, *Associations, Synagogues, and Congregations* (Minneapolis: Fortress Press, 2003).

[83] Note particularly Romans 16:1–16: Phoebe (16:1; deacon and patron/benefactor); Prisca, named before her husband Aquila (16:3); Junia (16:7; a prominent apostle); Mary, Tryphaena, Tryphosa, Persis (16:6,12; hard workers).

[84] The letters confirm the broad picture provided by Acts of a mission focusing principally around the Aegean.

[85] Acts 18:11, 19:10.

[86] See particularly Stephen Mitchell, *Anatolia: Land, Men and Gods in Asia Minor*, 2 vols. (Oxford: Clarendon, 1993), vol. 2, pp. 3–4; see also Cilliers Breytenbach, *Paulus und Barnabas in der Provinz Galatien*, AGAJU 38 (Leiden: Brill, 1996), particularly pp. 140–148.

[87] Acts 18:2; Romans 16:3; 1 Corinthians 16:19; see also Acts 18:18,26; 2 Timothy 4:19.

[88] The fact that Gallio's proconsulship in Corinth can be dated with confidence to 51–52 C.E. is one of the firmest points of attachment for a chronology of Paul's mission.

[89] Galatians 4:25; 2 Corinthians 11:22; Philippians 3:2–6.

[90] 1 Corinthians 16:1–4; 2 Corinthians 8–9; Romans 15:25–28.

[91] The description of "the man of lawlessness" echoes Ezekiel 28:2 (the prince of Tyre) and Daniel 11:31,36 (Antiochus Epiphanes); but "he who restrains" (2 Thessalonians 2:7) has baffled commentators for generations. Could it be a reference to Roman power?

[92] See endnote 35.

[93] Josephus provides an interesting parallel in his story of Izates, king of Adiabene. Attracted to Judaism, Izates was informed by a Jewish merchant that he could become a Jew without being circumcised. But he was subsequently rebuked by the

more scrupulous Eleazar from Galilee who insisted that circumcision was indispensable (*Antiquities* 20.38–46).

[94] The demand for circumcision went beyond the "apostolic decree" (Acts 16:4), but probably we have to infer that those whom Paul referred to as "false brothers" (Galatians 2:4) had gained more sway in Jerusalem or were pressing their understanding of the gospel on the daughter churches of Antioch anyway.

[95] There were no restaurants as such in ancient cities. The larger temple cults had dining facilities attached to the temple complex, where the meat would be provided from the sacrificial cult (only part of the sacrifice being burnt).

[96] A third letter, "the letter of tears," is indicated in 2 Corinthians 2:1–4,9; 7:8–12.

[97] Classically by Günther Bornkamm, "Die Vorgeschichte des sogenannten Zweiten Korintherbriefes," *Geschichte und Glaube: Gesammelte Aufsätze*, Band IV (München: Kaiser, 1971), pp. 162–194.

[98] The same considerations weigh against seeing Philippians as an amalgam of separate letters.

[99] "Wisdom"—Colossians 1:9,28, 2:3,23, 3:16, 4:5; "Knowledge"—Colossians 1:6,9–10, 2:2–3, 3:10.

[100] The new Jewish sect almost certainly became established in the Roman synagogues through visiting merchants and travelers. We do not know who founded the Roman churches—certainly not Paul or Peter. Two likely candidates are the apostles (and possible husband and wife) Andronicus and Junia (Romans 16:7), since Paul regarded apostles as church founders (1 Corinthians 9:1–2). As already noted, Paul's slight embarrassment at ministering to a church that he had not founded is evident in Romans 1:10–13 and 15:20.

[101] Eusebius, *Eccles. Hist.* 2.25.8, 3.1.1–3.

[102] *Antiquities* 20:200–203.

[103] Cf. Leviticus 24:13–16,23; Deuteronomy 23:6–10.

[104] Eusebius, *Eccles. Hist.* 2.23.13; cf. Mark 14:61–64; Acts 7:54–60.

IV. Judaism from the Destruction of Jerusalem to the End of the Second Jewish Revolt: 70–135 C.E.

[1] This chapter is an extensively revised version of its predecessor, especially the section dealing with the rabbinic traditions relating to the Yavnean era.

[2] See Lee I. Levine, *Jerusalem: Portrait of the City in the Second Temple Period (538 B.C.E.–70 C.E.)* (Philadelphia: JPS, 2002).

[3] *Siddur Sim Shalom (A Prayer-book for Shabbat, Festivals and Weekdays)*, ed. J. Harlow (New York: Rabbinical Assembly, 1985), pp. 462–463.

[4] It is generally accepted today that the Qumran sect is to be identified with the Essenes described in detail by Josephus (*War* 2.120–161) and Philo (*Quod Omnis Probus Liber Sit* 75–91; *Hypothetica* 11.1–18). A number of scholars have proposed a variety of other identifications for the site, including a pottery factory, a caravanserai, a military fortress, and a *villa rustica*, none of which has won wide support. See most recently Kenneth R. Atkinson and Jodi Magness, "Josephus's Essenes and the Qumran Community," *JBL* 129 (2010), pp. 317–342.

[5] See Martin Goodman, *Rome and Jerusalem: The Clash of Ancient Civilizations* (New York: Knopf, 2007), pp. 424–469.

[6] As claimed by Gedaliah Alon, *The Jews in Their Land in the Talmudic Age*, 2 vols. (Jerusalem: Magnes Press, 1980–1984), vol. 1, pp. 70–74; E. Mary Smallwood, *The Jews Under Roman Rule* (Leiden: Brill, 1976), pp. 339–345.

[7] Samuel G.F. Brandon, *The Fall of Jerusalem and the Christian Church: A Study of the Effects of the Jewish Overthrow of A.D. 70 on Christianity* (London: SPCK, 1978), pp. 167–184; Sidney Sowers, "The Circumstances and Recollection of the Pella-flight," *Theologische Zeitschrift* 26 (1970), pp. 305–320; John J. Gunther, "The Fate of the Jerusalem Church," *Theologische Zeitschrift* 29 (1973), pp. 81–94; Raymond Pritz, *Nazarene Jewish Christianity: From the End of the New Testament Period until Its Disappearance in the Fourth Century* (Jerusalem/Leiden: Magnes Press/Brill, 1988), pp. 122–127.

[8] See Dalia Trifon, "A Mishnah Fragment as Evidence of the Status of King Agrippa II," *Cathedra* 53 (1989), pp. 27–48 (in Hebrew).

[9] It is generally assumed that the Fourth Sybil was written around 80 C.E.; see Emil Schürer, *The History of the Jewish People in the Age of Jesus Christ (175 B.C.–A.D. 135)*, 3 vols., rev. and eds. Geza Vermes, Fergus Millar and Martin Goodman (Edinburgh: T & T Clark, 1973–1987), vol. 3, pp. 641–643. A sybil was a semimythical, semihistorical female figure from ancient Greek religion whose prophecies and oracles were dependent upon divine inspiration. Jews as well as pagans wrote books under the Sybil pseudonym. See also James H. Charlesworth, ed., *The Old Testament Pseudepigrapha: Apocalyptic Literature and Testaments*, 2 vols. (Garden City, NY: Doubleday, 1983), vol. 1, pp. 381–389.

[10] Schürer, *History of the Jewish People* (see endnote 9), vol. 3, pp. 325–331.

[11] For a useful summary of this spectrum of opinion, see George W. Nickelsburg, *Jewish Literature Between the Bible and the Mishnah: A Historical and Literary Introduction* (Philadelphia: Fortress Press, 1981), pp. 277–309.

[12] It is widely assumed that 4 Ezra dates to the very end of the first century C.E. See Schürer, *History of the Jewish People* (see endnote 9), vol. 3, pp. 299–300.

[13] See, for example, Jacob Neusner, "The Formation of Rabbinic Judaism: Yavneh (Yamnia) from AD 70 to 100," *ANRW* II.19.2 (1979), pp. 3–42; Hayim Lapin, "The Origins and Development of the Rabbinic Movement in the Land of Israel," *The Cambridge History of Judaism*, vol. 4: *The Late Roman-Rabbinic Period*, ed. Steven T. Katz (Cambridge: Cambridge University Press, 2006), pp. 206–229; Seth Schwartz, "The Political Geography of Rabbinic Texts," in *The Cambridge Companion to the Talmud and Rabbinic Literature*, eds. Charlotte E. Fonrobert and Martin S. Jaffee (Cambridge: Cambridge Univeristy Press, 2007), pp. 75–96.

[14] Robert Goldenberg, "The Broken Axis: Rabbinic Judaism and the Fall of Jerusalem," *JAAR* 45 (1977), pp. 869–882; Neusner, "Formation of Rabbinic Judaism" (see endnote 13), pp. 21–42; Peter Schäfer, "Die Flucht Joḥanan b. Zakkais aus Jerusalem und die Gründung des 'Lehrhauses' in Jabne," *ANRW* II.19.2 (1979), pp. 43–101.

[15] The periodization of these two stages is difficult to determine. It is generally considered to have taken place some time between 80 and 90–95 C.E.

[16] Later generations told of Yoḥanan's supposed mastery of scripture, Mishnah, Gemara (Talmud), *halakhah*, *aggadah*, and *midrash*, as well as the subtleties of the scriptural text, mysticism and metaphysical speculation (*Fathers According to Rabbi Nathan* A 14, B 28; BT *Sukkah* 28a; JT *Nedarim* 5,3,39b). The historical reliability of such traditions is questionable. On the other hand, somewhat more credible may be the early traditions reporting on Yoḥanan's engaging the Sadducees in numerous disputes (Mishnah *Yadayim* 4:6; Tosefta *Parah* 3:8; see also BT *Bava Batra* 115b–116a; BT *Menahot* 65a–b), although, for all we know, such conversations might have taken place in a pre-70 Jerusalem setting.

[17] This *takkanah* is problematic. Tosefta *Shekalim* 3:22 mentions it without attributing it to Yoḥanan, and it appears to have remained a matter of dispute among his students (*Sifre Zutta*, ed. Hayyim S. Horowitz [Leipzig: Gustav Fock, 1917], p. 283).

[18] On the difficulty of attributing this *takkanah* to Yoḥanan, see the talmudic discussion itself as well as Tosefta *Ma'aser Sheni* 5:15–16.

[19] Scholars are divided as to whether this office began to operate in some official capacity under Gamaliel himself, his son Simeon or his grandson Judah I. See David Goodblatt, *The Monarchic Principle: Studies in Jewish Self-Government in Antiquity* (Tübingen: Mohr Siebeck, 1994), pp. 131–175. It would seem that Gamaliel did enjoy some sort of official recognition (and thus one might refer to him as a proto-patriarch), although full-blown recognition came only in the time of his grandson, Rabbi Judah I, under the Severan dynasty.

[20] Goodblatt, *Monarchic Principle* (see endnote 19), pp. 176–231.

[21] Further suggestions as to the nature of the authority granted to Rabban Gamaliel include permission to travel abroad and an official appointment as patriarch of the Jews.

[22] For a full review of these sources and the arguments presented here, see Lee I. Levine, *The*

Ancient Synagogue: The First Thousand Years, 2nd rev. ed. (New Haven, CT: Yale University Press, 2005), pp. 540–557.

[23] Siegfried Stein, "The Influence of Symposia Literature on the Pesach Haggada," *JJS* 8 (1957), pp. 13–44.

[24] Schürer, *History of the Jewish People* (see endnote 9), vol. 1, pp. 534–557; Aharon Oppenheimer and Uriel Rappaport, eds., *The Bar-Kokhva Revolt—A New Approach* (Jerusalem: Yad Izhak Ben-Zvi, 1984) (in Hebrew); Shimon Applebaum, "The Bar-Kokhba Rebellion," in *Judea and Rome—The Jewish Revolts*, ed. Uriel Rappaport (Jerusalem: Am Oved, 1983), pp. 207–260; Smallwood, *Jews under Roman Rule* (see endnote 6), pp. 428–466; Peter Schäfer, *Der Bar Kokhba-Aufstand: Studien zum zweiten judischen Krieg gegen Rom* (Tübingen: Mohr Siebeck, 1981).

[25] Timothy D. Barnes, "Trajan and the Jews," *JJS* 40 (1989), pp. 145–162; William Horbury, "The Beginnings of the Jewish Revolt Under Trajan," in *Geschichte-Tradition-Reflexion: Festschrift für Martin Hengel zum 70 Geburstag*, ed. Peter Schäfer, vol. 1 (Tübingen: Mohr Siebeck, 1996), pp. 283–304; Miriam Pucci Ben Zeev, "The Uprisings in the Jewish Diaspora, 116–117," in Katz, *Cambridge History of Judaism*, vol. 4 (see endnote 13), pp. 93–104, and bibliography there.

[26] Victor Tcherikover and Alexander Fuks, eds., *Corpus Papyrorum Judaicarum*, 3 vols. (Cambridge, MA: Harvard University Press, 1964), vol. 3, p. 258, no. 450.

[27] See, for example, *Supplementum Epigraphicum Graecum* (Leiden: Sijthoff, 1938), vol. 9, p. 252.

[28] Smallwood, *Jews Under Roman Rule* (see endnote 6), pp. 412–415.

[29] Ibid., pp. 415–421.

[30] Schürer, *History of the Jewish People* (see endnote 9), vol. 1, pp. 534–557; Smallwood, *Jews Under Roman Rule* (see endnote 6), pp. 428–466; Schäfer, *Der Bar Kokhba-Aufstand* (see endnote 24); Benjamin Isaac and Aharon Oppenheimer, "The Revolt of Bar Kokhba: Ideology and Modern Scholarship," *JJS* 36 (1985), pp. 33–60; Hanan Eshel, "The Bar Kochba Revolt, 132–135," in Katz, *Cambridge History of Judaism*, vol. 4 (see endnote 13), pp. 105–127; Werner Eck, "Hadrian's Hard-Won Victory: Romans Suffer Severe Losses in Jewish War," *BAR*, September/October 2007, pp. 42–51; Yigael Yadin, *Bar-Kokhba: The Rediscovery of the Legendary Hero of the Last Jewish Revolt Against Imperial Rome* (London: Weidenfeld and Nicolson, 1971).

[31] Isaac and Oppenheimer, "Revolt of Bar Kokhba" (see endnote 30), pp. 57–58; Eshel, "Bar Kochba Revolt" (see endnote 30), pp. 109–111.

[32] Aharon Oppenheimer, "The Messianism of Bar-Kokhba," in *Messianism and Eschatology*, ed. Zvi Baras (Jerusalem: Zalman Shazar Center, 1983), pp. 153–165 (in Hebrew). Rabbi Akiva's many trips outside Judea have often been seen as an effort to galvanize support for Bar-Kokhba's plans. This assumption, however, is entirely gratuitous, for the sources report that these trips were associated only with legal questions or with sermons he delivered. Political concerns never appear in any of these traditions.

[33] Hugo Mantel, "The Causes of the Bar Kokba Revolt," *JQR* 58 (1968), pp. 274–296. See also Menachem Mor, *The Bar-Kochba Revolt: Its Extent and Effect* (Jerusalem: Yad Izhak Ben-Zvi, 1991), pp. 41–59 (in Hebrew).

[34] Israel Roll, "The Roman Road System in Judea," in *The Jerusalem Cathedra*, 3 vols., ed. Lee I. Levine (Detroit: Wayne State University Press, 1983), vol. 1, pp. 136–161.

[35] Isaac and Oppenheimer, "Revolt of Bar Kokhba" (see endnote 30), p. 53; Eshel, "Bar Kokhba Revolt" (see endnote 30), pp. 122–123.

[36] See Eck, "Hadrian's Hard-Won Victory" (see endnote 30).

[37] Saul Lieberman, "Persecution of the Religion of Israel," in *Jubilee Volume in Honor of Salo Baron* (Jerusalem: American Academy for Jewish Research, 1974), pp. 213–245 (in Hebrew); Moshe D. Herr, "Persecutions and Martyrdom in Hadrian's Days," *Scripta Hierosolymitana* 23 (1973), pp. 85–125. The historicity of these reports is somewhat compromised by the fact that only rabbinic literature notes these restrictions; neither Roman nor, more importantly, Christian authors make any reference to such decrees.

V. Christianity from the Destruction of Jerusalem to Constantine: 70–312 C.E.

[1] The Jewish historian Josephus (*War* 6.249–253) gives a graphic account of the event.

[2] The battle and its date are recorded by the Christian apologist Lactantius, in *On the Deaths of Persecutors* 44, and in Eusebius, *Eccles. Hist.* 9.9.2–10, where the inscription on Constantine's statue is mentioned. A description of the episode also appears in the *Life of Constantine* 1.28–29, 31, where Eusebius gives a detailed description of the sign used by Constantine, the *labarum*, a spear and a cross-bar topped by a wreath encircling the first two letters of Christ's name, *chi* and *rho*.

[3] For general histories of the early Church, see Philip Carrington, *The Early Christian Church*, 2 vols. (Cambridge: Cambridge University Press, 1957); Jean Daniélou and Henri Marrou, *The Christian Centuries*, vol. 1: *First Six Hundred Years* (London: Darton, Longman & Todd; New York: McGraw-Hill, 1964); Henry Chadwick, *The Early Church* (London: Penguin, 1967); Helmut Koester, *Introduction to the New Testament*, vol. 2: *History and Literature of Early Christianity* (Berlin: de Gruyter, 1982); W.H.C. Frend, *The Rise of Christianity* (Philadelphia: Fortress Press, 1984). A provocative study is Walter Bauer, *Orthodoxy and Heresy in Earliest Christianity* (rev. Georg Strecker; eds. Robert Kraft and Gerhard Krodel [Philadelphia: Fortress Press, 1971]); originally appeared as *Rechtgläubigkeit und Ketzerei im ältesten Christentum*, BHT 10 (Tübingen: Mohr Siebeck, 1934). On this work, see Daniel J. Harrington, "The Reception of Walter Bauer's *Orthodoxy and Heresy in Earliest Christianity* During the Last Decade," in *The Light of All Nations: Essays on the Church in New Testament Research*, Good News Studies 3 (Wilmington, DE: Glazier, 1982), and Thomas A. Robinson, *The Bauer Thesis Examined: The Geography of Heresy in the Early Christian Church*, Studies in the Bible and Early Christianity 11 (Lewiston, NY: Edwin Mellen, 1988).

[4] A comprehensive reference work is Johannes Quasten, *Patrology*, 3 vols. (Utrecht, Neth.: Spectrum, 1950–1960). Most of the literature is available in *The Ante-Nicene Fathers*, 10 vols., eds. Alexander Roberts and James Donalson (Edinburgh, 1885–1887; New York: Scribners, 1912–1927).

[5] Much of the relevant data are collected in Graydon F. Snyder, *Ante Pacem: Archaeological Evidence of Church Life Before Constantine* (Macon, GA: Mercer University Press, 1985). See also James Stevenson, *A New Eusebius: Documents Illustrative of the History of the Church to A.D. 337* (London: SPCK, 1957). For the artistic remains of the earliest Christians, see Paul Corby Finney, *The Invisible God: The Earliest Christians on Art* (New York: Oxford University Press, 1994).

[6] A text and translation is available in Kirsopp Lake, J.E.L. Oulton and H.J. Lawlor, *Eusebius, The Ecclesiastical History*, 2 vols., Loeb (Cambridge, MA: Harvard University Press, 1926–1932, frequently reprinted). For a translation and commentary, see H.J. Lawlor and J.E.L. Oulton, *Eusebius, Bishop of Caesarea, The Ecclesiastical History and the Martyrs of Palestine*, 2 vols. (London: SPCK, 1927–1928).

[7] See 1 Clement 5.7.

[8] For a sociological account of the spread of Christianity, see Rodney A. Stark, *The Rise of Christianity: A Sociologist Reconsiders History* (Princeton, NJ: Princeton University Press, 1996).

[9] For the texts and a commentary, see A.N. Sherwin-White, *The Letters of Pliny: A Historical and Social Commentary* (Oxford: Clarendon Press, 1966).

[10] The information is from Eusebius, *Eccles. Hist.* 5.10.1–4, and fits what is known of the trade routes of the time.

[11] For translations of the most important texts, often fragmentary, see W. Schneemelcher, *New Testament Apocrypha*, 2 vols. (Louisville: Westminster/John Knox Press, 1991–1992), vol. 2, pp. 322–411.

[12] With the purported discovery of an ossuary with an inscription naming "James the brother of Jesus," interest in the figure of James has surged in recent years. For reviews, see Bruce Chilton and Craig Evans, *James the Just and Christian Origins* (Leiden: Brill, 1999), and Bruce Chilton and Jacob Neusner, *Brother of Jesus, James the Just and His Mission* (Louisville: Westminster/John Knox Press, 2001).

[13] In general, see Martin Dibelius and Hans Conzelmann, *The Pastoral Epistles*, Hermeneia

Commentaries (Philadelphia: Fortress Press, 1972).

[14] Wayne Meeks (*The Moral World of the First Christians* [Philadelphia: Westminster, 1986]) usefully surveys the forms of ethical exhortation at work. Elisabeth Schüssler Fiorenza (*In Memory of Her: A Feminist Theological Reconstruction of Christian Origins* [New York: Crossroad, 1983]) treats perceptively the increasingly patriarchal character of Christianity in this period.

[15] A Greek text was discovered in 1875, in a codex dating to 1057 C.E. Text and translation are in Bart Ehrman, *The Apostolic Fathers*, 2 vols., Loeb (Cambridge, MA: Harvard University Press, 2003), 1.405–443. For a translation alone, see Robert A. Kraft, *Barnabas and the Didache*, ed. Robert M. Grant, Apostolic Fathers 3 (Camden, NJ: Nelson, 1965).

[16] Another example of teaching on the "two ways" appears in the Epistle of Barnabas 18–20.

[17] For the late first century, see Revelation 1:10; for the early second century, Ignatius, *Epistle to the Magnesians* 9 and Epistle of Barnabas 15.8. For the mid-second century data, cf. Justin Martyr, *1 Apology* 67.

[18] For a full treatment of the text, see Harold W. Attridge, *The Epistle to the Hebrews*, Hermeneia Commentaries (Philadelphia: Fortress Press, 1989) and Craig Koester, *Hebrews: A New Translation with Introduction and Commentary*, Anchor Bible (New York: Doubleday, 2001).

[19] An analysis is offered by Barbara Bowe, *A Church in Crisis: Ecclesiology and Paraenesis in Clement of Rome*, HDR 23 (Minneapolis: Fortress Press, 1988). On the issues of church order raised by the text, see John Fuellenbach, *Ecclesiastical Office and the Primacy of Rome*, Studies in Christian Antiquity 20 (Washington, DC: Catholic University of America, 1980). Dates ranging from 70 to 140 C.E. have been proposed. See the discussion of the issue in Attridge, *The Epistle to the Hebrews* (see endnote 18), pp. 6–8. On Roman Christianity in general, see Peter Lampe, *From Paul to Valentinus: Christians in Rome in the First Two Centuries*, trans. Michael Steinhauser, ed. Marshall Johnson (Minneapolis: Fortress Press, 2003).

[20] See Eusebius, *Eccles. Hist.* 3.4.9; 3.21.1; 5.6.2–3, citing Irenaeus, *Against Heresies* 3.3.3.

[21] 1 Clement 42.

[22] For text and translation, see Ehrman, *The Apostolic Fathers*, 1.203–353 (see endnote 15). Of the critical problems of these letters, see William R. Schoedel, *Ignatius of Antioch*, Hermeneia Commentaries (Philadelphia: Fortress Press, 1985). On the development of ecclesiastical office, see Hans von Campenhausen, *Ecclesiastical Authority and Spiritual Power in the Church of the First Three Centuries*, trans. J.A. Baker (Stanford, CA: Stanford University Press, 1969), and Eric G. Jay, "From Presbyters-Bishops to Bishops and Presbyters," *SC* 1 (1983), pp. 125–162.

[23] From Smyrna, modern Izmir, on the western shore of Asia Minor, he wrote to Ephesus, Magnesia and Tralles. From Troas, farther north on the coast, he wrote to Philadelphia, Smyrna and a personal letter to Polycarp, bishop of Smyrna.

[24] Ignatius, *Magnesians* 10; *Philadelphians* 6.

[25] Ignatius, *Trallians* 10; *Smyrneans* 2, 5. It is possible that Ignatius is in fact dealing with two facets of a single problem, people who wanted to continue the observance of Jewish customs and who discounted the significance of Jesus' suffering humanity.

[26] Cf., for example, Ignatius, *Ephesians* 3–5; *Magnesians* 4, 6–7; *Trallians* 7; *Smyrneans* 8–9.

[27] *Smyrneans* 8.2.

[28] *1 Apology* 65–67.

[29] On the development of the liturgy, see Josef A. Jungmann, *The Early Liturgy: To the Time of Gregory the Great* (Notre Dame, IN: University of Notre Dame Press, 1959). For recent recognition of the diversity of liturgical practices that remained through the first several centuries, see Paul Bradshaw, *Early Christian Worship: A Basic Introduction to Ideas and Practice* (London: SPCK, 1996) and Andrew McGowan, *Ascetic Eucharists: Food and Drink in Early Christian Meals* (Oxford: Clarendon Press, 1999).

[30] He was active from the time of Anicetus (c. 155–166 C.E.) through Eleutherus (174–189 C.E.), according to Eusebius, *Eccles. Hist.* 4.11.7. For discussion of his tendencies, see Gerd Lüdemann, *Opposition to Paul in Jewish Christianity* (Minneapolis: Fortress Press, 1989), pp. 155–168.

[31] Eusebius, *Eccles. Hist.* 4.8.2.

[32] The fragments are found at Eusebius, *Eccles. Hist.* 2.22.4–18; 3.20.1–6; 3.32.3–8; 4.8.2; 4.22.4–9. Reference to the succession of Christian leaders appears at *Eccles. Hist.* 4.22.3. Eusebius relied also on the *Chronographies* of Julius Africanus from the early third century. On the problems of early papal chronology, see Lawlor and Oulton, *Eusebius, Bishop of Caesarea* (see endnote 6), 2.37–46. For the importance of the succession lists for Eusebius, see Robert M. Grant, *Eusebius as Church Historian* (Oxford: Clarendon Press, 1980), pp. 45–59.

[33] A defense of the Quartodeciman practice and its apostolic basis, written by Polycrates, bishop of Ephesus, survives in Eusebius, *Eccles. Hist.* 5.24.2–8.

[34] See Eusebius, *Eccles. Hist.* 5.24.10–18.

[35] For Victor and the response to his action, see Eusebius, *Eccles. Hist.* 5.24.9–10.

[36] The fourth-century heresiologist Epiphanius (*Panarion* 48.1) gives a date of 157 C.E., but the date of Eusebius (*Eccles. Hist.* 5.4.3) is to be preferred. Cf. Hippolytus, *Refutation of All Heresies* 8.19.1–3.

[37] So Eusebius, *Eccles. Hist.* 5.18.2, according to an anti-Montanist named Apollonius. For a collection of Montanist oracles, see Ronald Heine, *The Montanist Oracles and Testimonia*, Patristic Monograph Series 14 (Macon, GA: Mercer University Press, 1989), and William Tabbernee, *Montanixt Inscriptions and Testimonia: Epigraphic Sources Illustrating the History of Montanism* (Macon: University of Georgia, 1997).

[38] In addition to the work of Apolinaris, Eusebius (*Eccles. Hist.* 5.16.1–17.4) preserves fragments of the major work of an anonymous writer.

[39] Note the letters preserved in Eusebius, *Eccles. Hist.* 5.19. The Roman bishop Eleutherus (c. 174–189) rejected Montanism in a written statement, to which Tertullian (*Adversus Praxean* 1) refers.

[40] See Gregory Dix, *The Treatise on the Apostolic Tradition of St. Hippolytus of Rome: Historical Introduction, Textual Materials and Translation* (London: SPCK; New York: Macmillan, 1937, reprinted, with corrections, preface and bibliography by Henry Chadwich, 1968), and Bernard Botte, *Hippolyte de Rome, La Tradition Apostolique: Texte Latin, introduction, traduction et notes*, Sources chrétiennes 11 (Paris: Cerf, 1946). For an English translation, see G.J. Cuming, *Hippolytus: A Text for Students*, Grove Liturgical Studies 8 (Nottingham: Grove, 1976). The most recent scholarship on the text is increasingly doubtful of the attribution to Hippolytus and recognizes in the text a compilation with materials ranging from the early third through the fourth century. See Paul Bradshaw et al., *The Apostolic Tradition: A Commentary*, ed. Harold W. Attridge, Hermeneia (Minneapolis: Fortress Press, 2002). For the ordination texts contained in this work and comparable liturgical sources, see Paul F. Bradshaw, *Ordination Rites of the Ancient Churches of East and West* (New York: Pueblo, 1990).

[41] The *Didascalia* survives in its entirety in Syriac and in translations from it into Ethiopic and Arabic. Portions were translated into Latin. The Greek original was incorporated in the fourth-century church order, the *Apostolic Constitutions*. See R.H. Connolly, *Didascalia apostolorum: The Syriac Version Translated and Accompanied by the Verona Latin fragments* (Oxford: Oxford University Press, 1929). Recent scholarship on the *Didache* has proliferated. See Clayton Jefford, *The Sayings of Jesus in the Teachings of the Twelve Apostles* (Leiden: Brill, 1989); Kurt Niederwimmer, *Didache*, trans. Linda Maloney, ed. Harold W. Attridge, Hermeneia (Minneapolis: Fortress Press, 1998); Aaron Milevec, *Didache: Text, Translation, Analysis and Commentary* (Collegeville, MN: Liturgical Press, 2003), and Marcello del Verme, *Didache and Judaism: Jewish Roots of an Ancient Jewish-Christian Work* (New York: T & T Clark, 2004).

[42] Hippolytus's charges against Callistus are in *Refutation of All Heresies* 9.12.20–26.

[43] On Roman Christianity and Hermas, see Carolyn Osiek, *Rich and Poor in the Shepherd of Hermas: An Exegetical-Social Investigation*, CBQ Monograph Series 15 (Washington, DC: CBA, 1983); and *The Shepherd of Hermas: A Commentary*, Hermeneia (Minneapolis: Fortress Press, 1999).

[44] In his treatise *On the Lapsed*. For translations, see *Ante-Nicene Fathers* (see endnote 4), 5.437–447; Maurice Bévenot, *St. Cyprian, the Lapsed: The Unity of the Church*, Ancient Christian Writers 25 (Westminster, MD: Newman, 1957), and Roy J. Defarrari, *St. Cyprian, Treatises*, Fathers of the Church 26 (New York: Fathers of the Church, Inc., 1958). For texts and translations, see Maurice Bévenot, *Cyprian, De Lapsis and De Ecclesiae*

Catholicae Unitate, Oxford Early Christian Texts (Oxford: Clarendon Press, 1971). For studies, see Peter Hinchliff, *Cyprian of Carthage and the Unity of the Christian Church* (London: Chapman, 1974), and J. Patout Burns, *Cyprian the Bishop* (London: Routledge, 2002).

[45] Novatian had established a reputation as a theologian, particularly for his work *On the Trinity*. See *Ante-Nicene Fathers* (see endnote 4), 5.611–644, and Herbert Moore, *The Treatise of Novatian on the Trinity* (London: SPCK, 1919). On Modalism, see the section of this essay on the development of doctrine.

[46] Eusebius (*Eccles. Hist.* 6.43.1–46.5) describes the controversy and the lively correspondence between Rome and various eastern bishops, although he calls the schismatic Roman Novatus.

[47] See *Ante-Nicene Fathers* (see endnote 4), 5.421–429, and the translations cited above, in endnote 44.

[48] A translation and useful commentary on Cyprian's extensive surviving correspondence is G.W. Clarke, *The Letters of St. Cyprian of Carthage*, 4 vols., Ancient Christian Writers 43–47 (New York: Newman, 1984–89).

[49] The attempt by J.A.T. Robinson (*Redating the New Testament* [Philadelphia: Westminster Press, 1976]) to date the Gospels much earlier has not won acceptance. Matthew 22:7 clearly alludes to the destruction of Jerusalem. Moreover, the cry attributed to the crowds at 27:25 is part of Matthew's attempt to explain the reason for the destruction of the city and Temple. See also Matthew 23:26.

[50] For these texts, see William H. Brownlee, *The Midrash Pesher of Habakkuk*, SBL Monograph Series 24 (Missoula, MT: Scholars Press, 1979), and Maurya P. Horgan, *Pesharim: Qumran Interpretations of Biblical Books*, CBQ Monograph Series 8 (Washington, DC: CBA, 1979).

[51] Like Matthew, Luke was clearly written after the destruction of Jerusalem in 70 C.E., as indicated by the handling of the prophecy in Luke 21:20 as a reference to Jerusalem's fate.

[52] On the literary qualities of Luke and Acts, see Charles H. Talbert, *Reading Luke: A Literary and Theological Commentary on the Third Gospel* (New York: Crossroad, 1982); Robert C. Tannehill, *The Narrative Unity of Luke-Acts*, 2 vols. (Philadelphia: Fortress Press, 1986, 1989); David Aune, *The New Testament in Its Literary Environment* (Philadelphia: Westminster Press, 1987), pp. 77–157, and Richard I. Pervo, *Profit with Delight: The Literary Genre of the Acts of the Apostles* (Philadelphia: Fortress Press, 1987).

[53] For example, the "Good Samaritan" (Luke 10:30–37) and the "Prodigal Son" (Luke 15:11–32).

[54] On the infancy narratives in general, see Raymond E. Brown, *The Birth of the Messiah* (Garden City, NY: Doubleday, 1977).

[55] The historical reliability of Acts continues to be debated. For opposing views, see Martin Hengel, *Acts and the History of Earliest Christianity* (London: SCM, 1979), and Ernst Haenchen, *The Acts of the Apostles: A Commentary* (Philadelphia: Westminster Press, 1971). A judicious assessment is offered by Gerd Lüdemann, *Early Christianity according to the Traditions in Acts* (Minneapolis: Fortress Press, 1987). Among recent critical commentaries, see Hans Conzelmann, *Acts of the Apostles*, Hermeneia Commentaries (Philadelphia: Fortress Press, 1987), and Joseph Fitzmyer, S.J., *Acts of the Apostles*, Anchor Bible 31 (New York: Doubleday, 1998).

[56] There has been considerable debate about Luke's attitudes toward the Jews. See Jacob Jervell, *Luke and the People of God* (Minneapolis: Augsburg, 1977); David Tiede, *Prophecy and History in Luke-Acts* (Philadelphia: Fortress Press, 1980); Donald Juel, *Luke-Acts: The Promise of History* (Atlanta: John Knox Press, 1983); Robert L. Brawley, *Luke-Acts and the Jews: Conflict, Apology, and Conciliation*, SBL Monograph Series 33 (Atlanta: Scholars Press, 1987), and Jack T. Sanders, *The Jews in Luke-Acts* (Philadelphia: Fortress Press, 1987).

[57] See, for example, Acts 16:35–40 (officials at Philippi); Acts 18:12–15 (Gallio in Corinth), and Acts 26:32 (Agrippa). Luke rationalizes contrary evidence. Thus, Felix left Paul in bondage merely to curry favor with the Jews (Acts 24:27).

[58] On the critical problems of Colossians, see Eduard Lohse, *Colossians and Philemon*, Hermeneia Commentaries (Philadelphia: Fortress Press, 1971).

[59] Numerous fine commentaries are available. See esp. Raymond E. Brown, *The Gospel According to*

John, 2 vols., Anchor Bible 29, 29A (Garden City, NY: Doubleday, 1966, 1970). For a less technical commentary, see R. Alan Culpepper, *The Gospel and Letters of John*, Interpreting Biblical Texts (Nashville: Abingdon, 1998), and D. Moody Smith, *John*, Abingdon New Testament Commentaries (Nashville: Abingdon, 1999).

[60] See, for example, Eusebius, *Eccles. Hist.* 3.23.1–4; 3.28.6, citing second-century sources, Irenaeus and Clement of Alexandria. For a discussion of the legend of the "Beloved Disciple," see R. Alan Culpepper, *John the Son of Zebedee: The Life of a Legend*, Studies on Personalities of the New Testament (Columbia: University of South Carolina Press, 1994; reprinted, Minneapolis: Fortress Press, 2000).

[61] Louis Martyn (*History and Theology in the Fourth Gospel*, 2nd ed. [Abingdon: Nashville, 1979]) has argued that the anti-Jewish polemic of the Fourth Gospel was occasioned by the *Birkat ha-Minim*, the "blessing (in reality an imprecation) on heretics." For skepticism, see Reuven Kimelman, "*Birkat Ha-Minim* and the Lack of Evidence for an Anti-Christian Jewish Prayer in Late Antiquity," in *Jewish and Christian Self-Definition*, vol. 2: *Aspects of Judaism in the Graeco-Roman Period*, eds. E.P. Sanders, A.I. Baumgarten and Alan Mendelson (Philadelphia: Fortress Press, 1981), pp. 226–244. On the overall placement of the Fourth Gospel in early Christianity, see Harold W. Attridge, "Johannine Christianity," in *The Cambridge History of Christianity*, vol. 1: *Origins to Constantine*, eds. Margaret M. Mitchell and Frances M. Young (Cambridge: Cambridge University Press, 2006), pp. 125–144.

[62] There is apparently an allusion to the tradition in Hebrews 11:37.

[63] Ascension of Isaiah 3:21–31.

[64] Ascension of Isaiah 3:23–24. For the text, see M.A. Knibb, "The Martyrdom and Ascension of Isaiah," in *Old Testament Pseudepigrapha*, 2 vols., ed. James H. Charlesworth (Garden City, NY: Doubleday, 1983–1985), vol. 2, pp. 143–176. A comprehensive thematic treatment of this sort of literature may be found in Jean Daniélou, *A History of Early Christian Doctrine Before the Council of Nicaea*, vol. 1: *The Theology of Jewish Christianity* (Chicago: Regnery, 1964).

[65] A translation with introduction may be found in Howard C. Kee, "The Testaments of the Twelve Patriarchs," in *Old Testament Pseudepigrapha* (see endnote 64), vol. 1, pp. 775–828.

[66] See *Antiquities* 20.197–203.

[67] For skepticism about the flight to Pella, recounted in Eusebius, *Eccles. Hist.* 3.5.3, see Gerd Lüdemann, "The Successors of Pre-70 Jerusalem Christianity: A Critical Evaluation of the Pella-Tradition," in *Jewish and Christian Self-Definition*, vol. 1: *The Shaping of Christianity in the Second and Third Centuries*, ed. E.P. Sanders (Philadelphia: Fortress Press, 1980), pp. 161–173.

[68] These works are part of the Nag Hammadi find, discussed below. Text and translation are in *Nag Hammadi Codices V, 2–5 and VI with Papyrus Berolinensis 8502*, 1 and 4, ed. Douglas M. Parrott, Nag Hammadi Studies 11 (Leiden: Brill, 1979), pp. 65–150. For translations alone, see *The Nag Hammadi Library in English*, 2nd ed., ed. James M. Robinson (San Francisco: Harper & Row, 1987).

[69] For reports on the Nazarenes and Ebionites, see Irenaeus, *Against Heresies* 1.26.2; Hippolytus, *Refutation of All Heresies* 7.34; Eusebius, *Eccles. Hist.* 3.27.1–2; Epiphanius, *Panarion* 29–30. That heresiological text is now available in Francis E. Williams, *The Panarion of Epiphanius of Salamis Book I (Sets 1–46)*, Nag Hammadi Studies 35 (Leiden: Brill, 1987).

[70] For the Jewish-Christian gospels, see Schneemelcher, *New Testament Apocrypha* (see endnote 11), vol. 1, pp. 134–178. The character and history of Jewish Christianity is much debated. Important discussions include: Hans Joachim Schoeps, *Jewish Christianity* (Philadelphia: Fortress Press, 1964); R.A. Pritz, *Nazarene Jewish Christianity: From the End of the New Testament Period Until Its Disappearance in the Fourth Century* (Jerusalem/Leiden: Magnes Press/Brill, 1988); Alan Segal, "Jewish Christianity," in *Eusebius, Judaism and Christianity*, eds. Harold W. Attridge and Gohei Hata (Detroit: Wayne State University Press, 1992); and Gerd Lüdemann, *Opposition to Paul in Jewish Christianity*, trans. M. Eugene Boring (Minneapolis: Fortress Press, 1989).

[71] Many of the fragments of the *Book of Elchasai* are in Hippolytus, *Refutation of All Heresies* 9.13–17; 10.29, translated in Schneemelcher, *New Testament Apocrypha* (see endnote 11), vol. 2, pp. 685–690.

[72] They are mentioned in a sermon of Origen, preserved in Eusebius, *Eccles. Hist.* 6.38.1, as a recent phenomenon.

[73] The circumstances of the discovery remain obscure. The codex was probably uncovered in Upper Egypt, perhaps around ancient Lycopolis, a Manichean center, in the middle of the 20th century, then acquired by the Cologne papyrus collection. For an account of the decipherment, see Albert Henrichs, "The Cologne Mani Codex Reconsidered," *Harvard Studies in Classical Philology* 83 (1979), pp. 339–367. The facsimile edition is Ludwig Koenen and Cornelia Römer, *Der Kölmner Mani-Kodex: Abbildungen und diplomatischer Text* (Bonn: Habelt, 1985). A translation is available in Ron Cameron and Arthur Dewey, *The Cologne Mani Codex (P. Colon. inv. nr. 4780) "Concerning the Origin of His Body,"* SBL Texts and Translations 15 (Missoula, MT: Scholars Press, 1979). On Manichaeism, see Geo Widengren, *Mani and Manichaeism* (New York: Holt, Rinehart & Winston, 1965).

[74] Eusebius, *Eccles. Hist.* 7.31.2.

[75] For the text and translation, see *Nag Hammadi Codex II,2–7, together with XIII.2*, Brit. Lib. Or. 4926(1), and P. Oxy. 1, 654, 655*, 2 vols., ed. Bentley Layton, Nag Hammadi Studies 20, 21 (Leiden: Brill, 1988–1989), vol. 1, pp. 37–93 (Coptic); vol. 1, pp. 95–128 (Greek fragments).

[76] Various dates for the work have been proposed, from the mid-first to the late second century. For an early date, see Stevan L. Davies, *The Gospel of Thomas and Christian Wisdom* (New York: Seabury, 1983). Among those who argue for a late second-century date is Jacques-É. Ménard, *L'Évangile selon Thomas*, Nag Hammadi Studies 5 (Leiden: Brill, 1975). For a review of the discussion, see the articles by Kenneth V. Neller, Klyne R. Snodgrass and Charles W. Hedrick in *SC* 7 (1989–1990), pp. 1–56.

[77] On the connection of the Gospel of Thomas and Edessa, see Helmut Koester, "GNOMAI DIAPHOROI: The Origin and Nature of Diversification in the History of Early Christianity," *HTR* 58 (1965), pp. 279–318, reprinted in Helmut Koester and James M. Robinson, *Trajectories Through Early Christianity* (Philadelphia: Fortress Press, 1971), pp. 114–157.

[78] Gospel of Thomas, Saying 12.

[79] In general, see Attridge, *The Epistle to the Hebrews* (see endnote 18).

[80] For texts, see Ehrman, *Apostolic Fathers* (see endnote 15), vol. 2, pp. 23–83, and Kraft, *Barnabas and the Didache* (see endnote 15).

[81] An allusion to a current attempt to rebuild the Temple in Epistle of Barnabas 16:4 has sometimes been taken to indicate a date around the time of the revolt, but the reference is quite vague.

[82] Eusebius (*Eccles. Hist.* 4.11.8) dates his activity to the period of the popes Pius (c. 141–156 C.E.) through Eleutherus (177–189 C.E.). On Justin in general, see Leslie W. Barnard, *Justin Martyr: His Life and Thought* (Cambridge: Cambridge University Press, 1967), and Eric F. Osborn, *Justin Martyr*, BHT 47 (Tübingen: Mohr Siebeck, 1973).

[83] See Justin Martyr, *Dialogue with Trypho* 2. His works are translated in Thomas B. Falls, *St. Justin Martyr*, Fathers of the Church (New York: Christian Heritage, 1949).

[84] For discussion of this genre of controversy literature, see A. Lukyn Williams, *Adversus Judaeos: A Bird's-eye View of Christian Apology until the Renaissance* (Cambridge: Cambridge University Press, 1935); James Parkes, *The Conflict of the Church and the Synagogue: A Study in the Origins of Antisemitism*, repr. (New York: Athenaeum, 1979 [1934]); and Rosemary Radford Ruether, *Faith and Fratricide: The Theological Roots of Anti-Semitism* (New York: Seabury, 1974).

[85] See Origen, *Contra Celsum* 4.52.

[86] See A. Pietersma and R.T. Lutz, "Jannes and Jambres," in *Old Testament Pseudepigrapha* (see endnote 64), vol. 2, pp. 427–442.

[87] For the Sibylline literature, see Schneemelcher, *New Testament Apocrypha* (see endnote 11), vol. 2, pp. 652–684, and John J. Collins, in *Old Testament Pseudepigrapha* (see endnote 64), vol. 1, pp. 317–472.

[88] For recent studies of the earliest stages of Christology, see James D.G. Dunn, *Christology in the Making: A New Testament Inquiry Into the Origins of the Doctrine of the Incarnation* (Philadelphia: Westminster Press, 1980); Marinus de Jonge, *Christology in Context: The Earliest Christian Response to Jesus* (Philadelphia: Westminster Press, 1988); Raymond E. Brown, "Christology" in *The*

New Jerome Biblical Commentary (Englewood Cliffs, NJ: Prentice Hall, 1990), pp. 1354–1359; and Larry W. Hurtado, *Lord Jesus Christ: Devotion to Jesus in Earliest Christianity* (Grand Rapids, MI: Eerdmans, 2003).

[89] Several passages (John 13:23–25, 20:2–10) contrast the Beloved Disciple and Peter to the detriment of the latter.

[90] A comprehensive treatment of the brief letters is Raymond E. Brown, *The Epistles of John*, Anchor Bible 30 (Garden City, NY: Doubleday, 1982). For a briefer treatment of Johannine Christianity, see his *Community of the Beloved Disciple* (New York: Paulist, 1979).

[91] For the former, see 1 John 4:1–3; for the latter, see 1 John 1:8–10.

[92] Justin Martyr, *Dialogue with Trypho* 35.5, 80.4; *1 Apology* 26.5, 58.1–2.

[93] Clement, *Stromateis* 3.12.1–25.4.

[94] Irenaeus, *Against Heresies* 1.27.

[95] Tertullian, *Against Marcion* and *Prescription of Heretics*.

[96] For a discussion of the significance of Ephraem's *Prose Refutations*, see Han J.W. Drijvers, "Marcionism in Syria: Principles, Problems, Polemics," *SC* 6 (1987–1988), pp. 153–172, reprinted in his *East of Antioch* (London: Varioroum Reprints, 1984).

[97] A brief but useful assessment of the evidence is Gerhard May, "Marcion in Contemporary Views: Results and Open Questions," *SC* 6 (1987–1988), pp. 129–152.

[98] For an reassessment of Marcion's career, putting his activity earlier than maintained here, see R. Joseph Hoffmann, *On the Restitution of Christianity: An Essay on the Development of Radical Paulinist Theology in the Second Century* (Chico, CA: Scholars Press, 1984). According to Hoffman, Luke-Acts and the Pastoral Epistles, among other products of the period, are a response to Marcion's radical Paulinism. Hoffmann restates his position in "How Then Know This Troublous Teacher? Further Reflections on Marcion and His Church," *SC* 6 (1987–1988), pp. 173–191.

[99] Marcion's Bible is not extant and reconstructing it is a delicate task. See John J. Clabeaux, *A Lost Edition of the Letters of Paul: A Reassessment of the Text of the Pauline Corpus Attested by Marcion*, CBQ Monograph Series 21 (Washington, DC: CBA, 1989).

[100] On the possible significance of Marcion in the development of the canon, see Hans von Campenhausen, *The Formation of the Christian Bible* (Philadelphia: Fortress Press, 1972). See also William R. Farmer and Denis M. Farkasfalvy, *The Formation of the New Testament Canon: An Ecumenical Approach*, ed. Harold W. Attridge (New York: Paulist, 1983).

[101] Translations may be found in Schneemelcher, *New Testament Apocrypha* (see endnote 11), vol. 1, pp. 34–37, and Stevenson, *A New Eusebius* (see endnote 5), pp. 144–147. A date after 172 C.E. is indicated by the reference to Montanism at the end of the Canon. A much later date has been proposed by Albert C. Sundberg, "'Canon Muratori: A Fourth-Century List," *HTR* 66 (1973), pp. 1–41, but not all have been convinced. See Everett Ferguson, "Canon Muratori: Date and Provenance," *Studia Patristica* 18 (1982), pp. 677–683.

[102] For the *Infancy Gospel of Thomas* and the *Protoevangelium of James*, see Schneemelcher, *New Testament Apocrypha* (see endnote 11), vol. 1, pp. 421–453.

[103] The best overall survey is Kurt Rudolph, *Gnosis: The Nature and History of Gnosticism* (San Francisco: Harper & Row, 1983). See also Pheme Perkins, *The Gnostic Dialogue: The Early Church and the Crisis of Gnosticism* (New York: Paulist, 1980), and Birger Pearson, *Gnosticism, Judaism, and Egyptian Christianity*, Studies in Antiquity and Christianity 5 (Minneapolis: Fortress Press, 1990). For further discussion, see Elaine Pagels, *The Gnostic Gospels* (New York: Random House, 1979); *The Rediscovery of Gnosticism*, ed. Bentley Layton, Proceedings of the International Conference on Gnosticism at Yale, New Haven, Connecticut, March 28–31, 1978, Studies in the History of Religions—Supplements to *Numen*, 40, 41, 2 vols. (Leiden: Brill, 1980–1981); A.H.B. Logan and A.J.M. Wedderburn, *The New Testament and Gnosis: Essays in Honour of Robert McL. Wilson* (Edinburgh: T & T Clark, 1983); *Nag Hammadi, Gnosticism, and Early Christianity*, eds. Charles W. Hedrick and Robert Hodgson, Jr. (Peabody, MA: Hendrickson, 1986); and *Images of the Feminine*

in *Gnosticism*, ed. Karen L. King, Studies in Antiquity and Christianity (Philadelphia: Fortress Press, 1988). Recent discussions have called into question the utility of the designation "Gnostic." See especially, Michael Williams, *Rethinking "Gnosticism": An Argument for Dismantling a Dubious Category* (Princeton, NJ: Princeton University Press, 1996), and Karen King, *What Is Gnosticism?* (Cambridge, MA: Belknap, 2003). While many of their critiques are important, there remains a social and intellectual phenomenon of the second century that is useful to identify and analyze as a phenomenon of religious history.

[104] The position of the church fathers is still defended by some scholars, especially Simone Pétrement, *Le Dieu separé: les origines du gnosticisme* (Paris: Cerf, 1984).

[105] See Justin Martyr, *1 Apology* 26.2; Irenaeus, *Against Heresies* 1.23.1–4; Eusebius, *Eccles. Hist.* 2.13.1–15.1.

[106] All of the texts are available in Robinson, *The Nag Hammadi Library in English* (see endnote 68). For a selection of annotated texts and evidence from the church fathers, see Bentley Layton, *The Gnostic Scriptures* (New York: Doubleday, 1987).

[107] Cf. Proverbs 8:22–31; Wisdom of Solomon 7:22–8:1.

[108] Versions of this myth appear in texts such as *The Apocryphon of John, The Hypostasis of the Archons* and *The Origin of the World* from the Nag Hammadi library. The outlines of the myth are also found in the reports of heresiologists such as Irenaeus, in the first book of his *Against Heresies*.

[109] For the possibility of such a process in the formation of Gnosticism, see Alan Segal, *Two Powers in Heaven: Rabbinic Reports About Christianity and Gnosticism* (Leiden: Brill, 1977).

[110] The major testimonies are in Irenaeus, *Against Heresies* 1.25.1–6; Clement of Alexandria, *Stromateis* 3.2.5,2–9,3; 3.2.10,1. Translations are collected in Werner Foerster, *Gnosis: A Selection of Gnostic Texts*, 2 vols., trans. R. Mcl. Wilson (Oxford: Clarendon Press, 1972), vol. 1, pp. 34–43. An extensive collection of evidence on the Carpocratians is to be found in Morton Smith, *Clement of Alexandria and a Secret Gospel of Mark* (Cambridge, MA: Harvard University Press, 1973).

[111] For an assessment of the principal fragments, from Clement of Alexandria and Irenaeus, see Layton, *The Gnostic Scriptures* (see endnote 106), pp. 417–444. A different account of Basilides's teaching, possibly reflecting the views of followers, is found in Hippolytus, *Refutation of All Heresies* 7.20.1–27.13. For a translation, see Foerster, *Gnosis* (see endnote 110), vol. 1, pp. 64–74.

[112] On Valentinus and contemporary philosophy, see G.C. Stead, "In Search of Valentinus," in *The Rediscovery of Gnosticism, I: The School of Valentinus* (see endnote 103), pp. 75–95, reprinted in Stead, *Substance and Illusion in the Christian Fathers* (London: Variorum, 1985). A comprehensive study of the Valentinian tradition is now available in Einar Thomassen, *Spiritual Seed: The Church of the Valentinians* (Boston: Brill, 2006).

[113] See Eusebius, *Eccles. Hist.* 4.11.1, "he flourished under Pius (c. 140–155) and remained until Anicetus (c. 155–166)."

[114] Cf. Tertullian, *Against the Valentinians* 4.

[115] See Layton, *The Gnostic Scriptures* (see endnote 106), pp. 229–248.

[116] For a critical edition and commentary, see Harold W. Attridge and George W. MacRae, "The Gospel of Truth," in *Nag Hammadi Codex I (The Jung Codex)*, ed. Harold W. Attridge, 2 vols., Nag Hammadi Studies 22–23 (Leiden: Brill, 1985), vol. 1, pp. 55–122 (text and translation), vol. 2, pp. 39–135 (notes).

[117] For the letter to Flora, see Layton, *The Gnostic Scriptures* (see endnote 106), pp. 306–315.

[118] Revisionist Valentinianism is found in another Nag Hammadi document, the *Tripartite Tractate.* The text and translation are in Harold W. Attridge and Elaine Pagels, "The Tripartite Tractate," in *Nag Hammadi Codex I (The Jung Codex)* (see endnote 116), vol. 1, pp. 159–337 (text and translation), vol. 2, pp. 217–497 (notes). A later dating of the work, and a different assessment of its relationship with Origen is offered by Einar Thomassen and Louis Painchaud, *Le Traité Tripartite (NH I,5) texte établi, introduit et commenté*, Bibliothèque copte de Nag Hammadi, Section "Textes" 19 (Québec: Presses de l'Université Laval, 1989).

[119] For the text, originally discovered at the end of the 19th century, see Karen L. King, *Gospel of*

Mary of Magdala: Jesus and the First Woman Apostle (Santa Rosa, CA: Polebridge, 2003).

[120] For a translation of the text, see Rodolphe Kasser, Marvin Meyer and Gregor Wurst, *The Gospel of Judas* (Washington, DC: National Geographic Society, 2006). For discussion of the discovery and its significance, see Herbert Krosney, *The Lost Gospel: The Quest for the Gospel of Judas Iscariot* (Washington, DC: National Geographic Society, 2006).

[121] The work, probably composed in Greek, survives in Coptic and Ethiopic. Both are translated into English in Schneemelcher, *New Testament Apocrypha* (see endnote 11), vol. 1, pp. 249–285.

[122] The anonymous homily is often associated with either Corinth or Rome. Only the association with 1 Clement suggests such a localization. For the Alexandrian possibility, see Koester, *Introduction to the New Testament* (see endnote 3), vol. 2, pp. 233–236.

[123] For reference to the work, see Justin Martyr, *1 Apology* 1.26, cited in Eusebius, *Eccles. Hist.* 4.11.10.

[124] On the debt to Philo among second-century theologians, see Henry Chadwick, "Philo and the Beginnings of Christian Philosophy," in *The Cambridge History of Later Greek and Early Medieval Philosophy*, ed. A.H. Armstrong (Cambridge: Cambridge University Press, 1967), pp. 137–192.

[125] See Justin Martyr, *Dialogue with Trypho* 61.2, for the notion, although not the technical Stoic terminology.

[126] Justin Martyr, *1 Apology* 46.2; *2 Apology* 13.3.

[127] Text and translation are in *Molly Whitaker, Tatian, Oratio ad Graecos and Fragments*, Oxford Early Christian Texts (Oxford: Clarendon Press, 1982). For a discussion of the critical problems, see Grant, *Greek Apologists of the Second Century* (Philadelphia: Westminster Press, 1988), pp. 112–132.

[128] On the original language, see William L. Petersen, "New Evidence for the Question of the Original Language of the Diatessaron," in *Studien zum Text und zur Ethik des Neuen Testaments*, ed. W. Schrage, BZNW 47 (Berlin: de Gruyter, 1986), pp. 325–343; on the Diatessaron's later influence, see Petersen's *The Diatessaron and Ephrem Syrus as Sources of Romanos the Melodist*, CSCO 475 (Louvain: Peeters, 1985).

[129] The Greek fragment was edited by Carl H. Kraeling, *A Greek Fragment of Tatian's Diatessaron from Dura*, Studies and Documents 3 (London: Christophers, 1935). For the *Diatessaron*'s place in the history of the New Testament text, see Bruce Metzger, *The Early Versions of the New Testament: Their Origin, Transmission, and Limitations* (Oxford: Clarendon Press, 1977), pp. 10–36.

[130] Reports on Tatian are found in Irenaeus, *Against Heresies* 3.23.8, and Eusebius, *Eccles. Hist.* 4.29.3. The latter reports on the *Diatessaron* at *Eccles. Hist.* 4.29.6.

[131] Irenaeus (*Against Heresies* 1.28.1) and Eusebius (*Eccles. Hist.* 4.29.1–2) associate the movement with Marcion and suggest that Tatian introduced doctrinal innovations. The general phenomenon of sexual asceticism is ably explored by Peter Brown, *The Body and Society: Men, Women, and Sexual Renunciation in Early Christianity* (New York: Columbia University Press, 1988).

[132] The translation is found in Robinson, *Nag Hammadi Library in English* (see endnote 68), pp. 199–207, and Layton, *Gnostic Scriptures* (see endnote 106), pp. 400–409.

[133] On Syrian asceticism, see Arthur Vöbus, *Celibacy: A Requirement for Admission to Baptism in the Early Syrian Church* (Stockholm: Almqvist, 1954); and *History of Asceticism in the Syrian Orient*, CSCO 184 (Louvain: Secrétariat CSCO, 1958).

[134] For a comprehensive review of the complex source-critical problems of the pseudo-Clementine literature, see F. Stanley Jones, "The Pseudo-Clementines: A History of Research," *SC* 2 (1982), pp. 1–34, 63–96. Selections of the texts, governed by an older theory of its development, may be found in Schneemelcher, *New Testament Apocrypha* (see endnote 11), vol. 2, pp. 483–541. See also Gerd Lüdemann, *Opposition to Paul* (see endnote 30), pp. 168–199.

[135] Eusebius, *Eccles. Hist.* 5.5.8.

[136] Eusebius (*Eccles. Hist.* 5.20.1–8, 5.23.3, 5.26) mentions various works. The *Demonstration of the Apostolic Teaching* survives in Armenian. See Joseph P. Smith, *St. Irenaeus, Proof of the Apostolic Preaching*, Ancient Christian Writers 16 (Westminster, MD: Newman, 1952).

[137] For a translation, see *Ante-Nicene Fathers* (see endnote 4), 1.315–578.

[138] He includes the Gospels, Pauline Epistles, Acts, Epistles of John and Revelation and 1 Peter. Unlike the Muratorian Canon, he also includes the Shepherd of Hermas, but does not recognize the Epistle to the Hebrews. Until the fourth century, East and West differed over Hebrews and Revelation. The East favored Hebrews; the West Revelation. Both were finally included.

[139] Irenaeus (*Against Heresies* 3.11.8) links John with the lion, Luke with the calf, Matthew with the man and Mark with the eagle. Later treatments will regularly reverse the beasts of Mark and John.

[140] Irenaeus, *Against Heresies* 1.10.102, 3.3.1, 4.26.2.

[141] The baptismal interrogation is attested for the early third century in Rome by Hippolytus, *Apostolic Tradition* 21–22. The practice was no doubt considerably older.

[142] Irenaeus, *Against Heresies* 1.9.4. On the formation of creeds, see J.N.D. Kelly, *Early Christian Creeds* (New York: McKay, 1960).

[143] Irenaeus, *Against Heresies* 3.18.1, 5.14.2, 5.21.2. For a sensitive assessment of the theology of Irenaeus, see Rowan Greer, *Broken Lights and Mended Lives: Theology and Common Life in the Early Church* (University Park: Pennsylvania State University Press, 1986).

[144] Irenaeus, *Against Heresies* 3.18.7.

[145] Origen (*Contra Celsum* 8.12.14) indicates that Celsus had lodged such a charge.

[146] Eusebius, *Eccles. Hist.* 5.28.10.

[147] Hippolytus, *Refutation of All Heresies* 9.7.1–10.12, and his *Against Noetus*.

[148] Hippolytus, *Refutation of All Heresies* 9.12.15–19; Eusebius, *Eccles. Hist.* 7.6.1, 7.26.1; Epiphanius, *Panarion* 72.1.

[149] George W. Butterworth, *Clement of Alexandria, The Exhortation to the Greeks, the Rich Man's Salvation and the Fragment of an address entitled To the Newly Baptized*, Loeb (Cambridge, MA: Harvard University Press, 1919, frequently reprinted). On Clement in general, see Eric Osborne, *Clement of Alexandria* (Cambridge: Cambridge University Press, 2005).

[150] For a translation, see *Ante-Nicene Fathers* (see endnote 4), 2.209–296; and Simon P. Wood, C.P., *Clement of Alexandria, Christ the Educator*, Fathers of the Church 23 (New York: Fathers of the Church, Inc., 1954).

[151] The work is incomplete. Book 7 promises a continuation, but Book 8 consists only of sketches. For a translation, see *Ante-Nicene Fathers* (see endnote 4), 2.299–567. Book 7, on Clement's notion of a Christian Gnostic, was edited and translated by F.J.A. Hort and J.B. Mayor, *Clement of Alexandria, Miscellanies, Book VII. The Greek text with introduction, translation and notes* (London/New York: Macmillan, 1902). Selections from *Stromateis* 3 and 7, on marriage and spiritual perfection, are in Henry Chadwick, *Alexandrian Christianity*, Library of Christian Classics (London/Philadelphia: SCM/Westminster Press, 1954), pp. 15–165.

[152] In general, see Timothy D. Barnes, *Tertullian: A Historical and Literary Study* (Oxford: Clarendon Press, 1971), valuable both for its critique of traditional views and for its constructive assessment of the man. On Tertullian's rhetoric, see Robert D. Sider, *Ancient Rhetoric and the Art of Tertullian* (New York: Oxford University Press, 1971). Translations are available in *Ante-Nicene Fathers* (see endnote 4), vols. 3 and 4. Barnes (*Tertullian*, pp. 286–291) provides fuller information on other texts and translations.

[153] For the former, see Tertullian, *Prescription of Heretics* 13; for the latter, see *Prescription of Heretics* 36.

[154] An example of a Valentinian effort to reinterpret belief in the resurrection is found in a Nag Hammadi tractate, *On the Resurrection*. See Robinson, *Nag Hammadi Library in English* (see endnote 68), pp. 52–57, and Layton, *Gnostic Scriptures* (see endnote 106), pp. 316–324.

[155] On Monarchianism, see above, on the early third-century doctrinal controversies in Rome.

[156] The outlines of Origen's life are given in Eusebius, *Eccles. Hist.* 6. A useful introduction to Origen is Joseph W. Trigg, *Origen: The Bible and Philosophy in the Third-Century Church* (Atlanta: John Knox Press, 1983). More technical is Henri Crouzel, *Origen: The Life and Thought of the First Great Theologian*, English translation (San Francisco: Harper & Row, 1989). For exploration

of topics of current scholarly interest, see Charles Kannengiesser and William L. Petersen, *Origen of Alexandria: His World and His Legacy*, Christianity and Judaism in Antiquity 1 (Notre Dame, IN: University of Notre Dame Press, 1988).

[157] Eusebius, *Eccles. Hist.* 6.8.1–3.

[158] Eusebius (*Eccles. Hist.* 6.21.3–4) discusses the visit to Julia Mammaea, which took place in 232.

[159] Henry Chadwick, *Origen: Contra Celsum, Translated with Introduction and Notes* (Cambridge: Cambridge University Press, 1965 [1953]). For a reconstruction of Celsus's work, see R. Joseph Hoffmann, *Celsus, On the True Doctrine: A Discourse Against the Christians* (Oxford: Oxford University Press, 1987).

[160] For the commentary on John, see *Ante-Nicene Fathers* (see endnote 4), 9.297–408. The commentary on Romans survives only in fragments.

[161] These works are available in Chadwick, *Alexandrian Christianity* (see endnote 151), pp. 171–429; and in Rowan A. Greer, *Origen, An Exhortation to Martyrdom, Prayer, First Principles: Book IV, Prologue to the Commentary on the Song of Songs, Homily XXVII on Numbers*, The Classics of Western Spirituality (New York: Paulist, 1979).

[162] G.W. Butterworth, *Origen, On First Principles*, repr., with an introduction by Henri de Lubac (New York: Harper & Row, 1966; repr., Gloucester, MA: Peter Smith, 1973 [1936]).

[163] On Origen's interpretative methods, expounded primarily in Book 4 of *On First Principles*, see Karen Jo Torjesen, *Hermeneutical Procedure and Theological Method in Origen's Exegesis* (Berlin and New York: de Gruyter, 1986). For the influence of his interpretation on later authors, see Joseph W. Trigg, *Biblical Interpretation*, Message of the Fathers of the Church 9 (Wilmington, DE: Glazier, 1988).

[164] Origin, *Homily on Jeremiah* 9.4; *On First Principles* 1.2.2.

[165] See, for example, the *Commentary on John* 10.37 (21), or *On Prayer* 15, where Origen insists that prayer is not directed to the Son, but to the Father.

[166] For a general discussion of these theological developments, see Aloys Grillmeier, S.J., *Christ in the Christian Tradition*, vol. 1: *From the Apostolic Age to Chalcedon (451)*, 2nd ed. (Atlanta: John Knox Press, 1975); and Jaroslav Pelikan, *The Christian Tradition: A History of the Development of Doctrine*, vol. 1: *The Emergence of the Catholic Tradition (100–600)* (Chicago and London: University of Chicago Press, 1971).

[167] For translations, see Robert T. Meyer, *St. Athanasius, The Life of Saint Antony*, Ancient Christian Writers (New York: Newman Press, 1950); and Robert C. Gregg, Athanasius, *The Life of Antony and the Letter to Marcellinus*, The Classics of Western Spirituality (New York: Paulist, 1980).

[168] For a review of the historical problems, see James H. Goehring, "The Origins of Monasticism," in *Eusebius, Judaism and Christianity* (see endnote 70).

[169] See *Ante-Nicene Fathers* (see endnote 4), 6.309–355; and Herbert Musurillo, S.J., *St. Methodius, The Symposium: A Treatise on Chastity*, Ancient Christian Writers 27 (New York: Newman, 1958).

[170] These works survive in fragments translated in *Ante-Nicene Fathers* (see endnote 4), 6.356–377.

[171] For this work, see particularly Adela Yarbro Collins, *Crisis and Catharsis: The Power of the Apocalypse* (Philadelphia: Westminster Press, 1984); and Elizabeth Schüssler Fiorenza, *The Book of Revelation: Justice and Judgment* (Philadelphia: Fortress Press, 1985).

[172] On Jewish apocalypticism, see especially John J. Collins, *The Apocalyptic Imagination: An Introduction to the Jewish Matrix of Christianity* (New York: Crossroad, 1984).

[173] This John, named at Revelation 1:9, is neither the son of Zebedee nor the author of the Fourth Gospel.

[174] See endnote 9.

[175] Hadrian did so in a letter to a proconsul, Minucius Fundanus, preserved in Justin, *1 Apology* 68, and Eusebius, *Eccles. Hist.* 4.9.1–3.

[176] See, for example, Tertullian, *Apology* 1.11–13.

[177] For a general survey of the persecution of Christians, see W.H.C. Frend, *Martyrdom and Persecution in the Early Church: A Study of a Conflict from the Maccabees to Donatus* (Oxford: Blackwell, 1965; repr., Grand Rapids, MI: Baker, 1981); and Marta Sordi, *The Christians and the Roman Empire* (Norman: University of Oklahoma Press, 1986).

[178] On the apologetic movement in general, see Robert M. Grant, *Greek Apologists of the Second Century* (Philadelphia: Westminster Press, 1988), with extensive bibliographies.

[179] See Eusebius, *Eccles. Hist.* 4.3.2

[180] On Quadratus and Aristides, see Grant, *Greek Apologists* (see endnote 178), pp. 35–39. The whole of Aristides's oration survives only in Syriac, published by J.R. Harris, *The Apology of Aristides*, Texts and Studies 1.1 (Cambridge: Cambridge University Press, 1893). There are Greek fragments: see J. van Haelst, *Catalogue des papyrus littéraires juifs et chrétiens* (Paris: Sorbonne, 1976), nos. 623 and 624; and H.J. M. Milne, "A New Fragment of the Apology of Aristides," *JTS* 25 (1923–1924), pp. 73–77.

[181] Eusebius (*Eccles. Hist.* 4.14.10–15.1) dates the event to 166–167, apparently in error. Grant (*Augustus to Constantine* [San Francisco: HarperSanFrancisco, 1990], pp. 106–107) discusses the date, with reference to other treatments.

[182] For the *Martyrdom of Polycarp*, see Ehrman, *Apostolic Fathers* (see endnote 15), vol. 1, pp. 357–401.

[183] Eusebius (*Eccles. Hist.* 4.18.1–3) mentions two apologies and the manuscripts do contain two separate works, although the second is now usually viewed as an appendix to the first. Translations are in the collection issued in two forms in Great Britain and the U.S.: *The Ante-Nicene Christian Library*, 24 vols. (Edinburgh: T & T Clark, 1868–1872); and *Ante-Nicene Fathers* (see endnote 4) 1.159–193. The American edition will be regularly cited here. On the date of Justin's apologies, see Grant, *Greek Apologists* (see endnote 178), p. 53.

[184] For a survey of Greco-Roman attitudes, see Robert L. Wilken, *The Christians as the Romans Saw Them* (New Haven, CT: Yale University Press, 1984).

[185] Variations on these charges occur frequently. They appear, for instance, in connection with the martyrs of Lyons, according to Eusebius, *Eccles. Hist.* 5.1.1–63, citing a report by the churches of Lyons and Vienne sent to Christians in the provinces of Asia and Phrygia.

[186] See, for example, Justin Martyr, *1 Apology* 27.

[187] On this traditional argument, see Arthur J. Droge, *Homer or Moses: Early Christian Interpretations of the History of Culture*, Hermeneutische Untersuchungen zur Theologie 26 (Tübingen: Mohr Siebeck, 1988).

[188] For a translation, see Stevenson, *A New Eusebius* (see endnote 5), pp. 28–30; and Herbert Musurillo, *The Acts of the Christian Martyrs* (Oxford: Clarendon Press, 1972), pp. 42–61.

[189] Gaius, in an anti-Montanist writing, according to Eusebius, *Eccles. Hist.* 1.25.7.

[190] The Vatican trophy competes with a site on the Via Appia that was venerated in the third century as the burial place of the apostles. For descriptions and bibliographies, see Snyder, *Ante Pacem* (see endnote 5), pp. 82–114. On the historical problems, see Henry Chadwick, "St. Peter and St. Paul in Rome: The Problem of the Memoria Apostolorum ad Catacumbas," *JTS* 8 (1957), pp. 31–52, reprinted in his *History and Thought of the Early Church* (London: Variorum, 1982).

[191] Lucian's account is found in his "Passing of Peregrinus," in *Lucian V*, Loeb (Cambridge, MA: Harvard University Press, 1926). Marcus Aurelius (*Meditations* 11.3) may have had the likes of Peregrinus in mind when he commented disdainfully on the stubbornness and histrionic display of Christian martyrs.

[192] Eusebius, *Eccles. Hist.* 5.5.1–7. Apolinaris's claim that the legion was thereby named "thundering" is mistaken. The name "Fulminata" occurs at least a century earlier.

[193] Recorded in Eusebius, *Eccles. Hist.* 4.26.12–14.

[194] In Eusebius, *Eccles. Hist.* 4.26.7–11. Tertullian (*Apology* 5.5–8) echoes the claim about bad emperors.

[195] Eusebius, *Eccles. Hist.* 5.1.1–63.

[196] For the account of the martyrdom, see Musurillo, *The Acts of the Christian Martyrs* (see endnote 188), pp. 86–89.

[197] Ibid., pp. 106–131.

[198] Eusebius, *Eccles. Hist.* 6.34.1. For a defense of the historicity of the report, see Sordi, *Christians and the Roman Empire* (see endnote 177), pp. 96–99.

[199] For examples, see Stevenson, *A New Eusebius* (see endnote 5), p. 228.

[200] Eusebius (*Eccles. Hist.* 7.13.1) preserves the text of Gallienus's letter to the Christian bishops.

[201] For the general political situation and the occasion of the persecution, see Timothy D. Barnes, *Constantine and Eusebius* (Cambridge, MA: Harvard University Press, 1981).

[202] Divergent descriptions of the sign are found in Lactantius, *On the Deaths of Persecutors* 44.5, and Eusebius, *Life of Constantine* 1.26–31.

[203] Two versions are extant, Eusebius, *Eccles. Hist.* 10.5.1–14, in Greek, and Lactantius, *On the Deaths of Persecutors* 48, in Latin.

[204] For an insightful assessment of the debt of Eusebius to Origen, see Charles Kannengiesser, "Eusebius of Caesarea, Origenist," in *Eusebius, Judaism and Christianity* (see endnote 70).

[205] On this massive undertaking, see Alden A. Mosshammer, *The Chronicle of Eusebius and Greek Chronographic Tradition* (Lewisburg, PA: Bucknell University Press, 1979); and William Adler, "Eusebius' Chronicle and Its Legacy," in *Eusebius, Judaism and Christianity* (see endnote 70).

[206] Various hypotheses have been advanced for the process of composition of the work. See Barnes, *Constantine and Eusebius* (see endnote 201), pp. 126–147. On Eusebius and his work, see also Robert M. Grant, *Eusebius as Church Historian* (Oxford: Clarendon Press, 1980).

[207] For a translation, see Lawlor and Oulton *Eusebius, Bishop of Caesarea* (see endnote 6).

[208] Eusebius, *Eccles. Hist.* 10.9.7–8; translation in *The Ecclesiastical History*, vol. 2 (see endnote 6), p. 479.

VI. Judaism to the Mishnah: 135–220 C.E.

[1] Edward Gibbon, *The Decline and Fall of the Roman Empire*, abridged ed., ed. D.M. Low (New York: Harcourt Brace, 1960), "Prologue," chapter 3, p. 1.

[2] Eusebius, *Eccles. Hist.* 4.6.2. The classic discussion is J. Rendel Harris, "Hadrian's Decree of Expulsion of the Jews from Jerusalem," HTR 19 (1926), pp. 199–206.

[3] Michael Avi-Yonah, *The Jews of Palestine: A Political History from the Bar Kokhba War to the Arab Conquest* (Oxford: Blackwell, 1976), pp. 79–81; and Joshua Schwartz, *Jewish Settlement in Jerusalem After the Bar Kochba War* (Jerusalem: Magnes Press, 1986), pp. 183–186 and 245–246 (in Hebrew).

[4] This impression is not disputed by Schwartz, ibid. See the graph of the number of settlements in Avi-Yonah, Jews of Palestine (see endnote 3), p. 20. See further Ze'ev Safrai, "The Bar-Kokhva Revolt and Its Effect on Settlement," and Joshua Schwartz, "Judaea in the Wake of the Bar-Kokhva Revolt," in *The Bar-Kokhva Revolt: A New Approach*, eds. Aharon Oppenheimer and Uriel Rappaport (Jerusalem: Yad Izhak ben Zvi, 1984), pp. 182–214 and 215–223 (in Hebrew).

[5] Aharon Oppenheimer, "Jewish Lydda in the Roman Era," *HUCA* 59 (1988), pp. 115–136, esp. p. 130.

[6] JT *Sanhedrin* 19a and BT *Berakhot* 63a-b. See Gedaliah Alon, *The Jews in Their Land in the Talmudic Age*, 2 vols., English ed. (Jerusalem: Magnes Press, 1980–1984), vol. 2, pp. 670–672.

[7] Sacha Stern, *Calendar and Community: A History of the Jewish Calendar* (Oxford: Oxford University Press, 2001). In general, see Isaiah M. Gafni, *Land, Center and Diaspora: Jewish Constructs in Late Antiquity*, JSP Supplement Series 21 (Sheffield, UK: Sheffield Academic Press, 1997).

[8] Emil Schürer, *The History of the Jewish People in the Age of Jesus Christ*, 4 vols., eds. Geza Vermes et al. (Edinburgh: T & T Clark, 1979), vol. 2, pp. 550–552; and John J. Collins, *The Scepter and the Star: The Messiahs of the Dead Sea Scrolls* (New York: Doubleday, 1995).

[9] BT *Sukkah* 52a.

[10]Joseph Heinemann, "The Messiah of Ephraim and the Premature Exodus of the Tribe of Ephraim," *HTR* 68 (1975), pp. 1–15.

[11] Tosefta *Avodah Zarah* 4(5).3–6; p. 466, in the edition by M.S. Zuckermandel.

[12] Isaiah Gafni, "The Status of Eretz Israel in Reality and in Jewish Consciousness Following the Bar-Kokhva Uprising," in *Bar-Kokhva Revolt* (see endnote 4), pp. 224–232.

[13] See Jonathan Goldstein's commentary on 2 Maccabees 6 and 7 in the Anchor Bible (Garden City, NY: Doubleday, 1983); *Die Entstehung der judischen Martyrologie*, ed. J.W. van Henten (Leiden: Brill, 1989). For a collection of ancient Jewish martyr texts, see Jan Willem van Henten and Friedrich Avemarie, *Martyrdom and Noble Death: Selected Texts from Graeco-Roman, Jewish, and Christian Antiquity* (London: Routledge, 2002). For a survey of Jewish martyrdom through the ages, see Shmuel Shepkaru, *Jewish Martyrs in the Pagan and Christian Worlds* (Cambridge: Cambridge University Press, 2006).

[14] *Apion* 1.42–45; cf. 1.191 (an excerpt from Hecateus or pseudo-Hecateus). See also 4 Maccabees.

[15] Saul Lieberman, "The Persecution of the Religion of Israel," *Salo Baron Jubilee Volume*, 3 vols. (New York: American Academy for Jewish Research, 1974), vol. 3, pp. 213–245 (in Hebrew); Peter Schäfer, *Der Bar Kokhba Aufstand* (Tübingen: Mohr Siebeck, 1981), chapter 7.

[16] BT *Sanhedrin* 74a; Moshe D. Herr, "Persecutions and Martyrdom in Hadrian's Days," *Scripta Hierosolymitana* 23 (1973), pp. 85–125.

[17] 1 Maccabees 1:15; Tosefta *Shabbat* 15:9, critical edition and commentary by Saul Lieberman, p. 71, and parallels.

[18] Shaye J.D. Cohen, *Why Aren't Jewish Women Circumcised?: Gender and Covenant in Judaism* (Berkeley: University of California Press, 2005), pp. 39–40 and 46.

[19] Amnon Linder, *The Jews in Roman Imperial Legislation* (Detroit: Wayne State University Press, 1987), pp. 99–102, no. 1; and Raanan Boustan, "Negotiating Difference: Genital Mutilation in Roman Slave Law and the History of the Bar Kokhba Revolt," in *The Bar Kokhba War Reconsidered: New Perspectives on the Second Jewish Revolt Against Rome*, ed. Peter Schäfer (Tübingen: Mohr Siebeck, 2003), pp. 71–91.

[20] See Appian, in Menahem Stern, *Greek and Latin Authors on Jews and Judaism*, 3 vols. (Jerusalem: Israel Academy of Sciences, 1974–1984) vol. 2, pp. 179–181, no. 343.

[21] Ammianus Marcellinus in *Greek and Latin Authors* (see endnote 20), vol. 2, pp. 605–607, no. 506.

[22] Galen, in *Greek and Latin Authors* (see endnote 20), vol. 2, pp. 306–328, nos. 376–394; Celsus, ibid., vol. 2, pp. 224–305, no. 375.

[23] Numenius of Apamea, in *Greek and Latin Authors* (see endnote 20), vol. 2, pp. 209–211, no. 363.

[24] JT *Ma'aserot* 3:8 50d; BT *Bava Mezia* 83b-84a; Pesikta de Rab Kahana, critical edition by Mandelbaum, p. 195. The essential truthfulness of the story is not doubted by Avi-Yonah, *Jews of Palestine* (see endnote 3), p. 71, or Alon, *Jews in Their Land* (see endnote 6), pp. 540–541. Shamma Friedman has persuasively argued that the Babylonian version of the story is secondary to the versions of the Yerushalmi and the Pesikta, but whether these versions are "true" is still in doubt. See Friedman, "On the Historical *aggada* in the Babylonian Talmud," *Memorial Volume for Saul Lieberman* (Jerusalem: Lieberman Institute of Talmudic Research, 1989), pp. 1–46, esp. pp. 4–14.

[25] I am not (yet) convinced by Seth Schwartz that Judaism "shattered" after the defeats of 70 and 135 C.E.; nor am I convinced by Martin Goodman that the Roman imperial government adopted a decidedly anti-Jewish policy after 70 C.E. (for the purpose of legitimating the rise of the Flavian house). See Schwartz, *Imperialism and Jewish Society, 200 B.C.E. to 640 C.E.* (Princeton, NJ: Princeton University Press, 2001); and Goodman, *Rome and Jerusalem: The Clash of Ancient Civilizations* (New York: Knopf, 2008).

[26] *Historia Augusta,* "Life of Septimius Severus," in *Greek and Latin Authors* (see endnote 20), vol. 2, p. 625, no. 515.

[27] For discussion, see Anthony R. Birley, *Septimius Severus the African Emperor,* 2nd ed. (New Haven, CT: Yale University Press, 1988), p. 135 with n. 12; Stern's discussion of "Life of Septimius Severus" (see endnote 26), pp. 623–625. For the chronology (195 C.E.), I follow Birley.

[28] Jean B. Frey, *Corpus Inscriptionum Judaicarum,* 2 vols. (Rome: Pontificio Istituto di archeologia cristiana, 1936–1952), vol. 2, pp. 157–159, no. 972.

[29] The passage from Jerome is quoted in Stern's commentary on the "Life of Septimius Severus" (see endnote 26), p. 624.

[30] Ibid., no. 514.

[31] Linder, *Jews in Roman Imperial Legislation* (see endnote 19), pp. 103–107, no. 2.

[32] Gedaliah Alon, "The 'Strategoi' in the Palestinian Cities During the Roman Epoch," in *Jews, Judaism, and the Classical World* (Jerusalem: Magnes Press, 1977), pp. 458–475.

[33] Jay Braverman, *Jerome's Commentary on Daniel* (Washington, DC: CBA, 1978), p. 120. The passage is also quoted by Stern in his commentary (see endnote 26). The identification of Severus with Septimius Severus and of Antoninus with Caracalla is beyond doubt; see Linder, *Jews in Roman Imperial Legislation* (see endnote 19), pp. 103–107, no. 2, which also refers to Severus and Antoninus. Braverman's discussion (pp. 120–121, esp. p. 121, n. 5) is wrong. Jerome also quotes other Jews who argue that the verse refers to the emperor Julian.

[34] Albert L. Baumgarten, "The Akiban Opposition," *HUCA* 50 (1979), pp. 179–197; and "Rabbi Judah I and His Opponents," *JSJ* 12 (1981), pp. 135–172.

[35] David Weiss Halivni, "The Reception Accorded to Rabbi Judah's Mishnah," in *Jewish and Christian Self-Definition,* vol. 2: *Aspects of Judaism in the Greco-Roman Period,* eds. A.L. Baumgarten et al. (Philadelphia: Fortress Press, 1981), pp. 204–212.

[36] Alon, "Those Appointed for Money," in *Jews, Judaism* (see endnote 32), pp. 374–435.

[37] These reasons are explored by Martin Goodman, "The Roman State and the Jewish Patriarch in the Third Century," in *The Galilee in Late Antiquity,* ed. Lee I.A. Levine (New York: JTSem, 1992), pp. 127–139.

[38] Harry J. Leon, *The Jews of Ancient Rome* (Philadelphia: JPS, 1960); Leonard Rutgers, *The Jews in Late Ancient Rome* (Leiden: Brill, 1995); and *The Hidden Heritage of Diaspora Judaism* (Leuven: Peeters, 1998); David Noy, *Jewish Inscriptions of Western Europe, vol. 2: The City of Rome* (Cambridge: Cambridge University Press, 1995); and Silvia Cappelletti, *The Jewish Community of Rome* (Leiden: Brill, 2006).

[39] Eric M. Meyers and A. Thomas Kraabel, "Archaeology, Iconography, and Nonliterary Written Remains," in *Early Judaism and Its Modern Interpreters,* eds. Robert Kraft and George W.E. Nickelsburg (Atlanta: Scholars Press, 1986), pp. 175–210, esp. pp. 184–185; Paul Trebilco, *Jewish Communities in Asia Minor* (Cambridge: Cambridge University Press, 1991). The chronology of the Sardis synagogue is disputed.

[40] Joyce Reynolds and Robert Tannenbaum, *Jews and God-Fearers at Aphrodisias* (Cambridge, UK: Cambridge Philological Society, 1987). On the date of the inscription (actually two separate inscriptions), see Walter Ameling, *Inscriptiones Judaicae Orientis, II Kleinasien,* Texte und Studien zum antiken Judentum 99 (Tübingen: Mohr Siebeck, 2004), no. 14, pp. 71–112, esp. pp. 78–82.

[41] *Diaspora Jews and Judaism: Essays in Honor of, and in Dialogue with, A. Thomas Kraabel,* eds. J. Andrew Overman and Robert S. MacLennan (Atlanta: Scholars Press, 1992).

[42] Shaye J.D. Cohen, "Epigraphical Rabbis," *JQR* 72 (1981), pp. 1–17, esp. pp. 15–16; Arye Edrei and Doron Mendels, "A Split Jewish Diaspora: Its Dramatic Consequences," *JSP* 16 (2007), pp. 91–137. Tannenbaum (*Jews and God-Fearers* [see endnote 40]) attempts to explain the Aphrodisias inscription in accordance with rabbinic norms, but the attempt is not successful.

[43] Bernard J. Bamberger, *Proselytism in the Talmudic Period* (Cincinnati: Hebrew Union College, 1939; repr. New York: Ktav, 1968), pp. 238–243; Saul Lieberman, *Greek in Jewish Palestine* (New York: JTSem, 1942; repr. 1965), pp. 17–20.

[44] Linder, *Jews in Roman Imperial Legislation* (see endnote 19), pp. 402–411, no. 66.

[45] See Jacob Neusner, *History of the Jews in Babylonia*, vol. 1 (Leiden: Brill, 1965).

[46] J. Kaplan, "Excavations at Jaffa," *IEJ* 12 (1962), pp. 149–150.

[47] For evidence and discussion, see Shaye J.D. Cohen, "The Place of the Rabbi in the Jewish Society of the Second Century," in *Galilee in Late Antiquity* (see endnote 37); and *Cambridge History of Judaism*, vol. 3: *The Early Roman Period*, eds. William Horbury et al. (Cambridge: Cambridge University Press, 1999), pp. 922–990.

[48] JT *Sotah* 7:1 21b.

[49] Mishnah *Demai* 2:2–3. I do not accept the emendation suggested by Jacob N. Epstein (*Introduction to the Text of the Mishnah* [Jerusalem: Magnes Press, 1964], p. 1210) and accepted by Chaim Rabin (*Qumran Studies* [Oxford: Clarendon Press, 1957; repr. New York: Schocken, 1975], p. 12, n. 9).

[50] On this transformation, see Alon, *Jews, Judaism* (see endnote 32), pp. 190–234; and Aharon Oppenheimer, *The 'Am Ha-Aretz: A Study in the Social History of the Jewish People in the Hellenistic-Roman Period* (Leiden: Brill, 1977), passim.

[51] Tosefta *Berakhot* 6:18, ed. Saul Lieberman, p. 38.

[52] *Fathers According to Rabbi Nathan* A 21 (37b in Schechter's edition); compare the prayer of Nehunyah ben Haqqanah in Mishnah *Berakhot* 4:2 with the amplifications in the Talmudim.

[53] The evidence for hatred between the rabbis and the *'amme ha'aretz* derives exclusively from the Babylonian Talmud (the major passage is BT *Pesahim* 49a–b) and seems not to reflect the social conditions of Palestine in the second and early third centuries. See Cohen, "The Place of the Rabbi" (see endnote 47). There was disdain but not hatred.

[54] For their observance of the Sabbath and priestly offerings, see Tosefta *Demai* 5:2, ed. Saul Lieberman, p. 85. For their observance of the sabbatical year, see Tosefta *Eruvin* 5:10, ed. Lieberman, p. 113. In general, see Mishnah *Bekhorot* 4:10.

[55] Horvat Ethri is a Jewish settlement of the Bar-Kokhba period that had at its center a large public building; it is reasonable to assume that synagogal functions (communal prayer and Torah study) will have taken place there, but the building is not yet a synagogue—it has none of the distinctive architectural elements that will come to characterize synagogues in the following centuries. See Boaz Zissu, "Village Razed, Rebel Beheaded: How Hadrian Suppressed the Second Jewish Revolt at Horvat 'Ethri," *BAR*, September/October 2007. Such public buildings have been discovered elsewhere, but they, too, are not synagogues. It used to be argued that the "monumental Galilean synagogues," the best known of which is at Capernaum, date from the second century C.E., but there is now growing consensus that they date from the fourth century at the earliest. See, for example, the extended discussion in chapter six of Lee I. Levine, *The Ancient Synagogue: The First Thousand Years*, rev. ed. (New Haven, CT: Yale University Press, 2005).

[56] *Avot* 3:10.

[57] Perhaps the most convenient collection of the material in English remains R. Travers Herford, *Christianity in Talmud and Midrash* (London: Williams and Norgate, 1903).

[58] On apostates, see the brief discussion by Lawrence Schiffman, *Who Was a Jew?* (New York: Ktav, 1985), pp. 41–49. On the "way of outsiders," see Mishnah *Megillah* 4:8; on "way of the Amorite," see Tosefta *Shabbat*, chapter 6.

[59] A good place to begin work on this topic is Reuven Kimelman, "*Birkat Ha-Minim* and the Lack of Evidence for an Anti-Christian Jewish Prayer in Late Antiquity," in *Jewish and Christian Self-Definition* (see endnote 35), vol. 2, pp. 226–244. By the third century there is good evidence for real contact and discussion between rabbis and (gentile) Christians, but that is outside the purview of this chapter. See the essays in *The Ways That Never Parted*, eds. Adam H. Becker and Annette Y. Reed (Minneapolis: Fortress Press, 2007; original edition Mohr Siebeck, 2003). I am not convinced by either the approach or the conclusions of *Border Lines* by Daniel Boyarin (Philadelphia: University of Pennsylvania Press, 2004).

[60] For an excellent account of the patriarchate and its history, see Lee I. Levine, "The Jewish Patriarch (*Nasi*) in Third Century Palestine," *ANRW* 19.2 (1979), pp. 649–688 and his follow-up article in *JJS* 47 (1996), pp. 1–32. For a full collection of material, see Martin Jacobs, *Die Institution des jüdischen Patriarchen* (Tübingen: Mohr Siebeck, 1995).

[61] Avi-Yonah, *The Jews of Palestine* (see endnote 3), pp. 39–42. Perhaps "Antoninus" had many identities, since rabbinic storytelling often combines several different historical personages to create a single archetype. The full collection of material is found in Samuel Krauss, *Antoninus und Rabbi* (Frankfurt: Sänger & Friedberg, 1910); see also Shaye J.D. Cohen, "The Conversion of Antoninus," *The Yerushalmi in Its Greco-Roman Context*, ed. Peter Schäfer (Tübingen: Mohr Siebeck, 1998), pp. 141–171.

[62] On Simonias, see JT *Yevamot* 12:7 13a = *Genesis Rabbah* 81:2, ed. Theodor-Albeck, p. 969; cf. JT *Hagigah* 1:7 76c and JT *Shevi'it* 6:1 36d. On Rabbi Romanus, see JT *Yevamot* 8:2 9b.

[63] According to one tradition, Rabban Gamaliel removed from office the "head" of Gader (Gezer?), but the Talmudim also record a conflicting tradition and the entire matter is very obscure. See JT *Rosh Hashanah* 1:6 57b = BT *Rosh Hashanah* 22a. In any case, Gamaliel is not said to have appointed anyone to a communal position.

[64] Shaye J.D. Cohen, "Patriarchs and Scholarchs," *PAAJR* 48 (1981), pp. 57–85 (with bibliography).

[65] For evidence and details, see Cohen, "The Place of the Rabbi" (see endnote 47).

[66] *Fathers According to Rabbi Nathan* A 6 and B 12–13, ed. Schechter, pp. 14b–17a, has a series of paradigmatic rags-to-riches stories meant to inspire students of Torah. They are not reliable "biographies."

[67] Prejudice against goatherds and shepherds, goats and sheep: Mishnah *Demai* 2:3 (see endnote 49); Mishnah *Bava Kamma* 7:7; Tosefta *Bava Kamma* 8:10–15, Lieberman edition, pp. 38–40; Tosefta *Bava Mezia* 2:33, Lieberman edition, p. 72; Tosefta *Sanhedrin* 5:5, M.S. Zuckermandel edition, p. 423; Mishnah *Rosh Hashanah* 1:8. By the third century, rabbinic views had shifted; Rabbi Yohanan preferred sheep to land (BT *Hullin* 84a).

[68] For evidence and discussion, see Cohen, "The Place of the Rabbi" (see endnote 47).

[69] On tension between the well-to-do and the rabbis, and appointment to salaried posts, see Gedaliah Alon, "Ga'on, Ge'im," and "Those Appointed for Money," both in *Jews, Judaism* (see endnote 32); Lee I. Levine, *The Rabbinic Class of Roman Palestine*, English ed. (Jerusalem: Yad Izhak ben Zvi, 1989), pp. 167–176. On distribution of poor tithe, see JT *Pe'ah* 8:8 21a. On amoraic testimonies about organized charity, see Levine, *Rabbinic Class*, pp. 162–167. In general, see pp. 139–151.

[70] On Judah and the cities, see Adolph Büchler, "The Patriarch Rabbi Judah I and the Graeco-Roman Cities of Palestine," in *Studies in Jewish History*, ed. I. Brodie and J. Rabbinowitz (Oxford: Oxford University Press, 1956), pp. 179–244; and Lee I. Levine, *Caesarea Under Roman Rule* (Leiden: Brill, 1975), pp. 64–68. On urbanization, see Levine, *The Rabbinic Class* (see endnote 69), pp. 25–33.

[71] The two standard English translations are by Herbert Danby (Oxford: Oxford University Press, 1933; frequently reprinted) and Jacob Neusner (New Haven, CT: Yale University Press, 1988).

[72] See, for example, Mishnah: *Shabbat* 7:1–2; *Kiddushin* 3:12; *Bava Kamma* 1:1; *Kelim* 1:5–9.

[73] The Mishnah says virtually nothing about the rabbinate: How does one become a rabbi, what does it mean to be a rabbi, what is the authority of a rabbi, etc.?

[74] Regular public prayer is discussed only briefly in tractates *Berakhot* and *Megillah*.

[75] I fully agree with Jacob Neusner that the Mishnah is not a law book, but Neusner has not convinced me that it is a book of philosophy. Of course, the Mishnah has a philosophy, or a worldview, inherent in its rulings and its mode of discourse, just as all works of literature, or for that matter, all creations of the human intellect, have an inherent philosophy, but this fact does not mean that the Mishnah was intended by its creators to be a work of philosophy (unlike the treatises of Plato and Aristotle, which clearly were intended by their creators to be works of philosophy). Neusner first propounded his thesis in *Judaism: The Evidence of the Mishnah*

(Chicago: University of Chicago Press, 1981), and has expanded on it in numerous later publications. Although I do not accept Neusner's "philosophy" thesis, I follow him in other points as the following paragraphs show.

[76] The evidence is assembled by Jacob N. Epstein, *Introduction to Tannaitic Literature* (Jerusalem: Magnes Press, 1957), p. 200 (in Hebrew).

[77] Of course there may have been implicit rules which were known to the Mishnah's readers and therefore did not need to be spelled out. The Talmudim and later rabbinic commentators, who read the Mishnah as a law book, invested great energy in determining those rules.

[78] See discussion in Catherine Hezser, *The Social Structure of the Rabbinic Movement in Roman Palestine* (Tübingen: Mohr Siebeck, 1997).

[79] David W. Halivni, *Midrash, Mishnah and Gemara* (Cambridge, MA: Harvard University Press, 1986).

VII. The World of the Talmud: From the Mishnah to the Arab Conquest

[1] For this shift, see Isaiah Gafni, *Land, Center and Diaspora: Jewish Constructs in Late Antiquity* (Sheffield, UK: Sheffield Academic Press, 1997), pp. 96–117; and "How Babylonia Became 'Zion': Shifting Identities in Late Antiquity," in *Jewish Identities in Antiquity: Studies in Memory of Menahem Stern,* eds. Lee I. Levine and D.R. Schwartz, Texts and Studies in Ancient Judaism (Tübingen: Mohr Siebeck, 2009), pp. 333–348.

[2] Population estimates for Palestine in late antiquity, as for much of the ancient world, are tenuous at best. The Jewish population of Roman Palestine has been estimated to have been as high as five to six million (see Jean Juster, *Les Juifs dans l'Empire Romain* [Paris: Librairie Paul Geuthner, 1914], vol. 1, pp. 209–212) and as little as half a million (see C.C. McCown, "The Density of Population in Ancient Palestine," *JBL* 66 [1947], pp. 425–436). For another estimate, based on a calculation of maximum agricultural yields for the land, see Magen Broshi, "The Population of Western Palestine in the Roman-Byzantine Period," *BASOR* 236 (1979), pp. 1–10 (Broshi's notes include a useful bibliography of demographic studies of Roman Palestine). The closest to a scholarly consensus on the population of the area in the late third century is somewhere between 1.1 and 1.5 million, with approximately one-half to two-thirds of a million Jews (see *The History of Eretz Israel, The Roman Byzantine Period,* ed. Moshe D. Herr [Jerusalem: Keter, 1985], p. 109 [in Hebrew]); Herr claims that the early third century, under the Severans, is probably the last stage during which Jews represented an outright majority of the total population. For a recent summary of the degree, stages and methodological issues involved in determining the extent of a possible demographic decline of the Jewish population during the period under discussion, see David Goodblatt, "The Political and Social History of the Jewish Community in the Land of Israel, c. 235–638," in *The Cambridge History of Judaism,* vol. 4, ed. Steven T. Katz (Cambridge: Cambridge University Press, 2006), pp. 405–410. (On population, see also endnotes 19 and 38 in Chapter I.)

[3] See E. Mary Smallwood, *The Jews Under Roman Rule* (Leiden: Brill, 1981), pp. 463–464.

[4] See Michael Avi-Yonah, *The Jews under Roman and Byzantine Rule* (Jerusalem: Magnes Press, 1984), p. 75; Gedaliah Alon, *The Jews in Their Land in the Talmudic Age* (Jerusalem: Magnes Press, 1984), vol. 2, pp. 562–565, 742–746. For Samaritans in the Roman-Byzantine period, see Alan D. Crown, *The Samaritans* (Tübingen: Mohr Siebeck, 1989), pp. 55–81; Menahem Mor, *From Samaria to Shechem: The Samaritan Community in Antiquity* (Jerusalem: Zalman Shazar Center, 2003), pp. 184–234 (in Hebrew); Yitzhak Magen, "The Samaritans in the Roman-Byzantine Period"; and "The Areas of Samaritan Settlement in the Roman-Byzantine Period," both in *The Samaritans,* eds. Ephraim Stern and Hanan Eshel (Jerusalem: Yad Ben-Zvi Press, 2002), pp. 213–271 (in Hebrew).

[5] The concentration of Christians primarily in the cities (Greek *poleis*) of Roman Palestine is apparent from the list of bishops who participated in the Council of Nicaea; see Louis Félix Abel, *Geographie de la Palestine* (Paris: Librairie Lecoffre, 1938), vol. 2, p. 198. One interesting "controlled" method for measuring the growth of the Palestinian Christian community is through a comparison of Eusebius's *Onomasticon* in the original Greek with the Latin

translation of Jerome completed a century later. Whereas Eusebius mentions only a few villages as populated primarily by Christians, the number rises dramatically in Jerome's rendition.

[6] See Yaron Dan, "Eretz Israel in the 5th and 6th Centuries," in *Eretz Israel from the Destruction of the Second Temple to the Muslim Conquest*, eds. Zvi Baras et al. (Jerusalem: Yad Ben-Zvi, 1982), vol. 1, p. 265 (in Hebrew); Avi-Yonah, *Jews Under Roman and Byzantine Rule* (see endnote 4), p. 241. See also Yoram Tsafrir, "Some Notes on the Settlement and Demography of Palestine in the Byzantine Period: The Archaeological Evidence," in *Retrieving the Past: Essays on Archaeological Research and Methodology in Honor of Gus W. Van Beek*, ed. Joe D. Seger (Winona Lake, IN: Eisenbrauns, 1996), pp. 269–283.

[7] See Goodblatt, "Political and Social History" (see endnote 2), pp. 409–410.

[8] See Reuven Kimelman, "*Birkat Ha-Minim* and the Lack of Evidence for an Anti-Christian Jewish Prayer in Late Antiquity," in *Jewish and Christian Self-Definition*, vol. 2: *Aspects of Judaism in the Graeco-Roman Period*, eds. A.L. Baumgarten et al. (Philadelphia: Fortress Press, 1981), pp. 226–244. For references to *minim* and *minuth* in early rabbinic literature, see also Martin Goodman, "The Function of *Minim* in Early Rabbinic Judaism," in *Judaism in the Roman World*, ed. Martin Goodman (Leiden/Boston: Brill, 2007), pp. 163–173.

[9] See Steven T. Katz, "The Rabbinic Response to Christianity," in *Cambridge History of Judaism*, vol. 4 (see endnote 2), pp. 259–298.

[10] This point is well taken by Adiel Schremer, "The Christianization of the Roman Empire and Rabbinic Literature," in *Jewish Identities in Antiquity* (see endnote 1), pp. 349–366.

[11] BT *Sanhedrin* 97a.

[12] *Antiquities* 18:310–379 (on Asineus and Anileus); 20:17–96 (on conversion of the royal family of Adiabene).

[13] See Jacob Neusner's comments, "Jews and Judaism Under Iranian Rule: Bibliographical Reflections," *History of Religions* 8 (1968), p. 164; also *Method and Meaning in Ancient Judaism* (Missoula, MT: Scholars Press, 1979), p. 6, and numerous other places; compare David M. Goodblatt, "Towards the Rehabilitation of Talmudic History," in *History of Judaism: The Next Ten Years*, ed. Baruch Bokser (Chico, CA: Scholars Press, 1980), p. 32.

[14] See Ramsay MacMullen, *Roman Government's Response to Crisis A.D. 235–337* (New Haven, CT: Yale University Press, 1976).

[15] See Doron Bar, "The Third Century Crisis in the Roman Empire and Its Relevance to Palestine During the Late Roman Period," *Zion* 66 (2001), pp. 143–170 (in Hebrew).

[16] See Smallwood, *Jews under Roman Rule* (see endnote 3), pp. 487–506; Alon, *Jews in Their Land* (see endnote 4), vol. 2, pp. 681–704.

[17] To be sure, some historians project the two centuries following the Bar-Kokhba war as one of Jewish decline, almost to the extent of disintegration (save for a small and as yet noninfluential rabbinic community); see Seth Schwartz, *Imperialism and Jewish Society, 200 B.C.E.–640 C.E.* (Princeton, NJ: Princeton University Press, 2001), pp. 104–161.

[18] The fullest treatment of the history of the patriarchate is Martin Jacobs, *Die Institution des jüdischen Patriarchen* (Tübingen: Mohr Siebeck, 1995); see also David M. Goodblatt, *The Monarchic Principle: Studies in Jewish Self-Government in Antiquity* (Tübingen: Mohr Siebeck, 1994), pp. 131–231. For a brief overview, see Goodblatt, "Political and Social History" (see endnote 2), pp. 416–423. On the patriarchate in the third and fourth centuries, see Lee I. Levine, "The Status of the Patriarch in the Third and Fourth Centuries: Sources and Methodology," *JJS* 47 (1996), pp. 1–32; for the suggestion of a more limited role, see Schwartz, *Imperialism and Jewish Society* (see endnote 17), pp. 104–128.

[19] BT *Gittin* 59a; BT *Sanhedrin* 36a; see Lee I. Levine, *The Rabbinic Class of Roman Palestine in Late Antiquity* (Jerusalem/New York: Yad Ben-Zvi/JTSem, 1989), pp. 33–38; and "The Period of Judah I," in *Eretz Israel from the Destruction* (see endnote 6), pp. 93–118. For a recent biography of Judah the Patriarch, see Aharon Oppenheimer, *Rabbi Judah ha-Nasi* (Jerusalem: Zalman Shazar Center, 2007, in Hebrew).

[20] Palestinian *aggadah* is replete with stories of patriarchs conducting correspondence with the emperors (e.g., *Genesis Rabbah* 75:5, p. 883 [on

Judah I and Antoninus]), or even appearing before them in person (e.g., *Genesis Rabbah* 63:8, pp. 668–670 [on Judah III before Diocletian]).

[21] See Lee I. Levine, "The Jewish Patriarch (Nasi) in Third Century Palestine," *ANRW* 2.19.2 (1979), pp. 649–688; also "The Status of the Patriarch" (see endnote 18). A synagogue inscription from Stobi (Macedonia) dating from 280/281 C.E. attests to the position of the patriarch even in the internal affairs of this Diaspora community. (A photo of this inscription may be found in Doron Mendels, "Why Paul Went West," *BAR*, January/February 2011, p. 52); see Levine, *The Rabbinic Class* (see endnote 19), p. 138, n. 29. See also Seth Schwartz, "The Patriarchs and the Diaspora," *JJS* 50 (1999), pp. 208–222; Isaiah Gafni, "Patriarchal Epistles," in *"Follow the Wise" (B. Sanhedrin 32b): Studies in Jewish History and Culture in Honor of L.I. Levine*, eds. Zeev Weiss, Oded Irshai, Jodi Magness and Seth Schwartz (Winona Lake, IN: Eisenbrauns/JTSem, 2010, in Hebrew).

[22] This diffusion of authority after the death of Judah I may also be reflected in the story of his last testament, BT *Ketubbot* 103b, wherein Judah divides his powers among three different individuals.

[23] JT *Sanhedrin* 1:19a. Judah I apparently used his control over ordination to punish sages perceived to have misbehaved toward the patriarchate; cf. JT *Ta'anit* 4:68a; JT *Mo'ed Katan* 3:81c.

[24] See Yehezkel Cohen, "The Time and Cause of the Transfer of the Patriarchate to Tiberias," *Zion* 39 (1974), pp. 114–122.

[25] See Reuven Kimelman, "The Conflict Between R. Yoḥanan and Resh Laqish on the Supremacy of the Patriarchate," *Proceedings of the 7th World Congress of Jewish Studies* (Jerusalem: Magnes Press, 1981), vol. 3, pp. 1–20. By the third century, the patriarchs apparently employed a private guard of Goths to be used against various opponents, including certain sages; cf. JT *Sanhedrin* 2:19d–20a (JT *Horayot* 3:47a).

[26] See, for example, the cynical statements regarding "those who are appointed for money," JT *Bikkurim* 3:65d; cf. BT *Sanhedrin* 7b. See also Gedaliah Alon, "Those Appointed for Money," in *Jews, Judaism and the Classical World* (Jerusalem: Magnes Press, 1977), pp. 374ff.; Ben-Zion Rosenfeld, "The Crisis of the Patriarchate in Eretz Israel in the Fourth Century," *Zion* 53 (1988), pp. 239–257 (in Hebrew).

[27] *Genesis Rabbah* 78:11, p. 931 and 80:1, p. 950; JT *Sanhedrin* 9:20c–d.

[28] The very use of rabbinic literature, and in particular the aggadic components of that literature, for historical purposes raises serious questions for all historians of this stage of Jewish history. For one perceptive introduction to the problem, see Hillel I. Newman, "Closing the Circle: Yonah Fraenkel, the Talmudic Story, and Rabbinic History," in *How Should Rabbinic Literature Be Read in the Modern World?* ed. Matthew Kraus (Piscataway, NJ: Gorgias Press, 2006), pp. 105–113; see also Isaiah M. Gafni, "The Modern Study of Rabbinics and Historical Questions: The Tale of the Text," in *The New Testament and Rabbinic Literature*, eds. Reimund Beiringer et al. (Leiden/Boston: Brill, 2010), pp. 43–61.

[29] See JT *Shevi'it* 5:36a (compare JT *Pe'ah* 1:15b). For a list of the various taxes, see Avi-Yonah, *Jews Under Roman and Byzantine Rule* (see endnote 4), pp. 93–104. For similarities between Jews and other provincials, even to the extent of similar complaints about taxes, see Saul Lieberman, "Palestine in the Third and Fourth Centuries," *JQR* 36 (1945–1946), pp. 356–357.

[30] *Genesis Rabbah* 24:1, p. 229; JT *Shevi'it* 9:38d; BT *Bava Batra* 8a. See also Daniel Sperber, *Roman Palestine 200–400: The Land* (Ramat-Gan, Israel: Bar-Ilan, 1978), pp. 102–118; on the pervasiveness of the Roman tax collector, unavoidable no matter where one goes, see also BT *Sanhedrin* 98b.

[31] JT *Sanhedrin* 15:26b.

[32] See Reuven Kimelman, *R. Yoḥanan of Tiberias: Aspects of the Social and Religious History of Third Century Palestine*, Ph.D. dissertation (Ann Arbor, MI: University Microfilms, 1980); and "Rabbi Yoḥanan and the Professionalization of the Rabbinate," *Annual of the Institute for Research in Jewish Law* 9–10 (1982–1983), pp. 329–358.

[33] See Levine, *Rabbinic Class* (see endnote 19), p. 194; Aharon Oppenheimer, "Batei-Midrash in Eretz-Israel in the Early Amoraic Period," *Cathedra* 8 (1978), pp. 80–89 (in Hebrew); the only material evidence relating explicitly to a *beth midrash* is the basalt lintel found at Dabbura in the Golan (now in the Golan Museum), with the inscription: "This

is the beth-midrash of Rabbi Eliezer Ha-Kappar," cf. Shlomit Nemlich and Ann Killebrew, "Rediscovering the Ancient Golan—The Golan Archaeological Museum," *BAR*, November/December 1988. Certain halls or buildings adjacent to ancient synagogues may also have served as *batei midrash*, but this is frequently no more than speculation; for literature, see Levine, *Rabbinic Class* (see endnote 19), p. 29, n. 17.

[34] The outstanding example of such a figure is Rabbi Abbahu of Caesarea, a late third-century sage who is referred to as "spokesman for his nation," cf. BT *Ketubbot* 17a; see also BT *Hagigah* 14a; JT *Avodah Zarah* 5:44d; cf. Lee I. Levine, "R. Abbahu of Caesarea," in *Christianity, Judaism and Other Greco-Roman Cults, Studies for Morton Smith at Sixty*, ed. Jacob Neusner (Leiden: Brill, 1975), vol. 4, pp. 56–76.

[35] See Catherine Hezser, *The Social Structure of the Rabbinic Movement in Roman Palestine* (Tübingen: Mohr Siebeck, 1997); Seth Schwartz, *Imperialism and Jewish Society* (see endnote 17), esp. pp. 103–128; for a recent debate on this issue, see "In the Wake of Destruction: Was Rabbinic Judaism Normative?" in *Jewish Identities in Antiquity* (see endnote 1), pp. 163–236. On questions relating to the degree of organized institutions within the rabbinic community, as well as their location and influence within the cities of Roman Palestine, see Hayim Lapin, "Rabbis and Cities: Some Aspects of the Rabbinic Movement in its Graeco-Roman Environment," in *The Talmud Yerushalmi and Graeco-Roman Culture*, vol. 2, eds. Peter Schaefer and Catherine Hezser (Tübingen: Mohr Siebeck, 2000), pp. 51–80.

[36] The current generation of scholarship has witnessed attempts at a major revision of our understanding of the nature, and chronological stages of the ultimate Jewish-Christian "parting of the ways." One direction has been to defer the final "schism" to the stages of late antiquity that coincided with the triumph of the Church; see, for example, Daniel Boyarin, *Dying for God: Martyrdom and the Making of Christianity and Judaism* (Stanford, CA: Stanford University Press, 1999); and also *Border Lines* (Philadelphia: University of Pennsylvania Press, 2004); see also Boyarin's article and others in *The Ways that Never Parted: Jews and Christians in Late Antiquity and the Early Middle Ages*, eds. Adam H. Becker and Annette Y. Reed (Tübingen: Mohr Siebeck, 2003); for an attempt to see the emergence of Rabbinic Judaism and many of its communal contexts as a response to Christianity (along with a Judaized appropriation of many of its trappings), see Schwartz, *Imperialism and Jewish Society* (see endnote 17), pp. 179ff. One recent study, however, has come out against attributing an overwhelming interest and response on the part of the rabbis to Christianity. See Adiel Schremer, *Brothers Estranged: Heresy, Christianity and Jewish Identity in Late Antiquity* (Oxford: Oxford University Press, 2009).

[37] See Samuel T. Lachs, "R. Abbahu and the Minnim," *JQR* 60 (1970), pp. 197–212. Levine ("R. Abbahu of Caesarea" [see endnote 34], p. 61) correctly notes, however, that the identification of Rabbi Abbahu's intended target is not always clear, for Samaritans and Gnostics, and sometimes even pagans, are also frequently addressed.

[38] JT *Ta'anit* 2:65b.

[39] *Exodus Rabbah* 29:5.

[40] BT *Avodah Zarah* 4a. It should be noted, however, that this confrontation between Rabbi Abbahu and the *minim* of Caesarea, and the rabbi's stress on what "we" in Palestine take upon ourselves, appears in a story attested only in the Babylonian Talmud, and thus scholars have suggested that it may in fact be a projection of Babylonian realities, where Christian-Jewish polemics were also not unknown, upon the Palestinian scene, where we might expect to find them more readily; see Adiel Schremer, "Stammaitic Historiography," in *Creation and Composition: The Contribution of the Bavli Redactors (Stammmaim) to the Aggada*, ed. Jeffrey L. Rubenstein (Tübingen: Mohr Siebeck, 2005), pp. 223–224; also "The Christianization of the Roman Empire" (see endnote 10), pp. 365–366, n. 66.

[41] Much scholarship has been devoted to these comparative studies; see, for example, Ephraim E. Urbach, "The Repentance of the People of Nineveh and the Discussion between Jews and Christians," *Tarbiz* 20 (1950–1951), pp. 118–122; and "Rabbinic Exegesis and Origen's Commentaries on the Song of Songs," *Tarbiz* 30 (1960–1961), pp. 148–170; Reuven Kimelman, "Rabbi Yohanan and Origen on the Song of Songs: A Third Century Jewish-Christian Disputation," *HTR* 73 (1980), pp. 567–595; Marc G. Hirshman,

A Rivalry of Genius: Jewish and Christian Biblical Interpretation in Late Antiquity (Albany: SUNY Press, 1996).

[42] JT *Shabbat* 6:7d.

[43] *Genesis Rabbah* 14:2, p. 127; cf. Saul Lieberman, *Hellenism in Jewish Palestine* (New York: JTSem, 1950), pp. 76–77.

[44] For a brief summary of the issue and citation to the major relevant scholarship, see Moshe D. Herr, "Hellenismos and the Jews in Eretz Israel," *Eshkeolot*, n.s. 9–10 (1977–1978), pp. 20–27 (in Hebrew). See also Lee I. Levine, *Judaism and Hellenism in Antiquity: Conflict or Confluence?* (Seattle/London: University of Washington Press, 1998), pp. 96–138.

[45] Saul Lieberman, *Greek in Jewish Palestine* (New York: JTSem, 1942); *Hellenism in Jewish Palestine* (see endnote 43); and "How Much Greek in Jewish Palestine," in *Biblical and Other Studies*, ed. Alexander Altman (Cambridge, MA: Harvard University Press, 1963), pp. 123–141.

[46] See Henry A. Fischel, *Story and History: Observations on Greco-Roman Rhetoric and Pharisaism*, American Oriental Society, Middle-Western Branch, Semi-Centennial Volume, ed. Denis Sinor (Bloomington, IN: Indiana University Press, 1968), pp. 59–88.

[47] *Sifre Deuteronomy* 343, pp. 394–395.

[48] *Genesis Rabbah* 80:1, pp. 950–953; JT *Sanhedrin* 9:20c–d.

[49] For the Greek synagogue inscriptions of Palestine, see Leah Roth-Gerson, *The Greek Inscriptions from the Synagogues in Eretz-Israel* (Jerusalem: Yad Ben-Zvi, 1987) (in Hebrew). The Hebrew and Aramaic inscriptions of Palestinian synagogues were published by Joseph Naveh in *On Stone and Mosaic* (Jerusalem: IES, 1978). The linguistic differences between Galilean and Judean synagogues were noted by Shmuel Safrai, "The Synagogues South of Mt. Judah," *Immanuel* 3 (1973–1974), pp. 44–50.

[50] For a possible explanation, see Herr, "Hellenismos and the Jews" (see endnote 44), pp. 26–27.

[51] For a summary of Diocletian's rule, see A.H.M. Jones, *The Later Roman Empire* (Oxford: Blackwell, 1964), vol. 1, pp. 37–76; on Diocletian and the Jews of Palestine, see Smallwood, *Jews Under Roman Rule* (see endnote 3), pp. 533–538.

[52] Diocletian passed through Palestine at least twice; he spent time in Tiberias in 286 C.E. (talmudic tradition places him in Paneas as well) and, following the winter of 296/297 C.E. and the suppression of a revolt in Alexandria, he again passed through the country to Antioch on his way to join Galerius for a counterattack against the Persians. On a possible third stay in Palestine, see Smallwood, *Jews Under Roman Rule* (see endnote 3), p. 536, n. 40.

[53] JT *Avodah Zarah* 5:44a. While this source exonerates Diocletian from anti-Jewish persecution, it specifically notes that the Samaritans were not exempted from forced participation in certain pagan rites. The rabbis point to Samaritan acquiescence to certain Roman demands, such as pouring libations on pagan sacrifices, as a justification for placing a distance between the Samaritans and the Jewish community "and therefore their wine was forbidden." For a discussion of the background and possible interpretations of this source, see Saul Lieberman, "The Martyrs of Caesarea," *Annuaire de l'Institut de Philologie et d'Histoire Orientales et Slavs* 7 (1939–1944), pp. 403–404.

[54] See, for example, Eusebius's description of a martyr in Nicomedia, who "was ... raised on high naked and had his whole body torn with scourges until he should give in ... But when he remained unmoved even under these sufferings, they proceeded to mix vinegar and salt together and pour them into the mangled parts of his body ... and as he despised these pains also, a gridiron and fire were then produced, and the remnants of his body ... were consumed by the fire, not all at once, in case he might find immediate release, but little by little ..."; *Eccles. Hist.* 8.2 (quoted in Naphtali Lewis and Meyer Reinhold, *Roman Civilization*, Sourcebook 2: The Empire [New York: Columbia University Press, 1955], pp. 599–600). For similarities and literary contacts between Jewish and Christian descriptions of martyrdom, see Boyarin, *Dying for God* (see endnote 36), pp. 93–126.

[55] Lieberman, "Martyrs of Caesarea" (see endnote 53), p. 410.

[56] For a survey of Roman legislation toward the Jews in the Roman and Byzantine periods, see Amnon Linder, "The Legal Status of the Jews in the

Roman Empire," in *Cambridge History of Judaism*, vol. 4 (see endnote 2), pp. 128–173.

[57] See Lieberman ("Palestine in the Third and Fourth Centuries" [see endnote 29], pp. 329ff.), who refutes the assumptions of Heinrich Graetz and others regarding the persecution of the Jews in the early stages of the Christian empire. Lieberman bases his argument primarily on the lack of any allusion to outright persecution in rabbinic literature; the same conclusion is arrived at by most scholars of Roman legislation in the fourth century; see Amnon Linder, *The Jews in Roman Imperial Legislation* (Detroit: Wayne State University Press, 1987), pp. 67–74; and "The Roman Imperial Government and the Jews Under Constantine," *Tarbiz* 44 (1974), pp. 95–143 (in Hebrew). See also Jeremy Cohen, "Roman Imperial Policy Towards the Jews from Constantine until the End of the Palestinian Patriarchate (ca. 429)," *BS* 3/1 (1976), pp. 1–29.

[58] See James W. Parkes, *The Conflict of the Church and the Synagogue* (London: Soncino, 1934), pp. 174–175; Cohen, "Roman Imperial Policy" (see endnote 57), p. 3, n. 10.

[59] Eusebius, *Life of Constantine* 3.18, PG 20, 1076. The Council of Nicaea determined that Easter would be the first Sunday following the full moon after the spring equinox; but not all Eastern churches agreed to sever the link between Easter and the Jewish Passover. For a summary of the entire issue, see Marcel Simon, *Verus Israel*, trans. H. McKeating (Oxford: Littman Library, Oxford University Press, 1985), pp. 310–321; on Constantine's role in raising the issue of Easter at Nicaea, see Timothy D. Barnes, *Constantine and Eusebius* (Cambridge, MA: Harvard University Press, 1981), p. 217; see also Lieberman, "Palestine in the Third and Fourth Centuries" (see endnote 29), p. 333.

[60] See Parkes, *Conflict of the Church* (see endnote 58), p. 176; Cohen, "Roman Imperial Policy" (see endnote 57), p. 4.

[61] Linder, *Jews in Roman Imperial Legislation* (see endnote 57), pp. 67ff.

[62] *Codex Theodosianus* 16.8.1 (October 18, 329); 16.8.5. All the relevant "Jewish" laws in the codex are quoted in the original and translated by Linder in *Jews in Roman Imperial Legislation* (see endnote 57). For the fifth century, see *Codex Theodosianus* 16.8.26, pp. 124–132.

[63] Cf. *Codex Theodosianus* 16.9.1; 16.9.2; 16.8.6. It is unclear whether Constantine or his successor Constantius was the originator of this law; see Linder, *Jews in Imperial Legislation* (see endnote 57), pp. 144–147.

[64] See Ephraim E. Urbach, "*Halakhot* Regarding Slavery as a Source for the Social History of the Second Temple and the Talmudic Period," *Zion* 25 (1960), pp. 175ff. (in Hebrew) (Eng. trans. in Papers of the Institute of Jewish Studies [Jerusalem: Magnes Press, 1964], vol. 1, pp. 1–95).

[65] Cf. *Codex Theodosianus* 16.8.3 (December 11, 321). Until this time the Jews might have backed demands for exemption from participation in the local councils by claiming that this would involve some contact with pagan activity; see Avi-Yonah, *Jews Under Roman and Byzantine Rule* (see endnote 4), p. 163.

[66] Cf. *Codex Theodosianus* 12.1.99; 16.8.13; 12.1.158; see Linder, *Jews in Roman Imperial Legislation* (see endnote 57), p. 121.

[67] The doubts regarding historical evidence for this prohibition under Constantine stem from the fact that the law is found nowhere in Roman legal corpora, but rather is mentioned by various Christian authors, who obviously had an interest not only in establishing Jerusalem as a Christian city, but also in stressing the ongoing removal of the Jews from the city as part of the religious argument; cf. Avi-Yonah, *Jews Under Roman and Byzantine Rule* (see endnote 4), pp. 163–165. On the prohibition from the days of Hadrian, see Rendel Harris, "Hadrian's Decree of Expulsion of the Jews from Jerusalem," *HTR* 19 (1926), pp. 199–206, but the historicity of that decree has also been doubted, see Linder, "Roman Imperial Government" (see endnote 57), p. 136, n. 227, for a summary of the arguments against the existence of the prohibition.

[68] This event would have served as the logical occasion for renewing the removal of Jews from Jerusalem, given the significance attached to the encaenia (consecration) of the Church of the Holy Sepulchre; see Joshua Schwartz, "The Encaenia of the Church of the Holy Sepulchre, The Temple of Solomon and the Jews," *Theologische Zeitschrift* 43 (1987), pp. 265–281. On the development of Christian pilgrimage to Jerusalem and the Holy Land, see endnote 120.

[69] Epiphanius, *Panarion*, 3.4–12; see Ze'ev Rubin, "Joseph the Comes and the Attempts to Convert the Galilee to Christianity in the Fourth Century C.E.," *Cathedra* 26 (1982), pp. 105–116 (in Hebrew).

[70] The historicity of this story has been examined (and questioned at times) by numerous scholars. For a recent attempt at a literary analysis, which projects the story as a "foundation story" of the early Galilean Church, see E. Reiner, "Joseph the Comes of Tiberias and the Jewish-Christian Dialogue of Fourth-Century Galilee," in *Continuity and Renewal: Jews and Judaism in Byzantine-Christian Palestine*, ed. Lee I. Levine (Jerusalem: Dinur Center, Yad Ben Zvi and JTSem, 2004, in Hebrew), pp. 355–386 (for a bibliography on the episode, see p. 356, n. 3).

[71] For a review of the sources and scholarship on this event, which in the opinion of many is hardly worthy of the title "revolt," see Günter Stemberger, *Jews and Christians in the Holy Land* (Edinburgh: T & T Clark, 2000), pp. 161–184; for previous research, see also Barbara G. Nathanson, "The Fourth Century Jewish 'Revolt' During the Reign of Gallus" (unpublished Ph.D. dissertation, Duke University, 1981); Peter Schäfer, "Der Aufstand gegen Gallus Caesar," in *Tradition and Re-Interpretation in Jewish and Early Christian Literature*, ed. J.W. Henten (Leiden: Brill, 1986), pp. 184ff.; recently Oded Irshai has posited a perceived weakness of Rome, accompanied by evidence of messianic agitation among Christians and pagans alike, as a possible catalyst for a limited outburst of violence; see Irshai, "Jewish Violence in the Fourth Century CE—Fantasy and Reality: Behind the Scenes Under the Emperors Gallus and Julian," in *Jewish Identities in Antiquity* (see endnote 1), pp. 402–410.

[72] Aurelius Victor, *De Caesaribus* 42.11.

[73] Jerome, *Chronicon* a.355, PL 27, 686.

[74] Socrates, *Ecclesiastical History* 2.33; Sozomen, *Ecclesiastical History* 4.7,5.

[75] See Benjamin Mazar, *Beit Shearim* (Jerusalem: IES, 1944), vol. 1, p. 26.

[76] For literature on Julian, see Oded Irshai, "Jewish Violence in the Fourth Century CE" (see endnote 71), pp. 410–411, nn. 57–59; for Julian and the attempt to restore the Jewish Temple, see Stemberger, *Jews and Christians in the Holy Land* (see endnote 71), pp. 198–216.

[77] For the influence of all these on Julian, see the literature cited by Menahem Stern, *Greek and Latin Authors on Jews and Judaism*, 3 vols. (Jerusalem: Israel Academy for the Humanities and Sciences, 1980), vol. 2, p. 506, n. 2.

[78] On this issue, see David Rokeah, *Jews, Pagans and Christians in Conflict* (Jerusalem/Leiden: Magnes Press/Brill, 1982); Rokeah concludes that while "the Jews were no party to it [the pagan-Christian confrontation] ... without the Jews' existence and independent attitude towards Christians and pagans alike, and without their holy scriptures and the writings of Hellenistic Jewry, the pagan-Christian polemic could not have taken the course and shape it did" (pp. 9–10).

[79] Much has been written about the silence in rabbinic literature regarding the events of Julian's day, which at times has been compared to their minimal reference to the Christianization of the empire under Constantine; see Martin Goodman, "Palestinian Rabbis and the Conversion of Constantine to Christianity," in *The Talmud Yerushalmi* (see endnote 35), pp. 1–9; and Irshai, "Jewish Violence" (see endnote 71), p. 392 and n. 5.

[80] Whether Julian had a knowledge of Judaism based only on the Bible is a point of contention among scholars; see Johanan H. Levy ("The Emperor Julian and the Building of the Temple," *Zion* 6 [1941], p. 3 [in Hebrew]; reprinted in Levy's collected *Studies in Jewish Hellenism* [Jerusalem: Mosad Bialik, 1960]), who limits Julian's knowledge to the Bible, and Gedaliah Alon, *Studies in Jewish History* (Tel Aviv: Hakibutz Hameuchad, 1958), vol. 2, pp. 313–334 (in Hebrew).

[81] The definitive study is Levy, *Studies in Jewish Hellenism* (see endnote 80); see also Mordechai Hak, "Is Julian's Proclamation a Forgery?" *Yavne* 2 (1940), pp. 118–139 (in Hebrew).

[82] *The Works of the Emperor Julian*, Loeb, trans. W.C. Wright, vol. 3, pp. 177–181; for a comprehensive commentary on the letter, see Stern, *Greek and Latin Authors* (see endnote 77), vol. 2, pp. 559–568; see also Linder, *Jews in Roman Imperial Legislation* (see endnote 57), pp. 154–160.

[83] *Against the Galileans*, in *The Works of the Emperor Julian* (see endnote 82), pp. 313–427; for the

sections relating directly to Jews in this work, see Stern, *Greek and Latin Authors* (see endnote 77), vol. 2, pp. 513–549.

[84] Julian, *Against the Galileans* (see endnote 83), 191D–E and 224E, p. 385; Porphyry had already attacked the Christians on this issue, claiming that they "are very much mistaken when they believe that God is angered if someone else is called god and thereby acquires his appellation, whereas even rulers do not begrudge their subjects', or masters their slaves', having the same name; it is therefore forbidden as regards religion to suppose that God is more petty minded than men" (*Gegen die Christen*, ed. Adolf von Harnack [Berlin: Koenigliche Akademie der Wissenschaften, 1916], p. 93, no. 78; quoted by Rokeah, *Jews, Pagans and Christians* [see endnote 78], p. 128).

[85] Julian, *Against the Galileans* (see endnote 83), 305D–306A, pp. 405–407.

[86] Ibid., 306A–B, p. 407.

[87] For Christian sources on this argument, see Stern, *Greek and Latin Authors* (see endnote 77), vol. 2, p. 506, n. 3; the issue came up frequently in connection with the developing Christian theology around the notion of a "heavenly Jerusalem." See Joshua Prawer, "Christianity Between Heavenly and Earthly Jerusalem" (in Hebrew), in *Jerusalem Through the Ages, The 25th Archaeological Convention* (Jerusalem: IES, 1968), pp. 179–192; for talmudic references to the term "heavenly Jerusalem," see Ephraim E. Urbach, "Heavenly and Earthly Jerusalem," in *Jerusalem Through the Ages*, pp. 156–171.

[88] Sozomen, *Ecclesiastical History* 5.22.

[89] Ammianus Marcellinus, *History* 23.1, Loeb, trans. John C. Rolfe, vol. 2, pp. 311f.

[90] The original connection between the inscription, situated under Robinson's Arch in the southern part of the Western Wall, was made by Benjamin Mazar, *The Mountain of the Lord* (Garden City, NY: Doubleday, 1975), p. 94; see, however, Yaacov Bilig and Ronny Reich ("A New Interpretation on the Inscription 'And ye shall see and your heart shall rejoice' on the Western Wall," *New Studies on Jerusalem*, vol. 3 [Ramat Gan: Bar Ilan University, 1997)], pp. 18–24 [in Hebrew]) who attribute the inscription to an 11th-century burial site on the premises.

[91] While we have noted above (see endnote 79) that explicit references to the event in rabbinic literature are lacking, some have pointed to various messianic deliberations in this literature as being influenced by the events under Julian. See Michael Adler, "The Emperor Julian and the Jews," *JQR* o.s. 5 (1893), pp. 591–651; Wilhelm Bacher, "Statements of a Contemporary of the Emperor Julian on the Rebuilding of the Temple," *JQR* o.s. 10 (1898), pp. 168–172; see also Lieberman, "Martyrs of Caesarea" (see endnote 53), p. 412; and "Palestine in the Third and Fourth Centuries" (see endnote 29), p. 243.

One common view is that the rabbinic leadership of Palestine, headed by the patriarch from the house of David, was naturally wary of the resurgence of the priesthood and concomitant weakening of its own position should the Temple actually be restored, cf. Avi-Yonah, *Jews Under Roman and Byzantine Rule* (see endnote 4), pp. 196–197. While doubts regarding Julian's promise may indeed have arisen at the time, it is questionable how much we can really conclude from the "silence" of the sources. Not only must we be constantly aware of the ahistorical nature of the Palestinian Talmud and midrashim, but, as pointed out by various scholars, we would do well to note how little information on the second half of the fourth century made its way into the Palestinian Talmud (even if Julian's name is mentioned there).

[92] *Codex Theodosianus* 7:8:2 (May 6, 368), pp. 161–164; this *hospitium*, known in rabbinic sources as *akhsania*, also interfered with certain Jewish legal steps taken for the purpose of creating a common domain on the Sabbath for all the residents of a courtyard. The issue is referred to in numerous talmudic texts, cf. Lieberman, "Palestine in the Third and Fourth Centuries" (see endnote 29), pp. 354–357.

[93] *Codex Theodosianus* 16.8.13 (July 1, 397) alludes to earlier legislation, including that of Valens and Valentinian, which has not survived.

[94] The nature of the correspondence between Libanius (a leading Greek rhetorician of the late fourth century, born and later taught at Antioch) and the patriarch of the period is evidence of the high regard in which the noted Greek rhetor of Antioch held the Jewish leader, cf. Stern, *Greek and Latin Authors* (see endnote 77), vol. 2, pp. 580–599. Another example of the power of

the patriarchate is suggested in the letter of Jerome (letter 57, PL 22, col. 570), in which we learn that Hesychius, governor of Palestine, was executed for certain improper behavior toward the patriarch. As late as 415 C.E., Gamaliel VI was still in possession of the rank of honorary prefect, cf. *Codex Theodosianus* 16.8.22, p. 271.

[95] For the definitive study on the history of the ancient synagogue, see Lee I. Levine's *The Ancient Synagogue: The First Thousand Years*, 2nd rev. ed. (New Haven, CT: Yale University Press, 2005).

[96] See Avigdor Shinan, "Sermons, Targums, and the Reading from Scriptures in the Ancient Synagogue," in *The Synagogue in Late Antiquity*, ed. Lee I. Levine (Philadelphia: ASOR, 1987), pp. 97–10. The synagogue also provided a framework for other communal services: The local school might be situated there, charity was pledged there, and the site served as a local gathering place for any number of other purposes. An impressive bibliography on synagogues in the talmudic period exists; for a helpful list, see Menahem Mor and Uriel Rappaport, "Bibliography on Ancient Synagogues," in *Synagogues in Antiquity*, eds. Aryeh Kasher et al. (Jerusalem: Yad Ben-Zvi, 1987), pp. 267–285; and also the comprehensive list at the end of Levine's study (*Ancient Synagogue* [see endnote 95], pp. 615–682).

[97] John Chrysostom, *Homily Against the Jews*, 4:3, PG 48, col. 847; see Wayne A. Meeks and Robert L. Wilken, *Jews and Christians in Antioch* (Missoula, MT: Scholars Press, 1978), p. 90. Many of Chrysostom's homilies against the Jews were delivered just prior to Jewish festivals, when the attraction of the synagogues was greatest. See Robert L. Wilken, *John Chrysostom and the Jews: Rhetoric and Reality in the Late Fourth Century* (Berkeley: University of California Press, 1983), pp. 66ff.

[98] Chrysostom, *Homily Against the Jews* (see endnote 97), col. 851; Meeks and Wilken, *Jews and Christians* (see endnote 97), p. 96. That Christians as well as others, including gentile "Godfearers," were attracted to the synagogue is widely attested both in literary sources as well as epigraphical evidence; see Levine, *Ancient Synagogue* (see endnote 95), pp. 272–277.

[99] Ambrosius, *Epistle* I 40–41, PL 16, col. 1101; see Avi-Yonah, *Jews Under Roman and Byzantine Rule* (see endnote 4), p. 212; Parkes, *Conflict of the Church* (see endnote 58), pp. 166–168. One of Ambrosius's arguments in demanding that the fine placed upon the Christian destroyers of the synagogue be rescinded alludes to the "many basilicas of the Church [that] were burnt by the Jews in the time of the reign of Julian." This claim, however, cannot be confirmed and, as shown by Irshai, is spurious. See Irshai, "Jewish Violence" (see endnote 71), pp. 410–415.

[100] *Codex Theodosianus* 16.8.9.

[101] *Codex Theodosianus* 16.8.21 (August 6, 420).

[102] *Codex Theodosianus* 16.8.25 (February 15, 423).

[103] Ibid.

[104] See Yoram Tsafrir, "The Byzantine Setting and Its Influence on Ancient Synagogues," in *Synagogue in Late Antiquity* (see endnote 96), p. 152.

[105] *Codex Theodosianus* 16.8.11.

[106] *Codex Theodosianus* 16.8.14.

[107] Chrysostom, *Homily Against the Jews* (see endnote 97), cols. 835 and 911.

[108] *Codex Theodosianus* 16.8.15.

[109] *Codex Theodosianus* 16.8.22; for a brief discussion of this law, see Linder, *Jews in Roman Imperial Legislation* (see endnote 57), pp. 267–272.

[110] *Codex Theodosianus* 16.8.29.

[111] See Linder, *Jews in Roman Imperial Legislation* (see endnote 57), p. 320–323; on the end of the patriarchate, see also Avi-Yonah, *Jews Under Roman and Byzantine Rule* (see endnote 4), pp. 225–229.

[112] See Yaron Dan, "Leadership of the Jewish Community in Eretz Israel in the Fifth and Sixth Centuries," in *Nation and History*, Papers Delivered at the Eighth World Congress of Jewish Studies, ed. Menahem Stern (Jerusalem: Zalman Shazar Center, 1983), vol. 1, pp. 211–217 (in Hebrew); and "Eretz Israel in the Fifth and Sixth Centuries" (see endnote 6), vol. 1, pp. 273–275. Dan posits a reverse scenario as well, i.e., that a possible attempt by the Romans to abolish the patriarchate might have in fact served as catalyst for the 418 rebellion. For Dan's collected essays on Jews in the Byzantine period, see *Studies in the History of Palestine in the Roman-Byzantine Period* (Jerusalem: Yad Ben-Zvi, 2006). For a survey of the literature on the cessation of the patriarchate, see Oded

Irshai, "The Priesthood in Jewish Society of Late Antiquity," in *Continuity and Renewal: Jews and Judaism in Byzantine-Christian Palestine*, ed. Lee I. Levine (Jerusalem: Dinur Center, Yad Ben-Zvi and JTSem, 2004), p. 68, n. 2 (in Hebrew).

[113] See Uzi Leibner, "Settlement Patterns in the Eastern Galilee: Implications Regarding the Transformation of Rabbinic Culture in Late Antiquity," in *Jewish Identities in Antiquity* (see endnote 1), p. 295; see also Zeev Safrai, *The Missing Century: Palestine in the Fifth Century: Growth and Decline* (Leuven: Peeters, 1998). For a rejoinder to both, see Jodi Magness, "Did Galilee Experience a Settlement Crisis in the Mid-Fourth Century?" in *Jewish Identities in Antiquity* (see endnote 1), pp. 296–313.

[114] See Dan, "Leadership of the Jewish Community" (see endnote 112), pp. 215–217.

[115] For a historical overview of the period, see Avi-Yonah, *Jews Under Roman and Byzantine Rule* (see endnote 4), pp. 232–265; on the Byzantine administration of Palestine in the fifth and sixth centuries, see Dan, "Leadership of the Jewish Community" (see endnote 112), pp. 275–299.

[116] See Naveh, *On Stone and Mosaic* (see endnote 49), pp. 72–73 (Beth Alpha), pp. 31–32 (Kfar Naburaya); Roth-Gerson, *Greek Inscriptions from the Synagogues* (see endnote 49), pp. 91ff. (Gaza).

[117] For Palestinian synagogues of the Byzantine period, see Levine, *Ancient Synagogue* (see endnote 95), pp. 194–231.

[118] The most prominent proponent of this later dating is Jodi Magness; see *Judaism in Late Antiquity, Part 3: Where We stand: Issues and Debates in Ancient Judaism*, vol. 4: *The Special Problem of the Synagogue*, eds. Alan J. Avery-Peck and Jacob Neusner (Leiden: Brill, 2001), pp. 1–92; see also the symposium (in Hebrew) entitled "The Disappearance of Synagogues in the Mishnaic-Talmudic Period," with a presentation by Magness, and responses by Gideon Foerster, James F. Strange (English) and Mordechai Aviam, in *Continuity and Renewal* (see endnote 112), pp. 507–553. See also Schwartz, *Imperialism and Jewish Society* (see endnote 17), pp. 208–212.

[119] See Michael Avi-Yonah, "The Economics of Byzantine Palestine," *IEJ* 8 (1958), pp. 39–51.

[120] On pilgrimage to Palestine, see E.D. Hunt, *Holyland Pilgrimage in the Late Roman Empire, AD 312–460* (Oxford: Clarendon Press, 1984); John Wilkinson, *Jerusalem Pilgrims Before the Crusades* (Jerusalem: Ariel, 1977); Jews in particular might serve as "tour guides" for Christian pilgrims, cf. Avi-Yonah, *Jews Under Roman and Byzantine Rule* (see endnote 4), p. 222.

[121] Eudocia remained for about one year, but subsequently left her husband and by 441/443 C.E. had returned to Palestine, where she remained until her death in 460 C.E.

[122] See Francois Nau, "Deux E'pisodes de l'histoire juive sous Theodose II (423 et 438)," *REJ* 83 (1927), pp. 184–202.

[123] See Francois Nau, "Résumé de Monographies Syriaques" *Revue de l'Orient chretien* 9 (1914), pp. 118ff.

[124] See Avi-Yonah, *Jews Under Roman and Byzantine Rule* (see endnote 4), pp. 251–253; *The Book of Himyarites*, ed. A. Moberg (Lund, Sweden: Gleerup, 1924), p. 7a (trans. on p. cv); see also Hayyim Z. Hirschberg, "Joseph, King of Himyar, and the Coming of Mar Zutra to Tiberias," in *All the Land of Naphtali*, 24th Archaeological Convention, October 1966, ed. Hirschberg (Jerusalem: IES, 1967), pp. 139–146 (in Hebrew). For this Jewish intervention into sixth-century Arabian affairs, see the literature cited by Irshai in *Continuity and Renewal* (see endnote 112), p. 72, n. 12 (in Hebrew). Irshai cites this testimony as evidence for a central role of social leadership still maintained by the Jewish priesthood hundreds of years after the destruction of the Second Temple.

[125] Ignazio Guidi, ed., "La lettera di Simeone vescovo di Beth Arsham," *Atti della R. Accademia de Lincei* 7 (1881), pp. 501ff.

[126] See Ephraim E. Urbach, "Mishmarot and Ma'amadot," *Tarbiz* 42 (1973), pp. 304–327 (in Hebrew).

[127] See David M. Goodblatt, *The Monarchic Principle* (Tübingen: Mohr Siebeck, 1994), pp. 274–276.

[128] See Adolf Neubauer, *Medieval Jewish Chronicles* (Oxford: Clarendon Press, 1895), vol. 2, p. 76; while the historicity of this account is problematic, an attempt has been made to insert the emigration of a descendant of the "House of David" to Palestine in the year 520 into Jewish (as

well as Christian) calculations regarding the "end of days," or coming of the Messiah; see Oded Irshai, "Dating the Eschaton," in *Apocalyptic Time*, ed. Albert I. Baumgarten (Leiden: Brill, 2000), p. 153.

[129] See Hayyim Z. Hirschberg, "Mar Zutra, Head of the Sanhedrin at Tiberias," in *All the Land of Naphtali* (see endnote 124), pp. 147–153; David M. Goodblatt, *Rabbinic Instruction in Sasanian Babylonia* (Leiden: Brill, 1975), p. 189.

[130] Greek *Novellae* no. 146; the *Novellae* contained the new laws and/or constitutions promulgated by Justinian after the publication of the Codex in 534 C.E.

[131] For a discussion of this law, see Linder, *Jews in Roman Imperial Legislation* (see endnote 57), pp. 402–411; Leonard V. Rutgers, "Justinian's Novella 146," in *Jewish Culture and Society under the Christian Roman Empire*, eds. Richard L. Kalmin and Seth Schwartz (Leuven: Peeters, 2003), pp. 385–407.

[132] See Linder, *Jews in Roman Imperial Legislation* (see endnote 57), p. 409; Albert I. Baumgarten, "Justinian and the Jews," in *Rabbi Joseph H. Lookestein Memorial Volume*, ed. L. Landman (New York: Ktav, 1980), pp. 37–44.

[133] This being the case, it is just as clear why the law goes on to threaten "the Archipherekitae, or possibly Presbyters or Didaskeloi"—for all three terms designate precisely those who preach. *Archipherekitae* is clearly a translation of *resh pirka*; *pirka* is a well-documented rabbinic term—mostly in BT but also found in JT—designating a popular type of sermon delivered in the synagogue. Thus the form *resh pirka* may be a secondary usage, designating some official or dignitary among the sages. (See Isaiah Gafni, *The Jews of Babylonia in the Talmudic Era* [Jerusalem: Merkaz Shazar, 1990], pp. 204–213 [in Hebrew].) The "preachers, elders and teachers" were, in the legislators' eyes and most probably following the lead of the Church, those spiritual leaders who "introduce ungodly nonsense."

[134] For an overview of this material, see Lee I. Levine, "Jewish Archaeology in Late Antiquity: Art, Architecture and Inscriptions," in *Cambridge History of Judaism*, vol. 4 (see endnote 2), pp. 519–555.

[135] Greek and Latin references to Jews are not much more helpful after the second century and, as noted by Martin Goodman, these authors "seem largely to have fallen into literary clichés when writing about Jews, and little that they wrote sheds any light on the Jews of their own day." See Goodman, "Jews and Judaism in the Mediterranean Diaspora," in *Judaism in the Roman World–Collected Essays* (Brill: Leiden, 2007), pp. 238–239.

[136] Levine, *Ancient Synagogue* (see endnote 95), pp. 232–263.

[137] See Leonard V. Rutgers, *The Jews in Late Ancient Rome: Evidence of Cultural Interaction in the Roman Diaspora* (Leiden: Brill, 1995); and *The Hidden Heritage of Diaspora Judaism* (Peeters: Leuven, 1998), pp. 45–71.

[138] For a concise overview of these divergent conclusions see Leonard V. Rutgers, "Recent Trends in the Study of Ancient Diaspora Judaism," in *Hidden Heritage of Diaspora Judaism* (see endnote 137), pp. 15–41.

[139] See A.T. Kraabel, "The Roman Diaspora: Six Questionable Assumptions," *JJS* 33 (1982), p. 459.

[140] Levine, *Ancient Synagogue* (see endnote 95), p. 283; Levine specifically notes that "The Torah shrine is prominent in most synagogues of late antiquity, appearing in a variety of settings in Palestine as well as in the Diaspora."

[141] See Paul R. Trebilco, *Jewish Communities in Asia Minor* (Cambridge: Cambridge University Press, 1991), p. 50; Goodman ("Jews and Judaism" [see endnote 135], p. 257) justifiably disagrees, and concludes that "it seems likely that the individual called "Somoe, priest and wise teacher" ... was a rabbinic Jew.

[142] Jonathan J. Price, "The Jewish Diaspora of the Graeco-Roman Period," *Scripta Classica Israelica* 13 (1940), p. 179.

[143] See Arye Edrei and Doron Mendels, "A Split Jewish Diaspora: Its Dramatic Consequences," *JSP* 16 (2007), pp. 91–137.

[144] On this I would concur with Martin Goodman's hypothetical observation: "It is worth asking what, if historians totally lacked the benefit of evidence from literary texts, they would deduce about Judaism from archaeology and inscriptions. I doubt if they would ever discover that Judaism was

distinguished from most other ancient religions by being a system, or a number of systems, with a complex mythology based on the covenant and revelation on Mount Sinai ... the nature of Jewish religious beliefs would surely be totally obscure from the iconography of *menoroth*, lions, incense shovels, birds, *lulavim* and so on" (see Goodman, "Jews and Judaism" [see endnote 135], p. 254).

[145] See Angelos Chaniotis, "The Jews of Aphrodisias: New Evidence and Old Problems," *Scripta Classica Israelica* 21 (2002), pp. 209–242.

[146] See Goodman, "Jews and Judaism" (see endnote 135), pp. 242–248.

[147] See Fergus Millar, "Christian Emperors, Christian Church, and the Jews of the Diaspora in the Greek East, A.D. 379–450," *JJS* 55 (2004), pp. 1–24, esp. pp. 18–19; and *Rome, the Greek World and the East*, vol. 3: *The Greek World, the Jews and the East*, eds. H.M. Cotton and G.M. Rogers (Chapel Hill: University of North Carolina Press, 2006), pp. 479–480.

[148] While isolated rabbinic statements or portions of traditions may have been put in writing at an early stage, the point here is that these "hidden scrolls," as the rabbis referred to them, played no part in the process of formal academic study and teaching, but were used only privately by individual sages; cf. the classic chapter on this by Lieberman ("The Publication of the Mishna") in *Hellenism in Jewish Palestine* (see endnote 43), pp. 83–99. The conclusive and definitive statement on the extreme degree of orality within the rabbinic learning community is Yaacov Sussmann, "Oral Torah, Its Literal Meaning: The Power of the Tip of an Iota," in *Meḥqerei Talmud* 3:1: *Talmudic Studies Dedicated to the Memory of Professor Ephraim E. Urbach*, eds. Ya'akov Zussman and David Rosenthal (Jerusalem: Magnes Press, 2005), pp. 209–384; for further literature on this issue, see Leibner, "Settlement Patterns" (see endnote 113), pp. 292–293 and nn. 64–65.

[149] See the brief survey by Moshe D. Herr (*EJ*, vol. 9, col. 1510), who refers to these works as "classical amoraic midrashim." For descriptions of the various amoraic midrashim, their content, structure and provenance, see G. Stemberger, *Introduction to the Talmud and Midrash*, 2nd ed. (Edinburgh: T & T Clark, 1996), pp. 276–325.

[150] One of the first and most important of these studies was conducted by Zacharias Frankel, *Mavo ha-Yerushalmi* (Breslau: 1870), pp. 18–40; see also Jacob N. Epstein, *Mevo'ot Le-Sifrut ha-Amora'im* (Jerusalem: Magnes-Dvir, 1962), p. 274. For a comprehensive bibliography on research of the Palestinian Talmud, see Baruch Bokser, "An Annotated Bibliographical Guide to the Study of the Palestinian Talmud," *ANRW* 2.19.2 (1979), pp. 139–256. For a more recent introduction to the Jerusalem Talmud, see Leib Moscovitz, "The Formation and Character of the Jerusalem Talmud," in *Cambridge History of Judaism*, vol. 4 (see endnote 2), pp. 663–677.

[151] See Epstein, *Mevo'ot Le-Sifrut ha-Amora'im* (see endnote 150), p. 274. For the last stages of the amoraic period in Palestine, see Ya'akov Zussman, "Again on Yerushalmi Nezikin," in *Meḥqerei Talmud*, vol. 1, eds. Ya'akov Zussman and David Rosenthal (Jerusalem: Magnes Press, 1990), pp. 132–133 and n. 187 (in Hebrew). Zussman sets the final years of the Palestinian amoraim in the late 360s C.E.

[152] See Jacob N. Epstein, *Mavo Le-Nusah ha-Mishnah*, 2nd ed. (Jerusalem: Magnes-Dvir, 1964), pp. 626ff. Numerous discrepancies between the two Talmudim can also be attributed to a variance in the text of the Mishnah used by the rabbis in the two lands, cf. Epstein, pp. 706ff. For the literary sources available to the Jerusalem Talmud, see Moscovitz, "Formation and Character" (see endnote 150), pp. 669–670.

[153] The Palestinian Talmud appears to be lacking the prolonged and aggressive editorial intervention that is so striking in the Babylonian Talmud, most notably in the anonymous strata of that corpus. Indeed, the distinction between earlier, attributed statements and later anonymous reformulations, so marked in the Babylonian Talmud, is far less apparent in the Palestinian Talmud, and thus the supposedly "abrupt" completion of the Yerushalmi need not be necessarily attributed to pressing external (political) pressures; see Moscovitz, "Formation and Character" (see endnote 150), pp. 670–673.

[154] For a careful study of this issue, see Christine E. Hayes, *Between the Babylonian and Palestinian Talmuds: Accounting for Halakhic Difference in Selected Sugyot from Tractate Avodah Zarah* (New York: Oxford University Press, 1997), esp. pp. 3–29.

. ne days were most terrible, and from the .ıme the new religion took over it was a period of distress for Israel ... and who cannot understand that in such a difficult time there is no leisure to arrange one statement after another as is fitting ... and let us not, therefore, be surprised if we sometimes do not find order in the Yerushalmi" (Frankel, *Mavo ha-Yerushalmi* [see endnote 150], p. 48). Some even suggested that the Palestinian Talmud underwent no redaction at all, but against this see Saul Lieberman, *The Talmud of Caesarea*, Tarbiz suppl., II, 4 (1931), pp. 20f.

[156] See, for example, Mishnah *Nedarim* 3:4.

[157] But note the qualifying tone to this in Shmuel Shiloh, *Dinah De-Malkhuta Dina, The Law of the State Is Law* (Jerusalem: Jerusalem Academic Press, 1975), p. 23, n. 91 (in Hebrew).

[158] See Hayes, *Between the Babylonian and Palestinian Talmuds* (endnote 154) for examples.

[159] The Palestinian Talmud has talmudic discourse for the Mishnaic orders: *Zera'im, Mo'ed, Nashim* and *Nezikin*, but not for *Kodashim* and *Tohorot*; whereas the Babylonian Talmud has no text for Zera'im, but has for most of *Kodashim*. On the question of the study of *Kodashim* in Palestine, see Epstein, *Mevo'ot Le-Sifrut ha-Amora'im* (see endnote 150), pp. 332–334. For the most comprehensive discussion on the question of *Sedarim*, for which we have no Talmud, see Ya'akov Zussman, "Babylonian Sugyot to the *Sedarim* of *Zera'im* and *Taharot*," unpublished Ph.D. dissertation, Jerusalem 1969 (in Hebrew).

[160] Lieberman, *Talmud of Caesarea* (see endnote 155).

[161] Epstein, *Mevo'ot Le-Sifrut ha-Amora'im* (see endnote 150), pp. 279–287ff.; Moshe Assis, "On the Question of the Redaction of Yerushalmi Nezikin," *Tarbiz* 56 (1987), pp. 147–170 (in Hebrew).

[162] See Moshe D. Herr, "On the Rabbinic Understanding of History," *Proceedings of the 6th World Congress of Jewish Studies* (Jerusalem: Magnes Press, 1977), pp. 129–142 (in Hebrew); Ephraim E. Urbach, "Halacha and History," in *Jews, Greeks and Christians: Religious Cultures in Late Antiquity: Essays in Honor of William David Davies*, eds. Robert Hamerton-Kelley and Robin Scroggs (Leiden: Brill, 1976), pp. 112–128; Isaiah M. Gafni, "Rabbinic Historiography and Representations of the Past," in *The Cambridge Companion to the Talmud and Rabbinic Literature*, eds. Charlotte E. Fonrobert and Martin S. Jaffee (New York: Cambridge University Press, 2007), pp. 295–312; the phenomenon described here does not, however, totally preclude the possibility of arriving at "talmudic history," cf. Goodblatt, "Towards the Rehabilitation of Talmudic History" (see endnote 13), pp. 31–44.

[163] *Sifre Deuteronomy* 49, p. 115.

[164] Numerous midrashic statements allude to the growing public preference for *aggadah* over *halakhah* in sermons, cf. *Song of Songs Rabbah* 2.5; BT *Sotah* 40a; JT *Horayot* 3:48c.

[165] For an overview of amoraic midrashim, see Stemberger, *Introduction* (see endnote 149), pp. 276–325; on the nature of *aggadah* and *aggadic* literature, see also Avigdor Shinan, "The Late Midrashic, Paytanic and Targumic Literature," in *Cambridge History of Judaism* (see endnote 2), vol. 4, pp. 681–691.

[166] For a survey of halakhic literature in Palestine following the redaction of the Palestinian Talmud, see Mordechai Margaliot, *Hilkhot Eretz Israel from the Geniza* (Jerusalem: Mossad Harav Kook, 1973), pp. 1–16.

[167] For an important study on *ma'asim* literature, see Mordechai A. Friedman, "Marriage Laws Based on Ma'asim Livne Erez Yisra'el," *Tarbiz* 50 (1981), pp. 209–242. No historical study has yet been produced on sifre hama'asim, save for an excellent M.A. thesis by Hillel Newman, "Ma'asim Livne Eretz Israel and Their Historical Background" (Jerusalem: The Hebrew University, 1987; this work, enhanced and completely updated, by Yad ben-Zvi in 2011).

[168] *Seder Eliahu Rabbah* 20, ed. M. Friedman, 3rd printing (Jerusalem 1969), p. 114.

[169] For messianic expectations on the part of the Jews, and concomitant fears for the fate of Jerusalem in Christian writings, see Günter Stemberger, "Jerusalem in the Early Seventh Century: Hopes and Aspirations of Christians and Jews," in *Jerusalem: Its Sanctity and Centrality to Judaism, Christianity, and Islam*, ed. Lee I. Levine (New York: Continuum, 1999), pp. 260–272.

[170] *Lamentations Rabbah* 1.

[171] BT *Yoma* 10a.

[172] See Zvi Baras, "The Persian Conquest and the End of Byzantine Rule," in *Eretz Israel from the Destruction* (see endnote 6), pp. 323–327 (in Hebrew).

[173] Quoted in *Histoire d'Héraclius par l'évèque Sebeos*, ed. and trans. Frédéric Macler (Paris, 1904), p. 68.

[174] See Avi-Yonah, *Jews Under Roman and Byzantine Rule* (see endnote 4), p. 260.

[175] The best-known collection of these works is in *Midrashei-Ge'ulah*, ed. Yehuda Even-Shmuel (Jerusalem-Tel Aviv: Mossad Bialik, 1954); see, for example, *Seder Eliahu*, p. 42, where the angel Michael describes to Elijah the various kings due to appear before the advent of the Messiah; the names all correspond with the various names of the Persian and Byzantine kings of the time.

[176] For the obvious prejudice incorporated into many of the Christian accounts of these events, and the ensuing care required in any attempt to use them for historical purposes, see Averil Cameron, "The Jews in Seventh-Century Palestine," in *Scripta Classica Israelica* 13 (1994), pp. 75–93.

[177] *Sefer Zerubavel, Midrashei Ge'ulah* (see endnote 175), p. 78.

[178] See *Histoire d'Héraclius* (see endnote 173), p. 71.

[179] *Sefer Zerubavel* (see endnote 177), pp. 80–81.

[180] Avi-Yonah, *Jews Under Roman and Byzantine Rule* (see endnote 4), p. 270.

[181] *Pesikta Rabbati*, ed. Meir Ish-Shalom (Vienna, 1880), p. 162; see Bernard Bamberger, "A Messianic Document of the Seventh Century," *HUCA* 15 (1940), pp. 425–431.

[182] For a critical text of the poem with an introduction and commentary, see Yosef Yahalom, "On the Validity of Literary Works as Historical Sources," *Cathedra* 11 (1979), pp. 125–133 (in Hebrew).

[183] BT *Kiddushin* 72b.

[184] The *geonim* (singular, *gaon*) were the heads of the Babylonian rabbinic academies. *Gaon* is probably a shortened form of *Rosh Yeshivat Ge'on Ya'akov*, with the final two words taken from Psalm 47:4—"the *pride* of Jacob"; see Robert Brody, *The Geonim of Babylonia and the Shaping of Medieval Jewish Culture* (New Haven, CT: Yale University Press, 1998), pp. 44, 49. Brody's excellent work is the definitive statement on the post-talmudic rabbinic world in Babylonia.

[185] For a survey of Jewish settlement in the Babylonian captivity, see Elias J. Bickerman, "The Babylonian Captivity," in *The Cambridge History of Judaism*, vol. 1, eds. William D. Davies and Louis Finkelstein (Cambridge: Cambridge University Press, 1984), pp. 342–358; see also the relevant chapters in *History of the Jewish People: The Restoration—The Persian Period*, ed. Hayim Tadmor (Jerusalem: Am-Oved, 1983) (in Hebrew).

[186] *Antiquities* 11.133, 15.39; Philo, *Legatio ad Gaium* 216.

[187] See, for example, *War* 1.5.

[188] For a history of Babylonian Jewry from just prior to the destruction of the Second Temple until the talmudic period, see David M. Goodblatt, "The Jews in Babylonia, 66-c. 235 CE," in *Cambridge History of Judaism* (see endnote 2), vol. 4, pp. 82–92.

[189] The date itself is supplied by Rav Sherira Gaon in his well-known tenth century *Iggeret*, ed. Lewin, p. 78; for the veracity of this date, see Gafni, *Jews of Babylonia* (see endnote 133), pp. 255–257.

[190] BT *Gittin* 6a; see H. Norman Strickman, "A Note on the Text of Babylonian Talmud Git. 6a," *JQR* 66 (1975–1976), pp. 173–175.

[191] See Josef Wiesehöfer, *Ancient Persia from 550 BC to 650 AD* (London/New York: L.R. Tauris, 1996), pp. 108–109, 133–134, 141–143.

[192] The major source for this claim is the medieval chronicle known as *Seder Olam Zuta* (see endnote 128); the precise date for this work is unclear, with most scholars ascribing it to the ninth century. The fullest and most recent discussion on this is by Geoffrey Herman, "The Exilarchate in the Sasanian Era," unpublished Ph.D. dissertation (Jerusalem: The Hebrew University, 2005), pp. 53–85; this excellent study is to be published shortly as Geoffrey Herman, *A Prince Without a Kingdom: The Babylonian Exilarch in the Sasanian Era* (Tübingen: Mohr Siebeck, 2011).

[193] This change of regime is alluded to in a fascinating talmudic story about a Babylonian rabbinic disciple, Rav Kahana, who was forced to flee

,ıonia after taking the life of a potential Jewish .ıformer; the story appears in BT *Bava Kama* 117a–b, and has been the focus of much scholarly attention in recent years; see the literature cited in Geoffrey Herman, "The Story of Rav Kahana (BT *Baba QaMMA* 117a–b) in Light of Armeno-Persian Sources," *Irano-Judaica* 6 (2008), pp. 56–59, nn. 13–18.

[194] See Herman, *Exilarchate* (see endnote 192), pp. 281–319.

[195] This had been the assumption of one of the major studies on the exilarchate; see Moshe Beer, *The Babylonian Exilarchate in the Arsacid and Sassanian Periods* (Tel Aviv: Bar-Ilan/Dvir, 1970) (in Hebrew); see also Jacob Neusner, *A History of the Jews in Babylonia*, 5 vols. (Leiden: Brill, 1965–1970), but note the reservations regarding taxes and control of the Jewish marketplace raised by Herman in *Exilarchate* (see endnote 192), pp. 267–280.

[196] Some scholars have posited a greater distance between Babylonian sages and commoners than what was described above regarding the Palestinian scene; see, for example Richard L. Kalmin, *The Sage in Jewish Society of Late Antiquity* (London/New York: Routledge, 1999), esp. chapter 2 ("Non-rabbinic Jews"), pp. 27–50.

[197] See Isaiah Gafni, "Babylonian Rabbinic Culture," in *Cultures of the Jews*, ed. David Biale (New York: Schocken Books, 2002), pp. 223–265; in recent years, Yaakov Elman has produced a major series of studies comparing rabbinic realities, legal reasoning and modes of thought with the surrounding Persian environment; for one example, see Yaakov Elman, "Middle Persian Culture and Babylonian Sages: Accommodation and Resistance in the Shaping of Rabbinic Legal Tradition," in *Cambridge Companion to the Talmud and Rabbinic Literature* (see endnote 162), pp. 165–197; for more references to Elman's work, see Adam H. Becker, "The Comparative Study of 'Scholasticism' in Late Antique Mesopotamia," *AJSR* 34, p. 100, n. 41.

[198] For a summary of recent scholarship on this issue, see David Goodblatt, "The History of the Babylonian Academies," in *Cambridge History of Judaism*, vol. 4 (see endnote 2), pp. 821–839.

[199] Determining the stages of the Babylonian yeshiva's development and initial literary appearance is inexorably linked to our dating of the numerous Babylonian talmudic passages that would appear to allude to this institutional development. David Halivni's claim that much of the anonymous strata of the Babylonian Talmud are the work of post-talmudic sages whom he refers to as "stammaim" (see a summary of his theory in David Halivni, "Aspects of the Formation of the Talmud," in *Creation and Composition* [see endnote 40], pp. 339–360) has led some scholars to conclude that the initial appearance of the academy coincides with this late stratum of post-talmudic text; see Jeffrey L. Rubenstein, *Talmudic Stories* (Baltimore: Johns Hopkins University Press, 1999), pp. 21–22. A comparison between the rabbinic *yeshivot* and Christian schools in the East points to some interesting parallels as well as major differences; see Becker, "The Comparitive Study of 'Scholasticism' in Late Antique Mesopotamia" (see endnote 197), pp. 91–113.

[200] See Isaiah Gafni, "'Staff and Legislator'—On New Types of Leadership in the Talmudic Era in Palestine and Babylonia," in *Priesthood and Monarchy*, eds. Gafni and G. Motzkin (Jerusalem: Merkaz Shazar, 1987), pp. 79–92; on relations between the exilarch and the rabbis, see Herman, *Exilarchate* (see endnote 192), pp. 217–266.

[201] BT *Yevamot* 63b.

[202] See Wiesehöfer, *Ancient Persia* (see endnote 191), p. 215; see also Robert Brody, "Judaism in the Sasanian Empire: A Case Study in Religious Coexistence," in *Irano-Judaica* 2, eds. Shaul Shaked and A. Netzer (Jerusalem: Ben-Zvi Institute, 1990), pp. 52–62.

[203] BT *Yoma* 10a; for a detailed discussion of this text, see Richard L. Kalmin, *Jewish Babylonia Between Persia and Roman Palestine* (New York: Oxford University Press, 2006), pp. 122–129.

[204] William Wright, *The Homilies of Aphraates, The Persian Sage* (London: Williams and Norgate, 1869), vol. 1, p. 394.

[205] BT *Kiddushin* 71a.

[206] BT *Ketubbot* 110b.

[207] See Gafni, "Expression and Types of 'Local Patriotism' among the Jews of Sasanian Babylonia," in *Irano-Judaica* 2 (see endnote 202), pp. 63–71; and "How Babylonia Became 'Zion'" (see endnote 1).

VIII. The Religion of the Empire: Christianity from Constantine to the Arab Conquest

[1] My thanks to Dr. Robert C. Gregg, emeritus professor of religious studies at Stanford University, for his close scrutiny of this chapter and his helpful suggestions, and to Dr. Constance DeYoung Groh for her invaluable help in assembling materials for the chapter's revision.

[2] In April 311, Galerius issued an edict reversing the policy of persecution; but it did not end there. The persecutions of 311/312 C.E. claimed the lives of two famous bishops, Peter of Alexandria (November 311) and Lucian of Antioch (January 312). See Timothy D. Barnes, *Constantine and Eusebius* (Cambridge, MA: Harvard University Press, 1981), p. 159.

[3] For an archaeological look at the regional diversity in Palestine and an overview of Christianity and Judaism across the Byzantine period, see Dennis E. Groh, "Palestine in the Byzantine Period," in *OEANE*, vol. 4, pp. 228–232; and "Byzantine Period," in *Dictionary of Judaism in the Biblical Period*, ed. Jacob Neusner (New York: Macmillan, 1996), vol. 1, pp. 105–107. For the epigraphic expressions of public and personal salvation across religions, see Jason Moralee, *"For Salvation's Sake": Provincial Loyalty, Personal Religion, and Epigraphic Production in the Roman and Late Antique Near East* (New York and London: Routledge, 2004). For a definitive history of the conflicts between Jews, Christians and Samaritans in late antique Palestine, see Hagith Sivan, *Palestine in Late Antiquity* (Oxford/New York: Oxford University Press, 2008).

[4] See Timothy D. Barnes, "The Emperor Constantine's Good Friday Sermon," *JTS* 27 (1976), pp. 414–422; and *Constantine and Eusebius* (see endnote 2), pp. 73–76.

[5] *To the Assembly of Saints* 26, in *NPNF*, 2nd series, vol. 1, *Eusebius* (New York: Christian Literature Co., 1890), p. 580, translation slightly altered.

[6] Richard Krautheimer, *Three Christian Capitals: Topography and Politics* (Berkeley: University of California Press, 1983), p. 41.

[7] For this and the plan of the new Christian city, see Krautheimer, *Three Christian Capitals* (see endnote 6), pp. 45, 51–55. However, it is important to note that the city was not as Christian as Eusebius portrayed it; see p. 61.

[8] Eusebius, *Life of Constantine* 4.60, in *NPNF*, vol. 1, p. 555.

[9] For this and the following, see Dennis E. Groh, "Jews and Christians in Late Roman Palestine: Towards a New Chronology," *BA* 51 (1988), pp. 85–86.

[10] Jeremy Cohen, "Roman Imperial Policy Toward the Jews from Constantine until the End of the Palestinian Patriarchate (ca. 429 C.E.)," *BS* 3 (1976), p. 8; Robert L. Wilken, "The Jews and Christian Apologetics After Theodosius I *Cunctos Populos*," *HTR* 73 (1980), pp. 464–465.

[11] Wilken, "The Jews and Christian Apologetics" (see endnote 10), p. 465.

[12] Cohen, "Roman Imperial Policy" (see endnote 10), p. 6; Wilken, "The Jews and Christian Apologetics" (see endnote 10), p. 464.

[13] *Codex Theodosianus* 16, 8.1 as translated in Cohen, "Roman Imperial Policy" (see endnote 10), p. 6. In fact, what Constantine has initiated is the legitimizing of "one-way conversion" (to Christianity only) and the beginning of the end of religious pluralism which will persist to the end of antiquity. See Leo Duprée Sandgren, *Vines Intertwined: A History of Jews and Christians from the Babylonian Exile to the Advent of Islam* (Peabody, MA: Hendrickson, 2010), p. 12.

[14] Glenn F. Chesnut, *The First Christian Histories: Eusebius, Socrates, Sozomen, Theodoret, and Evagrius*, 2nd ed. (Macon, GA: Mercer University Press, 1986), pp. 134–136. Chesnut thinks the signs were apparent only by 335 C.E.; but Barnes (*Constantine and Eusebius* [see endnote 2], p. 162) thinks they were already apparent by 315 C.E. See also Dennis E. Groh, "The Road More Traveled: The *Onomasticon* of Eusebius," *BAR*, March/April 2006, pp. 54–59.

[15] *Codex Theodosianus* 16.10.10. See James Stevenson, *Creeds, Councils, and Controversies: Documents Illustrative of the History of the Church A.D. 337–461* (New York: Seabury, 1966), p. 161. For subsequent edicts in the fifth and sixth centuries, see pp. 260, 261, 263, 358. See also J.R.

..ique et al., *The Church in the Christian Roman* ..*mpire*, vol. 1: *The Church and the Arian Crisis*, trans. Ernest C. Messenger (New York: Macmillan, 1953), pp. 705–709. The factors and subtle shifts that led from the noncoercive anti-pagan attitudes of Eusebius of Caesarea and other key fourth century theologians to the coercive state policies of the late fourth-century are detailed by H.A. Drake, *Constantine and the Bishops: The Politics of Intolerance* (Baltimore: Johns Hopkins University Press, 2000), pp. 402–440.

[16] See Noel Q. King, *The Emperor Theodosius and the Establishment of Christianity* (Philadelphia: Westminster Press, 1960), pp. 18, 30.

[17] Ibid., p. 31.

[18] Ibid., pp. 50–59.

[19] See Richard Lim, "Christian Triumph and Controversy," in *Late Antiquity: A Guide to the Postclassical World*, eds. Glen W. Bowersock, Peter Brown and Oleg Grabar (Cambridge, MA: Belknap Press of Harvard University, 1999), p. 197.

[20] Quoted from Moshe Sharon, "Islam on the Temple Mount," *BAR*, July/August 2006, p. 43.

[21] See Cohen, "Roman Imperial Policy" (see endnote 10), pp. 12–13. For a more comprehensive discussion of Theodosius I's laws as they relate to the Jews, see Sandgren, *Vines Intertwined* (see endnote 13), pp. 522–525.

[22] See Peter Brown, "Aspects of the Christianization of the Roman Aristocracy," in *Religion and Society in the Age of St. Augustine* (New York: Harper & Row, 1972), pp. 161–182, though Brown cautions us about overvaluing the importance of marriage and family in this process on p. 174. More significant is the fact that the laws of the 390s specified that all upper echelon bureaucrats had to be Christians. See Peter Heather, *The Fall of the Roman Empire: A History of Rome and the Barbarians* (Oxford/New York: Oxford University Press, 2006), p. 123.

[23] Chesnut, *First Christian Histories* (see endnote 14), p. 122.

[24] See Dennis E. Groh, "Grace and Backsliding in the Nicene Age: A Footnote on a Triumphalist Orthodoxy," *explor* 3 (1981), pp. 78–93.

[25] Groh, "Jews and Christians" (see endnote 9), pp. 85–86.

[26] See Libanius, *Funeral Oration Over Julian*, for the sad outcome of Julian's attempt to reestablish paganism and his tragic murder in the course of his campaign against the Persians.

[27] For the best reconstruction of events, see R.P.C. Hanson, *The Search for the Christian Doctrine of God: The Arian Controversy 318–381* (Edinburgh: T & T Clark, 1988), pp. 133–135; Lewis Ayers (*Nicaea and Its Legacy* [Oxford/New York: Oxford University Press, 2004]) offers a primarily theological look at the controversy. Eusebius's letter, *Epistle ad Paulin.*, can be found in *Anthanasius' Werke*, fasc. 3, *Urkunden zur Geschichte des arianischen Streits: 318–328*, ed. Hans-Georg Optiz (Berlin: de Gruyter, 1935), Urk. 8.7.

[28] He was, in fact, a distant relative of the future emperor Julian. See Barnes, *Constantine and Eusebius* (see endnote 2), p. 70, n. 79.

[29] Canon 15: see *The Trinitarian Controversy*, ed. William C. Rusch, Sources of Early Christian Thought (Philadelphia: Fortress Press, 1980), p. 54.

[30] Hanson, *Search for the Christian Doctrine* (see endnote 27), pp. 134–135.

[31] Ibid., pp. 148–149.

[32] The synodal letter of this council is available in Rusch, *Trinitarian Controversy* (see endnote 29), pp. 45–48.

[33] The Creed of the Council of Nicaea is not the creed said in current churches. That Nicene Creed, produced by the Council of Constantinople in 381 C.E., was called "Nicene" because it claimed to encapsulate the faith which the Synod of Nicaea promulgated.

[34] Alexander of Alexandria, *Epistle to Alexander of Thessalonica* 32–38, 47, in *Trinitarian Controversy* (see endnote 29), pp. 39–40, 42.

[35] Alexander, *Epistle to Alexander* 28, in *Trinitarian Controversy* (see endnote 29), p. 38; Athanasius *De Decretis* 3.6, in Optiz, *Anthanasius' Werke* 6.4 (see endnote 27), p. 6.

[36] For this view of Arianism, see Robert C. Gregg and Dennis E. Groh, "The Centrality of Soteriology in Early Arianism," *ATR* 59 (1977), pp. 260–278; and *Early Arianism—A View of Salvation* (Philadelphia/London: Fortress Press/SCM, 1981). For debates on this view of the controversy, see

Groh, "New Directions in Arian Research," *ATR* 68 (1986), pp. 347–355. For a quite contrary view, see Rowan Williams, *Arius, Heresy and Tradition* (London: Darton, Longman & Todd, 1987).

[37] The foregoing paragraph is from Groh, "Grace and Backsliding" (see endnote 24), p. 77. See also A.H.M. Jones, *The Roman Economy: Studies in Ancient Economic and Administrative History*, ed. P.A. Brunt (Oxford: Blackwell, 1974), pp. 202–203 (for the *solidus*), p. 403 (on the bureaucratic freeze). Though the Romans insisted on regular and defensible borders, they actually had no real strategy for resisting anything but territorial incursions and no interest in what lay beyond those borders. See James J. O'Donnell, *The Ruin of the Roman Empire* (New York: Ecco/HarperCollins, 2009), p. 87.

[38] *The Creed of the Synod of Nicaea* (June 19, 325), in *Trinitarian Controversy* (see endnote 29), p. 49.

[39] Eusebius of Caesarea's *Letter to His Church*, in *Trinitarian Controversy* (see endnote 29), p. 59.

[40] Gregory of Nazianzus, *Oration* XVIII. 17; quoted in H.M. Gwatkin, *Studies of Arianisim*, 2nd ed. (Cambridge: D. Bell, 1900), p. 46.

[41] Some research on Athanasius has tended to stress his tough-minded and even unfair political ploys. See Hanson, *Search for the Christian Doctrine* (see endnote 27), pp. 240ff. For Athanasius's literary quality, see Charles Kannengiesser, *Athanase d'Alexandrie: Evêque et écrivain* (Paris: Beauchesne Editeur, 1983).

[42] Hanson, *Search for the Christian Doctrine* (see endnote 27), pp. 268–273.

[43] Three excellent (but quite different) books allow the reader to trace these debates. Manlio Simonetti, *La Crisi Ariana nel IV Secolo* (Rome: Institutum Patristicum "Augustinianum," 1975); Thomas A. Kopecek, *A History of Neo-Arianism*, 2 vols., Patristic Monograph Series 8 (Philadelphia: Philadelphia Patristic Foundation, 1979); and Hanson, *Search for the Christian Doctrine* (see endnote 27).

[44] Probably a citywide (hence pagan) reaction. See J.W.C. Wand, *Doctors and Councils* (London: Faith Press, 1962), p. 25. For the wider political violence, see Richard E. Rubenstein, *When Jesus Became God: The Epic Fight over Christ's Divinity in the Last Days of Rome* (New York/San Diego/London: Harcourt Brace & Co., 1999).

[45] Hanson (*Search for the Christian Doctrine* [see endnote 27], pp. 678–679) also points out how independent of Athanasius was their theological tradition. I have followed Hanson in not giving the various parties names based on their favorite essence words for God and have avoided terms such as "Semi-Arian," in accordance with Hanson's warning about "labels" (p. 398).

[46] Hanson, *Search for the Christian Doctrine* (see endnote 27), p. 731. For this conflict of *will* and *nature* languages, see also Gregg and Groh, *Early Arianism* (see endnote 36), pp. 161–183.

[47] See Hanson, *Search for the Christian Doctrine* (see endnote 27), pp. 730ff.

[48] Ibid., pp. 688, 698–699.

[49] The Creed, said as the Nicene Creed in churches today (see endnote 33), was preserved in the statement of faith adopted by the Council of Chalcedon in 451 and can be found in Richard A. Norris, Jr., *The Christological Controversy*, Sources of Christian Thought (Philadelphia: Fortress Press, 1980), p. 157. For the debates about whether this derives from the Council of Constantinople, see Hanson, *Search for the Christian Doctrine* (see endnote 27), pp. 812–815.

[50] See Dennis E. Groh, "Hans von Campenhausen on Canon: Positions and Problems," *Interpretation* 28 (1974), pp. 331–343.

[51] See Albert C. Sundberg, "Canon Muratori: A Fourth Century List," *HTR* 66 (1973), pp. 1–41, whose results were sustained by Geoffrey Hahneman, "More on Redating the Muratorian Fragment," in *Studia Patristica*, vol. 19, *Papers Presented to the Tenth International Conference on Patristic Studies Held in Oxford 1987* (Louvain: Peeters, 1989), pp. 364–365.

[52] For this date and the process of canonization, see Albert C. Sundberg, "Canon of the NT," in *Interpreter's Dictionary of the Bible, Suppl. Vol.* (Nashville: Abingdon, 1976), pp. 136–140.

[53] Ibid., p. 140.

[54] *The Gospel of Judas*, eds. Rodolphe Kasser, Marvin Meyer and Gregor Wurst (Washington, DC: National Geographic, 2006).

[55] See Bart D. Ehrman, *Lost Christianities: The Battles for Scripture and Faiths We Never Knew* (Oxford/New York: Oxford University Press,

2003). Ehrman provides English translations for many of these texts.

[56] See the wall mosaic of the Mausoleum of Galla Placidia (Church of San Lorenzo) (discussed on p. 297 and in endnote 163) which depicts the *amarum* or "chest" with bound volumes of the four Gospels.

[57] See James J. O'Donnell, *Augustine: A New Biography* (New York: HarperCollins, 2005), pp. 126–133, though some Greek copies of the entire Bible were, apparently, available in his time (ibid., p. 127). Here it must be remembered that the cultural centrality of books and their interpreters was one of the most important contributions of late antiquity to the culture of subsequent ages. See O'Donnell, *Ruin of the Roman Empire* (see endnote 37), p. 206.

[58] Ramsay MacMullen, *Roman Social Relations 50 B.C.–284 A.D.* (New Haven, CT: Yale University Press, 1974), p. 38. See Heather, *Fall of the Roman Empire* (see endnote 22), pp. 133–139 for landowning and civic participation percentages.

[59] For references, see Groh, "Jews and Christians" (see endnote 9), pp. 80–81, 89–92; and the discussion of new findings concerning rural prosperity later in this chapter (pp. 300–301).

[60] *Potentiores* appear in the Severan age at the latest, but the term becomes the preferred way of designating the wealthier class in the fourth century. See Jean Gagé, *Les classes sociales dans Empire romain* (Paris: Payot, 1964), p. 284; G. Cardascia, "L'Apparition dans le droit des classes d''Honestiores' et 'Humiliores,'" *Revue historique de droit francais et Etranger* 28 (1950), p. 309.

[61] John Chrysostom, *Homily* 87 (John 20:24–21:14) in Saint John Chrysostom, *Commentary on St. John the Apostle and Evangelist: Homilies 48–88*, trans. Sister Thomas Aquinas Goggin, Fathers of the Church (New York: Fathers of the Church, 1960), pp. 467–468.

[62] *Phthonos* and its compounds. Based on the *Wisdom of Solomon* 2:23–24, the text is often applied to the envy of the devil (cf. Athanasius, *Life of Antony* 5; *De Incarnatione* 5. See also the delightful apotropaic inscriptions on Christian houses in the Golan Heights, erected to ward off "envy." Robert C. Gregg and Dan Urman, *Jews, Pagans, and Christians in The Golan Heights: Greek and Other Inscriptions of the Roman and Byzantine Eras*, South Florida Studies in the History of Judaism 140 (Atlanta: Scholars Press, 1996), no. 227, pp. 264–265. Eyes painted on amulets to ward off envy were commonly worn by both Christians and Jews in antiquity (Sandgren, *Vines Intertwined* [see endnote 13], p. 582), but their use, painted on walls, continued into the modern Palestinian village. See Yizar Hirshfeld, *The Palestinian Dwelling in the Roman-Byzantine Period* (Jerusalem: Franciscan Printing Press/IES, 1995), p. 183. The group of small objects excavated at the Isaurian coastal town of Anumurium illustrates common devices to protect against the evil eye: James Russell, "The Archeological Context of Magic in the Early Byzantine Period," in *Byzantine Magic*, ed. Henry Maguire (Washington, DC: Dumbarton Oaks Research and Library Collection, 1995), pp. 36–38. As a source of ecclesiastical discord, see Eusebius, *Eccles. Hist.* 7.1.7 and G.W.H. Lampe, *A Patristic Greek Lexicon* (Oxford: Clarendon Press, 1961), p. 1474; and Matthew W. Dickie, "The Fathers of the Church and the Evil Eye," in idem., *Byzantine Magic*, pp. 9–34.

[63] Peter Brown, *The Making of Late Antiquity* (Cambridge, MA: Harvard University Press, 1978), p. 57. This behavior stands, as Brown points out, in stark contrast to the aristocratic commitment to a "parity model" of the earlier empire.

[64] See Russell Meiggs, *Roman Ostia*, 2nd ed. (Oxford: Clarendon Press, 1973), p. 259. John E. Stambaugh (*The Ancient Roman City* [Baltimore: Johns Hopkins University Press, 1988], p. 274) calls Ostia in this period "an upper-class beach resort."

[65] Yvon Thébert, "Private Life and Domestic Architecture in Roman Africa," in *A History of Private Life*, ed. Paul Veyne, vol. 1, *From Pagan Rome to Byzantium* (Cambridge, MA: Belknap, 1987), pp. 344–345.

[66] Ibid., p. 338.

[67] For a depiction and discussion of the House of Julius mosaic, see Ibid., fig. 39, pp. 396 and 375. The mosaic depicts a fortified rustic manor house (with adjacent private bath house), whose archaeological accuracy has now been confirmed by recent finds. See Yizhar Hirschfeld "Habitat," in *Late Antiquity* (see endnote 19), pp. 264–265. For a full study of the private dwelling in the Holy

Land itself, see Hirshfeld, *The Palestinian Dwelling* (see endnote 62).

[68] Thébert, "Private Life and Domestic Architecture" (see endnote 65), pp. 335, 337 (figs. 7–9), 341, 344–345.

[69] See Mary G. Houston, *Ancient Greek, Roman, and Byzantine Costume and Decoration*, 2nd ed. (London: Adam & Charles Black, 1966), pp. 120ff. and endnote 70; and Lucille A. Roussin, "Women's and Children's Costumes: Indications of Social Status in the Piazza Armerina Mosaics," in *Studies on Patristic Texts and Archaeology. If These Stones Could Speak ... Essays in Honor of Dennis Edward Groh*, eds. George Kalantzis and Thomas F. Martin (Lewiston/Queenston/Lampeter: The Edwin Mellen Press, 2009), pp. 189–200, figs. 3–12.

[70] Quoted in Eunice Dauterman Maguire, Henry P. Maguire and Maggie J. Duncan-Flowers, *Art and Holy Powers in the Early Christian House* (Urbana: University of Illinois Press, 1989), p. 31; see fig. 28, p. 30 for an example of this kind of tunic.

[71] Ibid., pp. 81–82.

[72] See John Hayes, *Late Roman Pottery* (London: British School at Rome, 1972), African Red Slip Ware, crosses and saints, p. 222, type E (11) and p. 227, nos. 232–242; for Asia Minor wares, see Late Roman "C," pp. 363–368 (Groups II-III, nos. 61–80, for crosses) and p. 262 (no. 58, for a priest). For the way both Jews and Christians were able to purchase small objects from the same workshops and employ similar artistic motifs, see Leonard Victor Rutgers, "Archaeological Evidence for the Interaction of Jews and Non-Jews in Late Antiquity," *AJA* 96.1 (1992), pp. 104–109. Heather, *Fall of the Roman* Empire (see endnote 22), p. 278, for cost-cutting shipping measures.

[73] See Frederik van der Meer, *Augustine the Bishop: The Life and Work of a Father of the Church* (London: Sheed and Ward, 1961), pp. 389–390.

[74] Peter Brown, "Late Antiquity," in *A History of Private Life* (see endnote 65), p. 276.

[75] Ibid.

[76] The *penes* and the *ptochos*: Evelyne Patlagean, *Pauvreté économique et pauvreté sociale à Byzance 4e-7e sciècles* (Paris: Mouton & Ecole des Hautes Etudes en Sciences Sociales, 1977), pp. 25–29.

[77] These powerful verbal images are taken from Peter Brown, *Poverty and Leadership in the Later Roman Empire*, The Menahem Stern Jerusalem Lectures (Hanover, NH: University Press of New England, 2002), p. 12.

[78] Ibid., especially pp. 1–12. For the new role of the bishops, see pp. 1, 8–9, 72. To view Brown's groundbreaking work in a wider setting, see Brent D. Shaw, "Loving the Poor," *New York Review of Books* 49, no. 18, November 21, 2002, pp. 42–45.

[79] Brown, *Poverty* (see endnote 77), pp. 33, 36–37. At the end of the Byzantine period, some former forts in Israel's Negev and Sinai were even transformed into *xenodochia*. See Philip Mayerson, "The Desert of Palestine According to Byzantine Sources," in *Monks, Martyrs, Soldiers and Saracens: Papers on the Near East in Late Antiquity (1962–1993)* (Jerusalem: IES, 1994), p. 51. According to Sivan (*Palestine in Late Antiquity* [see endnote 3], p. 21), such a structure was found near Naaran in the Golan Heights. For the use of and activities in hospices, see Lionel Casson, *Travel in the Ancient World* (Baltimore: The Johns Hopkins University Press, 1994 [1974]), pp. 320–324.

[80] See Daniel Sperber, *Roman Palestine 200–400, The Land: Crisis and Change in Agrarian Society as Reflected in Rabbinic Sources* (Ramat Gan, Israel: Bar-Ilan University, 1978), pp. 96–118.

[81] Clive Foss, "The Near Eastern Countryside in Late Antiquity: A Review Article," in *The Roman and Byzantine Near East: Some Recent Archaeological Research, Journal of Roman Archaeology*, Supplemental Series 14 (1995), pp. 218–219. There is no perceptible decline in Syrian city-culture until the Muslims invade in 635 C.E. See Maurice Sartre, *The Middle East Under Rome*, trans. Catherine Porter and Elizabeth Rawlings, with Jeannine Routier-Pucci (Cambridge, MA: The Belknap Press of Harvard University Press, 2005), p. 365. For the blossoming of village culture in Syria, Turkey and even North Africa, see Heather, *Fall of the Roman Empire* (see endnote 22), p. 113.

[82] Foss, "The Near Eastern Countryside" (see endnote 81), pp. 222, 228–229.

[83] MacMullen, *Roman Social Relations* (see endnote 58), p. 38.

[84] Brown, *The Making of Late Antiquity* (see endnote 63), pp. 12, 56–57, 62–65.

[85] Athanasius, *Life of Antony* 3.

[86] E.A. Judge, *The Conversion of Rome: Ancient Sources of Modern Social Tension*, Macquarie Ancient History Association 1 (North Ryde, Australia: Macquarie Ancient History Association, 1980), pp. 2–4.

[87] Cf. Athanasius, *Life of Antony* 82–89. In Syria, the Holy Man tended to fill the time-honored place of the patron in village society. See Brown, "The Holy Man in Late Antiquity," in *Society and the Holy in Late Antiquity* (Berkeley: University of California Press, 1982), pp. 120–128.

[88] Palladius, *Historia Lausiaca* 38, quoted from Joseph Cullen Ayer, *A Source Book for Ancient Church History* (New York: Charles Scribner's Sons, 1913), p. 403.

[89] *Longer Rule* (7th Rule), quoted in Owen Chadwick, *John Cassian*, 2nd ed. (Cambridge: Cambridge University Press, 1968), p. 60.

[90] Yizhar Hirschfeld, *The Judean Desert Monasteries in the Byzantine Period* (New Haven, CT: Yale University Press, 1992), p. 79. The number of monasteries in the Judean desert alone (not counting Jericho and its surrounding countryside) stands at around 65. Idem., p. 10.

[91] Ibid., pp. 205–212 and maps 5–7. Alliance between the desert monks and the patriarchate of Jerusalem was the crucial factor in the victory of Christian orthodoxy over heresy in Judea. See Sivan, *Palestine in Late Antiquity* (see endnote 3), p. 229.

[92] Hirshfeld, *Judean Desert Monasteries* (endnote 90), pp. 196–199.

[93] Brouria Bitton-Ashkelony, *Encountering the Sacred: The Debate on Pilgrimage in Late Antiquity* (Berkeley: University of California Press, 2005), pp. 5–8. For the importance of the shrines in leading visitors to Christian baptism, see Robin M. Jensen, "Baptism *ad Sanctos*," in *Studies on Patristic Texts and Archaeology* (see endnote 69), pp. 93–110, figs. 1–3, 15–17.

[94] For the term, see Brown, *The Making of Late Antiquity* (see endnote 63), pp. 85–89.

[95] The recently found inscription (238–239 C.E.) from Hippos/Sussita on the eastern side of Lake Kinneret refers to a woman as a "matrona stolata" (Arthur Segal and Michael Eisenberg, "The Spade Hits Sussita," *BAR*, May/June 2006, p. 46). According to the site's excavators, the title indicates her especially conferred ability to manage her own affairs without a male guardian. The full publication of the inscription is less assertive that the *ius (trium) liberorum*, which was conferred on women who birthed at least three children, was also conferred by this title. See Arthur Segal, Jolanta Młynarczyk, Mariusz Burdajewicz, Mark Schuler and Michael Eisenberg, *Hippos-Sussita: Fifth Season of Excavations (September–October 2004 and Summary of All Five Seasons (2000–2004)* (Haifa: Zinman Institute of Archaeology, University of Haifa, 2004), pp. 44–48. But this inscription dated to the autumn of 238 lies much closer in time to the *matronaliter nupta* term applied to a Christian of senatorial rank (*honeste nata)*, Vibia Perpetua, than to the *femina stolata* which they offer as the translation of the Greek term "matrona stolata." *Femina* designates a person of high social class, especially when linked with *maior* (an *honestior)*; but *matrona* is a special title (deriving from the kind of marriage the woman underwent). See Dennis E. Groh, "Upper-Class Christians in Tertullian's Africa: Some Observations," in *Studia Patristica* 14, ed. Elizabeth A. Livingstone, Texte und Untersuchungen zur Geschichte der altchristliche Literatur 117 (1976), pp. 44–45. The aristocratic women of late antiquity who took up the ascetic life did receive dominion over their own property and business affairs.

[96] Paulinus of Nola, *Epistle* 29.7, quoted in Elizabeth A. Clark, *Women in the Early Church*, Message of the Fathers of the Church 13 (Wilmington, DE: Michael Glazier, 1983), p. 217. Sivan (*Palestine in Late Antiquity* [see endnote 3], pp. 34–35) sees a new kind of female virtue being created in such Christian rhetorical pieces as Jerome's eulogy of Paula.

[97] See *The Sayings of the Desert Fathers: The Alphabetical Collection*, trans. Benedicta Ward (London: A.R. Mowbray, 1975), pp. 117–121, for Moses' *dicta*. For his history and life, see Frank M. Snowden, Jr., *Blacks in Antiquity: Ethiopians in the Greco-Roman Experience* (Cambridge, MA: Belknap, 1970), pp. 209–211; for a more negative assessment of attitudes of some early Christians to Moses' blackness, see Peter Frost, "Attitudes Toward Blacks in the Early Christian Era," *SC* 8.1 (1991), pp. 5–6; and Philip Mayerson, "Anti-Black Sentiment in the *Vitae Patrum*," *Monks,*

Martyrs, Soldiers and Saracens (see endnote 79), pp. 140–147 (pp. 140–141 for instances of "prejudicial treatment" based on skin color against Abba Moses).

[98] As, for example, in the end of a villa in Britain around 353–354 C.E. See David S. Neal, *The Excavations of the Roman Villa in Gadebrid Park Hemel Hampstead 1963–8*, Society of Antiquaries of London (London: Thames and Hudson, 1974), p. 98.

[99] John Percival, "The Villa in Italy and the Provinces," in *The Roman World*, ed. John Wacher (London: Routledge and Kegan Paul, 1987), pp. 540–541. Trade between the continent and the eastern Mediterranean, however, was generally down in the late fourth century. See A.J. Parker, "Trade Within the Empire and Beyond the Frontiers," in idem, *The Roman World*, p. 653.

[100] Ibid.

[101] Research on the transition from the late Roman to the barbarian centuries now emphasizes how central the Roman Empire was in forming and sustaining the local "elites" on which that empire depended. The steady withdrawal from the west by the Roman state (beginning in the early fifth century with Britain) precipitated the dramatic collapse of "the Roman-style economy" which previously had fueled and maintained the cities, the armies and the enormous wealth on which the local elites depended. See Peter Brown, *The Rise of Western Christendom: Triumph and Diversity, A.D. 200–1000*, 2nd ed. (Malden, MA: Blackwell Publishers, 2003), p. 13. These are the mixed and continually changing peoples and centuries that will provide the grist for that mythical construct of the birth of various later European nations which Patrick J. Geary has so brilliantly detailed as *The Myth of Nations: The Medieval Origins of Europe* (Princeton, NJ: Princeton University Press, 2003), pp. 63–64, 141, 155–157, 173.

[102] J.H. Waszink, "Some Observations on the Appreciation of the 'Philosophy of the Barbarians' in Early Christian Literature," in *Melanges offerts à Mademoiselle Christine Mohrmann* (Utrecht-Anvers: Spectrum, 1963), pp. 41–56.

[103] See Lidia Storoni Mazzolani, *The Idea of the City in Roman Thought: From Walled City to Spiritual Commonwealth*, trans. S. O'Donnell (Bloomington: Indiana University Press, 1970), pp. 26, 184.

[104] E.A. Thompson, *The Visigoths in the Time of Ulfila* (Oxford: Clarendon Press, 1966), pp. 91, 98. For the overall progress and influence of the Goths, see Heather, *Fall of the Roman Empire* (see endnote 22), especially pp. 153–185, 210–213.

[105] Notably at Socrates Scholasticus, *Ecclesiastical History* 7.10; Sozomen, *Ecclesiastical History* 9.9.10.

[106] Stephen Johnson, *Later Roman Britain* (London: Granada, 1982), pp. 147–149, 162, 200. For western Britain, the picture is one of gradual decline of the towns to the end of antiquity there, about 500 C.E. (p. 202).

[107] O'Donnell, *Augustine* (see endnote 57), p. 341, n. 5: colonial Bône. The classic biography by Peter Brown (*Augustine of Hippo: A Biography*, 2nd ed. [Berkeley: University of California Press, 2000]) should now be supplemented by O'Donnell. For Augustine's religious development, see Dennis E. Groh, *Augustine: Religion of the Heart* (Nashville: Graded Press, 1988).

[108] *The Confessions of St. Augustine* 5.13, *Translated with an Introduction and Notes*, John K. Ryan (Garden City, NY: Image Books, 1960), p. 130. Our understanding of Ambrose's influence on Augustine has been significantly deepened and corrected by J. Patout Burns, "A Surprise for Simplician," in *Studies on Patristic Texts and Archaeology* (see endnote 69), pp. 7–9, 26. According to O'Donnell (*Augustine: A New Biography* [see endnote 57], pp. 33–34), the net effect of newly discovered letters of Augustine has been to shake up the chronology of Augustine's early years (395–411), extending the completion of the *Confessions* to 403 C.E. and emphasizing the years after 410 as the years of his greatest fame.

[109] On Augustine's developing notions of sexuality, see Peter Brown, *The Body and Society: Men, Women, and Sexual Renunciation in Early Christianity* (New York: Columbia University Press, 1988), pp. 387–427.

[110] F. Decret, *L'Afrique manicéene, IVe-Ve siécles* (Paris, 1978), pp. 241–242. It was only after 410 that Augustine returned again to an aristocratic connection, this time through the imperial legate Marcellinus. See O'Donnell, *Augustine* (see endnote 57), p. 34.

[111] See Alfred Warren Matthews, *The Development of St. Augustine from Neoplatonism to Christianity*

386–391 A.D. (Washington, DC: University Press of America, 1980).

[112] See Brown, *Augustine of Hippo* (see endnote 107), pp. 146–157.

[113] Augustine, *Confessions* 13.13.14 (see endnote 108), p. 343, alluding to 2 Corinthians 5:7.

[114] Brown, *Augustine of Hippo* (see endnote 107), p. 234.

[115] Ibid., p. 139.

[116] See W.H.C. Frend, *Donatist Church* (Oxford: Clarendon Press, 1985), pp. 15–24.

[117] W.H.C. Frend, *The Rise of Christianity* (Philadelphia: Fortress Press, 1984), pp. 653–654.

[118] Frend, *Donatist Church* (see endnote 116), pp. xxii, 333–336. Jean-Paul Brisson (*Autonisme et Christianisme dans l'Afrique romaine de Septime Sévère a l'invasion vandale* [Paris: E. de Boccard, 1958]) downplayed the Berber backgrounds (see pp. 5, 28, 413–414) in favor of political, economic and theological/ecclesiastical factors, which Frend now accepts (*Donatist Church*, p. xx). Mixed native and Roman names appear in North African families—even Augustine's, whose mother came from a Donatist background and whose name (Monica), as well as Augustine's son's (Adeodatus), derived from a Berber religious background. See O'Donnell, *Augustine* (see endnote 57), pp. 56, 116 (and p. 352, n. 209).

[119] Brown, *Augustine of Hippo* (see endnote 107), p. 226.

[120] Frend, *Rise of Christianity* (see endnote 117), p. 672.

[121] Ibid.

[122] Ramsay MacMullen, *Christianizing the Roman Empire A.D. 100–400* (New Haven, CT: Yale University Press, 1984), p. 119.

[123] O'Donnell, *Augustine* (see endnote 57), pp. 185–187. The severe and comprehensive measures brought to bear on the pagans wore them out. See Ramsay MacMullen, *Christianity and Paganism in the Fourth to Eighth Centuries* (New Haven, CT: Yale University Press, 1997), p. 73: "... paganism was dismantled from the top down."

[124] Peter Brown, "Pelagius and His Supporters: Aims and Environment," in *Religion and Society* (see endnote 22), pp. 185–193.

[125] Gerald Bonner, *St. Augustine of Hippo: Life and Controversies*, 2nd ed. (Norwich, UK: Canterbury Press, 1986), p. 320.

[126] Joseph T. Lienhard, *Paulinus of Nola and Early Western Monasticism* (Cologne: Peter Hanstein Verlag, 1977), pp. 113–114.

[127] Augustine, *Confessions* 10.29.40 and 10.37.60 (see endnote 108).

[128] See Brown, *Augustine of Hippo* (see endnote 107), pp. 351–352.

[129] See Brown, *Body and Society* (see endnote 109), pp. 405–406; see also *Augustine and Sexuality*, Protocol of 46th Colloquy, Center for Hermeneutical Studies in Hellenistic and Modern Culture (Berkeley: Graduate Theological Union and University of California, 1983), p. 7.

[130] Augustine, *On the Merits* 2.26, 33. Augustine shows life-long attachment to this chapter of Paul, in struggling with which he finds a "Christian" rhetoric to replace the old classical one. See Thomas F. Martin, *Rhetoric and Exegesis in Augustine's Interpretation of Romans 7:24–25A*, Studies in Bible and Early Christianity 47 (Lewiston, NY: The Edward Mellon Press, 2001), pp. 214–215.

[131] Elaine Pagels, *Adam, Eve, and the Serpent* (New York: Random House, 1988); and, more recently, O'Donnell, *Augustine* (see endnote 57), pp. 180–181, 295–303.

[132] Cf. the Synod of Orange of 529 in J. Patout Burns, *Theological Anthropology*, Sources of Early Christian Thought (Philadelphia: Fortress Press, 1981), pp. 109–128.

[133] O'Donnell (*Augustine* [see endnote 57], p. 247) points out the pagan aristocrats were from the first families of Rome.

[134] Augustine, *City of God* 1.9.24, trans. Marcus Dods (Edinburgh: T & T Clark, 1871), pp. 339–340.

[135] Augustine, *City of God* 14.13.

[136] Augustine, *City of God* 22.30, in *Saint Augustine: The City of God*, trans. Gerald C. Walsh (New York: Fathers of the Church, 1952), pp. 506–507.

[137] See Donald C. Earl, *The Moral and Political Tradition of Rome* (Ithaca, NY: Cornell University Press, 1976 [1967]), pp. 122–132.

[138] On envy, see endnote 62.

[139] *The Rule of St. Benedict* 7, in *Western Asceticism, Selected Translations with Introductions and Notes by Owen Chadwick*, Library of Christian Classics 12 (Philadelphia: Westminster Press, 1958).

[140] See Peter Brown, *The Cult of the Saints: Its Rise and Function in Latin Christianity* (Chicago/London: University of Chicago Press/SCM, 1981), pp. 86–127; and see endnote 91.

[141] Cf. Pope Leo I, *Sermo* 4.2–4.

[142] Pope Gregory, *Dialogue* 3.24, in *The Fathers of the Church: A New Translation* (New York: Fathers of the Church, 1959), p. 157.

[143] *The Definition of Faith*, quoted from Norris, *Christological Controversy* (see endnote 49), p. 158, italics added.

[144] See Judith Herrin, *The Formation of Christendom* (Princeton, NJ: Princeton University Press, 1987), pp. 72–75 for the bishops' role in the cities and p. 105 for the Roman Christian influence on the Franks.

[145] *Vita S. Caesarii Arelatensis a discipulis scripta* 1.28–34, in *The Conversion of Western Europe 350–750*, ed. J.N. Hillgarth (Englewood Cliffs, NJ: Prentice-Hall, 1969), pp. 37–39. Yet if we step outside the orthodox Church's view of the Arian rulers, we discover that Theodoric's long reign in Italy was also one of "civility" and that Vandal Africa experienced something of a late classical literary renaissance. See O'Donnell, *Ruin of the Roman Empire* (see endnote 37), pp. 127, and also 71, 107 and 251–253. The real danger to the empire and its religion lay in the landowners' need to come to accommodation with whoever ruled. See Heather, *Fall of the Roman Empire* (see endnote 22), pp. 139–140.

[146] See L. Michael White, *Building God's House in the Roman World: Architectural Adaptation Among Pagans, Jews, and Christians* (Baltimore: Johns Hopkins University Press, 1990), pp. 104–110; and Bradley Blue, "Acts and the House Church," in *The Book of Acts in Its First Century Setting*, vol. 2, *Graeco-Roman Setting*, eds. David W.J. Gill and Conrad Gempf (Grand Rapids, MI: Eerdmans, 1994), pp. 173–177, 183. For the development of architecture, see also Paul Corby Finney, "Churches," in *OEANE*, vol. 2, pp. 1–5.

[147] See Gradon F. Snyder, *Ante Pacem: Archaeological Evidence of Church Life Before Constantine* (Macon, GA: Mercer University Press, 2003), pp. 140–153. Snyder's book also provides a current review of Christian art and archaeology before the fourth century.

[148] Ibid., p. 128; see also L. Michael White, *The Social Origins of Christian Architecture*, vol. 2, *Texts and Monuments for the Christian Domus Ecclesiae in Its Roman Setting*, Harvard Theological Studies (Valley Forge, PA: Trinity Press International, 1997), pp. 4–6, for San Clemente, et al.

[149] Snyder, *Ante-Pacem* (see endnote 147), pp. 134–136.

[150] Based on the stratigraphic evidence presented by the excavator, I have accepted an earlier date for the structure in the first three decades of the third century, rather than the 250–300 C.E. date given by Tzaferis (see Vassilios Tzaferis, "Inscribed 'To God Jesus Christ'," *BAR*, March/April 2007, p. 44). Israeli excavators tend to add (incorrectly, I think) several decades to their stratigraphic evidence in order to provide the most conservative overall dating for a structure. See, for example, Zeev Weiss, *The Sepphoris Synagogue: Deciphering an Ancient Message Through Its Archaeological and Socio-Historical Contexts* (Jerusalem: IES, 2005), p. 39, where the synagogue's stratigraphically obtained foundation date of "no later than 400 C.E." becomes " ... the synagogue was built no later than the first or second decade of the fifth century C.E."

[151] Snyder, *Ante Pacem* (see endnote 147), pp. 127–134.

[152] For the details cited and plans, see ibid., pp. 132–134.

[153] White, *Building God's House* (see endnote 146), pp. 127–130.

[154] Ibid., p. 128.

[155] Snyder, *Ante Pacem* (see endnote 147), p. 139; and Blue, "Acts and the House Church" (see endnote 146), pp. 146–149, for Julianos and Aquileia, respectively.

[156] See James R. Strange, *The Emergence of the Christian Basilica in the Fourth Century, International Studies in Formative Christianity and Judaism*, Global Publications (Binghamton: State University of New York at Binghamton, 2000), pp. xi–xii, 15; p. 54 for the processional liturgical use of such spaces.

[157] See L. Michael White, "Architecture," in *The Encyclopedia of Early Christianity*, 2nd ed., ed. Everett Ferguson (New York: Garland Publishing, 1997), vol. 1, p. 105; and Gregory T. Armstrong, "Basilica," in *The Encyclopedia of Early Christianity*, vol. 1, pp. 172–175. Most convincing to me is Strange's thesis that Constantinian basilicas represent "grand processional halls" that derive from the Roman colonnaded street. See *Emergence of the Christian Basilica* (see endnote 156), pp. 54–55.

[158] Ibid., pp. 55–66.

[159] W.F. Volbach, *Early Christian Art* (London: Thames and Hudson, 1961), p. 336 and plate 131. Volbach's assertion that the building was an earlier pagan one must be corrected; it dates to 432–440 at the latest, see Richard Krautheimer, *Early Christian and Byzantine Architecture*, Pelican History of Art (Baltimore: Penguin Books, 1965), p. 324, n. 46.

[160] According to a new interpretation by Thomas F. Matthews, *The Clash of the Gods: A Reinterpretation of Early Christian Art*, rev. ed. (Princeton, NJ: Princeton University Press, 2003), pp. 98–111. Matthews argues that Christ as "the son of God" is the central emphasis of these huge mosaic images (see p. 96).

[161] John Beckwith, *Early Christian and Byzantine Art* (Baltimore: Penguin Books, 1970), pp. 14, 32 and plate 18.

[162] Sivan, *Palestine in Late Antiquity* (see endnote 3), pp. 189, 193, 200, 202; Sandgren, *Vines Intertwined* (see endnote 13), pp. 550–551, 591ff. For the struggle to take Jerusalem into Christian ownership, see the discussion "The growing Christian presence in the Holy Land" later in this chapter (pp. 321–327) and endnotes 188–189.

[163] Krautheimer, *Early Christian and Byzantine Architecture* (see endnote 159), pp. 337–338; Matthews, *Clash of the Gods* (see endnote 160), pp. 149 and 153, for its signaling the ascension of Christ over the old planetary dignities. If anyone deserved her rest, it was Galla Placidia. See Stuart Irvin Oost, *Galla Placidia Augusta: A Biographical Essay* (Chicago: University of Chicago Press, 1968) and Heather, *Fall of the Roman Empire* (see endnote 22), pp. 191, 251.

[164] Krautheimer, *Early Christian and Byzantine Architecture* (see endnote 159), p. 192.

[165] See Thomas A. Kopecek, "Neo-Arian Religion: The Evidence of the Apostolic Constitutions," in *Arianism: Historical and Theological Reassessments*, ed. Robert C. Gregg (Philadelphia: Philadelphia Patristic Foudation, 1985), p. 174.

[166] Guiseppe Bovini, *Ravenna Felix* (Ravenna, Italy: Edizione A. Longo, 1960), p. 31; for the processional mosaics, see Matthews, *Clash of the Gods* (see endnote 160), 164ff.

[167] Bovini, *Ravenna Felix* (see endnote 166), pp. 35–40; note an earlier Arian human hand still appears on the column of the representation of Theodoric's palace. See Alberto Busignani, *I mosaici ravenati*, forma e colore (Firenza: Sadea editore, no date), plate 26. For the significance of the Palatium mosaic, see Sabina G. MacCormack, *Art and Ceremonial in Late Antiquity* (Berkeley: University of California Press, 1981), p. 237.

[168] Busignani, *I mosaici ravenati* (endnote 167), pp. 31–32; MacCormack, *Art and Ceremonial* (see endnote 167), pp. 259–266, for the significance of the mosaics; Matthews (*Clash of the Gods* [see endnote 160], p. 171) insists that clergy "outrank" the imperials in this mosaic. For Justinian's biological age and his never having visited either the church or the city, see O'Donnell, *Ruin of the Roman Empire* (see endnote 37), p. 178.

[169] See John Julius Norwich, *The Middle Sea: A History of the Mediterranean* (New York: Doubleday, 2006), pp. 70–71, for this last moment of Rome's Mediterranean-wide unity.

[170] Cf. Fragments 74, 87, 93, 126, in Norris, *Christological Controversy* (see endnote 49), pp. 109–111.

[171] Frend, *Rise of Christianity* (see endnote 117), p. 635.

[172] For the "schools" of Alexandria and Antioch, see R.V. Setters, *Two Ancient Christologies* (London: SPCK, 1940).

[173] Guillet, "Les Exégèses d'Alexandrie et d'Antioche. Conflit ou maltendue," *Recherches de science religieuse* 34 (1947), pp. 257–302. Despite its obvious methodological flaw of comparing Theodore of Mopsuestia to Origen, the comments on exegetical differences between the two schools are useful.

[174] Herrin, *Formation of Christendom* (see endnote 144), pp. 119–120. For Theodore, see Richard A. Norris, Jr., *Manhood and Christ: A Study in the Christology of Theodore of Mopsuestia* (Oxford: Clarendon Press, 1963). The contemporary charges of the Alexandrians that Theodore taught two different and distinct Sons has been challenged on the basis of the recently translated and edited Greek fragments of his commentary on John. See George Kalantzis, *Theodore of Mopsuestia: Commentary on the Gospel of John*, Early Christian Studies 7 (Strathfield, Australia: St Paul's Publications, 2004), pp. 31–34.

[175] Socrates Scholasticus, *Ecclesiastical History* 7.34.

[176] *Third Letter of Cyril to Nestorius*, quoted from Edward Rochie Hardy and Cyril C. Richardson, *Christology of the Later Fathers*, Library of Christian Classics 3 (Philadelphia: Westminster Press, 1954), p. 350.

[177] Socrates Scholasticus, *Ecclesiastical History* 7.34; but see Francis M. Young (with Andrew Teal), *From Nicaea to Chalcedon*, 2nd ed. (Grand Rapids, MI: Baker Academic, 2010), pp. 288–298.

[178] For these, see R.V. Sellers, *The Council of Chalcedon: A Historical and Doctrinal Survey* (London: SPCK, 1961), pp. 3–129; Aloys Grillmeier, *Christ in Christian Tradition*, vol. 1: *From the Apostolic Age to Chalcedon (451)*, 2nd ed., trans. John Bowden (Atlanta: John Knox Press, 1975), pp. 520–539.

[179] Sellers, *Council of Chalcedon* (see endnote 178), pp. 109–110.

[180] Ibid., p. 116.

[181] For the text of Chalcedon on these points, see T. Herbert Bindley, *The Oecumenical Documents of the Faith*, 4th ed. (London: Methuen, 1950), p. 235. See also *Definition of Faith* (see endnote 143).

[182] Frend, *Rise of Christianity* (see endnote 117), pp. 639, 772–773.

[183] Sellers, *Council of Chalcedon* (see endnote 178), p. 125.

[184] See W.H.C. Frend, *The Rise of the Monophysite Movement: Chapters in the History of the Church in the Fifth and Sixth Centuries* (Cambridge: Cambridge University Press, 1972).

[185] For his attempts to "re-Chalcedonianize" the monasteries, see James E. Goehring, "Chalcedonian Power Politics and the Demise of Pachomian Monasticism," Institute for Antiquity and Christianity, Occasional Papers 15. (See also endnote 174.)

[186] Frend, *Rise of the Monophysite Movement* (see endnote 184), pp. 292–293.

[187] Aziz S. Atiya, *A History of Eastern Christianity* (London: Methuen, 1968), pp. 240–241.

[188] Asher Ovadiah, *Corpus of the Byzantine Churches in the Holy Land*, Theophaneia 22 (Bonn: Peter Hanstein Verlag, 1970), p. 188. Eudocian churches include St. John the Baptist (Corpus no. 67, pp. 78–79), St. Stephen (Corpus no. 66, pp. 77–78), the church at Silwan (Corpus no. 78a, pp. 90–91). To the Silwan basilica should now be added the public building just above it on Mount Zion from area H in the City of David Excavations, only a corner of which has been excavated. See Yigal Shiloh, *Excavations at the City of David I 1978–1982*, Qedem 19 (Jerusalem: The Institute of Archaeology, The Hebrew University of Jerusalem, 1984), p. 6. My preliminary study of the section, plans and pottery from area H (filed as a preliminary report with Dr. Yigal Shiloh before his untimely death) confirms a date compatible with a Eudocian founding reported in the Shiloh report (p. 6). The date proposed by Jodi Magness is much too early. See Jodi Magness, "The Late Roman and Byzantine Pottery from Areas H and K," *Excavations at the City of David I 1978–1985 Directed by Yigal Shiloh*, vol. III, eds. Alon De Groot and Donald T. Ariel, Qedem 33 (Jerusalem: The Institute of Archaeology, The Hebrew University of Jerusalem, 1992), p. 151. The empress Eudocia's building efforts developed the city in a direction north of the old walls. See Sivan, *Palestine in Late Antiquity* (see endnote 3), pp. 213–214.

[189] See Robert L. Wilken, "The Restoration of Israel in Biblical Prophecy in the Early Byzantine Period," in *"To See Ourselves as Others See Us,"* eds. Jacob Neusner and Ernest S. Frerichs (Chico, CA:

Scholars Press, 1985), pp. 460, 464–465; and "Byzantine Palestine: A Christian Holy Land," *BA* 51 (1988), p. 217. (See also endnote 162.)

[190] See King, *Emperor Theodosius* (see endnote 16), p. 118; Cohen, "Roman Imperial Policy" (see endnote 10), pp. 1–29; Wilken, "Jews and Christian Apologetics" (see endnote 10), pp. 451–471. (See also endnote 15.)

[191] King, *Emperor Theodosius* (see endnote 16), p. 177. See also S. Krauss, "The Jews in the Works of the Church Fathers," *JQR* 5 (1893), pp. 122–157; *JQR* 6 (1894), pp. 82–99.

[192] See Gedaliah Alon, *The Jews in Their Land in the Talmudic Age (70–640 CE)*, trans. and ed. Gershon Levi (Cambridge, MA: Harvard University Press, 1989), p. 740.

[193] See Socrates Scholasticus, *Ecclesiastical History* 7.16, 17, 38 and 13 respectively.

[194] For the Judaizers at Antioch, see Robert L. Wilken, *John Chrysostom and the Jews* (Berkeley: University of California Press, 1983), pp. 67, 75.

[195] *Adversus Judaeos Homily* 1.6 (PG 48, 852) as cited by Wilken, *John Chrysostom and the Jews* (see endnote 194), p. 160.

[196] For the frequency and nature of these references, see Robert L. Wilken, *Judaism and the Early Christian Mind: A Study of Cyril of Alexandria's Exegesis and Theology* (New Haven, CT: Yale University Press, 1971), pp. 59–61.

[197] See Dennis E. Groh ("The Road More Traveled" [see endnote 14]) for the beginnings of this Christian claim to the Holy Land as supplanting the Jews; see also "The *Onomasticon* of Eusebius of Caesarea and the Rise of Christian Palestine," *Studia Patristica XVIII Papers of the 1983 Oxford Patristics Conference*, ed. E.A. Livingstone, vol. 1: *Historica-Theologica-Gnostica-Biblica* (Kalamazoo, MI: Cistercian Publications, 1986), pp. 23–31; and Robert L. Wilken, *The Land Called Holy: Palestine in Christian History and Thought* (New Haven, CT: Yale University Press, 1992), pp. 97–100, 166–172. (See also endnotes 161–162.)

[198] See Steven Fine and Eric M. Myers, "Synagogues," in *OEANE*, vol. 5, pp. 118–123; Dan Urman and Paul V.M. Flesher eds., *Ancient Synagogues: Historical Analysis and Archeological Discovery*, 2 vols. (Leiden: Brill, 1995); Wilken, "Jews and Christian Apologetics" (see endnote 10), pp. 461–462; *Judaism and the Early Christian Mind* (see endnote 196), pp. 37, 53; *John Chrysostom and the Jews* (see endnote 194), p. 65; and Sandgren, *Vines Intertwined* (see endnote 13), pp. 569–573.

[199] On the lessened exegetical contact between contemporary Christians and Jews, see Judith R. Baskin, "Rabbinic Patristic Exegetical Contacts in Late Antiquity: A Bibliographical Reappraisal," in *Approaches to Ancient Judaism*, vol. 5: *Studies in Judaism in Its Graeco-Roman Context*, ed. William S. Green (Atlanta: Scholars Press, 1985), pp. 65–67; A.P. Hayman, "The Image of the Jew in the Syriac Anti-Jewish Polemical Literature," in *"To See Ourselves as Others See Us"* (see endnote 189), p. 440. See also Sandgren, *Vines Intertwined* (see endnote 13), pp. 569–573.

[200] Glanville Downey, "Caesarea and the Christian Church," in *The Joint Expedition to Caesarea Maritima*, vol. 1: *Studies in the History of Caesarea Maritima*, ed. Charles T. Fritsch (Missoula, MT: Scholars Press, 1975), p. 36.

[201] Glanville Downey, *Gaza in the Early Sixth Century* (Norman: University of Oklahoma Press, 1963), pp. 115–116.

[202] Robert Schick, *The Christian Communities of Palestine from Byzantine to Islamic Rule: A Historical and Archaeological Study* (Princeton, NJ: The Darwin Press, 1995), p. 12. Schick estimates the Jewish population at only 10 to 15 percent of the total population of Palestine by the sixth century; but Andre S. Jacobs ("Visible Ghosts and Invisible Demons: The Place of Jews in Early Christian *Terra Sancta*," in *Galilee Through the Centuries: Confluence of Cultures*, ed. Eric M. Meyers, Duke Judaic Studies Series, vol. 1: *Second International Conference on the Galilee in Antiquity* [Winona Lake, IN: Eisenbrauns, 1999], p. 361) indicates only that the Jewish population "dropped markedly."

[203] Wilken, "Byzantine Palestine" (see endnote 189), pp. 216–217; see also endnote 93. For the triumphalist campaign against paganism carried on at Gerasa in inscriptions on Christian monuments and through the use of epigraphic *spolia*, see Jason Moralee, "The Stones of St. Theodore: Disfiguring the Pagan Past in Christian Gerasa," *Journal of Early Christian Studies* 14.2 (2006), pp. 183–215.

[204] For agricultural technology, see Philip Mayerson, "The Ancient Agricultural Regime of Nessana and

the Central Negeb," in *Excavations at Nessana*, vol. 1, ed. H. Dunscomb Colt (London: British School of Archaeology in Jerusalem, 1962), pp. 211–269; "A Note on Demography and Land Use in the Ancient Negeb" and "The Wine and Vineyards of Gaza in the Byzantine Period," in *Monks, Martyrs, Soldiers* (see endnote 79), pp. 100–104 and 250–255, respectively.

[205] See *Ancient Churches Revealed*, ed. Yoram Tsafrir (Jerusalem/Washington, DC: IES/Biblical Archaeology Society, 1993). To the list of Christian monuments discovered in the Negev should now be added the Northern Monastery (Area P) and large Central Church (Area F) at Nessana. See Dan Urman, "Nessana Excavation 1987–1995," in *Nessana: Excavations and Studies*, vol. 1, ed. Dan Urman (Beer-Sheva: Ben-Gurion University of the Negev Press, 2004) (English version), pp. 11*–21* and 69*–101*.

[206] J. Shereshevski, *Byzantine Urban Settlements in the Negev Desert* (Beer-Sheva: Ben-Gurion University of the Negev Press, 1991).

[207] The prosperity in the West ended in the fifth century C.E., but continued in the East until the mid-sixth. See Yizhar Hirschfeld, "Habitat," in *Late Antiquity* (see endnote 19), p. 268.

[208] See Bellarmino Bagatti, *The Church from the Gentiles in Palestine: History and Archaeology* (Jerusalem: Franciscan Printing Press, 1971), pp. 71–72; Alon, *Jews in Their Land* (see endnote 192), p. 753, for the text. See especially Stephan Goranson, "Joseph of Tiberias Revisited: Orthodoxies and Heresies in Fourth Century Galilee," in *Galilee Through the Centuries* (see endnote 202), pp. 335–343.

[209] Eric M. Meyers, Ehud Netzer and Carol L. Meyers, "Sepphoris 'Ornament of All Galilee,'" *BA* 49 (1986), p. 6; Zeev Weis, "Sepphoris," in *NEAEHL*, vol. 4, p. 1325. For the full history of the site, see James F. Strange, Thomas R.W. Longstaff and Dennis E. Groh, *Excavations at Sepphoris: The USF Excavations*, vol. 1 (Leiden: Brill: 2006), pp. 9–33. But the city also had a spectacular synagogue built between previously existing structures which flourished from the early fifth into the seventh centuries. See Zeev Weiss, *The Sepphoris Synagogue: Deciphering an Ancient Message through Its Archaeological and Socio-Historical Contexts* (Jerusalem: IES/Institute of Archaeology, The Hebrew University of Jerusalem, 2005), p. 39. In fact, a small Jewish community continued there until the 11th century. See Seth Ward, "Sepphoris in Sacred Geography," in *Galilee Through the Centuries* (see endnote 202), p. 393.

[210] Eric M. Meyers and James F. Strange, *Archaeology, The Rabbis, and Early Christianity* (Nashville: Abingdon, 1981), pp. 128–137. For the overall presence of Christian churches in Galilee, see Mordechai Aviam, "Christian Galilee in the Byzantine Period," in *Galilee Through the Centuries* (see endnote 202), pp. 281–300.

[211] Alon, *Jews in Their Land* (see endnote 192), p. 576.

[212] James F. Strange, "Diversity in Early Palestinian Christianity, Some Archaeological Evidences," *ATR* 65 (1983), p. 22. See also the very recent identification of Mary imagery on a bread mold found at Mamre where Constantine had already built a basilica. Robert C. Gregg, "A Pagan and Christian 5th–6th Century Bread Mold?" *Studies on Patristic Texts and Archaeology* (see endnote 69), pp. 161–163.

[213] Stanislao Loffreda, *The Sanctuaries of Tabgha*, trans. Claire Fenaell (Jerusalem: Franciscan Printing Press, 1975); *Scavi di et-Tabgha*, Pubblicazioni dello Studium Biblicum Franciscanum, Collectio minor 7 (Jerusalem: Topographia dei PP. Francescani, 1970). For Kursi, see Dan Urman, "The Site of the Miracle of the Man with the Unclean Spirit," *Christian News from Israel*, n.s. 22 (1971), pp. 72–76; and Vassilios Tzaferis, "The Early Christian Monastery at Kursi," in *Ancient Churches Revealed* (see endnote 205), pp. 77–79.

[214] Krautheimer, *Early Christian and Byzantine Architecture* (see endnote 159), pp. 153–161, 180 (for St. Irene); William MacDonald, *Early Christian and Byzantine Architecture* (New York: George Braziller, 1971), pp. 34–36.

[215] Ovadiah, *Corpus of the Byzantine Churches* (see endnote 188), Corpus no. 78b, pp. 92–93.

[216] Nahman Avigad, *Discovering Jerusalem* (Nashville: Thomas Nelson, 1980), pp. 212–229, for the inscription, see p. 245; see also "The Nea: Justinian's Church of St. Mary, Mother of God, Discovered in the Old City of Jerusalem," in *Ancient Churches Revealed* (endnote 205), pp. 134–135. The crucial Christian ideological import of the

Madaba map is discussed by Sivan, *Palestine in Late Antiquity* (see endnote 3), pp. 255–257.

[217] Ovadiah, *Corpus of the Byzantine Churches* (see endnote 188), Tables 1 and 7.

[218] Pao Figueras, *Decorated Jewish Ossuaries* (Leiden: E.J. Brill, 1983), pp. 10–12. For a less clear contention that Jews ceased ossuary burial because of Christian imitation, see Byron H. McCann, "Bones of Contention? Ossuaries and Reliquaries in Early Judaism and Christianity," *SC* 8.4 (1991), pp. 235–246.

[219] See Groh, "Jews and Christians" (see endnote 9), pp. 84, 92; and "The Stratigraphic Chronology of the Galilean Synagogue from the Early Roman Period Through the Early Byzantine Period (ca. 420 C.E.)," in *Ancient Synagogues* (see endnote 198), vol. 1, pp. 67–68. Sivan (*Palestine in Late Antiquity* [see endnote 3], p. 46) emphasizes the rivalry that the side-by-side structures reveal; she (p. 24) wisely emphasizes that architecture could be used as a weapon by a religious community in its struggles with outsiders.

[220] See G. Foerster, "Beth-Shean at the Foot of the Mound," in *NEAEHL*, vol. 1, p. 233, who now considers the house with Homeric and Nilotic scenes to be a synagogue. For other Nilotic and Hellenic motifs, see also the house found at Sepphoris. Ehud Netzer and Zeev Weiss, "New Evidence for Late-Roman and Byzantine Sepphoris," in *Roman and Byzantine Near East* (see endnote 81), pp. 164–171.

[221] A couple of splendid examples of such amulets have been found at Sepphoris. One is a rare amulet that was thought to bring about "social magic." See C. Thomas McCollough and Beth Glazier-McDonald, "A Silver Amulet From Sepphoris, Israel," in *Studies on Patristic Texts and Archaeology* (endnote 69), pp. 201–218 (see also p. 204 for the more common amulets meant to protect a person against disease). Another is an amulet to bring about relief from a particular kind of fever. See C. Thomas McCollough and Beth Glazier-McDonald, "Magic and Medicine in Byzantine Galilee: A Bronze Amulet from Sepphoris," in *Archaeology and the Galilee: Texts and Contexts in the Graeco-Roman and Byzantine Periods*, eds. Douglas R. Edwards and C. Thomas McCollough (Atlanta: Scholars Press, 1997), pp. 143–149; though the stratigraphic context appears to date from the late fourth to the early fifth centuries (p. 144), it is a superb example of this kind of magical/medical amulet.

[222] Sandgren, *Vines Intertwined* (see endnote 13), p. 584; for the use of Jewish and Christian magical amulets, see pp. 581–583. A late Byzantine (sixth–seventh centuries) gold necklace has been found with two amulet cases mounted on either side of the central gold cross. See Maguire, *Art and Holy Powers* (see endnote 70), p. 165, n. 90.

[223] O'Donnell, *Ruin of the Roman Empire* (see endnote 37), pp. 286–287, for the Herodotus reference and start and progress of the plague; for the exact dates and precise course of the outbreaks, see Dionysios Stathakopoulos, "Crime and Punishment: The Plague in the Byzantine Empire, 541–749," in *Plague and the End of Antiquity: The Pandemic of 541–750*, ed. Lester K. Little (Cambridge: Cambridge University Press, in Association with the American Academy in Rome, 2007), pp. 102–103.

[224] Stathakopoulos, "Crime and Punishment" (see endnote 223), p. 105.

[225] See Eamon Duffy, "The First Great Pandemic in History," for a review article on *Plague and the End of Antiquity* (see endnote 223), in *New York Review of Books* 55, no. 9 (2008), pp. 17–19.

[226] Lester K. Little, "Life and Afterlife of the First Plague Pandemic," in *Plague and the End of Antiquity* (see endnote 223), pp. 3–15.

[227] Robert Sallares, "Ecology, Evolution, and Epistemology of Plague," in *Plague and the End of Antiquity* (see endnote 223), pp. 243 and 249.

[228] Duffy, "The First Great Pandemic in History" (see endnote 225), p. 17.

[229] See Little, "Life and Afterlife," (see endnote 226), p. 7; see also the numbers reported by the Syriac writer John of Ephesos, Michael G. Marony, "'For Whom Does the Writer Write?' The First Bubonic Plague Pandemic According to Syriac Sources," in *Plague and the End of Antiquity* (see endnote 223), pp. 72–78.

[230] Michael McCormick, "Toward a Molecular History of the Justinianic Pandemic," in *Plague and the End of Antiquity* (see endnote 223), p. 298. However, in central Italy, a cemetery of infants who died of malarial fever, dated to the fifth century, has

been discovered. See Sallares, "Ecology, Evolution, and Epistemology of Plague" (see endnote 227), p. 234. The difficulty of tracking the effects of empire-wide crises can be seen in the careful study of Peter Garnsey, *Famine and Food Supply in the Graeco-Roman World: Responses to Risk and Crisis* (Cambridge: Cambridge University Press, 1989), where the author notes, for example, the lack of records relating to the problems caused by the plague that struck Rome in 167 C.E. (p. 227).

[231] See Hugh N. Kennedy, "Justinianic Plague in Syria and the Archaeological Evidence," in *Plague and the End of Antiquity* (see endnote 223), pp. 87–95.

[232] Stathakopoulos, "Crime and Punishment" (see endnote 223), especially p. 110.

[233] Note that Sallares ("Ecology, Evolution, and Epistemology of Plague" [see endnote 227], p. 234) reports the use of magic rituals to combat malarial fever; the fourth/fifth century Sepphoris amulet was intended to cure such a fever (see endnote 221). Bodily healing could be sought through amulets, texts or appeal to Christian saints. See *Religions of Late Antiquity in Practice*, ed. Richard Valantasis (Princeton, NJ: Princeton University Press, 2000), pp. 9, 341–342. A complete survey of the types and scale of importance of miracles performed by saints has not been compiled; but Alexander Kazhdan's preliminary list does show that "healings were performed by each and every saint." See "Holy and Unholy Miracle Workers" in *Byzantine Magic* (see endnote 62), p. 76.

[234] Michael Avi-Yonah, *The Jews of Palestine: A Political History from the Bar Kokhba War to the Arab Conquest* (New York: Schocken, 1976), pp. 251, 254.

[235] Ibid., pp. 261–270; Sandgren, *Vines Intertwined* (see endnote 13), p. 610. For the devastating blow the fall of Jerusalem constituted for contemporary Christians, see Wilken, *Land Called Holy* (see endnote 197), pp. 218–224.

[236] Herrin, *Formation of Christendom* (see endnote 144), pp. 194–195, 203–204; Avi-Yonah, *Jews of Palestine* (see endnote 234), p. 266 (for church destruction). For the fact that the Christian communities never recovered from the Persian conquest and occupations, see Schick, *Christian Communities of Palestine* (see endnote 202), p. 47.

[237] For the dates, see Avi-Yonah, *Jews of Palestine* (see endnote 234), pp. 272–275. See Dennis E. Groh, "Judaism in Upper Galilee at the End of Antiquity: Excavations at Gush Halav and en-Nabratein," in *Studia Patristica* 19, ed. E.A. Livingston (Louvain: Peeters, 1990), pp. 62–71; Zvi Uri Ma'oz and Ann Killebrew, "Ancient Qasrin: Synagogue and Village," *BA* 51 (1988), pp. 10–11; Michele Piccirillo, "The Mosaics at Um er-Rasas in Jordan," *BA* 51 (1988), p. 213; public facilities also continued: see Yizhar Hirschfeld, *The Roman Baths of Hammat Gader* (Jerusalem: IES, 1997), pp. 478–479. However, the rate of new construction and rebuilding continued at a much slower rate than before the Muslim conquest. See Schick, *Christian Communities of Palestine* (see endnote 202), p. 162.

[238] A demand set forth in the Treaty of Umar, which regulated communal relations in newly conquered Palestine. See Sivan, *Palestine in Late Antiquity* (see endnote 3), p. 349.

[239] Schick, *Christian Communities of Palestine* (see endnote 202), p. 223.

[240] Among the last popular forms are African Red Slip Ware, Forms 103–104, and Late Roman C (= now Phocaean Red Slip Ware), Form 10. See John Hayes, *Late Roman Pottery* (London: British School at Rome, 1972), pp. 157–167, 343–347; *A Supplement to Late Roman Pottery* (London: British School at Rome, 1980), LIX–LXI (for the name change of Late Roman C).

[241] For example, the local rouletted bowls made in the Jerusalem area appear with frequency in Jerusalem and environs and a locally made "bag-shaped" storage jar (with a later variant) enjoyed a wider circulation in the sixth and seventh centuries. See Jodi Magness, *Jerusalem Ceramic Chronology circa 200–800 CE* (Sheffield, UK: JSOT Press, 1993), pp. 153–154, 160.

[242] See also the transitional coins (650–700 C.E.) found in the last floor of the synagogue at en-Nabratein: Eric M. Meyers et al., "Preliminary Report on the 1980 Excavations at en-Nabratein, Israel," *BASOR* 244 (1981), pp. 20–21. The Damascus mint was especially important for gold coins in the Umayyad period. See Vassilios Tzaferis, *Excavations at Capernaum*, vol. 1, 1978–1982 (Winona Lake, IN: Eisenbrauns, 1989), pp. 139, 142, 164.

[243] The often repeated truism that Alexander the Great marks the reversal of trade patterns from East to West has been pushed back to the Persian period for its beginnings. See Ephraim Stern, *Material Culture of the Land of the Bible in the Persian Period 583–332 B.C.* (Warminster, UK/ Jerusalem: Axis & Phillips/IES, 1982), p. 232. On the other hand, in late antiquity there was a long "pull" toward Persia, Arabia and points East exerted on the eastern provinces of the empire. See Brown, *Rise of Western Christendom* (see endnote 101), pp. 267–294.

IX. Christians and Jews in the First Six Centuries

[1] Søren Kierkegaard, *Attack Upon "Christendom,"* trans. W. Lowrie (Princeton, NJ: Princeton University Press, 1968), passim.

[2] 1QpHab[akkuk] 7.

[3] Pesikta 39b.

[4] 1QH[odayot] 16.4–40 [*olim* col. 8 according to Sukenik] (the *Thanksgiving Psalms*).

[5] *Antiquities* 13.13.5.

[6] *War* 1.4.6; *Antiquities* 13.14.2.

[7] See *Antiquities* 20; also see Hegesippus, as quoted in *Eccles. Hist.* 2.23.

[8] Except for the Samaritans, but this is another chapter in history.

[9] See the contributions in James D.G. Dunn, ed., *Paul and the Mosaic Law* (Grand Rapids, MI: Eerdmans, 2001).

[10] See Carlo Giordano and Isidoro Kahn, *The Jews in Pompeii, Herculaneum, Stabiae and in the Cities of Campania Felix*, 3rd ed., revised and enlarged by Laurentino García y García, trans. Wilhelmina F. Jashemski (Rome: Bardi, 2001, reprinted 2003).

[11] See especially Mishnah *Berakhot* 4:4; *Avot* 2:13.

[12] *Antiquities* 18.63–64.

[13] Origen, *Exhortation to Martyrdom*.

[14] See the bibliography, Greek text and English translation in *The Cologne Mani Codex*, eds. R. Cameron and A.J. Dewey, *SBL Texts and Translations* 15, *Early Christian Literature Series* 3 (Missoula, MT: Scholars Press, 1979).

[15] See, for example, Doron Mendels, *The Media Revolution of Early Christianity* (Grand Rapids, MI: Eerdmans, 1999).

[16] See Lee M. Mcdonald, *The Biblical Canon: Its Origins, Transmission, and Authority* (Peabody, MA: Hendrickson, 2007).

[17] John Chrysostom, *Homily Against the Jews* 48.844.

[18] Ibid., 48.847.

[19] Max I. Dimont, *Jews, God and History* (New York: Simon and Schuster, 1962), p. 154.

[20] Melito, *Peri Pascha* (Concerning Passover [or Easter]), 96.

[21] The earliest evidence of this fabricated account is in Origen's *Contra Celsum* (chapter 32), which dates from about 248. *Sefer Toledoth Yeshu* is a product of the early polemics that separated Jews and Christians. For Hebrew versions of the Toledoth Yeshu, see Samuel Krauss, *Das Leben Jesu nach Jüdischen Quellen* (Berlin, 1902); also see Krauss, "Une nouvelle recension hébraique du Toldot Yêsû," *REJ*, n.s. 3 (1938), pp. 65–88; and Krauss, "Jesus in Jewish Legend," *Jewish Encyclopedia* 7 (1907), pp. 170–173. A helpful work is Morris Goldstein, *Jesus in the Jewish Tradition* (New York: Macmillan, 1950), see esp. "Toledoth Yeshu," pp. 147–166.

[22] See the second-century tradition in *Justin Martyr's Dialogue with Trypho* 69; see BT *Sanhedrin* 43a.

[23] Martyrdom of Isaiah 5; Psalms of Solomon 17:37; 4 Ezra 14:22.

[24] Mishnah *Sotah* 9:6, 15.

[25] Dead Sea Scrolls, esp. 1QS, 1QSb, 1QH, CD, 4Q403–405.

[26] James H. Charlesworth, *Jesus and the Dead Sea Scrolls*, Anchor Bible Reference Library (New York: Doubleday, 1992).

[27] Tosefta *Sotah* 13:2.

[28] Tosefta *Pesahim* 4:14.

[29] Tosefta *Sotah* 13:3; *Seder 'Olam Rabbah* 6.

Index

Note: Page numbers in *italics* refer to illustrations, maps and charts.